CONFLICT
& UNITY

Capters
7
4 5 6 8

Tutorial Topics
Canadian / American Political culture
Dualism , Regionalism
Redistributive politics
Constitutional Politics
Party Discipline.

THIRD EDITION

CONFLICT & UNITY

An Introduction to Canadian Political Life

ROGER GIBBINS

Department of Political Science
University of Calgary

Nelson Canada

I⊤P⁻
International Thomson Publishing
The trademark ITP is used under licence

Published in 1994 by
Nelson Canada,
A Division of Thomson Canada Limited
1120 Birchmount Road
Scarborough, Ontario M1K 5G4

Canadian Cataloguing in Publication Data
Gibbins, Roger, 1947–
    Conflict and unity : an introduction to Canadian political life

3rd ed.
Includes bibliographical references and index.
ISBN 0-17-604244-X
1. Canada - Politics and government. I. Title.

JL65 1988.G52 1994   320.971   C94-930227-9

Acquisitions Editors   Dave Ward and Andrew Livingston
Editorial Manager   Nicole Gnutzman
Production Editor   Tracy Bordian
Developmental Editor   Joanne Scattolon
Art Director   Bruce Bond
Design   Stuart Knox
Cover Photo   COMSTOCK

Printed and bound in Canada
1 2 3 4 (WC) 98 97 96 95 94

CONTENTS

ACKNOWLEDGMENTS

Len Norris cartoon from *The Best of Norris* by Len Norris used by permission of the Canadian Publishers, McClelland and Stewart, Toronto.

Cartoon by Roy Peterson from *Swamped* by Stanley Burke and Roy Peterson, published by Douglas & McIntyre, 1987. Reprinted by permission.

Excerpt from *The Public Philosophy*. Copyright © 1955 by Walter Lippman. Copyright renewed © 1983 by Walter Lippman. By permission of Little, Brown and Company in association with the Atlantic Monthly Press.

"How Big is Big?" and "The Costs of Democracy" reprinted by permission of The Canadian Press.

Excerpt from James Eayrs, "Sharing a Continent: The Hard Issues," p. 93, *The United States and Canada*, James Sloan Dickey, ed. Englewood Cliffs, N.J.: Prentice-Hall, 1964. Reprinted by permission of The American Assembly, Columbia University, New York.

Duncan Macpherson cartoons reprinted with permission of the Toronto Star Syndicate.

Phil Mallette cartoon reproduced by permission of the artist.

Brian Gable cartoons reproduced by permission of the *Regina Leader Post*.

Andy Donato cartoons reproduced by permission of *The Toronto Sun* and Key Porter Books.

All material from Canadian government sources reproduced by permission of the Minister of Supply and Services Canada.

"Mending Wall," from *The Poetry of Robert Frost*, edited by Edward Connery Lathem. Copyright 1930, 1939, © 1969 by Holt, Rinehart and Winston. Copyright © 1958 by Robert Frost. Copyright © 1967 by Lesley Frost Ballantine. Reprinted by permission of Holt, Rinehart and Winston, Publishers.

Vince Rodewalt cartoon reproduced by permission of the artist and *The Calgary Herald*.

Malcolm Mayes cartoon reproduced by permission of the artist and *The Edmonton Journal*.

"W.L.M.K." from *Collected Poems of F.R. Scott*, reprinted by permission of McClelland and Stewart Ltd., The Canadian Publishers.

PREFACE

The first edition of this text was written as Canadians went to the polls in 1984 to elect a new Progressive Conservative government, led by Brian Mulroney. Since then, Canadians have been witness to a series of initiatives to refashion the nature of both their political community and the economic foundations upon which the community rests. Some of these initiatives, including the Free Trade Agreement, the Goods and Services Tax, and the North American Free Trade Agreement, have been successfully implemented, although their long-term impact remains to be seen. Others, including the Meech Lake and Charlottetown Accords, were unsuccessful but have left a deep mark on the political community nonetheless. The cast of players on the political stage has also changed dramatically. The Progressive Conservatives have gone from one of the most impressive landslide victories ever in 1984 to occupying only two seats in the current House of Commons; the Bloc Québécois and the Reform Party have emerged as robust and contentious players on the national stage; and Canadian voters themselves have had their role expanded and transformed by the 1992 constitutional referendum.

The intervening years between the first and third editions of *Conflict & Unity* have been anything but uneventful for Canadian political life. If we have failed to notice the rapidity and scope of the changes taking place around us, it has only been because we have been fascinated by the even broader currents of political and economic change that have been refashioning the international community during the same years. The most dramatic barometer of international change, of course, has been the transformation of the former Soviet Union, where events have been so dramatic that changes closer to home inevitably pale by comparison. However, we have also come to realize that the economic and political transformation of the international order is not remote to Canadian interests, but is rather something that reverberates immediately and powerfully throughout the Canadian community. The future of our community is inextricably linked to that of the larger international community of which we are a part.

Despite the change that swirls around us, the foundations of Canadian political life still stand. We confront the same geography, the same regional distribution of the national population, the same linguistic mix, and the same marginal location on the North American continent. As a consequence, many of the same problems and dilemmas keep reappearing, and keep being addressed within the same institutional forums that we have used over the past century and a quarter. The challenge, then, is to untangle the patterns of continuity and change, to understand at the same time where we came from and where we appear to be heading in order to appreciate how our hopes and aspirations for the future are anchored in the trials and tribulations of the past. It is to this challenge that the third edition of *Conflict & Unity* is directed.

Not surprisingly, the attempt to meet this challenge, and to grapple with recent changes in Canadian political life, has led to a number of changes in the text. The growing emphasis on the debt and deficit has led to an increasingly contentious debate on Canadian social programs, and on policies designed to address regional economic development. Thus a new chapter has been added on redistributive politics. The recent constitutional debate has forced Canadians to take a closer look at the operation and principled foundations of our political institutions, and this is reflected in a new chapter on the institutional landscape. New social movements, including environmentalism and feminism, have come to play a larger role in national politics, and hence have also come to play a larger role in the text. And finally, the third edition covers a series of major events that have taken place since the Meech Lake Accord, the Charlottetown Accord and the 1992 constitutional referendum, the North American Free Trade Agreement, the rise of the Bloc Québécois and the Reform Party, and the 1993 general election.

Finally, I should stress that any project such as this is much more than the product of a single author. To a large degree, this book is a distillation of the research and analysis of members of the political science community, and members of related disciplines, over the past twenty years. It is to them that I owe my thanks. In a more immediate sense, I would also like to thank the people at Nelson Canada for their remarkable patience and assistance in bringing this work to fruition, and both Valerie Snowdon and Sonia Arrison at the Calgary end for their support. Finally, I would like to thank my students over the past twenty-one years, men and women from whom I have learned so much. This book is a modest repayment for their contribution to my understanding of the political world, and life its own self.

SETTING THE STAGE

The political game is a great one to play. It is exciting even to watch; it brings with it disappointments and frustrations, but there are compensations in the acquaintances it brings, in the friendships formed, and in the knowledge acquired of humanity, sometimes at its worst, more often at its best.

Chubby Powers's memoirs, *A Party Politician*

This text provides an introduction to the complex and often tumultuous world of Canadian politics. Its focus is on the *dynamics* of politics, the issues and conflicts that drive the political process. Thus we will explore the historical and contemporary debate over language policies, the sharp clash of regional interests and the more muffled competition among social classes, the evolution of Canadian–American relations, and the ongoing, almost perpetual quest for constitutional reform. Woven into this analysis is a discussion of the institutional arenas within which political conflict takes place and the parties, leaders, and groups through which conflicting interests are mobilized.

It is useful in this context to compare politics with Canada's national game of hockey, although we have to stretch our imaginations a bit to include women players and less corporate control. We can think of hockey in quite different ways: as a set of rules for playing a game; as a network of professional and community arenas (not to forget backyard rinks and frozen prairie ponds); and as a vast army of referees, league officials, time-keepers, scorekeepers, coaches, parent helpers, skate-tiers, and rink-cleaners who make the game possible. In an analogous fashion the Canadian political system encompasses a set of rules and procedures that govern elections, the legislative process, and the conduct of public officials. It also encompasses a network of political arenas including Parliament, provincial legislatures, the courts, federal–provincial conferences, town councils, and school boards, all staffed by a multitude of federal, provincial, and municipal public servants. Yet hockey is much more than rules, arenas, and officials; it is competing teams, stars, and villains, traditional rivalries, the emotion of parents and fans, bodychecks, penalties, and questionable calls. While one must know the rules to understand the game, it is the teams, emotion, and conflict that bring the sport alive. In the chapters that follow, particular emphasis will be placed on the issues and conflicts that energize political life. Of course, the arenas and rules of the game will not be neglected, and the early chapters are devoted to mapping out the institutional landscape. However, this landscape will be brought to life through a study of the broader game of politics.

Like hockey, politics is a great spectator sport. We can read political news as we might read the sports pages, looking at the Gallup polls to determine the partisan point-spread and following political columnists as parties fire coaches, trade players, and combat dissension within their ranks. Politics, however, is much more than a spectator sport, for the political process moulds our lives and shapes our futures. It is therefore imperative that we be not only interested spectators, but also active players. If we are to be players, if we are to leave the sidelines and wade into the fray, we must first understand the game.

CONFLICT AND POLITICS

The study of politics is first and foremost the study of conflict. Political systems are systems of conflict management for dividing up the spoils of public life among competing interests. In the words made famous by Harold Lasswell, the study of politics is the study of who gets what, when, where, and how. However, in democratic political systems conflict is largely contained within well-established institutional arenas. The scope and intensity of conflict is limited by a general respect for the rules of the game and by an overarching set of values or "political culture" that most participants share. Democratic systems are thus characterized by their capacity to manage conflict without recourse to violence. In the words of American essayist H.L. Mencken, "voting is simply a way of determining which side is the stronger without putting it to the test of fighting."[1]

It is the conflictual character of politics that makes the political world not only so fascinating, but also so difficult to understand. Citizens are bombarded by competing and contradictory explanations for every event that takes place. The heroes and villains of the piece are a function of who is speaking, of the partisan lenses through which we see the political world, and of the ideological predispositions we bring to our analysis. Like beauty, much of the truth in politics lies in the eye of the beholder. It may be for this reason that the public school system conveys so little information about politics; educators choose to neglect political life rather than send students and teachers into a partisan and ideological morass. Although at the college and university level we have no choice but to plunge into this morass, the discipline of political science fortunately provides a set of survival skills that makes the enterprise less risky, more fruitful, and considerably more enjoyable.

The conflictual nature of politics contributes to one of the more intriguing democratic paradoxes. Canadians are generally proud to live in a democratic country; when we look at the world about us, our system of government is often seen as setting us apart from our less fortunate

Democratic politics has been the source of a good deal of sardonic commentary, as the following examples illustrate:

> "It is the nature of politicians to promise a bridge in one election and a river to run under it in the next."
>
> —Stephen Leacock

> "Political language ... is designed to make lies sound truthful and murder respectable, and to give an appearance of solidarity to pure wind."
>
> —George Orwell, *Politics and the English Language* (1950)

> "Politics and the fate of mankind are shaped by men without ideals and without greatness. Men who have greatness within them don't go in for politics."
>
> —Albert Camus, French author and philosopher

> "Government runs on two things: patronage and the hope of patronage."
>
> —George Ferguson, Ontario premier during the 1920s

> "Now I know what a statesman is; he's a dead politician. We need more statesmen."
>
> —Bob Edwards, *The Calgary Eye Opener*

> "You must learn that there are times when a man in public life is compelled to rise above his principles."
>
> —Arizona's Senator Ashurst

> "In the trackless wastes of politics, men lose their purpose, and the stars by which they once steered vanish in the bottomless sky of other men's aspirations. They wander like nomads, from oasis to oasis, quenching their thirst from the wells of power and warming themselves by the abandoned fires of those who have come and gone before."
>
> —Dalton Camp, *Gentlemen, Players and Politicians*

> "Democracy substitutes election by the incompetent many for appointment by the corrupt few."
>
> —George Bernard Shaw, British playwright

counterparts in other countries. Yet at the same time "politics" tends to be a very derogatory term in popular speech. How often have you heard something dismissed as "mere politics"; how often are terms such as "office politics" and "political connections" used to refer to the shady underside of life? (Robert Thompson, former leader of the national Social Credit Party, even complained that Parliament was being turned into "a political arena"!) How often do you find in novels, movies, and television programs that politicians are the villains, thwarting the more honest endeavours of police officials, community groups, and private detectives? The paradox inherent in this contempt for politics is that it extends to those very elements that make democratic government possible: election campaigns, political parties, interest groups, office-seeking politicians, and voting itself.

Popular Perceptions of Politicians

A 1979 survey of 840 students attending ten Ontario universities presented respondents with a list of thirty occupations and, for each, respondents were asked if they contributed a great deal to the general good of society, whether they contributed more good than harm, or more harm than good. Overall, politicians ranked 24th, coming ahead of corporate executives, bank presidents, oil company presidents, public relations experts, advertising executives, and bill collectors, but behind military generals, plumbers, musicians, actors, sports stars, lawyers, union leaders, and even professors! Only 4 percent of the students felt that politicians contributed a great deal to the general good of society; another 4 percent felt that they contributed more good than harm, while 92 percent felt they contributed more harm than good.

Source: *Saturday Night*, October 1979, pp. 35–40.

Given widespread cynicism toward things political, it is important to stress that there is a positive side to political life. Throughout history people have banded together in political communities in order to achieve goals collectively that they could not achieve alone. Political organization has provided an indispensable vehicle for the pursuit of collective security from external foes or internal disorder, economic expansion, cultural enlightenment, and a sense of group identity and mission that transcends and thus elevates the individual. It is because those things that transcend the individual are so integral to the human spirit that politics is so important. As Aristotle observed in the 4th century B.C., it is for this reason that man is a "political animal." William Lyon Mackenzie, an Upper Canadian reformer in the pre-Confederation period, picked up the same theme:

Politics is the science which teaches the people of a country to care for each other. If a mischievous individual were to attempt to cut off his neighbour's hand, would that neighbour's other hand and feet do well quietly to permit the amputation of the limb if they could hinder it? All will say, No. This then is politics. That part of our duty which teaches us to study the welfare of our whole country, and not to rest satisfied altho' our own household is well off when our neighbours are in difficulty and danger. The honest politician is he who gives all he can of his time and means to promote the public good, whose charity begins at home but does not end there. The man who says he is no politician, is either ignorant of what he is saying, or a contemptible selfish creature, unworthy of the country or community of which he is a part.[2]

Well-functioning democratic political systems do not eliminate conflict, but reduce its intensity and effects to a level compatible with a civil society. It should also be stressed, however, that conflict is not necessarily bad. As former prime minister Pierre Trudeau has urged, we should keep our differences: "creative tension, after all, gives society its very life and growth."[3] Thus to describe the Canadian political system as conflictual is to recognize its vitality and human face.

At the same time, there are a number of important questions about political conflict that merit consideration. Are there features of the political system that exacerbate rather than moderate conflict? Are there some forms of conflict that the system handles well, and others that it handles poorly or even creates? Have we become so preoccupied with certain conflicts that other important issues are pushed from the political agenda? Is the level of conflict so high that collective goals, including national unity and our survival as an independent country on the North American continent, are imperilled? Underlying such questions is a concern for the integrative capacity of the political system, its ability to knit together often disparate regional and linguistic communities into a national whole. Fortunately, the conclusion advanced in the chapters that follow is generally positive. Although the Canadian political system has been confronted with an array of very difficult problems, the national community has endured and prospered, and has done so while maintaining the strength and vitality of subnational linguistic and regional communities.

THE CONFLICT AGENDA

If you were to take a copy of a major newspaper and note all the political disputes and issues raised within its pages, your list would be formidable even if you excluded those occurring outside Canada. It is the sheer volume of political information and the complexity of so many issues that can make the study of politics so daunting to students. How can one hope to make sense out of a political world that is so complex and often so unfettered by logic or rationality? One answer is to go "back to" the basics, to

"What is in behind the little curtains … just in case anyone should ask me?"

Len Norris, *9th Annual*; originally published in the *Sun* (Vancouver), December 9, 1959.

address a relatively small handful of issues forming the bedrock of Canadian political life. In so doing, of course, many exciting and some important issues will be neglected, but the pedagogical premise of this text is that the "big issues" provide the essential backdrop against which one can place the welter of other issues forming the daily grist of politics.

What, then, are the big issues, the threads that must be followed if one is to untangle the Gordian knot of national politics? The selection of any set of issues will be contentious and idiosyncratic to a degree; both writers and readers will differ as to what issues should be included. I would argue, however, that the five pursued in this text—language politics and Quebec nationalism, regionalism, redistributive politics, Canadian–American relations, and constitutional politics—are fundamentally important to the Canadian political experience. While their relative importance can be debated and a case can undoubtedly be made for a more expansive set of issues, these five are essential to an understanding of Canadian political life. All share deep historical roots, and none is likely to slip from the nation's political agenda in the near future.

The format of the text follows directly from the selection of these central issues. Chapter 2 provides a historical backdrop by looking at the Confederation agreement and at the early emergence of the major axes of Canadian political life. Chapter 3 provides an overview of the institutional landscape upon which political conflict is played out. The five issues are then examined sequentially in Chapters 4 through 8. Chapter 9 looks at the Canadian party system and the extent to which it has been shaped by and reflects the principal lines of cleavage that have been identified. The concluding chapter looks ahead to the emerging political landscape and to the shape of Canadian political life in the years to come. Each chapter provides study questions and suggested readings. The former are designed not so much to test your comprehension of the chapter's material, but to expand that comprehension, to push against the limitations of the chapter's coverage. The latter provide not only avenues that might be pursued for term paper research, but also some modest acknowledgment of the parasitical nature of textbooks. A good text builds upon and to some extent pillages the wealth of facts, theories, and insights put together over time with great effort by the academic community. I am thus deeply indebted to my colleagues whose research cleared the land and broke the soil; this text is far more the fruit of their labours than my own.

By the time you reach the final chapter, there is little doubt that many questions will remain unanswered. For this I make no apologies; my hope is that your appetite for things political will have been whetted and not satiated. This text can do no more than create a portal upon the rich and fascinating vista of Canadian political life. As a student of politics, you must demand more. As a citizen, you must be prepared to use your increased understanding as a bridge to active political participation. Not to participate in the political process is to abandon your fate to those who do, and who may not share your goals, ambitions, and dreams. As Plato warned in *The Republic*, "the punishment which the wise suffer, who refuse to take part in the government, is to live under the government of worse men."

NOTES

1. *Minority Report*, 1956. Cited in Jonathon Green, *The Book of Political Quotes* (New York: McGraw-Hill, 1982), p. 213.

2. *The Colonial Advocate*, June 27, 1833.

3. Speech to the Confederation Dinner, Toronto, October 27, 1982.

IN THE BEGINNING

If the primary objective of this text is to introduce the reader to contemporary Canadian politics, why do we begin in the distant past? Why is it important to delve into the pre-Confederation politics of the 1850s and 1860s, and to dust off the Constitution Act of 1867? In part, we do so *because* Canadians tend to be a very ahistorical people believing, as one of my students wrote, that "Canada has very little history." Our reluctance to grapple with the past goes beyond the widely shared delusion that we are a new country—we are in fact one of the oldest countries in the world—to embrace two common assumptions. The first is that the past has little relevance for what is happening today; the second is that Canadian history is boring, lacking as it does the clash of armies and the fiery rhetoric of revolution. Neither assumption withstands serious examination. One has only to look at the slogan *Je me souviens* on Quebec licence plates to realize not only the relevance of the past, but also the way in which history is woven into the cloth of contemporary political life, in some cases with deliberate intent to shade our appreciation of current events and our perceptions of the political landscape. Thus our views of Canada, and of our province and its place in the national fabric, are to a degree historical artifacts that should be inspected carefully.

The past provides a useful guide for those interested in contemporary politics, highlighting as it does important landmarks and identifying the winners and losers in political combat. As Canadian historian Donald Creighton has written:

> The waves behind the vessel which is carrying humanity forward into the unknown ... can teach us where the winds of change are blowing and on what course the chief currents of our age are set. They can reveal to us the main direction of our voyage through time.[1]

For the political scientist, it is the currents rather than the details of the past that are of particular importance. They provide a clarity of perspective that is often difficult to find amid the complexities of contemporary events, and they allow us to identify the harmonies and conflicts that have shaped and continue to shape political life. If, as Creighton has written, there are no "tragic finalities" in Canadian politics but "only the endless repetitions of the same themes,"[2] then it is important to have some appreciation of the historical setting from which those themes emerged. Indeed, the argument will be made throughout this text that the principles embraced in the Confederation agreement, and the institutions put into place by that agreement, continue to set the terms of contemporary debate over such matters as regional representation, Québécois nationalism, and constitutional reform.

The reader who is prepared to go beyond the brief synopsis of this chapter to a deeper exploration of the Confederation era will find that Canadian political history is far from colourless. In Sir John A. Macdonald, the chief architect of Confederation and Canada's first prime minister, one finds a fascinating mix of political brilliance, statesmanship, chicanery, human frailty, and personal charm. Even if the personalities of the day are put aside, the Confederation era presents an intriguing tangle of political conflict and opportunity. The way that tangle was addressed provides as good an introduction to political craftsmanship and applied political science as one is likely to encounter.

The politicians who drafted the Confederation agreement and, in so doing, laid the foundations for the modern Canadian state, faced a formidable task. At the very least they had to accomplish the following:

- They had to dissolve the 1840 marriage between Canada East (now Quebec) and Canada West (now Ontario) while at the same time reuniting the two in a larger political community. Thus the instrument of divorce had also to be the instrument of reconciliation.

- They had to hold at bay an American military threat and the prospect of American territorial expansion in the West.

- They had to meet the demand from Canada West for representation by population while meeting the demand from Canada East that "rep by pop," and through it the domination of the Catholic francophone minority by the Protestant anglophone majority, not be imposed.

- They had to create a strong central government that would be able to take over colonial debt and attract the financing required for railway construction while at the same time recognizing the commitment to local autonomy in the existing British North American colonies.

- They had to entice the Maritime colonies into a transcontinental union centred far from the Atlantic coast, a union in which Maritimers would play at best a supporting role.

Quite remarkably, they were successful, and for this reason alone the Confederation agreement warrants our attention as a fine example of political craftsmanship. We also find in the agreement the emergence in elementary form of what have become perennial features of national political life: the tensions between anglophones and francophones, between the centre and the periphery, between Canada and the United States, between the provincial and federal governments, and between parliamentary institutions and federal principles. In short, for those readers trying to understand Canadian politics today, Confederation is a good place to start.

The Wit and Wisdom of Sir John A. Macdonald

There is no better advice for the after-dinner speaker in search of a humorous opening, or the student in search of some adornment for a term paper, than to rummage through the sayings of Sir John A. Macdonald. *Colombo's Canadian Quotations* (Edmonton: Hurtig, 1974) offers the following gems:

- "The task of the politician is to climb the tree and shake down acorns for the pigs below."

- In an exchange with Senator A.R. Dickey, who had promised to support Macdonald whenever he thought Macdonald was right, Macdonald replied: "That is no satisfaction. Anybody may support me when I am right. What I want is a man who will support me when I am wrong."

- "Given a Government with a big surplus, and a big majority and a weak Opposition, you could debauch a committee of Archangels."

- "I will have no accord with the desire expressed in some quarters by any mode whatever that there should be an attempt made to oppress the one language or to render it inferior to the other; I believe that would be impossible if it were tried, and it would be foolish and wicked if it were possible."

- "As for myself, my course is clear. A British subject I was born. A British subject I will die."

- "Let us be English or let us be French, but above all let us be Canadians."

- "Would you move away please, your breath smells terrible ... it smells like water."

FACTORS LEADING TO CONFEDERATION

The road to Confederation can only be summarized here, with the more detailed account being left to the historians.[3] Our discussion focuses upon four factors that played particularly important roles in bringing about the Confederation agreement: political stalemate in the Canadas, a two-pronged threat from the United States, economic imperatives, and for lack of a better phrase, what might be termed the "national dream."

Confederation was first proposed in 1858 by John A. Macdonald, left, and George-Étienne Cartier, one of the most famous teams of political leaders in Canada—Macdonald from Canada West and Cartier from Canada East.

Archives of Ontario.

Political Stalemate in the Canadas

The capture of Quebec in 1759 by British armed forces set in motion a complex colonial interplay between the French and English communities in British North America. In 1774 the British Parliament passed the Quebec Act, which provided recognition of the French language, institutions, and civil law in what had become *British* North America. (The 1992 report of the Beaudoin-Dobbie Special Joint Committee argued that the Quebec Act made legal provision "for a distinctive society in Quebec with institutions, laws and culture quite different from the surrounding English-speaking societies."[4]) Beyond recognizing what has been termed "the French fact," the act also extended the boundaries of the Quebec colony westward to the Great Lakes. Then, in the face of growing English settlement around the Great Lakes, the British Parliament passed the Constitutional Act of 1791, which divided Quebec into Upper Canada—now Ontario—and Lower Canada—now Quebec. The 1791 act also provided for elected assemblies in each colony, but not for responsible government; the appointed political executive could not be turned out of office by a majority vote of the legislative assembly. Thus by 1791 the French-speaking inhabitants of Lower Canada, although not those of the other British North American colonies, had received legislative recognition of their language and institutions along with an elected assembly in which they exercised majority control.

In 1837 political unrest in both Upper and Lower Canada led to an investigation of the colonial situation by Lord Durham. In his *Report on the Affairs of British North America*, Durham made his famous observation on Canadian political life:

> *I expected to find a contest between a government and a people: I found two nations warring in the bosom of a single state: I found a struggle, not of principles, but of races.*

Lord Durham's solution was straightforward: French Canadians should be assimilated into what was then a smaller English-Canadian community. It was a solution reflecting not only Durham's commitment to liberal principles,[5] but also his harsh assessment of French Canadians:

> *There can hardly be conceived a nationality more destitute of all that can invigorate and elevate a people, than that which is exhibited by the descendants of the French in Lower Canada, owing to their retaining their peculiar language and manners. They are a people with no history, and no literature.*

Durham's solution abandoned the political accommodation that had been put in place following the conquest of New France, an accommodation in which British colonial control and economic dominance co-existed in Lower Canada with the French language and the social dominance of the Catholic Church.

In partial response to the political unrest of 1837, Durham recommended that responsible government be implemented, that the executive's term of office be contingent upon continued majority support in the elected assembly. However, in order to ensure that responsible government did not fall under the control of French-Canadian nationalists and that responsible governments were not bounded by racial-linguistic identifications, and in order to promote the assimilation of French Canadians, Durham also recommended the colonial union of Upper and Lower Canada. This second recommendation was carried out through the 1840 Act of Union, which combined Upper and Lower Canada into a single British colony, the Province of Canada, with a single elected assembly. The act further promoted the linguistic assimilation of French Canadians by making English the only official language of the new legislative assembly and by giving Canada East and Canada West (as Lower and Upper Canada were now called) equal representation in that assembly even though only 432,000 people lived in Canada West compared to 717,000 in Canada East. Here it should be noted that although the population of Canada East included a significant number of anglophone Protestants, the francophone Catholic population in Canada East alone exceeded the total population of Canada West.

Had the assimilationist objectives of the act been achieved, Canada today would be a unilingual state with a fully assimilated French-Canadian minority. French Canadians, however, were able to protect their interests within the new legislative arena by acting as a bloc on matters of religion and language. French was reinstated as a language of legislative debate following an 1842 speech in French by Louis-Hippolyte Lafontaine. When faced with the demand that he speak in English, Lafontaine replied:

> I am asked to pronounce in another language than my mother tongue the first speech that I have to make in this House. I distrust my ability to speak English. But I must inform the honourable members that even if my knowledge of English were as intimate as my knowledge of French, I should nevertheless make my first speech in the language of my French Canadian compatriots, if only to protest against the cruel injustice of the Union Act in trying to proscribe the mother tongue of half the population of Canada. I owe it to my compatriots; I owe it to myself.[6]

Thereafter French was used in the House, although it was not to become an official language of parliamentary debate and record until 1848.

Even though the Lower and Upper Canadian colonies had been merged into a single political unit by the Act of Union, an informal linguistic and political duality emerged that foreshadowed the formal introduction of federalism in 1867. Indeed, as J.M.S. Careless argues, the continued existence of two Canadas, East and West, "destroyed Durham's very idea of a complete blending of the two peoples."[7] De facto coalition governments were headed by leaders from both Canada East and Canada West, with the team of George-Étienne Cartier and John A. Macdonald being the most famous. Legislation impinging upon linguistic or cultural interests required a double majority—a majority of members from both Canadas—to pass. The administration of the colony was carried out on a dual basis with separate ministries for Canada West and Canada East. Macdonald, for example, served as attorney general for Canada West, but not for the colony as a whole.

Practical as these adaptations were, the colonial marriage of the two Canadas proved to be unworkable within an atmosphere marked by cultural polarization, governmental instability, and a growing pettiness in public life. The introduction of responsible government in 1848 did little to improve the situation. Deadlock rather than accommodation set the tone of legislative politics, with eighteen different ministries holding office between 1841 and 1867. Double majorities were increasingly difficult to find as the linguistic and religious cleavage was reinforced by growing economic rivalry between the transportation, banking, and manufacturing interests of Montreal (supported to a degree by Toronto, Kingston, Hamilton, and London) and the agrarian interests of western Ontario championed with such force by George Brown, editor of *The Globe* (Toronto).

The most important factor eroding the Act of Union was the shifting demographic balance between Canada East and Canada West. By 1851 Canada East no longer had the larger population; approximately 952,000 people lived in Canada West compared to 890,000 in Canada East. By 1861 the imbalance was even greater: 1,396,000 lived in Canada West compared to 1,112,000 in Canada East. With some reason, Canada West became increasingly restive with the equal representation embedded in the Act of Union, and agitation grew for the introduction of representation by population in order to give Canada West the legislative clout that its numbers seemed to warrant. In 1861, for example, George Brown wrote the following editorial in *The Globe*:

> THE GLOBE is the unflinching advocate of REPRESENTATION BY POPU-LATION. By the present iniquitous system, Lower Canada sends the same number of Representatives to Parliament as Upper Canada, although Upper Canada has THREE HUNDRED THOUSAND SOULS more than Lower Canada, and contributes SEVEN DOLLARS to the general revenue for every THREE DOLLARS contributed by Lower Canada. By this system of injustice and the unanimity with which the French Canadians act together, the Representatives of the Lower Section not only administer the affairs of their own Province, but control those of Upper Canada as well.[8]

With equal reason and passion, French Canadians in Quebec rejected representation by population. Stuck in 1841 with the equal representation of the two Canadas despite their majority, they were quite happy to be stuck with it still when Canada East no longer formed a majority.

The failure of the Act of Union was clearly apparent by the late 1850s, but proposals for reform foundered on the issue of representation by population. Stalemated within the colony, Canadian politicians began to seek an escape through territorial expansion that would make possible a more workable federal structure than could be attained with only two provinces.[9] Such expansion was indeed to provide the solution, but only in the wake of civil war in the United States and growing economic distress north of the American border.

The American Threat

Throughout its history, Canada has been buffeted by events in the United States. Indeed, the landmarks of early American history such as the

Revolution of 1776, the War of 1812, and the Civil War were also landmarks in Canadian history, with the Civil War providing a major impetus for Confederation. When the Civil War broke out in 1861, Canadian attitudes could best be described as anti-Northern and anti-Southern.[10] If anything the former prevailed, not because Canadians sided with the South on the slavery issue, which they did not, but because the secession of the South would break up a growing American hegemony on the North American continent. When General Lee surrendered the Confederate forces in 1865, Canadian hopes for some future balance of strength on the continent were also lost. In the victorious northern states, where Britain's support of the South during the war had soured perceptions of the British North American colonies, Canada had come to be seen as decidedly pro-Southern and anti-Northern. This perception was reinforced in 1864 when a small Confederate raiding party crossed the border from the Canadian side and robbed the bank in St. Albans, Vermont. When the raiders fled back into Canada they were only briefly detained before being released with the bank's money. It was an admittedly minor event, but one that the North had by no means forgotten when the war ended a year later.

Postwar Canadian–American tensions were heightened on the Canadian side by the Fenian threat. The Fenians were Irish-American veterans of the Civil War who sought to free their native Ireland from British rule. Given that the Atlantic Ocean prevented any direct Fenian intervention in Ireland, the alternative of an attack on the British presence in Canada was considered. As the *Song of the Fenian Brotherhood* proclaimed:

We are the Fenian Brotherhood, skilled in the art of war,
And we're going to fight for Ireland, the land that we adore.
Many battles have we won along with the boys in blue,
And we'll go and capture Canada, for we've nothing else to do.[11]

In retrospect, the Fenians have a comic-opera character that belies the serious threat that Canadians perceived at the time. An anticipated Fenian invasion on St. Patrick's Day, 1866, led to the mobilization of 10,000 volunteers for the defence of Canada. A month later 1,500 Fenians did cross the border, to be repulsed in a brief battle in which nine Canadians were killed.

The Fenians, it should be stressed, constituted only the tip of a threatening iceberg; the largest army in the world was being demobilized in the American North, releasing thousands of trained soldiers who quite literally might have nothing else to do than "go and capture Canada." The American threat was further exacerbated by British indifference. Canadians had always assumed that any continental war with the United States would be an offshoot of a larger British–American conflict, and hence that Britain would come to Canada's defence. In the wake of the Civil War, however, a purely North American conflict seemed all too possible, for the

British government was more concerned with reducing the financial burden of colonial defence and resuming war-disrupted trading relations with the United States than with the defence of Canada. As Benjamin Disraeli, Chancellor of the Exchequer, wrote to the British prime minister, Lord Derby, in 1866:

> It can never be our pretense or our policy to defend the Canadian frontier against the United States.... What is the use of these colonial deadweights which we do not govern?

If the British North American colonies were to defend themselves, they had little alternative but to band together in defence of a common foe. External threat has played a significant role in the formation of most of the world's federal unions,[12] and Canada was no exception.

As things turned out, the American military intervention did not materialize. However, the resumption of American westward expansion across the continent following the end of the Civil War posed an equally serious threat to Canadian interests. The creation of new American states prior to the war had been checked by political deadlock over whether they would be slave-holding or free states, with neither the North nor the South prepared to accept any increase in the ranks of the other side.[13] With the slavery issue settled by the Civil War, unbridled western expansion began to threaten the unoccupied prairie land lying to the north of the 49th parallel. If American settlement were to pre-empt Canadian settlement on the prairies, Canadians would be boxed into the northeastern corner of the continent, and their absorption into the United States would be only a matter of time. Finally, it should be noted that quite apart from the specific threats of the Fenians, demobilization, and westward expansion, a more general fear of the United States lay behind Confederation. As S.F. Wise and Robert Craig Brown conclude, "it is not too much to say that the large measure of agreement among provincial leaders on the nature of and dangers from political *Americanism* constituted one of the unifying intellectual forces in the Confederation movement."[14]

Economic Imperatives

In the 1840s British economic policy swung toward international free trade and away from the preferential imperial tariffs that had been designed to promote trade between Britain and her colonial possessions. On the positive side, British liberalization of trade encouraged the establishment of responsible government in British North America. As J.M.S. Careless explains, "now that the Old Colonial System was being abandoned, now that trade was freed and the colonies' economic life was not to be controlled, there seemed little reason to control their political life either."[15]

Responsible government came to Nova Scotia and the Province of Canada in 1848, to Prince Edward Island in 1851, to New Brunswick in 1854, and to Newfoundland in 1855. On the negative side, the British abandonment of "imperial preferences" was a serious, almost devastating, economic blow. The repeal of the Corn Laws in 1846 ended a privileged British market for Canadian flour and grain, and preferential treatment for Canadian timber was also ended. In 1849 economic conditions were so bad in Montreal that over 1,000 merchants signed a manifesto urging annexation to the United States. In related riots the Quebec parliament buildings were burned and the British governor of the colony was pelted with stones.

Canadians sought reciprocal tariff reductions with the United States in order to replace lost British markets. Although Americans were initially cool to the idea, representations by the British government eventually brought them round to the Canadian side. The New England states were particularly enticed by promised access to the entire North American fisheries.[16] The southern states were persuaded by the British Colonial Secretary, Lord Elgin, that reciprocity, rather than bringing about the annexation of Canada and thus upsetting the delicate free state/slave state balance, would be the one thing that would allow the British North American colonies to resist the siren call of annexation. The eventual outcome was the 1854 Reciprocity Treaty, which, it was believed at the time, significantly increased north–south trade and revitalized the Canadian economy.[17] The treaty provided for free trade in natural products including grain, lumber, coal, livestock, meat, and fish.

While the Reciprocity Treaty cushioned the young Canadian economy from the impact of British trade liberalization, it also made the Canadian economy more vulnerable than it had been to events in the United States. With the outbreak of the Civil War in 1861 and the disposition of Canadian sympathies in that war, the prospects for the treaty's survival looked bleak. As a consequence, the treaty's anticipated termination and the economic consequences thereof became major considerations in the discussions leading toward Confederation. The British North American colonies, almost wholly dependent upon trade with Britain and the United States yet facing a hostile political climate in both countries, were caught between a rock and a hard place. The creation, through Confederation, of a free trade zone on the northern half of the continent offered the only prospect of economic relief. When the Reciprocity Treaty was indeed cancelled in 1866, the new Canadian economic community was largely in place.

Economic factors played a particularly important role in the Maritime colonies where they helped offset popular opposition to Confederation. The Reciprocity Treaty opened up lucrative Maritime trade with the United States and launched the golden age of "iron men and wooden ships," an age in which the colonies were oriented toward the sea, Britain, New England, and the West Indies. As G.A. Rawlyk and Doug

Brown explain,[18] "it is difficult to imagine a people less concerned in their enterprise or vision with the interior of North America than were the Maritimers at the mid-way point in the nineteenth century." However, with the looming loss of reciprocity, the onset of technological change that was making wooden ships (if not iron men) obsolete, escalating debts associated with extensive railway construction, and the ever growing importance of a rail-fed continental economy, Confederation became an increasingly attractive economic if not emotional enterprise.

Maritime Opposition to Confederation

In 1865 the pro-Confederation Tilley government in New Brunswick fought an election on the issue of Confederation and was soundly defeated. This lesson was not lost on the pro-Confederation government in Nova Scotia, which avoided any electoral confrontation until Confederation was in place. When provincial and federal elections were held in Nova Scotia during the fall of 1867, pro-Confederation candidates went down to massive defeat; anti-confederates captured 36 of the 38 provincial seats and 18 of the 19 federal seats. Yet while Confederation was far from popular, to many it seemed an economic necessity.

For many French Canadians, Confederation promised the economic growth that was essential if emigration from Quebec into the New England states was to be stemmed.[19] More generally, Confederation provided the political foundation for a dynamic and expansionist capitalist state. David E. Smith argues in this respect that "the impetus for Confederation lay in the need for greater public works as much as it did in providing increased security or an escape from political instability in the United Canadas."[20] Intrinsic to this vision was the construction of new railways that would connect the Maritimes to the continental economy, open up new markets for central Canadian manufacturers, and fend off the northward expansion of Americans in the West. Confederation would also enable existing railway debts to be taken over by the new central government; W.T. Easterbrook and Hugh Aitken go so far as to argue that the assumption of railway debts by the central government was "a prerequisite for the formation of the dominion."[21] As Eric Nicol and Peter Whalley note in their more irreverent history, "in Canada as in no other country the ties that bind are five feet long and creosoted."[22] More important is Pierre Berton's reminder, in the title of his history of the CPR, that the railways were part of a more encompassing "national dream."[23]

The National Dream

It is easy to emphasize the negative in discussions of Confederation, to conclude that it came about because of external threat from the United States and anti-colonial sentiment in Great Britain, because English and French Canadians could not work together within a single colonial government, because the economy was distressed and no one was willing or able to shoulder the debts associated with railway construction. Certainly this negative tone figures prominently in the writings of political scientists and historians. French-Canadian historian Jean-Charles Bonenfant, for example, writes:

> Confederation was achieved because English Canadians had to exist with French Canadians, and the latter could not then become independent. The great majority of nations have been formed, not by people who desired intensely to live together, but rather by people who could not live separately.[24]

Bonenfant's sentiment is echoed in historian Arthur Lower's now-famous comment on Confederation:

> Some peoples are born nations, some achieve nationhood and others have nationhood thrust upon them. Canadians seem to be among these latter.[25]

But the tone of this comment places insufficient emphasis on the positive appeal of Confederation, on the "national dream" of a new transcontinental state stretching from sea to sea—*a mari usque ad mare*—across the northern half of the continent. David Smith argues that "the goal of expansion more than any other motivated the Fathers of Confederation."[26] Thomas D'Arcy McGee, one of the Fathers who was particularly concerned with American expansion, gave expression to the national dream in an 1860 speech to the House of Assembly in Quebec City:

> I see in the not remote distance, one great nationality bound, like the shield of Achilles, by the blue rim of ocean—I see it quartered into many communities—each disposing of its internal affairs—but all bound together by free institutions, free intercourse, and free commerce;... I see a generation of industrious, contented, moral men, free in name and in fact, men capable of maintaining, in peace and in war, a constitution worthy of such a country.

It was a bold vision given that the British North American colonies contained just over three million people, and given that the much larger nation to the south had not abandoned its self-proclaimed manifest destiny of continental expansion.

Admittedly, the territorial expansion embodied in the national dream was championed primarily by the banking, transportation, and manufacturing interests of central Canada, which stood most to gain from the creation of new hinterlands to the east and west, and which sought a firmer governmental base to support the massive debt engendered by territorial expansion. There was, however, a grander vision than commercial exploitation, a vision bordering on imperialism. Note, for example, an editorial on western expansion that appeared in the Toronto *Globe* on January 22, 1863:

> If Canada acquires this territory, it will rise in a few years from a position of a small and weak province to be the greatest colony any country has ever possessed, able to take its place among the empires of the earth. The wealth of 400,000 square miles of territory will flow through our waters and be gathered by our merchants, manufacturers and agriculturalists. Our sons will occupy the chief places of this vast territory, we will form its institutions, supply its rulers, teach its schools, fill its stores, run its mills, navigate its streams. Every article of European manufacture, every pound of tropical produce will pass through our stores. Our seminaries of learning will be filled by its people. Our cities will be the centres of its business and education, its wealth and refinement. It will afford fields of enterprise for our youth.

While it may be difficult from our contemporary perspective to see Canadians as imperialists, the sentiment captured above played an important role in forging the national state. It was also a sentiment that failed utterly to incorporate aboriginal communities into the emergent national vision, and thus set the stage for the confrontations of recent years between those communities and the governments of Canada.

Those who sought to build a new transcontinental nation faced some harsh practical realities. There was a strong parochial attachment to local autonomy across the British North American colonies. In the Maritimes, where Prince Edward Island struggled to avoid the clutches of "imperialistic" Nova Scotia, there was little enthusiasm for being swallowed by the new Canadian whale. For Catholic francophones in Canada East, cultural autonomy and protection from the Canadian Protestant (and anglophone) majority were essential conditions for entry into Confederation. In Canada West "local control of local affairs"—or freeing the Protestant majority from the shackles imposed by the Act of Union—was a longstanding plank of the Liberal-Reform movement. The trick, then, was to maintain or, in the case of Canada East and West, enhance local autonomy while at the same time creating a new national government strong enough to deal with the awesome tasks of territorial expansion and defence, to create a new Canadian nationality without submerging its constituent cultural and regional parts. The solution was found in the marriage of British parliamentary institutions to the American innovation of federalism.

THE CONSTITUTION ACT OF 1867

On July 1, 1867, the British North America Act—now called the Constitution Act, 1867—was proclaimed and the embryonic Canadian state came into being. Although at the time Canada encompassed only Nova Scotia, New Brunswick, and the southern portions of what are now Quebec and Ontario, the act established the basic constitutional framework for the larger state that was to come. As new territories and provinces were added, that framework remained intact. Indeed, it continues to provide the country's basic constitutional skeleton, albeit augmented by the 1982 Constitution Act, which brought into play the Charter of Rights and Freedoms, an amending formula for the Constitution, and the constitutional recognition of aboriginal peoples. To understand the 1867 act, it is best to begin with what it was not.

Convention at Charlottetown, Prince Edward Island, to consider the union of the British North American Colonies, 1864. (John A. Macdonald seated, centre of photograph.)

Public Archives Canada/C733.

What Did Not Happen in 1867

The 1867 Constitution Act did not emerge suddenly as a dramatic or revolutionary document. It had roots in earlier constitutional documents including the Quebec Act and the Act of Union,[27] and its details emerged slowly through an extended series of intercolonial negotiations. The Confederation proposal was first broached in 1858 by the Macdonald-Cartier administration in the hope that the creation of a broader federal community would end the Union government's political impasse. When its major opponent, George Brown, finally endorsed the proposal in 1864, Canadian politicians sought an opportunity to present it to the Maritime colonies. The opportunity came that year when the Nova Scotia legislature called for a conference to discuss Maritime union. When the governments of New Brunswick, Nova Scotia, and Prince Edward Island decided to meet in Charlottetown in early September, the coalition government in Canada asked to send a delegation. Through Macdonald's leadership the Canadian delegation was able to have discussion of Maritime union shelved in favour of a debate on the proposal for a broader federal union. After ten days of talks the delegates agreed to continue the following month in Quebec City, and from the Quebec conference emerged a series of resolutions that were to form the core of the Constitution Act. Following approval of the Quebec resolutions by the governments of Nova Scotia, New Brunswick, and Canada, a final conference was held in London in December 1866, in which the details of the new legislation were worked out with the active participation of the British government.

The Constitution Act, it must be stressed, was not a declaration of Canadian independence; it was a British law passed by the Parliament of the United Kingdom. Canadians at the time did not seriously consider any alternative to remaining a colony within the British Empire, and did not chafe at the bonds of colonial administration. Indeed, David Smith notes that whereas imperial practices and modes of thought were expelled from the American system by the Revolution, in the Canadian case they were internalized in the new federal system.[28] The Constitution Act simply regrouped three British North American colonies into a single colony and provided means for the eventual absorption of other British colonial possessions in North America into the new Canadian colony. Independence was to evolve more slowly. While Canada's independence was acknowledged by the Balfour Declaration of 1926 and formally recognized by Britain in the 1931 Statute of Westminster, it was not until 1946 that the Canadian Citizenship Act was passed, 1949 that the Supreme Court of Canada became the final court of appeal, 1950 that the first Canadian governor general was appointed, 1965 that Canada had its own flag, and 1982 that the country's Constitution was patriated from Great Britain.

There was no ringing rhetoric in the Constitution Act, nothing analogous to the American Declaration of Independence—"We hold these truths to be self-evident, that all men are created equal, that they are endowed by their Creator with certain unalienable Rights, that among these are Life, Liberty and the pursuit of Happiness"—or the opening words of the American Constitution—"We the People of the United States, in Order to form a more perfect Union, establish Justice, insure domestic Tranquility, provide for the common Defence, promote the general Welfare, and secure the Blessings of Liberty to ourselves and our Posterity, do ordain and establish this Constitution for the United States of America." The Constitution Act began in a far more prosaic fashion: "Whereas the Provinces of Canada, Nova Scotia, and New Brunswick, have expressed their desire to be federally united into one Dominion under the Crown of the United Kingdom of Great Britain and Ireland, with a Constitution similar in principle to that of the United Kingdom: And whereas such a Union would conduce to the welfare of the Provinces and promote the interests of the British Empire: And whereas...." This is not the sort of phrase that one shouts from the barricades—"We will not conduce!"—or that school children memorize to give them a sense of their constitutional heritage. As Eric Nicol and Peter Whalley note, "in the entire history of literate man, no people has ever found endearing a document that began with 'Whereas.'"[29] As we will observe in Chapter 8, Canadians have been no more successful recently in attaching rhetorical flourishes to their constitutional documents than they were in 1867.

Confederation was not wrested from the unwilling hands of the British government. At that time colonial sentiment was weak in Britain; the consensus was that colonies were costing more than they were worth and should be encouraged to carry their own weight. Indeed, the British government played an important role in bringing about Confederation by closing off any alternative solution to the economic problems faced by the Maritime colonies. (The British government played essentially the same role in the negotiations leading to Newfoundland's entry into Confederation in 1949.) Britain was unwilling to negotiate a reciprocity agreement on their behalf with the United States that did not include Canada, and would not discuss Maritime union apart from some broader union with Canada. Thus Canadians were assuming responsibilities that Britain was only too willing to shed. The Canadian negotiators who came to London in December 1866 met with something between general indifference and active assistance, but not opposition. On March 1, 1867, a *Times of London* editorial stated that "we look to Confederation as the means of relieving this country from much expense and much embarrassment."[30] The contrast with the American Revolution in the 1770s could not be more stark.

Lastly, the Constitution Act did not provide a complete constitutional framework for the Canadian state; a large part remained unwritten, covered only by the act's opening phrase, "with a Constitution similar in principle to that of the United Kingdom." In practice this meant that Canada adopted British parliamentary institutions and conventions of responsible government, that provinces other than Quebec adopted British common law, and that Canadians were able to draw upon centuries of British parliamentary and democratic tradition. As former prime minister John Diefenbaker so nicely put it, "the warp and woof of our constitution are the golden threads of our British heritage."[31] Those threads were to become badly strained after Diefenbaker's time when the British heritage seemed less and less relevant to contemporary challenges to the country's constitutional framework.

What Did Happen in 1867: The Creation of a Federal State

The Constitution Act of 1867 divided the former colony of Canada into Quebec and Ontario, and then combined the two with Nova Scotia and New Brunswick in a single British colony, the Dominion of Canada. Section 146 also provided for the eventual entry of Newfoundland, Prince Edward Island, British Columbia, Rupert's Land, and the North-West Territories into the Dominion. The act spelled out Canada's colonial relationship in a detailed description of the powers of Britain's representative in Canada, the governor general. In general, the act was primarily concerned with those aspects of Canadian government that were not similar in principle to the United Kingdom, including the division of legislative powers and fiscal resources between the federal and provincial governments, the limited recognition of linguistic duality, and the protection of educational rights under specified conditions. New national legislative institutions—the House of Commons and the Senate—were created, and their methods of election and appointment were described. A national judicial system was created, and the financial obligations of the federal government to the provinces were described. Section 145 called for an immediate start to the construction of the Intercolonial Railway linking the St. Lawrence Valley to Halifax.

The key sections of the act were those that put into place a federal system of government. It is here that the act drew from American constitutional innovations and, to a degree, from the bifurcated administrative experience of the Province of Canada. It is here also that we find the most dramatic departure from British constitutional principles. Those principles were not fully rejected, but nor was federalism fully embraced. The Constitution Act was thus an awkward marriage of parliamentary institutions and federalism principles, a marriage that has survived with some difficulty and that has created a very distinctive Canadian style of intergovernmental relations.

The most fundamental characteristic of federal systems of government is that they divide the sovereign powers of the state between two orders or levels of government, both of which govern the same people and the same territory. As David Smith points out, the Sovereign, or Crown, not only "eludes the control of any single national institution,"[32] but also eludes the control of any one order of government. Thus, for example, the residents of Manitoba come under the jurisdiction of both the Parliament of Canada and the Legislative Assembly of Manitoba, and also elect representatives to both assemblies. In this context it is particularly important to stress that the federal government—the Government of Canada—is chosen by the people of Canada and not by the provincial governments or legislatures, and its impact on the Canadian people is not mediated by the provincial governments. In theory, each level of government in a federal state should have at least one area in which it is sovereign and in which the other level of government cannot legislate. There must also be a written agreement specifying the federal division of powers, one that cannot be unilaterally altered by either level of government. In Canada's case, this agreement is embedded within the Constitution Act of 1867 and, as we will see shortly, particularly within Sections 91 and 92 of that act. Finally, there must be some means of settling disputes that might arise over the meaning and interpretation of the federal agreement. In Canada this was provided first by a British institution—the Judicial Committee of the Privy Council—and then after 1949 by the Supreme Court of Canada. Whether either mechanism has been impartial is a matter of ongoing and contentious debate within the legal and political science communities.[33]

Of course, federalism involves more than the constitutional division of powers. Federal systems of government enhance citizen participation by providing more than one level of elected and responsible government. By encouraging competition among governments, federalism both limits the power of any one government and may, under some conditions, increase the power of the electorate. The competition among governments is also a healthy source of innovation and experimentation, and federalism enables public policies to be more finely tuned to the policy preferences of territorial communities. As a relatively decentralized form of government, federalism is seen as a means by which power is moved closer to the people and thus a means by which democracy is enhanced. However, and underlying many of these attributes, we still come back to the division of powers as the defining characteristic of federalism.

The federal division of powers in Canada was initially set forth in a number of sections within the 1867 Constitution Act of which the most important were Section 91, specifying the powers of Parliament, and Section 92, specifying those of the provincial legislatures. In a very general sense, the two sections gave Parliament control over national economic management including public debt, the regulation of trade and commerce, legal tender, and banking. These provisions, along with those relating to the federal acquisition of provincial debt and the prohibition of internal tariff barriers to trade,[34] put into place the promised economic union. The two sections also gave the provincial legislatures control over matters "of a merely local or private Nature in the Province." This division of powers was designed to free the new federal government from the sectarian

Municipal Governments and Federalism

People often refer to the *three* levels or "orders" of Canadian federalism—the *national* or *federal* government in Ottawa, *provincial* governments, and *local* or *municipal* governments in the cities and towns of Canada. However, municipal governments are not part of the federal system per se; the division of powers embedded in the Constitution Act of 1867 relates only to the national and provincial governments. Municipal governments, and indeed the territorial governments in the Yukon and Northwest Territories, are creatures of the provincial and federal governments respectively. They exercise delegated powers that are not constitutionally entrenched or defined, and that could, at least hypothetically, be diminished or withdrawn at the whim of the provinces (in the case of municipal governments) or Ottawa (in the case of territorial governments in the North). Nor do territorial or municipal governments have any formal status in the constitutional amending formula.

The distinction between delegated and constitutionally entrenched powers has come to play a very important role in deliberations over the character and form of aboriginal self-government. Some people envision aboriginal governments as being analogous to municipal governments, exercising a similar range of delegated powers. Others, and particularly those within the aboriginal communities, see aboriginal governments as being analogous to provincial governments, exercising a similar range of constitutionally entrenched powers. Still others see aboriginal governments as being analogous to national governments, exercising a broad range of sovereign powers and dealing on a government-to-government basis with other political communities in Canada.

conflict that had crippled the Union government while at the same time providing it with the economic leverage thought to be essential for territorial expansion. It was hoped that by assigning the major areas of French–English conflict to the jurisdiction of the provinces, Ottawa would be free to meet the challenges of national economic development.

Areas of sectarian conflict included "property and civil rights," which Section 92 assigned to the provinces, and education, which Section 93 also assigned to the provinces, albeit with important constraints imposed to protect the educational interests of the Protestant minority in Quebec. Section 95 gave Ottawa and the provinces concurrent jurisdiction—both could be legislatively active—over agriculture and immigration with the proviso that should provincial legislation be "repugnant to any Act of the

Parliament of Canada," the federal legislation would be paramount. Section 109 assigned "all lands, mines, minerals and royalties belonging to the several provinces" to the provinces. It is this section, along with article 5 in Section 92 ("the management and sale of the Public Lands belonging to the Province, and of the timber and wood thereon"), that established provincial ownership of natural resources, a constitutional principle that has played an important decentralizing role in the evolution of the Canadian federal state.

The federal division of powers is linked in theory and application to the anti-majoritarian impulse of federalism. The division of powers places some matters beyond the reach of the national Parliament and thus beyond the reach of the national majority. In the Canadian case, the division of powers was the means used to reconcile Canada West's demand for and Canada East's opposition to representation by population. The terms of that reconciliation can be illustrated by the treatment of education in the Constitution Act of 1867. By assigning education to provincial jurisdiction, the act put Quebec's educational system beyond the legislative reach, through Parliament, of a Canadian majority that was both anglophone and Protestant. This in turn meant that "rep by pop" *within Parliament* was acceptable to French Canadians because Parliament, with its anglophone Protestant majority, was constitutionally prohibited from infringing upon the provincial control of education. "Rep by pop" *within Quebec* was also acceptable as Catholic francophones made up a clear majority of the Quebec population, and were thus assured of political control in Quebec's National Assembly. This federal protection of local control was of similar appeal outside Quebec, and particularly to the reform tradition in Ontario. Thus to the extent that minority concerns were assigned to provincial jurisdiction, federalism blunted the inherent danger that majority rule poses to minority interests. Here W.L. Morton has placed the Confederation agreement in a more positive context by noting that "only in the provinces was the electorate homogeneous enough to allow the majoritarian principle to work without reserve."[35] It is "reserve" that federalism provides.

It should be stressed, however, that the federal division of powers protects only certain kinds of minority interests under certain conditions. It works only if *national minorities* are also *provincial majorities*, as was and is the case for francophones living within Quebec. The division of powers per se provides no protection for minority group members who live outside the province in which their group is a majority, such as francophones living outside Quebec or anglophones in Quebec. To the extent that the Constitution Act did provide protection of minorities embedded within provincial majorities, it did so through means other than the division of powers and it did so primarily for the anglophone, Protestant minority in Quebec; francophone minorities outside Quebec did not, at least initially, receive similar protection. As noted above, Section 93 provided protection for

Protestant schools in Quebec. Section 133 provided for the use of both French and English in the Quebec legislature and courts, and for the representation of the English minority in both the Canadian Senate and the Quebec National Assembly.

At the time of Confederation provincial autonomy for Quebec was seen as the key safeguard for French-Canadian interests, and little constitutional attention was paid to francophone minorities in other provinces. It was only after Confederation that these minorities were brought to the attention of Quebec by "the harassment of the Metis in the North-West, the dismantling of Catholic separate school systems in New Brunswick, Prince Edward Island and the prairie provinces, the disestablishment of the French language on the prairies, [and] the attempt to eliminate French from Ontario schools."[36] Even then, and as will be discussed in greater detail in Chapter 4, the *federal* response was inadequate. As Smith notes, "because Canada's principal minority is concentrated in one province (Quebec), the majoritarian principle has prevailed elsewhere, notwithstanding short, sharp but ultimately futile resistance from numerically small and declining French Catholic minorities."[37] The general point is that although federal systems are often designed to accommodate cultural, linguistic, religious, or geographic cleavages that are too deep or broad to be bridged by unitary systems of government, they are best able to handle cleavages that can be territorially delineated. In a constitutional sense, federal systems differentiate among political communities that can be demarcated by physical lines on a map. It is when the relevant communities cannot be so neatly separated, when they spill across geographical boundaries as linguistic communities do in Canada, that federal systems of government become more contentious and less effective means of minority protection.

The protection of minority interests through the federal division of powers is limited in a second way: it does not extend to minorities, even those who constitute provincial majorities, when minority interests differ sharply from those of the majority in matters of *national jurisdiction*. For example, and as discussed in Chapter 9, French Canadians during the First and Second World Wars opposed the introduction of military conscription for overseas service, a policy that their English-Canadian compatriots strongly supported. In this case jurisdiction resided with Parliament and thus the division of powers per se failed to provide any shelter for French-Canadian interests. A second example stems from the "energy wars" of the late 1970s and early 1980s, when Ottawa pursued a package of energy programs and policies strongly opposed by the Alberta government. Even though Alberta retained constitutional ownership of its resources, the federal government had sufficient leverage within its own legislative domain to pass the National Energy Program through Parliament. Alberta's MPs, all of whom sat on the opposition benches, were simply outgunned. The point to be emphasized is that well-designed federal states cannot rely exclusively on the division of powers for the protection of minority interests; other forms of protection must be built into the representational character and procedural norms of national political institutions. Hence, for example, the role played by upper chambers—the Senates in Australia, Canada, and the United States, the Bundesrat in Germany—in providing territorial representation.

Even when the primary means of protection is the constitutional division of powers, that division is seldom watertight. Take, for example, contemporary jurisdictional control of post-secondary education, a matter of particular concern for students and instructors. Initially, the issue may seem quite clear; Section 93 of the Constitution Act assigns education to the provinces. However, although the federal government cannot legislate in the educational field, there are no constitutional limitations on its capacity to spend. In the last thirty years the federal government has used its "spending power" to invade a number of jurisdictional domains reserved by the Constitution for the provinces, action precipitated by a structural imbalance in Canadian fiscal federalism. (Over much of the past 125 years, Ottawa's fiscal resources have exceeded its programmatic responsibilities, whereas just the opposite situation has prevailed in the provinces.) In this case, then, we find that since the early 1960s Ottawa has been paying approximately half the cost of post-secondary education provided through provincial institutions. Of the approximately $55 billion that Canadian governments spend annually on education, $13 billion comes from the federal government, including $4 billion in tax transfers to the provinces.[38] The research activities of Canadian academics are largely funded by Ottawa through such agencies as the Canada Council, the Medical Research Council, the National Research Council, and the Social Sciences and Humanities Research Council, an annual contribution that amounts to more than $500 million. To the extent that universities can be seen as providing *manpower training* rather than *education*, the constitutional door is further opened for direct involvement by the federal government. (It is interesting to note in this context that federal strategy papers refer to "learning" rather than "education" in order to avoid provincial sensitivities.[39]) Finally, both levels of government provide financial support for students, although perhaps not to the degree that readers might wish.

Thus contemporary federalism in most federal states is far more complex than one would suspect from an inspection of constitutional documents. In the United States, the Supreme Court has removed virtually all division of powers constraints on the national government,[40] and in Canada there are few policy areas today that in practice come under the exclusive control of either level of government. As the report of the Beaudoin-Dobbie Special Joint Committee observed:

> *The reality of our world, the central fact of which account must be taken,*
> *in the design of federalism and in the fate of nations, is not independence*

but interdependence. The complexity and scale of modern problems of public policy no longer permit, if they ever did, a "water-tight" division of powers.[41]

It is not surprising, incidentally, that the federal spending power has been a matter of considerable constitutional concern for provincial governments. This concern stems in part from Ottawa's capacity to distort provincial spending priorities by offering matching funds and in part from the justifiable fear that Ottawa may create expensive, shared-cost programs and then reduce its level of financial support, leaving provinces holding the bag. This fear has been amplified in the 1990s as Ottawa scrambles for ways to curb the federal deficit. Thus recent proposals for constitutional change have included restrictions on the federal spending power. The 1987 Meech Lake Accord, for example, would have enabled provinces to opt out of new federal programs in areas of exclusive provincial jurisdiction and to receive full financial compensation, provided that they initiated a provincial program "compatible with the national objectives" of the federal program. The 1992 Charlottetown Accord included a similar provision.

Our discussion of the federal division of powers should also note that some matters are not explicitly assigned by the Constitution to either level of government. The 1867 Constitution Act, for example, did not mention telecommunications or the disposal of nuclear wastes, lapses for which the politicians of the day can surely be excused. In Canada it is often argued that such *residual powers* are assigned to Parliament by the opening clause of Section 91: "It shall be lawful for the Queen, by and with the advice and consent of the Senate and House of Commons, to make laws for the peace, order, and good government of Canada, in relation to all matters not coming within the classes of subjects by this Act assigned exclusively to the Legislatures of the Provinces." Over time, however, the courts have interpreted the "peace, order, and good government" clause somewhat narrowly, restricting its application to emergency conditions or situations in which a clear national interest can be demonstrated. At the same time, the property and civil rights clause in Section 92 has been broadly interpreted so as to verge upon being a residual powers clause. Other clauses in Sections 91 and 92 can also be used to lodge powers that were not specified in the original constitutional document. For instance, consumer protection, which did not weigh heavily in the Confederation debates, can be seen as falling under Parliament's responsibility for trade and commerce or under the responsibility of provincial legislatures for property and civil rights.

As mentioned at the outset of this discussion, the 1867 Constitution Act sought to combine federal and parliamentary forms of government. One of the consequences of this uneasy marriage is that federalism acts as a constraint on the supremacy of Parliament. In the Westminster model of parliamentary government, Parliament—which in the British case includes the House of Commons, the House of Lords, and the Crown—is supreme:

"there is no higher legislative authority; no court can declare Acts of Parliament to be invalid; there is no limit to Parliament's sphere of legislation; and no Parliament can legally bind its successor, or be bound by its predecessor."[42] In Canada, however, parliamentary supremacy has been limited in a number of ways. Until the passage of the Statute of Westminster in 1931, Canada remained a British colony and thus the supremacy of the Canadian Parliament was in theory limited by Britain, although in practice this limitation was of little consequence. More importantly, the doctrine of parliamentary supremacy does not enable the Parliament of Canada to encroach legislatively upon provincial fields of jurisdiction. (As we have just seen, fiscal encroachment is another matter.) Within those fields, parliamentary supremacy rests with the provincial legislative assemblies. Finally and more recently, the Charter of Rights and Freedoms further restricts the supremacy of both Parliament and the provincial legislatures. The Charter permits court challenges to the constitutionality of Acts of Parliament (or acts passed by provincial legislatures) on grounds other than an alleged transgression of the federal division of powers. With respect to rights specified within the Charter, Parliament and the provincial legislatures are not supreme. At the same time, Section 1 of the Charter guarantees the rights and freedoms set forth within it "subject only to such reasonable limits prescribed by law as can be demonstrably justified in a free and democratic society." This clause resurrects the principle of parliamentary supremacy in that legislative action is central to any such demonstrable justification. Moreover, the "notwithstanding" provision of Section 33 enables legislatures to override some Charter rights for up to a five-year (renewable) period: "Parliament or the legislature of a province may expressly declare in an Act of Parliament or of the legislature, as the case may be, that the Act or a provision thereof shall operate notwithstanding a provision included in Section 2 or Sections 7 to 15 of this Charter."

The above discussion has provided a glimpse, but no more than a glimpse, of federal dynamics in Canada. As the remaining chapters of this text will demonstrate, federalism has had and continues to have a pervasive influence on Canadian politics, and it is difficult to understand virtually any contemporary issue without probing its federal aspects. At this point, however, it is useful to conclude by reiterating how federalism provided a solution to the perplexing problems politicians faced in the 1860s. Many of the factors that led to Confederation—political deadlock in the united Canadas, the American threat, economic distress, and the national dream—did not dictate a *federal* constitution. Federalism was dictated by the conflict over representation by population, by a widespread desire to protect local autonomy, and by the need to create a strong national government without mangling the cultural and regional components of the new Canadian state. Federalism permitted "rep by pop" while giving the French Catholic minority, or at least those living in Quebec, constitutional protection from the national English Protestant majority. It created a strong federal government while maintaining local autonomy in a number of important jurisdictional domains, and it laid the foundations for a new Canadian nationality without doing violence to the regional and cultural roots of the Canadian population. This was possible because of the federal division of powers and the constraint it imposed on the majoritarian impulse of national parliamentary institutions. While the founding fathers adopted the Westminster parliamentary model from Great Britain, they tempered its application by adopting and adapting federal principles originating in the United States.

THE CONFEDERATION LEGACY

In any country's history there are *formative events* that have an importance reaching far beyond their time and place.[43] Confederation was such an event, setting in place institutions that to this day shape the unfolding of national political life. Confederation also plays an important role in debates over the direction Canada should take in the years ahead, for we all try to anchor our claims and visions in the past, portraying them as the inevitable outcome of historical forces set in motion by older and, if our thinking concurs, wiser leaders. As Krasner has explained, there is a great deal of institutional inertia within the existing state system: "historical developments are path dependent; once certain choices are made, they constrain future possibilities."[44] It is therefore useful to examine the meaning of Confederation, to go beyond the terms of the 1867 Constitution Act to their intent. What vision guided the politicians of the 1860s? What aspirations were they trying to achieve through such dry and convoluted constitutional language? Here we must recognize, however, that most political events are ambiguous, open to widely divergent interpretations, and Confederation is no exception. The search for meaning is hobbled by a lack of consensus among the original participants, by an ambiguous historical record, and by a human tendency to bend the historical record to fit the political needs of today.

Evidence that the intent of Confederation was to create a federal system characterized by a strong central government and relatively subordinate provincial governments is provided by the terms of the Constitution Act and the argumentation on their behalf by Macdonald. Here it must be remembered that the Confederation agreement was reached against the tragic backdrop of the American Civil War. Although Canadians were prepared to adopt a federal system, and indeed had little choice in the matter, they were not prepared to adopt the specifics of an American model that had failed to prevent the calamity of civil war. Thus we find repeated references to the failure of American federalism and the lessons to be learned from that failure. At the 1864 Quebec conference Macdonald argued that "we must have a strong Central Government with all authority except what is given to the local governments in each Province, and avoid the errors of the American constitution."[45] The point where the American Constitution broke down, Macdonald argued, was in the assignment of residual powers to the states and to the people rather than to the national government. The "peace, order, and good government" clause was the product of Macdonald's concern.

To Canadians like Macdonald, the principal weakness of the American system was that the states had been given too much power; the lesson for Canada was that the federal government should be strengthened vis-à-vis the provinces. The architects of Confederation set out to achieve that end through a number of provisions in the 1867 Constitution Act:

- The act assigned to Parliament what were thought to be the "great subjects of legislation"; the provincial legislatures were restricted primarily to matters of a "merely local or private nature."

- Parliament was given the power to raise money by "any Mode or System of Taxation" while the provincial legislatures were restricted to direct taxation and federal subsidies.

- The act gave Parliament paramountcy in areas of concurrent jurisdiction.

- Parliament was given the declaratory power to make laws in relation to "such works as, although wholly situate within the province, are before or after their execution declared by the Parliament of Canada to be for the general advantage of Canada or for the advantage of two or more provinces."

- The act gave Parliament the power to make criminal law, with a national Criminal Code being the consequence, and gave the federal government the power to appoint all superior court justices.

- The federal government was given the power to appoint lieutenant governors who were to serve as a national check on the provincial governments, just as the governor general was to serve as an imperial check on the federal government of Canada. The lieutenant governor had the power to withhold assent from provincial legislation, and to reserve such legislation for acceptance or rejection by the federal government.

- Senators were to be appointed by the federal government and not by the provinces.

- The act gave Parliament the power to disallow provincial legislation—to prevent it from coming into effect—even when such legislation was wholly within the provincial legislative domain.

As Donald Smiley explains, "in terms of both the provisions of the Act and the expectations of those who framed it, the provinces were to be in precisely the same constitutional relationship to the federal government as the individual colonies of British North America had been to the Imperial authorities."[46] Indeed, the federal government's power to intervene in the constitutional domain of the provincial legislatures was so extensive that some federal scholars have been reluctant to describe the Constitution Act of 1867 as a federal document, preferring instead the term "quasi-federal."[47]

This view of Confederation has not gone unchallenged. After examining the historical record in Ontario, Paul Romney rejects the view that the 1867 act was, on balance, a centralist document:

> The centralist account of Confederation and the provincial rights controversy was not history but a vast fabric of myth. In reality the BNA Act had given force to that broad local autonomy which Upper Canadian Reformers had always claimed as a matter of constitutional right.[48]

A.I. Silver presents similar and persuasive evidence that French Canadians did not see Confederation "as a national unification transforming a scattered collection of colonies into a single people under a strong national government."[49] Rather, Confederation was endorsed because it was seen to protect the autonomy and separateness of Quebec. Silver points out that the assignment of issues of a "merely local or private matter" to the provinces was interpreted in Quebec as a recognition of, and not a diminution of, provincial autonomy. The mid-1860s attitude of the French-Canadian press toward Confederation can be encapsulated by the following editorial statement appearing in Le Courier de St-Hyacinthe: "We want a confederation in which the federal principle will be applied in its fullest sense—one which will give the central power control over only general questions in no way affecting the interests of each separate section, while leaving to the local legislatures everything which concerns our particular interests."[50] Confederation was supported, then, because it would free Quebec from Upper Canada, and give French Canadians autonomous control over their local affairs. As E.-P. Taché explained in 1864, the federal government would have enough power "to do away with some of the internal hindrances to trade, and to unite the Provinces for mutual defence," but it would be the provinces to which people would look for the protection of their liberty, rights, and privileges.[51]

Thus Romney and Silver argue that at the time of Confederation, Macdonald's vision was not characteristic of Ontario or French Canada respectively. More recently, *compact theories* have emerged to provide historical support for bicultural and province-centred visions of the Canadian federal state. Bicultural compact theorists do not dispute the letter of the Constitution Act, but focus instead on its spirit. Confederation, they suggest, was the result of an implicit but nonetheless very real bicultural compact between the French and English communities. Without that compact Confederation would not have occurred, and thus the meaning of Confederation is revealed more by the bicultural compact than by the letter of the Constitution Act. While there may admittedly be little evidence for the compact theory in the act itself, evidence can be found in subsequent legislation such as the 1869 Act for the Temporary Government of Rupert's Land, the Manitoba Act of 1870, and the North-West Territories Act of 1875.[52]

Bicultural compact theories emerged in Quebec during the 1930s and came to play a significant role in debates on the place of Quebec in Canada, and on the status of the French language outside Quebec. They have also been highly contentious, with critics charging that they distort, if not falsify, the historical record. One of the most outspoken critics has been historian Donald Creighton, who has concluded that the evidence against the two-nation theory of Confederation is overwhelming:

> It is obvious that the last thing the Fathers of Confederation wanted to do was to perpetuate duality; they hoped, through confederation, to escape from it entirely.... There was nothing in ... the British North America Act which remotely approached a general declaration of principle that Canada was to be a bilingual or bicultural nation.[53]

Nor have critics of the bicultural compact been confined to English Canada. In its background paper for the 1980 sovereignty-association referendum, the Parti Québécois government declared:

> Under the terms of the British North America Act, Quebec is not the homeland of a nation, but merely a province among the others.... Nowhere in the Act is there a talk of an alliance between two founding peoples, or of a pact between two nations.[54]

Compact theories have also been tied to classical models of federalism in which federal constitutions are seen as legal contracts. If the Constitution Act is seen as a contract, one can ask whom the contract was between or among. Since the federal government did not exist prior to 1867, it can be argued that the contract was among the provinces and that the provincial governments are its legitimate custodians. In this view there is no acknowledgment of a subordinate role for the provincial legislatures, as the letter of the Constitution Act might suggest. As Garth Stevenson points out, the lack of public ratification of the Confederation agreement has strengthened compact interpretations. Confederation, after all, was a governmental rather than a popular product, portrayed at the time as a treaty among governments.[55] As the only governments in existence at the time were the provincial governments, the compact interpretation gains weight.

If it remains a matter of debate whether the provinces created Confederation, there is no doubt that Confederation cemented into place provincial communities that have dominated the country's political landscape since that time. As David Smith explains in his discussion of Canada's imperial past, the initial strength of the provinces came not from their constitutional powers per se, but from their integrity as political communities:

> The provinces were the true beneficiaries of imperialism, for although Canada's federation was conceived as a highly centralized form of government, the provinces inherited cohesive societies which predated Confederation and monarchical forms of government to give those societies institutional expression. Unlike the nation, the provinces have never suffered an identity problem.[56]

Over time, the provinces used their governments and constitutional resources to strengthen the underlying communities and thus strengthen the federal character of the Canadian state and society.[57]

Of course, the boundaries of the Canadian state have greatly expanded since 1867. In 1870 Manitoba entered Confederation, and both the North-West Territories and Rupert's Land were acquired by Canada. On the promise of a transcontinental railway, British Columbia joined in 1871, as did Prince Edward Island two years later in the wake of a poor harvest, economic recession, and railway debt. In 1880 Canada acquired the Arctic islands, and in 1905 Alberta and Saskatchewan became the eighth and ninth provinces. In 1912 Ontario and Quebec nearly doubled in size as their boundaries were expanded to the north, and in 1949 Newfoundland became Canada's tenth province. The country has also changed in countless other ways. Our population has increased from just over three million at the time of Confederation to more than 27 million at the time of the 1991 census. No longer a frontier society, Canada has become a modern industrialized state. No longer rural and agrarian, Canadians live in a highly urbanized and technologically dependent society.

Yet these massive changes have not rendered Confederation irrelevant for an understanding of contemporary politics. The Constitution Act of 1867 continues to provide the federal skeleton for the Canadian state, and the political institutions it put into place continue to provide the arenas within which most of our political life occurs. While Confederation did not provide the script for the evolution of national politics, it set the stage, provided the institutional props, and supplied many of the dramatic themes. To an extent that the problems of the 1860s are still with us one might be tempted to conclude that Confederation was a failure, but such a conclusion would be too harsh. One must remember that the 1867 agreement created a political community that has experienced quite remarkable stability, domestic peace, and material prosperity. Moreover, the problems that Canadians confronted in the 1860s can never be eliminated; at best they can be moderated and contained, their burden on the community lightened, but not removed. As British Prime Minister James Callaghan said in 1978, you can never reach the promised land, but only march toward it. The fact that we are still here as a country to grapple with the same problems that faced the architects of Confederation pays no small compliment to their work.

SUGGESTED READINGS

1. Janet Ajzenstat, *The Political Thought of Lord Durham* (Kingston and Montreal: McGill-Queen's University Press, 1988).

2. Michel Brunet, "The Historical Background of Quebec's Challenge to Canadian Unity," in Dale C. Thompson, ed., *Quebec Society and Politics* (Toronto: McClelland and Stewart, 1973), pp. 39–51.

3. For a discussion of the compact theory, see Ramsay Cook, *Canada and the French Canadian Question* (Toronto: Macmillan, 1976). For an illustration of the historical debate on the compact theory, see Ralph Heintzman, "The Spirit of Confederation: Professor Creighton, Biculturalism, and the Use of History," *Canadian Historical Review* (September 1971), pp. 245–75, and D.J. Hall, "The Spirit of Confederation: Ralph Heintzman, Professor Creighton, and the Bicultural Compact Theory," *Journal of Canadian Studies* (November 1974), pp. 24–43.

4. For a discussion of Nova Scotia's opposition to Confederation, see Colin D. Howell, "Nova Scotia's Protest Tradition and the Search for a Meaningful Federalism," in David Jay Bercuson, ed., *Canada and the Burden of Unity* (Toronto: Macmillan, 1977), pp. 169–91.

5. Rod Preece, "The Political Wisdom of Sir John A. Macdonald," *Canadian Journal of Political Science*, 17:3 (September 1984), pp. 459–86.

6. G.A. Rawlyk and Doug Brown, "The Historical Framework of the Maritimes and Confederation," in G.A. Rawlyk, ed., *The Atlantic Provinces and the Problems of Confederation* (Breakwater Press, 1979), pp. 1–47.

7. A.I. Silver, *The French-Canadian Idea of Confederation, 1864–1900* (Toronto: University of Toronto Press, 1982).

8. Jennifer Smith, "Canadian Confederation and the Influence of American Federalism," *Canadian Journal of Political Science*, 21:3 (September 1988), pp. 443–64.

9. Garth Stevenson, *Unfulfilled Union: Canadian Federalism and National Unity*, 3rd ed. (Toronto: Gage, 1989).

10. Peter B. Waite, *The Life and Times of Confederation* (Toronto: University of Toronto Press, 1962); and *The Confederation Debates in the Province of Canada, 1865* (Toronto: McClelland and Stewart, 1963).

STUDY QUESTIONS

1. In light of the limited defence provided by the division of powers for francophones living outside Quebec, how would you assess the protection provided by the division of powers for anglophones living inside Quebec? In what ways are the two situations analogous? In what ways are they not?

2. If your province was entering Confederation today, would your provincial government seek a different division of powers? If so, what would be the difference? What about you personally? Would you favour a different division of powers, and if so, what would the differences be?

3. Take a careful look at the federal division of powers outlined in Sections 91 and 92 of the Constitution Act, 1867. Given that division, which level of government do you think should have primary responsibility in the following fields: language training for immigrants, the disposal of nuclear wastes, the regulation of professional sports, consumer protection, lotteries, medicare, and air pollution control? In each case, to what extent does the formal division of powers provide a useful practical guide?

4. What relevance, if any, does federalism have for aboriginal peoples? For women? For visible minorities? Is their political leverage enhanced, reduced, or unaffected by the federal character of the Canadian state?

NOTES

1. Donald Creighton, *The Passionate Observer: Selected Writings* (Toronto: McClelland and Stewart, 1980), p. 19.

2. Ibid., p. 51.

3. For example, see W.L. Morton, *The Critical Years: The Union of British North America, 1857–1873* (Toronto: McClelland and Stewart, 1964).

4. Hon. Gérald Beaudoin, Senator, and Dorothy Dobbie, MP, *A Renewed Canada*, Report of the Special Joint Committee of the Senate and House of Commons (Ottawa: February 28, 1992), p. 6.

5. Janet Ajzenstat, *The Political Thought of Lord Durham* (Kingston and Montreal: McGill-Queen's University Press, 1988).

6. Cited in Sheila McLeod Arnopoulos and Dominique Clift, *The English Fact in Quebec* (Montreal: McGill-Queen's University Press, 1980), pp. 56–57.

7. J.M.S. Careless, *Canada: A Story of Challenge*, rev. ed. (Toronto: Macmillan, 1963), p. 198.

8. *The Globe* (Toronto), December 27, 1861.

9. Garth Stevenson, *Unfulfilled Union: Canadian Federalism and National Unity*, 3rd ed. (Toronto: Gage, 1989), pp. 22–23.

10. R.W. Winks, *Canada and the United States: The Civil War Years* (Baltimore, 1960), pp. 210–11 and 220–29.

11. Cited in John Murray Gibbon, *Canadian Mosaic* (Toronto: McClelland and Stewart, 1938).

12. William H. Riker, *Federalism: Origin, Operation, Significance* (Boston: Little, Brown, 1964), pp. 12–13.

13. Stevenson, *Unfulfilled Union*, p. 24.

14. S.F. Wise and Robert Craig Brown, *Canada Views the United States: Nineteenth-Century Political Attitudes* (Toronto: Macmillan, 1967), p. 94.

15. Careless, *Canada*, p. 202.

16. John Bartlet Brebner, *North Atlantic Triangle* (Toronto: McClelland and Stewart, reprinted 1966), p. 158.

17. For a discussion of the economic impact of the treaty, see J.L. Granatstein, "Free Trade between Canada and the United States: The Issue That Will Not Go Away," in Denis Stairs and Gilbert R. Winham, Research Coordinators, *The Politics of Canada's Economic Relationship with the United States* (Toronto: University of Toronto Press, 1985), pp. 14ff.

18. G.A. Rawlyk and Doug Brown, "The Historical Framework of the Maritimes and Confederation," in G.A. Rawlyk, ed., *The Atlantic Provinces and the Problems of Confederation* (Breakwater Press, 1979), pp. 7–8.

19. A.I. Silver, *The French-Canadian Idea of Confederation, 1864–1900* (Toronto: University of Toronto Press, 1982), pp. 47–48.

20. David E. Smith, "Empire, Crown and Canadian Federalism," *Canadian Journal of Political Science*, 24:3 (September 1991), p. 457.

21. W.T. Easterbrook and Hugh G.J. Aitken, *Canadian Economic History* (Toronto: Macmillan, 1967), p. 376.

22. Eric Nicol and Peter Whalley, *100 Years of What?* (Toronto: Ryerson, 1966), p. 10.

23. Pierre Berton, *The National Dream: The Great Railway, 1871–1881* (Toronto: McClelland and Stewart, 1970). The "national dream" aspect of Canadian railways played a significant role in the late 1980s political debate over VIA Rail.

24. Jean-Charles Bonenfant, "Quebec and Confederation: Then and Now," in Dale C. Thompson, ed., *Quebec Society and Politics: Views from the Inside* (Toronto: McClelland and Stewart, 1973), p. 55.

25. Cited in J. Bartlet Brebner, *Canada: A Modern History* (Ann Arbor: University of Michigan Press, 1960), p. 277.

26. David E. Smith, "Party Government, Representation and National Integration in Canada," in Peter Aucoin, Research Coordinator, *Party Government and Regional Representation in Canada* (Toronto: University of Toronto Press, 1985), p. 17.

27. It is interesting to note that the Constitution Act did not draw from the Royal Proclamation of 1763, which recognized aboriginal rights. The Royal Proclamation was referenced in the Constitution Act, 1982.

28. Smith, "Empire, Crown and Canadian Federalism," p. 451.

29. Nicol and Whalley, *100 Years*, p. 6.

30. Cited in Brebner, *Canada*, p. 281.

31. John A. Munro, ed., *The Wit and Wisdom of John Diefenbaker* (Edmonton: Hurtig, 1982), p. 30.

32. Smith, "Empire, Crown and Canadian Federalism," p. 460.

33. For a recent summary of that debate, see André Bzdera, "Comparative Analysis of Federal High Courts: A Political Theory of Judicial Review," *Canadian Journal of Political Science*, 26:1 (March 1993), pp. 3–29.

34. Section 121 of the act states: "All Articles of the Growth, Produce, or Manufacture of any one of the Provinces shall, from and after the Union, be admitted free into each of the other Provinces."

35. W.L. Morton, "The Extension of the Franchise in Canada: A Study in Democracy," Canadian Historical Association *Report*, 1943, p. 79.

36. Silver, *The French-Canadian Idea of Confederation*, p. 220.

37. Smith, "Empire, Crown and Canadian Federalism," p. 462.

38. Jennifer Lewington, "Ottawa Seeks Role in Guiding Education," *The Globe and Mail*, April 13, 1993, p. A1.

39. Ibid., p. A5.

40. The abandonment of division of powers constraints began in the late 1930s, and was confirmed in the 1985 decision *Garcia v. San Antonio Metropolitan Transit Authority*.

41. Beaudoin and Dobbie, *A Renewed Canada*, p. 11.

42. R.M. Punnett, *British Government and Politics*, 4th ed. (London: Heinemann, 1980), p. 173.

43. The concept comes from Seymour Martin Lipset, *The First New Nation* (New York: Basic Books, 1963), p. 7.

44. Stephen D. Krasner, "Sovereignty: An Institutional Perspective," *Comparative Political Studies*, 21:1 (April 1988), p. 67.

45. Cited in Robert A. MacKay, *The Unreformed Senate of Canada* (Toronto: McClelland and Stewart, 1963), p. 35.

46. Donald V. Smiley, *The Canadian Political Nationality* (Toronto: Methuen, 1967), pp. 4–5.

47. K.C. Wheare, *Federal Government* (London: Oxford University Press, 1953), p. 19.

48. Paul Romney, "The Nature and Scope of Provincial Autonomy: Oliver Mowat, the Quebec Resolutions and the Construction of the British North America Act," *Canadian Journal of Political Science*, 25:1 (March 1992), p. 28.

49. Silver, *The French-Canadian Idea of Confederation*, p. 218.

50. Ibid., p. 35.

51. Ibid., pp. 48–49.

52. For an example of this line of thought see Ralph Heintzman, "The Spirit of Confederation: Professor Creighton, Biculturalism, and the Use of History," *Canadian Historical Review* (September 1971), pp. 245–75.

53. Donald Creighton, "John A. Macdonald, Confederation, and the Canadian West," in Donald Swainson, ed., *Historical Essays on the Prairie Provinces* (Toronto: McClelland and Stewart, 1970), p. 62.

54. Government of Quebec, *Quebec–Canada: A New Deal* (Editeur officiel du Québec, 1979), p. 9.

55. Stevenson, *Unfulfilled Union*, pp. 40–41.

56. Smith, "Empire, Crown and Canadian Federalism," p. 471.

57. Alan C. Cairns, "The Governments and Societies of Canadian Federalism," *Canadian Journal of Political Science*, 10 (December 1977), pp. 695–726.

THE INSTITUTIONAL LANDSCAPE

The chapters to come will discuss a number of issues that have shaped the Canadian political landscape. Although each has had its own particular political dynamics and constellation of social forces, all have been played out within a common institutional framework. The intent of the present chapter is to sketch in that framework, to assess its strengths, and more briefly, to explore ways in which it might be reformed.

This institutional framework would be of interest even if it were simply a neutral arena within which various policy issues were played out. It is important to know, for example, where final political authority rests within the federal state and how a public policy initiative emerges eventually as an Act of Parliament. However, we know that institutions are seldom neutral arenas; their configuration and composition have an impact, sometimes subtle and sometimes profound, on how political issues are handled and resolved or, for that matter, if they are handled and resolved. As Schattschneider has argued, politics entails the mobilization of bias; some issues are mobilized into politics and others out.[1] In this respect, institutions influence the mobilization of bias; they tip the scales and load the dice for some policy outcomes and against others. They determine who will be heard and with what effect. Thus it is impossible to understand how issues play out without coming to grips with the institutions through which those issues move.

This institutional analysis has already begun with last chapter's discussion of federalism, which is an essential part of the principled foundation upon which we have built complex institutional structures. Yet if our institutional life has been shaped in a fundamental way by the precepts and principles of federalism, it has also been shaped by the norms and traditions of parliamentary democracy. In this chapter we will discuss those norms and traditions, ones that are deeply embedded in the national political culture. Throughout, our primary focus will be on the institutions of the national government, but the reader should note that for the most part the principles that underlie those institutions find full reflection in provincial institutions. Although the latter are not federal in character, they are based on the same principles of parliamentary democracy. Thus, for example, an understanding of the House of Commons provides a good introduction to, albeit not a full understanding of, provincial legislative assemblies.

THE PRINCIPLED FOUNDATION OF CANADIAN PARLIAMENTARY DEMOCRACY

Chapter 2 mentioned that Canadian constitutional documents are relatively devoid of rhetorical flourishes. This should not suggest, however, that our political life is without a principled foundation. The commitment to both federalism and the conventions of parliamentary democracy have deep roots in the political culture. The opening line of the 1867 Constitution Act calls for "a Constitution similar in principle to that of the United Kingdom," and it is through this phrase that the historical traditions of British parliamentary democracy and a good deal of the formal rules and informal conventions governing parliamentary procedure have been transposed to Canadian soil. The present discussion focuses on four elements: representative democracy, responsible government, party government (and party discipline), and parliamentary sovereignty. In combination, the four provide a good introduction to the principled foundation of Canadian parliamentary democracy.

Representative Democracy

Canadian parliamentary democracy is *representative democracy*. Citizens elect representatives—Members of Parliament—who legislate on their behalf, provide parliamentary support for or opposition to the government of the day, and are answerable to the electorate in periodic elections. We have indirect rather than direct democracy; we elect MPs who in turn vote on our behalf, if not necessarily as we would like, on matters of public policy. The instruments of direct democracy—referenda, plebiscites, and initiatives—are seldom used in federal or provincial politics; the 1949 Newfoundland vote on entry into Confederation, the 1980 sovereignty-association referendum in Quebec, and the 1992 constitutional referendum are very much exceptions to the rule in which the policy preferences of citizens are filtered through elected assemblies. Rather than govern directly, we elect representatives who govern in our place. If we are unhappy with the way in which our representatives interpret our policy preferences, we can retaliate through the ballot, but we cannot directly assume legislative power. The Canadian electorate makes governments, not laws.

The principle of representative democracy also suggests that the composition of political institutions should be broadly reflective of the electorate, that politicians should not only represent their constituents in the sense of a lawyer representing his or her clients, but should also, in the aggregate, constitute a broad cross-section of Canadian society. To a degree this form of representation is provided by the structure of parliamentary institutions. There is regional equality of a sorts in the Senate, each province has a number of seats in the House roughly proportionate to its population, and a francophone majority in most Quebec ridings ensures that francophones within Quebec are well represented in the House. As will be discussed below, the federal cabinet is first and foremost a representative institution. In other respects, however, Parliament is much less representative; MPs and senators (and for that matter provincial legislators)[2] have higher incomes, more formal education, and higher-status occupations than do the citizens they represent. Nowhere is the House of Commons less representative of the Canadian population than in its gender composition. From 1867 through 1984 only 57 of the 3,371 MPs elected (or 1.6 percent) were women, and only 24 women were appointed during that period to the Senate. While more women MPs have been elected in recent years, their share of the total House membership is still small. In the 1980 election only 15 (5 percent) of the elected MPs were women; 28 women (10 percent) were elected in 1984, 40 (13.6 percent) were elected in 1988, and 53 (18 percent) were elected in 1993.

Responsible Government

Canadian parliamentary democracy embraces *responsible government* in that the government of the day holds office only so long as it is able to command majority support in the House of Commons. The House, then, is a *confidence chamber*; parliamentary convention dictates that if the government is unable to command the "confidence" of the House, if it is unable to secure majority support, the prime minister is expected either to tender his or her resignation to the governor general or to call for a general election. In the latter instance, the governor general can either dissolve the House or, much more rarely, refuse the prime minister's call for an election and ask another MP to form a government. Thus while the House can defeat a government, it cannot choose a new one. Conversely, the Senate is not a confidence chamber; the defeat of government legislation in the Senate does not force the government to resign. It should also be noted in this respect that governments have some latitude although not a monopoly in defining what bills should and should not be considered confidence measures. Nevertheless, the essential principle is clear; the right to govern rests upon the government's ability to command a legislative majority in the House of Commons.

As will be discussed below, the conventions of responsible government are linked inextricably to the strength of party discipline and the pervasiveness of partisanship in the House. They also define the relationship of cabinet ministers to the House, to the Crown, and to one another. The cabinet is collectively responsible to the House in that the government must maintain the support of a majority of MPs if it is to continue in office. Cabinet ministers are responsible individually for the conduct of their departments and must answer for their departments on the floor of

Parliamentary Defeat and Responsible Government

The convention requiring the resignation of the government following its defeat in the House is open to interpretation. In February 1968, the minority Liberal government was defeated in the House through carelessness. Prime Minister Pearson, who had earlier announced his impending retirement, was on holidays, and many prominent Liberal MPs were out of Ottawa campaigning for the upcoming leadership convention. When a vote was called in the House, the remaining Liberal MPs were outnumbered and the government was defeated. A strict application of the doctrine of responsible government would have dictated the resignation of the government and the dissolution of Parliament. This would have pitched the leaderless and ill-prepared Liberals into a national campaign against a rejuvenated Progressive Conservative Party and its new leader, Robert Stanfield.

The Liberals argued that the defeat in the House was a mistake, and did not constitute a true loss of confidence. To prove this point, the government introduced a formal vote of confidence in the House the next day. By this time Pearson was back from holidays, all leadership candidates and other absent MPs were in the House, and with the support of the Créditistes, the confidence motion was passed. If the opposition parties had boycotted the House when the vote of confidence was called, if they had insisted that the government had been defeated and that an election should be called, it is unlikely that the Pearson stratagem would have worked. However, Stanfield decided that an election should not be forced at that time. As a consequence, the House continued to sit, the Liberals chose a new leader less than two months later, and the new leader, Pierre Elliott Trudeau, promptly called a general election. The Liberals swept to victory and the Conservatives were to wait eleven years before briefly winning power in June 1979. In politics, nice guys finish last.

This episode could have provided an important precedent that might have loosened the bonds of party discipline for the House. If governments were deemed to fall only on explicit votes of nonconfidence, as has become the parliamentary convention in Great Britain, then government backbenchers would be less compelled to support government legislation "come hell or high water." However, the precedent was not picked up and the importance of party discipline was not eroded.

the House. Although they are not held personally responsible for everything that happens within their department, which might encompass thousands of employees, their resignation is expected in the event of major scandals or blunders.[3] Cabinet ministers are responsible to the Crown, which formally appoints them, and to the prime minister, who in reality appoints them. Finally, cabinet ministers are collectively responsible to one another. Like the Three Musketeers, cabinet ministers operate on the principle of one for all and all for one; cabinet speaks with a single voice, and thus an announcement by any one minister carries the full weight of cabinet. Collective responsibility requires that cabinet proceedings be secret, and ministers are bound to secrecy through their Privy Council oath. Secrecy in turn facilitates both frank discussion within cabinet and a facade of government cohesion for the external political environment; once a cabinet decision has been made all ministers are expected to endorse that decision publicly even though they may have strenuously opposed it within cabinet. Collective responsibility therefore means that the House cannot oust a single minister, but can only defeat the government as a whole; the prime minister alone can appoint or dismiss individual ministers. Collective responsibility in this context is all to the good for opposition parties because it allows them to tar the whole government with a bad ministerial brush.

Party Government and Party Discipline

The conventions of responsible government lead directly to strong and pervasive party discipline in the House of Commons. A cabinet unable to command the loyalty of its supporters in the House would run the risk of losing the confidence of the House and being forced to resign; MPs unwilling to support their cabinet colleagues "come hell or high water" would run the risk of having power fall into the hands of their partisan opponents. Hence the reality of responsible government; if the governing party controls a majority of seats in the House, it will not be defeated on a vote of confidence. The House is unable to change governments without an intervening election, and the government will remain in office until the prime minister decides to go to the people or until its five-year constitutional term expires. Thomas Hockin notes that "ever since the ascendancy of mass, disciplined political parties in Canada was confirmed in 1878, the notion of responsible government, except for its legal accuracy, has grown increasingly unhelpful as a way to understand day-to-day parliamentary activity and its role in policy-making."[4] As David Smith points out, "the achievement of responsible government was the achievement of party government."[5] Once the legislative process has been set in motion by the introduction of a government bill, there is little that government members can do but support the cabinet, and there is little that opposition members can do but delay and obstruct. In this sense, the function of the House and

MPs is to support and criticize the government of the day, but not to govern directly.[6]

The term "party discipline" may be misleading to some readers in that it draws too much attention to negative constraints on parliamentary behaviour. (Votes in the House are orchestrated by the party whips, a term that reinforces the negative connotations of party discipline.) Admittedly there are costs associated with breaking party ranks on matters of importance to the party's leadership; the prospects of a cabinet appointment may be hurt, access to key decision-makers may be curtailed, and in some cases projects and programs of interest to a dissident MP's constituency may be threatened. Nevertheless, MPs to a large extent impose party discipline on themselves because of the positive personal benefits that it might bring and because no matter what the disadvantages might be, MPs know in their bones that the country is better off with their party in power than it would be under *any* alternative arrangement. If party discipline is a yoke, it is one that rests lightly on the shoulders of most MPs. In writing about his experiences as a Liberal backbencher, Mark MacGuigan, former justice minister in the Trudeau government, dismissed heavy-handed pressure as a factor in maintaining party discipline, arguing that a more compelling factor was

> the desire to get along with and to be well thought of by one's closest associates. It is, in other words, an in-group feeling that is generated by constant association, a common philosophy, and the desire to keep the party strong.[7]

Party discipline follows from the conventions of responsible government, from peer pressure and the desire to be a good team player, from a willingness to follow the leader of one's party despite disagreement on particular policies, and from an understandable belief among longtime partisans that what is best for their party is also best for their country. As Peter Aucoin concludes, "party discipline is first and foremost a consequence of the pursuit and maintenance of political power, a discipline that is accepted by leaders and followers alike as a prerequisite to success in party competition."[8] Whether this discipline will be accepted by the new Reform MPs, wedded as they are to the principle of constituency control, remains to be seen.

The House, then, is organized along party lines, and the MP is first and foremost a party representative. As C.E.S. Franks explains:

> To party leaders, the function of the MP, like the function of the party outside, is to support. Though MPs find their party a source of strength and influence, they also submerge their identity within party. Party and party discipline have moulded the structure and process of parliament.... It is

the most dominant and pervasive force in parliament and the work world of MPs.[9]

In a classic commentary written shortly before the Second World War, Richard Crossman characterized the British House in the following terms: "one can say that the scale of ethics in parliamentary democracy today is roughly that your conscience comes last, your constituency second, and your party requirements come first."[10] There would be little quarrel in applying Crossman's characterization to the contemporary Canadian House, Reform MPs notwithstanding. As Robert Jackson and Michael Atkinson maintain, "the overriding fact of parliamentary life is the existence of persistent and powerful political parties, and members of parliament are encouraged to regard party cohesion as more important than freedom of action in the House."[11] It is perhaps not surprising, then, that Franks concludes that "the backbench member is all too often an unhappy, underpaid, overworked, and anonymous foot soldier in the battle between parties."[12]

However, it is not only the House that is organized along partisan lines; it is also the electorate:

> *The electorate votes on the basis of party and leader, not on the record or promises of local candidates. Public opinion surveys can, and do, find that the electorate might wish the individual member to be less obedient to party, but the same electorate does not vote in a way that permits the MP to be independent.[13]*

It is disciplined parties in the House that enable voters to hold governments responsible for their record; we know who to blame and punish, and who to reward. In this sense, party discipline is the hallmark rather than the curse of parliamentary democracy for it extends responsible government from the House to the electorate. Party discipline, and through it party government, also permits a more broadly based form of representative government that goes beyond individual interests and grievances. As Finer explains within the context of British parliamentary democracy, "the individual MP can press individual remedies for individual cases, but only a party system is capable of generating the collective policy necessary to redress the grievances of a category."[14]

The Supremacy of Parliament

The principle of parliamentary supremacy stems from British parliamentary tradition and means, quite simply, that no Parliament is bound by the decisions of its predecessors and no Parliament can bind Parliaments to come. There is, in effect, no greater source of political authority than the Parliament of the day. This principle is linked in turn to Parliament's symbolic and practical centrality to Canadian politics. It also played an important role with respect to the early relationship between Parliament and the judiciary, with the latter being reluctant to encroach upon parliamentary supremacy.

It should be stressed, however, that parliamentary supremacy is restricted in a number of important ways. First, Parliament is not supreme or sovereign in the sense of directing the legislative process and determining the nature of legislation; party discipline ensures that these functions remain in the hands of the political executive. Second, Parliament is supreme only with respect to those matters falling within its legislative competence as defined by the federal division of powers. In those areas falling within the legislative domain of the provinces, parliamentary supremacy comes to rest with the provincial legislative assemblies, subject in the past to the federal powers of disallowance and reservation. Third, parliamentary supremacy has been restricted since 1982, and for both Parliament and the provincial legislatures, by the Charter of Rights and Freedoms. The Charter sets forth rights that cannot be encroached upon by Parliament or the provincial legislatures, and thus parliamentary supremacy is restricted. Yet the 1982 Constitution Act also recognizes and reinforces parliamentary supremacy in two important ways. The "notwithstanding" clause (Section 33) permits legislatures to override the Charter in specific instances and for a renewable period of five years, provided that any override is explicitly identified in the legislation and is thereby highlighted for the electorate. Section 1 of the Charter also recognizes parliamentary supremacy to a degree by stating that "the Canadian Charter of Rights and Freedoms guarantees the rights and freedoms set out in it subject only to such reasonable limits prescribed by law as can be demonstrably justified in a free and democratic society." Clearly legislative assemblies will play an important role in setting such limits and in providing the demonstrable justification.

In summary, parliamentary democracy in Canada rests on a fairly comprehensive principled foundation. Those principles in turn shape, and are shaped by, the political institutions of the Canadian state.

THE INSTITUTIONAL PLAYERS

Parliament stands at centre stage in public perceptions of the political system, and therefore provides an appropriate point of departure for our institutional examination. More substantively, Canadian government is based on the rule of law, and it is within representative legislative institutions that laws are created and legitimized. It is therefore again appropriate to place Parliament at the centre of our discussion. Yet Parliament is not a single institution. Although many Canadians may equate Parliament with the House of Commons, it consists of three distinct, albeit interlocked,

The "Notwithstanding" Clause

The "notwithstanding" clause is found in Section 33 of the Constitution Act, 1982. This section sets forth the conditions under which the "notwithstanding" provision can be used. The provision is restricted to particular sections of the Charter of Rights and Freedoms and only has effect for a five-year period, although this period can be renewed.

33. (1) Parliament or the legislature of a province may expressly declare in an Act of Parliament or of the legislature, as the case may be, that the Act or a provision thereof shall operate notwithstanding a provision included in section 2 or sections 7 to 15 of this Charter.

(2) An Act or a provision of an Act in respect of which a declaration made under this section is in effect shall have such operation as it would have but for the provision of this Charter referred to in the declaration.

(3) A declaration made under subsection (1) shall cease to have effect five years after it comes into force or on such earlier date as may be specified in the declaration.

(4) Parliament or a legislature of a province may re-enact a declaration made under subsection (1).

(5) Subsection (3) applies in respect of a re-enactment made under subsection (4).

institutions; Section 17 of the 1867 Constitution Act states: "There shall be One Parliament for Canada, consisting of the Queen, an Upper House styled the Senate, and the House of Commons." The consent of all three is required before a "bill"—a proposed piece of legislation—becomes an Act of Parliament and thus part of the legal framework of the Canadian state. Our discussion begins with the House of Commons, by far the most important of the three.

The House of Commons

The House of Commons is the symbolic and representational centrepiece for Canadian politics; it is the primary stage upon which are played out the major dramas and many of the soap operas of political life. There are currently 295 seats in the House, distributed across the provinces and northern territories in approximate accordance with the spatial distribution of the national population. As Table 3.1 illustrates, the principle of representation by population holds with relatively minor exceptions. Prince Edward Island is overrepresented because of the "senatorial floor," a constitutional provision specifying that a province cannot have fewer members in the House than it has senators. The northern territories are overrepresented in a realistic concession to geography; even three northern MPs have a great deal of difficulty covering the remote and demographically complex northern constituencies sprawled across the top of Canada. Manitoba, New Brunswick, Newfoundland, Nova Scotia, and Saskatchewan are all overrepresented and are protected by legislative provisions that ensure that when redistribution occurs, their number of seats will not be reduced below the number to which they were entitled in 1974. As a result of all these exceptions to strict representation by population, three of the four largest provinces have small but significant deficits.

In general, departures from pure representation by population have not been particularly contentious in the conventional political arena. However, they became very contentious in the constitutional arena during the 1992 debate on the proposed Charlottetown Accord. The accord's provision that would have guaranteed Quebec 25 percent of the seats in the House of Commons even if the province's share of the national population

TABLE 3.1 *Representation by Population and Province in the House of Commons*

Province	% 1991 Population	1994 House of Commons # seats	1994 House of Commons % seats	If strict "rep by pop" # seats	If strict "rep by pop" difference
Ontario	36.9	99	33.6	109	+10
Quebec	25.3	75	25.4	75	0
British Columbia	12.0	32	10.8	35	+3
Alberta	9.3	26	8.8	27	+1
Manitoba	4.0	14	4.7	12	-2
Saskatchewan	3.6	14	4.7	11	-3
Nova Scotia	3.3	11	3.7	10	-1
New Brunswick	2.7	10	3.4	8	-2
Newfoundland	2.1	7	2.4	6	-1
Prince Edward Island	0.5	4	1.4	1	-3
Northern Territories	0.3	3	1.0	1	-2
	100.0	295	100.0	295	

Note: The distribution of seats in 1994 was determined by the Representation Act, 1985, which was based in turn on the 1981 census.

dropped below that figure was controversial in the extreme. At least in the West, it was this provision of the accord that attracted the greatest public opposition, and that contributed the most to the accord's ultimate defeat.

A more contentious issue has been the degree to which the composition of the House should mirror the social diversity of Canada beyond its regional and linguistic composition. To date, MPs have been overwhelmingly males, white, and from professional and business backgrounds, and the growing concern about the proportion of women MPs constitutes only the leading edge of a more general challenge to the representative character of legislative institutions, a challenge that brings into play gender, ethnicity, aboriginal status, disabilities, and sexual preference. The composition of the House is important because the task of political representation is so basic to the House. As Hockin has pointed out, the "essential day-to-day business of the Canadian House of Commons is not decision-making but representation."[15] To the extent that MPs are successful in this task and are seen to be successful, then the House is able to legitimate and support strong executive government. To the extent that the House does not mirror the national population, to the extent that important segments are excluded or are seen to be excluded, then the capacity of the House in these respects is constrained. These representational issues, it should be stressed, are also of relevance to the provincial sphere where, as Table 3.2 shows, the proportion of women in legislative assemblies is not much greater than the percentage in the House (13.2 percent at the time that Table 3.2 was put together).

TABLE 3.2 *Women in Provincial Legislatures*

Province	Women as % of province's federal MPs	Women as % of provincial candidates	Women as % of provincial legislators
Newfoundland	0	8	2
Nova Scotia	18	21	6
Saskatchewan	0	25	8
New Brunswick	0	16	12
British Columbia	19	21	13
Alberta	8	18	15
Manitoba	7	21	18
Quebec	17	18	19
Ontario	9	23	22
Prince Edward Island	25	25	22

Note: The information in this table was compiled by Professor Chantal Maille for her study *Primed for Power: Women in Canadian Politics*, prepared for the Royal Commission on Electoral Reform and Party Financing.

Representational concerns have resulted in challenges to the manner in which MPs are elected to the House. Canada uses a first-past-the-post, plurality electoral system. Each constituency elects a single MP, and the individual elected is the one who receives the most votes, a plurality, but not necessarily a majority of the votes. This system has led to significant and sometimes even dramatic regional discrepancies between the share of the popular vote received by political parties in federal elections and their share of seats in the House. For example, in the 1970s and early 1980s the Liberals were all but shut out of the West and the Progressive Conservatives were all but shut out of Quebec despite significant electoral support in each case. In the former case, western Canadians lacked significant elected representation on the government side of the House and within the cabinet when the National Energy Program was introduced in 1980. Not only was the legislation less sensitive to regional concerns than it might otherwise have been, but the Liberal government lacked elected members to sell the package in the West. Thus electoral distortions exacerbated regional alienation and further eroded the legitimacy of parliamentary institutions. In the latter case, similar distortions contributed significantly to the "Tory Syndrome"; Conservative efforts to build the party within Quebec and to convince Canadian voters at large that the party was truly national, capable of spanning linguistic divisions within the country, were bedevilled by the systematic underrepresentation of Quebec Conservative voters in the House of Commons.[16] The 1993 election provides an even more dramatic illustration of distortions stemming from the first-past-the-post electoral system. The Liberals were handsomely rewarded, winning 60 percent of the seats in the House of Commons with 41 percent of the popular vote. The Bloc Québécois also benefited, winning 18 percent of the seats with a regionally concentrated 14 percent of the popular vote. The Reform Party was slightly penalized, winning just 18 percent of the seats with just over 19 percent of the vote. The real losers, however, were the New Democrats, who won 7 percent of the vote but only 3 percent of the seats, and the Progressive Conservatives, who captured 16 percent of the popular vote but won only 2 of 295 seats in the House.

The physical design of the House reflects the principled foundation of parliamentary democracy. Its architecture reinforces the latter's adversarial nature; government and opposition MPs face one another across a neutral no-man's land, separated by the length of two swords, their physical disposition signalling that there are two opposing sides to the issue at hand and little if any common ground. The architecture of the House also dramatizes the important parliamentary principle identified by Franks:

Parliamentary government is a great simplifier, especially in creating a stark distinction between those who hold power and those who do not. In doing so it resolves one of the most difficult things to achieve in a political system: to ensure accountability by binding responsibility to power.[17]

The Speaker of the House, an MP elected to this position by all members of the House, sits at the head of the House and between the government and opposition benches. The Speaker serves as a referee, but not as a judge; the electorate is the judge, albeit only with respect to the global performance of the government and parties, and not with respect to specific pieces of legislation.

In its architecture, procedures, and adversarial format, the House in many ways resembles a court of law. The objective of the parliamentary game is not to reach a compromise solution, not to find the best possible outcome, but rather to present two vigorously opposing points of view with the electorate left to judge. Note the title of "Her Majesty's Loyal Opposition": the opposition has a constitutional mandate to oppose, rather than to cooperate. Indeed, it can be argued that the public is not well served when opposition parties reject this mandate and cooperate with the government. Certainly this argument was raised in recent constitutional debates when the opposition parties locked arms with the government in an effort to short-circuit the public debate. Unfortunately, the adversarial style of parliamentary politics, particularly as manifested in the daily Question Period (discussed below), finds a less appreciative public audience than does the adversarial style of the courts.

Before leaving the subject of the House, some mention should be made of the various roles played by MPs. To this point in the discussion, MPs may appear to be little more than markers for the outcome of the last election, a means by which decisions are made by counting hands and heads. However, MPs also play an important and ongoing representative role. The MP is the primary link between the electorate and the complex apparatus of modern government. The MP therefore spends a great deal of time and energy answering letters and phone calls from constituents with questions or complaints. Through caucus meetings, discussions with colleagues, contacts with the bureaucracy, and interaction with the media, the MP serves as a vitally important transmission belt for the conveyance of citizen demands, support, and criticism into the political process. At the same time, the MP serves as a transmission belt from the government to the electorate: through newsletters, town hall meetings, media appearances, and a variety of informal means, he or she acts to explain public policy developments to the electorate. All told, these representational activities consume a large proportion of the MP's time. What is left over is devoted to constituency events, to activities on behalf of the MP's party, to committee work in the House, and to attendance on the floor of the House. The workload can be staggering at times, and is only partially offset by the secretarial and administrative support MPs now receive.

In summary, the House of Commons brings together the essential elements of Canadian parliamentary democracy. It is the institutional home for both the political executive (the cabinet) and the opposition parties. It provides a vibrant stage for political debate and a means by which

The Speaker of the House of Commons

In the early history of the British Parliament, the Speaker of the House of Commons was the intermediary between the House and the monarch; he was quite literally "the speaker" and carried out this role at considerable personal risk. Today, the Speaker's primary role as the presiding officer of the House is to oversee parliamentary debate and procedure within the Commons. Parliamentary debate and procedure are governed by a set of written rules—the Standing Orders—and it is the Speaker who applies and interprets these rules. In a sense, the Speaker is the custodian of a long history of parliamentary norms and conventions, and the rulings of the Speaker play an important role in the gradual evolution of those same norms and conventions.

As the umpire or referee in legislative debate, the Speaker is expected to be neutral, to apply the rules of the game in a nonpartisan fashion, and to be an impartial source of appeal for MPs. The Speaker does not cast a vote unless there is a tie, and is forbidden from taking part in parliamentary debate. In the past the prime minister nominated an MP from the government side of the House to be Speaker, and thus the Speaker's neutrality was often in doubt. Since September 1986, the Speaker has been elected by all MPs through a secret ballot. However, given the ubiquitous influence of party discipline and the fact that it is impossible to remove all measure of partisanship from procedural wrangles in the House, the Speaker is still almost certain to be drawn from the ranks of the majority party in the House. It should be noted that the Speaker is a Member of Parliament with constituents to represent.

The Speaker has a number of other roles and responsibilities. He or she is the formal spokesperson for the House in communications with the Senate or the Crown. The Speaker is also responsible for the logistical operations of the House, a task that involves thousands of employees and a very substantial budget. Finally, the Speaker must be able to operate effectively in both official languages, although the position has alternated by convention between English- and French-speaking members. The Standing Orders of the House state that the Deputy Speaker "shall be required to possess the full and practical knowledge" of the official language which is not that of the current Speaker.

votes can be taken, decisions made, and support registered for the government of the day. It serves as the focal point for media coverage, and it provides the institutional framework within which MPs pursue their representational roles, party responsibilities, and career aspirations. In all of these respects, it differs dramatically from our second national legislative assembly.

The Senate

The Canadian Senate finds its roots in British parliamentary institutions and the American innovation of federalism. It was created to perform a *legislative* role similar to that performed by the House of Lords in Britain, even though the two institutions had quite different social and political foundations. At the time of Confederation the House of Lords was still well grounded in the aristocratic structure of British society; a powerful landed gentry, the titled aristocracy, and an influential clergy all found symbolic and practical representation within the House of Lords, which therefore had an important albeit shrinking political constituency. In Canada, there were no similar groups requiring institutional representation: the separation of church and state was an established political principle, and an aristocratic class or landed gentry had not emerged in the colonial conditions of the 19th century. Perhaps the closest the Senate came to the House of Lords in these respects was in the constitutional requirement that senators have "real and personal property" worth $4,000 over and above debts and liabilities, a very considerable sum in 1867. Nevertheless, the legislative role of the Senate was to parallel that of the House of Lords; the appointed Senate was to be a chamber of "sober second thought" within which legislation passed by the House of Commons could be reviewed. In part that review was meant to provide a check by men of property on possible democratic excesses by the elected House, for as Mallory points out, "few of the Fathers of Confederation can have viewed the rising tide of nineteenth-century democracy with much enthusiasm and the Senate must have seemed a natural obstacle to the excessive growth of democratic institutions, or of confiscatory legislation."[18] The Senate's more important function was to provide a technical review of legislation passed by the House rather than to question such legislation in principle.

However, even this role was not important enough to justify a bicameral national legislature. (Nor was it important enough to sustain bicameralism in the provinces, which has now disappeared from the central and eastern provinces and was never introduced in the West.) It was the federal role of providing regional representation that was decisive in the creation of the Senate, and it was here that the American institutional precedent came into play.[19] The American Senate, unlike the House of Lords, was a federal chamber within which each state, regardless of its population, had two representatives indirectly elected by the legislative assemblies of the states. (American senators were not directly elected until after a 1913 constitutional amendment.) The Canadian Senate reflected the same federal principles as its American counterpart, but it did not follow the specifics of the American model. Canadian senators were selected not by provincial legislatures or governments, but by the federal government; in practice, senators have been appointed by the prime minister, who has been under no obligation even to consult with provincial governments.[20] (Until 1965, senators were appointed for life; senators appointed after that date must retire at the age of 75.) Canadians also opted for equal representation by region rather than by province. Thus in 1867 Ontario, Quebec, and the Maritimes were each given twenty-four Senate seats. For the one region that was not a province, the Senate seats were divided between the two and then among the three Maritime provinces. When a 1915 constitutional amendment recognized Western Canada as a senatorial region, it too was assigned twenty-four seats divided equally among the four western provinces. Seats for Newfoundland and the two northern territories were added to the initial regional allocation of seats in 1949 and 1975 respectively. The final result is a distribution of Senate seats that has a residual historical logic but bears little relationship to the size of provincial populations or to any other rationale of political representation. As Table 3.3 demonstrates, it is Alberta and British Columbia rather than the two largest provinces that have the weakest proportional representation in the current Senate.

TABLE 3.3   *Current Distribution of Senate Seats*

Province	# of Senate Seats	Population per Senator
Newfoundland	6	94,745
Prince Edward Island	4	32,441
Nova Scotia	10	88,994
New Brunswick	10	72,390
Quebec	24	287,331
Ontario	24	420,204
Manitoba	6	181,990
Saskatchewan	6	164,821
Alberta	6	424,259
British Columbia	6	547,010
Yukon	1	27,797
Northwest Territories	1	57,649

Note: Population figures based on 1991 census.

Provincial inequities or at least peculiarities in the distribution of Senate seats are often overlooked in the belief that the Senate provides for equal *regional* representation, but even regional equality in the Senate takes on some odd twists. The West, for example, is underrepresented in the Senate commensurate to its share of the national population; the region has 29 percent of the 1991 national population, but only 23 percent of the Senate seats. It is Atlantic Canada, with 9 percent of the national population and 29 percent of the Senate seats, that is the primary beneficiary of Senate representation based on regional equality, a principle that was jettisoned in any event when Newfoundland's Senate seats were added to rather than drawn from the pre-existing Maritime allotment.

Although the Senate is an appointed chamber, it has formal powers that are virtually identical to those of the elected House. If the Senate does not pass legislation passed by the House, the legislation cannot be enacted. In other words, the Senate's veto cannot be overridden. The one exception is that the Senate has only a suspensive veto on constitutional amendments, and therefore cannot block its own reform or even abolition. Money bills cannot be introduced in the Senate, but the Senate must approve money bills initiated in the House. It should be stressed, however, that only on *very* rare occasions has the Senate attempted to block legislation passed by the House. Thus the potential democratic problems associated with an appointed chamber having formal powers roughly equivalent to those of the elected chamber have traditionally been avoided by the voluntary restraint shown by senators in the exercise of their formal powers. Such restraint ensured a relatively smooth working relationship between the two houses of Parliament, or at least did so until the 1984 election transformed this delicate but functional relationship. In the aftermath of that election a Liberal majority in the Senate faced an overwhelming Conservative majority in the House. Given that the Liberal opposition caucus in the House was both decimated and dispirited, the locus of partisan opposition to the Conservative government shifted to the Senate. On a number of key legislative initiatives, including the Canada–U.S. Free Trade Agreement and the Goods and Services Tax, the Liberal majority in the Senate set out to block the Conservative majority in the House. In the case of the FTA, the Senate gave way only after forcing a national election in which the Conservative government was returned to power; in the case of the GST, the opposition of the Senate was overcome only when the prime minister used an obscure constitutional provision (Section 26 of the Constitution Act, 1867) to appoint eight additional Conservative and pro-GST senators.

Senators have a much lighter representational load, and generally a much lighter workload overall, than do MPs. They are not seen by most voters as useful interlocutors in citizen interactions with government bureaucracies. Because they represent their provinces at large rather than more narrowly circumscribed constituencies, senators are more remote and difficult to contact than are MPs, who all have constituency offices and staffs. (Quebec senators do represent specific senatorial districts, but it is a safe bet that the vast majority of Quebec voters could name neither their district nor their senator.) Senators have a lower media profile, if any media profile at all, and unlike MPs are not deluged with requests to attend school events, reunions, golden anniversaries, and holiday celebrations. If senators are busy, it is because they choose to be so. MPs have little choice in the matter.

In summary, the Senate was designed to fulfil a legislative role similar to that fulfilled by the House of Lords in Britain and a federal role similar to that fulfilled by the American Senate. On balance, the Senate has had greater success with the first role than with the second, and over the past decade, it is the Senate's weakness as a federal institution that has been the primary force behind the movement for Senate reform. During the Mulroney governments, however, the Senate's more aggressive pursuit of the first role, a pursuit driven primarily by the partisanship of Liberal senators, brought the appointed and elected assemblies into greater conflict. While this conflict may have increased public support for Senate reform along the lines favoured by those seeking more effective regional representation, it is more likely to have generated public support for the abolition of the Senate. Thus a broadening public dissatisfaction with the Senate status quo is not linked to a growing consensus on the nature of reform. Perhaps the only firm conclusion is that the push for institutional reform will be irresistible in the long run.

The Crown and Governor General

The formal executive powers of the Canadian state are lodged with the Crown and governor general. Section 9 of the Constitution Act, 1867, states that "the executive government and authority of and over Canada is hereby declared to continue and be vested in the Queen." Section 12 goes on to specify that executive powers, authorities, and functions are to "be vested in and exercisable by the Governor General, with the advice or with the advice and consent of or in conjunction with the Queen's Privy Council for Canada, or any member therefore, or by the Governor General individually." This clause gives broad executive powers to the governor general, who is also, on behalf of the Queen, the "Commander-in-Chief of the Land and Naval Militia, and of all Naval and Military Forces" (Section 15). However, these vast formal powers are in practice exercised only upon *the advice and consent* of the cabinet. Constitutional practice makes an important distinction between the formal executive, comprised of the governor general and the Privy Council, and the political executive comprised of the prime minister and cabinet.

The governor general fits into the Westminster model of parliamentary government that Canada inherited from Britain; he or she is the structural although not the political equivalent of the early British monarchs. The governor general is the Crown's representative in Canada and for all but the most unusual occasions carries out the formal duties associated with the Crown. (When the Constitution was patriated in 1982, Queen Elizabeth II came to Ottawa on a rain-swept day in April to sign the new Constitution Act.) Prior to Confederation, the governor general was the Crown's representative in an active sense; he was appointed by the British government and was responsible for carrying out that government's colonial responsibilities in Canada. The executive power exercised by the governor general was real and immediate, although the achievement of responsible government in 1848 marked an important transfer of power from the formal to the political executive. In the decades following Confederation the governor general's role became increasingly ceremonial in character, and the political power of the incumbent extended little beyond moral suasion and the opportunity to offer advice. The cabinet acted formally by tendering advice to the governor general who, except in the most unusual circumstances, was expected to act on that advice. The power to appoint the governor general passed in practice from the British to the Canadian government, and from 1951 onward only Canadian citizens have been appointed.

The Crown and the governor general symbolize the separation of the government of the day from the Canadian state; they help "depoliticize the instruments of government."[21] Although the prime minister is the political head of the government, the formal executive authority of the state resides in the governor general and transcends the political personalities of the day. (By contrast, the president of the United States is not only the political head of the American government, but is also its formal and ceremonial head.) This important theoretical distinction between government and the state may not be salient to most citizens, but it has important practical consequences for the operation of government. The governor general is able to carry much of the ceremonial load—the greeting of lesser foreign dignitaries, presiding over public events held on holidays such as Remembrance Day, handing out awards and honours, meeting with Scouts and Guides, opening public buildings—that would otherwise fall on the shoulders of the prime minister. The prime minister is thus freed to address other more pressing problems, or at least to choose ceremonial opportunities with the greatest promise of partisan gain or impact on national unity goals.

As discussed below, the governor general also plays a significant formal role in the legislative process. Bills passed by the House and Senate must be presented to the governor general for the Queen's assent before they can become Acts of Parliament. The governor general can convey that assent, withhold it, or reserve the bill "for the signification of the Queen's pleasure." In this last case, the bill would not be proclaimed unless assent was attained within two years. While this potential hitch in the legislative process has not arisen with the governor general in this century, it arose frequently in the more recent past with the governor general's provincial counterparts. The lieutenant governor holds many of the same formal executive powers, plays the same ceremonial roles, and occupies the same position in the legislative process as does the governor general. However, lieutenant governors were historically much more likely to interfere in provincial politics than was the governor general to interfere nationally. The former were appointed by the prime minister and not necessarily with the advice, much less the consent, of provincial premiers. They were thus more prone to reserve provincial legislation for federal scrutiny, or to disallow provincial legislation on the advice of the federal government. Lieutenant governors did not suffer the liability of being British actors playing on a Canadian stage; they were drawn from the provincial political class and were therefore more likely to play an active role. Nonetheless, the lieutenant governors, like the governor general, now play an executive role that is almost exclusively formal and ceremonial. Moreover, the appointment of the lieutenant governor has passed in all but the most formal terms into the hands of provincial governments, thus parallelling the evolution of the appointment process for the governor general.

Finally, the Crown's representatives play an important symbolic role in the legislative process by delivering the speech from the throne at the opening of each session of Parliament or the provincial legislature. The throne speech is designed to outline the government's legislative intentions for the upcoming session, and it is therefore written by the government of the day and only delivered by the Crown's representative. Thus the governor general or lieutenant governor refers to "my government" even though, in a partisan sense, he or she is assumed to be neutral.

In summary, it is important to stress that the fact that Canada is a constitutional monarchy does not mean that the *British* Crown is at the formal apex of the Canadian state. The governor general represents the Canadian Crown, which just happens to reside in the same person, Her Majesty Queen Elizabeth II, as does the British Crown. In this hydra-like position the Queen plays an important symbolic role in the Commonwealth, serving as the formal head of state for most although not all of the member states. Within Canada, the governor general and the symbolic trappings of the Crown are significant elements in the formal institutional configuration of the Canadian state. The governor general also plays an important practical role by shouldering much of the ceremonial load for the prime minister. However, the governor general and Crown do not exercise political power; that responsibility resides within the more informal institutions of cabinet government.

The Cabinet and Political Executive
Canadian cabinet government finds its origins in early British parliamentary history where the initial cabinets were small groups of ministers who advised and were appointed by the sovereign of the day. As Parliament began to assert its independence from the sovereign, ministers began to be

drawn more and more from the elected House of Commons. Then, with the eventual full flowering of responsible parliamentary democracy, cabinet ministers were drawn almost exclusively from the House. However, they continued to serve as "Ministers of the Crown" and thus provided the essential link or *buckle* between the administrative apparatus of the state—the public service—and elected representatives in the House. When Canadians adopted a system of government "similar in principle to that of the United Kingdom," cabinet government was part of the British legacy. Canadian practice, at least at the start, departed little from British precedent as the cabinet came to provide the centrepiece of responsible government.

When the cabinet tenders formal advice to the Crown it does so as the Privy Council, and cabinet ministers serve in this capacity as Privy Councillors. Ministers are appointed to the Privy Council for life; the title continues even though the individual in question may no longer hold office or indeed be in public life. However, the Privy Council meets only in exceptional and ceremonial circumstances, such as on April 17, 1982, when the Constitution was patriated to Canada. The cabinet itself is an informal subcommittee of the Privy Council, that group of Privy Councillors who hold ministerial positions in the government of the day. Although the cabinet enjoys no formal constitutional recognition, it has an effective monopoly on the right to tender advice to the Crown. Indeed, this is the operational definition of responsible government: "those who command the support of the elected chamber alone advise the Crown."[22] The legal instruments through which the cabinet and individual ministers advise the Crown are called "orders-in-council." These in theory require, and in fact carry, the collective approval of cabinet.

Cabinet government rests upon the firm foundation of party discipline in the House of Commons.[23] The ability of the cabinet to *govern* depends upon its capacity to control the legislative agenda and output of the House and, secondarily to this point in time, of the Senate. This capacity, the assurance that cabinet decisions will find faithful reflection in legislation passed by Parliament, comes from party discipline in the House. The strength of party discipline in turn stems directly from the conventions of responsible government. If the defeat of a government bill in the House signifies that the cabinet has lost the confidence of the House and must therefore resign, the consequence is that government MPs must support government bills willy-nilly or risk losing partisan control of the government. To be sure, legislative proposals are subjected to extensive parliamentary debate, but this is not to be confused with parliamentary supremacy or control. Here it should be noted, however, that cabinet's control over the content of legislation is considerably greater than its control over the speed and timing of the legislative process. Cabinet is less likely to face legislative defeat than it is to face delays and obstruction in both the House and Senate, delays that in the end may prevent passage of significant components of the government's legislative agenda.

The cabinet fusion of executive and legislative power (and the concomitant strength of party discipline), one that concentrates power within the hands of cabinet and thus within the hands of the prime minister, is perhaps the most outstanding feature of Canadian parliamentary democracy. In the provinces it works in an identical fashion to concentrate power within the hands of provincial cabinets and their premiers. This facilitates, in turn, the emergence of executive federalism whereby federal and provincial governments can negotiate with one another secure in the knowledge that bargains reached are virtually assured of legislative ratification, should such be needed.[24] It is the fusion of executive and legislative power that most clearly sets Canadian national institutions apart from those in the United States. Executive and legislative powers in the United States are lodged in distinct branches of government—the presidency and Congress, respectively—with their own institutions and electoral mandates. This separation of powers is designed to prevent the very concentration of power that Canadian parliamentary institutions ensure. It, along with the sheer number of American states, also prevents the emergence of Canadian-style executive federalism in the United States.[25]

Although cabinet ministers are formally appointed as Ministers of the Crown and are sworn into the Privy Council by the governor general, they are in fact selected by the prime minister of the day and continue to serve in the cabinet only so long as they enjoy the prime minister's confidence. There is no legal or constitutional requirement that cabinet ministers have seats in either the House or Senate, but political convention dictates that a person appointed to the cabinet from outside Parliament will, if not appointed to the Senate, seek a seat in the House at the first available opportunity, and that he or she will resign from the cabinet if unsuccessful in the bid to be elected. This is the essence of parliamentary systems of government, whether British or non-British in inspiration; the executive is simultaneously part of the legislature and responsible to that legislature. The only exceptions are cabinet appointments drawn from the Senate. The Government Leader in the Senate is automatically a member of cabinet, but the principles of responsible government limit the extent to which the prime minister can draw from the Senate for other cabinet appointments. Senators cannot appear on the floor of the House and thus ministers from the Senate weaken the practical responsibility of ministers to the House. In special circumstances, however, additional senators have held cabinet posts. For example, Prime Minister Joe Clark drew upon Quebec Progressive Conservative senators to increase that province's cabinet representation after the 1979 general election in which only a single Progressive Conservative MP was elected from Quebec. In a similar fashion, Prime Minister Pierre Trudeau used western Canadian senators to provide regional representation in the cabinet when, following the 1980 election, only two Liberal MPs (both from Manitoba) were elected west of the Manitoba–Ontario border.[26]

The size of Canadian cabinets expanded considerably in the post-Confederation period. Only thirteen ministers, including the prime minister, sat in Sir John A. Macdonald's first cabinet, and provincial cabinets and their associated bureaucracies were even leaner. In 1881, for example, Manitoba had only five civil servants, including four deputy ministers; the provincial attorney general ran his department single-handedly without a deputy, clerk, or secretary.[27] By contrast, provincial cabinets until very recently averaged more than twenty ministers, and Brian Mulroney's largest cabinet had forty ministers, including himself. In part, this growth reflected the increased complexity and scope of contemporary government. At the time of Confederation no one could have imagined that the federal government would play a role in, much less have cabinet ministers responsible for, such fields as fitness and amateur sport, environmental protection, multiculturalism, and the status of women. Contemporary society is also much more diverse than it was at the time of Confederation, and this diversity generates pressures for larger and larger cabinets. There are now ten provinces to be represented rather than four, and there is a need that did not exist in the past to provide representation for women and multicultural communities. In short, the federal cabinet has come to be seen as a mirror, if an imperfect mirror, of the Canadian society. Citizens expect to find their reflection in the composition of the cabinet, and the size of the cabinet has grown accordingly as groups within an increasingly complex society jockey for both symbolic recognition and the practical political leverage that cabinet representation is thought to provide.

Provincial premiers experienced the same pressures to expand the size of their cabinets. Although provincial cabinets remain smaller in absolute numbers than the federal cabinet, they are proportionately much larger. While just over 13 percent of MPs sat in the federal cabinet during the Mulroney Progressive Conservative governments, Table 3.4 shows that during the same time period provincial cabinets ranged from 21 percent of elected members in Ontario to 42 percent in Nova Scotia. Thus the odds of securing a cabinet position are much better provincially than they are in Ottawa. The relatively large provincial cabinets have much greater weight in the governing party caucuses and in the legislative process than does the federal cabinet. Government members who are not cabinet ministers are almost the exception in provincial legislatures, whereas backbench MPs on the government side of the House of Commons outnumber their cabinet colleagues by a ratio of three or four to one.

The prime minister faces a host of representational principles and conventions in constructing a cabinet. The first principle, which has been applied more erratically than is often assumed,[28] is to represent all provinces around the cabinet table if it is at all possible to do so. As Smiley and Watts point out, prime ministers will sometimes go to extraordinary lengths to achieve this objective: after the 1921 election, in which the Liberals were shut out of Alberta, Prime Minister King appointed a former

TABLE 3.4 *Absolute and Proportionate Size of Provincial Cabinets*

Province	Cabinet size	% of Legislature
Quebec	30	24
Ontario	27	21
Alberta	27	33
New Brunswick	24	41
British Columbia	23	33
Nova Scotia	22	42
Saskatchewan	20	31
Manitoba	18	32
Newfoundland	15	27
Prince Edward Island	11	34
Mulroney's cabinet	39	13
Campbell's 1993 cabinet	25	8
Chrétien's first cabinet	23	8

Source: Provincial data from Rand Dyck, Provincial Politics in Canada *(Scarborough: Prentice-Hall, 1991), p. 623.*

Alberta premier to the cabinet and found him a Commons seat in Quebec.[29] At the Westminster Conference of 1866, which put into place the final details of the Confederation agreement, it was decided that the first Canadian cabinet would have five ministers (including the prime minister) from Ontario, four from Quebec, and two each from New Brunswick and Nova Scotia.[30] Today, the principle of representing provinces in a manner proportionate to their size still applies: Ontario generally has more ministers than any other province, Quebec more than any province other than Ontario, British Columbia and Alberta more than smaller provinces, and so on. If any province is likely to be left out it is Prince Edward Island, where the small pool of MPs increases the chances that the government will not have an elected member from the Island. Kim Campbell's short-lived 1993 cabinet captured this strategy perfectly; there were eight ministers from Ontario, seven from Quebec, three (including Campbell) from British Columbia, two from Alberta, and one each from the rest of the provinces, excluding Prince Edward Island. Jean Chrétien's first cabinet, however, departed from this formula; ten of the twenty-three ministers came from Ontario, five (including Chrétien) came from Quebec, two came from Alberta, Prince Edward Island was excluded, once again, and the remaining provinces, including British Columbia, contributed only a single minister.

The prime minister must also ensure that the country's two linguistic communities are adequately represented and that gender representation is addressed if not necessarily balanced; seven of the thirty-five members of Brian Mulroney's last cabinet were women, compared to five of twenty-five in Kim Campbell's cabinet and four of twenty-three in Chrétien's first cabinet. If possible, representation is provided for multicultural communities, visible minorities, linguistic minorities inside and outside Quebec, the major religious faiths, aboriginals, and the disabled. At the same time the prime minister must use the construction of the cabinet to promote internal harmony within the party and caucus. It was imperative, for example, that Kim Campbell offer Jean Charest a prominent role within her cabinet in order to heal the internal party wounds caused by the 1993 PC leadership race. The cabinet must represent the party's major ideological camps, and the prime minister must reward supporters without appearing to be too vindictive to enemies and rivals. It is difficult for the prime minister to avoid members of stature within the governing party even if they fail to share the prime minister's ideological outlook, policy dispositions, or friendship. The prime minister must give some attention to competence, particularly within key portfolios. Here the primary concern is not the minister's expertise in the department's sphere of operations, but rather his or her more general managerial competence and ability to withstand pressure.

Finally, it should be noted that all cabinet positions are not the same in stature and influence, and thus provinces and groups are concerned not only with being represented within cabinet, but also with the specific portfolio held by their "representative." Kim Campbell's cabinet nicely demonstrates the range of cabinet positions that can exist. Jean Charest was named deputy prime minister and the minister-designate for Industry and Science (which included corporate and consumer affairs); he was also given ministerial responsibility for the Federal Office of Regional Development (Quebec). Bernard Valcourt, minister-designate for the new superministry of Human Resources and Labour, was given responsibility for manpower training, some aspects of immigration, and everything the federal government does in connection with labour, welfare, and social services. At the other end of the spectrum, Gerry Weiner was minister-designate for Citizenship, for which virtually all responsibilities were being assumed by the new Department of Canadian Heritage. Mr. Weiner, the only Quebec anglophone and only Jew in the cabinet, was left with the right to attend cabinet meetings and a "department" consisting of a couple of ministerial assistants, a secretary, and a chauffeur.[31]

If the cabinet is to serve as a vehicle of political integration for the Canadian federal state, then we might expect ministers to be drawn from the ranks of those with extensive experience in provincial politics and government. This, however, is not the case. Of all individuals who served in federal cabinets between 1867 and 1984 inclusive, 75 percent had no

TABLE 3.5 Composition of Jean Chrétien's First Cabinet, 1993

Minister	Ministry
Jean Chrétien	Prime Minister
Herb Gray	Solicitor General and Government Leader in the House of Commons
André Ouellet	Foreign Affairs
Lloyd Axworthy	Human Resources
David Collenette	National Defence
Roy MacLaren	International Trade
David Anderson	National Revenue
Ralph Goodale	Agriculture and Agri-Food
David Dingwall	Public Works and Atlantic Canada Opportunities Agency
Ron Irwin	Indian Affairs and Northern Development
Brian Tobin	Fisheries and Oceans
Joyce Fairbairn	Government Leader in the Senate
Sheila Copps	Deputy Prime Minister and Environment
Sergio Marchi	Citizenship and Immigration
John Manley	Industry
Diane Marleau	Health
Paul Martin	Finance, with responsibility for Quebec regional development
Doug Young	Transport
Michel Dupuy	Canadian Heritage
Art Eggleton	Treasury Board and Infrastructure
Marcel Massé	Intergovernmental Affairs and Public Service Renewal
Anne McLellan	Natural Resources
Allan Rock	Justice and Attorney General

experience whatsoever in provincial politics.[32] Only 9.1 percent had served in a provincial legislative assembly, an additional 5.9 percent had also served in a provincial cabinet, and 4.8 percent had been provincial premiers; another 5.2 percent had provincial experience that was limited to running unsuccessfully in a provincial campaign. Provincial experience has thus been relatively rare among federal cabinet ministers and among the MPs from which they are recruited, and has been diminishing over time.

In media coverage it is commonplace to encounter such phrases as "the cabinet met to decide" or "cabinet deliberations continued," but the cabinet in such instances is little more than what columnist Jeffrey Simpson has described as an "amiable fiction." Since the early years of the

Trudeau governments the cabinet has been transformed from a "depart-mentalized" cabinet that brought together relatively autonomous ministers in a collegial, decision-making forum into an "institutionalized" cabinet characterized by an elaborate committee structure and supporting central agencies including Treasury Board and the Privy Council Office.[33] This transformation illustrates the prime minister's prerogative and capacity to restructure the machinery of government to fit his or her own leadership style. Indeed, Aucoin argues that "the leadership paradigms of prime min-isters—their philosophies of governance, their management styles and their political objectives—are the chief determinants in the organizational design of the central machinery of government."[34] In Trudeau's case, trans-formation meant the strengthening of central agencies—the Privy Council Office, the Treasury Board Secretariat, and the Prime Minister's Office—to provide a collective cabinet counterweight to the bureaucratic advice upon which individual ministers are inevitably reliant. The enhanced central agencies were also meant to increase interdepartmental coordination in policy planning.[35] In Mulroney's case, the transformation entailed an increased measure of political control achieved in part by a shift in power from central agencies to the Priorities and Planning Committee of cabinet, and to the prime minister himself. In the case of Kim Campbell and Jean Chrétien, it meant a smaller cabinet, a less elaborate cabinet committee structure, and the abolishment of the Priorities and Planning Committee.

The full cabinet thus provides an umbrella for a complex array of committees, agencies, and players. At best, it reviews decisions that have been taken elsewhere. In most cases, meetings of the full cabinet provide little more than an opportunity for the prime minister and other ministers to brief their colleagues and to exchange information rather than to make decisions. The full cabinet has become a "mini-caucus" of the governing party,[36] a body too large and cumbersome to be effective at deliberation or decision-making. The problem of size is further compounded by the fact that the government's most senior bureaucrats, including the Clerk of the Privy Council and the prime minister's Principal Secretary, attend and par-ticipate actively in cabinet meetings. Officials from departments relevant to the day's agenda may also attend, although their participation is more circumspect. A meeting of the full cabinet, chaired by the prime minister, may therefore include more than forty people over and above the transla-tion staff. (All cabinet documents are prepared in both official languages, and simultaneous translation is provided for all cabinet and cabinet com-mittee meetings.) It is not surprising, then, that the growth of the federal cabinet has spawned the evolution of an elaborate cabinet committee system.

Cabinet committees enjoy a good measure of autonomy. In many and perhaps most cases they act as the cabinet; decisions taken by committees need not be ratified or even discussed by the full cabinet, although all deci-sions taken are placed before the full cabinet for notification. At the same time it should be noted that the decentralization of decision-making within the cabinet has done nothing to decentralize power within the federal government more broadly conceived. The institutionalized cabinet retains and may even have strengthened its commanding presence at the apex of the federal government and the Canadian state. It should also be noted that the committee system has complicated the representation of regional interests within the national government. Given that the most representative body, the full cabinet, is no longer central to the process, the role of regional ministers has become more difficult: "to be effective, regional ministers now must not only convince the prime minister and their cabinet colleagues of the need to accommodate the regional interests which they represent, but must accomplish this within a decision-making system that has become more formal, structured and complex."[37]

The elaborate cabinet committee system requires extensive logistical support. This support is provided by the Privy Council Office (PCO), which also provides detailed policy analysis and strategic advice. The senior officials of PCO are at the heart of the federal decision-making process, and wield considerable policy and political influence. The deputy minister of the PCO, who carries the titles Clerk of the Privy Council Office and Secretary to the Cabinet, is the most senior public servant in the federal government. The Clerk of the PCO occupies three principal roles. First, he or she is in effect the prime minister's deputy minister, and in that capacity advises the prime minister with respect to overall policy direction, the functioning and organization of the government, and senior appointments. Second, the Clerk is Secretary to the Cabinet, and thus supplies both support and advice to the ministry as a whole. Finally, he or she is the formal head of the public service, and is ultimately responsible for its operation and for its protection from partisan interference.

When decisions are made within cabinet, formal votes are not taken. Voting makes sense as a decision-making technique when all participants are considered equal, but in the cabinet context this equality condition is not met. Some ministers will have a greater departmental stake in the issue at hand than will other ministers. We would expect, for example, that the ministers of energy and finance would carry more weight in a cabinet discussion of energy policy and taxation than would the ministers of agriculture or justice. Some ministers will have a greater regional stake than will others; a minister from Saskatchewan might be expected to contribute less to a discussion of fishing bans and the protection of cod stocks than would ministers from Atlantic Canada. Some ministers will be smarter, more seasoned, and more politically astute, or at least will be seen as such by their colleagues. Simply taking a vote would impose an artificial equality and would also weaken the quality of cabinet discussion by driving the discussion toward polar alternatives rather than the search for a middle ground. Ministers might refrain from useful critical commentary if they had to commit later to an unambiguous vote. Voting would produce clear winners and losers, logrolling, and possibly longstanding factions, and would thus disrupt the internal harmony of the cabinet. Perhaps most importantly, it would reduce the weight of the prime minister to one vote. This would not only undercut the prime minister's capacity for leadership, but would fly in the face of the very real differences in status, electoral importance, and power between the prime minister and ministers. Cabinet decisions are therefore taken by consensus, and it is the prime minister who articulates the consensus. Although the prime minister cannot consistently or wildly depart from the views of cabinet colleagues, there remains a large element of discretion through which prime ministerial leadership can be exercised.

In summary, the composition and operating rules of cabinet are linked to the more general principles of Canadian parliamentary democracy. Cabinet is a representative institution par excellence, and cabinets are built with representational issues as the central concern. The norms of secrecy and collective responsibility are a direct reflection of the conventions of responsible government. Whether widespread public discontent with many of the principles of representative and responsible government will penetrate the inner reaches of cabinet government remains to be seen.

The Prime Minister

In theory, the prime minister's relationship with his or her ministers is captured by the seemingly contradictory phrase *first among equals*. The equality aspect of this description derives from the facts that both are for the most part elected MPs and that the prime minister does not occupy a unique formal position within Canada's constitutional framework. In reality, however, equality is far from the case. Individuals become prime minister by being elected as party leader in a national party convention, one in which MPs and senators play an important but far from decisive role, and by having led their party to victory in a national election. (In some cases, of course, an individual may take on the office of prime minister before facing a general election; Pierre Trudeau, John Turner, and Kim Campbell all became prime minister by winning the leadership of the incumbent party.) Only the extra-parliamentary party can remove the individual as party leader, and this is unlikely to happen prior to electoral defeat. Thus the prime minister owes his or her position first to the party and second to the electorate, and at best only indirectly to support from cabinet colleagues. Bluntly put, the prime minister appoints ministers (and their deputy ministers); ministers do not appoint or select the prime minister. Ministers owe their cabinet appointment and their specific ministerial post to the prime minister who appoints them, subject of course to the host of representational constraints noted above. In addition, it is the prime minister alone who articulates the consensus of cabinet and who decides when an election will be called.

Only the prime minister has the authority and resources to energize and orchestrate the complex cabinet machinery described above. For political authority the prime minister can draw upon success at the polls—many MPs and ministers will be elected on their leader's coattails—and election as party leader by the extra-parliamentary party. The prime minister, more than any other individual, is able to define the election mandate and is able to link that mandate to his or her own leadership. For resources, the prime minister can draw upon the bureaucratic and strategic support of the Privy Council Office and Prime Minister's Office. The PCO serves principally as the prime minister's department, and provides the prime minister with information and policy advice on all issues of national importance. In this respect, its role overlaps and complements that of the PMO, which serves prime ministers in their capacity as both party leader and head of government.[38] Thus with regard to political and organizational resources the prime minister is much more than a single actor; he or she commands the immediate resources and personal loyalty of close to a thousand public servants and political aides. The prime minister also has unparallelled access to the media and to the public.

The power of prime ministers within cabinet government has been enhanced by the longevity in office that many have enjoyed, a longevity that has enabled them to put their stamp not only on the government of the day, but on political eras. William Lyon Mackenzie King, for example, was prime minister from 1921 through 1930, with one brief interruption, and again from 1935 to 1947; it is next to impossible to disentangle thirty years of Canadian political history from his leadership. Pierre Trudeau was prime minister from 1968 to 1979, and again from 1980 to 1984. During this same period the United States experienced the presidencies of Lyndon Johnson, Richard Nixon, Gerald Ford, Jimmy Carter, and Ronald Reagan, each of whom is identified in the United States with a unique political era. Even Brian Mulroney's nine years in office overlapped with the presidencies of Ronald Reagan, George Bush, and Bill Clinton.

In many ways the prime minister occupies a position in the Canadian political system similar to that of the American president. Admittedly, the prime minister does not have the same opportunity that the president has to refashion the federal bureaucracy in his or her own image; an incoming prime minister will make only a fraction of the roughly 2,600 appointments made by an incoming president. Over time, however, the prime minister has considerable capacity to shape the institutional environment by moving and promoting people within the public service, by recruiting new blood, by determining the staffing of key central agencies including the PMO and PCO, and by making a large number of appointments to government boards and agencies. (For example, Mr. Mulroney made close to 700 appointments, virtually all patronage in character, in the four months between when he announced his decision to retire and his replacement by Kim Campbell.) The prime minister, like the American president, is able to convert high-profile action on the international stage into political authority and resources at home. However, the most important point of contrast with the president is that the prime minister exercises much greater control over the legislative process. The fusion of executive and legislative power in Canada means that in most cases the prime minister will be able to secure legislative approval for policy initiatives; the cabinet dominates the House and the prime minister dominates the cabinet. The prime minister has no need to bargain with the House in the way in which the president must continually bargain with both houses of Congress.

In a rough sense, therefore, Canadian government can be seen as prime ministerial government rather than cabinet government. The prime minister is the focal point of the party's electoral strategy and the lightning rod for public discontent. At the same time, the federal government is too large and too complex to be directed by any single individual even when backed by the resources of the PCO and PMO. In the trench warfare of public policy formulation and administration, cabinet ministers retain real influence and discretionary power. The prime minister's time, energy, and attention are carefully rationed out to a relatively few areas of special interest, political sensitivity, or expertise. Beyond that, cabinet government flourishes and shapes the public policies of the federal government.

The Courts

Although many may think of the courts as standing beyond the pale of politics, it has long been recognized by political scientists that they play an important role within the political system. The judicial branch of government provides an opportunity for the authoritative adjudication of legislative enactments, a safeguard on the abuse of executive and—since the introduction of the Charter of Rights—legislative power, and a widely used arena for dispute resolution. Yet it is also fair to conclude that until quite recently Canadian political scientists paid much less attention to the judicial branch than did their counterparts in the United States. This neglect stemmed in part from the principle of parliamentary supremacy, which placed the courts in a somewhat subordinate institutional role, or at least a role subordinate to that of the American courts, which operated within an institutional environment characterized by constitutional supremacy. However, parliamentary supremacy does not apply to interpretations of the federal division of powers, and in this respect the political role of the Canadian courts has always been acknowledged. Not surprisingly, this focus on the constitutional impact of the judicial branch led in turn to a focus on the Supreme Court and, until very recently, a relative absence of scholarship on the lower courts.

The Supreme Court of Canada was created in 1875, but its initial establishment did not abolish the existing right of appeal to the Judicial Committee of the Privy Council in the United Kingdom. At the time,

Canada was still a British colony, and thus the Supreme Court became a link in the chain of appeal rather than the final arbiter. Only in 1949 was the right of appeal to the JCPC abolished and the court made supreme in fact as well as in name. This change opened the door for the court's more active participation in Canadian political life by ensuring that its decisions would be final. However, several decades would pass before the Supreme Court came to be generally recognized as a central feature of the Canadian institutional landscape. The court began to assume a more activist stance to public policy issues in the late 1960s and early 1970s, but the justices did not hit their full stride until the passage of the Charter of Rights in 1982.

The Supreme Court presents an interesting combination of the rule of law and the principle of representation. In theory, the rule of law is incompatible with the more political notion of representation; the law is assumed to possess an objective neutrality irrespective of the specific individuals who interpret it. Nevertheless, while it is expected that the decisions of the court will be guided by law, its structure, like that of other central government institutions, is based on representative principles. In order to diminish French-Canadian fears that the court would pose a threat to provincial rights and powers, the 1875 Supreme Court Act guaranteed Quebec representation on the court. At the same time, Parliament rejected a proposal that at least one of the judges come from British Columbia "because of the feeling on both sides of the House that the representative principle was not of the same importance to the other provinces as it was to Quebec."[39] By statute, the composition of the contemporary Supreme Court includes nine justices, three of whom must come from Quebec; by convention, three of the remaining six come from Ontario, two from the West, and one from Atlantic Canada. Under Section 41(d) of the 1982 Constitution Act, the composition of the court can only be changed with the unanimous consent of Parliament and the ten provincial legislative assemblies.

An important structural feature of the Supreme Court is that appointments are made by the federal government alone. Partly as a consequence, and as James Mallory explains, "the Supreme Court of Canada—like that of the United States—is capable of playing a role of a 'nationalizing' institution, which interprets and imposes the sense of the whole community even when that consensus is openly rejected by part of the community."[40] Provincial governments have been wary of that very nationalizing potential, and there has been a corresponding reluctance to have federal–provincial disputes settled in a judicial arena where the umpires have been appointed by one of the parties in the dispute. It has been an open question among judicial scholars whether the Supreme Court has been overly centralist in its interpretation of constitutional disputes; some have argued that the court's decisions have balanced out over time[41] while others have detected a systematic infringement on the provincial sphere.[42]

The Supreme Court of Canada, 1993–94.

The Supreme Court of Canada.

In any event, provincial fears on this account have not evaporated and were addressed by the Meech Lake Accord, which, if it had been ratified, would have required that the federal government make appointments to the Supreme Court from lists submitted by the provinces.

As noted above, the court's historical role in the political process was limited not only by the right of appeal to the JCPC, but also by the general subordination of Canadian courts to legislative assemblies. The doctrine of parliamentary supremacy limited the court's ability, and the inclination of its justices, to strike out in directions different from those established by Parliament or the provincial legislative assemblies. This changed dramatically in 1982 with the creation of a constitutionalized Charter of Rights and Freedoms binding on both levels of the government. With the Charter in place, legislation can now be struck down on grounds other than a violation of the federal division of powers. The court therefore has the constitutional authority and the public legitimacy to play a more central role in the evolution of public policy. In recent years the Supreme Court and the judicial system more broadly considered have played an important role in the recognition of aboriginal rights and the advancement of aboriginal land claims, the striking down of legislation regarding abortion, the extension of gay rights, the definition of minority education rights, and the procedural implementation of environmental impact assessment reviews, to name but a few of the affected areas of public policy. In short, the courts have become an increasingly important political arena, and judges have become active players, a role that some embrace and others have thrust upon them regardless.

There is no question that the Supreme Court and the judicial branch of government more broadly defined will play an even greater political role in the years to come. There is also no question that the courts will attract greater attention from political scientists. The growing importance of the courts to Canadian public policy, for example, is leading to greater scholarly interest in the recruitment of judges, the composition of the courts, and the impact of both on policy-related decisions, something that has been a longstanding interest of the American political science community.[43]

THE LEGISLATIVE PROCESS

The initial incentives for parliamentary action may arise from virtually anywhere; interest groups, royal commissions, special inquiries, court decisions, opinion polls, the actions of other governments, and world events can all come into play. The government caucus and caucus committees also play an important role by generating legislative initiatives and providing a sounding board for initiatives originating within the government. However, the translation of policy needs and initiatives into concrete legislative proposals takes place primarily in the interplay between cabinet and bureaucracy. Thus while MPs who are not in the cabinet may be active in the caucus committees and scrums, and may introduce legislation in the House as senators may do in the Senate, the great bulk of legislation brought before the House for serious debate is government legislation. Other legislative initiatives are inconsequential in volume and policy importance. Here it should also be noted that most government bills are *public* bills that have a general impact on Canadian citizens. The impact of *private* bills, such as those needed to incorporate private companies or charitable organizations, or to change the existing terms of incorporation, is limited to specific persons or corporations; these bills are dispatched with little if any parliamentary discussion or debate. Private bills are often introduced in the Senate and receive only perfunctory treatment in the House.

Legislative proposals, or "bills," are introduced into the House by the responsible minister or initiating MP and are then given *first reading*.[44] At this stage the bill is simply announced, numbered, and printed in both official languages for distribution; there is no discussion or debate. In effect, the government serves notice to the House, and through the House to the country, that the bill has been placed on the legislative agenda. Substantive debate begins with *second reading*, at which time the bill is discussed in principle. At the end of this stage a vote is taken on the bill as a whole; amendments are not permitted, and specific clauses or provisions are not discussed in detail. It is at this stage in the legislative process that the government defends the need for the legislation and outlines the legislation's general principles and intended effects.

If the bill is approved at second reading it is sent to committee for more detailed, clause-by-clause examination. The committee stage may involve one of the Standing Committees of the House, a special committee created for the specific legislative proposal, or the entire House sitting as a "committee of the whole." (While the first and third options were most likely in the past, the second has come to prevail in more recent years.) Committee hearings provide an opportunity for some measure of legislative independence from the bureaucratic advice woven into the proposed legislation; expert witnesses may be called and public hearings held. By this time, however, what is at issue is the fine print, although the line between principle and detail is not always easy to draw. Fidelity to the principle of the legislation is ensured by the fact that committees other than the Public Accounts Committee have a majority of members and a chairperson drawn from the government side of the House, and the constraints of party discipline that apply to the House as a whole apply with equal force to the votes of its committees. Admittedly, the style and tone of committee debate may be less partisan and more free-wheeling, in part because media coverage is much lighter. Amendments are moved, discussed, and voted upon, but this all takes place within the constraints of party discipline and with the understanding that the bill has already been approved in principle by the House.

After detailed committee examination, the bill is brought back to the floor of the House for the *report* stage. At this point all members of the House are able to discuss the details of the bill and any changes recommended from the committee stage. Committee amendments are considered and new amendments are proposed, all in the context that the bill has already been approved in principle and that amendments that would go to the principled core of the legislation are not permitted. Once all proposed amendments have been put to a vote, the bill as a whole is voted upon by the House. If the bill passes, it goes to *third reading*. At this last stage no further changes or amendments are entertained, and members must accept or reject the bill as it stands. The formal vote on third reading brings the legislative process in the House to a close. If the bill is approved on third reading, it is sent to the Senate.

For the most part, therefore, legislation reaching the Senate already carries the stamp of democratic legitimacy from the House. This stamp curtails Senate debate, which at times is little more than perfunctory.

Legislation within the Senate moves through the same stages as in the House, but the hurdles are lower at each stage; bills are given "sober second thought" rather than a more root-and-branch examination that would touch upon the principles of the legislation. Many bills reach the Senate so late in the parliamentary session that the delay entailed in any detailed examination would be tantamount to a veto, and thus detailed examination is avoided. The legislative coordination of the House and Senate has therefore been achieved by the joint institutional recognition of the House's greater democratic legitimacy. Despite the formal equality of the two legislative assemblies, the Senate is seen to play and indeed does play a decidedly secondary role.

The Senate can amend legislation passed by the House. In such instances, the House is informed in writing of the amendments and the amendments are put to a vote in the House. If the amendments are defeated and the Senate still insists upon amendments before passage, then a meeting of representatives from the two chambers is called by the Speaker of the House to see if the impasse can be sorted out. If a bill is to be passed it must be passed in exactly the same form by the two chambers. Defeat in the Senate is absolute; it cannot be overridden by the House, which explains in part why in the past the unelected Senate has rarely opposed the will of the elected House. As noted above, in some cases the legislative process will begin in the Senate and then move to the House. This might be the case with legislation incorporating companies, or legislation of limited general effect. It was also the case for the first cut at legislation establishing the Canadian Security and Intelligence Service; the government used Senate debate and hearings as a trial balloon, and when it became clear that the legislation needed a major overhaul it was withdrawn and then later reintroduced, this time in the House.

Passage in the Senate leads to the final step in the legislative process as the bill is sent to the governor general for royal assent, which has never been refused. (The same is not true for provincial legislation, which was frequently turned back by lieutenant governors in the decades following Confederation.) The title of the bill is read in the Senate by the Clerk of the Senate and in the presence of the Speaker and members of the House. The governor general or his or her representative, such as the chief justice or another judge from the Supreme Court, signals royal assent by a nod of the head. It should be noted, however, that although the bill becomes an Act of Parliament with royal assent, it does not have the force of law until it is proclaimed. There may often be a delay of months and occasionally even years between royal assent and proclamation. For example, although the Charter of Rights and Freedoms was passed by Parliament in 1982 as part of the Constitution Act, and was ratified as a constitutional amendment by nine of the ten provincial governments, Section 15 of the Charter was not proclaimed until 1985. The delay gave Parliament and the provincial legislatures time to bring existing legislation into line with the

Section 15 provisions and thus avoid unnecessary litigation following proclamation.

Not all legislation is government legislation, although only the government has the right to introduce money bills. MPs and, more rarely, senators have the opportunity to introduce private members' bills and thereby initiate legislative debate without the support of the government. At the beginning of the parliamentary session the names of all MPs who have introduced a private members' bill for first reading in the House are put in a drum and a number of names are chosen at random. Those MPs whose names are chosen are assured that their bill will receive at least one hour of parliamentary debate, thereby entering the public record. However, such bills are severely constrained because they cannot require the raising or spending of public funds. Very little time is allotted for the debate of private members' bills, and it is a rare event when they move through the entire legislative process and are proclaimed. Such bills are used primarily to float trial balloons or to convince the local electorate that the individual MP is actively engaged in the legislative process. (American senators and congressmen employ this tactic far more often than do Canadian parliamentarians.) Trial balloons that show some potential for lift-off may be co-opted by the government and brought back as government legislation. Yet exceptions to this general assessment do occur. On January 1, 1990, the Non-smoker's Health Act came into effect, prohibiting smoking in any workplace regulated by the federal government including the public service, radio stations, shipping companies, and crown corporations. This act had been introduced into the House not only as a private members' bill, but also by an opposition MP.

The speed with which the legislative process moves depends upon a number of factors including the determination and skill of opposition parties in frustrating the government. Opposition parties can draw from an impressive arsenal of procedural weapons, including legislative debate itself. As Franks points out:

> The function of much debate is not to state, convince, prove, persuade, rally, or support, but simply to occupy time. Time is a valuable commodity in the House of Commons, and it is in short supply. The consumption of time through prolonged debate is a weapon the opposition can use in its warfare with the government.[45]

The speed of the process depends in addition upon the priority the government attaches to the bill, the urgency of public concern, the number of other legislative initiatives competing for time and attention, and the degree to which the parties share a common interest in the legislation. Although it normally takes months to complete the process, speed is possible; in 1981, a bill to increase the salaries of MPs moved through all stages in the House in only five hours![46] Here it should also be noted that the government has resources other than public opinion at its disposal in determining the pace of parliamentary debate. At the extreme, closure can be invoked to terminate debate. In some circumstances, the purpose of prolonged debate may simply be to provoke the government into using closure, which in itself becomes another cause célèbre for the opposition. The use of closure is not without risk, given the potential appearance of a government riding roughshod over legitimate debate and concerns, but it appears nonetheless that closure is becoming an increasingly common and less controversial response by the government to prolonged opposition debate. What used to be extreme has now been routinized to a considerable degree.

This description of the legislative process does not capture many of the nuances of parliamentary procedure, nor does it capture the "theatre" of parliamentary government. The House provides the national stage upon which are played out the dramas, tragedies, and even comedies of Canadian political life. MPs are cast into roles—the Leader of the Opposition, the crusading backbencher, the indignant minister, the embattled prime minister—and in the forty-minute daily Question Period these roles are played to the hilt before partisan colleagues and foes, before the limited audience in the Visitors' Gallery and—through the media—before the electorate. Question Period provides a highly visible opportunity for MPs to hold the government responsible to the House. It is, moreover, Question Period that attracts the most media coverage—newspaper coverage of Question Period exceeds coverage of debate on government bills by a ratio of 35:1[47]—and that generates most of the ten-second clips for television news. MPs are able to question ministers about current events, about charges of corruption and misconduct, and indeed about any matter they may choose. Not surprisingly, Question Period is dominated by opposition MPs and by the leaders of the opposition parties, who have the option to lead off the daily assault; questions by government backbenchers are much less frequent and, when asked, are often used to set up favourable statements by ministers. Question Period is valued because it forces ministers, day in and day out, to respond to their critics, but it is not an unqualified blessing for parliamentary democracy. Ministers can evade most questions if they choose to do so, and the prime minister can slough off difficult questions to ministers. More importantly, media coverage captures MPs in their most adversarial and abrasive temper. The results of public inquiries such as the Spicer Commission suggest that the partisan and polemical character of Question Period has contributed to the erosion of public confidence in parliamentary institutions.

To bring this procedural discussion to a close, it should be noted that the parliamentary environment is very complex. Not surprisingly, MPs and senators take considerable time to learn the rules of the game and even longer to exploit them successfully to their own partisan and personal advantage. Parliamentarians go through a period of socialization and apprenticeship that includes committee assignments and, if fortunate, a position as parliamentary secretary to a cabinet minister or, if an opposition MP, a position in the shadow cabinet. Finally, it should be noted that involvement in the legislative process is only part of the MP's job, and indeed a minor part for many MPs. A great deal of time and energy is expended on constituency service—answering letters and phone calls, sorting out bureaucratic problems, attending constituency events, and hosting visitors in Ottawa. The MP serves as an informal ombudsman for constituents as they become entangled in disputes about pensions, unemployment insurance, passports, agricultural subsidies, and a myriad of other program areas in which the federal government plays a role. The MP is also involved in parliamentary committee work that may have little to do with legislation per se, and is responsible for the party organization in his or her constituency. Thus for many MPs it may be all to the good that what goes on in Question Period and legislative debate is little more than ritualistic combat, for they are freed as a consequence to get on with more important aspects of their political careers.

PARLIAMENTARY REFORM

Parliamentary institutions have come under a good deal of public criticism in recent years. That criticism in part has spilled over from the ongoing constitutional debate; the discussion of Senate reform, for example, has been driven as much by the broader constitutional debate as it has been by any detailed examination of the day-to-day operation of the Senate. In part the criticism has sprung from public dissatisfaction with particular pieces of legislation that have appeared to offer evidence of parliamentarians being out of touch with the views and preferences of their constituents. Here the GST provides perhaps the most outstanding example. In part it has sprung from a failure to appreciate the principled underpinnings of parliamentary democracy and, more specifically, to understand the positive contribution of party discipline to responsible and effective government.[48] However, many of the most cogent criticisms have come from within Parliament itself as parliamentarians have sought to grapple with the changing nature of democratic politics. These internal critiques have coincided with public attacks in that both focus particularly on problems associated with party discipline, and both seek to enhance the role and influence of the ordinary MP.

House of Commons Reform

There is no question that perceptions of party discipline are the major source of public dissatisfaction with the performance of parliamentary

institutions, and that party discipline is the least understood and appreciated aspect of parliamentary democracy. The role of party discipline in
providing responsible and effective government is largely overlooked by
citizens who perceive their MPs to be little more than trained seals prepared to place the interests of their party above the interests of their constituents, region, and even principles. Of course, appearances are not
totally deceiving, for when it comes to formal votes in the House, MPs
and particularly government MPs have little option but to toe the party
line. The loss of confidence that might follow from legislative defeat, and
thus the trials and uncertainties of a national election campaign, constitute too great a risk to place constituency interests or personal beliefs
above the interests of one's party. However, the appearance of trained
seals is also misleading in that MPs may be vigorous spokespersons for
constituency and regional interests behind the closed doors of party caucus and in lobbying efforts with cabinet ministers and bureaucrats. Unfortunately, this activity takes place almost entirely in private, is known to
only a few, and therefore does little to enhance the public's image of Parliament; representation takes place, but it is not transparent. In the case of
regional representation, more visible if not necessarily more effective representation is left to provincial premiers and the politics of executive
federalism.

Party discipline is often seen as an unfortunate contaminant in legislative debate, one that reduces what should be a serious, deliberative discussion to little more than a shouting match among partisan camps. While
this perception is not without foundation, we must also recognize that parliamentary debate serves a number of quite different purposes. Partisan
clashes help build party solidarity and morale: "a well-fought battle rallies
the opposition troops; the opposition does not expect to gain concessions
or make changes, but creates its own coherence and enthusiasm through
attack on the government."[49] As noted above, the purpose of much debate
is simply to consume time and thereby to frustrate the legislative timetable
of the government. In this context, John Reid has somewhat cynically
observed that "the purpose of most debates in the House of Commons is
not to enlighten but to beat one's opponents to death by dullness."[50] As
Franks points out, "the struggle in the House is not to change the minds
and votes of Members of Parliament, but to woo and win the voters in the
next election."[51] It is thus irrelevant that debate has no impact on decisions taken in the House, for the primary audience is external to the
House.

Party discipline has always been a particular bone of contention in
Western Canada where it is seen to choke off rather than facilitate regional
representation. Radical reform movements such as the Progressives in the
1920s, Social Credit in the 1930s, and the Reform Party more recently
have targeted party discipline as a priority for institutional reform. The
perceived problems of party discipline have also spilled over into regional

support for Senate reform; frustration with the constrained nature of regional representation in the House has prompted a search for other outlets. At the same time, the problems that any significant reduction in party discipline might pose for *responsible* government are largely ignored. It should be noted, however, that there may be ways in which the scope of party discipline could be reduced without serious damage to the canons of responsible government. It is interesting to observe, for instance, that party discipline is more relaxed in the much larger British House of Commons. (Size alone may weaken party discipline as a larger number of MPs reduces the odds of a cabinet appointment and promotes the emergence of "career backbenchers" who maintain electoral visibility by harassing the government.) Bills in the British Parliament are identified by the government at the start of the legislative process as one, two, or three-whip bills. In the first case the sponsoring minister may indicate a preference as to how his or her party members should vote, but government MPs are free to vote according to their conscience or constituency preferences. No penalties are applied to MPs who break party ranks, and the defeat of the legislation would not signify that the cabinet has lost the confidence of the House. In the case of two-whip bills, the cabinet and sponsoring minister indicate a considerably stronger preference, and government MPs are expected to follow party lines unless exceptional circumstances prevail. Even in this case, however, the defeat of the bill would not signify a loss of confidence; by designating the bill as a two-whip measure, the government has declared in advance that the parliamentary vote will not be interpreted as a confidence measure. Three-whip bills are confidence measures; party discipline is strictly enforced, defectors can expect to be sanctioned, and the defeat of the bill would force the resignation of the government and precipitate a general election. It is both ironic and frustrating that Canadian parliamentarians display greater fidelity to the Westminster model at the time of Confederation than they pay attention to the more contemporary British experience. As Esberey notes, the Westminster model has become "petrified" in Canada.[52]

The impression should not be left, of course, that Canadian MPs are little more than robots with little effective freedom of action, tied hand and foot by party discipline. Private channels of protest do exist, including the weekly caucus meeting where dissension can be safely and at times effectively vented behind closed doors. To a limited degree, public dissension is also possible in speeches outside the House, and MPs can lobby members of the cabinet on behalf of constituency interests. "Free votes" do occur in Parliament, although they are generally restricted to issues with a heavy moral content, such as capital punishment and abortion, where party discipline would be difficult to maintain even if imposed. The committee system also provides an opportunity for backbenchers to question the details of government legislation and to propose amendments. The fact remains, however, that much of the representational work that MPs do takes place in private, out of the sight of constituents. Although in private the MP may be an indefatigable champion of constituency and regional interests, the public image of the MP is that of a slave to party discipline at the expense of regional interests. It is not that party discipline prevents effective representation, but rather that it inhibits dramatic *public* displays of representation in action.

Recent internal reforms to the House of Commons have concentrated on enhancing the resources of individual MPs and strengthening the role of committees within the legislative process. MPs today are much better resourced than were their counterparts of twenty or thirty years ago, and committees play a more active role, if not necessarily a more visible or effective role, within the legislative process. Reform proposals currently under consideration would further strengthen the role of committees. For example, televised committee hearings would increase the visibility of parliamentary committees, would give additional media exposure to backbench and opposition MPs, and would provide an opportunity for less partisan media clips than that provided by the daily Question Period. A more important change would be for the government to send draft legislation to the committees for preliminary discussion before legislative proposals are formally introduced as bills in the House. Still, the reforms that have taken place to date and the reform proposals currently on the table should be seen as evolutionary in character, reforms that attempt to fine-tune parliamentary institutions without disrupting the basic principles of parliamentary government. Discussions of more fundamental, root-and-branch reform have generally been confined to the Senate.

Senate Reform

To say that the Senate has never been a popular institution in Canada would be to greatly overstate the degree of public support it has enjoyed. Part of what can only be described as public antagonism arises because senators are appointed and not elected; that senators are appointed by the federal government rather than by provincial governments has been of concern to provincial governments and academic commentators, but has not had a major impact on public perceptions. Who appoints senators is less important than the fact that they are appointed. Unfortunately, but perhaps inevitably, the appointment process, and hence the Senate, has fallen into disrepute. Senate appointments are seen primarily as a reward for party service, a means of paying off political debts and removing deadwood from active political life. While this perception is not always justified, it is correct often enough to tarnish even the most worthy Senate appointment. More importantly, an appointed Senate lacks political legitimacy within a democratic system and as a consequence is unable to fulfil its federal role of providing effective regional representation. There is no effective balancing of majority interests, expressed through the House of Commons, and regional interests, expressed through the Senate. Given the role that second chambers are designed to play in federal states, it is not surprising that the Canadian Senate has become a habitual target of reform for those promoting more effective forms of regional representation.

In the late 1970s and early 1980s, Senate reform was proposed as a solution to incessant intergovernmental conflict and, more positively, as a response to the need for more effective intergovernmental coordination. Reform proposals such as those recommended by the Pépin-Robarts Royal Commission envisioned a House of the Provinces to which provincial governments would send delegations. Those delegations would vote as a bloc on instructions from their government, thereby providing provincial governments with a general check on the legislative activities of the national government and, in some reform models, with a specific check on the use of the federal spending power in areas of exclusive provincial jurisdiction. Senate reform of this type would have had a decentralizing impact on the Canadian federal state, not by changing the constitutional division of powers, but by bringing provincial governments into the heart of the national legislative process without providing for any reciprocal national influence on provincial legislative assemblies. It was a reform model in keeping with the decentralist thrust of Quebec nationalism and with the more general support for decentralization that was characteristic of constitutional deliberations prior to the passage of the Constitution Act, 1982. The emphasis was on the representation of provincial governments rather than electorates within the national legislative process.

By the mid-1980s the House of the Provinces model began to lose ground to a model designed to address chronic problems of regional alienation rather than intergovernmental conflict. This new approach, which has been identified most closely with the "Triple E" vision of an elected, equal, and effective Senate, was built around very different representational concerns. Rather than providing an enhanced role for provincial governments, it would provide for the direct popular election of senators. The impact of such reform would be to diminish and not enhance the role of provincial governments and premiers on the national stage; the latter would have to compete for national attention and influence with elected senators from their province, senators who might enjoy a broader electoral mandate. Regional alienation would be addressed in a number of ways: the election of senators would strengthen ties between citizens and their national government; an equal number of seats for all provinces would give "outer Canada" sufficient legislative clout to counterbalance central Canadian domination of the House of Commons; and an effective Senate would ensure that regional representatives would in fact be heard in Ottawa. Just as the House of the Provinces model is decentralizing in principle, the Triple E model would be centralizing in effect. Its major

Rodewalt, *Calgary Herald*; reprinted from Guy Badeaux, ed., *Portfoolio 8* (Toronto: Macmillan, 1992), p. 16.

objective is to strengthen the legitimacy and clout of federal politicians and legislative institutions, and it is therefore a model of institutional reform that runs directly contrary to the decentralizing current of Quebec nationalism.

Support for an elected Senate, although not necessarily for an equal or effective Senate, gained additional momentum from the public discontent with parliamentary institutions documented by the Spicer Commission, and from the public dissatisfaction with executive federalism that grew out of the Meech Lake debacle. The 1991 constitutional proposal by the federal government, which neatly side-stepped House of Commons reform, called for an elected and equitable Senate armed with substantive powers. As the constitutional debate progressed through late 1991 and the first part of 1992, those Senate reform proposals remained reasonably intact, and in the end the Charlottetown Accord proposed an equal Senate in which every province would have six seats. The proposed Senate would have been elected, although not necessarily by the people; in a concession to Quebec, the proposal included the option of indirect election by provincial legislatures or, given the realities of Canadian legislative government, appointment by the provincial cabinet. The proposed Senate would have had an absolute veto on new taxes on natural resources, francophone senators would have had an absolute veto on legislation materially affecting the French language or culture, and aboriginal senators would have had an absolute veto on legislation materially affecting aboriginal peoples. In most cases, the defeat of legislation in the Senate would have triggered a joint sitting of the House and Senate in which a simple majority would be needed to pass the legislation. In this situation, an enlarged House of Commons would have meant that MPs would outnumber senators by a margin of greater than five to one in joint sittings.

The Senate reform debate exposed a number of important institutional tensions. First, the proponents of Senate reform challenged many of the fundamental tenets of responsible government by seeking to weaken executive control over the legislative process. Second, Senate reform of virtually any stripe would shift power to the regional peripheries lying to the east and west of the central Canadian heartland, and thus Senate reformers seek to redefine the power relationship among regional communities in Canada. Third, and not unrelated to the first two points, the quest for Senate reform posed serious complications for the representation of Quebec and the country's very sizable francophone minority within national parliamentary institutions. Any move toward provincial equality in the Senate ran up against the awkward demographic fact that Canada's linguistic minority is concentrated in one of the largest provinces. Approximately 87 percent of francophones live in Quebec, and therefore any reduction of Quebec's weight in the Senate would also be a reduction in francophone representation. Here it should also be noted that the threat Senate reform poses to cabinet dominance can also be seen as a threat to Quebec and thus to francophone representation. Bakvis shows that since the 1960s Quebec francophones have been slightly overrepresented in the federal cabinet and have occupied major economic portfolios. Quebec ministers, enjoying strong caucus support from Quebec MPs, "have given genuine meaning to the expression 'French power in Ottawa.'"[53] This, Bakvis argues, explains "the reluctance of Quebec to embrace Senate reform in so far as an elected Senate, in which the smaller provinces enjoy overrepresentation, could derogate power and influence from cabinet."[54]

Senate reformers maintained significant momentum throughout the late 1980s and early 1990s despite the fact that virtually all of the existing institutional actors would lose by Senate reform. The potential losers went beyond the two central Canadian provinces to include MPs in the House of Commons, who would have to share the stage with a second elected chamber; the cabinet and the prime minister, whose control over the legislative process would be weakened if the reformed Senate was effective;

provincial premiers, who would be eclipsed as the primary advocates and defenders of regional interests on the national stage; the existing senators; and perhaps provincial governments in general if, as has been the case in both Australia and the United States, more effective regional representation at the centre were to strengthen the role of national institutions. Yet despite this opposition among the very institutional actors whose support was required for constitutional amendment, the Senate reform bus kept rolling along until late 1992.

There is no question that the rejection of the Charlottetown Accord has stopped the movement for Senate reform in its tracks. However, the problems with the existing Senate remain. It is still appointed, not elected, and provincial governments have no role in the appointment process. It still has formal legislative powers virtually equal to those of the House, powers that the unelected senators seem increasingly inclined to exercise. It is still based on an antiquated formula of regional representation that makes little if any contemporary sense. And it is still an institution that attracts unrelenting public criticism and no discernible public support. Note, for example, the vehemence of *La Presse*'s Lysiane Gagnon's assessment:

> *In the post-Trudeau years, as Liberal senators began their childish vendettas against the Mulroney government, the Senate evolved from an innocuous, albeit expensive retirement home for old cronies and bagmen, to a vicious antidemocratic thorn in our parliamentary system. Whether one likes Tory legislation or not, the sight of unelected senators blocking or delaying laws approved by elected parliamentarians has been one of the worst political scandals of the last few years.[55]*

Therefore, it is hard to see how the status quo can hold despite the understandable reluctance of Canadians to tackle constitutional reform. Sooner or later the appointed Senate and elected House will clash again on a major policy issue, and at that point the only issue will be whether the Senate will be reformed or abolished.

THE INSTITUTIONAL LANDSCAPE

The intent of this chapter has been to sketch in the major features of the institutional landscape, to identify and briefly describe the primary institutional actors in Canadian political life. The reader should be aware, however, that the picture that has been presented is far from complete. Canadian governments are wide-ranging and complex organizations, and the discussion presented above has done no more than scratch the surface. The reader should also be aware that the institutional landscape is far from stable. Changes in government, and at times even changes of leaders within the same governing party, are analogous to earthquakes within the institutional landscape as new governments and leaders seek to transform that landscape to fit their own political visions. Quite apart from such major disruptions, a more subtle, incremental transformation is ongoing as institutions adapt to a rapidly changing political, economic, and social environment.

The internal procedures of the House of Commons have evolved considerably over time and will continue to evolve.[56] However, most of the reforms have only been apparent to MPs and to aficionados of the Hill. This is not to say that the reforms have been unimportant, for they have not. At the same time, they have not provided much purchase on public dissatisfaction with the House and the behaviour of MPs, or on more general discontent with the responsiveness and representativeness of parliamentary democracy. In the absence of more visible, root-and-branch reform to the House, it is not surprising that a good deal of the public's dissatisfaction has come to be focused on the Senate. As Mallory noted prior to the most recent constitutional debate, "because so few people seem to love the Senate, it seems all too easy to use it as a readily saleable part of a constitutional reform package."[57] It is also the case that MPs have been very resistant to fundamental reform to the House and have been more than happy to have the Senate serve as the lightning rod for public discontent. The irony is that if the Senate had been reformed along the lines proposed by the Charlottetown Accord, it may have acted as a goad rather than as an alternative to House reform as MPs scrambled to catch up to a revitalized second chamber and, for the most part, elected senators. In any event, we should now expect a revived and intensified public debate on House of Commons reform in the wake of the rejection of the Charlottetown Accord and its proposals for Senate reform. Should the Senate be abolished, pressure for House of Commons reform may intensify even more.

SUGGESTED READINGS

1. Michael M. Atkinson, *Governing Canada: Institutions and Public Policy* (Toronto: Harcourt Brace Jovanovich, 1993).

2. Herman Bakvis, *Regional Ministers: Power and Influence in the Canadian Cabinet* (Toronto: University of Toronto Press, 1991).

3. André Bzdera, "Comparative Analysis of Federal High Courts: A Political Theory of Judicial Review," *Canadian Journal of Political Science*, 26:1 (March 1993), pp. 3–29.

4. C.E.S. Franks, *The Parliament of Canada* (Toronto: University of Toronto Press, 1987).

5. Leslie A. Pal and David Taras, *Prime Ministers and Premiers: Political Leadership and Public Policy in Canada* (Scarborough: Prentice-Hall, 1988).

6. Peter H. Russell, *The Judiciary in Canada: The Third Branch of Government* (Toronto: McGraw-Hill Ryerson, 1987).

7. Donald V. Smiley and Ronald L. Watts, *Intrastate Federalism in Canada* (Toronto: University of Toronto Press, 1985).

8. David E. Smith, "Empire, Crown and Canadian Federalism," *Canadian Journal of Political Science*, 24:3 (September 1991), pp. 451–73.

9. Sharon L. Sutherland, "Responsible Government and Ministerial Responsibility: Every Reform Is Its Own Problem," *Canadian Journal of Political Science*, 24:1 (March 1991), pp. 91–120.

10. Paul G. Thomas, "The Role of National Party Caucuses," in Peter Aucoin, Research Coordinator, *Party Government and Regional Representation in Canada* (Toronto: University of Toronto Press, 1985), pp. 69–136.

STUDY QUESTIONS

1. You have been asked to appear in a public debate to defend the proposition that "Parliament provides a reasonably accurate reflection of Canadian public opinion." Your opponent notes that Canadians have consistently supported the death penalty while MPs have opposed it, that political parties opposing the Canada–U.S. Free Trade Agreement won almost 60 percent of the popular vote in the 1988 federal election, and that the GST was imposed despite overwhelming public opposition. How do you respond? How can you defend instances where major splits develop between public and parliamentary opinion? How can you link your defence to the underlying principles of Canadian parliamentary democracy?

2. There is no question that the 295 MPs do not capture the social diversity of the Canadian population; women, ethnic and racial minorities, aboriginal Canadians, and for that matter youth are only some of the groups that fail to find proportionate representation within the ranks of Canadian MPs. But to what extent should this be seen as a problem? What are the practical and symbolic consequences? If you do see it as a serious problem, what remedial steps

might you propose? If you do not see it as a problem, how would you defend your position to those groups who are at present underrepresented in the House of Commons?

3. One of the current options for Senate reform is the Triple A: Abolish, Abolish, Abolish. What would be the impact of this option on the principles of parliamentary democracy discussed in this chapter? What would be the impact on your region of the country? Given these assessments, would you support or oppose the Triple A option?

NOTES

1. E.E. Schattschneider, *The Semi-Sovereign People: A Realist's View of Democracy in America* (New York: Holt, Rinehart and Winston, 1960).

2. Allan Kornberg, William Mishler, and Harold D. Clarke, *Representative Democracy in the Canadian Provinces* (Scarborough: Prentice-Hall, 1982), p. 175.

3. For a complete discussion of ministerial responsibility, see S.L. Sutherland, "Responsible Government and Ministerial Responsibility: Every Reform Is Its Own Problem," *Canadian Journal of Political Science*, 24:1 (March 1991), pp. 91–120.

4. Thomas A. Hockin, "Adversary Politics and Some Functions of the Canadian House of Commons," in Richard Schultz, Orest M. Kruhlak, and John C. Terry, eds., *The Canadian Political Process*, 3rd ed. (Toronto: Holt, Rinehart and Winston, 1979), p. 315.

5. David E. Smith, "Party Government, Representation and National Integration in Canada," in Peter Aucoin, Research Coordinator, *Party Government and Regional Representation in Canada* (Toronto: University of Toronto Press, 1985), p. 5.

6. John B. Stewart, *The Canadian House of Commons* (Montreal and London: McGill-Queen's University Press, 1977), p. 14.

7. Mark MacGuigan, "Impediments to an Enlarged Role for the Backbencher," in Paul Fox, ed., *Politics: Canada*, 5th ed. (Toronto: McGraw-Hill Ryerson, 1982), p. 496.

8. Peter Aucoin, "Regionalism, Party and National Government," in Peter Aucoin, Research Coordinator, *Party Government and Regional Representation in Canada* (Toronto: University of Toronto Press, 1985), p. 146.

9. C.E.S. Franks, *The Parliament of Canada* (Toronto: University of Toronto Press, 1987), p. 115.

10. Richard Crossman, *Government and the Governed* (London: Christophers, 1939), p. 5.

11. Robert J. Jackson and Michael M. Atkinson, *The Canadian Legislative System*, 2nd ed. (Toronto: Macmillan, 1980), p. 113.

12. Franks, *The Parliament of Canada*, p. 258.

13. Ibid., p. 259.

14. S.E. Finer, *The Changing British Party System, 1945–1979* (Washington, D.C.: American Enterprise Institute, 1980), p. 178.

15. Hockin, "Adversary Politics," p. 361.

16. George C. Perlin, *The Tory Syndrome: Leadership Politics in the Progressive Conservative Party* (Montreal: McGill-Queen's University Press, 1980).

17. Franks, *The Parliament of Canada*, p. 265.

18. J.R. Mallory, *The Structure of Canadian Government* (Toronto: Macmillan, 1971), p. 248.

19. See Jennifer Smith, "Canadian Confederation and the Influence of American Federalism," *Canadian Journal of Political Science*, 21:3 (September 1988), pp. 443–64.

20. The brief exception to this rule came during the three years between the initial signing of the Meech Lake Accord in 1987 and its collapse in June 1990. During this interregnum, Prime Minister Mulroney agreed to make Senate appointments from lists submitted by provincial governments.

21. David E. Smith, "Empire, Crown and Canadian Federalism," *Canadian Journal of Political Science*, 24:3 (September 1991), pp. 451–73.

22. Ibid., p. 460.

23. Aucoin, "Regionalism, Party and National Government," p. 137.

24. The failure of the Meech Lake Accord to find legislative ratification has shaken this assumption.

25. For an extended discussion of this point, see Roger Gibbins, *Regionalism: Territorial Politics in Canada and the United States* (Toronto: Butterworths, 1982), ch. 4.

26. The Senate reforms proposed in the 1992 Charlottetown Accord would have removed this option by prohibiting senators from sitting in the federal cabinet.

27. Nelson Wiseman, "The Questionable Relevance of the Constitution in Advancing Minority Cultural Rights in Manitoba," *Canadian Journal of Political Science*, 25:4 (December 1992), p. 701.

28. Herman Bakvis, *Regional Ministers: Power and Influence in the Canadian Cabinet* (Toronto: University of Toronto Press, 1991).

29. Donald V. Smiley and Ronald L. Watts, *Intrastate Federalism in Canada* (Toronto: University of Toronto Press, 1985), p. 65.

30. Ibid., p. 4.

31. Hugh Windsor, "Slim Cabinet Offers Five Kinds of Ministers," *The Globe and Mail*, June 29, 1993, p. A4.

32. See Doreen Barrie and Roger Gibbins, "Parliamentary Careers in the Canadian Federal State," *Canadian Journal of Political Science*, 22:1 (March 1989), pp. 137–45.

33. J.S. Dupré, "The Workability of Executive Federalism in Canada," in H. Bakvis and W. Chandler, eds., *Federalism and the Role of the State* (Toronto: University of Toronto Press, 1987). See also Colin Campbell, *Governments Under Stress: Political Executives and Key Bureaucrats in Washington, London and Ottawa* (Toronto: University of Toronto Press, 1983), p. 351.

34. Peter Aucoin, "The Machinery of Government: From Trudeau's Rational Management to Mulroney's Brokerage Politics," in Leslie A. Pal and David Taras, eds., *Prime Ministers and Premiers: Political Leadership and Public Policy in Canada* (Scarborough: Prentice-Hall, 1988), p. 66.

35. Ibid., p. 54.

36. Jeffrey Simpson, "Operations Unlimited," *The Globe and Mail*, May 19, 1988, p. A6.

37. Aucoin, "Regionalism, Party and National Government," p. 146.

38. Aucoin, "The Machinery of Government," p. 63.

39. Frank MacKinnon, "The Establishment of the Supreme Court of Canada," in W.R. Lederman, ed., *The Courts and the Canadian Constitution* (Toronto: McClelland and Stewart, 1964), p. 112.

40. Mallory, *The Structure of Canadian Government*, p. 331.

41. For an example of this former conclusion, see Peter W. Hogg, "Is the Supreme Court of Canada Biased in Constitutional Cases?" *Canadian Bar Review* (1979).

42. For an example of this latter conclusion, see André Bzdera, "Comparative Analysis of Federal High Courts: A Political Theory of Judicial Review," *Canadian Journal of Political Science*, 26:1 (March 1993), pp. 3–29.

43. For a recent example of this trend in Canadian political science, see Andrew D. Heard, "The Charter in the Supreme Court of Canada: The Importance of Which Judges Hear an Appeal," *Canadian Journal of Political Science*, 24:2 (June 1991), pp. 289–308.

44. *Resolutions* of the House, including those used to propose constitutional amendments, need not go through the three stages outlined below; they can be introduced and voted upon without protracted committee hearings or debate.

45. C.E.S. Franks, "The 'Problem' of Debate and Question Period," in John C. Courtney, ed., *The Canadian House of Commons: Essays in Honour of Norman Ward* (Calgary: University of Calgary Press, 1985), pp. 4–5.

46. Ronald G. Landes, *The Canadian Polity: A Comparative Introduction* (Scarborough: Prentice-Hall, 1983), p. 165.

47. Canada, House of Commons Standing Committee on Organization and Procedure, *Minutes*, November 20, 1975, 9:10.

48. This point is made emphatically by Franks in *The Parliament of Canada*, pp. 257ff.

49. Franks, "The 'Problem' of Debate and Question Period," p. 7.

50. Ibid., p. 9.

51. Ibid., p. 9.

52. Joy E. Esberey, "The 'Maple Leaf' Mutation," paper presented to the Annual Conference of the British Association for Canadian Studies, Nottingham, April 12–14, 1991, p. 2.

53. Bakvis, *Regional Ministers*, p. 287.

54. Ibid., p. 287.

55. Lysiane Gagnon, "A Word We Long to Hear from the Senate: Adieu," *The Globe and Mail*, July 3, 1993, p. D3.

56. There exists a large literature on parliamentary reform. For example, see Thomas D'Aquino, G. Bruce Doern, and Cassandra Blair, *Parliamentary Democracy in Canada: Issues for Reform* (Toronto: Methuen, 1983); Magnus Gunther and Conrad Winn, eds., *House of Commons Reform* (Ottawa: Parliamentary Intern Program, 1991).

57. J.R. Mallory, *The Structure of Canadian Government*, rev. ed. (Toronto: Gage, 1986), p. 269.

THE POLITICS OF LANGUAGE AND QUÉBÉCOIS NATIONALISM

Two features of Canadian society have been of unsurpassed importance in shaping the contours of political life. The first is the existence of a large *francophone minority* that, over the last 125 years, has constituted between a quarter and a third of the Canadian population. The second is the concentration of that minority within Quebec, where a solid *francophone majority* controls the provincial government. In conjunction, these two features have generated a complex pattern of language politics that weaves together the tensions between the anglophone national majority and the francophone national minority, between the federal and Quebec governments, between the francophone majority and anglophone minority within Quebec, and between francophone minorities and anglophone majorities within the other provinces. The resultant pattern is not only fascinating in its own right, but also provides a useful window through which to view the broader dynamics of Canadian politics.

The exploration of language politics can be compared to opening a carved set of Russian dolls; within the first doll is another, and within that another, and so forth until one is left with a table covered in doll parts but

FIGURE 4.1 *Linguistic Composition (Mother Tongue) of Canada and Quebec (1991)*

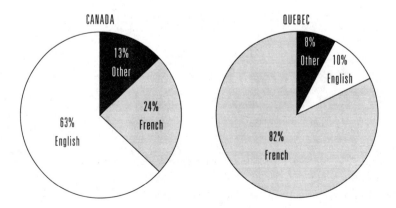

no doll. Because the components of language politics, like the dolls, are nested within one another we must consider not only each one in turn, but also their interaction in coming to grips with the language policies pursued by the governments of Canada, Quebec, and the other nine provinces. At the same time, the reader should be aware that language forms only part of the complex relationship between the French and English communities in Canada. The historical relationship was based in large part on the religious division between Catholics and Protestants; language per se was important primarily as a carrier of religious and cultural values. Then, as both social and political life became more secular in tone and substance, language itself came increasingly to the fore. As René Lévesque wrote in 1968:

> At the core of the Québécois personality is the fact that we speak French. Everything else depends on this one essential element and follows from it or leads us infallibly back to it.[1]

While cultural, class, and religious differences between the two communities are by no means absent today—hence the recent constitutional attempts to recognize Quebec as a "distinct society"—the place of Quebec and francophones within the broader fabric of Canadian life is largely defined in linguistic terms. Here it should also be noted that although conflict emerges as the dominant theme in any discussion of language politics, the two linguistic communities have co-existed for more than two centuries without either bloodshed or the assimilation of the francophone minority. The survival of the "French fact" speaks well not only for francophones' tenacious defence of their language and culture, but also for the political system's ability to forge and maintain relatively stable compromises in very contentious areas of public policy.

LINGUISTIC COMPOSITION OF CANADA AND QUEBEC

Over the years the linguistic composition of Canada has been reasonably stable. Figure 4.2 shows that since 1931 the percentage of Canada's population whose mother tongue (the language first spoken and still understood) is French has varied within a range of only 4 percent. (These data were not available prior to the 1931 census.) Figure 4.2 also shows that Quebec's share of the national population, a share roughly equivalent to the combined population of seven provinces—Newfoundland, Prince Edward Island, Nova Scotia, New Brunswick, Manitoba, Saskatchewan, and Alberta—has also been reasonably stable over time, although between 1961 and 1991 its share dropped from 28.8 to 25.3 percent.

In many ways it is remarkable that Quebec has retained a quarter of the national population and that almost one Canadian in four is of French

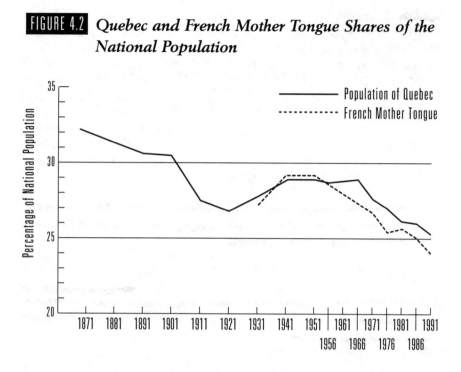

FIGURE 4.2 *Quebec and French Mother Tongue Shares of the National Population*

Population of Quebec

French Mother Tongue

mother tongue. The present francophone population of over six million can be traced almost entirely to the 70,000 French settlers who remained in Canada after the capture of New France by British forces in 1759–60.[2] Immigration from France virtually ceased in 1760 just as immigration from other countries was getting under way. Soon francophones became a minority within the British North American colonies, although they remained a clear majority in what is now Quebec. Immigrants from countries other than France tended to settle outside Quebec, in part because economic opportunities were better and land was more readily available, in part because of the relatively homogeneous and therefore closed nature of the French-Canadian community, and in part because English was of greater economic currency in North America than was French. (For many immigrants, Canada was little more than a stop-over on their way to the United States.) For every immigrant who settled in Quebec during the first 100 years after Confederation, three to four settled in Ontario.[3] As Table 4.1 illustrates, that pattern has continued. Of all immigrants living in Canada in 1991, 54.6 percent lived in Ontario while only 16.6 percent lived in Quebec.

TABLE 4.1 Distribution of Canada's Immigrant Population, 1991

Province	# of immigrants	% prov. population	% all immigrants
Newfoundland	8,465	1.5	0.2
Prince Edward Island	4,105	3.2	0.1
Nova Scotia	39,110	4.4	0.9
New Brunswick	23,975	3.3	0.6
Quebec	591,210	8.7	13.6
Ontario	2,369,175	23.7	54.6
Manitoba	138,595	12.8	3.2
Saskatchewan	57,815	5.9	1.3
Alberta	381,510	15.1	8.8
British Columbia	723,170	22.3	16.6
Yukon	2,965	10.7	0.1
Northwest Territories	2,795	4.9	0.1
Canada	4,342,890	16.1	100.0

After 1760, and regardless of where they settled, immigrants were almost entirely anglophones to start with or overwhelmingly adopted English rather than French upon their arrival in North America. Richard Joy found that by the 1961 census 91 percent of the prewar immigrants spoke English only, 7 percent spoke both French and English, and only 1 percent spoke only French, the same proportion that spoke neither official language.[4] Between 1966 and 1976, 52.6 percent of the immigrants who settled in Canada were anglophones, only 6.7 percent were francophones, and 40.7 percent were neither.[5] Overall, then, immigration has worked in the past, and is likely to work in the future, to erode the proportionate contribution of both Quebec and francophones to the national population.

Here it should also be noted that immigration has not only reduced Quebec's share of the national population. To the limited extent that immigrants have come to Quebec they have sustained the province's non-francophone minority by assimilating into the anglophone community. (To the extent that immigrants have assimilated into the francophone community, they have weakened the cultural homogeneity of that community.) Historically, the proportion of immigrants adopting English rather than French was only slightly less in Quebec than in Canada as a whole; René Lévesque estimated that of the 620,000 immigrants who came to Quebec between 1945 and 1966, of whom only 8 percent came from France, 80 percent were absorbed into the anglophone population.[6] More recently, the percentage of immigrants opting for French rather than English as their first official language has increased from 28 percent in 1981 to 37 percent in 1991, but still remains a minority. (It should also be noted that 60 percent of the immigrants arriving in Quebec over the past twenty years have since left the province.) Quebec's principal linguistic "battleground" has been and remains Montreal island, the primary locale for immigrant settlement. It is here that the important choice between Canada's official languages is being made and where the political debate over provincial sign laws has been most intense. In recent years the demographic struggle for linguistic dominance in Montreal has been further intensified by the exodus of many middle-class francophones to the suburbs, a development that has made the language choice of immigrants even more critical to the linguistic future of the city. Today only a bare majority of the Montreal school population is of French mother tongue.[7]

Quebec, like other provinces, has experienced a steady loss of population through out-migration, a loss attesting to the geographical mobility that Canadians enjoy. In Quebec's case, however, out-migration was primarily to the United States rather than to other provinces, and thus most of those who left were lost not only to Quebec, but to French Canada more broadly defined. Quebec migrants, for instance, played a relatively minor role in the settlement of the Canadian West; for every one person who moved from Quebec to the West before 1931, six moved to the West from Ontario and eight moved from Quebec to the United States.[8] Without infusion from Quebec, francophone communities in the West and outside Quebec more generally were left exposed to the assimilationist pressure of the anglophone majority. As Joy concludes, "the great exodus of French Canadians toward the United States was one of the decisive factors contributing to the supremacy of the English language in Canada."[9]

In Quebec's case, out-migration was offset not by immigration from abroad or from other provinces, but by a high birthrate reflecting the rural character of early 20th-century Quebec, the dominance of the Catholic religion, and a cultural ethos that linked a high birthrate to the very survival of French Canada. With respect to this last point, Joy cites the eulogy in a Beauce County newspaper for a Monsieur Philippon who, when he died at the age of 96, left 600 descendants: "the grandfather of Mr. Philippon met an honorable death at the Battle of the Plains of Abraham; his grandson has well revenged this death by adding, through his own efforts (sic!), an entire parish to French Canada."[10] This "revanche des berceaux" or "revenge of the cradle" played a critical role in maintaining Quebec's share of the national population in the face of the "fatal hemorrhage" of French Canadians into the New England states and the steady flow of overseas emigration into Ontario and the West. By the 1960s, however, this demographic balance was upset by a number of changes of which the most important was a dramatic decline in the birthrate. In 1931 Quebec's birthrate had been 40 percent greater than that for the country as a whole, but this advantage declined to 35 percent in 1941, 26 percent in 1951, 9 percent in 1961, and 6 percent in 1966.[11] By 1971 Quebec's birthrate had fallen below the national average, and by the mid-1970s it was the lowest in Canada. By the late 1980s the birthrate in Quebec had fallen to 1.4 children per fertile woman (1.2 among anglophones), well below the national rate of 1.8 and even further below the replacement rate of 2.1 required for a stable population. Indeed, Quebec's birthrate is now one of the lowest in the world. Although in 1989 the Quebec government introduced special financial incentives designed to reduce the financial burden imposed by young children,[12] these incentives have had little impact. In fact, the province's birthrate fell between 1990 and 1991.

At the same time that Quebec's birthrate was plummeting, provincial language legislation and intensified Québécois nationalism increased emigration from the anglophone community and reduced even further in-migration from other provinces and countries. In the wake of the Quiet Revolution in the early 1960s and the coming to power of the Parti Québécois in 1976, Quebec anglophones underwent a dramatic transformation. Historically, they had carried far greater economic and political weight than their numbers warranted. Although a minority within Quebec, albeit one with deep historical roots, they were able to draw upon the political power of the anglophone national majority, and upon the cultural and economic power of an overwhelming continental majority. Anglophones formed the economic elite in Quebec, although by no means were all Quebec anglophones part of that elite. They were the representatives of Anglo-Canadian and American capital, and in a crude sense, they had the power and political protection that money can buy.[13] Anglophones also formed a sizable electoral constituency in Quebec that could be ignored only at considerable political risk. Furthermore, anglophone or, more accurately, Protestant educational institutions were constitutionally protected through Sections 93.2 and 93.3 of the Constitution Act, 1867. Finally, Section 133 of the same act stated that "either the English or the French language may be used by any Person in the Debates of the Houses of the Parliament of Canada and of the Houses of the Legislature of Quebec; and both those Languages shall be used in the respective Records and Journals of those Houses; and either of those Languages may be used by any Person or in any Pleading or Process in or issuing from any Court of Canada established under this Act, and in or from all or any of the Courts of Quebec."

Yet despite all such advantages, the political position of the anglophone minority was precarious in the long run. It was inevitable that the francophone majority would use its democratic control of the provincial political system to redress the linguistic disparities in wealth and economic opportunity. What was needed before this could occur was a more positive outlook toward state intervention in the economic order and an altered political perspective in which Anglo-Quebeckers were seen less in a Canadian context (as part of the national majority) and more in a Québécois context (as a provincial minority). As we will see below, the Quiet Revolution provided both. As a result, Quebec anglophones became strangers, if not imperialists, in their own land, "les autres" in a province vibrating to the themes of Québécois nationalism. Anglophones took up the uncomfortable garments of minority status being shed by francophones; their relative wealth became a political stigma, and their contribution to the province was stripped of symbolic recognition as Quebec was increasingly recast as a Québécois and francophone society. Their grip on the province's business community was loosened, if not broken, by language legislation and educational reform. Not surprisingly, many left Quebec to seek a more hospitable social and linguistic climate; between 1976 and 1986, 147,000 more anglophones left Quebec for other provinces than moved to Quebec from other provinces.[14] Anglophones have been twenty-three times more likely than francophones to leave Quebec, whereas francophones in the rest of Canada have been twenty-six times more likely than their anglophone compatriots to move to Quebec.[15]

The remaining "allophone" community in Quebec is no longer *English* Canadian, as it had largely been in the past. Somewhat ironically, this diverse ethnic population, composed of those whose mother tongue is not French, is bound together primarily by the province's language legislation. Here it is also interesting to note parenthetically that Quebec's language legislation has at the same time increased the heterogeneity of the francophone community. The legislation has separated language and culture by making French the principal language of communication for *all* cultures in Quebec. Whereas in the past francophones shared a common history, culture, and religious orientation, this will be less and less the case in the future as the francophone community expands to encompass the totality of Quebec society. Historical events like the "conquest" may lose their integrative and symbolic force as a growing proportion of the increasingly heterogeneous francophone community comes to find its roots in quite different historical settings.

The demographic changes outlined above have not only deepened the country's linguistic divide and eroded Quebec's share of the national population; they have also strengthened nationalist arguments in Quebec. In its 1979 proposal for sovereignty-association, the Quebec government stated that it would be an illusion to believe that francophones could, in the future, play a determining role in the Government of Canada:

> On the contrary, they will be more and more a minority and English Canada will find it increasingly easy to govern without them....Given these prospects ... Quebecers feel it is urgent to take action before it is too late.[16]

From this perspective, the longer Quebec stays in Canada, the weaker its demographic position will be and thus the more difficult it will be to negotiate favourable terms through which Confederation might be restructured or dissolved. More recently, Quebec's concern over the impact of immigration found expression in the immigration provisions of the Meech Lake and Charlottetown accords, provisions designed to ensure that Quebec would receive a proportionate share of immigration to Canada, that the Quebec government would have a significant degree of influence on immigration policy, and that immigrants to Quebec would be assimilated into the francophone community.

As Table 4.2 shows, however, the French language has more than held its own throughout Quebec despite the challenges posed by immigration. Anglophones, who are more likely than in the past to be recent immigrants, are increasingly confined to the Montreal area although significant enclaves still exist in the eastern townships, the upper Ottawa Valley, and Hull. Between 1971 and 1986, the proportion of Quebeckers with English mother tongue declined from 13.1 to 10.4 percent. The proportion of students attending French schools increased from 83.4 percent in 1976–77 to 87.5 percent in 1982–83, and is expected to reach between 91 and 92 percent by 1993–94.[17] Here it should be noted, however, that some of the very factors that are strengthening the French language in Quebec, such as the anglophone exodus, are undercutting the demographic strength of Quebec in Canada.

TABLE 4.2 *Percentage of Quebec Population with French Mother Tongue*

1931	79.7
1941	81.6
1951	82.5
1961	81.2
1971	80.7
1976	80.0
1981	82.4
1986	82.8
1991	83.2

Note: 81.2 percent of Quebec residents in the 1991 census listed French as their only mother tongue; another 2 percent listed French as one of their mother tongues.

The Canadian population outside Quebec is often referred to as "English Canada," a term that neglects both anglophones inside Quebec and francophones outside Quebec—groups that play critically important roles in Canadian language politics. It also distorts our perception of the non-French community, which has become progressively less English, more ethnically diverse or multicultural, and more *Canadian* over time. While 88 percent of the non-French population was of British descent in 1871, that proportion has fallen to less than 60 percent today. Yet, while "English Canada" is much more heterogeneous in its regional, ethnic, and religious composition than is "French Canada," this greater heterogeneity has not affected the supremacy of the English language outside Quebec; in the 1991 census, 78 percent of Canadians living in provinces other than Quebec reported English as their only mother tongue.

Canadians of French mother tongue living outside Quebec at the time of the 1991 census constituted only 4.4 percent of the non-Quebec population, a decline from 7.8 percent in 1941, 6 percent in 1971, and 5 percent in 1986. In the past, Canada was sprinkled with French-Canadian communities whose relatively self-contained educational, social, and religious institutions preserved the French language. Today, that insularity has disappeared in the face of social and technological change, and the linguistic assimilation of francophones has been progressive and far-reaching. While Canadians of French mother tongue constitute a fairly stable one-third of New Brunswick's population, their proportion falls to approximately 5 percent in Ontario, Manitoba, and Prince Edward Island, 4 percent in Nova Scotia, 2 percent in the three westernmost provinces, and less than 1 percent in Newfoundland. Even the small proportion of non-Quebec residents whose mother tongue is French overstates the strength of the French language outside Quebec since many such Canadians have been or are being assimilated into the anglophone community. When anglophones and francophones have come into contact anywhere across the country, linguistic assimilation has favoured anglophones except in those cases where francophones make up more than 95 percent of the population.[18]

The trends described above demonstrate that linguistic segregation is increasing in Canada; what began as national linguistic duality is increasingly becoming a territorial duality.[19] The francophone proportion of Quebec's population is increasing, and will continue to increase, while the francophone proportion of the non-Quebec population is decreasing, and will continue to decrease. As a consequence, Canada's francophone population is increasingly concentrated within Quebec. (In the 1991 census, 86.1 percent of those whose mother tongue was French and 90.2 percent whose home language was French resided in Quebec.) The bilingual "belt" that used to surround Quebec is being reduced to a series of "pockets."[20] This trend of linguistic segregation threatens francophone minorities outside Quebec and the anglophone minority inside that province, and raises concerns about the long-term viability of national policies to promote bilingualism. As Donald Smiley noted back in 1980:

> The ongoing territorial separation ... means that a decreasing proportion of Canadians experience duality as an important circumstance of daily life.... Because of this, the resistance of most non-francophones to a view that the essential nature of their country is dualistic is understandable.[21]

Little has happened since to reduce the problem that Smiley identified. While the national linguistic split may be approximately three to one, anglophones to francophones, very few people live in such a community. As Table 4.3 shows, we live in provincial communities where the linguistic balance is much more lopsided, and our local communities are likely to be even more homogeneous than our provinces in their linguistic composition. Only New Brunswick resembles the national average. Beaujot concludes that 89 percent of francophones and 95 percent of anglophones live in communities where their language is in the majority; only between 5 and 7 percent of francophones and anglophones combined live in minority language situations.[22] Thus the national "average" bears little resemblance to the linguistic reality that most Canadians experience.

TABLE 4.3 *Home Language, 1991 Census*

	English[a]	French[b]	English & French[c]	Other
Canada	68.7%	23.1%	0.5%	7.7%
Newfoundland	99.3	0.2	0.1	0.5
Prince Edward Island	97.2	2.3	0.2	0.3
Nova Scotia	96.4	2.4	0.1	1.1
New Brunswick	67.9	30.8	0.7	0.6
Quebec	10.9	82.8	1.0	5.3
Ontario	85.9	3.0	0.4	10.7
Manitoba	88.5	2.2	0.3	9.0
Saskatchewan	94.8	0.6	0.2	4.4
Alberta	92.1	0.7	0.2	7.0
British Columbia	90.3	0.4	0.2	9.1
Northern Territories	77.8	1.1	0.3	20.8

[a] Includes those whose "home language" is English or English and a nonofficial language.
[b] Includes those whose "home language" is French or French and a nonofficial language.
[c] Includes those whose "home languages" are both English and French, or English, French, and a nonofficial language.

Figure 4.3 presents a set diagram incorporating two overlapping segments of the Canadian population—those living in Quebec and those whose mother tongue is French. In combination, those segments identify the three principal linguistic groups upon which Canadian language politics has centred. The largest group is the Québécois, defined here as the francophone residents of Quebec. Of course, this is a rather barren definition, and the reader should be aware of the emotional baggage associated with the term. René Lévesque, for example, began his independence manifesto with the statement "We are *Québécois*," and then elaborated: "what that means first and foremost—and if need be, all that it means—is that we are attached to this one corner of the earth where we can be completely ourselves: this Quebec, the only place where we have the unmistakable feeling that 'here we can really be at home.'"[23] The second group is composed of those persons of French mother tongue living outside Quebec. With the emergence of "Québécois" as a group identity, the term "French Canadian" has sometimes been identified with these non-Quebec francophones. Interestingly, the federally funded organization for this group is called *Francophones hors Québec*, a label that describes the group by what it is not rather than by reference to the more positive, national affiliation embodied in the term French Canadian. Nonfrancophone Quebeckers, a residual category composed of Quebec residents whose mother tongue is other than French, form the increasingly heterogeneous third group, which encompasses the descendants of United Empire Loyalists whose roots in the province go back to the 1770s, more recent immigrants to Quebec who have assimilated into the anglophone rather than into the franco-

FIGURE 4.3 *The Three Nodes of Linguistic Politics*

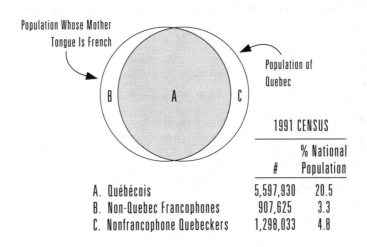

	#	% National Population
		1991 CENSUS
A. Québécois	5,597,930	20.5
B. Non-Quebec Francophones	907,625	3.3
C. Nonfrancophone Quebeckers	1,298,033	4.8

phone community (or into neither), and anglophones who have moved to Quebec from other provinces.

There is also a fourth group, not shown in Figure 4.3, which is coming to play an increasingly important role in language politics, and that is the group composed of bilingual Canadians whose mother tongue is English rather than French. Historically, only a small fraction of the Canadian population—12.7 percent between 1931 and 1971—has been bilingual. Of those, 60 percent lived in Quebec, and only 8 percent of the non-Quebec population was bilingual.[24] The vast majority of bilinguals were Canadians of French mother tongue who had learned English for reasons of employment or who were in the process of being assimilated into the English-Canadian community. English mother tongue bilinguals were a rare breed until the passage of the Official Languages Act in 1969, when knowledge of French became an economic asset for anglophones and unilingualism suddenly offered the prospect of "a life sentence to job immobility."[25] An explosive growth in French immersion programs occurred as a result across the country—programs that cater largely to an English mother tongue clientele. By the end of the 1980s, over 200,000 Canadian students were in French immersion programs, although francophones are still four times as likely to be bilingual as are anglophones.[26] In the lower grades outside Quebec, anglophone immersion students now outnumber French mother tongue students who are receiving their education in French. It is interesting to note, however, that at the same time immersion enrolments have been increasing, the overall proportion of students outside Quebec

Bilingualism in Canada

In the 1991 census, 4,398,655 Canadians stated that they could conduct a conversation in both English and French. This figure represents 16.1 percent of the national population, up from 15.3 percent in 1981 and 13.4 percent in 1971. However, it should be noted that the prevalence of bilingualism varies dramatically across Canada's linguistic communities. More than half (55 percent) of the bilingual population lives in Quebec, where 58.4 percent of anglophones and 31.3 percent of francophones declared themselves bilingual in the 1991 census. Outside Quebec, 81.2 percent of francophones but only 6.3 percent of anglophones were bilingual. Overall rates of bilingualism ranged from 35.4 percent in Quebec and 29.5 percent in New Brunswick to 11.4 percent in Ontario and 3.3 percent in Newfoundland.

Source: 1991 census, *Knowledge of Languages*.

who are taking French has been decreasing. Thus French language education has become a more intensive experience for a smaller proportion of the student body.[27] As a consequence, we may be developing for the first time in our history "a distinct social elite of young, upper middle-class, bilingual graduates."[28] This elite will form a powerful lobby for the national bilingualism policies from which it derives its elite status, and may also reinforce class cleavages within the body politic. As Donald Smiley explains, "because in anglophone Canada it is the more prosperous parents who are most insistent about their children's becoming bilingual, the issue has the potentiality of dividing English-speaking Canadians along class lines."[29]

Now that a rough linguistic profile of the Canadian population has been sketched, we can turn to the manner in which that profile has shaped the evolution and current dynamics of language politics in Canada. Our discussion begins with linguistic tensions outside Quebec, and then turns to the more recent linguistic debate within that province.

LANGUAGE POLITICS OUTSIDE QUEBEC

Political conflict often turns upon symbolic events. The execution of Louis Riel in 1885, following the North-West Rebellion, provides an excellent if unfortunate example, for it came to symbolize the relationship between the English and French communities outside Quebec. In English Canada, Riel's execution was seen as just and deserved. Prime Minister Macdonald's statement that "he shall hang though every dog in Quebec bark in his favour" captured the more moderate reaction, while *The Toronto Star* (May 18, 1885) wrote: "Strangle Riel with the French flag! That is the only use that rag can have in the country." In Quebec, the reaction was dramatically different. Israel Tarte, a prominent Quebec Liberal, predicted that "at the moment when the corpse of Riel falls through the trap and twists in convulsions of agony, at that moment an abyss will be dug that will separate Quebec from English-speaking Canada, especially Ontario."[30] Tarte's prediction was borne out immediately as 40,000 people took to the streets of Quebec to burn Macdonald in effigy. In the longer run it is often assumed in political folklore that the reaction to Riel's execution set in motion a partisan realignment that persisted into the 1980s when Brian Mulroney recaptured Quebec for the Conservatives. Honoré Mercier, who declared that "the murder of Riel was a declaration of war upon French-Canadian influence in Confederation," formed the Parti National and, in 1886, drove the provincial Conservatives from power in Quebec.[31] Wilfrid Laurier, who said "had I been born on the banks of the Saskatchewan I myself would have shouldered a musket," became leader of the national Liberal Party and, in 1896, inaugurated a Quebec-based Liberal dynasty that was to dominate Canadian politics for most of the next century.[32] While electoral statistics suggest that the role of Riel's execution has been exaggerated in explanations of both Liberal success and Conservative failure in Quebec,[33] the execution has nonetheless become an important symbol in the mythology of Canadian language and partisan politics.

Language politics outside Quebec has been largely dominated by nonviolent albeit acrimonious conflict centring on the educational rights of French-Canadian minorities. Here the "Manitoba Schools Question" provides an early and still instructive example. In 1890 the Manitoba legislature abolished the existing denominational school system, which included Catholic schools using French as the language of instruction, and replaced it with a nonsectarian public system in which English was the sole language of instruction. Franco-Manitobans, with ecclesiastical support from the Catholic Church in Quebec, urged the Conservative government in Ottawa to disallow the Manitoba legislation. The government demurred, pending an appeal to the Judicial Committee of the Privy Council. When that appeal upheld the provincial legislation, Ottawa was then urged to pass remedial legislation to restore the dual school system. This demand was deflected to the Supreme Court, which ruled that Parliament could not pass such legislation, and then to the JCPC, which ruled that it could. All this set the stage for the 1896 general election campaign in which the Conservatives promised remedial legislation, believing that the consequent losses in English Canada (twenty-one Conservative seats were in fact lost) could be offset by gains in Quebec where remedial legislation was strongly supported. However, although the Liberals opposed remedial legislation and incurred the wrath of the Catholic Church by so doing, Wilfrid Laurier's appeal to his fellow French Canadians was too great; the Liberals captured forty-nine Quebec seats, a gain of fourteen from 1891, and won the election.

Laurier charted a constitutional course in this conflict similar in principle to that followed by Quebec governments over the next 100 years. Because Laurier attached great importance to the federal division of powers for the protection of French Canada, he opposed remedial legislation as a threat to provincial autonomy. If remedial legislation was used in the short term to protect Franco-Manitobans by breaching the federal–provincial division of powers, in the longer term it could lead to the intrusion of the English-Canadian national majority into the internal affairs of Quebec. Thus on constitutional grounds Laurier was prepared to sacrifice Franco-Manitobans to the greater good of provincial autonomy, although he subsequently worked out a practical compromise with the Manitoba government that met many but certainly not all of the educational concerns of Franco-Manitobans.

The resolution of the Manitoba schools question also set the course to be followed by most provincial governments outside Quebec until late in this century, a course marked by at best reluctant and grudging support for minority language education. These governments have generally been far less sympathetic toward provincial francophone minorities than has the Quebec government been toward the anglophone minority in Quebec, or than Ottawa has been toward the national francophone minority. Perhaps this should not be surprising, given that the francophone provincial minorities have been proportionately much the smallest of the three. What is more surprising, and more lamentable, has been the reluctance of the federal government to defend the interests of francophone minorities against anglophone and Protestant provincial majorities.[34] Historian W.L. Morton has argued that this reluctance forced French Canadians to turn to the Quebec provincial state for protection and thus made an important contribution to the ongoing constitutional tension between the Quebec and federal governments.[35]

The conflict over minority education rights brings us back to a basic limitation in the protection federalism provides for minority interests. The federal division of powers provides protection to national minorities that can be recast as provincial majorities, but it provides no constitutional protection per se within the legislative domain of the national government and no protection for linguistic minorities within the legislative domain of the provincial governments. (As we will see shortly, Quebec is an exception here.) The federal government's power of disallowance and its capacity to enact remedial legislation provide a second theoretical line of defence, but one that has not been used. Thus federalism itself fails to protect the educational interests of francophone minorities outside Quebec. Given these limitations, it is not surprising that, in their quest for "la survivance," many French Canadians have sought protection within "Fortress Quebec," and have sought to defend and where possible expand the powers of *their* government. Nor should it be surprising that this strategy has been largely rejected by francophones living in other parts of Canada, for whom Quebec has been a fickle ally at best. However, it has also been rejected by a significant number of francophones within Quebec who see the fulfilment of French Canada taking place within the country as a whole rather than within the more narrow confines of Quebec. It is this perspective that came to be closely associated with the writings and political leadership of Pierre Elliott Trudeau, and it is both this perspective and Trudeau himself that propelled minority language rights to the centre of the Canadian political stage.

The Emergence of Official Bilingualism

In reaction to the claustrophobic Duplessis years (discussed below), many French Canadians sought an expanded national vision in which French and English Canada would co-exist in an equal partnership rather than as the "two solitudes" so vividly portrayed by novelist Hugh MacLennan in 1945. This vision was captured by the Royal Commission on Bilingualism and

Biculturalism, which had been established in 1963 by Prime Minister Lester Pearson "to inquire into and report upon the existing state of bilingualism and biculturalism in Canada and to recommend what steps should be taken to develop the Canadian Confederation on the basis of an equal partnership between the two founding races." Chaired by André Laurendeau and Davidson Dunton, the B & B Commission laid the foundations for the official bilingualism that was to follow. However, while the commission's call for the equality of the English and French languages—for a *bilingual* Canada—was accepted, its call for the equality of the English and French societies—for a *bicultural* Canada—was not. In its response to the commission, the federal government separated the threads of language and culture that the commissioners had woven into a single strand, and argued that *multiculturalism within a bilingual framework* was a vision that better captured the demographic and political realities of modern Canada.

Prime Minister Pearson started the federal public service down the rocky road toward bilingualism in 1966. Then, in July 1969, Parliament passed the Official Languages Act, which declared English and French to be Canada's official languages, granted all citizens the right to communicate with the federal government in the official language of their choice, enabled employees of the federal government to work in the official language of their choice, provided funds for second language education across Canada, and established the Commissioner of Official Languages. Official bilingualism had arrived. In 1982 the principal features of the Official Languages Act were "constitutionalized" in Sections 16 through 20 of the Charter of Rights and Freedoms. The passage of Bill C-72 in the summer of 1988 amended the Official Languages Act by formally establishing English and French as the official languages of the federal courts (but not of provincial courts presided over by federally appointed judges), extending the bilingual provision of federal government services where a "significant demand" exists, committing the federal government to ensuring that anglophones and francophones have equal access to appointment and promotion in the federal public service, and increasing the powers of the Commissioner of Official Languages. As a consequence, there has been some expansion, particularly in Western Canada, in the number of public service positions designated as "bilingual-imperative." When Bill C-72 was initially introduced it provoked considerable opposition in Western Canada and even among western Progressive Conservative MPs, and opposition to it formed a major plank in the 1988 campaign platform of the nascent Reform Party of Canada. However, after relatively minor amendments in committee the bill was passed by the House of Commons with only nine MPs, all Conservatives, voting against it.

National bilingualism has been closely identified with the personality and career of Pierre Trudeau, even though it was set in motion by the Pearson government. It was Trudeau's government that introduced the 1969 Official Languages Act and was the motive force behind the 1982

Language Provisions in the Canadian Charter of Rights and Freedoms

The 1969 Official Languages Act has now been "constitutionalized" in Sections 16 to 20 of the Charter of Rights and Freedoms.

Section 16(1) of the Charter states that "English and French are the official languages of Canada and have equality of status and equal rights and privileges as to their use in all institutions of the Parliament and government of Canada." Section 16(2) extends this provision to the legislature and government of New Brunswick.

Sections 17 and 18 establish the equality of English and French in the proceedings of Parliament and the New Brunswick legislature (debate, statutes, records, journals), while Sections 19(1) and 19(2) state that "either English or French may be used by any person in, or in any pleading in or process issuing from" any court established by Parliament or any court of New Brunswick.

Section 20(1) states that "any member of the public in Canada has the right to communicate with, and to receive available services from, any head or central office of an institution of the Parliament or government in English or French, and has the same right with respect to any other office of any such institution where (a) there is a significant demand for communications with and services from that office in such language; or (b) due to the nature of the office, it is reasonable that communications with and services from that office be available in both English and French."

Section 23 of the Charter goes beyond the Official Languages Act to state that, where numbers warrant, "citizens of Canada (a) whose first language learned and still understood is that of the English or French linguistic minority population of the province in which they reside, or (b) who have received their primary school instruction in Canada in English or French and reside in a province where the language in which they received that instruction is the language of the English or French linguistic minority population of the province, have the right to have their children receive primary and secondary school instruction in that language in that province." Section 23(2) states that "citizens of Canada of whom any child has received or is receiving primary or secondary school instruction in English or French in Canada, have the right to have all their children receive primary and secondary school instruction in the same language."

Charter of Rights and Freedoms. Trudeau's flawless command of both official languages epitomized the bilingual Canadian ideal, and the promotion of bilingualism was a central concern, at times even a preoccupation, of the governments he led. In *Grits*, Christina McCall-Newman nicely captures Trudeau's image at the time: "above all he was perfectly bilingual, with his French father and his English mother, his Jesuit education at home and his post-graduate education abroad, the pan-Canadian the country had been looking for, who fused the French and English into one, a kind of racial hermaphrodite, the unmatchable bicultural man."[36] Bilingualism was to Trudeau "as the CPR was to John A. Macdonald, his instrument for building a continent-wide country out of a huddled group of provinces."[37]

Bilingualism was well received initially in English Canada as a necessary and appropriate response to the Quiet Revolution in Quebec and to the growing independence movement in that province. Given the role that young francophones were beginning to play as a nationalist force within the Quebec public service, it seemed essential that countervailing career opportunities be opened up for francophones in Ottawa. More generally, if francophones were to be bottled up in Quebec by their language, the appeal of independence would be difficult to counter. Bilingualism thus appeared to be not only an acceptable price for national unity, but came to be seen as a significant component in the resurgent Canadian nationalism of the period. At a time when the British connection no longer played a useful role in setting Canada apart from the United States, Canada's bilingual character came to satisfy the same nationalistic need. Bilingualism symbolically distinguished Canadians from Americans even though most of the former were in fact no more bilingual than the latter.

For many English Canadians growing uneasy about the independence movement in Quebec, Trudeau was seen as a leader who could stand up to the separatists and defend Canada in a way that no anglophone of the times could do in Quebec. This role was dramatically illustrated on the eve of the 1968 federal election when Trudeau reviewed Montreal's St. Jean Baptiste Day parade. As separatist demonstrators threw bottles at the reviewing stand and other dignitaries fled, Trudeau stood alone, unmoved and defiant. It was a moment of personal courage and dramatic political symbolism, one that anointed the new prime minister as Canada's champion against the "indépendantistes." Yet this role was easily misunderstood, for although Trudeau opposed the indépendantistes and the more extreme constitutional demands of Quebec governments, he vigorously promoted the extension of the French presence throughout the institutional fabric of the Canadian society and state. In its own way, Trudeau's vision of Canada was no less sweeping in the demands that it would make upon English Canadians than was the vision held by René Lévesque. As Richard Gwyn argued at the time, although "Trudeau and Levesque are the heroes of opposing armies ... each has fought for his people, the French Canadians, even though Levesque's francophones are limited to those within Quebec while Trudeau's vision encompasses all in Canada whose mother tongue is French."[38] Trudeau sought to extend the French fact across Canada while Lévesque sought to consolidate and defend it within Quebec, objectives that were by no means incompatible. Both leaders brought English Canadians face to face with the linguistic transformation of their society.

This is not to say that official bilingualism was completely new in Canada. Section 133 of the 1867 Constitution Act provided for the use of both English and French in Parliament, in federal courts created through the act, and in the legislature and courts of Quebec. Thus both languages were used in parliamentary debate and Hansard, all Acts of Parliament were printed in both languages, and even the prayer beginning each sitting day was read by the Speaker in English and French on alternate days. Bilingual stamps appeared in 1927, bilingual currency in 1936, and in 1962 Prime Minister Diefenbaker introduced bilingual federal cheques and simultaneous translation in Parliament. Still, in many respects the rate of change was glacial. When Trudeau worked in the Privy Council Office in the early 1950s, at the time when Louis St. Laurent was serving as Canada's second French-Canadian prime minister, he witnessed what Christina McCall-Newman has described as an "unbelievable fight" to have a sign put up in the East Block reading *Bureau du Premier Ministre* as well as *Prime Minister's Office*.[39] In retrospect, and given the extent to which the Official Languages Act has transformed the linguistic face of Canada, opposition to such an innocuous proposal almost defies comprehension, particularly when such forms of bilingualism were virtually cost-free and invisible to most English Canadians. However, the Official Languages Act had a more problematic impact by extending the parliamentary equality of the two languages into the wider society, by broadening the scope of state intervention in the language field, and thus by intruding in a more direct and visible fashion into the lives of Canadians. All federal government signs and publications began to appear in both languages, consumer products were required to carry bilingual labels, and airline passengers were told to buckle up in English and French. In short, Ottawa was increasing the visibility of French across Canada, albeit in a bilingual context, in a manner analogous to the Quebec government's efforts to increase the visibility of French in Quebec.

Bilingualism had its most immediate impact on the federal public service. The institutional bilingualism put into place by the Official Languages Act was designed so that individual Canadians would not have to be bilingual—they would be able to communicate with the federal government in the official language of their choice. Yet bilingual institutions necessitated a bilingual public service. Before the reforms launched by Prime Minister Pearson, English had been *the* language of work in the federal public service. Francophones were proportionately underrepresented in Ottawa, with underrepresentation increasing as one moved up through the ranks, and virtually the only bilingual public servants were those of

French mother tongue. As senior positions demanded a skilled and even artful use of language, francophones were placed at a double disadvantage. Not only did they have to absorb the costs of learning a second language, but in having to function in their second language, they often appeared less subtle, less sensitive, and thus less competent than their anglophone compatriots. Then, with the introduction of bilingualism, knowledge of French became a career asset rather than a liability, and anglophones faced limited career mobility unless they learned French. Although the majority of public service positions were not designated as bilingual, the senior positions and therefore in effect the middle-rank positions from which senior managers were drawn were so designated. To ease the transition to bilingualism, French language training was made available in 1973 for anglophones holding positions that had been designated as bilingual. For thousands of anglophones, many of whom were senior officials at the peak of their careers, this meant months of being reduced to the status of secondary students, struggling with the acquisition of a new language.

By the early 1980s French language training began to be phased out, with greater reliance being placed on an adequate knowledge of both official languages prior to initial recruitment. Nonetheless, as late as 1991–92 the Public Service Commission was still spending more than $31 million on internal language training programs. In total the federal government spent $661 million on official language programs during that year. Almost 40 percent of the total ($264 million) was in the form of transfer payments to the provinces and territories for language programs. The Official Language Service of the Secretary of State absorbed another $102 million while $66 million was spent on language programs within the Armed Forces, $94 million on programs within other departments of the federal government, $45 million on transfer payments to official language minority groups and for bilingualism development programs, and $25 million on programs within crown corporations. The budget for the Commissioner of Official Languages was $13 million, and $8 million was spent by the Official Language Branch of Treasury Board.

Bilingualism has resulted in an increase in the number of francophones employed within the federal public service, where proficiency in both official languages is now a requirement for close to a third of the positions. This increase reflects the fact that beginning with the Trudeau period and extending through the Mulroney governments, bilingualism was associated with the growth of "French Power" in Ottawa, a phenomenon marked by the emergence of highly visible and influential francophone ministers, deputy ministers, heads of crown corporations, and senior advisers. At the same time, a knowledge of both official languages became increasingly useful outside the government for the leaders of professional organizations, interest groups, and cultural associations claiming to be national in character. In short, bilingualism became a virtual prerequisite for individuals hoping to scale the peaks of Canadian public life.

"Darling, I am just a poor civil servant ... cheri, je ne suis qu'un pauvre fonc-tionnaire ... but I love you ... mais je vous aime beaucoup ... will you ... voulez-vous..."

Len Norris, *15th Annual*; originally published in the *Sun* (Vancouver), April 15, 1966.

Bilingualism was also associated with the widespread symbolic transformation of Canadian public life that began in the mid-1960s with the creation of a Canadian flag to replace the Union Jack and Red Ensign. Symbols grounded in only one of the two linguistic communities, such as the royal coat-of-arms on mail boxes, were replaced by ones that might include not only French Canadians but also Canadians of neither British nor French descent. The names of government departments and agencies were changed to ones that could be easily expressed in either official language, and thus we had Transport Canada/Transports Canada, Canada Post/Postes Canada, Lotto Canada, and so forth. The national anthem was now sung in its bilingual version, to the initial accompaniment of boos from some sports fans in English Canada. During the same period Canada began to convert to the metric system of measurement, a system described

"I know what I'd tell Quebec ... the Plains of Abraham are still there and I'll even make it best two out of three."

by both its opponents and opponents of bilingualism as the "French system of measurement."

The Official Languages Act and the promotion of bilingualism captured an important if contentious tenet of Canadian life. If French Canadians were to be *Canadians,* then not only Quebec but also Canada would have to be the home of the French language. As Henri Bourassa wrote in 1912:

> We deserve better than to be considered like the savages of the old reservations and to be told: "Remain in Quebec, continue to stagnate in ignorance, you are at home there; but elsewhere you must become English." No, we have the right to be French in language; we have the right to be Catholics in faith; we have the right to be free by the constitution. We are Canadians before all; and we have the right to be as British as anyone. And we have the right to enjoy these rights throughout the whole expanse of Confederation.[40]

More recently, Raymond Breton has argued that "individuals expect to recognize themselves in public institutions."[41] Unfortunately, while the symbolic transformations noted above made it easier for French Canadians to find their reflection in public institutions, it had the opposite impact on segments, and particularly older segments, of the English-Canadian population. The national majority was being asked to accept extensive symbolic change for the sake of the national minority, change that included a significant redistribution of status between the English and French communities. To many, bilingualism was seen not as the foundation for a stronger pan-Canadian nationalism, but as an assault on the country's British heritage. Opposition was particularly intense in the more multicultural West where the French-Canadian minority tended to be seen in a regional rather than national context. In the latter context French Canadians made up a quarter of the national population, but in a regional context they were outnumbered by many of the ethnic groups who had settled the West and who had adopted the English language in the process.

Regional Differences in Support for Bilingualism

An April 1988 survey for Southam News by Angus Reid Associates found strong national support for official bilingualism. Across the country, 67 percent of the respondents supported official bilingualism, with 32 percent offering strong support and 35 percent more moderate support. Only 31 percent opposed official bilingualism; 17 percent did so strongly and 14 percent moderately.

There were, however, sharp regional variations in this national pattern. Support for official bilingualism, be it strong or moderate, ranged from 88 percent in Quebec to 67 percent in Atlantic Canada, 63 percent in Ontario, 58 percent in British Columbia, and only 47 percent on the prairies. Conversely, opposition ranged from 49 percent on the prairies to 40 percent in British Columbia, 34 percent in Ontario, 30 percent in Atlantic Canada, and only 9 percent in Quebec. Of those respondents whose mother tongue was French, 87 percent supported official bilingualism compared to 62 percent of those whose mother tongue was English.

A very different picture of public support emerged in a Gallup survey conducted in February 1992. At that time, 64 percent of respondents in a national survey stated that official bilingualism has been a failure, and only 26 percent maintained that it has been a success. Once again, there were sharp regional differences: the proportion concluding that bilingualism has failed was 42 percent in Atlantic Canada, 61 percent in Quebec, 63 percent on the prairies, 68 percent in Ontario, and 74 percent in British Columbia.

Although bilingualism affected career opportunities for a substantial number of anglophones, it may have been the perceived status threat that best explains the intensity of opposition among individuals who were untouched in any practical or objective sense by the introduction of bilingualism. For others, opposition was not to bilingualism per se, but to what they saw as Ottawa's excessive preoccupation with bilingualism and the consequent neglect of economic and regional concerns. In this respect Dalton Camp argues that the politics of bilingualism intensified regional and intergovernmental strains within the national community:

> The persistence and growing pervasiveness of bilingualism had alienated English Canadians from their federal government, turning them inwards to more familiar, compatible and nearer political jurisdictions in the provinces.... The government of Canada had lost its constituency.[42]

However, and somewhat surprisingly, opposition to bilingualism failed to find a significant champion within the party system. Apart from a few dissenting voices among Progressive Conservative MPs, the major parties locked arms on the original Official Languages Act and, with the exception of the Reform Party and another handful of Conservative MPs, on the 1988 Bill C-72 amendments. In elections subsequent to 1969 voters were not given a choice between parties supporting and opposing bilingualism. Conservative leaders Robert Stanfield and Joe Clark, whose party potentially had the most to gain from catering to anti-French sentiment given its then-bleak electoral prospects in Quebec, were adamant in their support of bilingualism. Opponents of bilingualism outside the party system who found their way into the media encountered a consistently hostile reception; they were dismissed as bigots and political Neanderthals rather than treated as citizens with legitimate concerns about the direction of national policy.

Within the political science literature, the deliberate exclusion of potentially divisive issues from public debate and electoral competition by political and social elites is termed *consociationalism*. A consociational democracy is one "with subcultural cleavages tending towards immobilism and instability but which is deliberately turned into a stable system by the leaders of the major subcultures."[43] In the case of French–English relations, consociationalism has shaped an asymmetrical national debate over bilingualism and Quebec's place within the Canadian federal state. Although the latter debate in Quebec has ranged freely from support for the federal status quo to the advocacy of complete independence, the debate in English Canada has been far more restricted. Rarely has it encompassed the creation of a unilingual anglophone state including Quebec, the use of force to suppress Quebec's independence, or the welcomed departure of Quebec. Persons holding such views have not been encouraged to join the debate over Quebec's place in Canada; they confront an elite consensus that national unity must be maintained and that bilingualism is essential if this is to happen.

This elite consensus, however, has not completely escaped critical commentary. When Newfoundland MP John Crosbie ran for the leadership of the national Progressive Conservative Party in 1983, his lack of French proved to be an insurmountable problem. Crosbie's reaction on the campaign trail is worthy of note:

> *There are over 20 million of us who are unilingual English or French.... I don't think that the 3.7 million who are bilingual should suddenly think themselves some kind of aristocracy and leaders can come only from their small group.*[44]

Don Braid of *The Edmonton Journal* called Crosbie's comments a "burst of insight." For this "self-satisfied ruling elite," Braid charged,

> *bilingualism has become a ritual chant ... they demand it of national leaders, thus guaranteeing their continued membership in the club. They dismiss dissenters as red-necked bigots and intellectual lightweights, while exercising a powerful bigotry of their own.*[45]

Opposition to bilingualism has also been associated with the rise of several small protest parties, including the Confederation of Regions party, but only one of these has been a significant player on the electoral stage. This exception is the Reform Party, which rejects existing bilingualism policies and instead supports a form of territorial bilingualism: French as the official language in Quebec, and English as the official language outside Quebec. Although it is not clear whether this policy has played a particularly important role in generating either support for or opposition to the Reform Party, the election of fifty-two Reform MPs in 1993 will undoubtedly shake the consociational consensus on official bilingualism.

The Provincial Response

Perhaps the most acute political tensions stemming from official bilingualism have arisen within the provincial arenas as minority language communities and governments have wrestled with the provincial implications of the federal policy, and with the entrenchment of aspects of that policy in the Charter. There is no question that national language legislation and the Charter have increased pressure from francophone minorities for bilingual access to provincial programs and, in some cases, recognition of French as an official language. In New Brunswick, English and French are now constitutionally entrenched as official languages. In Ontario, where francophones make up less than 5 percent of the population, most government services are provided in both English and French, and every French-speaking student has been guaranteed the right to an education in French. French-language rights, however, are enshrined in provincial statutes only and not in the Constitution. The Ontario government has resisted calls for constitutional entrenchment, arguing that the backlash that might result could jeopardize francophone interests within the province.

In 1979 the Supreme Court of Canada ruled that 1890 Manitoba legislation making English the province's only official language was unconstitutional, that it violated the terms of the 1870 Manitoba Act, passed by the Parliament of Canada, which had brought Manitoba into Confederation and which now forms part of the Canadian Constitution. This ruling threw into question the constitutionality of 14,000 pages of laws passed since 1890 and written only in English, and thus forced Manitoba to translate its provincial statutes and to restore French as an official language in the legislative assembly and courts. The provincial government also designated 500 public service positions as ones to be filled eventually by bilingual employees.

In February 1988, the Supreme Court ruled that the 1877 language provisions in the North-West Territories Act (Section 110), added at a time when there was a substantial francophone population in the prairie West, remained in effect in Saskatchewan. Those provisions held that either English or French could be used in the legislature and in the courts, and that the records, journals, and ordinances of the legislature were to be in both languages. The government and legislature of Saskatchewan had functioned in English only since the province was created in 1905. In the eighty years that followed, the francophone population had declined steadily; today approximately 25,000 francophones constitute less than 3 percent of the provincial population. However, the court ruled that the Saskatchewan Act of 1905, which established the province, provided for the "continuation of all laws governing the Legislature," and therefore that Section 110 remained in force until replaced by another law. Thus the ruling potentially voided all provincial statutes passed since 1905, although the court also decreed that, to prevent a legal vacuum, the statutes would temporarily remain in effect until the provincial government had a chance to respond to the court's ruling. Here the court presented two options. First, the province could comply with Section 110 by translating, re-enacting, and printing all statutes in both French and English. Alternatively, the province could pass new legislation declaring that all existing statutes were valid even though they had been enacted and printed in English only. This option was possible because the court ruled that Section 110 was not constitutionally entrenched and therefore that the Saskatchewan legislative assembly was free to repeal or amend the existing legislation. Not surprisingly, the provincial Progressive Conservative government, led by Premier Grant Devine, chose the minimalist option and introduced legislation reducing the legal status of French within the province. At the same time, the provincial government stated that some of the more important existing statutes would be translated, at the discretion of the provincial government; that some future legislation might be translated; that translation facilities would be provided to francophones in court; and that the use of French would be permitted within the provincial legislature, although no translation would be provided. For its part, the federal government agreed to provide Saskatchewan with $60 million to cover the costs of translation and to enrich educational programs for francophones. Ottawa also gave Saskatchewan's francophone community an additional $17 million to help them protect and encourage the use of French.

Although the Supreme Court ruling applied directly only to Saskatchewan, it had inevitable consequences for Alberta given that the North-West Territories Act also applied to Alberta prior to the province's creation in 1905. Thus in June 1988, Premier Don Getty's Progressive Conservative government moved to pre-empt similar judicial intervention in Alberta. The legislative assembly passed legislation, ironically written in both English and French, that retroactively validated English-only legislation. Unlike the case in Saskatchewan, the Alberta legislation did not provide for the selective translation of provincial satutes nor for the translation of future legislation, although it did remove restrictions on the use of French in the provincial legislative assembly. Alberta's 60,000 francophones, who constituted less than 3 percent of the provincial population, expressed anger and dismay at the government's very limited recognition of linguistic rights.

Provincial language policies in the western provinces are inextricably linked to language policies in Quebec. If the rights and interests of the anglophone minority in Quebec are to be protected, then it is imperative that those of francophone minorities in the other provinces also be protected. At the same time, Quebec's drift toward a more unilingual society weakens political incentives for protecting linguistic minorities elsewhere in the country. Here it should also be stressed that language policies in Quebec and the other provinces do not interact directly; it is the federal government that plays a mediative role by offering political support for francophones outside Quebec and anglophones inside Quebec. Yet in most such cases Ottawa must rely upon moral suasion and financial incentives rather than legislative authority. As the Saskatchewan and Alberta experiences have shown, there are very real limits to Ottawa's influence even when the federal and provincial governments are of the same partisan stripe.

To summarize briefly, national bilingualism draws its political support from a diverse constituency that includes French Canadians living outside Quebec, Anglo-Quebeckers, a substantial proportion of francophones living inside Quebec, new anglophone bilinguals who have invested heavily in their own bilingualism or that of their children, and those English Canadians who believe that bilingualism, like it or not, is essential to the survival of Canada. It is a powerful coalition that, at least in the past,

Bilingualism in Canada

The line heard from some people outside Quebec runs this way: why bother providing French-language services for francophone Canadians in other parts of the country when Quebec won't even let merchants post bilingual signs? Why go forward when Quebec is going backward?

There are a few quick responses: that Quebec has moved slightly forward from the existing law by permitting bilingual signs inside shops; that anglophone Quebeckers enjoy a wide range of services in their mother tongue; that Mr. Bourassa's Liberals brought in laws in 1987 to give English-speaking Quebeckers social services and health care in their own language, and amnesty to students illegally registered in English schools; that Quebec remains bound by constitutional obligations which cannot be overridden by the Charter's "notwithstanding" clause, including the right of parents educated in English in Canada to have their children educated in English.

But the broader response is that two official languages are not some artificial construct imposed on the country by the Pearson/Trudeau Liberals, to be endured only as long as everything goes smoothly. They are a reflection of the social contract between English and French which gave birth to this country, a bond maintained not because it is easy—heaven knows it's not—but because to a significant extent it defines the Canadian national identity. That remains so despite the many other linguistic groups who have helped build this country and remain prominent in many parts of it.

D'Iberville Fortier, Canada's Official Languages Commissioner, put the point eloquently in his report last March. Most Canadians, he wrote, "remain firmly opposed to a straight territorial solution to Canada's special linguistic dilemma, as being, in the end, a recipe for national suicide. With all its imperfections, some form of official bilingualism is the only answer that does not point toward a progressive dismemberment of Canada."

Source: Editorial from *The Globe and Mail*, January 12, 1989.

commanded support from the major parties and the social, economic, and cultural elites from which those parties in turn drew their support. There are, however, two critically important complications. The first is that the coalition addresses the linguistic concerns of, and draws its primary electoral support from, *minorities*—francophones in Canada and provinces other than Quebec, and anglophones in Quebec. The relevant linguistic and electoral *majorities*—anglophones in Canada and nine provinces, and francophones in Quebec—are a tougher sell for the proponents of bilingualism. The second and related complication is that the coalition often finds itself confronting the Quebec government. While it might be thought that federal legislation to protect the francophone national minority and, to a lesser degree, francophone provincial minorities outside Quebec would complement legislation to protect the francophone majority in Quebec, this has not always been the case.

UNILINGUALISM AND THE POLITICS OF NATIONALISM IN QUEBEC

In order to set the stage for a discussion of contemporary language politics in Quebec, and to explain the tension that often exists between provincial and federal language legislation, some historical background is required. This will be provided by a brief look at the Union Nationale government of Maurice Duplessis, the Quiet Revolution, and the emergence of the Parti Québécois.

Duplessis and the Union Nationale

Revolutionary change must be measured against the benchmark of the past, the essence of the new being the negation of the old. For the Quiet Revolution of the 1960s, that benchmark became the Duplessis years, "la Grande Noirceur" (the "great darkness" or "dark ages"). Yet we also find in the Duplessis governments one of the more enduring features of Quebec life—the use of the provincial state to protect Québécois interests and to hold at bay the national anglophone community and its perceived political agent, the Government of Canada.

The Duplessis years began with the victory of the Union Nationale in the 1936 provincial election. The victory was put together by a coalition of nationalist and Conservative elements, with control of the new party quickly coming to rest in the hands of Maurice Duplessis, who was to lead the party until his death in 1959. Although the Union Nationale was defeated in 1939, it rebounded to win large majorities in 1944, 1948, 1952, and 1956 before narrowly losing to the Liberals in 1960. With a platform stressing Quebec nationalism, Catholic values, and strident anti-communism, the party's electoral appeal extended outward from its heartland in rural and small-town Quebec to encompass a majority of the francophone constituencies in Montreal and Quebec City.

The Union Nationale's first defeat in 1939 helped to establish its long-term success. Duplessis called the election three weeks after the outbreak of the Second World War, contending "that the federal government was using the sweeping powers it possessed under the War Measures Act as a pretext for curtailing the rights of the province under the British North

Le Chef, Maurice Duplessis, leader of the Union Nationale from 1936 until his death in 1959.

Canapress Photo Service.

America Act."[46] (Here we have an example of the Canadian tendency to perceive the world through the narrow prism of federal–provincial relations!) Quite rightly, Duplessis's campaign was seen as a direct challenge to the national war effort, and Ottawa was quick to respond. The Quebec ministers in Mackenzie King's Liberal government took the unusual step of campaigning in the provincial election, stating that they were the only barrier to military conscription (see Chapter 9) and would resign from the federal cabinet if Duplessis won. Faced with this prospect and the certainty of conscription should the Conservatives form the federal government, Quebec voters elected sixty-nine Liberals and only fourteen Union Nationale candidates. However, it proved to be a Pyrrhic victory for the provincial Liberals when the King government was eventually forced to impose conscription despite intense opposition from Quebec. In the 1944 provincial election the Union Nationale became the nationalist vessel into which anti-conscription sentiment was poured, and the party captured forty-eight seats compared to thirty-seven for the Liberals.

The Second World War and the postwar expansion of the federal government threatened the constitutional autonomy of Quebec, the protection of which has been a primary objective for Quebec governments from Confederation through to the 1990s. In the face of an expansionist federal government, Duplessis promoted a classic vision of federalism, albeit one garbed in the clothing of Quebec nationalism. The provinces, he argued, should be sovereign and autonomous within their own constitutional domain. At the 1950 federal–provincial conference, Duplessis stated: "I definitely and firmly believe that Canada is and should always be a federation of autonomous provinces,"[47] a stance he placed before the provincial electorate in the campaigns of 1948, 1952, and 1956.

Duplessis sought to defend provincial autonomy from a variety of federal incursions including unemployment insurance, family allowances, a national plan of hospital insurance, and the construction of the Trans-Canada Highway. Following the expiration of wartime tax agreements, Ottawa and Quebec clashed on the collection and share of personal and corporate income taxes. Duplessis also campaigned against federal immigration policy, postwar loans to the United Kingdom, and foreign aid to developing countries. The Union Nationale slogan in the 1948 provincial campaign was "Les liberaux donnent aux étrangers; Duplessis donne à sa province." It should be stressed, though, that Duplessis's opposition to the expansion of government was not restricted to federal programs originating in Ottawa. In step with most nationalist intellectuals in the Quebec of his time, Duplessis opposed the expansion of the provincial state on ideological grounds as much as he opposed the expansion of the federal state on constitutional grounds. Schools, hospitals, and social services remained almost entirely in private—mostly church—hands. The growth of the Quebec provincial state, a quite different matter from the constitutional defence of its legislative domain, was to await and characterize the Quiet Revolution.

Although Duplessis was vigilant to the point of extremism in warding off constitutional intrusions by Ottawa, his governments actively encouraged the expansion of Anglo-Canadian and American capital in the Quebec economy. A combination of low taxes, minimal royalties on natural resources, and legislation that crippled provincial trade unions created a receptive investment environment, and the Duplessis government and anglophone business elite came to enjoy a close and mutually beneficial working relationship. The business community did not challenge Duplessis's authority within the political arena in return for freedom from state intervention and a restrained trade union movement.[48] The relationship was cemented by generous campaign contributions that fuelled the legendary Union Nationale patronage machine.[49] "Duplessisme," which Clift describes as "the corruption of the social and personal bonds which people in traditional societies have towards one another," was part of the Union Nationale legacy.[50]

Close relationships between the business community and provincial governments were not unusual in Canada, but in Quebec's case the relationship had the unique effect of reinforcing linguistic segmentation in the provincial economy, segmentation captured by the expression "capital speaks English and labour speaks French." Capital and labour were bridged by bilingual supervisors and foremen drawn almost exclusively from the francophone community. Thus the class division inherent in any industrialized society and the linguistic cleavage in Quebec were mutually reinforcing. Here it should be stressed, however, that Duplessis was not without supporters among the francophone elite, many of whom believed that distinctive French-Canadian cultural values could only be preserved through insulation from the secular and anglophone world of commerce. Duplessis, in an explicit political alliance with the Catholic Church, stuck to the tacit bargain that followed the Treaty of Paris: economic control would rest in English hands while control over social and cultural affairs would rest with the Catholic Church. The consequence was a restricted economic horizon for Quebec francophones.

For the many Quebec intellectuals and labour leaders radicalized during the 1949 Asbestos strike, and for those Canadians outside the province who followed Quebec affairs, Duplessis symbolized an old, almost archaic Quebec. His death in 1959, followed by the defeat of the Union Nationale government a year later, strengthened this symbolic role; he became the antithesis to, and thus helped define, the Quiet Revolution. The excesses of his administration—the authoritarianism, the patronage machine and electoral corruption, the political influence of the Catholic Church, the antediluvian approach to trade unions—were highlighted during the euphoria of the Quiet Revolution. Yet with the passage of time important threads of continuity in his constitutional stance have been recognized, threads reaching back to the Confederation agreement and forward to Quebec governments of the past three decades. Duplessis is now seen less of an anomaly and more as one in a series of premiers who shared an autonomous vision of Quebec.

The Quiet Revolution

The 1960 election of Jean Lesage's Liberal government marked the onset of the "Quiet Revolution," an event of mythological proportions in Quebec. The "revolution" was not so much in the social and economic underpinnings of Quebec, which had been in a state of transition since the 1930s, as it was in the province's state of mind. It was in the "beliefs about the purpose and character of society and polity," as McRoberts describes it, that the change was "so profound and far-reaching that we can see how many would have found it 'revolutionary.'"[51] Yet even in this respect the extent of change should not be exaggerated.[52] To call the Quiet Revolution the "springtime of Quebec," a now commonplace phrase, is to exaggerate the seasonal change and to understate the threads of continuity that link Quebec's past, present, and future.

The Quiet Revolution entailed an acceptance of the modern economic order and an enthusiasm for urban life. Gone was the cultural nostalgia for the values of a rural society long since departed. More importantly for the present discussion, the Quiet Revolution addressed the linguistic stratification of Quebec. In a province where 80 percent of the population was of French mother tongue, those who spoke only English earned substantially more on average than those who spoke only French or those who were bilingual. One could debate whether this reflected a host of cultural values and economic choices made by generations of francophone and anglophone Quebeckers, whether it reflected economic reality on a continent where the vast majority of the population was anglophone, or whether it reflected the raw edge of corporate power. But whatever the reason, it is clear that the perceived injustice of a situation in which the language of the majority was an economic burden lay at the root of the language legislation that was to emerge from the Quiet Revolution.

Linguistic tension grew in step with the Quiet Revolution's secularization of Quebec society. In the past, the Catholic Church had played a dominant role in the province; it had controlled the educational system (apart from the Protestant schools) and most social services, it was a central actor in the trade union movement, and it had a pervasive influence in political affairs. By 1960 this influence was on the wane as the church withdrew from an active role in political affairs and as many Quebeckers withdrew from the church. At the onset of the Quiet Revolution, more than 80 percent of the Catholic population of Quebec, which was more than 80 percent of the Quebec population, went to Mass every Sunday; by 1983 the attendance rate had fallen to only 25 percent.[53] With the decline of the church, the protection of the French language and cultural values passed from clerical hands to the secular hands of the provincial state.

Perhaps the most important impact of secularization came with the 1964 transfer of control over education from the church to the Quebec Ministry of Education, a transfer associated with the modernization of the educational curriculum and a rapid growth in the proportion of students pursuing post-secondary education. No longer were post-secondary students channelled through the classical colleges into the three traditional francophone occupations—law, medicine, and the clergy—where they could work in French and without entanglement in the anglophone business community. Graduates began to emerge with degrees in business administration, the social sciences, engineering, and communications. The modern economy was no longer rejected, but was embraced. English, however, was the language of work in that economy, at least at the levels to which the new graduates aspired. If one chose to or could work only in French, the limited employment opportunities in the private sector were not commensurate with the skills newly acquired from the secularized educational system. Immersion in the English work environment was equally unattractive given the personal cost of learning a second language, the handicap of operating in a second language, and the perceived danger of absorbing anglophone cultural values embedded in the workplace. From this dilemma came the pressure for legislation that would turn the ability to speak French into an economic asset, and that would shift the burden of bilingualism from the francophone majority in Quebec to the anglophone minority.

Another alternative for young francophone graduates was to pursue a career within the Quebec public service where French was the language of work. In the face of limited employment prospects in the private sector, educational reform thus promoted a rapidly expanding public service staffed with young, aggressive, well-trained, and highly ambitious people, similar in most respects to the reader. They were to spearhead Quebec's bureaucratic assault on the Canadian federal system, one designed to shift jurisdictional responsibilities and the accompanying career opportunities from Ottawa to Quebec City.[54] In a related move, Réne Lévesque, then Minister of Natural Resources in the Lesage government, created Hydro-Québec in 1962 through the nationalization of the province's privately owned electric power companies. Upon nationalization, French replaced English as the language of work in the corporation, and Hydro-Québec became both the showpiece for francophone managerial and technological competence and an important employment pole for nationalist francophones.[55]

It was the new Québécois middle class—the bureaucrats, writers, artists, intellectuals, teachers, musicians, technocrats, communications experts, and business managers—that derived the greatest personal benefits from the Quiet Revolution and who stood the most to gain from independence.[56] (In a similar fashion, such individuals outside Quebec are the ones who have stood to gain the most from Canadian policies of cultural nationalism vis-à-vis the United States.) The benefits of nationalism are rarely distributed evenly across social classes, and Quebec was to prove no exception. Within the province, trade union leaders have argued that the replacement of an anglophone managerial class with a francophone managerial class is not enough, that for a true revolution to occur there must also be a redistribution of wealth across social classes. To date, however, the primary redistribution of income and economic opportunity arising from the Quiet Revolution has been between anglophones and francophones rather than among social classes within the francophone community.

Before the Quiet Revolution, Québécois nationalism had been defensive in character, a bulwark for "la foi, la langue, la race" (faith, language, and race). Distinctive cultural values embedded in the Catholic religion and French language were to be protected by the federal division of powers, and by the insulation of francophones from the commercialism of the English world. By 1960 both forms of protection were breaking down. The federal government was encroaching upon Quebec's political autonomy, the modern mass media had breached the cultural walls of "Fortress Quebec," and the provincial economy had been thoroughly modernized. In this environment, nationalism based on "la survivance" was not enough and the theme of the Quiet Revolution became "la rattrapage," the desire to catch up to the modern world, to make up for the winter of the Duplessis years. Here Jean Blain referred to the "déblocage" of the sixties, "the progress of Quebec at a more normal rate towards the ideals familiar to every modern society."[57] For some, particularly those associated with the Quebec Liberal Party, the rejection of the Duplessis era led to the rejection of nationalism itself. For others, nationalism became more outward looking, expressing a new sense of confidence that Quebec could compete on equal terms in the modern social and economic order. For all, "la langue" rather than "la foi" or "la race" became the overarching concern.[58]

The Quiet Revolution initially had a positive reception outside Quebec where it was assumed that "rattrapage" would strengthen national unity by moving Quebec into the Canadian and North American mainstreams, and that the language divide could be bridged by a national commitment to bilingualism. In fact, the Quiet Revolution exacerbated language conflict both inside and outside the province as francophones sought to establish French as one of the two national languages in Canada and the dominant language in Quebec. Because of its "étatist" orientation, in which the provincial state was seen as the principal vehicle for "rattrapage," the Quiet Revolution also posed a fundamental challenge to the Canadian federal system. As James Mallory explained in 1971, it was to the provincial state that Quebec leaders looked for economic development, social change, and career opportunities; "for them, these things must be done by their own French-Canadian state of Quebec, and not by Ottawa."[59]

The Liberal campaign slogan in the 1962 provincial election—"maîtres chez nous" or "masters in our own house"—became the slogan of the Quiet Revolution. For some, this meant the rollback of federal intrusions into the provincial legislative domain and greater fiscal transfers from Ottawa to the Quebec government so that the latter could meet its growing legislative commitments. Yet for many others such rollbacks were not enough; the existing "house," as defined by the federal division of powers, was simply too small. If, they argued, the Quebec government was to meet its responsibilities as the "national" government for French Canada, then at the very least Quebec needed a restructured federal system with expanded provincial powers. This would still mean, however, that some important decisions would continue to be made by the federal government in which francophones were a minority, and a shrinking minority at that. For those who believed that "national" decisions should be made within the context of Quebec rather than Canada, any federal limitation on "maîtres chez nous" was unacceptable. In this sense, the independence movement can be seen as a logical although not a necessary extension of the Quiet Revolution.

Growing unrest with the federal status quo began to cause considerable unease outside Quebec. There were no comfortable answers to *the* political question of the late 1960s and 1970s: "What does Quebec want?"[60] Francophones who defended the federal system and who sought to exercise the power of French Canada through the government in Ottawa—people like Jean Chrétien, Marc Lalonde, Jean Marchand, Gérard Pelletier, and Pierre Trudeau—asked for a national commitment to bilingualism that many English Canadians were not prepared to make. Demands from the government of Quebec for a radically restructured federal system aided and abetted a broader assault by other provincial governments on the powers of the federal government. Of greatest concern was the growing support in Quebec for independence, for the dismantling of the Canadian state. The independence movement was driven by events within Quebec, but it was by no means a Quebec issue alone for it posed a direct threat to the very survival of Canada. As such, it was far from an abstract or remote issue for English Canadians. As John Meisel wrote in 1973, "for many English Canadians the internal threat to the continuation of Canada is emotionally and in every other way the equivalent of the challenge to their own survival experienced by most French Canadian nationalists."[61]

Independence and the Parti Québécois

Although there had been sporadic agitation for Quebec's independence since the Rebellion of 1837, only in the 1960s did independence emerge as a serious option commanding a reasonable degree of popular support, a broad intellectual following, and the backing of organized political parties. Indeed, the 1960s witnessed a plethora of separatist groups, some of which sought Quebec's independence as a means to a fundamental transformation of the social and economic order. Such groups, and indeed the Quiet Revolution itself, reflected a broader current of social and political unrest sweeping across North America and Western Europe, a current incorporating student radicalism, the American civil rights movement, opposition to the war in Vietnam, and early manifestations of the ecology and feminist movements.

The first and most important of the early independence groups, the *Rassemblement pour l'indépendance nationale* (RIN), emerged only months after the Liberal victory in 1960. Other groups, while enjoying less popular support, achieved a high public profile through the use of terrorist tactics. Quebec politics during the 1960s were marked by bombs, politically motivated robberies, and extremist rhetoric borrowing heavily from radical movements in the United States, Cuba, and across the Third World.[62] Quebec was portrayed as a colony (or as a colony within a colony, depending upon one's perception of the Canadian–American relationship) destined like other colonies in the Third World for national liberation.[63] Repeated reference was made to the fact that the General Assembly of the

United Nations was rapidly filling up with countries that were smaller, less populous, and much poorer than Quebec.

This radical stage of the independence movement was brought to a close by two events. The first was the founding of the Parti Québécois in 1967. The PQ, led by René Lévesque, grew out of the *Mouvement souveraineté-association* and retained sovereignty-association as the foundation for its political platform. After the RIN was disbanded and largely absorbed by the PQ in 1968, the PQ dominated the independence movement, although smaller, more radical groups remained. In Lévesque, a former broadcast journalist, the independence movement found an inspired and inspiring leader. A seasoned politician and master of modern mass communications, Lévesque was able to orchestrate the ideologically diverse independence movement. Lévesque was also effective in carrying the case for independence into English Canada where he was the ideal foil for the province's most popular federalist spokesman, Pierre Trudeau. Unlike most of his contemporaries, Lévesque tried to show that Quebec's independence would be to the advantage of English Canada, that it would free the anglophone majority from continual compromise with the francophone minority. The rejection of independence, he argued, would mean perpetual wrangling "over everything and over nothing"; it would mean "the sterilization of two collective personalities which, having squandered the most precious part of their potential, would weaken each other so completely that they would have no other choice but to drown themselves in the ample bosom of 'America.' "[64]

The second event was the October 1970 kidnapping of James Cross, British Trade Commissioner in Montreal, and Pierre Laporte, Quebec's Minister of Labour, by the FLQ (Front de Libération du Québec). Cross was eventually freed, but Laporte was killed in Canada's first political murder since the 1868 assassination of MP Thomas D'Arcy McGee by an Irish nationalist. The kidnappings and associated political turmoil came to be known as the "October Crisis," in response to which the federal government imposed the War Measures Act. In conjunction with the act, which gave law enforcement agencies extraordinary powers of search and arrest, the Canadian Armed Forces took on a highly visible role guarding political leaders and public institutions. Membership in the FLQ was declared a post facto crime and over 400 people were arrested in Quebec, none of whom were ultimately linked to the kidnappings. Although the imposition of the War Measures Act enjoyed strong public support at the time both inside and outside Quebec, it has subsequently been the topic of intense and generally critical debate.[65] Yet regardless of the merits of the federal response, the October Crisis did mark the disappearance of terrorist factions within the Quebec independence movement. Whether violence was dropped for strategic reasons, given Ottawa's demonstrated willingness to counter force with superior force,[66] or out of a sense of revulsion toward the excesses of the FLQ is not clear. What is clear is that in the wake of the

October Crisis the electoral success of the PQ became virtually the exclusive concern of what had been an ideologically and tactically fragmented independence movement.

In the 1970 provincial election the PQ captured 23 percent of the popular vote, but elected only 7 members in the 110-seat National Assembly. In 1973 the PQ won only 6 seats, compared to 102 seats for the Liberals, even though its share of the popular vote increased to 30 percent. On November 15, 1976, the PQ increased its vote to 41 percent and captured 71 seats; 26 seats were won by the Liberals, 11 by the Union Nationale, and 1 each by the *Ralliement créditiste* and *Parti national populaire*. For the first time a government had been elected that was committed to the withdrawal of Quebec from the federation. Ironically, however, the PQ's initial success stemmed as much from its promise *not* to secede, or at least not to interpret its election as an endorsation of independence, as it did from the party's support for independence.[67] In the 1976 campaign the PQ had promised that a referendum on sovereignty-association would be held before any steps were taken toward independence. This strategy of "étapisme" (independence by stages) was based on public opinion polls that showed support for the PQ and its leader ran consistently ahead of support for independence. The strategy, then, would enable voters to support the PQ while reserving judgment on independence. The PQ assumed that by postponing the decision on independence, time and demography were on its side given that opposition to independence was most widespread among older voters and that support was strongest among the younger Québécois, many of whom were not yet in the electorate.

For almost four years after the election of the PQ government, Canadians inside and outside Quebec waited for the referendum shoe to drop. In late 1979, Premier Lévesque set the stage with an emotional call to the people of Quebec, describing a yes vote in the forthcoming referendum as "the only road that can open up the horizon and guarantee us a free, proud and adult national existence."[68] When the referendum was held on May 20, 1980, voters were not asked if they supported independence per se, but whether they supported the Quebec government entering into sovereignty-association negotiations with Ottawa, with the final and at that point unknown pact being left for voter approval in a subsequent referendum. However, the intense referendum campaign inevitably addressed the broader issue of independence rather than the specific question posed by the ballot.[69] The "oui" forces favoured independence in some fashion and at some time, although the immediate consequences of a yes vote were not at all clear. The "non" forces, united by the slogan "mon non est québécois," favoured the retention of Canadian federalism, although not necessarily the federal arrangements in place at the time.[70] Indeed, the "non" campaign explicitly linked a no vote in the referendum to the promise of a "renewed federalism," an unspecified promise that was to ripple through subsequent national debates on the 1982 Constitution Act, and on the

Sovereignty-Association

The term sovereignty-association binds together the goal of political independence (or sovereignty) for Quebec with both a recognition and acceptance of Quebec's economic integration with the rest of Canada. Its closest model comes from the European Community, wherein still-sovereign states pursue coordinated and integrated economic policies.

The proposal for sovereignty-association called for Quebec and Canada-minus-Quebec to negotiate a series of agreements designed to preserve the existing benefits of economic association. Such agreements might yield a common tariff union, a common currency, the free flow of goods, people, and capital, and joint economic institutions such as a central bank. These agreements, however, would take the form of treaties between sovereign states, and hence would be flexible and adaptable rather than constitutional in character. The government of Quebec would be the only national government for Quebeckers. Quebec residents would not elect representatives to Parliament, but instead would be represented in Ottawa by the Quebec government.

Sovereignty-association would provide an equal partnership between Quebec and the rest of Canada, a partnership based on diplomatic norms of equality between sovereign states. Quebec would continue to enjoy the economic benefits of the larger Canadian union (as would other provinces) without being reduced to minority status within the Canadian state. In essence, then, sovereignty-association would preserve economic linkages while creating a new form of political association.

There was never much enthusiasm for sovereignty-association outside Quebec where many Canadians were convinced that sovereignty-association was simply independence by another name, that it had no more to offer Canadians than did outright independence. Others were uneasy with the continuing political linkages that were implied by sovereignty-association, linkages that might actually increase Quebec's power in any political institutions held in common. More fundamentally, the concept of sovereignty-association was largely overtaken by the Canada–U.S. Free Trade Agreement and the North American Free Trade Agreement (NAFTA), both of which appeared to put into place a continental economic union that reduced the need for any formalized economic association between an independent Quebec and what would be left of Canada.

Meech Lake and Charlottetown accords. Speaking during the campaign, Trudeau declared:

I can make the most solemn commitment that following a No, we will start immediately the mechanism of renewing the Constitution, and we will not stop until it is done. We are staking our heads, we Quebec MPs, because we are telling Quebecers to vote No. And we are saying to you in other provinces that we will not accept having a No interpreted as an indication that everything is fine, and everything can stay as it was before. We want change....[71]

The campaign engaged all political forces within Quebec including the seventy-four Quebec Liberal MPs, led by Jean Chrétien and Prime Minister Trudeau. To an important degree the contest was personalized— Lévesque against Trudeau and, to a lesser extent, Quebec Liberal leader Claude Ryan—making it a battle not only between competing visions of Quebec's future, but also between leaders who had come to symbolize those competing visions.

In the end, 60 percent voted no and 40 percent voted yes; the sovereignty-association proposal had been defeated. (Although the "oui" camp captured close to 50 percent of the francophone vote, little attempt was made to claim a moral victory.) However, the independence forces were not routed. In April 1981, the PQ government was re-elected with an increased majority and an 8 percent gain in its popular vote. In March 1982, an opinion poll conducted for *La Presse* found 28 percent of Quebeckers supported sovereignty-association and an additional 13 percent supported outright independence; among francophones alone the total reached 48 percent.[72] Yet in the longer run the referendum decision emerged as a decisive turning point. Regardless of the apparent contradiction of the 1981 election, the nationalist cause had been dealt a devastating blow; the PQ won despite its support for independence.[73] Then, in the 1985 provincial election following Lévesque's retirement, PQ support fell to 38 percent of the vote and only twenty-four seats in the National Assembly. The provincial Liberals, with former premier Robert Bourassa at the helm, received 56 percent of the vote and ninety-eight seats.

This change in government was an important event in Quebec, but it did not put an end to constitutional tension within the Canadian federal state. Indeed, Bourassa's Liberal government was to be a key player in the Meech Lake Accord and subsequent constitutional debate stretching through 1992. Nor did the change in government fundamentally disrupt the major public policy issue of the time, which was the role to be played by the provincial state in the preservation and promotion of the French language in Quebec.

Quebec Language Legislation

Although francophones in Quebec made up 80 percent of the population and controlled the electoral process at the onset of the Quiet Revolution, they earned considerably less than anglophones in the province and shouldered virtually the entire burden of bilingualism. Initially, little was done in the 1960s to overcome the linguistic income gap, and anglophone domination of the provincial economy continued unabated.[74] Yet the discrepancy between the political power and economic disadvantage of the Québécois was inherently unstable, making some legislative response inevitable. In essence, that response would be to make French the language of work within the province and to make French more visible on signs, billboards, and advertisements; it would also try to ensure that immigrants to Quebec assimilated into the francophone majority. All of these objectives were seen as essential if francophones were to enjoy a full range of economic opportunities and if the French language and culture were to be kept afloat on the North American anglophone sea. The primary concern lay with the francophone majority in Quebec and not with francophone minorities in other provinces who were, in any event, beyond the legislative reach of the Quebec National Assembly.

The first major piece of language legislation was steered through the National Assembly by Robert Bourassa's Liberal government in 1974. Bill 22, Quebec's Official Language Act, declared French to be the "official language" of Quebec and required students who wished to enrol in schools where English was the language of instruction to pass an English proficiency test, the latter measure being designed to channel the children of immigrants into French schools. Although businesses were not required to adopt French as the language of work, Bill 22 encouraged the use of French in the workplace by stating that contracts with the provincial government might hinge upon "francization." Bill 22 also required the use of French on all signs; other languages were permitted, but French had to predominate.

Bill 22 was strenuously attacked by Québécois nationalists who argued that it did not go far enough, and by the English and immigrant communities who argued that it went too far. The most contentious aspect of the legislation was the English proficiency requirement that limited the freedom of parents to send their children to the school of their choice. As it turned out, Bill 22 had little impact on the pattern of school enrolments, in part because the English proficiency barrier could be overcome by immigrant parents and their children who made the effort, and in part because the legislation did not prevent francophone parents from enrolling their children in English schools. In the 1973–74 school year, before Bill 22 came into effect, 16 percent of pre-college students were enrolled in schools where the language of instruction was English; with the passage of Bill 22, this proportion marginally *increased* over the next three years.[75]

Pierre Elliott Trudeau, elected in 1968 as the leader of the Liberal Party and the Prime Minister of Canada, was a strong advocate of a bilingual Canada and a forceful opponent of the independence movement in Quebec.

Canapress Photo Service.

René Lévesque, founder of the Parti Québécois, led his party to victory in the 1976 Quebec provincial election, but failed to carry Quebec in the 1980 referendum on sovereignty-association.

Canapress Photo Service.

In 1977 the new Parti Québécois government passed Bill 101, Quebec's French Language Charter (*Charte de la langue française*). Bill 101 did not depart from the principles of Bill 22 so much as it strengthened both their application and extension into Quebec society.[76] French was reaffirmed as the official language of Quebec, official bilingualism was rejected, and the only legislative reference to English was the passing mention of "other languages" in use in Quebec. Bill 101 abolished English as an official language of the legislature and courts, a provision overturned by the Supreme Court of Canada in 1979. English language schooling was restricted to children with at least one parent educated in English *in Quebec*, children who were attending an English school when Bill 101 came into effect, children who had a brother or sister already in an English school, and children whose parents were living in Quebec in 1977 but were educated in English elsewhere. Thus immigrants, people moving into Quebec from elsewhere in Canada, and Quebec francophones were denied educational freedom of choice. In order to strengthen the visibility of French, all public signs and advertisements were to be in French only. Municipalities, school boards, and hospitals, many of which were in English communities serving a largely anglophone clientele, were required to use French as the internal language of communication. The right to work in French was given legislative support, and firms employing more than 100 people were required to establish labour–management francization committees. (The legal requirements for francization, however, could be met by improving the French language skills of anglophone employees rather than by hiring or promoting francophones.) *L'Office de la langue française* was established to oversee the legislation, and its more zealous officials became known as the "tongue troopers."

In late 1983 the Quebec National Assembly moved to relax some of the provisions of Bill 101. Limited recognition was given to Quebec's English community by an addition to the bill's preamble stating that the National Assembly pursues the objective of making French Quebec's official and working language "in a spirit of justice and openness, and showing respect for the institutions of the English Quebec community and of ethnic minorities, whose precious contribution to the development of Quebec it recognizes." English educational rights were extended to children from those provinces that offered French schooling similar to the level of English schooling provided in Quebec. Only New Brunswick qualified at the time, but Ontario, the province from which Quebec employers would be most likely to recruit, could well qualify in the future. Students who had spent at least three years in an English-language high school in Quebec no longer had to pass a French proficiency test to practise as professionals in the province. Local institutions were no longer required to operate internally in French or to ensure that all employees spoke French as long as French language services could be provided. Bilingual signs were allowed, but only for stores specializing in products "typical of a foreign country or particular ethnic group," terms under which English Canadians did not qualify.

There is little question that Quebec's language policies were successful in many respects, and that the French language in Quebec enjoys greater security in the 1990s than it did in the 1960s and 1970s. However, those policies also became entangled in a series of conflicts with the bilingualism policies of the Canadian government and the embodiment of those policies in the Charter of Rights. On July 26, 1984, a unanimous ruling of the Supreme Court struck down the "Quebec clause" in Bill 101, which required parents (or at least one parent) to have received their primary education *in English in Quebec* before their children could attend English schools in Quebec. In upholding the 1982 decision by the Quebec Court of Appeal, the Supreme Court ruled that the Bill 101 provision was inconsistent with Section 23 of the Charter, which guarantees the educational rights of linguistic minorities—whether French or English—across the country, where numbers warrant. In making its case before the Supreme Court, the government of Quebec recognized this inconsistency, but argued that the Bill 101 provision was consistent with Section 1 of the Charter, which states that the rights and freedoms guaranteed by the Charter are subject to "such reasonable limits prescribed by law as can be demonstrably justified in a free and democratic society." The Quebec submission concluded that the limitation placed on English education in Quebec "is reasonable because it is the expression of a collective right of the francophone majority—vulnerable because it is a minority in Canada and only constitutes 2.5 per cent of the population of North America—to assure its rightful cultural security." The Supreme Court did not concur, ruling that Canadian citizens (and Quebec residents) who have themselves been educated in English elsewhere in Canada retained the right to have their children educated in English in Quebec, should numbers warrant.

The Supreme Court ruling did not have a dramatic impact on Quebec's linguistic profile or educational system. Bill 101's provisions were not altered for immigrant children, nor has the educational situation been altered for francophone families in Quebec as the Charter provisions do not extend the right to an English education to the children of francophone parents. Prior to the Supreme Court ruling, a study for the *Conseil de la langue française* by demographer Michel Paille predicted that the application of the Canada clause would increase the proportion of Quebec students attending English schools only from 13.1 to 13.5 percent.[77] As Liberal MNA Richard French said at the time of the ruling:

> *The future of the French language is not going to be played out in the courtroom or in the classroom—but in front of a TV set and a computer screen. If you compare the importance of this decision with the importance of cablevision in Chicoutimi with American TV channels, or the impact of Boy George and Michael Jackson on the Quebec record industry,*

*or the importance of English as the language of international technology,
you are talking about another order of magnitude.*[78]

Nevertheless, the Supreme Court ruling was of considerable symbolic importance. In a policy area of vital concern to the Quebec government, the Charter prevailed over legislation passed by the Quebec National Assembly.

This situation was repeated on December 15, 1988, when the Supreme Court of Canada overturned provisions of Bill 101 requiring that all signs, posters, and commercial advertising in the province be only in French. In upholding earlier decisions by the Quebec Superior Court in 1984 and the Quebec Court of Appeal in 1986, the Supreme Court ruled that such provisions violated freedom of expression guarantees in both the Quebec Charter of Rights and Freedoms and the Canadian Charter of Rights and Freedoms. The court ruled that while the province could require the use of French in public signage, it could not prohibit the use of other languages along with French:

> *Whereas requiring the predominant display of French language, even its
> marked predominance, would be proportional to the goal of promoting and
> maintaining a French* visage linguistique *in Quebec and therefore justified
> under Section 9.1 of the Quebec Charter and Section 1 of the Canadian
> Charter, requiring the exclusive use of French has not been so justified.*

In this case, however, Section 33 of the Constitution Act, 1982, enabled the Quebec government to override the Supreme Court decision. The Supreme Court's 1984 decision on minority education rights had been based on Section 23 of the Charter, a section to which the "notwithstanding" provisions of Section 33 do not apply, but the court's 1988 decision was based on Charter protection for freedom of expression to which the "notwithstanding" provisions can be applied. Therefore, the Quebec government responded with Bill 178, which, notwithstanding Charter guarantees with respect to freedom of expression, prohibited businesses from using bilingual signage or advertising outside their establishments while permitting limited bilingual signage inside. The regulations accompanying Bill 178 required that with respect to indoor signs, French letters be bigger than English letters, that the space around the French letters be larger, that the French message be placed to the left of or above the English message, and that the colours of the French and English messages be the same. If they are not, the colour of the French message must be stronger.

Quebec's use of the "notwithstanding" clause was roundly condemned outside the province, where it spilled over into the constitutional debate on the Meech Lake Accord, while the inside-outside solution received a mixed reception at best inside Quebec. If nothing else, the episode demonstrated how difficult it can be to find a consensual middle ground in the emotionally charged arena of language politics. In 1993, with the five-year limitation of the "notwithstanding" clause about to expire, Quebec's Liberal government again sought this middle ground through legislative amendments (Bill 86) designed to bring the public signage regulations into line with the Supreme Court decision. In essence, the amendments extended the existing regulations regarding indoor signage to external advertising; English was permitted, but French would have to be predominant with respect to location, size, and colour. The fact that such amendments could be entertained spoke to the success of previous language legislation and the enhanced security of the French language in Quebec. Not surprisingly, however, this attempt to soften the language provisions stemming from Bill 101 met with outspoken opposition from nationalist groups within the province. The passage of Bill

Setback in Quebec

The signs issue carries heavy symbolic freight, and this thumping decision [to introduce Bill 178] sends a clear message to the anglophone minority in Quebec. It is the brutal message of Camille Laurin, father of Law 101, the man who actually wanted to raze the Quebec countryside of all English place names. The message says: you are intruders here, you don't belong and never did, you are illegitimate, your language pollutes the atmosphere and even to see it on a sign is an insult; pack up and go. Sadly, many of them will.

The consequences outside Quebec are equally grave. As of yesterday, Meech Lake was dead in the water, perhaps simply dead.

Worse, the generous vision of Canada that has transformed public policy in the last quarter century will come under renewed attack. From Lester Pearson through Pierre Trudeau to Joe Clark and Brian Mulroney, support for a bilingual country that respects its minorities has been painstakingly stitched together. Federal politics and institutions have been entirely transformed. Provincial governments have improved the lot of francophones outside Quebec. There have been setbacks, God knows, but overall progress has been tremendous.

What now? Almost certainly a hardening of hearts, a less generous attitude, an unwillingness to spend precious political capital on bilingualism and francophones, tougher questioning of the primordiality granted to Quebec's concerns; in sum, a quiet, unspectacular but undeniable backlash that will do us all no good.

Source: Editorial in *The Globe and Mail*, December 20, 1988.

86 marks only the continuation and not the end of language controversy in Quebec.

LANGUAGE LEGISLATION IN COLLISION

To understand why the language policies of Ottawa and Quebec collide, we must go back to basic policy objectives. The 1969 Official Languages Act was designed to create a sense of security for francophones within Canada comparable to their sense of security within Quebec. This was to be achieved by strengthening the French language within national institutions and by increasing the visibility of French in the Canadian society at large. The act and subsequent entrenchment of language rights within the Charter of Rights were designed to protect the language rights of *individuals*; all Canadians, inside or outside Quebec, anglophone or francophone, were to have the same language rights based on their common Canadian citizenship. In practice, however, the federal language guarantees are of greatest relevance for linguistic *minorities*, be they francophones outside Quebec or anglophones inside the province. They are of much less relevance for the francophone *majority* in Quebec, to whom Bills 101 and 178 are addressed. Indeed, federal guarantees may even threaten the linguistic interests of the francophone majority by protecting the anglophone minority in Quebec and thus tempering provincial language legislation.

The language policies of Ottawa and Quebec therefore rest on different philosophical foundations. Ottawa's policies assert language rights as individual rights, indeed as fundamental human rights, and the primary concern is with the protection of anglophone and francophone linguistic minorities across the country. As a political and constitutional corollary, it is the federal government that should have ultimate responsibility for such minorities. Quebec's policies, on the other hand, promote collective interests even to the point of restricting the linguistic choices of individuals; the primary concern is with the protection of the province's francophone majority. The constitutional corollary is that provincial governments, and not Ottawa, should be vested with ultimate legislative responsibility with respect to language. While Ottawa's policies promote a bilingual Canada and respect for individual rights, those of Quebec promote a unilingual Quebec and the collective security of the province's francophone majority. Unfortunately, the latter policies may erode public support for bilingualism in English Canada where the language policies of the federal government already rest uneasily with support within the prevailing culture for multiculturalism and, potentially, linguistic pluralism. Any such backlash could in turn further support the rationale of Bill 101, compounding the vicious circle that bedevils language politics.

As noted at the start of this chapter, two linguistic features are of vital importance to an understanding of federalism and the broader dynamics of Canadian politics: first, that in the country at large one Canadian in four is of French mother tongue, and second, that francophones constitute a clear majority in the second largest province. Hence the ongoing and inevitable conflict between the linguistic majorities of Canada and Quebec. There is, however, a basic question underlying this conflict: Which government best speaks for French Canada? Is it the Government of Canada, which represents all French Canadians, but does so through institutions within which francophones are a minority, albeit a large and influential minority? Or is it the Government of Quebec, which represents only 80 percent of the French-Canadian population, along with a significant nonfrancophone element, but does so through institutions within which francophones form a majority?

In many respects, of course, both governments do and must speak for French Canada. The problem is that they speak for overlapping but nonetheless quite distinct linguistic communities. The linguistic concerns of French Canadians (primarily the protection of minority interests, in the face of an anglophone national majority and nine provincial anglophone majorities) are quite different from the linguistic concerns of the Québécois (primarily the promotion of majority interests, which may run counter to those of the linguistic minority in Quebec). Yet the latter constitute 80 percent of the former. It is perhaps surprising, then, that the governments of Canada and Quebec often articulate conflicting visions of French Canada. When the two visions differ as dramatically as they did under the governments of Pierre Trudeau and René Lévesque, the question inevitably arises: Who speaks for Quebec? Here it is useful to note that within the space of little more than a year the Quebec electorate elected Liberals in seventy-four of the seventy-five federal ridings in the 1980 federal election, defeated the sovereignty-association proposal in the 1980 referendum, and re-elected the PQ government in 1981 with an increased majority. During this period Trudeau and Lévesque both enjoyed strong personal and political support in Quebec, as did their competing visions of French Canada.

A number of factors have combined to create chronic uncertainty over the place of French Canada within the broader Canadian community. Quebec's declining share of the national population has raised fears that, over the long run, Quebec's and therefore French Canada's power within the national political community will be eroded. The demolinguistic transformation of Canada, in which Quebec is becoming progressively francophone and the rest of Canada is becoming progressively anglophone, raises concerns about the long-term survival of Anglo-Quebeckers, French Canada outside Quebec, and the bilingual policies of the federal government. Finally, there is ongoing constitutional tension arising from the conflicting demands for a strong federal government that can protect linguistic minorities outside Quebec and a strong provincial government that can more fully protect and promote the francophone majority inside Quebec.

SUGGESTED READINGS

1. Sheila McLeod Arnopoulos and Dominique Clift, *The English Fact in Quebec* (Montreal: McGill-Queen's University Press, 1980).

2. David V.J. Bell, *The Roots of Disunity: A Study of Canadian Political Culture*, rev. ed. (Toronto: Oxford University Press, 1992).

3. For excellent overviews of much of the material covered in this chapter, see David R. Cameron, "Dualism and the Concept of National Unity," in John Redekop, ed., *Approaches to Canadian Politics*, 2nd ed. (Scarborough: Prentice-Hall, 1983), pp. 233–50; and Kenneth McRoberts, "Quebec: Province, Nation, or 'Distinct Society,'" in Michael S. Whittington and Glen Williams, eds., *Canadian Politics in the 1990s*, 3rd ed. (Toronto: Nelson, 1989), pp. 98–118.

4. For a chronology and analysis of Quebec language policy, see William D. Coleman, "From Bill 22 to Bill 101: The Politics of Language Under the Parti Québécois," *Canadian Journal of Political Science*, 14:3 (September 1981), pp. 459–86. See also Coleman, *The Independence Movement in Quebec, 1945–1980* (Toronto: University of Toronto Press, 1984).

5. John F. Conway, *Debts to Pay: English Canada and Quebec from the Conquest to the Referendum* (Toronto: James Lorimer, 1992). Dominique Clift, *Quebec Nationalism in Crisis* (Montreal: McGill-Queen's University Press, 1982).

6. Richard Fidler, *Canada, Adieu? Quebec Debates its Future* (Lantzville and Halifax: Oolichan Books and the Institute for Research on Public Policy, 1991).

7. Alain-G. Gagnon, ed., *Quebec: State and Society*, 2nd ed. (Toronto: Nelson, 1993).

8. Richard Gwyn, *The Northern Magus: Pierre Trudeau and Canadians* (Toronto: McClelland and Stewart, 1980).

9. For an excellent overview of Quebec politics and society, see Kenneth McRoberts, *Quebec: Social Change and Political Crisis*, 3rd ed. (Toronto: McClelland and Stewart, 1988).

10. Herbert F. Quinn, *The Union Nationale: A Study in Quebec Nationalism* (Toronto: University of Toronto Press, 1963).

11. For a vigorous Québécois nationalist perspective on the material covered in this chapter, see Marcel Rioux, *Quebec in Question*, trans. James Boake (Toronto: James Lorimer, 1978).

12. Charles Taylor, *Reconciling the Solitudes: Essays on Canadian Federalism and Nationalism* (Montreal and Kingston: McGill-Queen's University Press, 1993).

13. Susan Mann Trofimenkoff, *The Dream of Nation: A Social and Intellectual History of Quebec* (Toronto: Macmillan, 1982).

STUDY QUESTIONS

1. The last twenty years have witnessed extensive discussion of the federal division of powers. Are there powers that the people of Quebec would like to see transferred to the provincial governments, and that residents of other provinces would like to see remain with the federal government in Ottawa? If so, how would you explain such different perspectives on the division of powers?

2. In the late 1970s, David R. Cameron described dualism as "the view which holds that the most significant cleavage in Canadian society is the line dividing English from French, and which identifies as the major challenge to domestic statecraft the establishment of harmonious and just relations between the English-speaking and French-speaking communities of Canada" ("Dualism and the Concept of National Unity," in John Redekop, ed., *Approaches to Canadian Politics* (Scarborough: 1978), p. 237). As we enter the 1990s, do you feel that a dualist view is still appropriate? If so, why? If not, what other cleavages rival that between the English and French communities?

NOTES

1. René Lévesque, *An Option for Quebec* (Toronto: McClelland and Stewart, 1968), p. 14.

2. The capture of Quebec by British forces was one of many military campaigns during prolonged hostilities between Britain and France. Hostilities were brought to a close by the Treaty of Paris, which ceded New France to Great Britain. The treaty also contained guarantees for the freedom of religious worship in the ceded territory.

3. Richard Joy, *Languages in Conflict* (Toronto: Macmillan, 1972), p. 86.

4. Ibid., p. 58.

5. Rejean Lachapelle and Jacques Henripin, *The Demolinguistic Situation in Canada* (Montreal: Institute for Research on Public Policy, 1982), p. 233.

6. Lévesque, *An Option*, p. 93.

7. Roderic Beaujot, *Population Change in Canada: The Challenges of Policy Adaptation* (Toronto: McClelland and Stewart, 1991), p. 296.

8. Ibid., p. 123.

9. Ibid., p. 69.

10. Ibid., p. 51.

11. Daniel Kubat and David Thornton, *A Statistical Profile of Canadian Society* (Toronto: McGraw-Hill Ryerson, 1974), p. 38.

12. As of May 1989, the Quebec government has paid a special allowance of $500 for the first child, $1,000 for the second, and $4,500 for the third child and subsequent children. The allowance is paid in instalments ending at age 3.

13. See Pierre Fournier, *The Quebec Establishment: The Ruling Class and the State* (Montreal: Black Rose, 1976).

14. Luc Albert, "Language in Canada," *Canadian Social Trends* (Spring 1989), p. 11.

15. Beaujot, *Population Change in Canada*, p. 293.

16. Government of Quebec, *Quebec–Canada: A New Deal* (Editeur officiel du Québec, 1979), p. 30.

17. *The Globe and Mail*, National Edition, October 20, 1983, p. 8.

18. Lachapelle and Henripin, *The Demolinguistic Situation*, p. 174.

19. Beaujot, *Population Change in Canada*, p. 291.

20. Don Cartwright, "Linguistic Territorialization: Is Canada Approaching the Belgium Model?" *Journal of Cultural Geography*, 8 (1988).

21. Donald V. Smiley, "Reflections on Cultural Nationhood and Political Community in Canada," in R. Kenneth Carty and W. Peter Ward, eds., *Entering the Eighties: Canada in Crisis* (Toronto: Oxford University Press, 1980), p. 33.

22. Beaujot, *Population Change in Canada*, p. 296.

23. Lévesque, *An Option*, p. 14.

24. Lachapelle and Henripin, *The Demolinguistic Situation*, pp. 32 and 39.

25. Richard Gwyn, *The Northern Magus* (Toronto: McClelland and Stewart, 1980), p. 223.

26. Beaujot, *Population Change in Canada*, p. 294.

27. This decline is in part attributable to the disappearance of French language entrance and exit requirements in most English-Canadian universities. Gwyn, *The Northern Magus*, p. 230.

28. Ibid., p. 225.

29. Donald V. Smiley, *The Federal Condition in Canada* (Toronto: McGraw-Hill Ryerson, 1987), p. 146.

30. Cited in Raymond Reid, *The Canadian Style* (Toronto: Fitzhenry and Whiteside, 1973), p. 93.

31. J.W. Dafoe, *Laurier: A Study in Canadian Politics* (Toronto: McClelland and Stewart, reprinted 1963; first printed 1922), p. 26.

32. Ibid., p. 26.

33. In the general election of 1882 the Conservatives captured 51 seats in Quebec with 52.3 percent of the popular vote. In 1887, two years after Riel's execution, they won only 33 seats after a very modest erosion of their popular vote to 49.6 percent. In the 1891 general election, the Conservative vote marginally increased to 50.8 percent while the number of Conservative seats fell to 28. The major drop did not occur until 1896 when the party won only 16 seats with 45.8 percent of the vote.

34. Smiley, *The Federal Condition*, p. 29.

35. W.L. Morton, "Confederation, 1870–1896: The End of the Macdonaldian Constitution and the Return to Duality," in Bruce Hodgins and Robert Page, eds., *Canadian History Since 1867: Essays and Interpretations* (Georgetown: 1972), pp. 195–200.

36. Christina McCall-Newman, *Grits: An Intimate Portrait of the Liberal Party* (Toronto: Macmillan, 1982), p. 62.

37. Gwyn, *The Northern Magus*, p. 220.

38. Ibid., p. 236.

39. McCall-Newman, *Grits*, p. 79.

40. Cited in Mason Wade, *The French Canadians, 1860–1967*, vol. II (Toronto: Macmillan, 1968), pp. 618–19.

41. Raymond Breton, "Multiculturalism and Canadian Nation-Building," in Alan Cairns and Cynthia Williams, eds., *The Politics of Gender: Ethnicity and Language in Canada* (Toronto: University of Toronto Press, 1986), p. 31.

42. Dalton Camp, *Points of Departure* (Toronto: McClelland and Stewart, 1979).

43. W.A. Matheson, *The Prime Minister and the Cabinet* (Toronto: Methuen, 1976), p. 22. Matheson uses consociationalism as a conceptual framework in this insightful look at cabinet government in Canada. For a more extended conceptual treatment, see K.D. McRae, ed., *Consociational Democracy: Political Accommodation in Segmented Societies* (Toronto: McClelland and Stewart, 1974).

44. Patrick Martin, Allan Gregg, and George Perlin, *Contenders: The Tory Quest for Power* (Scarborough: Prentice-Hall, 1983), p. 120.

45. *The Toronto Star*, June 5, 1983, p. F3.

46. Herbert F. Quinn, *The Union Nationale: A Study in Quebec Nationalism* (Toronto: University of Toronto Press, 1963), p. 105.

47. Cited in C. Nish, *Quebec in the Duplessis Era* (Toronto: Copp Clark, 1970), p. 36.

48. Kenneth McRoberts and Dale Posgate, *Quebec: Social Change and Political Crisis*, rev. ed. (Toronto: McClelland and Stewart, 1980), p. 74.

49. For a fascinating discussion of UN patronage and the electoral manipulation with which it was associated, see Quinn, *The Union Nationale*, ch. VII.

50. Dominique Clift, *Quebec Nationalism in Crisis* (Kingston: McGill-Queen's University Press, 1982), p. 15.

51. Kenneth McRoberts, *Quebec: Social Change and Political Crisis*, 3rd ed. (Toronto: McClelland and Stewart, 1988), p. 128.

52. Both trade union and intellectual discontent had been brewing since the early 1950s, with the latter finding expression in the small but politically influential magazine *Cité Libre*, to which Pierre Trudeau was a frequent contributor.

53. Report by the Quebec Assembly of Bishops to the Pope, *The Globe and Mail*, National Edition, November 28, 1983.

54. For a discussion of this point, see Albert Breton, "The Economics of Nationalism," *Journal of Political Economy* (August 1964), p. 385.

55. McRoberts, *Quebec*, pp. 132–33.

56. For a discussion of the new middle class and the consequent restructuring of class politics in Quebec, see Herbert Guidon, "The Modernization of Quebec and the Legitimacy of the Canadian State," in D. Glenday, H. Guidon, and A. Turowetz, eds., *Modernization and the Canadian State* (Toronto: Macmillan, 1978). See also Henry Milner, *Politics in the New Quebec* (Toronto: McClelland and Stewart, 1977).

57. Cited in Lévesque, *An Option*, p. 9.

58. Sheila McLeod Arnopoulos and Dominique Clift, *The English Fact in Quebec* (Montreal: McGill-Queen's University Press, 1980), p. 61.

59. J.R. Mallory, *The Structure of Canadian Government* (Toronto: Macmillan, 1971), p. 397.

60. For a discussion, see Andre Bernard, *What Does Quebec Want?* (Toronto: James Lorimer, 1978).

61. John Meisel, *Working Papers on Canadian Politics* (Montreal: McGill-Queen's University Press, 1973), p. 205.

62. The most influential American analogy was drawn by Pierre Vallières in *White Niggers of America*, trans. Joan Pinkham (Toronto: McClelland and Stewart, 1971).

63. For an English-language expansion of this theme, see Sheilagh Hodgins Milner and Henry Milner, *The Decolonization of Quebec* (Toronto: McClelland and Stewart, 1973).

64. Lévesque, *An Option*, p. 26. Writing in *Le Devoir* (September 19, 1967), Lévesque argued that Quebec's independence "would allow our two majorities to extricate themselves from an archaic federal framework in which our two very distinct 'personalities' paralyze each other by dint of pretending to have a third personality common to both."

65. See Ron Haggart and Aubrey E. Golden, *Rumors of War* (Toronto: New Press, 1971); and Denis Smith, *Bleeding Hearts–Bleeding Country: Canada and the Quebec Crisis* (Edmonton: Hurtig, 1971).

66. For a discussion of this point see Pierre Vallières, *Choose!*, trans. Penelope Williams (Toronto: New Press, 1972).

67. See Maurice Pinard and Richard Hamilton, "The Parti Québécois Comes to Power: The 1976 Election," *Canadian Journal of Political Science*, 11 (December 1978), pp. 739–75.

68. Government of Quebec, *Quebec–Canada*, p. 109.

69. For a discussion of the campaign, see McRoberts, *Quebec*, ch. 9.

70. As Louis Balthazar points out, "paradoxically, people had to be brought to vote for Canada in the name of Quebec." "Quebec at the Hour of Choice," in Carty and Ward, *Entering the Eighties*, p. 73.

71. Cited in McRoberts, *Quebec*, p. 326.

72. *The Globe and Mail*, National Edition, May 20, 1983, p. 8.

73. McRoberts, *Quebec*, p. 342.

74. McRoberts and Posgate, *Quebec*, p. 107.

75. William D. Coleman, "From Bill 22 to Bill 101: The Politics of Language Under the Parti Québécois," *Canadian Journal of Political Science*, 14:3 (September 1981), p. 468.

76. Ibid, p. 459.

77. *The Globe and Mail*, National Edition, July 27, 1984, p. 2.

78. Ibid.

REGIONAL POLITICS

To many foreign observers, the fact that Confederation is widely evaluated from the particular point of view of how given provinces have fared over the years is a remarkable feature of Canadian life. In other countries, cleavages such as social class, religion, race or creed have been of decisive importance to the collective lives of citizens. In Canada, how much the people of any given province have participated in the benefits of the federation, or shared its losses, has been at the forefront of our politics.[1]

It is not surprising that Canadians are acutely aware of geography and territory. Many of the symbols used to convey a sense of the country to non-Canadians and Canadians alike are rooted in geography: Peggy's Cove, Niagara Falls, the Great Lakes, the solitary splendour of the Canadian Shield captured in the paintings of the Group of Seven, the sweep of the prairies, the majestic Rocky Mountains, the blending of sea and air along the rain forest of the West Coast, and the vast silence of the North are intrinsic to the Canadian identity. Other national symbols such as the maple leaf, Canada goose, and beaver are drawn from the land itself rather than from its human population. Yet many of the geographical features that give definition to the country also carve it up into territorially defined subnational communities and thereby contribute to the strength of regional identities. Geographical barriers and the related scale of the country make it difficult for Canadians to come to grips with the nation as a whole. It is difficult, for example, for residents of the East Coast to have an emotional handle on the "miles and miles of miles and miles" that make up the prairie West, or for prairie residents to appreciate the soft beauty of the Laurentians. Given, then, a vast, transcontinental society with a federal Constitution designed explicitly to provide political expression for territorial communities, it seems only reasonable to expect regional identities and conflict to play a major role in political life. As former prime minister William Lyon Mackenzie King observed, "if some countries have too much history, we have too much geography."[2]

On closer inspection, however, this line of argument is not fully convincing. It does not explain why regional conflict in Canada increased[3] as other Western, industrialized countries were experiencing a marked and progressive decline in territorially based political conflict.[4] The existence of regional identities does not explain why or how those identities are politicized, or why they have been politicized to a greater extent than identities based on gender, ethnicity, or colour. It is also difficult to attribute the strength of regionalism to the simple facts of size and diversity, and to the not so simple fact of federalism, given that in the equally vast, diverse, and federal society to the south, regional conflict is less prevalent and disruptive.[5] A further complication is that regional differences within the society have waned at the same time that they have waxed within the political system. While lifestyles in Toronto, Halifax, Charlottetown, and Brandon are by no means identical, the differences are less acute today than they were in the past. With few exceptions, Canadians can watch the same news programs, shop at Canadian Tire, eat at McDonald's, subscribe to the same pay-TV channels, drink the same beer, and read *The Globe and Mail* no matter where they might happen to live. Thus the argument that political regionalism reflects regional divisions within the underlying society has become less tenable with the passage of time.

Just as the Quiet Revolution led Quebec into the mainstream of Canadian economic and social life while at the same time increasing political conflict between Quebec and the broader national community, so too has the regional homogenization brought about by technological change often been associated with increased regional conflict. The implication of this line of thought is that the primary roots of regional conflict are not to be found among regional variations in social characteristics, but rather in the nature of the political system itself. While there are pronounced regional variations in the distribution of natural resources and the nature of economic activity, the thesis to be pursued in this chapter is that even here the study of regional conflict is essentially a study of *political* cause and effect.

Before this thesis can be explored further, some guidelines must be established. First, the principal focus of the chapter will be on the intrusion of territorial identifications and conflicts into *national* political life; little attention will be paid to intraprovincial regional conflicts such as those between Vancouver and the interior communities of British Columbia, between northern Ontario and the "golden horseshoe" stretching along the shore of Lake Ontario, or between St. John's and the outports of Newfoundland. While these conflicts can be of critical importance in shaping the contours of provincial politics, their national impact is less pronounced. Second, Quebec, which was discussed at some length in Chapter 4, will not be brought into the regional analysis. This exclusion, however, should not blind us to the fact that in many respects Quebec is a region analogous to others. It can be argued, for instance, that Quebec, by facilitating the spatial organization of linguistic conflict, has thereby enhanced the salience of other forms of territorial conflict throughout the national community. Third, the chapter will not address the northern territories, which, despite their great size, contain only 0.3 percent of the Canadian population. The emerging impact of the North on national political life will be discussed in Chapter 10.

Here we should note a troublesome conceptual problem that comes from the unavoidable confusion between "province" and "region." Although terms such as "Western Canada," "Atlantic Canada," and "the Maritimes" imply the existence of transprovincial communities sharing at the very least common territorial interests, political perspectives, or economic orientations, the reality of such regional communities is a matter of contentious debate. As the former premier of Prince Edward Island, Alex Campbell, stressed in a 1977 address, the regional community is in many ways an artifact:

The only people who consider Atlantic Canada as a region are those who live outside Atlantic Canada, the planners and bureaucrats in Ottawa, the newscasters in Toronto, and the airline executives in Montreal. We in Atlantic Canada have not yet made the decision to develop as a region. We are four separate, competitive, jealous, and parochial provinces.... I suggest to you that we do not have a regional identity; we do not have regional bonds; we do not have regional strategies....

With respect to Western Canada, British Columbia is often portrayed by its residents as a region quite apart from the prairie West, one with a very different physical terrain, economic base, settlement pattern, and political history.

The related complexities and some of the pitfalls of a regional analysis can be illustrated by the three prairie provinces.[6] Initially they were bound together as a regional community by a common wheat economy and by the shared experiences, characteristics, and frustrations of an agrarian frontier. They constituted a distinctive and relatively well-integrated region not only because of what they had in common, but because what they shared clearly set them apart from other regions. Then, in the decades following the Great Depression and the Second World War, the prairie region began to come unstitched as the importance of the wheat economy declined and as the regional economy diversified. Heterogeneity among the three prairie provinces increased while at the same time differences between the prairies and other regions decreased. Yet, while Alberta and Manitoba may have less in common today than in the past, and while life in Edmonton, Saskatoon, or Winnipeg may be more like life in Toronto, Hamilton, or Halifax than in the past, regional commonalities have not totally disappeared. The prairie provinces continue to share a sense of alienation from the federal government, an economic reliance on the exploitation of natural resources, and a marked dependency on unstable foreign markets for those resources. In a similar fashion, one can identify points of commonality across the Atlantic provinces including but not limited to a concern with out-migration, a fragile and often depressed economic base, a coastal environment, and to a degree, an economic reliance on the sea that is not shared by other Canadians, even those on the West

Coast. A regional analysis must therefore be alert to shared characteristics among provinces, and in particular to shared characteristics that set one region apart from another. Yet it must also be alert to provincial variations within commonly used regional units of analysis such as "the West" or "the Maritimes," variations that often appear quite pronounced to people living within the regions.

DEMOGRAPHIC PROFILE

Figure 5.1 plots the regional composition of the Canadian population from 1871 to the 1991 census. The most dramatic change came with the settlement of the Canadian West when, between 1901 and 1931, the region's share of the national population rose from 12.1 percent to 29.5 percent. Then, with the onset of the Great Depression, accompanied on the prairies by drought, grasshoppers, and the collapse of foreign grain markets, the West's share of the national population began a slide that was not arrested until the mid-1960s. Although the region's share of the national population increased between 1971 and 1991, it has yet to reach the 1931 peak. The westward shift in population at the turn of the century was reflected in part by the relative decline in population along Canada's East Coast, with the proportion of the national population living in the three Maritime provinces falling from 16.7 percent to 9.6 percent between 1901 and 1931. The addition of Newfoundland in 1949 proved only a temporary respite in the progressive, albeit modest, demographic decline of

FIGURE 5.1 *Regional Distribution of the Canadian Population*

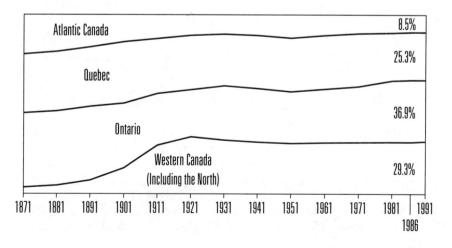

Atlantic Canada. In the twenty-five-year period from 1966 to 1991, Atlantic Canada's share of the national population fell from 9.9 percent to 8.5 percent.

Perhaps the most striking feature about Figure 5.1 is the demographic strength and resiliency of the centre. While Quebec's share of the national population has declined somewhat in recent years, dropping from 28.9 percent in 1966 to 25.3 percent in 1991, and while Ontario's share was eroded by the growth of the West in the early part of the 20th century, the centre has held. Ontario's share of the national population has rebounded from a low of 32.8 percent in 1951 to almost 37 percent in 1991. Quebec and Ontario's combined share reached its lowest point— 60.3 percent—in 1921. Since then it has fluctuated between 61 and 63 percent, and at the time of the 1991 census, 62.2 percent of Canadians lived in either Ontario or Quebec. Overall, then, Canada's regional demography has been surprisingly stable since the Depression brought the agricultural settlement of the prairie West to a close.

Such stability has been less evident within Atlantic Canada and particularly within the West. As Figure 5.2 illustrates, a major change in the Atlantic region came with Newfoundland's entry into Confederation in 1949. The other shifts, including the gradual erosion of Prince Edward Island's share of the regional population, have been very modest in recent decades. Within the West, however, there have been dramatic provincial differences in growth rates and a steady westward shift in population since the onset of the Depression. From 1931 to 1991, British Columbia's population increased by 473 percent and Alberta's by 349 percent, while

FIGURE 5.2 *The Provincial Distribution of Regional Populations*

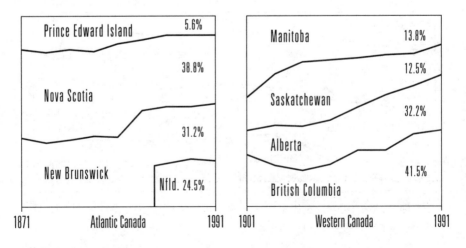

Manitoba's population grew by only 56 percent and Saskatchewan's by a minuscule 7 percent. (This translates into a net increase of 68,000 people in Saskatchewan compared to 2,590,000 in British Columbia!) As a consequence of this westward shift, 73.7 percent of the regional population resided in the two westernmost provinces in 1991, compared to only 46.8 percent in 1931.

ATLANTIC CANADA

"Atlantic Canada" did not exist at the time of Confederation. It would be another six years before Prince Edward Island joined the Dominion and eighty-two years before Newfoundland would expand "the Maritimes" to "Atlantic Canada." In the early years after Confederation, the geographic region was marked by strong local and provincial loyalties that precluded any regional sense of community. As Ernest Forbes has noted, "there was relatively little in the long history of the Maritimes to provide a truly collective historical experience, either actual or mythological, through which the people might develop a strong regional consciousness."[7] In the short run, Forbes argues, Confederation was an alternative to regional unity or consciousness; "the identification with the nation at the higher level and with the cultural group, economic interest, province, or local community at the lower seemed to leave little reason for interest in or loyalty to a Maritime region."[8] Over the longer run, however, Confederation and the ongoing struggle over "better terms" were to provide just such a regional bond.

The Maritimes in Historical Perspective

Confederation was greeted with a general lack of enthusiasm in Nova Scotia and New Brunswick. Opposition was particularly pronounced in the former colony, where a government pledged to repeal Nova Scotia's entry was elected almost before the ink was dry on the 1867 Constitution Act. However, the repeal movement was short-lived. Joseph Howe, its leading spokesperson, joined Macdonald's national cabinet after failing to win British support for repeal, and by 1870 the movement had collapsed. The entry of Prince Edward Island into the Dominion in 1873 was also accompanied by little enthusiasm: "most Islanders met the end of their independent history with bitter resignation and, as was the case in the other two Maritime Provinces, the legacy of resentment against those responsible remained."[9] The end came in the wake of British pressure, an economic recession coupled with a poor harvest, an impending financial crisis precipitated by overly ambitious plans for a provincial railway, and the patient courtship of the Canadian government.

The years between Prince Edward Island's entry into Confederation and the First World War saw the progressive "Canadianization" of the

Maritime economy. On balance, regional integration into the national economy appeared to yield substantial benefits even though that economy's centre of gravity came increasingly to rest in Ontario and Quebec. Maritime manufacturing industries shared in the economic prosperity generated by the settlement of the West. The protective tariffs of the National Policy and favourable freight rates on the Intercolonial Railway gave a particular impetus to the Nova Scotia coal and steel industries that was sustained by the industrial demands of the First World War. However, Canadianization was not complete. Other sectors of the Maritime economy—agriculture, forestry, and fisheries—were less successfully integrated into the national economy; because they relied on American and international markets, they benefited less from the protective tariffs of the National Policy, discussed in Chapter 7. Partly as a consequence of this imbalance, tensions developed between indigenous entrepreneurs and industries, on the one hand, and the increased presence of national economic interests, based in Ontario and Montreal, on the other. It should also be noted that the region was not bound together by a dominant economic interest, as the prairies were to be bound together by the grain trade. When common economic interests did exist, they frequently resulted in intense intraregional rivalry and jealousy; the conflicts between the ports of Halifax and Saint John took on legendary proportions. In combination, the diversity of economic interests and intraregional competition reduced the leverage of the Maritimes on national economy policy and hampered efforts to achieve better economic terms within Confederation. As Forbes explains:

> In trying to represent the diverse interests of their constituents Maritime politicians were often found quarrelling among themselves and attempting to influence national policy in different directions. This left them at a definite disadvantage in competing with regions having more clearly defined communities of interest.[10]

Such regions included both Ontario, with its manufacturing sector, and the emerging agricultural West.

The early years of Confederation also witnessed the political integration of the Maritimes into the broader party system, with the Conservative and Liberal parties sinking deep roots into the region. The major exception to this integration, although not to the dominance of the national parties, came with a flare-up of the Nova Scotia Repeal Movement in 1886–87. Faced with economic distress and federal reluctance to endorse better terms for the province, W.S. Fielding's Liberal government introduced and passed a resolution proposing that "the financial and commercial interests of the people of Nova Scotia, New Brunswick and Prince Edward Island would be advanced by these provinces withdrawing from the Canadian federation and uniting under one government." While the repeal agitation reflected the provinces' "deep and widespread, though not perhaps over-whelming, sense of grievance with their place in the new nation,"[11] the call for secession was largely a matter of rhetoric and ritual, born out of frustration. Certainly regional unification had very limited appeal in Nova Scotia, or elsewhere for that matter.

Although the Fielding government was re-elected shortly after the legislative resolution was passed, its re-election was not widely interpreted as a mandate for secession. Nor was secession taken up by Nova Scotia's MPs, and within the year it had fallen from the political agenda. The lack of support from the province's federal representatives is of particular importance. G.A. Rawlyk and Doug Brown argue that "in the only arena where regional grievances could be effectively redressed, the House of Commons in Ottawa, Nova Scotians as well as other Maritime Members of Parliament willingly sacrificed their regional interests on the altar of party loyalty."[12] This clash between party loyalty in the House and effective regional representation was to become a focal point of western political discontent in the years ahead; during the 1920s it was to result in a major challenge to and transformation of the national party system, and more recently it has found reflection in regional support for Senate reform. However, no such challenge to the party system, much less popular enthusiasm for Senate reform, emerged in the Maritimes as a legacy of the repeal movement.

The first two decades of the 20th century were prosperous ones for the Maritimes as the explosive rate of prairie settlement created a strong demand for the industrial products of central Canada and the Maritimes. Yet the settlement of the West also opened up interregional conflict between the West and the Maritimes, conflict fed from several sources. First, western population growth led to a regional redistribution of seats in the House of Commons, which had the appearance and to a degree the reality of *taking* seats from the Maritimes and *giving* them to the West. Here Figure 5.3 shows the growth of western representation in the House and the corresponding decline, both proportionate and absolute, in Maritime parliamentary representation. As seats disappeared, Maritimers were provided with dramatic evidence of their declining role in the national political community and of their eclipse by the rapidly ascendant West. (Between 1901 and 1911 the population of the three Maritime provinces increased only from 894,000 to 938,000 while the population of the four western provinces increased from 598,000 to 1,721,000.)

The two regions were also at loggerheads over the transfer of federal crown lands in the North-West Territories, which took place in 1905 when Saskatchewan and Alberta were created and the provincial boundaries of Manitoba were greatly expanded. As Ernest Forbes explains, the West and the Maritimes lodged mutually exclusive claims: "the prairie case rested on the contention that the public lands had always belonged legally to the provinces, the Maritime one on the assumption that they belonged to the

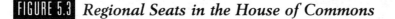

FIGURE 5.3 *Regional Seats in the House of Commons*

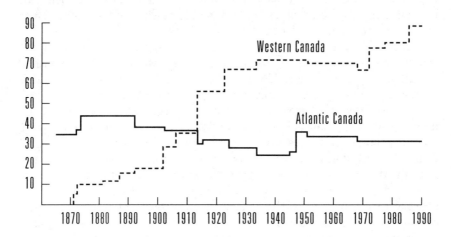

Western Canada

Atlantic Canada

90 80 70 60 50 40 30 20 10

1870 1880 1890 1900 1910 1920 1930 1940 1950 1960 1970 1980 1990

Dominion."[13] Maritimers argued that the original members of the Dominion were entitled to compensation for the "loss" of public lands, a *national* resource, to the prairie provinces. This argument was linked to a broader sense of regional grievance, for it was not only the prairie provinces that benefited from the transfer of crown lands: so too did Quebec and Ontario in 1912 when their provincial boundaries were expanded. For their part, the Maritime provinces were left without new land, because there was none available on the East Coast, and with a diminished share of a diminished national resource. In addition, Maritimers felt that the federal government had provided unreasonably generous financial subsidies to the new western provinces. For example, and quite apart from land transfers, the federal subsidy to the Saskatchewan government was set at approximately three times that of the Nova Scotia subsidy even though at the time Nova Scotia had twice Saskatchewan's population.[14] In a more general sense, the mythology that grew up around western settlement grated upon Maritimers. As Forbes explains, "the thesis which was then becoming widely accepted, that independence, economic and social progress, and even democracy itself were the products of a new and dynamic agrarian frontier, implied an unflattering role for the Maritimes."[15]

There was, then, a not unfounded feeling that the settlement of the West was occurring at the expense of the Maritimes and that the long-term consequence would be a diminished role for the Maritimes in the national community. This concern aroused little interest or empathy among western Canadians who focused their attention instead on regional conflict with central Canada, conflict in which the West could be unambiguously portrayed as the victim. When disputes arose over freight rates, western politicians vigorously pursued their own regional interests with little regard to the potentially negative impact on Maritime industries. The fact that western growth came in part at the expense of the Maritimes, and that the interests of the western regional periphery were at times at odds with those of the eastern periphery, received and indeed still receives little attention.

Regional unease with the ascendancy of the West and the consequent decline of the Maritimes was combined with other sources of political discontent—including labour unrest and a widespread interest in social reform—in the *Maritime Rights Movement*, a broad-gauged movement of regional protest that swept across the Maritimes between 1919 and 1927. While regional discontent was accentuated by the onset of an economic recession in 1920, its roots were "firmly grounded among the deepest concerns and aspirations of the people—aspirations of a political, economic, social, and cultural nature which were seriously threatened by the relative decline of the Maritime provinces in the Canadian Dominion."[16] It was hoped that the political strength that might come through regional unity could correct the injustices being inflicted upon the Maritimes by the federal government and, through the federal government, by other regions. The Maritimes Rights Movement was a continuation of the long-running quest for better terms within Confederation, and for the protection of a region being eroded by both the growth of the West and the increased concentration of economic activity in the central Canadian provinces.

The regional plight of the Maritimes came to be symbolized by the Intercolonial Railway. The ICR, which linked the Maritimes to central Canadian markets and trade, was a direct legacy of Confederation. Headquartered in the Maritimes, it was well attuned to the special economic and political interests of the region, and its rate structure was designed to further those interests. However, the ICR was dependent upon federal subsidies, which in turn were attacked by competing regional interests outside the Maritimes. In 1919 the federal government was instrumental in moving the Intercolonial headquarters from Moncton to Toronto, and in 1923 the ICR was absorbed into the new Canadian National Railway system. The transfer of the ICR headquarters was a stunning blow not only because of the loss of employment, but also because of the more important loss of regional control. The operation of the railway and its freight rate structure would now be determined by external management remote from the myriad regional interests clustered around the ICR. Rawlyk and Brown conclude that "the integration of the Intercolonial into a national railway system, in which management was neither sympathetic nor knowledgeable concerning Maritime problems, spelled disaster for Maritime business."[17]

The Maritime Rights Movement culminated in the 1925 appointment of a federal royal commission to provide a full hearing on regional grievances. The commission, chaired by Sir Andrew Rae Duncan, was successful in venting regional discontent. In 1926 it released a generally sympathetic report, which, together with promises by the federal government to act on its recommendations and the economic recovery of 1927, brought the Maritime Rights Movement to a close. At a federal–provincial conference held that year, interregional tensions were also eased as the Maritime provinces supported the West's demand for the provincial ownership of natural resources,[18] and the western provinces supported the Maritime quest for enhanced freight rate subsidies and intergovernmental fiscal transfers. While the Movement did not result in any significant progress toward the political unification of the Maritimes, it did help foster a regional consciousness and identity that were to persist.

Newfoundland

Whether this regional consciousness and identity extended to Newfoundland is a matter of ongoing and contentious debate. In the 1860s Newfoundlanders, faced with a vulnerable economy and widespread poverty, came up against the Canadian drive for Confederation. Although Newfoundland delegates did not attend the 1864 Charlottetown conference, they did attend the subsequent conference in Quebec City. There Newfoundland was offered generally favourable financial terms of entry, but Canadian politicians were not as insistent in their courtship of Newfoundland as they were in their courtship of Nova Scotia and New Brunswick. Given opposition to Confederation by economic elites in St. John's, and given the fact that little of Newfoundland's trade was with the Canadian mainland, Newfoundlanders rejected Confederation despite considerable British pressure. In 1869 an election was fought on the issue, with Confederation supporters winning nine seats and their opponents twenty-one. The island's sentiment was nicely captured by a song popularized during the campaign:

> Hurrah for our own native isle, Newfoundland!
> Not a stranger shall hold one inch of its strand!
> Her face turns to Britain, her back to the gulf.
> Come near at your peril, Canadian wolf![19]

The Canadian wolf took heed, and union was not considered again until 1895 when a severe recession led to unsuccessful talks with the Canadian government on financial terms of entry. When responsible government in Newfoundland came to an end in 1934 in the midst of near economic collapse, union with Canada, which at the time was itself in the throes of the Great Depression, was not considered. Instead, the reins of government were passed to an appointed six-man commission, with three of the commissioners coming from Newfoundland and three from Great

Britain. The commission remained in place to steer Newfoundland through the wartime prosperity brought by American and Canadian airfields, prosperity that also brought an end to Newfoundland's isolation. As Terry Campbell and G.A. Rawlyk conclude, the war years "forced Newfoundland into the mainstream of North American life and ... resulted in both a dramatic rise in the existing standard of living and also in the benchmark of expectations."[20]

With the end of the war and the departure of Allied airmen, the British government took a major step down the road to union with Canada. The decision was made to hold a referendum on Newfoundland's future and a convention was called to set the terms of the referendum. Initially, the convention did not propose union with Canada as one of the options for the referendum. However, in the face of protest mobilized by broadcaster Joey Smallwood and sympathetically received by the British government, union was included along with retention of commission government and a return to responsible government under the British crown. The first round of the referendum narrowed the choice to union with Canada or a return to responsible government. On July 22, 1948, 52.4 percent of those voting opted for confederation with Canada, and on March 31, 1949, Newfoundland became Canada's tenth province. Eighty-five years after the Charlottetown conference, Confederation was complete.

Smallwood went on to dominate Newfoundland politics for the next twenty years. His passionate support for Canada and his success in entrenching the Liberal Party were to cement the relationship between Newfoundland and the broader community. Yet that relationship was not without difficulties as Newfoundland came to epitomize the pattern of dependency that was increasingly characteristic of Atlantic Canada. Fiscal transfers from the federal government accounted for roughly half the provincial budget, and individual Newfoundlanders were the net beneficiaries of federal government social support programs such as unemployment insurance. These intergovernmental and interpersonal transfers to Newfoundland, and to the Atlantic region in general, could be borne by the national community because of the region's small and declining share of the Canadian population. At the same time, such transfers stopped well short of providing economic prosperity. Newfoundland, for example, chronically suffers from the country's highest unemployment rates.

The end of dependency has been a persistent but elusive goal for Newfoundland's political leaders. Prospects brightened considerably in the 1970s with the discovery of the Hibernia oil field off the east coast of Newfoundland, but the discovery also touched off a bitter jurisdictional battle stretching through to the mid-1980s between the Newfoundland and Canadian governments. Premier Brian Peckford's Progressive Conservative government claimed the same ownership and thus control of offshore resources that other provinces, and most particularly Alberta, exercised over continental resources. It was hoped that the revenues that would eventually flow from Hibernia could be used to lift Newfoundland from the ranks of the "have-not" provinces and transform Newfoundland as oil had transformed Alberta. For its part, the Liberal government in Ottawa claimed that offshore resources fell under federal jurisdiction, that oil revenues should replace rather than build upon equalization payments, and that once Newfoundland's provincial revenues reached the national average, the federal share of natural resource revenue should be increased.

The offshore dispute bounced around in the political arena for some time. Prior to victory in the 1979 federal election, Joe Clark stated that, if elected, a Progressive Conservative government would transfer ownership of offshore resources to the provinces. However, no action was taken before the Clark government was replaced by a less sympathetic Liberal government in the 1980 general election. At that point the offshore dispute became thoroughly entangled with the broader constitutional debate set in motion by the sovereignty-association referendum in Quebec. With the resolution of that debate in 1981–82, a resolution that did not address jurisdictional control over offshore resources, the Newfoundland government referred the offshore dispute to the provincial Supreme Court. When the Newfoundland court ruled in favour of Ottawa, the ruling was

Reprinted from Guy Badeaux, ed., *Portfoolio 8* (Toronto: Macmillan, 1992), p. 105.

appealed to the Supreme Court of Canada. In February 1984 the Supreme Court ruled that jurisdiction over offshore resources lay with the federal government. Newfoundland's claim that it had retained ownership of the continental shelf upon entering Canada in 1949 was rejected.

The court's decision put the dispute back into the federal–provincial arena, and into the 1984 federal election campaign. Shortly after the Progressive Conservative victory in September, Ottawa and Newfoundland endorsed the Atlantic Accord, which largely met Newfoundland Premier Brian Peckford's conditions for provincial control over and benefit from offshore development. However, the accord was no sooner in place than falling world oil prices threw Hibernia's development into doubt. The political debate shifted from constitutional ownership to the extent and timing of federal subsidies for the Hibernia project, subsidies that became increasingly critical to the project's realization as private players began to fall by the wayside. The storm clouds that began to gather around Hibernia intensified further as the governments of Newfoundland and Canada collided on constitutional issues and conservation measures for the northern cod fishery. Indeed, the personal relationship between Premier Clyde Wells and Prime Minister Mulroney became poisonous as the two locked horns over the Meech Lake Accord and subsequent constitutional initiatives. As the province moved toward the 21st century in the face of harsh economic realities and political discord, the end of dependency seemed to be as illusive a goal as it had ever been.

The Atlantic Region

Public opinion polls seldom provide a very reliable snapshot of the political culture in Atlantic Canada, in part because national samples do not include enough Atlantic respondents for provincial comparisons to be made. Thus public opinion in Atlantic Canada is generally served up as a homogeneous lump with no regard to provincial differences. Table 5.1 is therefore unusual in that it presents the results of a detailed regional survey conducted in 1978. The table demonstrates a very high level of support for Confederation among Atlantic Canadians. While a significant number agreed that "the way Confederation was set up gives all the advantages to Ontario," they were outnumbered more than two to one by those who disagreed. Fewer than 30 percent agreed that they belonged to "a group that hasn't got a fair deal out of federal government policy," even though 61 percent felt that people in Ontario were better off than were people in their own province. A majority of respondents also supported the federal status quo, with only 32 percent supporting a more decentralized federal system in which more power would be given to the provincial governments. Finally, it is interesting to note the very limited intraregional variation in the table. Opinion varied little from one province to the next, suggesting a regional perspective on political life that transcended

The Northern Cod Fishery

The early 1990s brought Newfoundlanders devastating news with respect to the northern cod fishery. The collapse of the northern cod stock came about through a variety of factors including unusually cold water conditions, lower salinity, predation by and competition from seals, the emigration of cod out of the region, and overfishing by Canadians and Europeans. The collapse led first to the closing of the fishery in the summer of 1992 and then to a two-year moratorium on fishing. The moratorium led to the largest layoff in Canadian history as 20,000 fishery workers were idled. By mid-1993, more than 40,000 fishery workers across Atlantic Canada had lost their jobs. Cod stocks are not expected to rebound until at least the late 1990s.

The federal government responded with the Northern Cod Adjustment and Recovery Program. The program, with an annual cost of approximately $1 billion, pays fishery workers between $225 and $406 a week. However, it was designed to provide short-term relief rather than to address the long-term unemployment problem should cod fishing not resume.

As the crisis deepened, federal–provincial conflict intensified over the management of the fishery, with Newfoundland seeking greater control. But, as federal Fisheries Minister John Crosbie said in June 1993, "the real issue today is not whether there should be joint management of the fishery, the real issue is whether or not we are going to have a fishery at all" (*The Globe and Mail*, June 19, 1993, p. A1).

The Department of Fisheries and Oceans also released a report in June 1993 that raised concerns about the future of fish stocks across the Atlantic region, stocks upon which 50,000 Atlantic Canadians depend for their livelihood. The report suggested that catches of cod and haddock might have to be reduced to 10 percent of traditional levels for a period of at least five years in order to allow stocks to replenish.

provincial residence. As we will see shortly, such a transcendent regional perspective is increasingly rare among the four western provinces.

Since the end of the Second World War Atlantic Canada has become increasingly marginal to the national economy.[21] Interlocking economic and demographic decline have in turn eroded the region's position within the national political community. While the development of offshore resources, if it takes place, may forestall any further erosion, the prospects for a dramatic reversal in the region's fortunes are not bright. To date,

TABLE 5.1 *Regional Sentiment in Atlantic Canada*

In the fall of 1978 the Task Force on National Unity commissioned a comprehensive public opinion survey of the Atlantic region. Directed by Professors George Perlin and George Rawlyk, both from Queen's University, the survey encompassed 1,939 respondents. Although a number of years have since passed, it still stands as the most detailed snapshot available of political opinion in the region. While there has undoubtedly been some change in opinion since 1978, there is little reason to expect that the broad parameters sketched in by the questions below have been altered to any substantial degree.

		Atlantic Canada	Nfld.	P.E.I.	N.S.	N.B.
1. "Overall, would you say that Confederation has been a good thing or a bad thing for this province?"	Good thing	84%	90%	80%	80%	84%
	Bad thing	7	4	10	8	6
	Both	1	1	1	1	1
	D.K./N.O.	9	4	10	12	9
2. "Some people say that the way Confederation was set up gives all the advantages to Ontario. Other people say that is not true. What do you think?"	True	24%	17%	21%	25%	27%
	Not true	59	60	60	59	58
	D.K./N.O.	17	22	19	16	15
3. "Do you feel you belong to a group that hasn't got a fair deal out of federal government policy?"	Yes	28%	29%	22%	29%	27%
	No	67	65	74	65	68
	D.K./N.O.	6	6	4	6	5
4. "In terms of their incomes and standard of living, on average, do you think people in Ontario are better off, about the same or worse off than people here in (name of province)?"	Better off	62%	61%	73%	63%	59%
	About the same	27	23	22	28	30
	Worse off	5	7	1	4	6
	D.K./N.O.	6	9	4	4	5
5. "Some people think that more of the power to make decisions should be taken from the federal government and given to the provincial governments. Other people would rather keep things as they are. What do you think?"	Decentralize	38%	32%	38%	41%	39%
	Status quo	50	55	47	50	49
	D.K./N.O.	11	14	14	9	12

though, the national fabric has not been seriously strained by regional discontent. As G.A. Rawlyk and Doug Brown conclude, "in a fascinating twist of a complex relationship, the region of Canada which was once most vociferously opposed to Confederation has become one of its most ardent and committed supporters."[22] Atlantic Canadians have not challenged the basic institutional or constitutional structure of the federal state, and have not allowed regional discontent to dampen their electoral support for the two mainline national parties. (In the 1993 general election, the Liberals and Conservatives between them captured 83 percent of the regional vote; Reform received only 8 percent, and the New Democrats less than 6 percent.) Economic competition among the Atlantic provinces,[23] a declining share of the national population, widespread dependency on transfer payments from the federal government, and powerful regional spokesmen within the federal cabinet have all served to contain regional discontent. It should also be stressed, however, that the region's political agenda is now heavily laden with issues that pit specific provincial governments, and at times the region as a whole, against the federal government. Conflict over issues such as federal subsidies for offshore resource development, the potential closure of military bases, changes in the unemployment insurance system, the management of fisheries and the control of foreign fleets, and the preservation of equalization payments in the face of growing fiscal constraints all portend intensified regional discord in the years ahead.

WESTERN CANADA

In a narrow sense, Confederation was the amalgamation of four existing British North American colonies into a single colonial unit, but in a broader sense it was also the vehicle through which a new and unsettled region could be developed, a region whose resources were believed to be immense. This region was the prairie West, stretching over a thousand miles from the western edge of the Canadian Shield to the Rocky Mountains.

Even before Confederation, the prairie West assumed an important place in the Canadian national vision. Note, for instance, an editorial that appeared in the Toronto *Globe* on March 6, 1862:

> *When the territory [the West] belongs to Canada, when its navigable waters are traversed for a few years by vessels, and lines of travel are permanently established, when settlements are formed in favourable locations throughout the territory, it will not be difficult by grants of land to secure the construction of a railway across the plains and through the mountains.... If we set about the work of opening the territory at once, we shall win the race [against the United States, which was pushing steadily westward].... It is an empire we have in view, and its whole export and*

import trade will be concentrated in the hands of Canadian merchants and manufacturers if we strike for it now.[24]

To a large degree, the West has fulfilled even the most optimistic visions of early Canadians. Yet it has done so through prolonged and often acrimonious regional conflict, the seeds of which are to be found in the above quotation. The conflict between *national* interests and the more narrow economic interests of central Canada, on the one hand, and the regional aspirations of those who settled the prairie West, on the other, has not been easily resolved. Indeed, the chronic character of western alienation provides ample testimony that a resolution still eludes Canadians over 100 years after European settlement began to spread across the prairies.

To explain the contemporary nature of political life in Western Canada we must first sketch in, using very broad strokes indeed, the region's historical evolution. In doing so we must also recognize that there have been two quite different Wests—the prairie West encompassing Manitoba, Saskatchewan, and Alberta, and, across the mountain divide, British Columbia. The settlement pattern, economic foundations, and political history of British Columbia have been very different from those of the prairie provinces, just as the same features have been very different for Newfoundland than for the three Maritime provinces. For this reason, our initial discussion focuses on the prairie West alone and its incorporation into the Canadian union.

The Prairie West in Historical Perspective

For many Canadians, Confederation was the key that would unlock the riches of the vast northwest territories and, in so doing, stimulate economic growth and prosperity in central Canada. However, settlement was slow and prosperity elusive in the first thirty years after Confederation. A worldwide economic depression in the 1870s and 1880s stemmed the tide of immigration to the New World, and for those who did come, open land was still available in the United States. There was also considerable scepticism as to whether the prairie climate and terrain would even support agricultural settlement, a scepticism that many prairie residents still share in the winter months! Nevertheless, the rail system that was to transport western resources to world markets and settlers to the West was put in place while incremental settlement spread across Manitoba and westward along the CPR tracks and the North Saskatchewan Valley. The long-anticipated settlement boom finally began in the late 1890s as the depression lifted, large-scale immigration resumed, and free land in the United States all but disappeared. The success of early settlers, and the introduction of new and hardier strains of wheat, put the earlier scepticism about prairie agriculture to rest. In the single decade from 1901 to 1911 the prairie population rose from 419,000 to 1,328,000, an increase of over 317 percent in only ten years. When Prime Minister Wilfrid Laurier declared in 1904 that the 20th century belonged to Canada, his optimism fully reflected the spirit of the "last, best West," as the prairies were described in promotional literature put out by the Canadian Pacific Railway and federal government.

While the settlement of the West is a saga that cannot be recounted in any detail here, a number of features should be noted for their impact on Canadian political life. Although the West was settled in large part by the westward migration of Canadians, and in particular by those from Ontario, many settlers came from Europe and the United States. These latter settlers had spent little if any time in other parts of Canada, and had limited exposure to the political values, institutions, and parties of the central Canadian heartland. Therefore, a substantial portion of the prairie population had relatively shallow roots in Canadian political soil and, more particularly, in the mainstream Conservative and Liberal parties. As a result, in the economic crises to come western Canadians were open to new political ideas and were quite prepared to abandon the traditional parties for more radical, regional parties.

The prairie population was also set apart by its ethnic composition. In the 1931 census, which marked the ethnic crystallization of the prairie community, only 56.5 percent of the residents were of British or French descent, compared to 80.1 percent for Canada as a whole and 82.7 percent for Ontario. The prairie population was marked by large numbers of German, Scandinavian, Ukrainian, Dutch, Polish, Russian, and American settlers. With that diversity came a multiplicity of religions, languages, and cultures, all giving the prairies a uniquely multicultural cast. French Canadians made up only 5.8 percent of the prairie population in 1931, a proportion surpassed by those of German, Ukrainian, and Scandinavian descent. This demographic feature helps explain why French Canadians were often seen as simply another ethnic minority, and a relatively small one at that, and why the *regional* rather than *national* size of the francophone population has dominated prairie reactions to bilingualism and biculturalism. Moreover, in the historical process of assimilating a linguistically diverse immigrant population, the protection of the French language was frequently viewed as an unwelcome shield behind which other ethnic groups might seek protection from assimilationist pressures. In combination, these demographic features help account for widespread opposition in the West to bilingualism and to more broadly conceived dualistic interpretations of Canadian life.

Although the prairie population may have been demographically diverse, it was pulled together by a wheat economy that touched the lives of virtually every prairie resident. Unlike the Maritime provinces, the prairie provinces shared a common and overriding set of economic interests. The wheat economy bound the prairie provinces into a single economic unit and forged a "regional way of life,"[25] one that facilitated the political integration of the prairie West and set the region apart from central Canada to the east and British Columbia to the west. Yet the wheat economy was a precarious undertaking at the best of times. Farmers were dependent upon an uncertain and often harsh climate, and upon volatile foreign markets lying beyond their control. (While the economy at large was also very dependent upon unpredictable foreign markets, no other region exported as much or was dependent upon such a narrow market base.) Wheat was not a crop that could be sold to any great extent on the local or even Canadian market. It had to be sold—through the middlemen in the grain trade—on distant foreign markets, and then shipped across Canada and the Atlantic Ocean on a monopolistic transportation system. The wheat economy was also afflicted by cycles of boom and bust determined by weather conditions in Europe and Western Canada, conditions that determined the demand from European markets and the size of the Canadian crop. Thus grain farmers rode an erratic, unpredictable roller coaster over which they had little control and which destabilized economic and political life on the prairies.

The nature of prairie agriculture led to a litany of economic grievances. At the top of the list came tariff protection for central Canadian manufacturers, which increased the price western Canadians had to pay for consumer goods and farm machinery while their own crops sold on the unprotected international market. Other grievances included transportation bottlenecks; freight rates, which were seen to be excessive; inequities in the grading and marketing of grain; and the frustrations of a debtor frontier toward central Canadian financial institutions that loaned badly needed capital, collected the interest, and when times were tough, foreclosed on the family farm. These economic grievances generated in turn a regional set of political grievances embodied in the term *western alienation*.[26] Apart from the specific economic grievances mentioned above, western alienation reflected the belief that the West's contribution to the national economy was not being sufficiently acknowledged. After all, wheat in the early part of this century was a mainstay of the national as well as the regional economy. As James Mallory has pointed out, "almost the whole Canadian economy was vitally affected by, and organized around, the movement of the annual grain crop into world markets."[27] Although that movement supported the national railway system, which in turn bound the new country together and provided essential western markets for central Canadian industries, the West received few compensations from national policies on tariffs and freight rates. At the heart of regional alienation lay the belief, and essentially the reality, that western Canadians lacked political muscle commensurate with their contribution to the national economy. The region found itself in a quasi-colonial position vis-à-vis central Canada and the federal government, and thus many of the specific economic problems confronting the West were attributed to the

Economic Alienation

It is a longstanding tenet of western alienation that the federal government has been at best indifferent to the economic woes of the West, and at worst a major contributor to those woes through national tariff and freight rate policies.

As economist Kenneth Norrie has pointed out, however, the West is a relatively sparsely populated economic hinterland within both the Canadian and North American market economies. Many of its economic grievances, such as the lack of secondary manufacturing and economic diversification, arise from the region's location in these market economies and "must be interpreted as dissatisfaction with a market economy rather than with discriminatory policies of the federal government." Norrie goes on to argue that the negative effects of federal policies have been exaggerated, and to question whether even the most supportive national policies would be able to overcome market forces and encourage any substantial increase in manufacturing and secondary industry in the prairie West. While extensive government intervention in the market economy would be a necessary condition, it may not prove to be a sufficient condition.

Here it should be noted that the free trade agreements should enhance the impact of market forces in Western Canada. If Norrie is correct, there is little prospect that the freer play of continental markets will promote economic diversification in Western Canada, although it may prompt further development in the resource sector.

Source: Kenneth H. Norrie, "Some Comments on Prairie Economic Alienation," in J. Peter Meekison, ed., *Canadian Federalism: Myth or Reality?* 3rd ed. (Toronto: Methuen, 1977), p. 325.

region's political impotence. Their solution was seen to require a regional assault on the political and institutional status quo.

The quest for political reform followed a number of paths including support for national opposition parties; the creation of new, regionally based parties that it was hoped would be more attuned to western Canadian interests; the rejection of the party system altogether and the advocacy of nonpartisan forms of government; and the advocacy of procedural changes in the House of Commons that would weaken party discipline and make MPs the agents of their constituents rather than of their parties. There was no clear focus or target; westerners were divided among those who sought no more than a change in government, those who sought new, regionally based parties, and those who rejected the party system altogether. The regional critique of parliamentary institutions was hesitant and inconsistent; although party discipline was assailed, Parliament itself was venerated without a clear recognition that party discipline was an essential feature of parliamentary democracy. The desire to weaken party discipline was not coupled with practical proposals for alternative institutional arrangements to sustain parliamentary democracy once the prop of party discipline was removed.[28]

Perhaps the most significant thing about western agrarian protest is that it failed to have any substantive impact on the *institutional* fabric of the Canadian federal state before Western Canada was transformed by the calamitous events of the 1930s. The Great Depression began in 1929, reached its peak in the early 1930s, and lingered on until the start of the Second World War. Although the Depression was a major economic shock for the entire country, its impact on the prairies was catastrophic. The collapse of world trade devastated the export-based prairie grain economy. Accompanying the collapse in markets came drought, grasshoppers, and high winds that stripped the top soil from the land, creating the immense duststorms of the "dirty thirties." Debt that had been undertaken in the good years, when farmers expanded their holdings and improved their equipment, became a crushing burden in the 1930s. When crops could be grown they often could not be sold, or could be sold only at a price insufficient to cover the costs of production and transportation. Farmers frequently had no choice but to plough their crops under and hope for better times. For many others in "next year country" the only alternative was to leave the land and the region as debts mounted and the banks foreclosed.

The Depression redefined the place of the prairie West in the national community. Prior to the 1930s the prairies had been the magnet drawing immigration into Canada. Then, with the onset of the Depression and the Second World War, immigration slowed to a trickle; when it resumed after 1945 the prairies were bypassed. Unsettled agricultural land had all but disappeared and grain prices were low. The grain economy had become more capital-intensive, offered fewer employment opportunities, and was costly to enter for new farmers. Most postwar immigrants, moreover, came primarily from urban backgrounds and lacked the skills and interest needed for prairie agriculture. In addition, the prairie West, struggling to recover from the devastation of the Depression, was no longer seen as a region of promise and new beginnings. Even a passing familiarity with the Depression was sufficient to deter all but the most masochistic immigrants from settling on the prairies. The end of in-migration to the region, the out-migration of hundreds of thousands of prairie residents during the Depression, and the increasing mechanization of prairie agriculture all combined to undercut the region's population base and political power. Western agriculture also became less central to the Canadian economy; even though more grain than ever was being produced, the grain economy's proportionate contribution to the national economy steadily declined. As fewer people produced more and more with less and

The Mulroney Grain Elevator

Andy Donato, *Gucci Blues: Political Cartoons* (Toronto: Key Porter Books, 1988).
Originally published in *The Toronto Sun*.

less economic impact, the prairie West drifted toward the margins of Canadian life.

The "New West"

Yet even as the "old" agrarian West declined, a "new West" was beginning to emerge, its birth marked by the discovery and commercial development of the Leduc oil field in Alberta during the late 1940s and early 1950s. The new West, like the old, was based on natural resources, but these now included oil, natural gas, potash, coal, and uranium. The *relative* although not *absolute* decline of agriculture and the expanded resource base brought the prairie economy more into line with that of British Columbia and laid the foundation for a broader political region than had existed in the past. (British Columbia's resource base encompassed not only forestry and the Pacific fisheries, but also coal, natural gas, hydroelectric power, and a variety of minerals including copper, lead, molybdenum, and zinc.) However, the new regional economy was similar to the old in that it was heavily dependent upon foreign markets and highly variable world prices. The "boom and bust" problems of the wheat economy were inherited, moderated to a degree by diversification *within* the resource sector, but not surmounted.

The new West developed slowly at first, with British Columbia as the primary growth pole and population magnet. Then, after 1973, escalating world prices for oil fuelled rapid growth in the Alberta and, to a lesser degree, Saskatchewan economies. The face of the new West was urban rather than rural, its features the skylines of Vancouver, Calgary, and Edmonton rather than the silhouettes of grain elevators against the prairie sky. The spirit of the region was marked by the aggressive boosterism of communities on the move and on the make. Migration into the region accelerated as thousands of Canadians packed their belongings into U-haul trailers and moved west in search of a slice of the natural resource pie. While the population of Canada increased by 12.9 percent between 1971 and 1981, the West's population increased by 21.8 percent, nearly twice the national average. In the same decade the population of Alberta increased by 37.5 percent and that of British Columbia by 25.6 percent. Once again the West seemed to be at the cutting edge of Canadian society, and the smouldering coals of political discontent burst into flame.

During the 1970s and early 1980s western alienation was fuelled from a number of sources. Provincial governments in the West, growing rapidly in size and bureaucratic expertise, challenged the federal government's management of national economic policy and sought to roll back federal intrusions into provincial fields of jurisdiction. In this respect, political developments in the West closely parallelled those occurring in Quebec. At the same time, national bilingualism policies found an unsympathetic and at times hostile audience in the multicultural West. This

Brian Gable, *The Globe and Mail*; reprinted from Guy Badeaux, ed., *Portfoolio 8* (Toronto: Macmillan, 1992), p. 103.

reaction was symptomatic of more general frustration stemming from Ottawa's apparent preoccupation with national unity problems originating in Quebec, a preoccupation that pushed western concerns off the nation's political agenda. Note a 1979 speech by Stan Roberts, then president of the Canada West Foundation:

> *The new fury of the Westerner demonstrates itself when it strikes home that Quebec's six million plus citizens have turned the country on its collective ear and created an enormous attention to their problems by the election of a pequiste government, while the West's six million plus citizens (still) can't be heard over the rush and scramble to accommodate Quebec. Sometimes the West's frustration and rage is misconstrued as antiQuebec in nature. It is not. It is, in most cases, envy of Quebec's political prowess combined with fury at the West's own impotence on the national scene.*[29]

Of perhaps greatest importance was the lack of elected western representation within the federal government and thus the inability of westerners to see their own regional reflection in national institutions. As Figure 5.4 illustrates, there have been dramatic swings in western Canadian representation on the government side of the House of Commons, dramatic at least in comparison with the more stable pattern in Atlantic Canada. The high water mark came in 1958 when the West moved overwhelmingly into

FIGURE 5.4 MPs Elected to the Government Side of the House

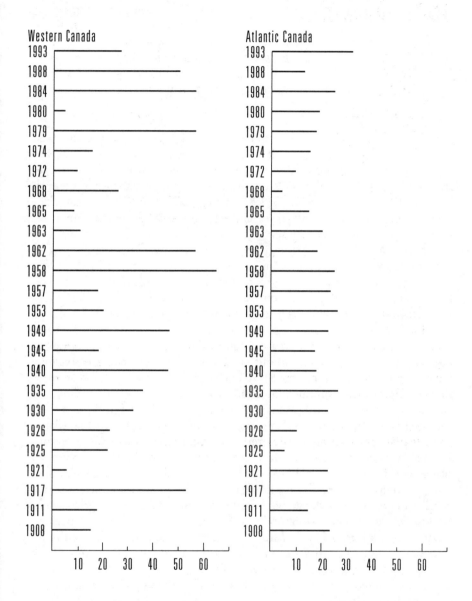

the Progressive Conservative camp as John Diefenbaker swept the region and the country in the largest Canadian electoral landslide ever. While Diefenbaker's appeal in that election was undeniably national in scope, it was particularly strong in the prairie West. As Denis Smith explains:

> He gave to the Prairies for the first time in their history the same sense of dynamic and central participation in nation-building that his predecessor, John A. Macdonald, had given to central Canada after 1867.... [His policies] were policies of national integration that typified the prairie conception of Canada.[30]

When other regions swung back to the Liberals in the early 1960s the West stood pat, and with Diefenbaker's defeat in 1963 western representation on the government side of the House fell to precariously low levels. The situation was particularly bleak on the prairies. Of the sixty-five western Liberal MPs elected in the 1963, 1965, 1968, 1972, and 1974 general elections combined, only twenty-three came from the three prairie provinces. In 1979 the Progressive Conservatives formed a minority government in which the West enjoyed strong representation. The Conservative leader, Joe Clark, was the first Canadian prime minister born in the West. Only nine months later, however, the Conservatives were defeated and replaced by a majority Liberal government. In that election only two Liberal MPs were elected west of Ontario, both in Manitoba. The West had been all but shut out.

The lack of elected representation in the federal government was at odds with the growing economic muscle of the West and the region's increasing share of the national population. It was irksome to westerners that a majority government could be elected before a single ballot was counted west of Ontario, as happened in 1980. (When this happened again in 1984, but with the West on the winning side, it provoked little comment!) The practical cost of regional exclusion from the federal government was driven home, at least to Albertans, by the federal response to rising world oil prices in 1973–74, by the introduction of the National Energy Program in the fall of 1980, and by the related and acrimonious conflict between the federal and Alberta governments over the price structure for Canadian oil and natural gas. As Figure 5.5 shows, at the peak of western alienation nearly a third of western Canadians agreed with the statement that "Western Canadians get so few benefits from being part of Canada that they might as well go it on their own." Levels of western alienation tended to be higher in Alberta and British Columbia than they were in Saskatchewan and Manitoba, but the sentiment was far from absent in the eastern half of the region. Alienation was also much more pronounced among Conservative voters, whose party formed the official opposition in Ottawa, than among Liberals; New Democrats tended to occupy an intermediate position.

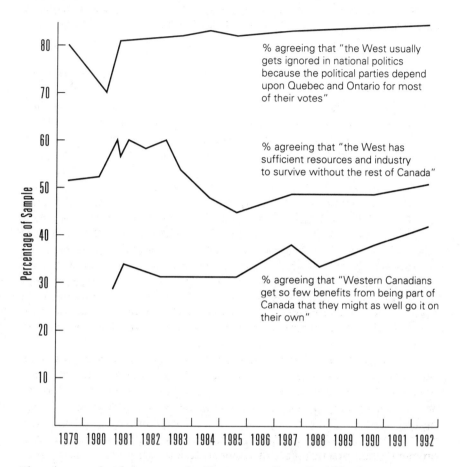

FIGURE 5.5 *Western Alienation*

% agreeing that "the West usually gets ignored in national politics because the political parties depend upon Quebec and Ontario for most of their votes"

% agreeing that "the West has sufficient resources and industry to survive without the rest of Canada"

% agreeing that "Western Canadians get so few benefits from being part of Canada that they might as well go it on their own"

Percentage of Sample

1979 1980 1981 1982 1983 1984 1985 1986 1987 1988 1989 1990 1991 1992

These data are taken from a series of public opinion polls conducted for the Canada West Foundation, Calgary, Alberta. For details, see the Foundation's *Opinion Update* series.

Western alienation, it should be stressed, cannot be equated with support for western separatism. Although western separatist parties did emerge for the first time following the 1980 federal election, they attracted only marginal support. In the absence of an immediate federal election, separatist candidates ran provincially where they played a minor role at best in elections held in Saskatchewan and Manitoba, and no role whatsoever in British Columbia. Only in Alberta did the Western Canada Concept party make a mark by electing an MLA in a provincial by-election and by capturing 11 percent of the popular vote in the subsequent provincial election. In that election, however, the sitting WCC member was defeated as the governing Progressive Conservatives picked up seventy-five of seventy-nine seats. In ten surveys tracked by the Canada West Foundation between mid-1979 and mid-1980, support for separatism averaged only 6.6 percent across the region. Even this figure may overstate the true level of separatist support as some respondents used the question to express the intensity of their frustration rather than to endorse an independent West.

Western Canadians sometimes drew a tactical parallel between their own situation and that faced by the residents of Quebec who, the argument went, had used the threat of separatism to extract political and economic concessions from the federal government. Only if western Canadians were prepared to play the same game, the argument continued, would Ottawa pay attention to their complaints and aspirations. However, the Quebec analogy failed to recognize that many Québécois had more than a tactical commitment to independence—that for many independence was a positive goal and not simply a club with which to beat concessions out of Ottawa. More importantly, the analogy failed to recognize the essential core of western alienation. Unlike the Québécois, who have sought to ward off assimilation, western Canadians have sought greater integration into the national political, economic, and social mainstreams. In the words of the late W.L. Morton:

> The West has been defined as a colonial society seeking equality in Confederation. That equality was sought in order that the West should be like, not different from the rest of Canada.[31]

Western alienation captures the frustration that comes from incomplete integration, from the belief that the region has failed to play a role in the nation's life commensurate with its resources, potential, and aspirations. As the early slogan of the Reform Party proclaimed, "The West Wants In!" Even among separatists the cry has been: "We are not separating, it's Canada that is abandoning the West." Thus western alienation has been not so much a vociferous expression of a regional or provincial identity as it has been the expression of a frustrated Canadian identity.

At its peak, western alienation represented a demand by the new West for greater recognition within the nation's political and economic fabric. This demand came to a head in the political struggle over the patriation of Canada's Constitution, a struggle that took place when the federal government had but two elected representatives from Western Canada. It was also a time when the West's economy was strong, its population was growing relative to the nation as a whole, and its provincial governments were led by popular and articulate leaders. Yet, when the dust finally settled on the patriation battle and the Constitution Act of 1982 had been proclaimed, little had been done to redress longstanding western grievances.[32] Admittedly, provincial control over natural resources had been strengthened through the addition of Section 92A—"Non-Renewable Natural Resources, Forestry Resources and Electrical Energy"—to the Constitution Act, and the new amending formula was modelled after western proposals. However, parliamentary institutions had not been reformed so as to provide more visible and effective regional representation in Ottawa. More generally, the West had not been able to impose its own political and institutional vision upon the Canadian federal state despite a nearly unbroken tradition of regional political discontent reaching back 100 years.

There is an important lesson to be learned from the western Canadian experience in the late 1970s and early 1980s. When all was said and done, once the price of oil had gone up and down again, once thousands had moved into the region and left again, *the centre held*. The West remained on the national periphery, a region rich in resources and territory, but with a relatively small and widely dispersed population. The lesson is that regional discontent will not be overcome by dramatic shifts in the regional location of people and industry. In the short and intermediate run, the Canadian economic and demographic landscapes are immutable; marked regional differences in the distribution of natural resources, population, and industry will remain and will continue to generate tension within the national political system. We must therefore look for solutions to regional discontent in the way we conduct our political affairs. Part of that search must embrace political parties, for as David Smith argued in the mid-1980s, the Liberal neglect of Western Canada during the Trudeau years was a matter of choice:

> *The provinces today see no defenders of their interests at the centre. That is the source of the demand for institutional change: the belief that the central government does not understand the regions, that it does not hear them. On this, however, the regions are wrong. They do not see the real issue. The governing party can court the regions at any time, just as governing parties did in the past. The truth is that the Liberals under Mr. Trudeau chose not to do so, and the reason was that the governing party held a different view of Canada.[33]*

In short, the Liberals chose to set the nation ahead of region. Elsewhere Smith has argued that internal reforms within the Liberal Party further undermined the party's sensitivities to regional concerns and aspirations.[34] Others have suggested that the solution might be found in more regionally attuned development policies.[35] However, it is not clear that either solution will be sufficient or even likely without complementary institutional reform.

During the 1970s and early 1980s, Pierre Trudeau served as the lightning rod for western Canadian political discontent. It is thus appropriate that in one of his last speeches as prime minister, Trudeau should

The Political Economy of Regionalism

The argument that regionalism has institutional rather than geographical roots is one that is developed at length within the political economy literature. Note, for example, the following discussion by Wallace Clement (p. 89):

> Regionalism is but one expression of more deeply rooted inequalities and social problems in Canada. Any dominant class creates problems through its very existence and actions; one such problem is regionalism. To suggest that regional inequalities are "natural" ignores the realities of power and the control some men have over the lives of others. Thus a detailed analysis of the current structure of regionalism would show that it is not the product of some natural phenomenon like geography or resources or even historical accident; rather, it is the product of a series of actions and institutions created and alterable by man.

Clement goes on to argue that primary importance should be attached to economic institutions and the impact of class. Thus it is not "Ontario" that dominates Canada: "it is the capitalist class and its operating arm in the economy, the economic elite, which has always performed and continues to perform this task" (p. 94). Political factors, such as the federal structure of the Canadian state, take on a somewhat secondary role (p. 99):

> But do ... political boundaries really explain regionalism in Canada? Are the real regional splits not based more on economics than politics?... While political fragmentation aggravates regionalism, it is not itself the cause of regionalism. That cause must be found in the uneven economic development of the country and the branch-plant structure of corporate capitalism.

Source: Wallace Clement, "A Political Economy of Regionalism in Canada," in Daniel Glenday, Hubert Guindon, and Allan Turowetz, eds., *Modernization and the Canadian State* (Toronto: Macmillan, 1978).

capture the essence of western Canadian discontent. Speaking before the Quebec wing of the federal Liberal Party on March 31, 1984, Trudeau said:

> No Canada can exist without the support of this province. Remind yourselves of that during the leadership race to elect my successor, during the coming election. Quebec is strong. Quebec can decide who will govern this country, but more importantly how this country will be governed.

Western Canadians would not challenge that statement. Their frustration stems from the fact that Canadian leaders could and would not make a similar statement about the West even though more people live in the four western provinces than in Quebec. (At the time of the 1991 census, 6,896,000 people lived in Quebec compared to 7,908,000 in the four western provinces.) The result is not discontent with Canada per se, but with the political system, discontent that in the past bound four rather disparate provinces into a single regional community and made regionalism a pervasive and enduring feature of Canadian political life.

Perceptions of How the Federal Government Treats Quebec and the West

In a national survey conducted by Angus Reid Associates for Southam News in late August 1988, 1,506 respondents were asked if they thought Brian Mulroney's Progressive Conservative government was doing too much, too little, or about the right amount for Quebec (*Calgary Herald*, September 3, 1988, p. A1). Including Quebec respondents, 47 percent of the national sample felt that the federal government was doing too much for Quebec, 13 percent too little, and 34 percent about the right amount. Among English Canadians alone, 60 percent felt that too much was being done for Quebec compared to only 29 percent who felt that the federal government was doing about the right amount.

In Western Canada, 71 percent of the respondents thought that the federal government was doing too much for Quebec while 73 percent felt that too little was being done for the West. Nationally, 46 percent of the respondents said that too little was being done for the West, 37 percent said that the West was being treated about right, and 7 percent said Ottawa was doing too much for the West.

Within the context of western alienation, the results of the 1984 federal election provided an important test for parliamentary institutions. Following that election western Canadian representation on the government side of the House of Commons surged from two to fifty-eight MPs, and the West had a strong voice in the federal cabinet through such ministers as Joe Clark, Jake Epp, Ray Hnatyshyn, and Don Mazankowski. Thus western Canadians were able to see how parliamentary institutions worked in the best rather than the worst of times. There is little question that the new Progressive Conservative government initially met the admittedly high regional expectations. The Western Energy Accord, signed by Ottawa and the three oil-producing provinces on March 27, 1985, brought an end to the protracted energy wars between the federal and western provincial governments. The accord removed or began to phase out most of the contentious tax provisions imposed by the National Energy Program, deregulated the price and sale of oil, eliminated the Petroleum Incentive Program, and created a better atmosphere for foreign investment. Through the Western Grain Stabilization Fund and a variety of other measures, $10 billion was spent over the first four years of the Mulroney government to protect western farmers facing drought, falling world grain prices, and a crushing debt load.[36] In August 1987, the federal government created the Department of Western Economic Diversification in order to help diversify the western economy.

It might have seemed, therefore, that parliamentary institutions did in fact perform well under the "right conditions." And yet, as Figure 5.5 illustrates, western alienation did not only persist, but flared up in even more virulent forms. In the 1988 election the Progressive Conservatives lost substantial ground in the West, dropping from 58 of 77 seats (75 percent) in 1984 to 48 of 86 seats (56 percent) in 1988. The new Reform Party of Canada, campaigning on its slogan "The West Wants In," fought an energetic campaign across the region and in Alberta picked up 15.3 percent of the popular vote, finishing second in nine of the province's twenty-six constituencies. Reform candidates, led by Preston Manning, provided a forceful and at times articulate expression of both traditional western grievances and more contemporary concerns including Senate reform and opposition to the Meech Lake Accord. Although the Reform Party had some trouble getting its concerns onto a campaign agenda dominated by the debate over the free trade agreement, and although no Reform candidates were elected until a March 1989 by-election in the Alberta riding of Beaver River, the party nonetheless made a significant mark on regional politics. At the very least, the 1988 campaign demonstrated that the ghost of western alienation had not been laid to rest by four years of Conservative government in Ottawa, a government within which the West had been well represented and through which economic policies favourable to the West had been pursued.

Nor was it laid to rest during the next five years of Conservative government, years in which the West still enjoyed strong and vigorous representation within cabinet and on the government side of the House. The Reform Party continued to grow in strength, and opposition across the region to the prime minister, the GST, and the Meech Lake and Charlottetown constitutional packages was emphatic. However, it is less clear that the West stood apart from the rest of English Canada in any of these respects; even the Reform Party decided to pursue a national mandate and began to play down the regionally idiosyncratic aspects of its platform and appeal. (Regional differences in the 1992 constitutional referendum are discussed in Chapter 8.) Thus regional discontent blended into a more general national discontent with politicians, parliamentary institutions, and specific policy initiatives of the Mulroney government. If western Canadians were still alienated from the political process, it was a characteristic that they shared with many other Canadians.

In 1993, the Reform Party won 51 seats across Western Canada, including 22 of 26 seats in Alberta, and 24 of 32 seats in British Columbia. The Reform Party picked up 38 percent of the regional vote, while the Progressive Conservatives were crushed, winning no seats and picking up only 13 percent of the regional vote. Clearly, Kim Campbell's attraction as a western Canadian leader was no match for that of Preston Manning's. It should be noted, however, that the Liberals also did well across the four western provinces, rebounding from the 1988 election to win 27 seats and 30 percent of the regional vote. The Liberals did particularly well in Manitoba and Saskatchewan, winning 12 of 14 seats in Manitoba and 5 of 14 in Saskatchewan.

Reform support among the electorate extended well beyond the West, even though the Reform Party captured only a single seat east of Manitoba. The Reform Party received more votes in Ontario than it did in the three prairie provinces combined; 33 percent of the total Reform vote came from Ontario, compared to 23 percent from British Columbia and 25 percent from Alberta. Thus while the Reform Party was in part an expression of traditional regional discontent, its message of fiscal constraint, populist unrest, and social conservatism found a much broader national audience. To some measure, the 1993 election results suggest the "nationalization" of western Canadian discontent.

ONTARIO

Embodied within western alienation lies a polarity that is fundamental to an understanding of both political life in Western Canada and the dynamics of regionalism more broadly conceived. That polarity pits the regional peripheries against "central Canada," "the East," or in the rubric of Atlantic regional discontent, "Upper Canada." While such terms are often used to include Quebec, it is Ontario that forms the regional pivot for Canadian politics.

By any measure other than geographical size, Ontario is Canada's largest "region." Moreover, we find within Ontario a concentration of people, wealth, industry, and cultural activity that sets Canada apart from the more geographically dispersed federal system to the south. Ontario contains 37 percent of the national population whereas California, the largest state in the United States, contains slightly more than 10 percent of the American population. Ontario not only forms the economic heartland of Canada, but its domination of the national economy far surpasses that exercised by any single state in the United States. For its part, Toronto dominates English-Canadian cultural life to a far greater extent than any one city is able to do in the United States; there is no ready Canadian equivalent to the cultural competition between New York, Boston, Los Angeles, San Francisco, and Washington, to name but a few. Ontario, furthermore, is the site of Canada's largest city and the national capital. Ottawa's location reinforces Ontario's position at the centre of Canadian life, whereas the capitals of Australia and the United States are located in special districts outside the boundaries of any state.

It may seem odd, then, that discussions of regionalism generally neglect Ontario. When the term is used in reference to Ontario, the focus is usually upon territorial divisions within the province—on conflict, for example, between northern Ontario and the "golden triangle"—rather than upon Ontario's position in and impact upon national political life. Conventional political discourse rarely treats Ontario as one of the many Canadian regions. In this respect, Joe Clark is considered to have made a major strategic blunder in his 1983 bid to retain the leadership of the national Progressive Conservative Party when he declared that, should Ontario Premier Bill Davis run for the leadership, Davis would be seen as "a regional candidate." Ron Graham concluded in a retrospective look at the leadership campaign that "however true that observation was, the heart of Ontario is not won by treating it as less than the centre of the universe."[37] Ontario politicians have certainly been reluctant to cast Ontario in mere regional terms, although Premier Bob Rae has been more prone than his predecessors to do so. In any event, the study of regionalism has been primarily the study of the Atlantic and western peripheries, with the central Canadian linchpin placed aside.

But how do we explain a regional analysis that all but ignores the largest and most influential region? Why is Ontario little more than a residual term in any regional analysis? In part, the answer has to do with how regionalism is conceived. The analytical focus is not on the relationship *among* the various regions that make up the Canadian community, but rather on the relationship *between* the centre and the periphery. In this context, the centre ceases to be a region like other regions and instead takes on the colouration of the whole. It is the *metropolis* to the regional *hinterlands*.[38] Given Ontario's size, electoral weight, and central location within the national community, the identification of the regional part—Ontario—with the national whole—Canada—is understandable. To illustrate the point in very simplistic terms, it is at least conceivable to imagine Quebec, Newfoundland, or the West separating from Canada, but it is inconceivable to imagine Ontario doing so; Ontario *is Canada* to a degree that no other region can claim.

To cast the argument in more political terms, Ontario's share of the national electorate is sufficient to ensure at least adequate representation within the federal government. Since the end of the Second World War there has not been a governing party elected with fewer than 35 Ontario MPs, and the average has been close to 50. In 1984 and 1988 federal elections respectively, 67 and 47 Progressive Conservative MPs were elected from Ontario; in 1993 the Liberals won 98 of the 99 seats in Ontario! Ontario traditionally has more representatives in the federal cabinet than any other province, including ten of twenty-three in Jean Chrétien's first cabinet, and the majority of Canadian prime ministers, including Macdonald, Mackenzie, Borden, King, Meighen, and Pearson, have held seats in Ontario. There is, then, a ready identification of Ontario with the federal government, an identification reinforced by the location of the national capital. This does not mean a lack of intergovernmental conflict between Ottawa and the Ontario provincial government in Queen's Park, nor does it mean that the direction of the federal government always follows the wishes of the Ontario electorate. What it does mean is that Ontario cannot be shut out of the federal government in the way in which both Quebec and the West have been in the past. It means, furthermore, that the "national interest" as articulated by Ottawa will not deviate widely from the national interest as perceived by the voters of Ontario. In this vitally important respect Ontario is not a region like the others, and the difference tends to place the province outside the framework of regional analysis.

REGIONAL AND NATIONAL IDENTIFICATIONS

Lodged within the above discussion is the assumption that regional and national identifications in Ontario overlap to such an extent that there is no conflict between being an "Ontarian" and being a Canadian, that one identity is the expression of the other. To some degree the same assumption was embedded in the discussion of Atlantic Canada, where strong regional and provincial identities co-existed with a strong attachment to Canada. However, in the West and certainly within Quebec the situation is more complex; there is a real and at times palpable tension between political identities. These somewhat divergent situations suggest that our understanding of regional politics might be strengthened by a closer look at the relationship between regional and national identifications.

Conflicting Expectations

There is little reason to doubt that the great majority of Canadians are strongly attached to their country. While it might be argued that nationalism in Canada is less intense than in some other countries, this is not to question the existence of a strong emotional bond between Canadians and their country. There is also little reason to doubt that Canadians are characterized by strong regional attachments, that where we live *within* Canada shapes our personal identity, our sense of who and what we are. What is less clear is how national and regional identifications interrelate, and how they combine to shape our political personalities.

For many observers, regional identities form the building blocks of the Canadian identity. Historian J.M.S. Careless, for example, writes that "what has been sought and to some degree achieved [in Canada] is not really unification or consolidation, but the articulation of regional patterns in one transcontinental state."[39] Regional identities, in other words, are found at the core of the *national* identity. This line of thought finds political expression in former prime minister Joe Clark's description of Canada as a "community of communities." It also found expression, to cite but one of many possible examples, in speeches by former Alberta premier Peter Lougheed in the political debate leading up to the patriation of the Constitution in 1982. Rankled by the charge that his vigorous defence of Alberta was "un-Canadian," Lougheed asserted that to defend Alberta was to defend Canada, that one's Canadian identity could be legitimately expressed through a strong provincial identity. To the premier there was no intrinsic conflict between regional and national identities; they were more appropriately seen as complementary means for expressing one's attachment to Canada.

This conclusion is not universally accepted. The counter-argument is that regional identities, or at the very least *strong* regional identities, constitute a corrosive influence on the strength and vitality of Canadian nationalism. It is as if individuals have only so much loyalty to parcel out, that there is a "zero-sum" relationship between national and regional identifications in which a gain by one means a corresponding loss by the other. While one can from this perspective be both a British Columbian and a Canadian, one can only be strongly attached to British Columbia at the expense of one's sense of attachment to the country as a whole. In this context, those who are concerned about a relatively weak sense of Canadian nationalism often finger regionalism as the cause; Canadians are accused of putting the regional cart before the national horse, of being preoccupied with narrow regional interests while the larger interests of Canada are ignored. For others the strength of regional identifications is seen as the consequence rather than the cause of a weak sense of Canadian nationalism; regional identifications fill the vacuum left by the absence of a more dynamic Canadian nationalism.

The Evidence

By far the clearest survey research finding from explorations into citizen identifications is that *regional* identities, as opposed to either *provincial* or *national* identities, are very weak. In the Perlin and Rawlyk study of opinion in Atlantic Canada, respondents were asked the following question: "Do you think of yourself first as a Canadian, as a Maritimer or as a (Newfoundlander, Prince Edward Islander, Nova Scotian, New Brunswicker)?"

Across the region, only 6 percent of the respondents first chose a Maritime identity. When a similar question was posed to western Canadian respondents in 1982, a time of intense regional angst, less than 8 percent identified themselves as "western Canadians."[40] Although neither finding demonstrates that respondents lack regional identities, the evidence suggests that regional identities pale compared to identifications with province and country. It also suggests that pan-provincial regional identities may come into full blossom only within the political environment, that the terms "Western Canada" and "Atlantic Canada" have a political resonance that they lack in other spheres of life.

It is not coincidental that identifications that lack a corresponding governmental structure are also the weakest. As Alan Cairns has argued, governments are not passive reflectors of their social environment.[41] They are actively involved in shaping that environment, in moulding the contours of citizen identifications as they seek to maximize political support. Thus one's sense of being a Canadian, and of being a resident of a specific province, is nurtured by our federal and provincial governments respectively. However, no government exists to nurture one's sense of being a western Canadian or an Atlantic Canadian. There are no *regional* flags, holidays, ceremonies, capitals, licence plates, or symbols. There is not even a regional structure to the Canadian Football League now that Winnipeg plays in the eastern conference and American teams have been added. It is not surprising, then, that few western Canadians or Atlantic Canadians see themselves *first* in regional terms. The only political institution that is formally organized along regional lines is the Senate, and even here it is now recognized that regional representation no longer squares with citizen identifications. Note, for example, the conclusion of the Beaudoin-Dobbie constitutional committee with respect to Ottawa's September 1991 constitutional proposal:

> The federal proposal argues that the reality of contemporary Canadian politics is that people identify primarily with their provinces or territories, rather than their geographical regions. The Senate should therefore represent people on a provincial or territorial rather than a regional basis.[42]

Repeated surveys have found that when respondents are asked to choose between national and provincial identifications, the former prevail by a wide margin. In the Perlin and Rawlyk study, 62 percent of those selecting either a national or a provincial identification selected the former while only 38 percent said that they thought of themselves first in provincial terms. In a 1980 national telephone survey, the Carleton School of Journalism asked 1,275 respondents the following question: "Where does your first loyalty lie—with Canada or with the province in which you live?" Nationally, 74 percent chose Canada and 26 percent their province. The ratio was 66 percent to 34 percent in the Atlantic provinces, 53 to 47 percent in Quebec, 90 to 10 percent in Ontario, and 80 to 20 percent in the West.

A final illustration of this point is provided by Table 5.2. The data in the table are derived from a national survey conducted by the author in April 1983. Overall, 73 percent of the respondents said that they thought of themselves first as Canadians, 17 percent first as provincial residents, 8 percent refused to choose or stated an equal preference, and 2 percent did not have an opinion. The interesting aspect of Table 5.2 is the marked provincial variation. Thus we find, for example, that while 93 percent of the Ontario respondents identified themselves as Canadians first, a plurality of Newfoundland respondents identified themselves as Newfoundlanders first. Although Table 5.2 should not suggest that provincial identities are absent in Ontario, it does support the conclusion that provincial and national identifications overlap to a greater extent in Ontario than they do elsewhere in the country. At the same time, national identities elsewhere are far from weak. In the West, 74 percent of the respondents identified themselves as Canadians first even though western alienation was very pronounced at the time of the survey.

TABLE 5.2 *Provincial Variation in Citizen Identifications, April 1983*

"Do you think of yourself first as a Canadian or as a Newfoundlander/Nova Scotian/New Brunswicker/Prince Edward Islander/Quebecker/Ontarian/Manitoban/Saskatchewanian/Albertan/British Columbian?"

	Canadian	Provincial Identification	Both Equally
Newfoundland	42%	47%	11%
Prince Edward Island	57	38	5
Nova Scotia	65	30	5
New Brunswick	78	18	3
Quebec	50	34	15
Ontario	93	5	1
Manitoba	85	11	2
Saskatchewan	73	14	12
Alberta	71	12	16
British Columbia	72	14	14

Note: Table excludes the 0.7% of the sample who failed to answer the question, and the 1.2% who cited identifications other than national or provincial.

The finding that national rather than provincial identifications prevail in most parts of the country is an important one, but it does not address the relationship between the two identifications. Although hard information on the nature of that relationship is neither abundant nor clear-cut, what there is suggests that national and provincial identifications are not in conflict and may even be mutually reinforcing to a modest degree. In an analysis of the 1974 national election survey, the "feeling thermometer" scores assigned by respondents to Canada and the various provinces were *positively* correlated; relatively positive assessments of one's country and province tended to hang together, as did relatively negative assessments of the two.[43] As the relationship was weak and, under some statistical conditions, inconsistent, the authors stopped short of concluding that national and provincial identifications were mutually reinforcing. However, they did conclude that "in simple affective terms, liking one's own region does not seem to be a deterrent to liking Canada as a whole."[44]

This conclusion was supported in a subsequent analysis of the 1974 data by David Elkins. While Elkins notes that Canadians have a "deep and abiding" sense of place extending to their local area, province, and country at large, and that this sense of place has heightened over time, the various identities are not competitive.[45] Indeed, respondents in the 1974 survey who were the most sensitive to regional considerations had the strongest sense of themselves as Canadians. Thus Elkins concludes that the assumption that provincial identities override a sense of nationalism or national identity "is totally unwarranted, except in the case of a minority of Quebec French respondents with separatist sentiments."[46] Thus regional identifications, far from precluding a sense of national identity, can best be seen as identifications within a grander, more diverse whole. Here it is also interesting to note that regional sensitivity in the 1974 survey was positively correlated with generally high levels of knowledge about Canada, with a familiarity with several parts of Canada, and with a preference for the federal government over provincial governments.

To conclude this discussion a number of methodological points should be noted. The first is that research to date may have distorted reality by asking the wrong questions. When, for example, respondents are asked if they "first think of themselves as Canadians or New Brunswickers," they are being placed in a forced-choice situation. Yet if national and provincial identifications are not competitive, the forced choice does not square with the psychological reality of respondents. For many and perhaps most Canadians, national and regional identities may be two sides of the same coin. This point was captured in the slogan of those Quebeckers opposed to the 1980 Quebec referendum on sovereignty-association; "mon non est Québécois" emphatically rejects the proposition that one must or can choose between Canadian and provincial identities. In the words of John Holmes, "it is in the Canadian tradition for citizens to want to preserve the Canadian framework in order to live more securely as Quebeckers or Nova Scotians or British Columbians."[47]

Second, regional identities often take on a poetic, almost mythical character that makes empirical measurement difficult. Richard Allen, for example, has described the Canadian West as "a region of the mind," an evocative and in many ways compelling phrase that nevertheless provides little guidance for empirical research.[48] Historian Douglas Francis invokes the same imagery, arguing that there is an aspect of the West's history

> ... which transcends the decisions of politicians, the intricate workings of the economy, and the daily activities of its peoples; it exists in the mind. The history of the West has often been governed as much by what people imagined the region to be as the "reality" itself.[49]

Survey researchers have yet to design instruments of sufficient sensitivity to capture the richness of regional imagery and identification implied in this passage. Until they do, a firm understanding of the relationship between national and regional identifications will have to wait.

Third, it should be noted that regional and/or provincial variations in public opinion are often not very pronounced. Admittedly, the empirical evidence here can be contentious for, within the mountain of public opinion data generated every year, one can select particular surveys and particular questions within particular surveys to support virtually any argument. Nonetheless, there are many issues for which regional differences in policy preference are small or for which significant variation is limited to single provinces or regions. Put somewhat differently, in many and perhaps even most cases, knowing where a person lives provides little indication of his or her policy preferences. Table 5.3 provides an illustrative snapshot of this point. It shows no regional variation with respect to public opinion on party discipline, but central Canadian respondents and in particular Quebec respondents were more likely than others to see the lack of women in the House of Commons as a serious or very serious problem. The same pattern was replicated to a degree when respondents were asked about the lack of visible minorities within the House, although on this occasion it was only the prairie West, and particularly Alberta, that stood apart. Limits on campaign contributions and spending found greater support in central Canada than elsewhere, but the regional differences were not pronounced. Finally, Quebec and prairie respondents differed significantly with respect to MPs following the public interest in their votes on controversial issues such as the death penalty.

What, then, do we conclude from all of this? First, public opinion data offer greater support for dualistic conceptions of Canada than they do for regional fragmentation. In general, differences between respondents inside and outside Quebec, or between anglophones and francophones, tend to be greater than regional differences *within* English Canada. If in the

TABLE 5.3 *Regional Variation in Public Opinion*

	Atl.	Que.	Ont.	Man./Sask.	Alta.	B.C.
% agreeing that "we would have better laws if MPs were allowed to vote freely rather than having to follow party lines"	78	80	77	81	80	77
% saying that it is a serious or very serious problem that "there are many more men than women in the House of Commons"	29	37	33	23	26	27
% saying that it is a serious or very serious problem that "there are very few members of visible minorities in the House of Commons"	43	47	39	34	28	41
% opposed to any ceiling on individual financial contributions to political parties	45	36	40	46	46	48
% supporting a limit on what political parties can spend in a federal election campaign	88	92	87	90	85	84
% saying that when MPs vote on a controversial issue such as the death penalty, they should follow what they believe to be the public interest rather than the views of people in their ridings	39	45	36	29	25	32

Source: *The data in this table come from a 1990 survey of 2,947 Canadian respondents, conducted for the Royal Commission on Electoral Reform and Party Financing. See André Blais and Elisabeth Gidengil,* Making Representative Democracy Work: The Views of Canadians *(Toronto: Dundurn Press, 1991).*

murky realm of public opinion data there is a "distinct society," it is Quebec and quite likely Quebec alone. A second and perhaps more speculative conclusion is that regional disputes within the political arena need not and often do not reflect regional differences in policy preferences within the general electorate. Canada's regional communities are not sharply divided in terms of their basic political values or policy preferences. Thus conflict may stem from weaknesses in our political institutions and from the electoral, bureaucratic, and constitutional self-interest of political elites as much as it does from differences in policy preferences across provincial electorates.

INSTITUTIONAL ROOTS OF REGIONAL DISCONTENT

National communities such as Canada are made up of countless competing and frequently overlapping groups, and the political system provides an arena within which group competition is played out. In some respects, however, the political system is more than an arena, more than a passive reflector of social conflict, for it actually shapes the pattern of conflict and shades the odds for specific outcomes. As Chapter 3 illustrated, political institutions are seldom if ever neutral in their impact on group competition. Thus we might ask, in the specific context of this chapter, whether there is an institutional bias to the way in which the political system handles regional conflict. Do political institutions moderate conflict by building bridges across regional divisions and thereby integrating a large and territorially diverse national community, or do they exacerbate regional conflict? Is regional conflict more intense and more pervasive within the political system than within the society itself?

To address such questions, we must revisit the concept of federalism and explore in more detail how federal institutions handle and mishandle regional conflict. As Chapter 2 explained, federalism provides an institutional means by which the potentially conflicting interests of national majorities and territorially bounded minorities can be reconciled. It provides a check on the national majority in some instances while permitting reasonably unfettered majority rule in others. To understand more precisely how this is accomplished, it is useful to draw a distinction between *interstate* and *intrastate* federalism.

The term interstate federalism refers initially to the federal division of powers. Minority interests, or at least the interests of those minorities that can be reconstituted as provincial majorities, can be protected from the national majority through the division of powers. The weight of that majority cannot be brought into play to the extent that provincial governments have jurisdiction over matters of concern to regional minorities. In practice, however, a watertight division of powers has been impossible and inconvenient to maintain. Thus, interstate federalism has been extended to include the protection of minority interests by provincial governments in the intergovernmental arena. The First Ministers' Conference, for example, is an interstate device par excellence. Indeed, it is prominence of this second form of interstate federalism that sets Canadian federalism apart from its institutional counterparts in Australia and the United States. The distinctive characteristic of contemporary interstate federalism in Canada is the representation of regional interests *to* the federal government by provincial governments rather than the representation of such interests *within* the institutions of the federal government by MPs and senators. This latter form of representation is referred to as intrastate federalism.

In part, interstate and intrastate federalism can be seen as alternative forms of territorial protection. The need for provincial governments to represent regional interests, as opposed to their more narrow governmental interests, to the federal government is reduced when such interests find full expression within national institutions. However, intrastate federalism can also be seen as an essential complement to interstate federalism. While the federal division of powers provides significant protection for minority interests, communities may still have important regional stakes in fields falling within the jurisdiction of the federal government. An example here might be a decision by the federal government to alter the eligibility requirements for unemployment insurance or to close military bases. If effective means of intrastate representation are not built into national institutions, regional conflict can be intensified by national policies that fail to take full account of regional interests, sensitivities, and peculiarities. Here it should also be noted that intrastate and interstate federalism shape political conflict in quite different ways. Intrastate federalism emphasizes the national dimension of conflict by channelling it through the institutions of the central government, whereas interstate federalism emphasizes the regional dimension of conflict by channelling it through intergovernmental relations. As a general rule of thumb, there are more incentives for conflict resolution in the intragovernmental arenas of intrastate federalism than exist within the intergovernmental arenas of interstate federalism.

As Chapter 2 discussed, the Constitution Act of 1867 tried to marry British parliamentary institutions, which had evolved within a small and relatively homogeneous country, to the American innovation of federalism, which had evolved to meet the political demands of a large and territorially segmented society. The marriage was not fully consummated. While the federal division of powers—interstate federalism—was put into place, national parliamentary institutions were not adequately modified to accommodate the needs of intrastate federalism—to provide for the representation of regional interests by national politicians within national institutions. The result has been a political system that does not handle regional conflict as well as it might.

The institutional discussion in Chapter 3 has demonstrated that parliamentary institutions frustrate intrastate federalism in a number of ways, with the nature of the Senate leading the list. A Senate that is unelected, that is appointed by the federal government without formal input from the provinces, and that has a distribution of seats that is increasingly bizarre cannot provide effective intrastate regional representation. Party discipline and the conventions of responsible government within the House of Commons make it all but impossible for MPs to place the interests of their region above those of their party, should the two conflict. While MPs may toil energetically behind the scenes on behalf of their constituents and region, little of this work is transparent to the electorate. Intrastate regional representation takes place not in the public arena, but behind closed doors—in cabinet, caucus, and endless meetings with colleagues and bureaucrats. Party discipline does not prevent regional representation so much as it renders it invisible; regional representation may be done, but it is not seen to be done.

In any discussion of the manner in which parliamentary institutions and conventions inhibit public forms of regional representation, the nature of the federal cabinet inevitably comes to the fore. Although from the time of the Confederation debates in the 1860s the cabinet has been seen as the first line of regional defence in Ottawa,[50] the evolution of the cabinet has hindered regional representation. As Peter Aucoin notes, "the growing dominance of the prime minister over the cabinet and governing party and the establishment of a more functionally structured cabinet have reduced the capacity of ministers individually and collectively to represent and accommodate regional interests in cabinet decision making."[51] Moreover, while the appearance of the cabinet, and particularly the emphasis on inclusive provincial representation, conveys an overriding concern with regional representation, the reality of regional representation again takes place far from the public eye. Ministers are bound not only by party discipline, but also by the cabinet conventions of secrecy and collective responsibility. Thus, while vigorous regional representation may take place behind the closed doors of cabinet, in public all ministers support cabinet policy. This places regional residents in a difficult position should the cabinet announce policies at odds with their perceived regional interest. In public, their "representative" in cabinet has no alternative but to endorse and defend the government. In private, any number of things could have happened: the minister may have fought hard for his or her region but lost, have traded a regional loss on one policy for a regional gain on another, have been convinced that on this particular issue the national interest or the interest of some other region should prevail, have been asleep at the switch, or may have sold his or her region and constituents down the river. Voters have no way of determining what in fact took place. Thus, with respect to the *public* defence of regional interests, voters are likely to receive more satisfaction from their provincial premier who is unhampered by party discipline, collective responsibility, or cabinet secrecy.

When the problems attendant upon regional representation in the Senate, House, and cabinet are taken together, and when they are considered in conjunction with the frequent inability of parties to elect candidates from all regions of the country, it seems fair to conclude that intrastate federalism is at best impaired. Partly although not entirely as a consequence, there has been a growing emphasis on the interstate representation and protection of regional interests. The provincial premiers and their governments have come to be seen as the primary line of regional defence *within the national political process*. This emphasis on interstate fed-

Cabinet Representation

In 1978, when the Liberal government of Pierre Trudeau had been in power for over ten years with largely the same cast of ministers, a Gallup survey asked a national sample of Canadians the following question: "Apart from Prime Minister Trudeau, do you happen to recall the name of a cabinet minister in Ottawa?"

Only 33 percent of the respondents could name a minister and correctly identify his or her portfolio. A further 14 percent were able to name a minister, but could not correctly identify the portfolio. Nineteen percent mentioned the name of an individual who was not in the cabinet, and 34 percent would not even venture a guess! (*The Gallup Report*, October 28, 1978.)

These findings raise some doubt as to the importance Canadians attach to regional representation within the federal cabinet. If many Canadians are unaware as to who is even in the cabinet, it is doubtful that they think of a particular minister as "their spokesperson in Ottawa." This suggests, in turn, that the much higher profile of provincial premiers, relative to that of cabinet ministers, greatly enhances the representative role of premiers within the national political process.

eralism inflates the role of provincial premiers by giving them a national prominence not envisioned in the original federal design. An overreliance on interstate federalism undermines the role of MPs, stripping them of an important function that is then transferred to the premiers. It can inflame intergovernmental conflict by allowing governments to package what may be a governmental struggle over resources, programs, and prestige as a regional conflict. All this is not to deny that premiers have the responsibility to speak out for their provinces and to do so on the national stage whenever possible. The problem arises from the lack of an effective counterbalance from national politicians. Instead of a multiplicity of regional voices articulating a variety of regional perspectives, the stage is dominated by the premiers. The regional voices of senators and MPs have been muted by the institutional constraints within which they must work. Thus parliamentary institutions, despite their other virtues, often fail to provide an effective forum for the resolution of regional conflict, which consequently has been deflected into the intergovernmental arena.

Frustration with impaired intrastate channels of regional representation and the resultant intergovernmental conflict was one of the factors that lay behind the search for institutional reform that preoccupied governments, task forces, policy institutes, and political scientists from the late

1970s to the early 1990s. If significant institutional reform on the scale of an elected Senate is to be attained, two conditions will have to be met. The first is that the costs of regional conflict must come to be seen as intolerable, or at least sufficiently onerous as to impair seriously the performance of the federal government and to threaten the stability of the political community. Second, Canadians must come to believe that only institutional reform offers a solution to regional discontent—that a solution is not to be found in a new leader, a new party, or a new government. Given our constitutional experience of the last decade, it is unlikely that either condition will be met. It is certainly unlikely that regional discontent alone will create an irresistible demand for institutional and constitutional reform. If reform is to be achieved, the driving force is likely to come from other dynamics within the Canadian political community, and more specifically from nationalist unrest in Quebec. Reform to address regional discontent may be achieved in tandem with reform to address other constitutional dilemmas, but it is unlikely to be achieved alone.

In summary, to describe regional conflict as something akin to a cancer in the body politic that should be removed by institutional surgery would be to overstate the problem that most Canadians perceive. Yet to describe it as a mere wart would be to understate the problem. Perhaps, then, an analogy might be found in arthritis. The condition can be painful and limiting, but with no satisfactory cure in sight, we can get by. If, moreover, the political community continues to change along the lines outlined in Chapter 10, it is at least possible that the intensity and pervasiveness of regional conflict may decline even without large-scale institutional reform.

THE NATIONAL INTEREST

While it is important to understand the institutional roots of regional conflict in Canada, the impression should not be given that such conflict is entirely the product of flawed institutions and flawed political leadership. The regions of Canada continue to differ in their resource base, demography, and industrial organization. These differences produce conflicting regional interests and aspirations that percolate in turn within the political system.[52] Many features of the Canadian landscape, furthermore, lie beyond the reach of political institutions, reformed or otherwise. Institutional reform will not move oil from the prairie sedimentary basin to the Canadian Shield, nor the pulp forests of Ontario and Quebec to Prince Edward Island. Nor will it dramatically affect the regional location of the Canadian population, the rate of unemployment in Newfoundland, or the concentration of industrial activity in central Canada.[53]

As Paul Phillips notes, "for most of the country outside of the industrial heartland, economic fortunes rest directly on the fortuitous distribution of climate, geography and natural wealth, and on the state of foreign markets, none of which respond much to Canadian policies."[54] The dependency on volatile foreign markets exposes the Canadian economy to sharp and unpredictable dislocations that are often regionally specific in their effects, both positive and negative. For example, the impact of the Great Depression was more catastrophic on the prairies than it was elsewhere, just as escalating world prices for oil in the 1970s conveyed widely divergent benefits and costs to the Canadian provinces. As Richard Simeon explains:

> Exogenous economic factors like the energy crisis have a highly differential regional impact. Because the domestic economy is so regionalized, this impact sharpens internal divisions; it is disintegrative rather than unifying ... the territorially specific location of resources combines with their allocation to the provinces to maximize regional conflict.[55]

Although governments cannot move resources and can do little to control foreign markets, they can, at least in the abstract, transfer the revenues that come from resource development and cushion the impact of foreign markets. Within the context of a national economy, regional dislocations need not be as severe as they might otherwise be nor economic specialization as risky. Regions whose markets have gone soft can ride out the storm, sheltered by those sectors of the national economy that remain strong. However, the redistributive mechanisms that are required, and that are discussed at some length in the next chapter, are complex and politically contentious. They also bring us up against conflicting visions of the national interest.

Discussions of regionalism often boil down to arguments over which should prevail: regional interests or the national interest? When the question is put in this blunt form, the answer in a democratic country seems obvious. The national interest should prevail, given that it reflects the aspirations of a larger number of citizens. However, the simple juxtaposition of regional and national interests obscures a more interesting and difficult debate. There are essentially three issues at stake in discussions of the national interest. The first is the extent to which the national majority should prevail, an issue that arose in last chapter's discussion of English–French relations. On this point, Pierre Trudeau has been an emphatic spokesman for the supremacy of the national will:

> If Canada is indeed to be a nation, there must be a national will which is something more than the lowest common denominator among the desires of the provincial governments. And when there is a conflict ... between the national will and the provincial will, the national will must prevail. Otherwise, we are not a nation.[56]

Brian Gable, *The Globe and Mail*, January 7, 1989, p. D7.

Yet federalism in principle rejects the assumption that the national majority should always prevail. The essence of federalism is that for at least some issues in some circumstances, the will of the national majority should be *constitutionally frustrated*. A political system is not federal if it is predetermined that national majorities will prevail over provincial majorities, should the two collide. As the Canadian political system is thoroughly federal in principle and design, it cannot be assumed that the national majority *should* prevail. The perception that the national majority *will* prevail, notwithstanding the principles of federalism, lies close to the heart of regional discontent. Note, for example, Dalton Camp's distillation of the political sentiment he found in British Columbia:

> *Where the wealth is found, the numbers are still few; where the numbers are found, so too are the looters, carpetbaggers and welfare indolents. And since democracy is the rule of numbers, the pillage of the West seems certain.*[57]

In federal systems, numbers alone should not rule.

The second issue is who should articulate the national interest or, if there are several articulations, which one should prevail. The House of Commons, with representatives elected from every nook and cranny of the country through a system that ensures the equal weighting of individuals and the proportionate weighting of provincial populations, is certainly a claimant. Yet how do we deal with the facts that Ontario and Quebec jointly determine the composition of the national government, that the

House is organized along party lines, that when the House speaks it is actually the governing party speaking, that important groups may lack adequate representation on the government side of the House, and that francophones constitute a permanent minority? Should provincial and territorial governments be involved in the articulation of the national interest? Should the national interest be articulated by the governments of Canada rather than by the federal government alone? If so, what would be the appropriate institutional mechanism for orchestrating the collective voice of the national, ten provincial, two and soon to be three territorial, and perhaps scores of aboriginal governments? How would we handle conflicts between governments, such as those that arose during the early 1980s when the Alberta government argued that higher oil prices were in the national interest and the federal government argued just the reverse? And how do we deal with groups such as women who fail to find adequate representation in elected governments, or with aboriginal communities that seek a direct voice in any articulation of the national will? If the constitutional failures of the early 1990s demonstrated nothing else, they demonstrated the immense complexities of trying to articulate the national will.

The third issue has to do with the way in which we conceptualize the "national interest." Is it something that transcends regional interests, or is it best seen as something that faithfully reflects regional interests? Is the whole greater than the sum of its parts, or is the whole equal to the sum of its parts? Ironically, one of the most colourful statements in support of a transcendent national interest came from the West's most successful politician, John Diefenbaker:

> We shall never build the nation which our potential resources make possible by dividing ourselves into anglophones, francophones, multicultural phones, or whatever kind of phoneys you choose. I say Canadians, first, last and always.[58]

This issue takes us back to the nature of Canadian society. Is Canada best seen as a community of communities, or is there a national community that in some meaningful way transcends its regional components? These are not easy questions to answer. They do show, however, that the articulation of the national interest in a regionally diverse federal state is never straightforward and seldom noncontentious. To appeal to the national interest in the resolution of regional conflict is to avoid a set of issues that adds much of the flavour and spice to Canadian political life.

SUGGESTED READINGS

1. David G. Alexander, *Atlantic Canada and Confederation: Essays in Canadian Political Economy*, compiled by Eric W. Sager, Lewis R.

Fischer, and Stuart O. Pierson (Toronto: University of Toronto Press, 1983).

2. Herman Bakvis, *Federalism and the Organization of Political Life: Canada in Comparative Perspective* (Kingston: Institute of Intergovernmental Relations, Queen's University, 1981).

3. Herman Bakvis, "Regional Politics and Policy in the Mulroney Cabinet, 1984–88: Towards a Theory of the Regional Minister System in Canada," *Canadian Public Policy*, 15:2 (June 1989), pp. 121–34.

4. J.F. Conway, *The West: A History of a Region in Confederation* (Toronto: James Lorimer, 1983).

5. David J. Elkins and Richard Simeon, eds., *Small Worlds: Provinces and Parties in Canadian Political Life* (Toronto: Methuen, 1980).

6. Ernest R. Forbes, *The Maritime Rights Movement, 1919–1927: A Study in Canadian Regionalism* (Montreal: McGill-Queen's University Press, 1979).

7. Roger Gibbins, *Regionalism: Territorial Politics in Canada and the United States* (Toronto: Butterworths, 1982); and *Prairie Politics and Society: Regionalism in Decline* (Toronto: Butterworths, 1980).

8. G.A. Rawlyk, ed., *The Atlantic Provinces and the Problems of Confederation* (Breakwater Press, 1979).

9. John Richards and Larry Pratt, *Prairie Capitalism: Power and Influence in the New West* (Toronto: McClelland and Stewart, 1979).

STUDY QUESTIONS

1. How would *you* answer the survey question discussed in this chapter: "Do you think of yourself first as a Canadian or as a Manitoban, Ontarian, Nova Scotian, or whatever?" What does your answer suggest about the relationship between national and provincial identifications in your own case?

2. How would you characterize your own province in terms of the costs and benefits of Confederation? Compared to other provinces, has your own province done relatively well or relatively poorly? Do you find the cost-benefit approach to be a useful one, or do you find it difficult to apply to your own or to other provinces?

3. Trace out the history of your province's representation on the government side of the House of Commons and within the federal cabinet. How has your province fared compared to others?

4. Have there been occasions in the past when the national interest, as articulated by Parliament, has been clearly at odds with the majority interest within your province? If so, how was the conflict resolved? Are there such conflicts at present, or can such conflicts be seen on the political horizon?

5. What would you propose as the best method of articulating the national interest? Within what institutional framework should this responsibility be lodged? How would you defend your choice?

NOTES

1. Task Force on National Unity, *A Future Together* (Hull: Supply and Services Canada, 1979), p. 29.

2. June 1936. Cited in Warner Troyer, *The Sound and the Fury* (Toronto: John Wiley and Sons, 1980), p. 11.

3. See Robert W. Jackman, "Political Parties, Voting and National Integration: The Canadian Case," in Richard Schultz, Orest M. Kruhlak, and John C. Terry, eds., *The Canadian Political Process*, 3rd ed. (Toronto: Holt, Rinehart and Winston, 1979), pp. 130–44; and Richard Johnston, "Federal and Provincial Voting: Contemporary Patterns and Historical Evolution," in David J. Elkins and Richard Simeon, eds., *Small Worlds: Provinces and Parties in Canadian Political Life* (Toronto: Methuen, 1980), pp. 131–78.

4. See Seymour Martin Lipset and Stein Rokkan, "Cleavage Structures, Party Systems, and Voter Alignments: An Introduction," in Lipset and Rokkan, eds., *Party Systems and Voter Alignments: Cross-National Perspectives* (New York: The Free Press, 1967), pp. 1–64; and Herman Bakvis, *Federalism and the Organization of Political Life: Canada in Comparative Perspective* (Kingston: Institute of Intergovernmental Relations, Queen's University, 1981), pp. 40–48.

5. For an expansion of this contrast, see Roger Gibbins, *Regionalism: Territorial Politics in Canada and the United States* (Toronto: Butterworths, 1982).

6. For an expansion of this discussion, see Roger Gibbins, *Prairie Politics and Society: Regionalism in Decline* (Toronto: Butterworths, 1980).

7. Ernest R. Forbes, *The Maritime Rights Movement, 1919–1927: A Study in Canadian Regionalism* (Montreal: McGill-Queen's University Press, 1979), p. 2.

8. Ibid., p. 2.

9. G.A. Rawlyk and Doug Brown, "The Historical Framework of the Maritimes and Confederation," in G.A. Rawlyk, ed., *The Atlantic Provinces and the Problems of Confederation* (Breakwater Press, 1979), p. 14.

10. Forbes, *Maritime Rights Movement*, p. 8.

11. Rawlyk and Brown, "The Historical Framework," p. 18.

12. Ibid.

13. Forbes, *Maritime Rights Movement*, pp. 20–21.

14. Ibid.

15. Ibid.

16. Ibid.

17. Rawlyk and Brown, "The Historical Framework," p. 26.

18. When Alberta and Saskatchewan were created in 1905, the ownership of natural resources was retained by the federal government. Ownership was not transferred to the western provinces until 1931.

19. Raymond Reid, *The Canadian Style* (Toronto: Fitzhenry and Whiteside, 1973), p. 105.

20. Terry Campbell and G.A. Rawlyk, "The Historical Framework of Newfoundland and Confederation," in Rawlyk, *The Atlantic Provinces*, p. 70.

21. Rawlyk and Brown, "The Historical Framework," p. 31.

22. Ibid.

23. See Anthony Careless, *Initiative and Response: The Adaptation of Canadian Federalism to Regional Economic Development* (Montreal: McGill-Queen's University Press, 1977).

24. Cited in Frank H. Underhill, *In Search of Canadian Liberalism* (Toronto: Macmillan, 1960), p. 55.

25. Vernon C. Fowke, *The National Policy and the Wheat Economy* (Toronto: University of Toronto Press, 1957), p. 282.

26. For an expanded discussion of western alienation, see Gibbins, *Prairie Politics and Society*, ch. 5.

27. J.R. Mallory, *Social Credit and the Federal Power in Canada* (Toronto: University of Toronto Press, 1953), p. 39.

28. See W.L. Morton, *The Progressive Party of Canada* (Toronto: University of Toronto Press, 1950).

29. Stanley C. Roberts, "Canadian Federalism and the Constitution: What is at Stake in the West," Alan B. Plaunt Memorial Lecture, Carleton University, April 6, 1979, p. 2. For empirical data on the relationship between western alienation and antipathy to Quebec, see Roger Gibbins, "Models of Nationalism: A Case Study of Political Ideologies in the Canadian West," *Canadian Journal of Political Science* (June 1977), pp. 341–73.

30. Denis Smith, "Liberals and Conservatives on the Prairies, 1917–1968," in David P. Gagan, ed., *Prairie Perspectives* (Toronto: Holt, Rinehart and Winston, 1970), p. 41.

31. W.L. Morton, "The Bias of Prairie Politics," *Transactions of the Royal Society of Canada*, series III, vol. XLIX (June 1955), section II, p. 66.

32. For an elaboration of this point, see Gibbins, "Constitutional Politics and the West," in Keith Banting and Richard Simeon, eds., *And No One Cheered: Federalism, Democracy and the Constitution Act* (Toronto: Methuen, 1983), pp. 119–32.

33. David E. Smith, "Party Government, Representation and National Integration in Canada," in Peter Aucoin, Research Coordinator, *Party Government and Regional Representation in Canada* (Toronto: University of Toronto Press, 1985), p. 51.

34. David E. Smith, *The Regional Decline of a National Party: Liberals on the Prairies* (Toronto: University of Toronto Press, 1981), ch. 6.

35. For a discussion, see Ralph Matthews, *The Creation of Regional Dependency* (Toronto: University of Toronto Press, 1983), and Paul Phillips, *Regional Disparities*, rev. ed. (Toronto: James Lorimer, 1982).

36. "Painting the Farm Tory Blue," *Alberta Report*, October 17, 1988, p. 49.

37. Ron Graham, "The Legacy of Joe Clark," *Saturday Night*, September 1983, p. 19.

38. The metropolitan–hinterland model dates from the work of economic historian Harold Innis. See *Empire and Communications* (Toronto: University of Toronto Press, 1950).

39. J.M.S. Careless, " 'Limited Identities' in Canada," *Canadian Historical Review*, 50 (1969), p. 9.

40. This survey, conducted by the author in June 1982, encompassed 1,402 randomly selected respondents from the four western provinces.

41. Alan C. Cairns, "The Governments and Societies of Canadian Federalism," *Canadian Journal of Political Science*, 10 (1977), pp. 695–726.

42. Hon. Gérald Beaudoin, Senator, and Dorothy Dobbie, MP, *A Renewed Canada*, Report of the Special Joint Committee of the Senate and House of Commons (Ottawa: February 28, 1992), p. 42.

43. Harold D. Clarke, Lawrence LeDuc, Jane Jenson, and Jon Pammett, *Political Choice in Canada* (Toronto: McGraw-Hill Ryerson, 1979). In "feeling thermometer" questions, respondents are handed a cardboard thermometer with values ranging from 0 (very negative) through 50 (indifferent) to 100 (very positive). They are then asked to locate various objects, such as Canada, their province, or political leaders, on this scale. Although the thermometer may seem somewhat crude, it has proved to be a valuable tool in measuring the degree of respondent affect or emotional predisposition toward a wide range of political objects.

44. Ibid., p. 64.

45. David J. Elkins, "The Sense of Place," in Elkins and Simeon, *Small Worlds*, p. 16.

46. Ibid., p. 21.

47. John W. Holmes, "Impact of Domestic Political Factors on Canadian–American Relations: Canada," in Annette Baker Fox, Alfred D. Herd, Jr., and Joseph S. Nye, eds., *Canada and the United States: Transnational and Transgovernmental Relations* (New York: Columbia University Press, 1976), p. 32.

48. Richard Allen, ed., *A Region of the Mind* (Regina: Canadian Plains Study Centre, University of Saskatchewan, 1973).

49. R. Douglas Francis, "Changing Images of the West," *Journal of Canadian Studies*, 17:3 (Fall 1982), p. 5.

50. Robert A. MacKay, *The Unreformed Senate of Canada* (Toronto: McClelland and Stewart, 1963), p. 44.

51. Peter Aucoin, "Regionalism, Party and National Government," in Peter Aucoin, Research Coordinator, *Party Government and Regional Representation in Canada* (Toronto: University of Toronto Press, 1985), pp. 144–45.

52. For an overview of this line of argument, see Phillips, *Regional Disparities*.

53. For a discussion of this last point, see N.H. Lithwick, *Regional Economic Policy: The Canadian Experience* (Toronto: McGraw-Hill Ryerson, 1978), p. 144.

54. Phillips, *Regional Disparities*, p. 130.

55. Richard Simeon, "Natural Resource Revenues and Canadian Federalism: A Survey of the Issues," paper presented to the Conference on the Alberta Heritage Savings and Trust Fund, Edmonton, October 18–19, 1979, p. 2.

56. Speech at the Liberal Party of Canada Fund Raising Dinner, Vancouver, November 24, 1981.

57. Dalton Camp, *An Eclectic Eel* (Ottawa: Deneau, 1981), p. 84.

58. June 4, 1973. Cited in John A. Munro, ed., *The Wit and Wisdom of John Diefenbaker* (Edmonton: Hurtig, 1982), pp. 80–81.

REDISTRIBUTIVE POLITICS

Governments provide many programs that are of roughly equal benefit to all citizens. The security benefits provided by national defence, for example, vary little across regions, gender groupings, or generations. Many other programs, however, provide more selective benefits: assistance for the disabled, low-cost student loans, Canadian content regulations for television stations, and income support for parents with dependent children provide but a few examples. Even in the field of national defence, significant selective benefits flow from the location of bases and the procurement of military supplies. While we all may benefit from one form or another of such selective benefits, this is not to say that on balance government largesse is equally or randomly dispersed across the population. Indeed, it is more realistic to assume that benefits are not equally dispersed, and that an essential element of political life is the contest over how such benefits are divided up among competing groups.

Government programs are supported by taxation, and just as the benefits of government are not evenly distributed, neither is the tax load. Some pay more, both absolutely and relative to the benefits they receive in return, while some pay less. Thus a second essential element in political life is the contest over the burden of government. Just as citizens, corporations, and regions try to maximize their return from government programs, so too do they try to minimize their tax load, shifting that burden where possible onto other shoulders.

Both of these elements blend into the *redistributive activities* of government. Simply put, governments no longer accept, if they ever did, the distribution of wealth that would occur through an unhindered free market. The market is constrained in countless ways: individuals too old or too incapacitated to work are provided with a minimal income, universities are subsidized so that students do not have to pay the market cost of their education, domestic industries continue to be protected to a degree from "unfair" foreign competition, and regional development incentives are used to induce firms to locate where they would not do so in the absence of such incentives. In Chapter 4 we discussed the redistributive impact of language policies in Quebec and within the federal public service, and in Chapter 5 we touched on regional perceptions of the redistributive aspects of national policies. In this chapter our primary focus is on the redistribution of income and economic opportunities among individuals and across regional communities, two policy domains widely recognized as central to Canadian political life. As a 1970 position paper on income security stated:

> We believe the Government of Canada must have the power to redistribute income, between persons and between provinces, if it is to equalize opportunity across the country.... The "sense of a Canadian community" is at once the source of income redistribution between people and regions in Canada and the result of such measures.[1]

This chapter addresses three basic topics in its exploration of redistributive politics. The first is the evolution and redistributive impact of the welfare state. Given that this redistributive impact turns out to be very modest for individuals, the chapter then examines why disparities in income and economic opportunities have not played a larger role in Canadian political life. The third topic is the redistribution of income and economic opportunities across regional communities. Throughout, the primary focus will be upon the redistributive role of the national government and national policies. However, it should be borne in mind that provincial governments are also actively involved in redistributive policies, and are central players in the administration and guidance of the welfare state. Furthermore, the territorial dispersion of economic activity, both across Canada and within provincial boundaries, is of acute concern to provincial governments. Thus the national focus of this chapter provides but the flavour of redistributive politics in the Canadian setting.

THE CANADIAN WELFARE STATE

The emergence of the welfare state[2] was marked by a shift in social responsibility from the private to the public sector. Prior to its emergence, individuals were dependent upon their own resources, the support of an extended family, and in the extreme, private charity in meeting the contingencies of unemployment, illness, injury, and old age. Today, while private means of support have not disappeared, they have been supplemented and in some cases dwarfed by state activity. The emergence of the welfare state has been associated with greatly increased public expenditures on education, health care, and social assistance. This growth, it should be stressed, has been characteristic of all Western, industrialized states; it is not a phenomenon restricted to Canada alone.

The Evolution of the Welfare State

Only a very limited redistributive role had been prescribed for government prior to the Great Depression of the 1930s. It was assumed that most people could thrive in the free market, and that those who did not had largely themselves to blame. Both success and failure were attributed to characteristics of the individual. Those who succeeded did so because they were frugal, restrained in their passions, and committed to the work ethic. Those who failed did so because of a lack of hard work, because they squandered their financial and human resources, or because their lack of self-restraint led to alcohol abuse and the crippling financial load of large families. Although it was recognized that some individuals could not compete for reasons beyond their control, including physical and mental disabilities and extreme old age, it was assumed that they were small enough in numbers to be sustained through private charity and the support of extended families. In essence, then, the free market was to run its course; the strong were to survive and thrive, and the weak were to fall by the wayside.

The Depression had a profound impact on such ideological predispositions. The 1929 collapse of the American stock market signalled the onset of a prolonged economic depression that lasted until the start of the Second World War and afflicted all industrialized countries. Per capita income in Canada fell by 50 percent, export prices fell to a fraction of 1929 prices, and the number of unemployed rose from 107,000 in 1929 to 646,000 at the height of the Depression in 1933. In Western Canada the Depression's impact was intensified by ruinous agricultural markets, drought, and crop infestation. By the millions, North Americans who believed in the work ethic, who believed that only the lazy need go without work, were unable to find employment. In the face of the magnitude of this economic collapse, explanations of success and failure based on individual characteristics lost much, though not all, of their force. It became increasingly evident that the root problem lay beyond the control of the individual, that in the throes of the Depression individuals were not the captains of their fate. Government intervention in the economic order became more acceptable when it came to be perceived that the economy could not cure its own ills, or could do so only at an unacceptable social and political cost.

The Depression was finally brought to a close by the onset of the Second World War and resultant massive governmental intervention in the economy. Somewhat unexpectedly, that intervention coincided with economic prosperity and a reasonably equitable sharing of the war's economic burden. Thus at the war's end, government intervention was seen in a more positive ideological light. Indeed, it was called for by many in order to ward off both an expected postwar recession and the growing left-of-centre electoral threat to the incumbent Liberal government posed by the Co-operative Commonwealth Federation, discussed in Chapter 9. When this acceptance of government intervention and the altered views of poverty that emerged from the Depression were combined with the new Keynesian emphasis on interpersonal transfers as an essential tool for economic management, the stage was set for the emergence of the modern welfare state.

John Maynard Keynes (1883–1946)

When the Great Depression struck in 1929, the initial response of Western governments was based on the economic model of the family. Just as families were expected to curtail expenditures when times were bad, governments were expected to slash public expenditures. Thus funds for social assistance became increasingly scarce just as the need for such assistance increased. As public spending was cut, the Depression only deepened.

Then, in 1936, John Maynard Keynes published *The General Theory of Employment, Interest and Money*, a book that crystallized a radical alternative approach to public expenditures. Keynes argued that government spending should not be seen as analogous to family spending, and that it should be *increased* when the private economy faltered. By increasing public spending and/or decreasing taxes when times were bad, and by decreasing public spending and/or increasing taxes when times were good, governments could moderate the inevitable swings in the business cycle. Public spending in the first case, the case that prevailed in the Depression, could compensate for a decline in private demand. It could stimulate the economy, create jobs, and eliminate troughs in the business cycle, troughs that in the past had been exaggerated by government cutbacks.

If governments wanted to provide an immediate stimulus to the economy, social programs provided a convenient way of transferring purchasing power to those who, in Creighton's words, "could be counted on to spend and keep on spending." Thus payments to the poor, the elderly, and the unemployed became important tools of economic management. As it turned out, however, it was much easier to increase program spending when times were bad than it was to cut back on such spending, and indeed on any government spending, when times were good.

Although the welfare state is usually seen as a collection of social programs, it also has an important economic component. James Rice argues that acceptance of the welfare state, particularly by business interests, hinged upon the prior acceptance of Keynesian economics, that the welfare state was born at the end of the Second World War when "the government realized that it could use social policies as a means of economic management."[3] It was the marriage of the welfare and economic management functions, Rice maintains, that created business support for the expansion of social programs that the welfare state entailed.[4] In 1945, the federal government's White Paper on Employment and Income recommended the stabilization and, in some cases, the subsidization of consumer expenditures through transfer payments to persons. Large-scale social programs, it was argued, would allow the government to stimulate the economy when private demand faltered, as it was feared would happen at the end of the war. Here historian Donald Creighton argues that the social programs of the new welfare state—veterans' benefits, family allowances, unemployment insurance, increased old age pensions—were designed to distribute purchasing power as widely as possible, to "put money into the hands of people who could be counted on to spend and keep on spending."[5] The welfare state therefore came to provide much of the fuel, if not the engine, for postwar economic growth.

A variety of other factors, rooted in a rapidly changing social and economic environment, also contributed to the emergence of the Canadian welfare state. For example, Marxist interpretations of the welfare state go beyond recognizing its role in economic management; Finkel argues that the welfare state "was devised by governments that wished to preserve the power of the ruling class but saw that power threatened by working-class militancy directed against an economic system that seemed unable to provide jobs or security."[6] Whether or not one chooses to accept this interpretation, it is clear that the economic stability fostered by the welfare state made an important contribution to postwar political stability, for with urbanization and industrialization came a new set of social problems that overwhelmed the resources of the family and private charity. In an urban setting and wage economy, those who could not earn a wage—the elderly, children, and the handicapped—became economic burdens within the family unit.[7] As the modern economy came to require a well-trained labour force, the state moved to create wider access to post-secondary education through a massive increase in funding for public universities, colleges, and technical institutes. Ideological changes set in motion by the Depression also continued to shape the evolution of the welfare state. It was increasingly accepted that old age, mental or physical disability, the poverty of one's parents, or the inability of the economy to provide full employment should not deny individuals adequate food, shelter, and medical attention.

In short, it came to be accepted that the government should provide assistance to those unable to fend for themselves, and that basic educational and medical services should be universally available to citizens regardless of their income or that of their parents. While the welfare state did not provide "cradle to grave" security, it left individuals much less exposed to the vagaries of the economy and the afflictions of life. As Carolyn Tuohy notes, however, the Canadian welfare state has been much more generous in protecting individuals and families against the cost of health care than it has been in protecting them against poverty.[8] Tuohy also notes that "Canada does not have a generous welfare state in comparison with other advanced industrialized nations."[9]

The embryonic Canadian welfare state can be seen in the 1914 Ontario Workmen's Compensation Act, the 1916 Mother's Allowances in

Manitoba, the federal Old Age Pensions Act of 1927, which provided modest pensions to those in need, and the introduction of national unemployment insurance, first unsuccessfully in 1935 and then successfully in 1941. However, the full flowering of the welfare state came with the end of the Second World War and the introduction of Family Allowance payments to the mothers of dependent children (1944),[10] universal old age pensions (1951), national hospital insurance (1958),[11] the Canada and Quebec Pension Plans (1965), national medicare (1971), progressive expansion in the coverage of Unemployment Insurance and Workers' Compensation, and growing public expenditures on schools, universities, and technical institutes. In 1966 the Canada Assistance Plan was instituted to provide an umbrella for a variety of social assistance programs including Old Age Assistance, Blind Persons Allowances, Disabled Allowances, child care, and aid for needy mothers. The federal government committed itself to pay 50 percent of the cost for all provincial programs falling under this umbrella, with the terms of coverage being set by the provincial governments. In total, these and other programs created an array of safety nets that protected Canadians from the more extreme hardships that might otherwise be imposed by injury, sickness, unemployment, and old age.

The emergence of the welfare state had a significant impact on Canadian federalism. The fields of government that were most germane to the welfare state—education, health care, and social services—fell largely within the jurisdictional domain of the provinces. Thus the consequent growth of government in those fields tipped the programmatic balance of the federal state toward the provinces as their governments came to supply a host of new programs and services. However, the federal government was also a major player as a source of funds and national standards, although its financial contributions had to be channelled through federal–provincial programs. The net result was increased intergovernmental friction over federal intrusions into the provincial domain, an increasingly complex set of federal–provincial fiscal arrangements, and growing fears on the part of the federal government that its contributions to the programs of the welfare state were not sufficiently appreciated by the electorate. (These results are explored in more detail in Chapter 8.) In addition, the central role of provincial governments meant that if the programs of the welfare state were to be available in roughly equal measure to all Canadians, discrepancies among the provinces' fiscal resources would have to be ironed out. We return to this point later in the chapter.

The Growth of Government

The emergence of the welfare state took place in step with a dramatic increase in the size of government. Government spending as a percentage of the country's Gross National Product—the total of all goods and services produced within the country—increased from 23.1 percent in the immediate postwar period to 38.7 percent by the mid-1970s.[12] There was a corresponding rise in both the tax load and the governmental contribution to personal income; during the same period the share of all personal income originating directly from the government increased from 3.7 to 13.9 percent.[13] The tax load as a percentage of the GNP increased from 25 percent in 1966 to 31.8 percent in 1976, 33.7 percent in 1986, and 37.3 percent in 1991.[14] Public sector employment also increased, though by much more modest proportions. From 1961 to 1975, the share of the Canadian labour force employed by all governments, including school boards and hospital boards, increased from 22.2 percent to 23.8 percent.[15] This compares to an increase from 18.9 percent to 20.6 percent in the United States, and from 22.4 percent to 27.4 percent in the United Kingdom over the same period. In the Canadian case there was actually a proportionate decline in public sector employment at the federal level, which was offset by growth at the provincial and municipal levels. This reflects a more general Canadian trend in which, by any measure, the growth of government has been greater at the provincial and municipal levels than it has at the federal level.

There are a number of points to keep in mind in assessing the linkage between the emergence of the welfare state and the growth of government. The first is that modern governments have grown for many reasons quite apart from the emergence of the welfare state. In the United States, for example, though not in Canada, much of the growth has been attributable to rising military expenditures. More generally, much of what we think of as "big government" entails government regulation of and intervention in the economy, and in the social sector. Neither is necessarily associated with the welfare state, though both serve to blunt what might otherwise be the raw edge of capitalism. It should also be noted that much of the growth has come about through an increase in transfer payments rather than exhaustive expenditures. This distinction is an important one. (There is also an important distinction between transfer payments to *persons*, which are under discussion here, and *intergovernmental* transfers, which are discussed later in the chapter.) Transfer payments entail monies that are redistributed by, but not ultimately spent by, governments. Pensions and social assistance constitute government expenditures, but the money involved is ultimately spent by private citizens in a manner that they determine. Exhaustive expenditures, on the other hand, entail monies that are ultimately spent by governments on salaries, roads, equipment, or whatever. From 1947 to 1977, 22.6 percent of all government expenditures in Canada were transfer payments to individuals, a proportion that has been increasing over time.[16] Indeed, in a rather complex economic argument, Bird maintains that since 1967 the growth of government has been somewhat of an illusion, that "the proportion of the economy's real goods and services 'used up' by the government sector [exhaustive expenditures] in the course of its activities has actually *declined* slightly."[17]

Income Redistribution and the Welfare State

It is a common assumption that the creation of the welfare state shifted income from the relatively affluent to the relatively poor, and that income disparities have been reduced though by no means eliminated. The very term "welfare" carries this connotation. In fact, however, *the emergence of the welfare state and the growth of government with which the welfare state has been associated have not led to any significant redistribution of income.* The popular image of the welfare state as Robin Hood writ large is not supported by the available evidence. The distribution of income among individuals remained virtually unchanged over the first thirty years of the postwar welfare state.[18] Despite the growth of government and the profusion of social programs that collectively make up the welfare state, the poorest fifth of the Canadian population received the same proportion of the national income in 1981—4 percent—as it did in 1951.[19] Nor was the income position of the wealthiest fifth significantly eroded; they received 42 percent of the total personal income in 1981 compared to 43 percent in 1951. Social benefits, it is important to note, did increase over this period and came to play a larger role in the income of relatively impoverished Canadians. They accounted for 57 percent of the 1981 income for the poorest fifth of Canadians, as opposed to only 29 percent in 1951. This increased flow of social benefits, however, did not result in any greater equality among income groups.

In an extensive analysis of income redistribution, Gillespie concluded that "in Canada, at least, a larger state has not led to a more egalitarian state."[20] Transfer programs have stabilized rather than significantly altered the distribution of income. Gillespie argues that while the poor gained ground in the 1960s, they lost ground during the 1970s. The rich, on the other hand, not only gained ground during the 1960s, but held that ground during the 1970s. (As we will see shortly, the tax position of the relatively well-to-do *improved* significantly during the 1980s.) The relative improvement of the rich, Gillespie finds, has been at the expense of the median and upper-middle income groups.[21] Gillespie's findings are supported by St. Laurent, who found that between 1951 and 1971 the distribution of income in Canada became *less* rather than more equal.[22] Hence Smiley's critically important conclusion: "the extension of the public sector has no inevitable disposition to further communitarian and egalitarian values."[23]

Perhaps the most striking change that has occurred with respect to income distribution has been a shrinkage or "hollowing out" of the middle class. If we define the middle class as those earning between 75 percent and 150 percent of the average wage, then the size of the Canadian middle class shrank from close to 40 percent of the population in the late 1960s to 32 percent in 1990.[24] This shrinkage has been accompanied more recently by an absolute decline in the after-tax income of the average Canadian family, a decline of 4.3 percent between 1980 and 1991.[25] Rising taxes

"Burglar? How d'you know it isn't just some Ottawa civil servant taking from the rich to give to the poor?"

Len Norris, *20th Annual*; originally published in the *Sun* (Vancouver), December 2, 1970.

played the major role in this decline, with tax increases since 1984 falling most heavily on middle-income earners. For example, the federal taxes paid by those earning from $45,000 to $75,000 increased by 6.7 percent between 1984 and 1993, whereas federal taxes increased by only 3 percent for those earning over $150,000 and by less than 4 percent for those earning less than $25,000.[26] In short, the tax system became more regressive. Here it should also be noted that the proportion of all government revenues coming from taxes on corporate profits declined from 11.6 percent in 1980 to 8.2 percent in 1986 and only 5.5 percent in 1991.[27]

There is still, then, a vast gulf between the rich and the poor. Peter C. Newman, who has chronicled Canadian wealth in his books *The Canadian*

Establishment and *The Acquisitors*, offers example after example of a level of affluence beyond the wildest dreams of most Canadians: the Ontario magnate who had his own private eighteen-hole golf course constructed, complete with resident pro, after being grazed by a duffer's ball on a less exclusive course; the Vancouver millionaire who donated $275,000 to the YMCA for two racquetball courts that would be reserved exclusively for him at 5:00 p.m. for the rest of his life; and another Vancouver millionaire who paid Billy Carter, brother of the then U.S. president Jimmy Carter, $28,000 to jump off a diving board with a red rose clenched in his teeth. In more academic analyses, Canadian sociologists have documented a small, homogeneous, and relatively cohesive corporate elite in Canada that enjoys great wealth and exercises even greater economic power.[28] At the other end of the scale we find that approximately four million Canadians—or one Canadian in six—live on incomes below the "poverty line."

The poverty line used in Canada is defined as the point below which 58.5 percent or more of family income is spent on the essentials of life: food, shelter, and clothing. The actual dollar figure varies according to family size and location, with higher incomes being required for large families and in urban areas. For example, the current poverty line income for a single individual living in rural Canada is $10,179; it is $29,661 for a family of four living in a metropolitan area with a population of 500,000 or more. The poverty line for a family of three ranges from $17,539 for a family living in a rural area to $25,761 for one located in a large metropolitan area.[29] Poverty is thus defined in relative rather than absolute terms; to be poor in this sense is not necessarily to be destitute or to be without adequate shelter, food, and clothing. In a relative sense, of course, the poor will always be with us as relative poverty cannot be eliminated.

It should be noted that the location of the official poverty line can be a contentious matter; the line defines how many Canadians are poor, and this establishes the extent of "the problem." As a consequence, there can be considerable debate as to whether individuals near the poverty line are in fact "poor," and whether the line should be moved up or down. In 1993 a House of Commons subcommittee on poverty, chaired by Conservative MP Barbara Greene and boycotted by opposition MPs, recommended that the poverty line be revised to reduce the number of the poor by almost 40 percent. Greene argued that the ranks of the poor were exaggerated by social advocacy groups and opposition parties, and that "there are quite a number of people in the counts now who shouldn't be there."[30] Here it is useful to note an important observation made by the National Council of Welfare:

> *The debate over what is the right poverty line and the real number of poor people contributes little if anything to an understanding of the economic situation of low-income Canadians. Poverty lines only establish the upper limit of the low-income population. Most poor Canadians—all welfare*

recipients, almost all minimum wage workers, and the majority of single elderly persons and single-parent families led by women—live on incomes that are hundreds and more often thousands of dollars under the poverty line. Few people would regard these incomes as adequate by any standard.[31]

Debate over the placement of the poverty line should not obscure the reality of poverty in Canada, or the fact that a significant number of Canadians would fall below even the most frugal placement.

Poverty is not randomly distributed. It is twice as prevalent in rural areas as it is in urban areas, though most of the poor live in urban areas because that is where most Canadians reside.[32] As Table 6.1 shows, the incidence of poverty varies considerably from province to province, though in absolute terms there are more low-income Canadians living in Ontario than in any other province.[33] The incidence is particularly high among the elderly—20 percent of those aged 65 and over were classified as poor in 1991.[34] By far the most impoverished group by any measure is the aboriginal population, although even here it is important to note that general impoverishment masks considerable variation in income and economic opportunities among aboriginal communities.

Many of the factors associated with poverty apply with particular force to women, with the consequence that over two-thirds of Canada's poor are women.[35] Since women live longer and are generally entitled to lower pension benefits, old age poses a greater threat to their income security. The loss of a spouse through death or divorce carries a greater income threat to women than to men. As Bryan observes, more than half of all married women between the ages of 55 and 64 have no income at all, and have been described as being "only one man away from poverty."[36] Women who do work generally earn lower incomes than do men. Single-parent families are more likely to be headed by women than by men, and to experience a high incidence of poverty. The 1991 poverty rates were 61.9 percent for single-parent mothers, 47.4 percent for unattached women 65 years of age or over, and 37.5 percent for unattached women under 65, all compared to an overall national poverty rate of 16 percent.[37]

Variations in the incidence of poverty are important to note, but we should do so in the context of the more general observation that the creation of the welfare state has not had a significant impact on the distribution of income and wealth. The lack of any significant redistributive impact can be traced to a number of factors. Many of the programs associated with the welfare state are social *insurance* programs that are supported by taxpayer contributions and have not been designed to redistribute income. Unemployment Insurance, Workers' Compensation, and the Canada and Quebec Pension Plans, for example, are designed to provide protection against income loss due to temporary unemployment, injury, or age. They are not designed to shift income from the relatively affluent to the rela-

TABLE 6.1 *Poverty by Province, 1991*

	Families		Unattached Individuals		All Persons	
	Number of Poor Families	Poverty Rate	Number of Poor Unattached	Poverty Rate	Number of Poor Persons	Poverty Rate
Newfoundland	25,000	16.4%	14,000	41.3%	100,000	17.6%
Prince Edward Island	3,000	9.9	6,000	40.5	17,000	13.2
Nova Scotia	31,000	12.9	34,000	35.6	134,000	15.5
New Brunswick	25,000	12.3	23,000	35.6	100,000	14.3
Quebec	300,000	15.9	403,000	44.2	1,296,000	19.2
Ontario	303,000	11.2	380,000	31.8	1,327,000	13.5
Manitoba	47,000	17.1	54,000	38.2	218,000	21.1
Saskatchewan	35,000	13.4	40,000	34.5	161,000	17.1
Alberta	87,000	13.1	106,000	33.4	396,000	15.9
British Columbia	93,000	11.1	197,000	35.7	479,000	15.1
Canada	949,000	13.1	1,258,000	36.5	4,227,000	16.0

Source: National Council of Welfare, Poverty Profile Update for 1991 *(Ottawa: Winter 1993), p. 10.*

tively poor, and thus we should not be surprised if they fail to do so. The redistributive impact of other programs such as Veterans' Allowances and Old Age Security is blunted by the fact that such programs are universalistic in their coverage; payments are made to the rich as well as to the poor. (Recent changes to the OAS program have ended universality for the high-income elderly.) While government spending overall provides greater benefits to those at the bottom of the income scale than to those at the top,[38] some programs may actually provide greater benefits for the relatively well-to-do. As Li concludes, "there is mounting evidence to suggest that the state, through its policies of taxation and welfare, subsidizes the rich and not the poor."[39] For example, government support for post-secondary education can also be seen as a transfer payment from the relatively poor to the relatively affluent; in theory a university education is available to all at a cost well below its market value, but in practice it is the sons and daughters of the relatively affluent who are most likely to attend university. Thus, to the extent that programs associated with the welfare state are used more extensively by the well-to-do, such programs may actually redistribute wealth in the opposite direction to what we might expect. Finally, it should be stressed that many, and in some estimates the majority, of Canadian poor are the "working poor," those who experience close to full employment and yet do not earn enough to raise themselves and their families above the poverty line.[40]

Any discussion of the redistributive impact of the welfare state must take into account how program expenditures are financed through the tax system, for expenditures and taxation are two sides of the same redistributive coin. Until the end of the Second World War and the emergence of the welfare state, income taxes played a relatively modest role in the Canadian tax picture. They had been introduced as a "temporary measure" during the First World War, and few taxpayers fell within their reach. In 1930, for example, only 3 to 4 percent of Canadians earned enough to be subjected to income taxes.[41] Then, as the costs of government increased, so too did the reach of income taxes. They have become the most visible form of taxation and a major source of revenue for both the federal and provincial governments. They have also become the symbol of a national commitment to the redistribution of wealth, to the principle that the relatively well-to-do should carry a proportionately larger share of the burden of government than should the relatively disadvantaged. The reality, however, is more complex than the principle would suggest, for income taxes are only one form of tax paid by Canadians. There are also property taxes (paid directly by homeowners and indirectly by renters), provincial sales taxes, excise taxes, licence fees, user fees for such things as national parks, special taxes levied on selected consumer items, and of course, the Goods and Services Tax. Taxes, for example, increase the cost of a litre of gas by about 60 percent, alcoholic beverages by about 100 percent, and cigarettes by approximately 140 percent. When all taxes are taken into account, income taxes alone account for only 30 to 35 percent of the total Canadian tax load.

The income tax is a *progressive* tax; the tax rate increases with income. As people make more money, they pay more taxes not only in an absolute sense, but also in a proportionate sense. Most other forms of taxation are *regressive*; as incomes rise, individuals pay a smaller and smaller share of their incomes in taxes. For example, an individual who smokes a package of cigarettes a day pays approximately $3 a day or $1,100 a year in taxes. If that individual makes $20,000 a year, the effective "tax rate" is 5.2 percent; if he or she makes $50,000 a year, the tax rate drops to 2.2 percent. Our *tax system* combines the progressive income tax with a wide variety of regressive taxes. Income taxes not only form the smaller of the two components of the system, but are also less progressive than is often assumed. Many of the tax breaks that are in theory open to all in fact convey far greater benefits to those with high incomes. For example, the tax savings from registered retirement savings plans, research development tax credits, and child-care expenses all increase as income increases. Marginal tax rates increase more slowly in fact than they do on paper, and may actually fall among individuals with very high incomes. On balance, income taxes have little redistributive effect. In 1981, for example, income taxes alone reduced the income share of the top fifth of Canadian families from 42 percent to 40 percent, and increased the income share of the bottom fifth from 4 percent to 5 percent.[42]

Given that income taxes are not as progressive as they appear on paper, and that the bulk of the tax load borne by Canadians comes through a variety of regressive taxes, it should not be surprising that the tax system as a whole does not redistribute income from the relatively affluent to the relatively poor. Indeed, the tax system is regressive over the upper- and lower-income brackets—the higher one's income, the lower the tax rate— while being mildly progressive across middle-income groups.[43] On balance, then, the mildly progressive impact of government expenditures— the programs and services of the welfare state—are cancelled out by a mildly regressive tax system. As Bryan concludes, it is these offsetting effects that help explain why there has been so little change in the distribution of income over the past thirty years.[44]

The discussion to this point should not leave the impression that there has been no improvement in the lot of the poor as a consequence of the welfare state. In absolute terms, the poor are better off in Canada today than they were in the past, even though their relative position has not changed. Numerous programs significantly enhance the quality of life of the relatively disadvantaged even if they do not shift income per se. Such programs would include medicare, assistance in many provinces for the purchase of pharmaceutical drugs, counselling programs of various kinds, rental assistance, employment training grants, and subsidized day-care facilities. Nor should we understate the importance of income security programs and the protection they provide against injury, illness, unemployment, and old age. Indeed, it is primarily such protection that the welfare state was designed to provide. That the welfare state has not redistributed income is not a mark of failure. The welfare state was never intended to remove inequality from the society, but rather to ensure that those near the bottom were spared destitution, that Canadians would enjoy a reasonable degree of security against the contingencies of life, and that all Canadians would have access to such things as medical care and educational opportunities.

THE ABSENCE OF CLASS CONFLICT

In the *Communist Manifesto*, published in 1848, Karl Marx argued that class conflict was *the* basic feature of political life. "Political power," the *Manifesto* declared, "is merely the organized power of one class for oppressing another." Marx traced out the critical linkage between economic and political power, and argued that the latter was a reflection of the former. Yet in Canada, the disparities in income and economic opportunities, and the nexus between economic and political power, have *not* played a central role in political life. To be sure, class conflict has not been entirely absent; radical parties such as the Communist Party of Canada and the Marxist-Leninists, the 1919 Winnipeg General Strike,[45] labour unrest in Quebec, and agrarian unrest in Western Canada provide only a few examples of its emergence onto the political stage. Nevertheless, when one looks at the major issues that have dominated political life, class conflict has not been among them. As Janine Brodie observes, "unlike other countries with similar levels of economic development, the spatial dimension of Canadian politics overshadows most other social cleavages, such as social class, in our collective political experience."[46] It is important, therefore, to ask *why* class conflict has played a relatively insignificant role. The answer is complex, and embraces a wide range of factors.

The Political Economy of Party Competition

For those associated with the political economy tradition in political science, the absence of more robust class politics is explained in part by the nature of the Canadian state. The state is seen not as a neutral arena within which class interests compete, but rather as an instrument of the dominant capitalist class. As such, the state acts to restrict the full expression and political organization of class interests, apart from those of the dominant class, and thereby moderates class conflict. From this perspective, the welfare state becomes an effective means of "pacifying" disadvantaged individuals within the society.[47] When this fails, the coercive power of the state is brought into play.

A substantial body of literature in this tradition has examined the Canadian economic elite and its proximity to the centres of political power.[48] This literature confirms a good deal of mobility between corporate and political elites, who share extensive interpersonal ties based on kinship, marriage, club memberships, and common ethnic and educational backgrounds. The strength of economic elites within both the Conservative and Liberal parties, it could be argued, effectively precluded the expression of class interests, other than those of the capitalist class, in party competition. Hence the lack of class conflict in the electoral arena may not reflect the reality of class tensions among voters, but rather the reality of the capitalist state and the linkage between economic and political power that it embodies.

Throughout this century, parties have existed that have offered a class analysis of political life and programs of reform based upon that analysis. On the whole, however, they have been bit players on the political stage. Although some, such as the Communist Party of Canada, have endured over time, most have not touched the political lives of the great majority of Canadians in any meaningful way. To the extent that the political left has had a significant impact on party politics, that impact has come through the New Democratic Party and its predecessor, the Co-operative Commonwealth Federation. While there is no questioning the radical stance adopted by the early CCF, there is also no question that the CCF mellowed over time, and that the radical legacy inherited by the NDP had been diluted by the end of the Depression and by the frustration of electoral defeat. The NDP, which replaced the CCF in 1961, stands to the political left of its major partisan rivals, but it would be incorrect to assume that the NDP embraces a radical critique of Canadian society. Although the NDP has provided a political vehicle for organized labour, the unions themselves have seldom offered a radical challenge to the economic order, and the majority of union members support the Liberal and Conservative parties rather than the NDP. In the late 1960s the Waffle faction within the NDP called for "an independent socialist Canada" and "a truly socialist party," but the Wafflers failed to carry the NDP, much less the country. Brodie and Jenson conclude that the political analysis put forward by the NDP owes more to populism—to the defence of the ordinary individual against corporate interests—than it does to social democracy, much less to any more radical socialist analysis.[49] Brodie and Jenson argue that in its 1972 federal campaign the NDP offered Canadians "a fairer, more just, and more equitable capitalism" while launching a populist attack on "corporate welfare bums."[50] In the 1974 federal election the NDP campaign slogan was "People Matter More," not exactly the kind of phrase revolutionaries might hurl from the barricades. The 1984 campaign, with its slogan "Mainstreet not Bay Street," was built around the NDP's role in protecting the "average Canadian," a category from which few voters were excluded.

The Conservative and Liberal parties, which until recently routinely attracted more than 75 percent of the popular vote between them (a figure that fell to 58 percent in 1993), have not differed historically with respect to redistributive policies.[51] Nor have they drawn upon different bases of class support within the electorate. The correlates between voting behaviour and social class have been modest at best, and have been dwarfed by the correlates with regional, religious, or ethnic characteristics.[52] Thus Brodie and Jenson conclude that while the politics of class may be part of the Canadian reality, the electoral organization of classes is not.[53] Interestingly, however, they take the very absence of class differences among the parties as evidence for the existence of class politics more broadly defined.[54] "Political parties," they argue, "shape the interpretation of what aspects of social relations should be considered political, how politics should be conducted, what the boundaries of political discussion most properly may be and what kinds of conflicts can be resolved through the political process."[55] From this perspective, the Conservative and Liberal parties have in the past structured the political agenda so as to conceal class conflict behind an artificial emphasis on linguistic, religious, and regional conflict. Brodie and Jenson maintain that "the most successful exercise of capitalist

The Regina Manifesto

At its first national convention, held in July 1933, the Co-operative Commonwealth Federation (CCF) set forth its program in the *Regina Manifesto*. The *Manifesto* began with a ringing condemnation of the status quo:

> We aim to replace the present capitalist system, with its inherent injustice and inhumanity, by a social order from which the domination and exploitation of one class by another will be eliminated, in which economic planning will supersede unregulated private enterprise and competition, and in which genuine democratic self-government, based upon economic equality, will be possible. The present order is marked by glaring inequalities of wealth and opportunity, by chaotic waste and instability; and in an age of plenty it condemns the great mass of the people to poverty and insecurity. Power has become more and more concentrated into the hands of a small irresponsible minority of financiers and industrialists and to their predatory interests the majority are habitually sacrificed.... We believe that these evils can be removed only in a planned and socialized economy in which our natural resources and the principal means of production and distribution are owned, controlled and operated by the people.

The *Manifesto* closed with equal fire:

> No CCF government will rest content until it has eradicated capitalism and put into operation the full program of socialized planning which will lead to the establishment in Canada of the Co-operative Commonwealth.

class domination occurs when conflict between the classes is simply 'defined away' by ethnic, religious or other social differences."[56] Thus the absence of any conclusive evidence of class politics in studies of voting behaviour confirms the existence of class politics:

> The electoral organization of class relations occurs if the bourgeois parties, for whatever reasons, can successfully maintain an ideological and organizational dominance which defines politics in non-class terms. It is precisely non-class definitions of politics which disorganize the subordinate classes and place some limits on their demands on private capital.[57]

The Ambiguity of Class Lines

If political life were to be organized along class lines, we would need a workable class division of the population. For a number of reasons, such a division is difficult to accomplish whether we employ subjective or objective definitions of social class. As Johnson points out, this definitional distinction is a critical one:

> There is, in all likelihood, no greater point of division between non-Marxist and Marxist intellectuals in North America than that which arises over the definition, importance, and purpose of the study of class. Primary to this division is the degree to which the non-Marxist (or "liberal") intellectual depends upon the measurement of the subjective attitudes of individuals as his basis of analysis. In contrast, the Marxist measures or defines his categories by the objective situation of those studied.[58]

Let us look first at the measurement of subjective attitudes.

Most Canadians have at best a weak "class consciousness." They do not think of themselves in class terms and do not identify with a particular social class.[59] For example, in the 1968 and 1974 national election studies, only 39 percent and 45 percent of the respondents respectively said that they considered themselves as belonging to a social class.[60] Immediately after the 1979 federal election, respondents in the national post-election survey were asked the following question: "Which of the five social classes would you say you were in—upper class, upper-middle class, middle class, working class, or lower class?"[61] Fully 58.5 percent of the respondents refused to or could not locate themselves within one of the five class categories provided. Of those who did answer the question, 58.4 percent described themselves as middle class, 25 percent as working class, 13.3 percent as upper-middle class, 2.8 percent as lower class, and 0.5 percent as upper class. In total, then, 82 percent of the national respondents either did not adopt a class location or used the most innocuous and indistinct class category—the middle class.

Admittedly, survey questions that ask respondents to identify their subjective class position are fraught with a number of methodological problems.[62] Respondents may use the class terminology provided by the question without it having any real meaning or resonance. In the social setting of the interview, it is easier simply to seize upon one of the answers provided than to admit that you do not understand what the interviewer is talking about. What are termed "ego effects," or the respondent's use of the survey question to enhance his or her own social standing, may distort class measurements if respondents attribute a higher class position to themselves than others would accord them.[63] In more general terms, there is reason to suspect that forced-choice questions, in which respondents are asked into which of three, four, or five classes they fall, probably overstate the degree of class consciousness within the population. Although such problems do not negate the usefulness of the concept of social class, they do complicate its empirical application.

The understandable tendency of respondents to inflate their class position takes us to objective definitions of social class, for only if we have objective criteria can we argue that individuals are "wrong" in their self-placements. In part, what is at issue here is whether our social status is as we perceive it to be or as others perceive it to be. If I see myself as "middle class" but others see me as "lower-middle class" or "working class," am I wrong or are they wrong? Perhaps more importantly, if I fail to see myself in class terms at all, am I reflecting the reality of contemporary social life, or am I displaying "false consciousness" by failing to see the class structures that are in fact in place?

Objective definitions of social class are structural; an individual's class position is defined by reference to his or her relationship to the means of production. In the initial Marxist terminology, three basic classes were identified in capitalist societies: (1) the bourgeoisie or capitalists, who owned the means of production and purchased labour; (2) the petite bourgeoisie, such as craftsmen and farmers, who both owned and operated the means of production, but who did so on a relatively small scale; and (3) the proletariat, who did not own the means of production and who sold their labour in the marketplace. This classification is of much less use within modern industrial societies. It provides little assistance, for example, in enabling us to make analytical distinctions among stockbrokers, teachers, veterinarians, models, bureaucrats, rock stars, hockey players, plumbers, chartered accountants, lawyers, real estate agents, consultants, academics, computer programmers, car salesmen, ministers (either clerical or political), doctors, and pharmacists. In short, the very complexity of modern societies makes it difficult to draw class lines. While the top and bottom of the class structure may be relatively easy to identify, there remains a very large and poorly differentiated middle.

The problems associated with objective definitions of social class can be illustrated by the methodological problems that confront survey researchers trying to measure the social class of respondents. Here it is useful to pause for a moment and think of those attributes that contribute in some significant way to the class position of individuals. At the very least we would want to include income, occupation, and education. Even these three, however, are not perfectly correlated. Thus we must deal with individuals with high formal educations but relatively modest incomes (academics and clerics might be included here) and those with modest educations but high incomes, a group that includes many businessmen, professional athletes, and some skilled tradesmen. We might also want to include some assessment of the respondent's dwelling place and personal possessions, and perhaps even more subjective measures such as the respondent's use of language or knowledge of the arts. Combining such multiple and inconsistent measures into a single index of social class is an extremely difficult task.

Nor do the problems end there. If occupation is used as a measure of class, what do we do about the woman who is employed within the house? Simply assigning her a class position equal to her husband's seems iffy—

Does a judge's spouse have the same social standing as a judge?—but then neither is her husband's occupation irrelevant to her own class position. How does one handle retired people: Do they carry the status of their previous occupation (or occupations), or is their status fundamentally altered by retirement? What do we do with the tremendous variance that can exist within occupational groupings? Certainly business people are not interchangeable in their class position, nor are lawyers, doctors, mechanics, athletes, musicians, civil servants, or construction workers. Dividing up the population also means deciding how many classes are to be used—deciding into how many pieces the social pie should be cut—and how cutpoints between the various classes are to be determined. These and other methodological problems confound the use of class concepts for the analysis of political life, be that analysis by academics or by the average Canadian trying to make some sense out of a complex social and political reality. Such problems only increase when we acknowledge that, to a significant degree, class lines are fluid rather than fixed.

Social Mobility

The political importance of social class depends in large part on the rigidity or permeability of class lines. If individuals feel trapped at birth, if they feel that no matter how hard they work their chances to rise in the world are restricted by their social background and that of their parents, then class-based political action becomes more likely. People may decide that the only way their own position in the world will be improved is if the position of all people like themselves is improved, and that will require collective political action. If, on the other hand, the society is seen to be relatively open, if individuals can climb to or at least toward the top on the basis of their own effort, if the channels of upward mobility such as educational institutions are open to all, then class-based politics becomes less likely. If solo ascent is possible, there is little point in dragging along one's class compatriots.

The belief in social mobility—the belief that class boundaries are fluid, that individuals rise and fall in the social order because of their own effort, that the peaks of social and economic life are relatively accessible to individuals with talent and ambition—forms an important part of our cultural mythology. Like all myths that survive over time, those embedded within the notion of social mobility enjoy some correspondence to reality, although, like all myths, they simplify that reality and brush aside conflicting details. Figure 6.1 presents three forms of social mobility that, in combination, capture a good part of the Canadian mythology and reality. The first panel illustrates individual social mobility, or the ability of individuals to rise through social strata by their own efforts, pulling themselves up by their own bootstraps. (The "strata" lines in the figure are used only to position the individual relative to the surrounding society; they are not meant

Income and the Determination of Social Class

Measurement problems in survey research are particularly acute when it comes to income, a variable of critical importance in any discussion of social class.

For a start, many respondents will not reveal their income to interviewers. Other respondents, the number of which is impossible to estimate, will lie or at least exaggerate. Sometimes a researcher may suspect a lie, as I did when one of my respondents—an unemployed, 19-year-old male living in a run-down boarding house—reported a yearly income of $60,000. It is difficult, however, for the interviewer simply to fill in the "correct" income.

Considerable confusion can arise from the differences between before-tax and after-tax income, and between personal and family incomes. To many wage-earners, income before taxes or before other deductions means little; it is the take-home pay that counts. Many people keep count of their income by their hourly, weekly, or monthly wage, and experience some difficulty converting this into the annual income requested by interviewers.

Even when income figures are eventually obtained, and assuming that they are accurate, they must then be adjusted to take into account the age of the respondent and the number of dependents that he or she is supporting. Many retired respondents have relatively low incomes but enjoy substantial wealth; they may own their own homes whereas younger respondents with similar incomes are carrying large mortgages or are paying substantial rent. A young, unattached man earning $35,000 has a very different class position than does a single mother in her mid-30s earning the same salary but supporting three dependent children.

---

to suggest distinct class lines or divisions.) As Li points out, the flip-side to the belief that individuals rise through their own efforts is the belief that individuals who fail to do so have only themselves to blame:

> *If the system is guided solely by rational and competitive forces of supply and demand, then the only factor which can determine social failure is the lack of self-effort, or the inability of individuals to respond to opportunities. In either event, it is the individuals' flaws and deficiencies, and not the way the capitalist system operates, which account for social inequality.*[64]

It is this first form of mobility that is central to the prevailing social mythology in Canada, but it is the second panel that captures a larger part of the reality. In that panel, the position of the individual improves over time because the entire society moves upward over time. For example, individuals today live in a far wealthier society than did their grandparents; they have access to a wider range of private and public goods than did people in the past. Thus individuals can gain in an absolute sense without any *relative change* in their social position. Therefore, in the second panel of Figure 6.1, the individual has "moved up in the world" only because the world has moved up; he or she has been swept along by the general improvement in the society.

In third panel of Figure 6.1, we find mobility across generations; the parents' position does not change over time, but that of their child does. Parents may find a great deal of satisfaction in seeing their sons and daughters move up in the world. Thus the parents who work hard at manual jobs in order to send a son or daughter to university can believe that "the system works" when the child graduates as a doctor, an engineer, or even a political scientist! Children may also measure their own progress by reference to their parents; have they come up or down in the world from the social status achieved by their parents?

It should be stressed that the three forms of social mobility illustrated in Figure 6.1 may be difficult for individuals to untangle. An individual who appears to be moving up in the world through his or her own efforts may in fact be carried along by the upward movement of the society, the absolute gain of the society being misinterpreted as relative gain for the individual. Societal mobility may be mistaken for generational mobility; the father who takes pride in the fact that his daughter received a university degree while he himself received only a Grade 12 education may not realize that today's university degree is the functional equivalent of his high school diploma. The father who worked as a labourer may be pleased to see his daughter pursuing a white-collar career as a data-entry specialist, without realizing that the labouring jobs of his generation are disappearing and that data-entry may be the new functional equivalent. Thus while both individual and generational mobility unquestionably exist, their importance tends to be exaggerated under conditions of general societal improvement. As our lives improve we are likely to attribute that improvement to our own efforts rather than to broader patterns of social change, just as when our children succeed we are likely to attribute that success to their own stellar characters and to the upbringing that they were so fortunate to receive.

Mobility, it should be stressed, can run both ways. Individuals can fall as well as rise in the world, the general standard of living for the society can fall as it did during the Great Depression, and many children will be less successful than their parents. Individual mobility may also be dependent upon collective action. Organizations such as trade unions, ethnic associations, feminist groups, and provincial governments can play an important role in determining the success or failure of group members.

FIGURE 6.1 *Models of Social Mobility*

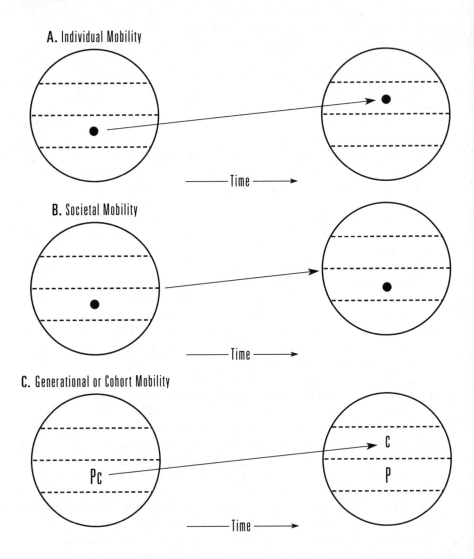

A. Individual Mobility

B. Societal Mobility

C. Generational or Cohort Mobility

Here Strauss points out the importance of collective factors in the mobility experienced by individual Americans: "while many citizens have shrewdly hitched their individual stars to rising industries, towns, and regions, other Americans have been caught in the decline of entire regions, towns, and industries."[65] To regard individuals in either case as masters of their own fate, Strauss argues, turns a blind analytical eye to the important role of collective factors.

Social mobility in its various forms contributes to the appearance of a classless society, or at least of a society in which social status is fluid. With respect to that fluidity, a great deal of importance is attached to education. If educational opportunities are open to all, and if education is the golden key to social mobility, then the educational system in general and the universities in particular come to play a central role. Here reality conveys a more sombre message. Forcese, for example, concludes that

> *the educational system favours the already privileged, and screens out the already disadvantaged. Rather than defeating stratification, formal education is a cause of persisting and increasingly rigid stratification.*[66]

Li is even more damning in his assessment, concluding that the school system

> *perpetuates the myth of mobility by upholding a meritocratic ideology which promotes the notion that societal rewards are linked to individual merits. The end result is that the educational system maintains the class inequality which exists prior to the educational process, and socializes individuals to an ideology which is supportive of the existing class structure.*[67]

More generally, there is little question that the reality of social mobility is less than the mythology suggests. It is not clear, however, that the mythology has been seriously eroded by the critical conclusions of social scientists, or that its moderating impact on class conflict has abated; the mythology of social mobility continues to blunt the appeal of those who would try to organize political life along class lines. The very broad perceptual image of the "middle class" also moderates class conflict; most class conflict is intraclass conflict as we jockey for position within a vast and amorphous middle class. The greatest potential threat to the mythology of social mobility could come through a decline in societal wealth, and thus a decline in the mobility captured by the second panel in Figure 6.1. Here it is interesting to note that while the annual wage for Canadians (measured in current dollars) grew from $11,249 in 1950 to $16,031 in 1960, and grew again to $21,298 in 1970, more recent growth has been very modest. By 1980 the average annual wage had grown by less than $2,000 to $23,791, and over the next decade it grew by only $468, reaching $24,259 by 1990.[68]

Cross-Cutting Cleavages

One explanation for the relative weakness of class politics is that voters and political parties have been preoccupied with other issues. Thus, for example, one might argue that linguistic and/or regional conflict have pushed class conflict down, if not off, the political agenda. While at first

Lotteries and Social Mobility

The mythology of social mobility holds out the promise that anyone can become a millionaire, can climb to the top of the heap. In fact, of course, very few can, and those most likely to do so are those born to wealth. Today, however, the dream has been rekindled and is vigorously marketed by lotteries run in large part by governments and public authorities.

Lotteries were legalized by a 1969 amendment to the Criminal Code, and the first major lottery was launched by the federal government in 1973 in order to raise revenue for the 1976 Olympic Games held in Montreal. Since the termination of the federal government's Sports Pool in 1984, provincial governments have had exclusive control over this lucrative form of voluntary taxation.

Lottery regulations require that winners be publicly identified, and one consequence is that players can see that people like themselves have won. To date, few winners have been found among prominent business people, doctors, and engineers. (In part this is because lotteries are a very bad investment risk, often paying out as little as 30 percent of the money paid in for tickets.) Thus the public image of lotteries is one in which "ordinary Canadians" can suddenly be catapulted into the ranks of the millionaires. Lottery advertising plays upon this image, and indirectly upon the mythology of social mobility; winners are shown enjoying a lifestyle that could never be attained through waged employment. In fact, anyone can become a millionaire by winning a lottery, although the odds of winning the grand prize in the 6/49 Lottery are 13,983,816 to one.

Lotteries diminish class conflict by providing a few people with the means, and large numbers of people with the dream, of dramatic social mobility. As long as some people can make it, perhaps for as little as a $1 investment, then the fact that most do not becomes more tolerable. The random chance of the lottery even introduces an element of fairness into a system that, in other ways, may not provide equal rewards for equal labour. The irony is that lotteries draw their revenue disproportionately from the relatively poor; they are perhaps the most regressive form of taxation we have, albeit a form of voluntary taxation.

glance this explanation may not seem to take us very far, as it does not say *why* other issues have been more important, it takes on additional weight when we consider how other issues have tended to *cross-cut rather than reinforce* class cleavages.

Figure 6.2 presents three models of hypothetical societies in which individuals differ from one another in only two respects: income and religion. In all other respects—age, gender, place of residence—individuals are indistinguishable from one another. In the first model, the income and religious cleavages *cross-cut* one another. The fact that an individual is a Catholic tells you nothing about that individual's income, just as knowledge of the individual's income provides no indication of religious preference. Low-income individuals are as likely to be Protestant as they are to be Catholic. In this model, class conflict is moderated by the cross-cutting religious cleavage, assuming that the religious cleavage is politically salient. Low-income Protestants find their hostility to the high-income individuals

FIGURE 6.2 *Cross-Cutting and Reinforcing Cleavages*

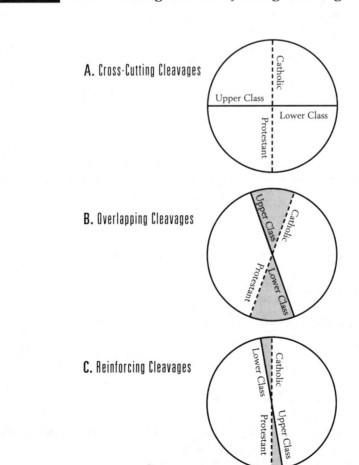

A. Cross-Cutting Cleavages

B. Overlapping Cleavages

C. Reinforcing Cleavages

moderated by the fact that many of their religious compatriots also enjoy high incomes. If one shares a common bond with members of one's class (defined here by income alone) and one's religion, then either intense class or religious conflict would be disquieting. Thus cross-cutting cleavages moderate conflict.

In the second model, the income and religious cleavages *overlap* to a significant degree. The majority of Catholics have high incomes, just as a majority of Protestants have low incomes. Thus to a degree religious and class conflicts within the political system will tend to reinforce one another; Protestants will conflict with Catholics not only because the latter are of a different religion, but also because they have higher incomes. However, conflict will also be moderated by those individuals who fall within the shaded segments of the model. While the majority of low-income individuals are Protestants, and a majority of high-income individuals are Catholics, there are significant minorities of high-income Protestants and low-income Catholics. These minorities signify the extent to which the two cleavages are cross-cutting rather than reinforcing. If we turn to the third model in Figure 6.2, the income and religious cleavages *reinforce* one another to a much greater degree. Virtually all low-income individuals are Protestants, and virtually all high-income individuals are Catholics. As a consequence, political conflicts are likely to be more intense than in the other two models. Religious conflict will also be class conflict, and class conflict will also be religious conflict.

In the Canadian case, cleavages within the social order tend to be cross-cutting rather than reinforcing. For example, there are a number of cleavages that have tended to cross-cut that arising from social class. Prior to the Quiet Revolution in Quebec, for example, the linguistic cleavage effectively immobilized class-based politics within the province. As Quinn has observed:

> In a society where an ethnic minority [within Canada] has reason to believe that its interests as a distinct cultural group are threatened, the struggle to defend and protect those interests tends to become the domi-nant issue in politics and encourages the growth of strong nationalistic sentiments. As a result, purely economic issues, which ordinarily play an important role in any capitalist society, are likely to be pushed into the background.[69]

With the onset of the Quiet Revolution, class and linguistic conflict became reinforcing as political attention was focused on the income differ-ential between francophones and anglophones. For Canada at large, how-ever, linguistic and class cleavages are predominantly cross-cutting. It is unlikely, for instance, that a blue-collar worker in British Columbia feels more in common with francophone blue-collar workers in Quebec than with other British Columbians occupying different class positions. At least within the political realm, there has been little evidence of individuals across the country putting aside linguistic differences in order to pursue class interests held in common.

Within English Canada, regional conflict cross-cuts class conflict. When, for example, there is conflict between the energy-producing and energy-consuming provinces on the price of oil or natural gas, the class interest that a white-collar professional in Alberta might share with a white-collar professional in Toronto tends to be submerged beneath a common regional interest shared with other Albertans of whatever economic status. In a related example, oil workers in Alberta, Saskatchewan, Newfoundland, and the Northwest Territories may share a common class position, but the issue of more immediate concern may well be the regional location of oil exploration. In general, when class lines are cross-cut by regional cleavages, the mobilization of class interests within the *national* political system is rendered difficult. Given the pervasiveness and saliency of regional conflict, this conclusion is of considerable importance.

Federalism further complicates the orchestration of class politics by introducing intergovernmental conflict into the political system, conflict that can cross-cut and overshadow political conflict based on class interests, and that can reinforce the regional effects noted above. It is for this reason, Richards and Pratt argue, that the Canadian left has been marked by impatience with both provincialism and federalism itself: "indeed, [the left's] dominant tradition, apart from its incorrigible penchant for sectarianism, is one of unabashed centralism, expressed as the belief that only a powerful federal government armed with overriding legislative and financial powers can regulate modern industrial capitalism and set in motion the transition towards a socialist society."[70] In recent years this tradition has abated somewhat as provincial New Democrats in the West have sought a greater reconciliation between social democratic principles and the political realities of a federal state with strong subnational loyalties and provincial governments.

In a landmark article on regional conflict, Richard Simeon pointed out that disadvantaged citizens face a choice among competing explanations for their status: "a poor New Brunswick logger may explain his poverty by saying he is disadvantaged because he is a New Brunswicker, or because he speaks French, or because loggers everywhere always get a poor deal."[71] The choice, Simeon argues, will have important consequences for which axis of political conflict—regional, linguistic, or class—will come to the fore. To date, the first two choices facing Simeon's logger have prevailed, and in doing so have pre-empted political conflict based more on class than on regional or linguistic lines. Although the 1984 and 1988 elections of national governments with strong support across the regions and within both linguistic communities set the stage for a more ideologically structured political agenda by reducing the saliency of regional and linguistic cleavages, party competition has yet to be characterized by a more free-wheeling ideological debate. Such a debate may have been set in motion by the 1993 general election campaign, with its focus on the deficit and social programs, and by the election of more than fifty Reform MPs.

Political Resources

In democratic political systems it is reasonable to expect that governments will be responsive to the pressure exerted upon them by citizens. Yet if the old cliché is true that the squeaky wheel gets the grease, it is also true that effective squeaking requires political resources. Such resources are not evenly distributed across the population.

Numbers do count in democratic politics, and the force of numbers is a key political resource. However, relatively small groups can offset a lack of numbers through other resources, including an educated and articulate leadership, ready access to and favourable treatment by the media, geographical concentration so that the group's vote is brought to bear in specific constituencies rather than being thinly dispersed across the country, the support of provincial governments, alliances within the domestic political arena, foreign allies, and economic power. Perhaps the key resource is money, which can be parlayed into a variety of other political resources. This is not to suggest that money can be equated with political power, but rather that it plays a critical role in the mobilization and effective use of other political resources. This suggests in turn that the relatively affluent have the financial wherewithal and hence other resources to protect their interests within the political system. There is nothing surprising about such a conclusion. Yet it is important to stress that the poor in Canada are poor not only in financial terms, but also in terms of other resources that are essential to the exercise of political power. In part this explains why their interests are not fully articulated, and why the debate on income redistribution has not played a larger role in political life. Although organizations representing the poor, such as the National Anti-Poverty Organization, the Canadian Council on Social Planning, the Child Poverty Action Group, and the Canadian Association of Food Banks, are increasingly active on the political stage, they do not command anywhere near the same resources as do other segments of the political community.

The political system does not compensate individuals for their lack of economic resources, but rather compounds their problem. It is not that the system is stacked against the poor per se. It is stacked against those who lack political resources, and such people are far more likely to be poor than to be rich. Harold Laski, a famous British political scientist and major figure in the London School of Economics, once wrote that "the meek will not inherit the earth unless they are prepared to fight for their meekness." Within the conventional political arena, that fight is a difficult one to wage for economically and hence politically impoverished groups.

The Political Organization of Welfare Recipients

A group was formed several years ago in Calgary to promote the rights and interests of local welfare recipients. The organizational problems faced by this group, problems that led shortly to its demise, illustrate in microcosm the political problems facing the economically disadvantaged.

One of the first problems the group faced was identifying its clientele. Many potential members were difficult to contact because they did not have telephones or fixed addresses. Others did not want it to be known by neighbours that they were receiving social assistance, and shunned any public identification with a welfare rights group. Still others did not want to associate with the "sort of people" who were welfare recipients. They saw their own dependency on social assistance as a temporary condition, and they shared with the broader society a negative perception of the "typical" welfare recipient.

Meetings were difficult to arrange. People could not be reached due to a lack of a telephone or irregular hours. Many single parents could not get or could not afford babysitters. A meeting place was difficult to find as most group members did not have large enough homes or enough chairs, coffee cups, and so forth. Meeting times were hard to find as many members had part-time employment at irregular hours.

If all these hurdles could be overcome, meetings were difficult to conduct. Few members had any experience running meetings, and few were familiar with conventional rules of order. Procedural and substantive criticisms were often taken as personal attacks, and tempers frequently ran high. Effective chairpersons were hard to find.

Decisions made by the group were difficult to implement. Implementation often required money, a detailed knowledge of the relevant political and bureaucratic environments, and well-honed interpersonal skills, all of which were in short supply. Throughout, then, the group was hobbled by severe organizational handicaps that were largely a consequence or manifestation of the economic position of the group's members, and that precluded any effective political action. Because of their disadvantaged economic position in society, group members lacked the political resources to challenge that position.

External Influences

The Canadian society is open to the external world, not only in terms of trade and immigration, but also with respect to ideological currents and the flow of political ideas. As a consequence, the way in which Canadians see the political world is strongly influenced by American and, to a lesser extent, Western European ideologies. With the United States, the world's largest and most successful capitalist society, Canada shares a dominant liberal ideology that emphasizes personal freedom and individual rights. Liberalism assumes that the primary allocation of wealth within the society occurs through the private sector, although liberals recognize that an unregulated free market can deny individuals equal opportunity to pursue private gain. Thus market intervention is accepted in order to promote equality of opportunity, to shelter those who cannot compete for reasons of age or incapacity, and to correct for distortions that might occur as a result of racial, religious, or sexual discrimination. Liberalism, then, accepts a substantial redistributive role for government while relying upon the private sector as the primary mechanism for the generation and distribution of wealth. At the same time, liberalism is resistant to class analysis in any form. To the extent that Canadians see the political world through such ideological spectacles, the class organization of political life along class lines is impeded.

The influence of both Britain and the United States has tended to obscure Canadian extremes of wealth and poverty. Britain's aristocratic heritage has generated a host of class symbols including titles, landed estates, the Oxbridge accent, and school ties that have no ready equivalent in Canada. It is not that wealthy Canadians do not exist, but rather that they are not so readily identified. Because the wealthy individuals featured in the mass media followed by most Canadians are Americans, we know far more about the comings and goings of the American rich than we do of the Canadian rich. The very obscurity of Canadian wealth, it can be argued, diminishes class conflict. The most visible targets of class hostility are found outside rather than inside the country. In a similar fashion, many of the images Canadians have of poverty are lodged outside the country, in the slums of London, the urban decay of the United States, and the appalling poverty of many Third World countries. The reality of Canadian poverty is thus obscured, and its impact on political life diminished.

In the international community there have been many countries that have offered radically different models of redistributive politics, but such models have played little role to date in Canadian political life. In part this is attributable to the military tension that existed between the Soviet Bloc and the NATO alliance. More importantly, American hostility to socialism in general and to the former Soviet Union in particular was so intense that it washed over into the Canadian political culture. While Canadians may not have accepted the American world view holus bolus, it had sufficient credibility and penetration to significantly weaken the impact of socialist models on conventional Canadian political discourse.[72] In summary, much of Canada's external environment consisted of an impoverished Third World, a continental neighbour within which class-based political cleavages were relatively weak and anti-communism was very strong, socialist states posing a serious military threat, and Great Britain with its aristocratic symbols of wealth and power. Within this international context, the Canadian extremes of poverty and wealth tended to pale. Perhaps more importantly, neither end of the domestic income spectrum was exposed to the full light of the media, light that reflected instead images of wealth and poverty lodged beyond Canadian borders.

Inequality in the distribution of human talent and resources is inevitable. Some individuals will always be stronger, quicker, more intelligent, and more aggressive. Largely as a consequence, inequality in the distribution of wealth is also inevitable, and indeed there is no evidence that Canadians would prefer an egalitarian or even a more egalitarian society. There is no expectation that the modest political equality of one person/one vote should be transformed into economic equality. However, there appears to be public support for at least a modest redistributive role for governments. Equality of opportunity is a highly prized value, and thus government intervention to ensure that everyone has an equal chance to compete is endorsed. While there is no expectation that everyone can or should win, it is assumed that everyone should at least be in the race and should be as unencumbered as possible by discrimination stemming from race, national or ethnic origin, colour, religion, sex, age, or mental or physical disabilities. There is also widespread political support for greater security for those at the bottom of the economic scale, for the basic programs of the welfare state (and particularly medicare), and for the principle of the progressive income tax.

At the same time, there appears to be little support for any substantial redistribution of wealth among individuals, and little concern that no such redistribution has taken place over the past thirty years. While the welfare state has provided greater security for all Canadians, it has not redistributed wealth to any significant degree, and there is little evidence that many voters see this as a failure. For the reasons discussed above, class conflict has not energized the political process despite acute and persistent disparities in the distribution of income and wealth. Indeed, Canadians appear to be more willing to tolerate large income disparities among individuals than they have been to tolerate more modest income disparities among regions.

THE REDISTRIBUTION OF WEALTH ACROSS REGIONS

The regions of Canada differ significantly in their natural and human resources. Not surprisingly, such differences are reflected in marked variations both in personal income and in the fiscal resources available to provincial governments. In the absence of government intervention, the mobility of people and capital would be the natural consequence of such regional variations. Other things being equal, people would tend to move to those locations where employment prospects were the most promising, where government programs were the most richly endowed, and where tax rates were the lowest. In regions where resources were limited, both wages and the level of government services would fall, encouraging further out-migration until some equilibrium was established, with low wages drawing in new investment capital. In this manner the United States has experienced pronounced internal shifts in the regional distribution of its population. These have included not only the westward shift involved in the initial settlement of the continent, but also shifts from the rural South to the industrial cities of the Northeast and then, in more recent years, the shift from the Northeast and "frost-belt" states to the "sun-belt" states of the American South and Southwest. The mobility of both people and capital has been an acknowledged feature of the American experience, and an accepted response to changing economic circumstances across the country.

Canada has also experienced substantial interregional migration. As Chapter 4 noted, out-migration, albeit mostly to the United States rather than to other parts of Canada, has played an important role in the demographic evolution of Quebec, and regional migrations have been of great importance in the histories of both Atlantic Canada and the West. However, there has been less acceptance in Canada than in the United States of individual mobility as the appropriate response to regional differences in economic potential. Federal and provincial governments have intervened in a variety of ways to shore up the economies of regional communities and thus reduce the need for mobility. Three broad strategies have been employed: fiscal transfers from the national treasury to provincial governments in relatively depressed regions; redistributive programs run through the departments of the federal government; and "province-building" strategies pursued by provincial governments. Each of these will be examined briefly in turn.

Intergovernmental Transfers and Equalization

Intergovernmental transfers have been an integral part of the federal system since the passage of the Constitution Act in 1867. Initially they resulted from a fundamental imbalance between the federal division of legislative powers, on the one hand, and the division of fiscal resources, on the other. Ottawa's power to raise monies by "any Mode or System of Taxation" gave the federal government access to revenues well in excess of its expenditure obligations under the legislative division of powers, while the provincial governments had access to less revenue than their expenditure obligations required. Thus Sections 118 and 119 of the 1867 Constitution Act provided for federal subsidies to provincial governments, subsidies that were constantly under review and that served as a permanent source of contention between the two levels of government.[73] The "subsidy question" was of particular importance in the Maritimes where, as Chapter 5 discussed, the search for "better terms" played a major role in the Nova Scotia Repeal Movement of 1886–87 and the Maritime Rights Movement of the 1920s. It should be stressed, however, that the initial provincial subsidies were intended to correct the fiscal imbalance stemming from the federal division of powers, rather than to redistribute wealth from "have" to "have-not" regions, although the latter aspect came into play when subsidies began to assume much greater importance in the Maritime provinces than elsewhere in the country. Interregional redistribution came more to the fore in an array of conditional grant programs launched by the federal government in the 1950s and early 1960s, as discussed in more detail in Chapter 8.

Conditional grant programs were shared-cost programs in which Ottawa picked up half the cost of provincially administered programs in provincial fields of jurisdiction, provided that minimum national standards were observed. Through such assistance the federal government made a very substantial contribution to provincial programs in health care, post-secondary education, and social assistance. Conditional grant programs enabled "have-not" provinces to supply a level of social services roughly equivalent to that provided by the "have" provinces in those program areas covered by conditional grants. There was, as a consequence, some significant redistributive effect as basic social services were provided at a roughly equivalent level to all Canadians, regardless of where they happened to live. The redistributive effect was blunted, however, by the fact that the provinces received *matching* grants. By spending more, the wealthier provinces were able to receive more from Ottawa. They were also able to use the federal funds to free up previously committed provincial funds, and thus launch new program initiatives.[74]

Unconditional equalization payments, which were specifically directed toward the have-not provinces rather than toward all provinces, found their conceptual roots in the 1940 *Report of the Royal Commission on Dominion–Provincial Relations*. In its report, the Rowell-Sirois Commission recognized that the regional structure of the Canadian economy, with its concentration of corporate head offices in Montreal and Toronto, gave Ontario and Quebec disproportionate access to corporate taxes. The commission therefore recommended a system of National Adjustment Grants paid by the federal government "to enable each province (including its municipalities) without resort to heavier taxation than the Canadian average to provide adequate social, educational and developmental services."[75] Although this recommendation was not implemented at the time, the *principle* of equalization endured, and governments began to move toward a system of fiscal transfers that would ensure that citizens of similar economic status would have equal access to government services and face equal tax loads no matter where they happened to live. This principle is now constitutionally entrenched in Section 36 of the Constitution Act, 1982.

Equalization

Section 36 of the 1982 Constitution Act captures the national commitment to equalization that began with the 1940 Rowell-Sirois recommendations:

36 (1) Without altering the legislative authority of Parliament or of the provincial legislatures, or the rights of any of them with respect to the exercise of their legislative authority, Parliament and the legislatures, together with the government of Canada and the provincial governments, are committed to (a) promoting equal opportunity for the well-being of Canadians; (b) furthering economic development to reduce disparity in opportunities; and (c) providing essential public services of reasonable quality to all Canadians.

(2) Parliament and the government of Canada are committed to the principle of making equalization payments to ensure that provincial governments have sufficient revenues to provide reasonably comparable levels of public services at reasonably comparable levels of taxation.

The equalization principle was first put into practice through the Federal–Provincial Tax Sharing Arrangements, 1957–62. Provincial governments were provided with unconditional grants[76] from the national treasury totalling $139 million in the first year, and designed to bring their yield from individual taxes, corporate taxes, and succession duties up to the average per capita yield for the two wealthiest provinces, British Columbia and Ontario. In the 1962–67 fiscal agreement the equalization formula was extended to include provincial revenues from natural resources, and the British Columbia/Ontario average was replaced by the national average. In 1967 the formula was expanded to include sixteen provincial revenue sources, and in the Federal–Provincial Fiscal Arrangement and Established Program Funding Act of 1977 this was further expanded to include twenty-nine revenue sources, or virtually all the revenue sources available to provincial governments. At that time the formula was amended to include only 50 percent of the revenue accruing to provincial governments from nonrenewable natural resources, a modification to which we shall return shortly. The formula was also amended to tie any increase in funding directly to growth in the GNP and the respective provincial populations. In 1991–92 equalization payments totalled $8.4 billion. By way of comparison, benefits to the elderly totalled $18.9 billion in the same year, Unemployment Insurance payments totalled $17.2 billion, and aboriginal peoples received $1.6 billion.[77]

The application of the equalization formula is a complex undertaking. For each province, the per capita revenue yield is calculated for each of the twenty-nine revenue sources. If, across the twenty-nine sources, the provincial yield is less than the average yield of Ontario, Quebec, Manitoba, Saskatchewan, and British Columbia, the federal government makes up the difference. If the provincial yield is more than this average, no equalization payments are made. The point to be stressed is that equalization payments are made from the federal treasury. The equalization formula does *not* take money from the richer *provincial governments* and redistribute it to the poorer ones. Provincial revenues per se are not redistributed; they are used only in the calculation of equalization payments to be made by Ottawa to the have-not provincial governments. Thus the "burden" of equalization is carried by all Canadian taxpayers, including those in the have-not provinces.

Table 6.2 provides one snapshot showing how equalization payments are distributed across the provinces. There you will note that Quebec receives the largest total payment, whereas the largest per capita payments are received by Prince Edward Island and Newfoundland. As can be seen from the table, the general purpose transfers to the smaller Atlantic provinces are, on a per capita basis, very substantial. Table 6.2 also records specific purpose transfers from Ottawa to the provincial governments, transfers that cover the federal contribution to medicare, hospital care, advanced education, and social assistance. Again on a per capita basis, these payments are not equal across the ten provinces. The northern territories constitute a special case in that there are no provincial governments in the North, and thus the total transfers from the federal government are much greater than in the case of the provinces.

One of the reasons for equalization payments is that the Constitution gives provincial governments primary access to revenues derived from natural resources, revenues that are not evenly dispersed across the provinces. In the 1970s the concentration of oil reserves in Alberta and, to a much lesser extent, Saskatchewan severely disrupted the equalization formula. When the price of oil escalated after 1973, and the Alberta government imposed higher royalties, the revenues accruing to Alberta grew enormously. When this increase was fed into the equalization formula, the national treasury faced a significant leap in equalization payments. Yet Ottawa had no access to the oil revenues that were generating the increased equalization payments. Although Alberta's revenues were driving equalization payments upward, it was not those revenues that were being redistributed.[78]

A number of important consequences flowed from the resulting fiscal crisis. The Alberta government diverted a substantial portion of its oil revenues into the Alberta Heritage Savings and Trust Fund. This portion was not included in the equalization formula, and thus reduced the strain on the federal treasury. The formula itself was amended so that no province

TABLE 6.2 *Fiscal Transfers from the Federal Government to Provincial and Territorial Governments, 1992–93*

		Millions of Dollars			
	Equalization	Other General Purpose	EPF*	CAP*	Other Specific Purpose Transfers
Nfld.	953.0	24.3	333.3	135.0	83.4
P.E.I.	202.0	5.4	78.2	32.0	12.3
N.S.	1,001.0	17.9	589.7	230.0	47.4
N.B.	928.0	15.1	453.5	214.0	49.3
Que.	3,935.0	116.9	4,767.1	2,320.0	439.9
Ont.	—	254.1	7,680.5	2,243.3	344.5
Man.	977.0	23.5	720.1	260.0	135.5
Sask.	565.0	12.0	626.0	183.0	349.3
Alta.	—	171.8	1,946.1	599.9	204.0
B.C.	—	46.8	2,492.2	799.7	100.9
N.W.T.	—	826.6	42.0	22.0	77.6
Yukon	—	225.7	20.7	7.8	19.5
Total	8,561.0	1,740.1	19,749.7	7,046.9	1,863.4

*Includes cash transfers and tax transfers.

Source: Canadian Tax Foundation, The National Finances, 1992 (Toronto, 1992), pp. 16:18–19.

could receive equalization payments if its per capita income was above the national average. This amendment pre-empted equalization payments to Ontario, which under the old rules would have qualified as a have-not province from 1977 to 1982. As noted above, the formula was changed to include only 50 percent of nonrenewable natural resource revenues. The federal government also moved to keep Canadian oil prices below world levels. Finally, in 1980 Ottawa introduced the National Energy Program, which was designed in part to give the federal government access to oil revenues through which it could finance the increased equalization payments that the rise in oil prices had brought about.

The redistribution of resource revenues poses a very thorny problem for the Canadian political system. If revenues were to go primarily to individuals or to corporations, as is the case with oil revenues in the United States, redistribution would be relatively easy as the federal government would have access to such revenues through personal and corporate income taxation. However, to the extent that revenues go to provincial governments in the form of royalties, they are not accessible to Ottawa through personal or corporate taxation, although the federal government is

"This year, in the spirit of national equalization, Reggie and I feel we should spend our vacation in the have-not provinces ..."

Len Norris, *23rd Annual*; originally published in the Sun (Vancouver), January 25, 1974.

still faced with the bill for equalization. This leads in turn to attempts by the federal government to capture a share of resource revenues, attempts that were incorporated in the controversial National Energy Program. In this narrow sense, the equalization program can promote federal raids on provincial treasuries even though, more generally, equalization does not entail any expropriation or redistribution of provincial government revenues.

Equalization payments alter the dynamics of individual mobility by reducing the costs of staying in relatively depressed regions: they both reduce the tax load and improve the quality of public services in the have-not provinces. At the same time, equalization payments have altered the dynamics of federalism in the have-not provinces. In conjunction with other federal subsidies, they have transformed the Atlantic provinces into virtual client states of the federal government.[79] The extreme case is Prince Edward Island, where nearly 60 percent of the provincial budget comes from federal transfer payments of one kind or another, and where the provincial treasury has become little more than an agent for the distribution of federal funds.[80] Somewhat ironically, equalization payments may also contribute to intergovernmental conflict. Hugh Thorburn maintains that they have enabled the have-not provinces to strengthen their bureaucracies and thus challenge the federal government across a broader front: "in short, the improved financial capacity of the provinces may well have served to accentuate the rivalries between provinces, and between federal and provincial authorities, because it has made possible a level of provincial intervention that could not have occurred without such improved financial capacity."[81] In a crude sense, equalization payments enable the have-not provinces to bite the federal hand that feeds them.

Redistributive Effects of Federal Programs

Although equalization payments provide the centrepiece for federal efforts to redistribute wealth across provincial communities, various other federal programs also have significant redistributive effects. In 1961 Parliament passed the Agricultural Rehabilitation and Development Act, which was designed to address rural poverty. The act provided for joint federal–provincial funding of rural development projects and the coordination of federal and provincial programs in the policy field. In 1965 the terms of the act were expanded by the passage of the Agricultural and Rural Development Act (ARDA), followed by the creation of the Fund for Rural Economic Development in 1966. ARDA was later expanded to include development programs in tourism and fisheries. In 1962 Ottawa also established the Atlantic Development Board to coordinate the developmental activities of federal departments and the four provincial governments in the region. While these legislative initiatives were not designed to redirect economic activity from one region to another, they were designed to promote economic development in rural as opposed to urban Canada.

The major federal initiative came with the creation of the Department of Regional Economic Expansion (DREE) in 1969.[82] DREE's mandate was to ensure that economic growth was widely dispersed across Canada, and that employment and income prospects in slow-growth regions were brought up to the national average.[83] Building on the precedents of the Area Development Agency (1963) and the Area Development Incentives Act (1965), DREE was designed to give Ottawa a direct and high-profile role in regional economic development, a role well beyond the provision of equalization payments, which were then spent solely at the discretion of provincial governments. In 1982 the Liberal government created the Ministry of State for Economic and Regional Development (MSERD), which was disbanded by Prime Minister John Turner in 1984, and DREE was merged with the Department of Industry, Trade and Commerce to form DRIE, the Department of Regional Industrial Expansion.

On the one hand, DRIE was to maximize industrial competitiveness and efficiency, while on the other hand it was to reduce regional disparities brought about in part by the operation of market forces. In 1987 DRIE was merged with the Ministry of State for Science and Technology to form the Department of Industry, Science and Technology (DIST). Much of DRIE's former involvement in regional economic development was taken up by new agencies (discussed below) with specific mandates for Atlantic Canada, Western Canada, and northern Ontario.

The DREE-DRIE-DIST initiative represents only one of many strategies the federal government has taken or could potentially take to alleviate regional disparities. The drilling incentives in the National Energy Program, for example, were designed to shift drilling activity onto federal crown lands in the Canadian North and off the east coast of the Atlantic provinces, much to the outrage of the Alberta government. Federal support for energy megaprojects on the East Coast and in Western Canada has been designed to promote development that the market alone would not support. The federal government may pick up infrastructure costs in the hope that improved ports, roads, and airports will promote private economic development. Ottawa may also move federal agencies to specific areas in the hope that the agencies will bring business development in their wake. An example here is provided by Ottawa's decision to locate the new Space Agency in Montreal. Finally, the government may intervene in countless ad hoc ways to provide financial support for existing firms or new development.

All such programs are designed to influence the locational decisions of private firms. The starting assumption is that market-determined locational decisions may not be optimal from a social or political perspective. Thus an array of public incentives is brought into play to affect locational decisions. These incentives can include tax breaks, the public provision of infrastructure support, subsidized land, and preferential government services. Unfortunately, their impact on regional economic development is very difficult to assess. In some cases, grants go to firms that may have located in the region anyway. In other cases, new firms may not survive, or may displace existing firms in the region. New firms may discourage additional investment by driving up the costs of wages and services. Finally, Ingrid Bryan argues, "firms that need to be 'bribed' to invest in an area may be less likely than other firms to reinvest, and therefore the long-term benefits of subsidized investments may be small.[84] Thus, while public expenditures may be clearly redistributive, flowing from the national treasury to disadvantaged regions within the country or from the provincial treasury to disadvantaged regions within the province, it is less clear that such expenditures significantly alter the regional distribution of investment and employment opportunities.

When the Progressive Conservatives came to power in 1984, the emphasis of the new Mulroney government was on a market-driven economy, and on improving Canada's international competitiveness. Regional development incentives were difficult to square with this commitment, given that they constituted direct intervention in the market, and thus the Conservative government displayed little initial enthusiasm for regional economic development. In 1987, however, and following widespread dissatisfaction with DRIE, Ottawa introduced a series of new initiatives. In June the federal government announced the creation of the Atlantic Canada Opportunities Agency (ACOA) with a staff of 300 and an annual budget of $200 million for each of the next five years. (In 1989, Ottawa announced that the same amount of money would be spread over seven and not five years.) ACOA was to assume responsibility for the bulk of existing regional economic development programs in the Atlantic provinces and, significantly, was headquartered in Moncton, rather than in Ottawa. In July, Ottawa announced the creation of FED-NOR, a development program for northern Ontario with an initial budget of $55 million. Then, in August, the picture was rounded out with the creation of the Western Diversification Office (WDO), a parallel agency to ACOA. WDO is headquartered in Edmonton, with suboffices in Vancouver, Saskatoon, and Winnipeg, and has a budget of $1.2 billion spread over five years. In the first eighteen months it provided grants and loans to 765 diversification projects across the West, including a special $45 million fund to promote the sale of low sulphur coal. Per capita expenditures amounted to $37 in Manitoba, $35 in Saskatchewan, $26 in Alberta, and $22 in British Columbia.[85]

Other federal programs, including transfers to individuals, can have redistributive regional effects even though they have not been designed with any redistributive intent. If the need that a program is designed to address is more prevalent in one region than another, or if the clientele of a particular program is disproportionately located in one region rather than another, some regional redistribution will occur. For example, if the birthrate in one region is higher than in others, as it was in Quebec prior to the Quiet Revolution, then a universal program such as Family Allowance will benefit that region more than others. The beneficiaries of the Canada Assistance Plan are not evenly dispersed across the country, and thus some modest regional redistribution occurs to the benefit of the Atlantic provinces. Canada's Unemployment Insurance program also results in a net transfer of resources into Atlantic Canada. Ottawa's procurement of goods and services, the location of military bases, research centres, mints, and head offices of crown corporations, and in some instances, the location of government departments, all have potential redistributive effects.[86] As Herman Bakvis points out in a more general sense, it is rarely the case that the effects of *any* government policy or development program are distributed evenly across geographical space.[87]

While expenditure patterns often provide unequal regional benefits, and while specific programs exist to encourage the regional dispersion of economic activity, the net effect on the regional distribution of wealth and employment opportunities is difficult to determine. It is not clear whether the distributional objectives of public policy are being met and, if they are, at what cost to the growth objectives of public policy, assuming that some tension between the two is inevitable.[88] What is clear is that the effective management of regional economic development is dependent upon extensive intergovernmental coordination and cooperation. This is not easily achieved given the zero-sum character of locational decisions, where the gain of any one province is the loss of its provincial competitors.

Province-Building and Redistributive Politics

It is of little concern within the context of the national economy if individuals from depressed regions "go down the road" to seek employment in other regions. Indeed, such mobility may be a useful form of adjustment to changing economic conditions. It may alleviate unemployment in depressed regions, raise wages for those left behind, and reduce the costs of social assistance. From the perspective of provincial governments, however, out-migration is a matter of considerable concern. In part, the concern stems from the fact that it is the young and the best educated who are most likely to migrate, leaving behind an impoverished pool of human resources.[89] Out-migration can further depress the local economy by decreasing the size of local markets, and can erode the local tax base to the point where the quality of public services will deteriorate.[90] Thus, while out-migration may not be damaging to the national economy, it is resisted by provincial governments who seek to convince voters that their sons and daughters will be able to live and work within their home province no matter what career they may wish to pursue.

Provincial governments seek to ward off out-migration by province-building strategies designed to strengthen the provincial economy. Provincial businesses are shored up through tax breaks, infrastructure support, and preferential purchasing and contracting policies. Extensive efforts are made to attract investment from outside the province and the country, efforts that may entail a "beggar-thy-neighbour" policy of luring investors away from neighbouring provinces. Economic strength alone, however, is not sufficient to prevent out-migration if that strength rests on a capital-intensive rather than labour-intensive base, and if the provincial economy lacks sufficient economic diversification. In the latter case, out-migration can still be forced upon those who choose to pursue careers falling beyond the parameters of the provincial economy. In Western Canada, economic diversification has been the primary focus of province-building strategies given the somewhat narrow natural resource base of the regional economy, the concentration of labour-intensive industries in central Canada, and the historical lure of a more complex labour market outside the region.[91]

Province-building strategies can have a somewhat contradictory effect in that provincial economic strength may weaken the national economy. As Hugh Thorburn explains, the understandable effort by provincial governments to curtail out-migration

> has counteracted the natural adjustment process by which movements of people and capital would take place in response to variation in wages, job opportunities, production costs, and so forth. The result was the creation of ten provincial economies rather than one Canadian economy.[92]

This suggests in turn that economic management can be a very complex task in a federal state when one level of government tries to ensure a healthy and vital national economy while the second level tries to ensure healthy provincial economies, even to the extent of inhibiting the mobility of capital and labour within the national economic community. The management task is not only complex from the standpoint of intergovernmental relations; it is also complex for the federal government alone when it tries to ensure both national economic growth and an equitable regional distribution of economic activity.

CONCLUSIONS

In the decades following the end of the Second World War, Canadians put into place an extensive welfare state. Although the extent of that state was particularly evident with respect to medicare, it also entailed a wide range of income support programs. However, the welfare state was not accompanied by any extensive or even significant redistribution of income or wealth across the population. Whatever the reasons, and including the success of the welfare state itself, class conflict and the associated redistributive politics had at best a limited impact on postwar political life. To the extent that redistributive politics claimed a significant place on the nation's political agenda, it was primarily concerned with the distribution of wealth across provincial communities. Redistributive politics, like so many other aspects of Canadian politics, was spatially oriented.

In many respects, the political system has coped well with redistributive conflict and issues. However, in the years to come we can expect increased strain on the arrangements put into place in the postwar years. Growing public concern with the deficit and debt, and the aging of the population, will put increasingly acute strain on social programs, and particularly on the medicare flagship of the Canadian welfare state. The embrace of continental free trade will also make it more difficult to sustain support for national and provincial programs designed to enhance regional economic development. As Brodie explains in the context of the FTA:

The free-trade agreement does, in fact, limit the ability of provincial gov-
ernments to reintroduce the kind of province-building strategies employed
in the 1970s. Differential pricing in energy, subsidized industrial diversifi-
cation policies, and preferential purchasing are all contrary to the terms
of the agreement.[93]

With the implementation of NAFTA, the constraints on both the provincial and federal governments will only increase.

It would appear, then, that current redistributive arrangements will
become more and more difficult to sustain. On the surface, this would suggest that political conflict over redistributive policies will increase, and that
the political arena will be energized more by class and regional conflict.
Some evidence to this effect was provided by the 1992 debate over the
Social Charter, which had been proposed by the Ontario government as an
addition to the constitutional package. At the same time the constraints on
the mobilization of class conflict discussed in this chapter are still in place.
It is by no means clear, therefore, that budgetary constraint and globalization of the economy will fundamentally restructure the Canadian political
agenda.

SUGGESTED READINGS

1. Keith Banting, *The Welfare State and Canadian Federalism*, 2nd ed.
   (Toronto: University of Toronto Press, 1987).

2. Janine Brodie, *The Political Economy of Canadian Regionalism* (Toronto: Harcourt Brace Jovanovich, 1990).

3. Alain-G. Gagnon, "The Dynamics of Federal Inter-Governmental
   Relations: Delivery of Regional Development Programs in Canada,"
   Regional Politics and Policy, 1:1 (1991), pp. 1–24.

4. Peter S. Li, *Ethnic Inequality in a Class Society* (Toronto: Wall and
   Thompson, 1988).

5. M. Patricia Marchak, *Ideological Perspectives on Canada*, 3rd ed. (Toronto: McGraw-Hill Ryerson, 1988).

6. James J. Rice and Michael J. Prince, "Lowering the Safety Net and
   Weakening the Bonds of Nationhood: Social Policy in the Mulroney
   Years," in Susan D. Phillips, ed., *How Ottawa Spends: A More Democratic Canada ...?* (Ottawa: Carleton University Press, 1993), pp.
   381–416.

7. Donald J. Savoie, *Regional Economic Development: Canada's Search for
   Solutions*, 2nd ed. (Toronto: University of Toronto Press, 1992).

8. Carolyn Tuohy, "Social Policy: Two Worlds," in Michael M. Atkinson, ed., *Governing Canada: Institutions and Public Policy* (Toronto: Harcourt Brace Jovanovich, 1993), pp. 275–306.

STUDY QUESTIONS

1. How would you characterize the pattern of social mobility within your own family tree? What has been the role played by societal and generational mobility, as opposed to the individual mobility discussed in this chapter?

2. If you were asked to conduct an attitudinal survey and were told that you could allocate five questions to the measurement of respondents' social class, which five would you ask? How would you justify the questions that you included and the potential questions that you chose to exclude?

3. To what extent do class and gender politics overlap? In what ways are they quite different phenomena?

4. What arguments might you develop to support an *increase* in federal subsidies to "have-not" provinces? What arguments might you develop to support a *decrease* in such subsidies?

5. The proponents of liberalized continental and global trade argue that governments should not interfere with the decisions by firms about where to locate. What case might you develop for regional economic development incentives in the face of this argument? Does free trade spell the end of such incentives?

NOTES

1. Government of Canada, *Income Security and the Social Services* (Ottawa: 1970), pp. 60, 68.

2. For a conceptual and historical discussion of the Canadian welfare state, see Carolyn Tuohy, "Social Policy: Two Worlds," in Michael M. Atkinson, ed., *Governing Canada: Institutions and Public Policy* (Toronto: Harcourt Brace Jovanovich, 1993), pp. 275–306.

3. James R. Rice, "Social Policy, Economic Management, and Redistribution," in G. Bruce Doern and Peter Aucoin, eds., *Public Policy in Canada* (Toronto: Macmillan, 1979), p. 115.

4. Ibid., p. 117. For a discussion of business support for and opposition to the rudimentary welfare state put into place between 1930 and 1945, see Alvin Finkel, "Origins of the Welfare State in Canada," in

Leo Panitch, ed., *The Canadian State: Political Economy and Political Power* (Toronto: University of Toronto Press, 1977), pp. 344–70.

5. Donald Creighton, *The Passionate Observer: Selected Writings* (Toronto: McClelland and Stewart, 1980), p. 36.

6. Finkel, "Origins of the Welfare State," p. 345.

7. Rice, "Social Policy, Economic Management, and Redistribution," pp. 109–10.

8. Tuohy, "Social Policy," p. 275.

9. Ibid., p. 282.

10. In 1993 the Child Tax Benefit replaced Family Allowances.

11. Government hospital insurance was first introduced by the CCF Saskatchewan government in 1944.

12. Richard M. Bird, in collaboration with Meyer W. Bucovetsky and David K. Foot, *The Growth of Public Sector Employment in Canada* (Montreal: Institute for Research on Public Policy, 1979), pp. 9 and 23. The growth of social spending as a proportion of GDP then levelled off in the late 1970s and early 1980s. See Tuohy, "Social Policy," p. 280.

13. Bird, *The Growth of Public Sector Employment*, p. 23.

14. Drew Fagan, "Tax Promises Hard to Keep," *The Globe and Mail*, August 31, 1993, p. A6.

15. Bird, *The Growth of Public Sector Employment*, p. 49.

16. Ibid., p. 11.

17. Ibid., p. 19.

18. Ingrid Bryan, *Economic Policies in Canada* (Toronto: Butterworths, 1982), p. 188.

19. Statistics Canada, *Income Distribution in Canada* (Ottawa: May 1984).

20. W. Irwin Gillespie, *The Redistribution of Income in Canada* (Toronto: Gage, 1980), p. 173.

21. Ibid., p. 169.

22. Joan St. Laurent, "Income Maintenance Programs and Their Effect on Income Distribution in Canada," in John Harp and John R. Hofley, eds., *Structured Inequality in Canada* (Scarborough: Prentice-Hall, 1980), p. 430.

23. Donald Smiley, "Reflections on Cultural Nationhood and Political Community in Canada," in R. Kenneth Carty and W. Peter Ward, eds., *Entering the Eighties: Canada in Crisis* (Toronto: Oxford University Press, 1980), p. 37.

24. Edward Greenspon, "The Incredible, Shrinking Middle Class," *The Globe and Mail*, July 31, 1993, p. D1.

25. Ibid.

26. Ibid., p. D5.

27. Fagan, "Tax Promises," p. A6.

28. For example, see Wallace Clement, *The Canadian Corporate Elite: An Analysis of Economic Power* (Toronto: McClelland and Stewart, 1975); and John Porter, *The Vertical Mosaic* (Toronto: University of Toronto Press, 1965).

29. National Council of Welfare, *Poverty Profile Update for 1991* (Ottawa: Winter 1993), p. 2.

30. Geoffrey York, "Lower Poverty Line Urged," *The Globe and Mail*, June 9, 1993, p. A1.

31. National Council of Welfare, *1984 Poverty Lines* (Ottawa: Government of Canada, March 1984), p. 4. This document provides a good discussion of the technical complexities entailed in the construction of poverty lines.

32. Dennis Forcese, *The Canadian Class Structure*, 2nd ed. (Toronto: McGraw-Hill Ryerson, 1980), p. 64.

33. Ibid., p. 3.

34. National Council of Welfare, *Poverty Profile*, p. 6.

35. Bryan, *Economic Policies*, p. 191.

36. Ibid., p. 191.

37. National Council of Welfare, *Poverty Profile*, p. 22.

38. W. Irwin Gillespie, "On the Redistribution of Income in Canada," in Harp and Hofley, *Structured Inequality in Canada*, p. 36.

39. Peter S. Li, *Ethnic Inequality in a Class Society* (Toronto: Wall and Thompson, 1988), pp. 130–31.

40. St. Laurent, "Income Maintenance Programs," p. 435.

41. Finkel, "Origins of the Welfare State," p. 354.

42. Statistics Canada, 1984.

43. Gillespie, *The Redistribution of Income*, pp. 30–66 and 172.

44. Bryan, *Economic Policies in Canada*, p. 188.

45. Canada's only general strike began in Winnipeg in May 1919, with a strike in the metal and building trades over wages and union recognition. The Winnipeg Trades and Labour Council then called for a general strike in support of the metal and building trades. The city was all but paralyzed in a six-week strike. The strike climaxed with, and was brought to a close by, a clash between parading strikers and police on "Bloody Sunday," June 21, in which two people were killed and scores injured.

46. Janine Brodie, *The Political Economy of Canadian Regionalism* (Toronto: Harcourt Brace Jovanovich, 1990), p. 3.

47. Forcese, *The Canadian Class Structure*, p. 153.

48. For example, see Clement, *The Canadian Corporate Elite*, and Dennis Olsen, "The State Elites," in Panitch, *The Canadian State*, pp. 199–224.

49. M. Janine Brodie and Jane Jenson, *Crisis, Challenge and Change: Party and Class in Canada* (Toronto: Methuen, 1980), p. 263.

50. Ibid., p. 287.

51. See Douglas McCready and Conrad Winn, "Redistributive Policy," in Conrad Winn and John McMenemy, *Political Parties in Canada* (Toronto: McGraw-Hill Ryerson, 1976), pp. 206–27.

52. This conclusion holds whether class is measured by occupation, education, occupational prestige, or subjective assessments of class position. For a detailed analysis of the relationship between social class and voting behaviour in the 1965, 1968, and 1974 general elections, see Harold D. Clarke, Jane Jenson, Lawrence Leduc, and Jon H. Pammett, *Political Choice in Canada* (Toronto: McGraw-Hill Ryerson, 1979), pp. 107–19. For supporting evidence see Donald Blake, "The Measurement of Regionalism in Canadian Voting Patterns," *Canadian Journal of Political Science*, 5 (1972), pp. 55–81; and Jane Jenson, "Party Systems," in David J. Bellamy, Jon H. Pammett, and Donald C. Rowat, eds., *The Provincial Political Systems: Comparative Essays* (Toronto: Methuen, 1976), pp. 118–31.

53. Brodie and Jenson, *Crisis, Challenge and Change*, p. 299.

54. Their argument is developed at length in *Crisis, Challenge and Change*. A shorter synopsis appears as "The Party System," in Michael S. Whittington and Glen Williams, eds., *Canadian Politics in the 1980s*, 2nd ed. (Toronto: Methuen, 1984), pp. 252–70.

55. Brodie and Jenson, *Crisis, Challenge and Change*, p. 8.

56. Ibid., p. 11.

57. Ibid., p. 3.

58. Leo A. Johnson, "The Development of Class in Canada in the Twentieth Century," in Harp and Hofley, *Structured Inequality in Canada*, p. 99.

59. For some contrary evidence, see John Leggett, "The Persistence of Working-Class Consciousness in Vancouver," in John Allan Fry, ed., *Economy, Class and Social Reality* (Toronto: Butterworths, 1979), pp. 241–62.

60. E.M. Schreiber, "Class Awareness and Class Voting in Canada," *Canadian Review of Sociology and Anthropology*, 17:1 (1980), p. 37.

61. Variable 1383 in "The 1974–1979–1980 Canadian National Elections and Quebec Referendum Panel Study," Harold Clarke, Jane Jenson, Lawrence LeDuc, and Jon Pammett, principal investigators.

62. For a discussion of measurement problems, see Forcese, *The Canadian Class Structure*, pp. 14–20.

63. J. Goyder and P. Pineo, "The Accuracy of Self Assessment of Social Status," *Canadian Review of Sociology and Anthropology*, 14:2 (May 1977), p. 236.

64. Li, *Ethnic Inequality*, p. 130.

65. Anselm L. Strauss, *The Context of Social Mobility: Ideology and Theory* (Chicago: Aldine, 1971), p. 250.

66. Forcese, *The Canadian Class Structure*, p. 95.

67. Li, *Ethnic Inequality*, p. 131.

68. Greenspon, "The Incredible, Shrinking Middle Class," p. D5.

69. Herbert F. Quinn, *The Union Nationale: A Study in Quebec Nationalism* (Toronto: University of Toronto Press, 1963), pp. 192–93.

70. John Richards and Larry Pratt, *Prairie Capitalism: Power and Influence in the New West* (Toronto: McClelland and Stewart, 1979), p. 5.

71. Richard Simeon, "Regionalism and Canadian Political Institutions," in Richard Schultz, Orest M. Kruhlak, and John C. Terry, eds., *The Canadian Political Process*, 3rd ed. (Toronto: Holt, Rinehart and Winston, 1979), p. 294.

72. In the early part of this century, Canadian socialists themselves were often mired in imported models and ideas that had little relevance to

Canadian experience. It has only been more recently that socialism has become "a viable and distinctive element in Canadian political thought." Norman Penner, *The Canadian Left: A Critical Analysis* (Scarborough: Prentice-Hall, 1977), p. 260.

73. Donald V. Smiley, *Canada in Question: Federalism in the Eighties*, 3rd ed. (Toronto: McGraw-Hill Ryerson, 1980).

74. Anthony Careless, *Initiative and Response: The Adaptation of Canadian Federalism to Regional Economic Development* (Montreal: McGill-Queen's University Press, 1977), p. 169.

75. See ibid., p. 166, for a discussion.

76. Unconditional grants have no federal "strings" attached. The money can be spent as the provinces see fit, without the necessity of meeting federal program conditions or spending priorities.

77. James J. Rice and Michael J. Prince, "Lowering the Safety Net and Weakening the Bonds of Nationhood: Social Policy in the Mulroney Years," in Susan D. Phillips, ed., *How Ottawa Spends: A More Democratic Canada ...?* (Ottawa: Carleton University Press, 1993), p. 389.

78. For a discussion of the impact of higher oil revenues on equalization, see I.A. McDougall, *Marketing Canada's Energy* (Toronto: James Lorimer, 1983), pp. 66ff.

79. T.W. Acheson, "The Maritimes and 'Empire Canada,'" in David Jay Bercuson, ed., *Canada and the Burden of Unity* (Toronto: Macmillan, 1977), p. 103. See also Donald V. Smiley, *Canada in Question: Federalism in the Seventies*, 2nd ed. (Toronto: McGraw-Hill Ryerson, 1976), p. 192.

80. Frank MacKinnon, "Prince Edward Island: Big Engine, Little Body," in Martin Robin, ed., *Canadian Provincial Politics* (Scarborough: Prentice-Hall, 1972), p. 256.

81. H.G. Thorburn, *Planning and the Economy: Building Federal–Provincial Consensus* (Toronto: James Lorimer, 1984), p. 150.

82. For a discussion of DREE see Careless, *Initiative and Response*.

83. Bryan, *Economic Policies*, p. 210.

84. Ibid., p. 211.

85. *The Calgary Sun*, December 6, 1988, p. 4.

86. In 1976 the Department of Veterans Affairs was moved from Ottawa to a new $50 million headquarters in Charlottetown.

87. Herman Bakvis, *Federalism and the Organization of Political Life: Canada in Comparative Perspective* (Kingston: Institute of Intergovernmental Relations, Queen's University, 1981), p. 44.

88. Richard W. Phidd and G. Bruce Doern, *The Politics and Management of Canadian Economic Policy* (Toronto: Macmillan, 1978), p. 317.

89. T.J. Courchene, "Interprovincial Migration and Economic Adjustment," *Canadian Journal of Economics*, 3 (1970), pp. 550–76; and Economic Council of Canada, *Living Together: A Study of Regional Disparities* (Ottawa: Supply and Services, 1977).

90. Bryan, *Economic Policies*, p. 207.

91. Larry Pratt, "The State and Province-building: Alberta's Development Strategy," in Panitch, *The Canadian State*, pp. 133–62. For an examination of province-building in Ontario and Quebec, see the special issue of the *Journal of Canadian Studies*, 18:1 (Spring 1983).

92. Thorburn, *Planning and the Economy*, p. 120.

93. Brodie, *Canadian Regionalism*, p. 221.

CANADIAN–AMERICAN RELATIONS

Perhaps the most striking thing about Canada is that it is not part of the United States. Somehow more than half of North America has escaped being engulfed by its immensely more powerful neighbor although that neighbor has expanded fairly continuously in North America and else-where from 1776 to the present day.[1]

Canadian–American relations have been symbolized by the "world's long-est undefended border," a phrase that brings to mind a poem by one of America's foremost poets, Robert Frost. The narrator of "Mending Wall," who is helping his neighbour repair the stone wall separating their proper-ties, questions the very need for such a wall. The neighbour, however, insists that "good fences make good neighbours," and against this insistence Frost's narrator makes no headway:

Before I built a wall I'd ask to know
What I was walling in or walling out,
And to whom I was like to give offence.
Something there is that doesn't love a wall,
That wants it down. I could say "Elves" to him,
But it's not elves exactly, and I'd rather
He said it for himself. I see him there
Bringing a stone grasped firmly by the top
In each hand, like an old-stone savage armed.
He moves in darkness as it seems to me,
Not of woods only and the shade of trees.
He will not go behind his father's saying,
And he likes having thought of it so well
He says again, "Good fences make good neighbours."[2]

In this poem Frost has captured a fundamental tension in the Canadian–American relationship. The walls between the two countries are cumber-some and to some extent anachronistic; they are continually under attack by a continental economy, technological innovations such as the cable and satellite delivery of television signals, a continental approach to military defence, shared social movements such as environmentalism and femi-nism, and the massive flow of people and personal communications across the border. As a consequence, however, the building of "good fences" in order to maintain some independent national existence from the United States has been a major preoccupation of Canadian public policy-makers.

Maintaining those fences in a continental environment has proved to be an ongoing and daunting task.

Canadians, and English Canadians in particular, have not been sheltered from the American society by differences in language, race, or religion. Even the physical features that cross the continent have done more to separate Canadians from one another than from Americans. The international border has been breached by countless corporations, trade unions, service clubs, professional societies, sports leagues, and cultural organizations. With three out of four Canadians living within 150 kilometres of the border, and a majority living farther south than the 49th parallel, the United States is readily accessible. Canadians and Americans by the millions cross the border each year to visit friends, vacation, and pursue business interests. Kinship ties, fostered by extensive migration between the two countries, span the international border as readily as they do provincial borders within Canada. And yet because the border is so permeable, its defence has taken on great importance within the Canadian political system. Given the lack of physical, cultural, linguistic, religious, or racial defences, political defences have come to the fore.

The focus on political boundary maintenance that has been adopted for the present chapter runs a risk of painting Canadian–American relations in overly conflictual hues. Thus it should be stressed at the outset that the longstanding preoccupation with "good fences" does not arise because the Canadian–American relationship is predominantly ill-spirited or conflictual. To the contrary, it is precisely because the relationship has generally been so harmonious that boundary maintenance presents such a difficult challenge. It should also be stressed that boundary maintenance is more complex than simply building fences; it may take the form of active cooperation in order to ward off more damaging alternatives. In this respect, for example, some supporters of the Canada–U.S. Free Trade Agreement argued for closer economic integration in order to strengthen the Canadian economy and thereby shore up other distinctive features of Canadian culture, public policy, and social orientation. Boundary maintenance is therefore concerned with controlling rather than preventing American access to the Canadian society—with regulating access so as to maximize Canadian gains and minimize Canadian losses across the countless interchanges that take place between the two countries. Finally, it should be noted that governmental concern with boundary maintenance is subject to considerable variation over time and across parties. There is no question, for instance, that the Progressive Conservative government during the late 1980s and early 1990s was less preoccupied with boundary maintenance than its Liberal predecessor had been, nor that the tone of Canadian–American relations was much better as a consequence.

If Americans were not so much like Canadians, if there were not such a broad range of common values and interests, boundary maintenance would be far easier. It will, moreover, become an increasingly interesting and contentious aspect of public policy in the face of globalization and ideological change within Canada, both of which call into question the continued value of national boundaries as the 21st century approaches. If the proponents of globalization are correct, if international boundaries are becoming increasingly permeable throughout the world, then it will be more and more difficult to mount a reasoned defence for the continued existence of the border between such similar national communities.

HISTORICAL BACKGROUND

Over the past two centuries the United States has had a great impact on Canada while Canada has had a much more modest impact on the United States. This asymmetry, which is fundamental to an understanding of the Canadian–American relationship, reflects the basic demographic fact underlying that relationship—Americans outnumber Canadians by approximately ten to one.

The American War of Independence in 1776 created not one country but two, for it helped lay the foundations for Canada.[3] Of the approximately 100,000 United Empire Loyalists who fled the American Revolution, over 40,000 came north into an existing population of only 110,000 people. More than 30,000 settled in Nova Scotia, tripling the colony's population and spilling into New Brunswick, which was consequently established as a separate colony in 1784. Others formed the bedrock of what is now Ontario where their settlement led to the Constitutional Act of 1791, dividing what had been the single territory of Quebec into Upper and Lower Canada. In what is now Quebec, "the influx of Anglophone loyalists, pushed by expropriation or drawn by good farmland, changed Quebec once and for all from a homogeneous French-Canadian society to one with a prosperous and vocal English minority."[4] It is in this sense, then, that historian A.R.M. Lower has described Canada as a "by-product" of the American Revolution.[5]

The United Empire Loyalists—anti-American Americans—helped put in place the cornerstone of Canadian nationalism. As J.M.S. Careless explains, they

> represented a declaration of independence against the United States, a determination to live apart from that country in North America. As a result, they helped to create not only a new province [Ontario], but a new nation.[6]

By rejecting Britain, the Americans allowed Canadians to carve out a distinctive niche on the North American continent. Canadians stood apart by virtue of their attachment to things British and in particular by their attachment to parliamentary institutions and a deep aversion to republicanism. It should be stressed, however, that the emerging national division was based on more than ideological differences, for the American Revolution also raised fears of military conquest that were to remain with Canadians until Confederation. In 1776 John Adams, who was to become the second president of the United States, declared that "the Unanimous Voice of the Continent is Canada must be ours; Quebec must be taken."[7] In 1775 American forces had captured Montreal and, over the winter, had besieged Quebec until that garrison was relieved by the British fleet in the spring of 1776. Even with the subsequent withdrawal of American forces, the fear persisted that the Americans would not rest until the British had been expelled from the continent. The invitation in Article IV of the American Articles of Confederation, that Canada "join us in Congress and complete the American Union," was seen by Canadians more as a threat than as an act of generosity.

Thirty-seven years after the American Revolution, Canadians again found themselves at war with the United States. Although Britain and the United States were the principal players in the War of 1812, some of the fighting took place on Canadian soil as Americans invaded the Niagara Peninsula and burned the city of York (now Toronto), for which Washington was burnt in retaliation by the British. Former president Thomas Jefferson declared at the start of the conflict that "the annexation of Canada this year as far as the neighbourhood of Quebec will only be a mere matter of marching, and this will give us experience for the assault on Halifax next, and the final expulsion of England from the American continent."[8] As events turned out, it was not merely a matter of marching, and the American forces were repelled, but war nonetheless left a strong mark. The invading American forces had destroyed more than homes, barns, and crops: they had also destroyed any lingering sense among the United Empire Loyalists that the Loyalists were exiled Americans rather than British subjects and, in a nascent sense, Canadians. Despite the Rush-Bagot Convention of 1817, which demilitarized the Great Lakes, subsequent years saw the construction of the Rideau canal and an impressive string of military fortifications including Kingston's Fort Henry, the Quebec Citadel and its companion forts on the south shore at Lévis, and the Halifax Citadel.

The military threat from the United States remained dormant until the aftermath of the American Civil War when, as discussed in Chapter 2, it reappeared to play a significant role in Confederation. After 1867 the military threat subsided and then disappeared, to be replaced by new forms of American expansionism. The most immediate threat was in the largely unoccupied Canadian West as Americans spread westward and then, as free land disappeared, northward. The more general threat came from the American assertion of a "manifest destiny," which appeared to preclude sharing the continent with an independent Canada. In 1871 The Globe warned its readers that "we are divided only by an imaginary border

Manifest Destiny

The phrase "manifest destiny" was coined in 1845 by John L. O'Sullivan, an American journalist and diplomat. Writing in the *US Magazine and Democratic Review*, O'Sullivan described America's "manifest destiny to overspread the continent allotted by providence for the free development of our yearly multiplying millions."* The theme came to be applied with special force to the northern half of the continent:

- In 1867, the same year in which he acquired Alaska for the United States, Secretary of State W.H. Seward declared that "nature designs that this whole continent, not merely these thirty-six states, shall be, sooner or later, within the magic circle of the American Union."

- In 1889 James G. Blaine, U.S. Secretary of State, said that Canada was like "an apple on a tree just beyond reach. We may strive to grasp it, but the bough recedes from our hold just in proportion to our effort to catch it. Yet let it alone, and in due time it will fall into our hands."

- Champ Clark, Speaker of the U.S. House of Representatives, declared in 1911, "We are preparing to annex Canada.... I hope to see the day when the American flag will float on every square foot of British North American possessions clear to the North Pole."

Such American aspirations did not end with Speaker Clark. In 1952 Timothy Sheehan of Illinois proposed in the House of Representatives that the United States buy Canada from Great Britain! However, despite the American belief in a manifest destiny, the ten-to-one American edge in population, and the far greater economic and military power of the United States, Canadians ended up with more than half of the continent, albeit the colder part.

*Cited in Jonathon Green, compiler, *The Book of Political Quotes* (New York: McGraw-Hill, 1982), p. 59.

... from a people ... [who] have before now proved themselves aggressive—a people who believe in 'manifest destiny,' 'universal sovereignty,' and other ideas not very reassuring to their neighbours."[9] French-Canadian assessments were even harsher. Olivar Asselin declared that "the amiable Nation of Pirates which stole Texas, Cuba, Porto Rico and the Philippines cannot be depended upon to act justly towards a weaker nation,"[10] while

Henri Bourassa maintained that the United States was "waiting to gobble us up."[11]

As the 20th century unfolded, Canadian fears of absorption were replaced by anxieties over the growing American presence *within* Canada. Whereas in the past Britain had served as a counterweight to American influence in Canada, that role was now weakened as Britain's position in the international order declined, Canada shed its colonial ties, and the English-Canadian community diversified and drew away from its British roots. British investment in Canada was supplanted by American investment, trade with the United States far surpassed trade with Britain, and American cultural patterns began to prevail over those from the United Kingdom. By the 1960s, British influence on Canadian society had "evaporated."[12] Even by the end of the Second World War, the North Atlantic triangle formed by the United States, Britain, and Canada had been transformed. At least from the Canadian perspective, the Canadian–American side of the triangle was now dominant. The relationship between Canada and Great Britain had not only declined in relative importance, but had become increasingly irrelevant to the Canadian–American relationship. To an extent unknown in the past, Canada now faced the United States alone. This new continental relationship was highlighted in a speech to the Canadian Parliament by President John F. Kennedy on May 17, 1962:

> Geography has made us neighbours. History has made us partners. And necessity has made us allies. Those whom nature hath so joined together let no man put asunder.

If anything, however, history made the two countries antagonists rather than friends. As James Eayrs wrote in response to Kennedy's speech, "if they are friends today, it is in spite of history, not because of it."[13]

THE ECONOMIC RELATIONSHIP

In 1891, when Canadians were grappling with proposals for greater free trade between Canada and the United States, Goldwin Smith wrote what has become a classic statement of support for continental integration:

> Let any one scan the economical map of the North American continent with its adjacent waters, mark its northern zone abounding in minerals, in bituminous coal, in lumber, in fish, as well as in special farm products, brought in the north to hardier perfection, all of which the southern people have need: let him then look to its southern regions, the natural products of which as well as the manufactures produced in its wealthy centres of industry are needed by the people of the northern zone: he will see that the continent is an economic whole, and that to run a Customs line

*athwart it and try to sever its members from each other is to wage a des-
perate war against nature.*[14]

Smith's description of continentalism as a "force of nature" has become
common currency in discussions of Canadian–American relations. John
Holmes, for example, argues that "the threat of continentalization comes
not from governments but from forces beyond the control of governments."[15] James Eayrs asserts that the border between Canada and the
United States is political rather than geographic, that "what nature joined
together, Canadians have sought to sunder."[16] More recently, the "natural
forces" favouring continentalism have been supplemented in arguments for
free trade by the "forces of globalization," forces that are again portrayed as
falling beyond the control of governments. From wherever the pressures
for continentalism spring, they have been readily acknowledged as a fact of
Canadian life; the only matter of contention has been whether they should
be resisted or embraced. However, to address this question it is useful to
express the "force of nature" in the more prosaic language of trade flows,
tariff barriers, and foreign investment.

Continental Trade Flows

Britain was Canada's most important trading partner and primary source of
the nonresident investment capital needed to build the Canadian economy
in the early decades after Confederation. By the turn of the century, however, Britain was being rapidly replaced by the United States as Canada's
principal trading partner. Trade between the two continental neighbours
was facilitated by proximity, and by a complex and growing web of corporations spanning the border. Today, Canada and the United States are each
other's largest trading partners, with Canadian exports to the United States
exceeding $100 billion per annum and American exports to Canada run-
ning close to that figure. The United States accounts for approximately 70
percent of Canadian exports, with approximately the same proportion of
Canadian imports originating in the United States.

Of course, it is a mistake to discuss "continental" trade without bringing Mexico into play, although at the present time Canadian trade with
Mexico is minuscule compared to trade with the United States. For every
dollar in goods and services that Canada exports to Mexico, $235 in goods
and services is exported to the United States. For every dollar in goods and
services that Canada imports from Mexico, $34 is imported from the
United States. (American imports from Mexico amount to approximately
30 percent of American imports from Canada; American exports to Mexico amount to approximately 39 percent of American exports to Canada.)
Whether these proportions will be significantly altered by the North
American Free Trade Agreement (NAFTA) remains to be seen. In the short
term, the most immediate impact of NAFTA is likely to come from any

Trading Perceptions

In early 1989, Decima Research conducted a survey of 1,000 Canadian and 1,000 American respondents for *Maclean's* (July 3, 1989). Not unexpectedly, the survey showed that Canadians were more aware of the Canadian–American trading relationship than were Americans. For example, 97 percent of the Canadian respondents were "aware that Canada and the United States had recently signed a Free Trade Agreement," an awareness shared by only 57 percent of the American respondents. When Canadians were asked to identify Canada's largest trading partner, 83 percent correctly named the United States, 9 percent named Japan, and 1 percent each named China and Europe. When American respondents were asked to identify the United States' largest trading partner, only 12 percent correctly identified Canada; 69 percent named Japan, 3 percent named China, and 2 percent each named Britain, the Soviet Union, and Europe.

impact it might have on existing provisions of the FTA and on locational decisions by American investors.

Foreign trade is more important in proportionate terms to the Canadian economy than it is to the American economy. Canada's exports accounted for approximately 28 percent of its Gross Domestic Product compared to approximately 13 percent for Japan and only 7 percent for the United States. Even in absolute terms, Canada is a major player in world trade; in 1987 Canadian exports amounted to 43 percent of Japan's exports and 39 percent of American exports. This heavy reliance on trade means that the Canadian economy is very dependent upon the condition of foreign markets in general and the condition of American markets in particular. If the American economy and therefore the demand for Canadian imports softens, the impact on Canada can be severe. Hence the expression, "when the American economy catches cold, the Canadian economy catches pneumonia."

One of the chronic problems in Canadian–American trade has arisen from the imbalance between natural resources and semiprocessed goods, on the one hand, and manufactured products, on the other. While the former have constituted the bulk of Canadian exports to the United States, the latter constitute the great bulk of Canadian imports. This imbalance was addressed by the Canada–United States Automotive Products Trade Agreement, or Autopact, of 1965. Prior to the Autopact, the Canadian automobile industry was ailing with short production lines, inefficient plants, competition from European producers, and a heavy reliance on

Constable, *Union Art Services*; reprinted from Guy Badeaux, ed., *Portfoolio 8* (Toronto: Macmillan, 1992), p. 57.

imported American parts. The Autopact addressed these problems by opening up the American market to Canadian plants and thereby allowing longer production lines, more specialization, and greater efficiency. The Autopact, which created a qualified free trade arrangement for automobiles and automobile parts, greatly increased Canadian–American vehicle trade, although the larger volume of trade in automotive parts was less affected.

Tariff Protection

Trade between Canada and the United States has been the subject of ongoing and often intense political debate in Canada. In 1849 it was entangled with the annexation riots in Montreal, and the feared termination of the 1854 Reciprocity Treaty played a major role in the movement for Confederation. The debate has turned historically on the degree to which tariffs should be imposed on imports from the United States and, more contemporarily, on the extent to which a variety of nontariff barriers should impinge upon the Canadian–American trading relationship. In 1879 the

Government of Canada erected a 30 percent tariff wall between Canada and the United States in order to achieve a number of objectives:

> to provide for growth of Canadian manufacturing; to provide revenue to finance transportation development needed to encourage western settlement; to retard emigration to the United States by maintaining higher wages in Canada; to prevent dumping of foreign goods in Canadian markets; to encourage interprovincial trade; and to provide a bargaining chip for tariff negotiations with the United States.[17]

Tariffs, the construction of a transcontinental railway system, and the settlement of the prairie West formed the interlocking pillars of Sir John A. Macdonald's *National Policy*. The tariff wall, it was hoped, would promote an east–west axis for the Canadian economy to counteract the north–south pull of continental forces, an axis that would sustain the transcontinental railway system then being put in place. In introducing the tariff legislation, the Minister of Finance declared that "the time has arrived when we are to decide whether we will simply be hewers of wood and drawers of water." With the National Policy, the choice was made; an industrialized economy was to be developed behind the protective tariff wall.

The tariff wall was designed to raise the price of American imports to the point where goods manufactured in Canada would be competitive; it was to act as a barrier to imported goods and not as a barrier to American investment. Indeed, the tariff actually encouraged foreign investment as American firms wishing to sell to the Canadian market found it more profitable to establish branch plants in Canada, and thus enjoy the protection of the tariff wall, than to try to export goods to Canada from American plants. (American investment was also promoted by proximity, profitability, the desire for a secure source of raw materials, and the basic similarity of the two countries, which reduced the anxieties attendant upon investing outside one's own country.) Thus the National Policy laid the foundations for an American-dominated branch-plant economy and, as a consequence, for the extensive intrusion of American labour unions into Canada. The former outcome was by no means inadvertent; Canadian governments and private organizations actively courted American branch plants through vigorous promotional activities in the United States.[18] The goal was a healthy economy in Canada rather than a healthy Canadian economy; the question as to who owned Canada's industrial plant was not to become a concern until much later.

The National Policy tariff structure provided the basic framework for Canadian–American trade well into the 20th century. Although there were abortive attempts in 1891 and 1911 to dismantle the tariff component of the National Policy, attempts discussed in Chapter 9, the framework remained essentially intact. Then, following the end of the Second World War, both Canada and the United States participated in a collective move by Western industrialized countries to reduce tariff and nontariff barriers to international trade. Both countries are signatories to the General Agreement on Tariffs and Trade (GATT) and have reduced bilateral tariffs as part of more global tariff reductions negotiated through GATT. With the 1987 completion of the Tokyo round of GATT tariff reductions, approximately 80 percent of Canadian–American trade was tariff-free, and the tariff rate on the remaining 20 percent had been significantly reduced; the average tariff on imports from the United States was approximately 10 percent while the average American tariff on imports from Canada was approximately 5 percent. The remaining tariff-protected trade then became the target of the Canada–U.S. Free Trade Agreement, which will virtually eliminate tariffs on Canadian–American trade when fully implemented in 1999. In this sense, then, the FTA climaxed, although it did not bring to a close, a long and often very contentious political debate on Canadian tariff policy with respect to the United States, a debate that still ripples through discussions of NAFTA and analyses of the long-term impact of the FTA on the Canadian economy. It should be stressed, however, that changes in continental trade policy have been in large part a response to broader changes in the international trading environment. It should be stressed in addition that a multitude of nontariff barriers to trade remain, including quotas, technical standards, valuation and dumping procedures, and government procurement practices, many of which also pose significant barriers to interprovincial trade within Canada.[19]

Foreign Investment

At the turn of the century British investment in Canada surpassed that from the United States by a margin of nearly six to one. Then, with the First World War came an acceleration of American investment abroad, particularly in Canada, coupled with a parallel decline in British overseas investment. By 1926, American investment in Canada surpassed British investment; by the early 1960s it accounted for more than 80 percent of all foreign investment in Canada, and by the mid-1980s it surpassed British investment in Canada by a margin of more than eight to one. In 1985, 75.5 percent of all direct foreign investment in Canada originated in the United States, 9.3 percent in the United Kingdom, 2.9 percent in West Germany, 2.4 percent in the Netherlands, and 2.1 percent in Japan. American-controlled firms accounted for 53.6 percent of the assets, 66.9 percent of the revenue, and 65.8 percent of the profits of all foreign-controlled corporations in Canada.[20]

Here it should be noted parenthetically that the decline in British investment reflected a general deterioration in the place of Britain and the British Empire in the international order. As a consequence of both this decline and the ongoing continental pull of the United States, Canada's economic, cultural, and strategic focus shifted to the United States. That shift, and the altered international balance between Britain and the United States that lay behind it, had an important impact on English-Canadian nationalism. In its formative stages, English-Canadian nationalism had enthusiastically embraced imperial themes, drawing its confidence and expansionist thrust from Canada's tie to the British Empire.[21] Thus, Denis Smith argues, "as the Empire faded away in the fifties and sixties and as Britain turned inward to agonize over her own domestic problems, English Canada lost one—perhaps the most profound—of her spiritual props."[22]

The extent of foreign ownership in Canada, which far surpasses that in any comparable industrialized country, is highly variable across sectors of the economy. Foreign investment has been most prevalent in the manufacturing, mining, and energy sectors, and least prevalent in textiles, transportation, communications, and financial services. The extent of foreign ownership can also be quite variable over relatively short periods of time. Between 1985 and 1988, for example, Canadian ownership of the oil and gas industry slipped from 48.2 percent to 42.5 percent while Canadian control slipped from 42.7 percent to 34 percent.[23] Overall, foreign investors control approximately a third of the assets of the leading 500 economic enterprises in Canada and, among nonfinancial corporations, capture approximately 30 percent of Canadian sales and profits.[24] Finally, and as with most things Canadian, foreign investment is not evenly distributed across the provinces. Foreign investment has the greatest impact on the provincial taxable income of Alberta and the least impact on Prince Edward Island.

Foreign control of the Canadian economy reached a historic high in 1971 when 37 percent of the nonfinancial corporations were foreign (largely American) controlled. Not coincidentally, this period witnessed a virtual flood of publications championing economic nationalism. The forerunner was *Lament for a Nation* (1965) in which George Grant not only mourned the end of Canada as a sovereign nation, but elevated anti-Americanism to a conservative virtue in the face of an advancing continental and indeed global technological culture. In the early 1970s nationalists advanced the argument that foreign investment not only threatened Canada's political sovereignty and the survival of a distinctive national identity, but that it also *harmed* the Canadian economy. Book after book hammered away at the belief that foreign investment was beneficial. Works such as D.W. Carr's *Recovering Canada's Nationhood* (1971), James Laxer's *The Energy Poker Game* (1970), Kari Levitt's *Silent Surrender* (1970), Ian Lumsden's *Close the 49th Parallel Etc.* (1970), W.H. Pope's *The Elephant and the Mouse* (1971), Abraham Rotstein's *The Precarious Homestead* (1973), Rotstein and Gary Lax's *Independence: The Canadian Challenge* (1972), Philippe Sykes's *Sellout: The Giveaway of Canada's Resources* (1973), and John W. Warnock's *Partner to Behemoth* (1970) contributed to the nationalist cause. It is interesting to note that this nationalist outpour-

Who Is To Blame?

While nationalists have lamented the American domination of the Canadian economy, they have placed the blame squarely on Canadian rather than American shoulders:

- Donald Creighton (historian): "Canadians, themselves, half converted to the belief that economic development is the only sure road to happiness, have grown accustomed to selling out their birthright for a quick buck."

- Lester Pearson (while Leader of the Official Opposition in 1960): "The dependence of Canada on the United States market for trade and on U.S. capital for development is an increasing threat to our independence.... But, if we lose our national purpose and identity, it will be by our own default, not by the design of anybody else."

- Myrna Kostash (author and journalist) describes Canada as "a nation whoring on the sidelines of the world's biggest dollar bonanza while plotting all the time a cultural get-away that will astound the Pharisees and renew the hope of the exploited everywhere."

- The late W.L. Morton (historian) argued that the present degree of American investment "is solely the work and fault of Canadians, particularly of provinces and regions competing for foreign investment in any guise and at any cost. These Canadian harlots, having sold their bodies usually at a cheaper price than they could have got, will find they have also sold their souls."

- George Bain (*The Globe and Mail*): "If there is one thing that worries Canadians more than economic domination, it is that someone, sometime, will try to do something about it."

- Minutes after endorsing a United Auto Workers' resolution calling for Canadian content restrictions on foreign cars, the town council of Tilbury, Ontario, voted to buy a Japanese-made tractor because the dealer knocked $4,500 off the regular price.

ing, written largely by English-Canadian academics, coincided with the Quiet Revolution in Quebec. "Maîtres chez nous," the slogan of the Quiet Revolution, was also the implicit slogan for the economic nationalists of English Canada.

Economic nationalists rejected the argument that freer trade with the United States would benefit the Canadian economy. While Canadian firms would have access to the American market, American firms with their longer production lines and lower per unit costs would gain access to the Canadian market. In the exchange, Canadian-owned firms would be swamped while Canadian-based American subsidiaries would be unlikely to enter the American market. As Peter Newman argued:

> It is Alice in Wonderland economics to expect branch plants in Canada to compete with their U.S. parent companies on their home ground. Indeed, the reverse phenomenon is more likely: free trade will encourage the dismantling of Canadian branch plants.[25]

Of particular concern to economic nationalists was the fear that foreign ownership would dilute Canada's *political* control over its economy. From the nationalist perspective, the economy is an instrument for the attainment of not only individual consumptive goals, but also collective, social goals. Economic policy can be used to redistribute income among individuals or across regions, to promote employment, or to create nationally distinct social institutions and public services. However, to the extent that the Canadian economy is integrated into a continental scheme of things, the ability of governments to direct the economy toward social ends may be weakened. It is in this sense, Kari Levitt argued, that continentalism "is fundamentally destructive of Canadian unity because it rejects the maintenance of a national community as an end in itself."[26]

The fears of economic nationalists on this count were crystallized in an often quoted passage by George Ball, the Undersecretary of State for presidents Lyndon Johnson and John Kennedy. Canada, Ball believed, was fighting a "rearguard action against the inevitable":

> Sooner or later, commercial imperatives will bring about free movement of all goods back and forth across our long border; and when that occurs, or even before it does, it will become unmistakably clear that countries with economies so inextricably entwined must also have free movement of the other vital factors of production—capital, services and labor. The result will inevitably be substantial economic integration, which will require for its full realization a progressively expanding area of common political decision.[27]

For economic nationalists, it was this "expanding area of common political decision" that posed the threat. As Ian Wahn concluded in 1970:

> Oh sure, all our political paraphernalia would continue—the changing of the guard, the opening of Parliament—and it wouldn't be entirely form. There would be some substance to it. We could make all sorts of useful

regulations, just as municipal governments do. We'd be doing all sorts of useful things in the Parliament of Canada, but they wouldn't be the vital, important, basic things. The decision on those things would be made south of the border.[28]

In the twenty years since Ball's prediction and Wahn's sardonic observation, there has been little movement toward an expanding area of common political decision, although the same fears played a central role in the 1988 FTA debate, and in the more subdued NAFTA debate, as opponents charged that environmental and social program standards would be effectively set in the United States. The intervening years actually witnessed an overall decline in direct foreign investment in, and ownership of, the Canadian economy. The intervening years also witnessed significant moves to assert greater political control over the economy, and then to relax such control. Here FIRA, the Foreign Investment Review Agency, provided the symbolic centrepiece for an ongoing debate.

FIRA's creation had been recommended in the 1972 Gray Report[29] as an essential response to expanding foreign ownership. The agency was put into place in 1974 in response to growing nationalist pressure and to growing political pressure on the Liberal minority government by the federal New Democrats. The intent of FIRA was to screen rather than to block foreign investment, to ensure that takeovers and new investment were of "significant benefit" to Canada. As the Minister of Finance explained to a New York audience when FIRA was introduced, "it's not a dam, it's a filter."[30] Whether FIRA in fact served as an effective gatekeeper was a matter of considerable debate. While some claimed that the only firm likely to be denied entry by FIRA would have been Murder Incorporated, FIRA's regulations did force foreign investors to address the issue of Canadian benefit. They also generated a good deal of red tape, confusion as to what was and what was not of "significant benefit" to Canada, and delays of up to two years in the approval of investment proposals.

FIRA was not unique to Canada, as most countries, including the United States, imposed analogous if less formalized restrictions on foreign investment.[31] Nevertheless, for Canadian nationalists FIRA served as an important symbol of political control over the economy. For those with a more continentalist orientation, it served as an equally important symbol of misguided nationalism and excessive state intervention in the economy. In the early 1980s, as the Canadian economy worsened and unemployment rose, FIRA's nationalist mandate was subordinated to the overarching goal of maintaining a healthy economy. The welcome mat was thrown out to any foreign investment that might generate jobs; in the face of growing unemployment the fear was not that foreign investors would flood into Canada, but rather that they might not come at all. After the 1984 election, FIRA was renamed Investment Canada by the new Progressive Conservative government, and its primary mandate became to attract rather than to screen foreign investment. With the passage of the FTA, restrictions on American investment and the legacy of FIRA have been all but abolished. American investors are assured of "national treatment" no less favourable than that extended to domestic investors. Apart from some exceptions for cultural industries, there is no screening of most new investment, no screening of direct acquisitions valued at less than $50 million, and no new policies on minimum levels of Canadian equity holdings.

A second important nationalist initiative came with the creation of Petro-Canada in 1974 and the introduction of the National Energy Program in 1980. Petro-Canada, a crown corporation, became a major presence in all aspects of the oil industry from service stations to exploration in the Arctic and off the East Coast. The NEP was introduced to increase Canadian ownership of the oil industry from approximately 10 percent in 1980 to a target of 50 percent in 1990, to protect Canadians from rapidly rising world oil prices, and to promote energy self-sufficiency. While FIRA had sought to regulate foreign investment, the NEP constituted a more dramatic assertion of Canadian sovereignty in an important sector of the economy. It was introduced at a time when the new Reagan administration in the United States was attempting to reduce state intervention in the economy, and thus not surprisingly it ruffled ideological feathers in both countries and contributed to a general deterioration in Canadian–American relations.[32] American oil interests were upset at the NEP "back-in" provisions, which allowed Petro-Canada to acquire up to 25 percent ownership in frontier and offshore oil leases held by multinational corporations. These provisions were seen as confiscatory and were attacked because they were a post facto change in the rules governing foreign investment in Canada. The companies argued that if they came into Canada under one set of rules, the rules should not be changed once the investment was in place, a guarantee that has now been provided by the FTA. The NEP was also criticized vociferously by western Canadians and particularly Albertans as a federal raid on provincial resource revenues.

In drawing this discussion to a close, note should be made of the association between economic nationalism and the political left. Just as the case for continentalism is a case for a market-driven economic order in which the flow of capital, resources, and labour would be unimpaired by political constraints, the case for economic nationalism is a case for harnessing the economy to broader national and social goals. The association was central to George Grant's argument in *Lament for a Nation*:

> *After 1940, nationalism [in Canada] had to go hand in hand with some measure of socialism. Only nationalism could provide the political incentive for planning; only planning could restrain the victory of continentalism.[33]*

Or again, later in the same work:

> *No small country can depend for its existence on the loyalty of its capitalists. International interests may require the sacrifice of the lesser loyalty of patriotism. Only in dominant nations is the loyalty of capitalists ensured.*[34]

At the extreme, economic nationalism can be seen as a means of creating a more socialist economic order.[35] In its more moderate forms, economic nationalism prompts government intervention in the economy in order to regulate foreign investment and to ensure that such investment serves the national interest. Thus the debate over economic nationalism becomes entangled in a broader ideological debate over the appropriate role of the state in the economy, and in a broader political debate over how and by whom the national interest is to be defined. Economic nationalists have argued that foreign ownership would dilute Canadians' political control over their economy, but this result is a benefit rather than a problem to free-market continentalists who object to political interference in economic decisions. Indeed, free trade is supported in part because it will make state intervention in the economy more difficult.

The political tension between continentalism and economic nationalism will likely endure even in the wake of the FTA and NAFTA. With the trade agreements in place, the terms of debate will shift to an examination of the free trade balance sheet: Has American investment increased or decreased as a consequence, has employment risen or fallen, has the economy prospered or not? When, in 1968, Prime Minister Trudeau was asked if he was worried about the influx of American capital, he replied: "Well, I am not worried in the sense that I don't worry over something which is somewhat inevitable, and I think the problem of economic domination is somewhat inevitable ... these are the facts of life, and they don't worry me." In this respect at least, Trudeau did not reflect an important strand of Canadian political thought; economic nationalists have worried about and will continue to debate the inevitability of economic domination.[36] The emergence of the National Party in the 1993 election provides but one illustration of that continuing concern and debate.

CULTURAL NATIONALISM

Canada's nascent culture in the 19th century was shielded from American influence by the primitive state of communications technology. In addition, the political barrier between the two countries served as a reasonably effective cultural barrier; the main cultural influences followed political loyalties and flowed from Great Britain rather than from the United States. However, with the introduction of mass circulation magazines, wire ser-

Raeside, *Times-Colonist* (Victoria); reprinted from Guy Badeaux, ed., *Portfoolio 8* (Toronto: Macmillan, 1992), p. 58.

vices, motion pictures, records, radio, and television, and with the above-noted decline of British influence in Canadian affairs, the greater proximity of the United States was brought to bear on increasingly permeable cultural barriers. Cultural influences flowed from south to north, but *not* from north to south, through a multitude of channels. The air waves in particular, which were at first envisaged as "highways of national cultural integration," became "agents of denationalization by serving as roadways for foreign, largely American, cultural values."[37]

The response to American influence in the cultural realm was patterned after the response in the economic realm. Barriers were erected to shelter the Canadian culture and, more specifically, Canadian cultural artisans including authors, publishers, film and television producers, recording artists, and directors of dance and theatre. The intent was to create a protected domestic market for the producers of cultural artifacts, although in this case there was no anticipation that American artisans would leap the "tariff wall" as American manufacturing firms had done by establishing branch plants. Canadian content regulations for radio and television broadcasts provided a protective barrier for Canadian performers; "unfair" foreign competition was legislatively restricted although by no means excluded. It was hoped that a healthy cultural "industry" would flourish behind the protective wall of cultural tariffs, and that as a consequence a distinctive national culture would survive and even flourish.

For Canadian nationalists the cultural threat from the United States has been no less important than the economic threat, as the following quote from John Holmes illustrates:

> We are in danger of becoming a zombie nation, our physical structure intact but our souls and minds gone abroad. Having gloriously resisted with our loyal muskets the Yankee invader on the slopes of Quebec and Queenston, Canada may well be conquered by American television.[38]

While it can be argued although not assumed that foreign investment brings in its wake employment and economic growth, the benefits of the American mass culture are more elusive and contentious. As a result, nationalists have contested the American presence on the cultural front with greater moral conviction than they have possessed on the economic front.

Two principal themes of Canadian cultural nationalism were established by a series of royal commissions conducted during the 1950s and early 1960s: "that Canada's capacity for meaningful nationhood is somehow being thwarted and undermined by the proximity and potency of the cultural output of the United States," and that state intervention was essential "to create and support a countervailing cultural force to the unrelenting flow of Americana across the border."[39] Such intervention took the form of sticks and carrots. The "sticks" were regulations restricting the influx of American culture into Canada, regulations facilitated by the 1932 Supreme Court decision in the *Radio Case*, which gave jurisdiction over the air waves to the federal government. Examples of regulatory initiatives include the 1968 establishment of the Canadian Radio-Television Commission; the Canadian content regulations that the CRTC (now the Canadian Radio-television and Telecommunications Commission) spawned; the elimination of tax deductions for firms advertising in the Canadian edition of *Time* (now defunct as a consequence) or on American border television stations transmitting into Canada; the "Baie Comeau" policy to promote Canadian ownership in the publishing industry;[40] and immigration restrictions that require artistic companies and universities seeking to hire outside Canada to demonstrate first that no suitable Canadian candidates are available. The "carrots" generally involved financial support for cultural artisans. Examples here would include the 1957 creation of the Canada Council, public funding for the CBC, and current requirements that cable television firms plough some of their revenue back into the production of Canadian programming. There is little doubt that the CBC has been the flagship for all such endeavours, which explains in part why any attempt by the federal government to reduce the CBC's funding sets off such a strong nationalist response.

"...To comply with government regulations this picture will be displayed for 7 minutes and 32 seconds to bring our Canadian content to the required 60 percent. Please do not adjust your set. To comply with ..."

Len Norris, *19th Annual*; originally published in the *Sun* (Vancouver), February 14, 1970.

Policies to shelter Canadian culture face serious technological constraints. Canadians living in major metropolitan centres close to the American border have for decades been able to receive American radio and television signals. Now, for a modest fee, most Canadians have access to unimpaired American programming through cable television. While the content of cable television can be regulated to a degree by restricting the number of channels carrying American programming, recent advances in cable capacity and satellite delivery threaten the survival of any form of Canadian content regulation. The proliferation of channels has fragmented an already small viewing audience, and has further reduced the market penetration of Canadian broadcasters, both public and private. In the future, as in the past, technological innovation is likely to progressively erode cultural barriers between Canada and the United States.

At this point it is still difficult to determine what impact, if any, the FTA will have on Canadian culture and on the politics of cultural nationalism. Article 2005, paragraph 1, of the agreement states that "cultural industries are exempt from the provisions of this Agreement," but paragraph 2 goes on to state that, "notwithstanding any other provision of this agreement, a Party may take measure of equivalent commercial effect in response to actions that would have been inconsistent with this Agreement but for paragraph 1." In short, American economic retaliation is not precluded. The Canadian supporters of the FTA have argued that the agreement addresses only goods and services, not culture, and therefore that the protection of Canadian culture is not threatened. Opponents have argued that the exemption of cultural industries does not mean that the agreement will be without cultural impact. For their part, Americans insist that "goods and services" includes culture, and that cultural industries cannot be distinguished analytically from other forms of commercial enterprise.

It is important to note in this context that American cultural influences flow almost entirely from private sources. The American government has not been involved except for its role in the negotiation of the FTA and except, on rare occasions, when its help has been enlisted by private American interests affected by Canadian regulations. (Border television broadcasters provide an example of the latter case.) It should also be noted that restrictions on the influx of American culture necessarily restrict the freedom of Canadians to watch, read, and listen to whatever they like, just as public support for cultural industries necessarily entails government intervention in the marketplace. Cultural nationalism thus protects collective values—the survival of a distinctive national culture—through the curtailment of individual freedom, much as Quebec's language policy protects a collective value—the survival of the French language—through similarly modest restrictions on individual freedom. The limited tolerance of Canadians for such curtailment in turn limits the potential height of cultural barriers between Canada and the United States. Cultural barriers in this sense are analogous to economic tariffs; we all pay a modest price in terms of restricted access while a few—recording artists, film and television producers, actors—reap substantial economic benefits. This creates both a vigorous lobby for cultural nationalism and countervailing consumer pressure for freer trade in cultural artifacts.

Unfortunately, more effective cultural barriers exist between the linguistic communities within Canada than between Canada and the United States. While technological change has eroded cultural barriers in the latter case, it has done little to erode language barriers within the country. Even the CBC, with its mandate to foster national unity, operates through linguistically differentiated organizations (Radio-Canada is the francophone voice) that have little in common. Arthur Siegel concludes that "the structural arrangement within CBC encourages the 'two solitudes' of Canada, reinforcing differences in outlook by such creative elements as journalists and entertainment producers rather than bridging them," and that, more generally, "television has played an almost insignificant role in explaining the French and English societies to each other."[41] Thus modern technology may erode cultural differences between Canada and the United States while strengthening cultural differences within Canada. In either case, government intervention is a minor factor, at best, in the tendency of a common language to unite and different languages to divide.

As we look ahead it appears likely that the Canadian debate over cultural nationalism will wane in the face of increased globalization. The impact of globalization has meant that the American culture has a less monolithic presence in Canada, and is therefore less threatening. It may well be the case, then, that Canadians will be able to enjoy the benefits of open cultural borders without facing the same threat of Americanization that generated protective policies in the past. If nothing else, the "globalization" of the Canadian culture has a nicer ring to it than does the "Americanization" of that culture.

BORDER DISPUTES

John Holmes has written that "the great epic of North America is not the sharing of a continent; we only share a border."[42] It should come as no surprise, then, that sharing a border has given rise to numerous disputes. Given the simple length of the border, and that it crosses the Great Lakes and is crossed in turn by rivers and winds, the potential for environmental conflict alone is staggering. As Arthur Meighen, former leader of the national Conservative Party, stated in a 1937 address on Canadian–American relations, "we are not in the same boat but we are pretty much in the same waters." Thus we might expect border disputes to provide a source of ongoing irritation between the two national communities. And yet, perhaps because they are inevitable, border disputes rarely disrupt the broader Canadian–American relationship. The border exists primarily as a state of mind and only secondarily as a physical demarcation with its own unique set of problems. It should also come as no surprise that the national impact of border disputes is asymmetrical. Although 90 percent of Canadians live within 300 kilometres of the border, the American population is broadly dispersed well south of the border region. Few even moderately large American cities are close to the border whereas Montreal, Kingston, Toronto, Hamilton, Windsor, and Vancouver are within a proverbial stone's throw of the United States. Thus border disputes such as that over acid rain may potentially touch most Canadians while relatively few Americans are affected. For most Americans, the Canadian–American border and the disputes it generates have about as much relevance to their immediate lives as does the border separating Portugal and Spain.

Over the years border disputes have taken a variety of forms, with those relating to water predominating. Disputes over offshore fisheries have been present since the Convention of 1818 set limits on the right of

Fish — coast
— salmon

Americans to fish in British North American waters. With the extension of national control over coastal waters from 3 miles to 12 miles in 1970, and to 200 miles in 1977, disputes concerning overlapping fishing claims and the need to manage a diminishing resource were further compounded. On the Pacific coast, for example, the inability of the two countries to reach an agreement on salmon fisheries stems in large part from a dispute on whether or not fish stocks should be conserved. The Canadian government has spent millions on salmon propagation and habitat enhancement, and favours reduced fishing quotas to protect both salmon stocks and the survival of the domestic salmon industry. According to Stephen Clarkson, "American fishermen have retained a free market approach to fisheries, claiming that an exhaustion of the stocks will automatically reduce the number of vessels in the fishery and so allow the fish population to regenerate itself."[43] It should also be noted, however, that contemporary fishing disputes with the United States pale in importance when compared to those between Canada and the European Community.

Disagreements over the precise location of the international border still persist. A seven-year dispute over the maritime boundary through the Gulf of Maine was finally taken to the International Court of Justice in The Hague. At issue was fishing access to Georges Bank, an area rich in scallops, cod, and halibut, and upon which some 3,500 Canadian fishing jobs depend. Canada had claimed about a third of Georges Bank, while the United States had claimed it all. On October 12, 1984, the International Court fixed a boundary giving Canada about one-sixth of Georges Bank. By prior agreement between Canada and the United States, the new boundary is binding on both sides and cannot be appealed. Other boundary disputes are still outstanding. There is disagreement, for example, on where to set the maritime boundary in the Arctic's Beaufort Sea, a boundary that could affect national ownership of offshore oil resources associated with the Prudhoe Bay oil field in Alaska. Maritime disputes of a more environmental character have arisen over the passage of American oil tankers among the Arctic islands and down the Strait of Juan de Fuca between Vancouver Island and the British Columbia mainland.

On the continent, the management of shared river basins has been contentious at times. Hydroelectric development of the Columbia River Basin in Washington State touched off a forty-two-year argument over the potential flooding of the Skagit River Valley, running northward into British Columbia. The dispute was finally settled in 1984 when the Canadian and American governments signed an eighty-year treaty prohibiting the flooding of Canadian land in exchange for a Canadian guarantee of extra electrical power to Seattle. For Manitobans, the planned Garrison diversion irrigation project, which would irrigate 1.5 million acres in North Dakota, has been a source of conflict since it was first proposed in 1965. The Garrison diversion would introduce water from the Missouri River into Canada's Hudson Bay river basin and thus transfer foreign fish, microorganisms, and pollutants that could damage Manitoba's fishing industry. Looking ahead, a growing water shortage in the American southwest is likely to reactivate American interest in massive water-diversion projects to move "unused" Canadian water south across the border. The supporters of one such project, the 1963 North American Water and Power Alliance, proposed spending $150 billion to send Canadian water south through the Rocky Mountain Trench.

In recent decades environmental border disputes have become more common in the wake of greater environmental degradation and stronger environmental lobbies on both sides of the border. Disputes have ranged from efforts to clean up the Great Lakes to the dumping of raw sewage by Victoria into the Strait of Juan de Fuca to the construction of the world's largest garbage incinerator in Detroit. (In this last case, Ontario protested that the incinerator, which will burn 2,000 tonnes of garbage a day to provide heat and electricity for the Detroit area, does not contain adequate air pollution control devices.) The overriding environmental issue, however, has been the damage to Canadian lakes and rivers stemming from acid rain. Although Canadian industrial emissions of sulphur dioxide contribute substantially to the acid rain problem in Canada, industries and utility plants in the Ohio Valley states (Indiana, Illinois, Ohio, and Pennsylvania) also play a substantial role through emissions carried hundreds of miles north by prevailing winds. Canadian emissions contribute to the acid rain problem in the New England states, and Americans have expressed concern about environmental damage arising from the Inco smelter in Sudbury and from Canadian thermal-power plants at Poplar River, Saskatchewan, and Atikokan, Ontario. Yet on balance, and due in large part to the pattern of prevailing winds, the northward drift of acid rain across the international border appears to exceed the southward drift by a margin of three or four to one.[44]

Acid rain proved to be a particularly troublesome issue during the presidency of Ronald Reagan. Repeated Canadian calls for joint action on acid rain were met with indifference by the American administration or at most with the response that the issue warranted further scientific study before an appropriate policy response could be formulated. While Canadian research teams repeatedly stressed the environmental hazards of acid rain, American research teams tended to produce more equivocal results. In short, little headway was made throughout most of the 1980s despite concerted efforts by the Canadian government. Then, in June 1989, President George Bush unveiled a major acid rain initiative that went a long way toward meeting Canadian environmental concerns and standards. The Bush initiative was part of a more comprehensive clean-air package, which led to the Acid Rain Treaty between Canada and the United States. While the treaty will not quickly solve the acid rain problem, it did remove one of the few major irritants in the contemporary Canadian–American relationship.

American reluctance to address the problem of acid rain helped convince many Canadians that American environmental standards were lower and less rigorously enforced. This in turn led to some apprehension concerning the free trade agreement, which, with the passage of time, can be expected to harmonize environmental standards north and south of the border. To the extent that this occurs, Canadians can expect to do the harmonizing. However, the assumption that American environmental standards are lower is just that—an assumption. There is little evidence that Americans are less conscious of environmental degradation than are Canadians or that they are less supportive of environmental standards. In the *Maclean's* survey mentioned earlier in this chapter, respondents were asked the following question: "Would you favor or oppose shutting down a major company that provided many jobs in your community if it was polluting the environment?" Sixty-four percent of the American respondents would favour shutting down the company, an option favoured by 60 percent of the Canadian respondents.[45]

In summary, border disputes between the two countries are not uncommon. Some arise from the simple act of passage: a rock star is denied entry into Canada for drug-related reasons, a union official is denied entry to the United States because of a criminal record, a tourist is subjected to apparently unnecessary harassment by customs officials. Yet such incidents, when placed against the millions of uneventful border crossings that occur every month, constitute an extremely minor source of irritation. More serious disputes have been handled in part by the International Joint Commission (IJC), which was established in 1909 to deal with border-related issues arising from the Boundary Waters Treaty, signed in the same year. Canada and the United States are equally represented on the IJC, which is composed of a three-member commission in each capital. The IJC is empowered to make recommendations to the respective national governments rather than to impose solutions, but it can act as a judicial body if the two governments so decide. Although the IJC has been the principal institutional mechanism for handling border disputes, it has by no means supplanted more conventional diplomatic and political relations between Canada and the United States.

TRANSNATIONAL AND INTERGOVERNMENTAL RELATIONS

Although Canada and the United States are not unique in sharing an international border, the border they share has some interesting and perhaps even unique features. It is an "international" border only in the most formal sense as there is little perception that one's neighbours are "foreign" to any significant degree. The Canadian–American relationship is more familial than international; perceptually, the international environment begins offshore, somewhere beyond the North American continent. This feeling stems in part from the ease with which the border can be crossed and, in most cases, from the absence of geographical features that might reinforce the political boundary. It also stems from the multitude of linkages that span the border and tie together families, friends, business associates, corporations, trade unions, professional associations, fraternal societies, voluntary organizations, and sports leagues. Even in its physical characteristics the Canadian–American border is different from the international borders North Americans are likely to encounter in films, news reports, and spy novels; there is little in the way of barbed wire or guard dogs. If it is not quite a domestic border, it is certainly domesticated.

Canadian–American relations are primarily *transnational* rather than *international* in character, transnational being defined as "contacts, coalitions, and interactions across state boundaries that are not controlled by the central foreign policy organs of government."[46] Transnational relations encompass interactions among a vast array of private actors, which in their sheer volume overwhelm intergovernmental relations. The American penetration of Canada, around which so much of the Canadian–American relationship revolves, has been almost entirely nongovernmental in character, which may account for the lack of more acute Canadian concern.[47] The dominance of transnational interaction is reflected in the lack and indeed the impossibility of any coherent "American policy" in Ottawa or "Canadian policy" in Washington. Even though Canadian–American relations are Canada's most important foreign policy concern, they are too vast and involve too many issues and actors to be neatly packaged within a single policy perspective. Thus when Ottawa published a major review of foreign policy options in 1970, Canadian policy toward the United States was only obliquely addressed.[48] Nor is any greater coherence readily apparent in American policy toward Canada. As Robert Keohane and Joseph Nye point out:

> Neither country has found it possible to list formally, with meaningful consensus, its priorities toward the other in any specific form. It could not be done without simultaneously applying corresponding priorities to aspects of domestic policy, and consequently to constituent groups.[49]

The reality is that Canada and the United States are more affected by each other's domestic policies than by their respective foreign policies. The American deregulation of natural gas prices, for example, has had a marked impact on Canadian gas exports, just as American air pollution standards have an impact upon Canadian problems with acid rain. American events entirely within the private domain ripple through Canadian life as American cultural patterns, entertainment trends, and consumer developments wash ashore in Canada. In a similar fashion, American jurisprudence has had a growing impact on Canadian jurisprudence. Manfredi notes that until the 1970s "American cases played a negligible role in the development of Canadian jurisprudence," but that the American influence began to grow during Chief Justice Bora Laskin's term on the Supreme Court of Canada.[50] With the introduction of the Charter of Rights in 1982, American cases have been cited more frequently, particularly with respect to Charter decisions, and the ratio of British to American case citations has fallen from 11:1 in the pre-Charter period to less than 2:1 in the post-Charter period.[51] In general, then, Canadian–American relations touch upon so many aspects of Canadian life, and are therefore so entangled with both national and provincial governments, that they can often be seen as an extension of Canadian domestic politics rather than as a form of international relations.

Nonetheless, it is important not to lose sight of the international dimension. While in many respects the two countries have a "special relationship" that falls outside the boundaries of conventional international relations, they also interact with one another as they interact with other states. Intergovernmental relations remain important, and there is no evidence, even in the most embryonic form, of an emerging continental state that would supplant the international relationship. Even with the free trade agreement in place there are no institutions that imply, to use Ball's phrase, "a progressively expanding area of common political decision." As John Redekop concludes, "North American integration, such as it is, remains a low-level, uncoordinated, almost haphazard phenomenon."[52] Here John Holmes argues that the rules, commitments, and institutions that govern the bilateral relationship are not intended to bring the two countries closer together. On the contrary, their purpose "is to regulate forces which, unless a Canadian place is staked out, would inevitably erode our sovereignty and our identity."[53]

Before the appointment of Vincent Massey as the first Canadian ambassador to the United States, Canadian affairs were handled by the British embassy in Washington. Since his appointment Canada has maintained a vigorous diplomatic presence in the American capital, a presence recently capped by a new embassy and a $650,000 lobbying campaign. The use of congressional lobbyists—paid professionals who keep their fingers on the pulse of the American Congress, alerting Canadian officials to both threats and opportunities and presenting Canadian views to Washington politicians—is a diplomatic response to both the complexity of American government and the impact that congressional legislation can have on Canadian interests. The point to be stressed is that intergovernmental contact alone between the Canadian Department of External Affairs and the American State Department cannot sufficiently protect Canadian interests; there is a growing realization that direct penetration of the congressional arena is required.

Apart from the lobbying efforts of the Canadian embassy, there are over fifty "foreign agents" representing Canadian interests in the United States.[54] This rather melodramatic term for what are generally law firms, public relations agencies, or specialists in governmental affairs comes from the need for such lobbyists to register with the U.S. Department of Justice under the Foreign Agents Registration Act. The agents represent a variety of interests: private firms; industry organizations such as the Canadian Softwood Lumber Committee, the Canadian Manufacturers' Association, and the Independent Petroleum Association of Canada; public interest groups such as the Canadian Coalition on Acid Rain; provincial trade offices in the United States; provincial departments such as Ontario's Ministry of the Environment; and federal agencies such as the National Film Board of Canada. In all cases their tasks are essentially the same: alerting clients to opportunities created by changes to the legislative environment, warning them about potentially harmful congressional legislation—legislation that often arises in response to private American interests and not to policy initiatives from the president or State Department—and representing their clients' case within the congressional process.

Canada Ninth in Importance to United States

The US State Department has come up with a ranking system for its 50 largest and most important missions. Rankings are based on the size of the mission and the country's degree of importance to American economic and security interests.

The 1992 rankings placed Canada ninth in importance behind Germany, France, Britain, China, Japan, Russia, Mexico and Israel, in that order. Canada placed just ahead of Iraq (10th) and Italy (11th). Canada ranked 28th in terms of the size of its US mission; Saudi Arabia was first, with the largest American mission, and Germany ranked 7th.

Source: Graham Fraser, "Canada Ranked Ninth in Importance to U.S.,"
The Globe and Mail, July 8, 1993, p. A7.

This lobbying activity reflects a fact of American politics: the State Department cannot guarantee congressional support for bilateral deals struck with Canada. The American Senate, unlike the Senate in Canada, must approve any treaties negotiated by the executive branch. (The Canadian Senate, however, did play a very significant role in the debate over the FTA.) Senators can thus use the threat of veto to force modifications in the terms of treaties brought before them. Therefore, if Canadian interests are to be protected, Canadians must be prepared to wade into congressional combat on their own behalf and not rely on the State Department alone to carry the Canadian flag. In a somewhat analogous development, provincial governments are increasingly active participants in Canadian–American relations. They too have been unwilling to let External Affairs carry the flags of provincial interest, and premiers have engaged in frequent political sorties to Washington, New York, and the capitals of border states while provincial trade offices in the United States expanded in number and scope throughout the 1980s. However, in the more fiscally constrained environment of the 1990s many of these provincial initiatives have been rolled back, and there is a greater degree of cooperation and coordination among provincial and federal trade officials.

The American embassy in Ottawa, like its Canadian counterpart in Washington, is not involved in the great bulk of Canadian–American transnational interactions. Only rarely do American multinationals seek backing from the U.S. government in disputes with Canadian governments.[55] Admittedly, American ambassadors in the early 1980s were more prone to publicly criticize Canadian domestic policies, a change in diplomatic style that was also evident for Canadian ambassadors in the United States. In more recent years, ambassadorial commentary has once again become more subdued.

Calgary Herald, July 9, 1993, p. A4.

In many ways Canadian–American relations resemble a vast seamless web within which it is easy for different issues and disputes to become entangled. Somewhat paradoxically, this very interdependence traditionally led to a mutual avoidance of "linkage politics" whereby the settlement of one issue is tied to or is dependent upon the settlement of other, often substantively unrelated issues. As John Holmes has pointed out, not only have Canadians sensed that "linkage was a game that would inevitably be won by the stronger power," but that "the American government machine was too incoherent to formulate a coordinated Canadian policy in which fish or pork would be bargained for gas or relations with Cuba."[56] However, Stephen Clarkson argues that in the early 1980s Congress embraced linkage politics, retaliating in one sector of the bilateral relationship when American interests were hurt in another.[57] Canada, Clarkson suggests, should also embrace linkage politics in order to knit together a more coherent stance toward the bilateral relationship.

Despite the ten-to-one difference in population and economic power, Canada has not fared badly in the bilateral relationship. Canadians have not won on all issues, but certainly have won more frequently

Jeffrey Simpson on Linkage Politics

Linkage, which sometimes exists in the real world, is a strategy both Canada and the United States have tried hard to avoid in their bilateral dealings. The explanation for this avoidance is simple: relations are so extensive, complicated and close that linking issues would soon become a nightmare. If we don't like their farm policy, we decide to be ornery about energy. If they don't like that, they get nasty about our defence spending. And so on.

It is also in the interests of the smaller country in a bilateral relationship to avoid linkage, since linkage is essentially a power play—if you don't do what we want on this issue, we'll make life difficult for you on other issues. Unfortunately, Canada's capacity to make life difficult for the Americans is considerably less than their ability to do us harm. So linkage is a perilous game for Canada.

It is also a difficult game to play with the United States, given that country's division of powers. Even if we can turn the administration to our way of thinking, there is no guarantee that the Congress will agree. If we threaten the administration, we are implicitly insisting that it deliver the Congress, something a president would love to do but sometimes cannot.

Source: "Playing with Fire," *The Globe and Mail*, February 17, 1988.

than the odds might predict. This success has encouraged a strategy of "quiet diplomacy" through which Canadians protect their "special relationship" with the United States by refraining from public criticism of American world leadership. And yet American activities in the international arena impact directly upon long-term Canadian interests, including the avoidance of nuclear war. As a consequence, the norms of quiet diplomacy can be strained when Canada is drawn into international disputes in which Canadian and American interests or world views do not coincide.

INTERNATIONAL RELATIONS AND MILITARY DEFENCE

Canada has been an active international player although not a major international power since the Second World War. Through participation in the United Nations, including its peace-keeping forces and specialized agencies such as the UN World Food Program and UNESCO, and through multilateral organizations such as GATT, the North Atlantic Treaty Organization (NATO), the British Commonwealth, and the International Emergency Food Reserve, Canada has made and continues to make important contributions to the international order.

International involvement beyond the North American continent can take many forms, all of which may heighten the sense of belonging to a distinctive national community. It may be as personal as travelling abroad, in wearing the maple leaf on the back of one's jeans, in taking pride that strangers recognize the symbol and are able to distinguish Canadians from Americans. It may come through international hockey competition as Canadian teams challenge and, alas, too often fail to beat the world's best. And it may involve governmental participation in international organizations, participation that provides a valuable counterweight in our bilateral relationship with the United States. As John Holmes explains, "Canadian governments, if not always the Canadian people, have recognized that international institutions ... are essential for a country our size to act effectively vis-à-vis a great power."[58] The assertion of Canadian sovereignty in the international arena thus protects Canadian sovereignty in the bilateral relationship with the United States. It is interesting to note, however, that the United States, like Canada, is also willing to use international institutions such as GATT to provide leverage on the bilateral relationship. It should also be noted that, while international activity may strengthen Canada's continental position, it is not unencumbered by the Canadian–American relationship. The two countries share many important characteristics that propel them, willy-nilly, into the same international camp: both are Western, northern, nonsocialist, and industrialized states, linked together in a continental trading system. Where they differ dramatically is that the

United States is a superpower with a global set of strategic interests, obligations, and entanglements that Canada shares only to a limited degree. This difference, and the fear of being overshadowed by and ineffectual in the presence of the United States, explains in part why Canada took so long to join the Organization of American States.

Canada is firmly and unavoidably in the American military camp. In the Ogdensburg Declaration of June 1940, Canada and the United States declared that the "defence of the two countries constituted a single problem," a declaration backed by the establishment of the Permanent Joint Board of Defence to provide a common forum for the discussion and coordination of continental defence. In 1941 the two countries signed the Hyde Park Agreement, which all but erased the border as far as defence production was concerned.[59] The 1959 Defence Production Sharing Agreements updated and expanded the Hyde Park Agreement by allowing Canadian firms to compete without handicap for American defence contracts. Given that Canada requires modern weapons of war, that these have generally become too costly to produce for Canada's use alone, and that success as an international arms dealer may be both economically difficult and morally repugnant, the arrangement with the United States allows Canada to at least share in the economic benefits of defence production. Over the first twenty years of the DPS agreements, American military procurements in Canada totalled $5,195 million while Canadian procurements in the United States totalled $5,535 million.[60]

Canada, with the United States, is a member of NATO, and since 1958 has been a partner with the United States in the North American Air Defence Command (NORAD), rechristened the North American *Aerospace* Defence Command in March 1981. The creation of NORAD recognized a basic reality of the nuclear age; in any nuclear exchange, Canada and the United States would be a common continental target. Over the years, however, NORAD's importance has declined, first with the diminished threat of a Soviet bomber attack and, second, with the collapse of the Soviet Union and hence the greatly diminished threat of nuclear attack. NORAD's atrophy has shifted the focus of Canadian defence strategy from the bilateral Canadian–American relationship, in which the United States was overwhelmingly dominant, to the multilateral forum of NATO.

Canada's military alliance with the United States reflects not only its continental location, but also a basic agreement between Canadians and Americans on the desired shape of the international order. Yet, even if that agreement did not exist, Canada would still lie across the northern flank of the United States. If Canadians were not prepared to defend that flank, the United States would have no choice but to do so itself. Thus the Canadian military not only defends Canada against potential foreign aggression, but also defends Canadian political sovereignty from the United States. In this "defence against help," we encounter what has been termed the "sover-

TABLE 7.1 Public Support for a Common National Policy on Defence and Foreign Affairs

"Would you strongly support, support, oppose or strongly oppose Canada and the United States adopting common and identical policy on all matters relating to defence and foreign affairs?"

	Canada	United States
% strongly oppose	24	4
% oppose	36	19
% support	33	58
% strongly support	5	15
% no opinion	2	3

Source: Maclean's survey of 1,000 Canadian and 1,000 American respondents, July 3, 1989, p. 49.

eignty paradox." To protect its sovereignty, Canada must participate in bilateral defence arrangements with the United States, arrangements that in turn restrict Canadian sovereignty given that Canada will be a junior, not equal, partner.[61] Fortunately, the diminished bomber threat and technological advances in satellite surveillance, over-the-horizon radar systems, and airborne warning-and-control systems (AWACS) have all but eliminated the need for an American military presence on Canadian soil. At the same time and for the same reasons, Canadians have even less leverage on American defence policy than they had in the past.

Despite the basic complementarity of national views, there has been little public support on the Canadian side of the border for common national policies on defence and foreign affairs. As Table 7.1 shows, little more than a third of Canadian respondents in a 1989 survey supported the adoption of a common policy, and even then did so with little enthusiasm. However, there was considerably more support for a common policy on defence and foreign affairs among American respondents to the same survey. In this context it is useful to note that conflicts between Canada and the United States over military and foreign affairs policy are not uncommon, although such conflicts undoubtedly have a higher public profile in Canada than they do in the United States. For example, at times Canada has been accused by American officials of spending too little on defence or, more specifically, of making an insufficient military contribution to NATO. In proportionate terms, Canada's contribution to NATO ranks above only those of Luxembourg and Iceland, and only Luxembourg spends a smaller proportion of its Gross Domestic Product on defence. In 1988, the size of Canada's Armed Forces, as a proportion of the national labour force, reached its lowest level (0.9 percent) in fifty years. The gulf between Canadian and American defence expenditures is immense. In rough terms, American military expenditures are forty times those of Canada.

In the late 1950s and early 1960s disagreement arose between the two countries and within Canada over the acquisition of nuclear weapons for Canadian interceptor aircraft and anti-aircraft missiles (the Bomarc) based in Canada and with Canadian forces in Europe. Progressive Conservative Prime Minister John Diefenbaker came to symbolize nationalist resistance to American military policy, a resistance that extended to Canada's delay in putting its forces on alert during the 1962 Cuban missile crisis. The nuclear weapons issue played a significant role in the 1963 general election, in which the pro-warhead Liberals defeated the Conservatives to form a minority government. The warheads were subsequently installed, although they remained under American control. In the early 1970s the warheads were withdrawn, leaving the Canadian forces without nuclear weapons of any sort.

American military intervention abroad has occasionally provoked public and, more rarely, government criticism in Canada. American involvement in the Vietnam War received a generally negative press in Canada, although official opposition to the war was both muted and, if expressed, resented in the United States. When Prime Minister Pearson criticized the American bombing of North Vietnam in a 1965 speech at Temple University, President Lyndon Johnson bluntly rebuked Pearson, saying "you peed on my carpet."[62] The 1983 American invasion of Grenada, an island in the Caribbean, was widely criticized in Canada and demonstrated some significant national differences in perceptions of the communist threat and in preferred strategies for coping with that threat. The American invasion of Panama received at best mixed reviews in Canada, but there was widespread public support for the American-led United Nations intervention in Kuwait and Iraq. In comparison to the United States, Canada has attached less importance to the global threat of communism, and has generally opposed military intervention as a response to communist threats in the Third World. Incidents such as the American involvement in Nicaragua have occasionally provided the Canadian government with the opportunity to put some distance between Canada and the United States on the international stage without undermining the broader strategic principles of American foreign policy.

During 1983 and 1984 there was considerable protest in Canada over the testing of the Cruise missile guidance system in northern Alberta. To some, the Cruise testing implicated Canada in the international arms race and impaired the prospects for arms reduction, a nuclear freeze, and world peace. For others, the testing was seen as a modest contribution to a strengthened nuclear deterrent, and therefore to nuclear stability and world peace. Perhaps more importantly, it was also seen as a necessary fulfilment of Canadian alliance commitments under NATO. In an open letter to Canadians published in newspapers across the country on May 10, 1983, Prime Minister Trudeau stressed the alliance commitment:

> *It is hardly fair to rely on the Americans to protect the West, but to refuse to lend them a hand when the going gets rough. In that sense, the anti-Americanism of some Canadians verges on hypocrisy. They're eager to take refuge under the American umbrella, but don't want to help hold it.*

Since the election of the Mulroney Conservative government in 1984, domestic discussion of defence policy has focused largely on its economic implications. The purchase of new tanks, frigates, and helicopters, the closing of bases in Canada, and the withdrawal of Canadian forces from Europe have been discussed within the context of growing fiscal constraint more than within a broader foreign policy context. Foreign policy conflict between Canada and the United States has been primarily over the appropriate means to common ends rather than over those ends per se. The question remains, however, as to just how much independence Canada enjoys on the international stage. A firm answer would require a situation in which Canada and the United States had clearly conflicting international interests, and in which Canada's pursuit of its own interests would be actively opposed by the United States. To date, such conflicts have not emerged, and given that the two countries have so much in common, they are unlikely to emerge in the years to come. In the absence of such a test, Canadians may be too quick to assume that Canadian sovereignty is tightly constrained.

The relatively nuanced evolution of the international and defence relationship between Canada and the United States has been overshadowed in recent years by the far more dramatic transformation of the international order. The end of the cold war, the unification of Germany, and the emergence of democratic states in Eastern Europe have all contributed to the declining importance of the military alliances in which Canada and the United States have both participated. As a result, there are fewer opportunities for conflict between the two countries on matters of defence policy. At the same time, both Canada and the United States have become increasingly involved in United Nations activities in the Middle East, Somalia, and the former Yugoslavia. While these activities have been contentious in many respects, they have yet to open up significant cleavages between the two North American allies. In the new and destabilized world order of the 1990s, the Canadian–American international relationship is dominated almost exclusively by issues of continental and global trade, issues where the two countries share largely common but not completely compatible interests.

CANADIAN NATIONALISM AND THE UNITED STATES

Canada's history has been intimately tied to the two great English-speaking countries of the world and two of the world's great imperial states. When British influence waned in Canada and around the world during the 20th century, that of the United States waxed. It is not surprising, then, that Canada's colonial past has been used to model Canada's relationship with the United States. Harold Innis, Canada's most famous economic historian, first described Canada's progression from a British colony, to a brief period of national independence bounded by the two world wars, and then to a new colonial relationship with the United States. Historian Donald Creighton has written that, as Canada was growing apart from Great Britain, its "links with the United States became so numerous and so powerful that they threatened to convert the nation into a political vassal, an economic tributary, and a cultural colony of the American Empire."[63] Walter Gordon, then President of the Privy Council, developed the colonial theme in a 1967 interview:

> During the last fifty years we have freed ourselves of traces of colonial status insofar as Britain is concerned. But having achieved our independence from Britain, we seem to have slipped, almost without knowing it, into a semi-dependent position in relation to the United States.[64]

The colonial model is meant to be more than descriptive; it also embodies a sense of anger and despair. To quote again from Gordon's 1967 interview, "it is sadly ironic that in a world torn asunder by countries who are demanding and winning their independence, our free, independent and highly developed country should be haunted by the spectre of a colonial or semi-colonial future."[65] It should be stressed, however, that the colonial model understates Canada's political independence. It fails to recognize the lack of continental political institutions while at the same time directing insufficient attention to nongovernmental relations. It may also understate the common values that work to integrate the Canadian and American societies, and that lead many Canadians to embrace the continental relationship. To the extent that a colonial relationship does exist, it has been largely self-imposed. As John Redekop points out, "if the Canadian–American relationship constitutes colonialism, it must surely be the strangest colonial relationship extant."[66]

Redekop goes on to offer a comprehensive survey of concepts that have been used to model the Canadian–American relationship, concepts that include domination, dependency, partnership, interdependence, hegemony, continentalism, satellite, client state, neocolonialism, and "continental subsystemic dominance," his own preference. Canada has also been described as an American hinterland, a term that suggests interesting parallels between Canadian–American relations and regionalism within

Canada. Clearly the relationship can be modelled in many different ways, each of which directs our attention to different aspects of the relationship and distorts the reality of the relationship in different ways. Perhaps the most ubiquitous term, at least in American usage, has been "neighbours." Here it is worth citing at length a passage by James Eayrs that has retained its relevance through the years:

> If the Canadian–American relationship is to flourish to the mutual benefit of its partners, it will be because statesmen of both countries resist the temptation ... of believing their politics to be neighbourly rather than international. They must realize that the two nations of North America are of the states-system, not beyond and above it, and shape their policies accordingly. President Johnson, with the best intentions in the world, observed ... that "Canada is such a close neighbor and such a good neighbor that we always have plenty of problems there. They are kind of like problems in the hometown." They are kind of not like that at all. They are the problems not of neighbours but of friendly foreign powers.[67]

One of the best summaries of the Canadian–American relationship came in a speech to the House of Commons (February 4, 1963) by Robert Thompson, leader of the Social Credit Party. "The Americans," Thompson declared, "are our best friends whether we like it or not." Of course, if Canadians were able to choose their continental neighbour, most would choose the United States. It is ironic, then, that no country poses a greater threat to Canada's survival as a distinct and independent national community. It is because the United States is Canada's best friend that it is also Canada's "worst enemy."

The acknowledged friendship between the two countries has not fostered much support among Canadians for political union. This, of course, is an issue that has been on the table in Canada since the Montreal annexation riots in 1849, and there are probably few Canadians who have not at some time in their lives debated the merits of joining the United States. However, as Table 7.2 shows, political union enjoys very little public support among Canadians, and certainly not enough to propel the issue onto the nation's political agenda. Americans were certainly much more supportive of political union, but this finding should not be taken as evidence of any active American inclination in this respect. Political union with Canada is not on the American agenda and is unlikely to be so without some initiative from the Canadian side. It is interesting to note in this last respect that support for political union was significantly higher in Quebec, where 23 percent favoured the idea, than it was outside Quebec, where only 11 percent did so. It is also interesting to speculate on how respondents might have reacted to the prospect of Canada forming not the 51st state, but the 51st through 60th states. Would Canadians have been more enthusiastic and Americans less?

TABLE 7.2 *Support for Political Union Among Canadian and American Respondents*

"Would you favor or oppose Canada becoming the 51st state of the United States with full congressional representation and the rights of American citizenship?"

	Canada	United States
% strongly favor	2	12
% favor	12	54
% oppose	31	22
% strongly oppose	54	10
% no opinion	1	3

Source: Maclean's *survey of 1,000 Canadian and 1,000 American respondents, July 3, 1989, p. 49.*

Not surprisingly, perceptions of the United States and Americans have played an important role in the evolution of Canadian nationalism. As Hans Kohn explained in a classic work on the subject, nationalism is double-faced: "intranationally, it leads to a lively sympathy with all fellow members within the nationality; internationally, it finds expression in indifference to or distrust and hate of fellow men outside the national orbit."[68] Nationalism thus has two core components: in-group loyalty or patriotism, and out-group hostility toward other nationalities. Although this conceptualization of nationalism is not without its limitations,[69] it does identify the important role played by anti-Americanism in Canadian nationalism and particularly in English-Canadian nationalism.

Survival vis-à-vis the United States has been a central theme of English-Canadian nationalism,[70] just as "la survivance" has been a central theme of French-Canadian nationalism. Not surprisingly, that quest for survival has often found expression in anti-Americanism that has been directed at both the American presence within Canada and American perceptions of Canada. Canadians have not been aggravated by American hostility, for there is little measurable "anti-Canadianism" within the United States, but rather by American indifference to things Canadian, by the too-ready assumption that Canadians and Americans are essentially the same under their different national skins. Northrop Frye links this reaction to Canadian fears about annexation, arguing that what is resented

> *... is not annexation itself, but the feeling that Canada would disappear into a larger entity without having anything of any real distinctiveness to*

contribute to that entity: that, in short, if the United States did annex Canada it would notice nothing except an increase in its natural resources.[71]

To be disliked is one thing; to be ignored is something else entirely.

The United States, as Canada's only neighbour, necessarily becomes the mirror in which Canadians see themselves. As a consequence, Canadian nationalism waxes and wanes in response to conditions in the United States as much as in response to conditions in Canada. In the distant past, the strength of Canadian nationalism was sapped by the national comparison. When Canadians looked at their own country they saw a poorer, colder, less developed, and less vibrant United States. They saw Americans with overshoes and colds, a country whose national symbol was not the soaring eagle but rather a large rodent noted for its ability to run for cover. Canadian nationalism thus seemed an irrational emotion that flew in the face of any objective national comparison. It was not coincidental, then, that Canadian nationalism bloomed during the 1960s when the American society was experiencing deep distress. Looking south at racial conflict, a

"I do hope Americans don't think of us as ugly Canadians ... stuffy, dull, slow, mundane, colorless, bland, self-righteous hypocrites ... but not ugly."

Len Norris, *Sun* (Vancouver).

spiralling crime rate, deteriorating cities, student unrest, and the horror of the Vietnam War, and drawing upon radical American critiques of the American society, Canadians could objectively and somewhat smugly conclude that life was better in Canada than it was in the United States. As Canadian Senator John Nicol somewhat unkindly observed at the time, just as Americans "have seen their sense of destiny falter, we have picked up the torch of plastic nationalism and are dashing off at a dead run."[72]

This dependency means that any improvement in American conditions can have a corrosive impact on Canadian nationalism. The price of a healthy America is self-doubt among Canadians as to the worth of an independent country on the northern tier of the continent. Furthermore, to the extent that Canadian nationalism feeds off blemishes on the American society, Canadians may be too tolerant of blemishes on their own society and remain unaware of the excellence Canada has attained. It is here that Canada suffers from having but a single point of national comparison, and that being the wealthiest and most powerful country in the world. As Margaret Atwood points out:

> One of Canada's problems is that it's always comparing itself to the wrong thing. If you stand beside a giant, of course you tend to feel a little stunted.[73]

It is not coincidental that Canadian nationalism was at a low ebb, and that continentalism was enthusiastically embraced by many, during the mid-1980s when the American economy was booming and Americans were experiencing a revival of patriotic pride fed by the nostalgic nationalism of President Ronald Reagan. With everything looking so good in the United States, Canada appeared to pale by comparison.

An ironic feature of Canadian nationalism comes from the pride Canadians take in the very weakness of their nationalism. The more fervent displays of American nationalism such as one encounters during half-time shows in college football games are often denigrated by Canadians who refuse to sing their own national anthem in public, or who would like to sing but are no longer sure of the words. Moving beyond the American comparison per se, John Meisel has discussed the absence of a vigorous and active nationalism in Canada, "an absence, incidentally, which in the eyes of many who have elsewhere experienced the parochialism and inhumanity of chauvinism, bestows on Canada one of its most attractive characteristics."[74] While this point is well taken, the question remains whether Canadian nationalism is sufficiently strong to counterbalance the centrifugal forces inherent in a regionally diverse national community.

The anti-American component of Canadian nationalism has been an important current within the Canadian political culture. Somewhat paradoxically, this is in part because the United States has been the source of new and at times disruptive political ideas since the arrival of the United

"Your problem of course is that you're too nationalistic..."

Roy Peterson, *Sun* (Vancouver).

Empire Loyalists. Prior to the 1837 rebellions, radical reformers in both Upper Canada (the Clear Grits) and Lower Canada (the supporters of Louis-Joseph Papineau) drew much of their political inspiration from the United States, just as the later agrarian radical reformers in Western Canada drew upon American populist thought. As James Mallory points out, "Canada has been nourished by the same stream of constitutional ideas, and in many respects, the same constitutional atmosphere, as the United States."[75] At the same time, there has been a countervailing reluctance to imitate American political institutions. Wise and Brown argue that "the real puzzle in the history of Canadian ideas about the United States is why the bulk of Canadians, standing on the very threshold of liberty, were so little susceptible to American institutions, a seeming contradiction of nature, environment, and proximity."[76] It was a contradiction, they claim, with an unfortunate impact on Canada:

> *The urgent necessity for a small people, in the overwhelming presence of a supremely confident neighbour, to insist not merely upon their*

separateness and distinctiveness, but even upon their intrinsic political and moral superiority, had a paralytic effect upon the Canadian mind and upon the quality of Canadian thought. The rigidities established by the compulsion to maintain identity narrowed the range of political debate, channeled political thought along familiar paths, and discouraged the venturesome, the daring, and the rash. There is an imprecision and superficiality, a lack of progression and proliferation, about Canadian thought with respect to the United States that mirrors the general state of Canadian political thought in this era.[77]

Although one would have to be cautious in projecting this assessment of late-19th-century Canada onto the contemporary political scene, Canadians have not been sufficiently attentive to the American experience in coping with political conflict in a vast, transcontinental society more like Canada than any other in the world.[78]

Canadian–American relations and the politics of nationalism have often become entangled with other sources of political conflict in Canada. For example, the tariffs of Macdonald's National Policy soon became an enduring symbol of regional discontent, one associated with exacerbated provincialism and regional conflict:

The alleged "unfairness" of the tariff has always served as a potent argument for spokesmen, mainly provincial politicians, from the non-manufacturing regions of Canada when they have been seeking measures to promote their own self-interest. The resulting rampant regionalism has been antithetical to Confederation.[79]

Canadian–American relations have also been entangled with the relationship between the English- and French-speaking communities. In the absence of an effective language barrier between Canada and the United States, English-Canadian nationalists have sought to erect economic and cultural barriers. However, such barriers rely upon a relatively strong and activist federal government, and have therefore been viewed with suspicion by Quebec. Although English-Canadian attempts to fend off assimilationist pressures from the United States parallel Québécois attempts to fend off assimilationist pressures from English-speaking North America, the two goals have at times come into conflict. When English-Canadian nationalists promote a Canadian identity that obscures the French fact, such as occurred with John Diefenbaker's vision of "one Canada," they intensify the assimilationist threat to French Canada. Thus, while both Quebec and Ottawa have tried to build effective cultural walls, they have done so along quite different borders.

On the more positive side, French Canada makes a valuable contribution to English-Canadian nationalism as it is Canada's bilingual character that, more than anything else, sets it apart from the United States.

Canada and Quebec's extensive participation in La Francophonie has given Canada a distinctive presence on the international stage. The question that arises is what has English Canada to offer in return? As Kari Levitt wrote in 1970, why should French Canadians

> remain within Confederation when the dominant English-Canadian majority appear to put such a low value on Canada's national independence? What is being offered? To wander hand-in-hand, biculturally and bilingually, into the gravitational orbit of the American empire?[80]

The catch is that a more vibrant Canadian nationality could itself pose a threat to French Canada if it does not fully embrace French-Canadian culture and tradition. More specifically, it will be difficult to merge such a nationality with the concerns of Quebec so long as the former relies upon a strong federal government as its primary vehicle of expression and defence.

In summary, Canadian–American relations are not only of intrinsic importance; they are also entangled with the other major strands of Canadian political life. Moreover, while conflict between Canada and the United States will wax and wane over time, and will shift in focus from one set of issues to another, it will never disappear. Nor will the debate between nationalist and continentalist options disappear. Canada's location on the North American continent ensures continued American penetration, and continued Canadian efforts both to embrace and resist that penetration. Here it is useful to refer to a characterization of Canada advanced by Mason Wade. Writing in 1964, Wade asserted that "Canada has always been a willed nation, existing despite the conscious and unconscious forces which have sought to absorb it into its much more populous and powerful neighbour."[81] The notion of a "willed nation" seems particularly powerful, even if it is by no means unique to the Canadian case. It points to the importance of nationalism in Canadian life, for it is by the strength of nationalism that we can measure the will of Canadians to resist a continental future. It also suggests that if the strength of Canadian nationalism is unduly sapped by regional conflict, if a national vision cannot be found that embraces the bilingual realities of Canadian life, if political institutions fail to articulate a national interest that is truly national, then Canada's continued independence on the North American continent may be imperilled. In this sense, effective boundary maintenance with the United States depends upon fences coming down and staying down within Canada.

SUGGESTED READINGS

1. Charles F. Doran, *Forgotten Partnership: U.S.–Canada Relations Today* (Baltimore: Johns Hopkins University Press, 1984).

2. Terence J. Fay, "Canadian Studies on the American Relationship, 1945–1980," *American Review of Canadian Studies*, 13:3 (Autumn 1983), pp. 179–200. The appendix to this article contains a bibliography of 326 articles, books, and professional papers, grouped by historical period.

3. D.H. Flanerty and W.R. McKercher, eds., *Southern Exposure: Canadian Perspectives on the United States* (Toronto: McGraw-Hill Ryerson, 1986).

4. Marc Gold and David Leyton-Brown, eds., *Trade-Offs on Free Trade: The Canada–U.S. Free Trade Agreement* (Agincourt, Ontario: Carswell, 1988).

5. Although now twenty-five years old, George Grant's *Lament for a Nation: The Defeat of Canadian Nationalism* (Toronto: McClelland and Stewart, 1965) still provides a provocative ideological analysis of the Canadian–American relationship.

6. Alfred Olivier Hero, Jr., and Louis Balthazar, *Contemporary Quebec and the United States, 1960–1985* (Boston: University Press of America, 1988).

7. For an excellent overview of Canadian–American relations, see John W. Holmes, *Life with Uncle: The Canadian–American Relationship* (Toronto: University of Toronto Press, 1981); for a more extended treatment, see Graeme S. Mount and Edelgard Mahant, *An Introduction to Canadian–American Relations* (Toronto: Methuen, 1984).

8. For an analysis of the Autopact, see James F. Keeley, "Cast in Concrete for All Time? The Negotiation of the Auto Pact," *Canadian Journal of Political Science*, 16:2 (June 1983), pp. 281–98.

9. Denis Stairs and Gilbert R. Winham, Research Coordinators, *The Politics of Canada's Economic Relationship with the United States* (Toronto: University of Toronto Press, 1985), ch. 2.

10. Glen Williams, *Not for Export: Toward a Political Economy of Canada's Arrested Industrialization* (Toronto: McClelland and Stewart, 1983).

STUDY QUESTIONS

1. In the early 1980s Francis Fox, at that time the federal minister responsible for Canadian communication policy, warned that by 1985 the spread of U.S. television channels through satellite delivery could make Canada "an occupied land, culturally." To what extent has this come to pass? To what extent can and should the Government of Canada impose controls on television reception by Canadian

citizens? What risks do we run if such controls are not or cannot be imposed?

2. Where do you stand on the question of "free trade"? What are the *political* arguments that you would amass in defence of your position, and what are the *political* counter-arguments that you might expect?

3. To what extent, if any, might you expect residents of your own province to have a different perspective on Canadian–American relations than that held by the residents of other provinces? How would you explain such differences, should they exist?

NOTES

1. J. Bartlet Brebner, *Canada: A Modern History* (Ann Arbor: University of Michigan Press, 1960), p. ix.

2. F.O. Matthiessen, *The Oxford Book of American Verse* (New York: Oxford University Press, 1950), pp. 547–48.

3. David E. Smith, "Empire, Crown and Canadian Federalism," *Canadian Journal of Political Science*, 24:3 (September 1991), p. 454. As Robert Hughes points out, the American Revolution was also instrumental in the creation of Australia, for it eliminated the United States as a location for convicts being shipped overseas to relieve pressure on British penal institutions. *The Fatal Shore* (New York: Random House, 1986), p. 41.

4. Dale Posgate and Kenneth McRoberts, *Quebec: Social Change and Political Crisis* (Toronto: McClelland and Stewart, 1976), p. 19.

5. A.R.M. Lower, *Colony to Nation* (London: 1953), p. 109.

6. J.M.S. Careless, *Canada: A Story of Challenge*, rev. ed. (Toronto: Macmillan, 1963), p. 113.

7. Cited in Joseph Barber, *Good Fences Make Good Neighbours* (Toronto: McClelland and Stewart, 1958), p. 31.

8. Ibid., p. 31.

9. *The Globe*, June 1, 1871. Cited in S.F. Wise and Robert Craig Brown, *Canada Views the United States: Nineteenth-Century Political Attitudes* (Toronto: Macmillan, 1967), p. 109.

10. Olivar Asselin, *A Quebec View of Canadian Nationalism* (Montreal: 1909), p. 19.

11. Henri Bourassa, *Great Britain and Canada* (Montreal: 1901), p. 7.

12. Smith, "Empire, Crown and Canadian Federalism."

13. James Eayrs, "Sharing a Continent: The Hard Issues," in James Sloan Dickey, ed., *The United States and Canada* (Englewood Cliffs, N.J.: Prentice-Hall, 1964), p. 60.

14. Goldwin Smith, *Canada and the Canadian Question*, reprinted with an introduction by Carl Berger (Toronto: University of Toronto Press, 1971), pp. 223–24.

15. John W. Holmes, "In Praise of National Boundaries," *Saturday Night*, July 1974, p. 14.

16. Eayrs, "Sharing a Continent," p. 81.

17. John Whalley and Irene Trela, *Regional Aspects of Confederation* (Toronto: University of Toronto Press, 1986), p. 201.

18. Herbert Marshall, Frank Southard, Jr., and Kenneth W. Taylor, *Canadian–American Industry* (Toronto: McClelland and Stewart, 1936; reprinted 1976), pp. 274–77.

19. H.G. Thorburn, *Planning and the Economy: Building Federal–Provincial Consensus* (Toronto: James Lorimer, 1984), pp. 11 and 119.

20. *Corporations and Labour Unions Returns Act, Report for 1988* (Ottawa: Supply and Services, 1991).

21. Carl Berger, *The Sense of Power: Studies in the Ideas of Canadian Imperialism, 1867–1914* (Toronto: 1970).

22. Denis Smith, "Political Parties and the Survival of Canada," in R. Kenneth Carty and W. Peter Ward, eds., *Entering the Eighties: Canada in Crisis* (Toronto: Oxford University Press, 1980), p. 139.

23. *Report of the Federal Petroleum Monitoring Agency*, August 1988.

24. For extensive graphic illustrations of the extent and character of foreign investment in Canada, see Nydia McCool, *Canadian Facts and Figures* (Edmonton: Hurtig, 1982), pp. 85ff.

25. Peter C. Newman, "The High Cost of Free Trade," *Maclean's*, January 16, 1984, p. 38.

26. Kari Levitt, *Silent Surrender: The Multinational Corporation in Canada* (Toronto: Macmillan, 1970), p. 149.

27. George Ball, *Discipline of Power* (Boston: Little, Brown, 1968), p. 113.

28. *Eleventh Report of the Standing Committee on External Affairs and National Defence Respecting Canada–U.S. Relations* (Ottawa: Queen's Printer, 1970).

29. *Foreign Direct Investment in Canada* (Ottawa: Information Canada, 1972).

30. John W. Holmes, "Impact of Domestic Political Factors on Canadian–American Relations: Canada," in Annette Baker Fox, Alfred O. Hero, Jr., and Joseph S. Nye, Jr., eds., *Canada and the United States: Transnational and Transgovernmental Relations* (New York: Columbia University Press, 1976), p. 25.

31. For a cross-national comparison, see Nicholas J. Patterson, "Canada–U.S. Foreign Investment Regulation: Transparency Versus Diffusion," in Earl H. Fry and Lee H. Radebaugh, eds., *Regulation of Foreign Direct Investment in Canada and the United States* (Salt Lake City: Brigham Young University, David M. Kennedy International Center, 1983), pp. 47–62.

32. Stephen Clarkson, *Canada and the Reagan Challenge: Crisis in the Canadian–American Relationship* (Toronto: James Lorimer, 1982), pp. 87ff.

33. George Grant, *Lament for a Nation: The Defeat of Canadian Nationalism* (Toronto: McClelland and Stewart, 1965), p. 15.

34. Ibid., pp. 69–70.

35. See "The NDP 'Waffle' Manifesto: For an Independent Socialist Canada," in Paul Fox, ed., *Politics: Canada*, 3rd ed. (Toronto: McGraw-Hill, 1970), pp. 242–45.

36. J.L. Granatstein, "Free Trade Between Canada and the United States: The Issue That Will Not Go Away," in Denis Stairs and Gilbert R. Winham, Research Coordinators, *The Politics of Canada's Economic Relationship with the United States* (Toronto: University of Toronto Press, 1985), ch. 2.

37. Arthur Siegel, *Politics and the Media in Canada* (Toronto: McGraw-Hill Ryerson, 1983), p. 1.

38. Holmes, "In Praise of National Boundaries," p. 14.

39. Eayrs, "Sharing a Continent," p. 89.

40. Proclaimed in the summer of 1985, the Baie Comeau policy requires that Canadian-based and foreign-owned subsidiaries in the publishing industry must, if sold, divest 51 percent control to Canadian investors within two years of the takeover. The policy has not been enforced with a great deal of rigour or enthusiasm on the part of the federal government.

41. Siegel, *Politics and the Media*, p. 183. Siegel also shows (pp. 180–81) that the French-language broadcast media is much more Canadian in content than is the English-language media.

42. Holmes, "In Praise of National Boundaries," p. 16.

43. Cited in Patrick Nagle, "Border Disputes Still Pending," *Calgary Herald*, October 20, 1984, p. A4.

44. Clarkson, *Canada and the Reagan Challenge*, p. 185.

45. *Maclean's*, July 3, 1989, p. 49.

46. Joseph S. Nye, Jr., and Robert O. Keohane, "Transnational Relations and World Politics: An Introduction," in Robert O. Keohane and Joseph S. Nye, Jr., eds., *Transnational Relations and World Politics* (Cambridge: Harvard University Press, 1972), p. ix.

47. John Redekop, "A Reinterpretation of Canadian–American Relations," *Canadian Journal of Political Science*, 9:2 (June 1976), p. 237.

48. Government of Canada, *Foreign Policy for Canadians* (Ottawa: 1970). This was remedied somewhat by a special issue of *International Perspectives*, "Canada–U.S. Relations: Options for the Future," published in 1972.

49. Robert O. Keohane and Joseph S. Nye, Jr., *Power and Interdependence: World Politics in Transition* (Boston: Little, Brown, 1977), p. 170.

50. Christopher Manfredi, "The Use of United States Decisions by the Supreme Court of Canada Under the Charter of Rights and Freedoms," *Canadian Journal of Political Science*, 23:3 (September 1990), p. 503.

51. Ibid., p. 505.

52. Redekop, "A Reinterpretation," p. 233.

53. John W. Holmes, *Life with Uncle: The Canadian–American Relationship* (Toronto: University of Toronto Press, 1981), p. 43.

54. Peter Moon, "Agents Look Out for Canada's Interests," *The Globe and Mail*, National Edition, August 15, 1983, p. 5.

55. David Leyton-Brown, "Canada and Multinational Enterprise," in Norman Hillmer and Garth Stevenson, eds., *A Foremost Nation: Canadian Foreign Policy and a Changing World* (Toronto: McClelland and Stewart, 1977), p. 81.

56. Holmes, *Life with Uncle*, p. 54.

57. Clarkson, *Canada and the Reagan Challenge*, p. 289.

58. Holmes, *Life with Uncle*, p. 7.

59. Eayrs, "Sharing a Continent," p. 66.

60. Clarkson, *Canada and the Reagan Challenge*, p. 261.

61. Michael Tucker, *Canadian Foreign Policy: Contemporary Issues and Themes* (Toronto: McGraw-Hill Ryerson, 1980), pp. 149–50.

62. Clarkson, *Canada and the Reagan Challenge*, p. 8.

63. Donald Creighton, *The Passionate Observer: Selected Writings* (Toronto: McClelland and Stewart, 1980), p. 23.

64. Cited in Levitt, *Silent Surrender*, pp. 1–2.

65. Ibid., p. 2.

66. Redekop, "A Reinterpretation," p. 230.

67. Eayrs, "Sharing a Continent," p. 93.

68. Hans Kohn, *The Idea of Nationalism* (New York: Macmillan, 1944), p. 20.

69. See Roger Gibbins, "Models of Nationalism: A Case Study of Political Ideologies in the Canadian West," *Canadian Journal of Political Science* (June 1977), pp. 341–73.

70. For a discussion of this theme's expression in Canadian literature, see Margaret Atwood, *Survival* (Toronto: Anansi, 1972).

71. Northrop Frye, *The Bush Garden* (Toronto: Anansi, 1971), p. iv.

72. The *Sun* (Vancouver), January 27, 1972, p. 6.

73. Margaret Atwood, *Second Words: Selected Critical Prose* (Toronto: Anansi, 1982), p. 380.

74. John Meisel, *Working Papers on Canadian Politics* (Montreal: McGill-Queen's University Press, 1973), p. 208.

75. J.R. Mallory, *The Structure of Canadian Government* (Toronto: Macmillan, 1971), p. 1.

76. Wise and Brown, *Canada Views the United States*, p. 94.

77. Ibid., p. 96.

78. For an expansion of this point, see Roger Gibbins, *Regionalism: Territorial Politics in Canada and the United States* (Toronto: Butterworths, 1982), p. 196.

79. J.H. Dales, "'National Policy' Myths, Past and Present," *Journal of Canadian Studies*, 14:3 (Fall 1979), p. 93.

80. Levitt, *Silent Surrender*, p. 148.

81. Mason Wade, "The Roots of the Relationship," in Dickey, *The United States and Canada*, p. 53.

INTERGOVERNMENTAL RELATIONS
AND CONSTITUTIONAL POLITICS

This chapter has three closely related objectives. The first is to trace the post-Confederation evolution of the Canadian federal state, picking up the story from where it was left at the end of Chapter 2. The second is to outline the growth of intergovernmental relations, a growth that has both shaped and been shaped by the more general evolution of the Canadian federal state. The third objective is to discuss the evolution of constitutional politics over the past fifteen or twenty years, with particular emphasis being placed on the 1982 Constitution Act, the 1987 Meech Lake Accord, the 1992 Charlottetown Accord, and the 1992 constitutional referendum. These three objectives can be seen as strands of a single rope or, to stretch a metaphor, as three sides of the same coin.

EVOLUTION OF THE CANADIAN FEDERAL STATE

Confederation created a highly centralized federal system in which the principal legislative responsibilities of the day were assigned to the federal government, and in which the powers of reservation and disallowance placed Ottawa in a quasi-imperial relationship with the provinces. If we imagine a continuum of hypothetical federal systems, anchored at one end by highly centralized systems and at the other by very decentralized systems in which provincial or state governments are pre-eminent, the Constitution Act of 1867 clearly lodged Canada at the centralized end of the continuum. However, the subsequent evolution of federalism has been characterized neither by entrenched centralization nor by steady progression toward decentralization. Instead, the federal system has oscillated across this continuum. Within the bounds of a constitutional division of powers largely untouched by formal amendment, Canadians have experienced a variety of quite different federal arrangements.

Centralizing Factors

The centralized federal system put into place by Confederation was reinforced in the early years by a massive migration of political talent to Ottawa. With the exception of Ontario's Oliver Mowat, who went on to become the province's premier, all the politicians voting for Confederation opted for elected or appointed national office.[1] The action for the political movers and shakers was in Ottawa, not in the provinces, and the new provincial governments, all but denuded of political talent, were in no position to challenge Ottawa's dominance. However, it was not long before the provincial governments, led by Mowat,[2] began to develop as centres of political gravity and to emerge as increasingly effective counterweights to Ottawa. Federal–provincial conflicts emerged over language and education issues in Ontario and Manitoba, over the search for "better terms" in the Maritimes, and over boundary extensions for Ontario and Quebec. Nevertheless, the extent of intergovernmental conflict was contained by the small size and limited scope of the governments of the day. Given that neither level of government penetrated very extensively into the lives of citizens, there was little need for governmental interaction or coordination with respect to programs and services, and thus little opportunity for intergovernmental conflict. The federal and provincial governments had yet to occupy fully their own legislative domains, much less encroach upon the domain of the other order of government.

As the 19th century drew to a close, Ottawa's stature within the federal system was eroded by the country's sluggish economic growth. The federal government, caught in the midst of a prolonged worldwide depression, failed to deliver on the economic promise of Confederation. The West remained largely unsettled, and Canadians by the tens of thousands emigrated to seek their fortunes in the United States. Relief finally came in the mid-1890s. Coincident with the victory of Sir Wilfrid Laurier and the national Liberal Party in the election of 1896 came a lifting of the depression, the depletion of free land in the American West, and a spectacular increase in immigration to the "last, best West." The result was an unprecedented economic boom that spurred the agricultural settlement of the West and the industrialization of central Canada. Both the federal and provincial governments shone in the reflected light of the boom, and in the embryonic intergovernmental arena, the Laurier years were "characterized by a more constructive and harmonious pattern of relations between the federal and provincial governments than prevailed in the previous decades or was ever established again."[3]

The First World War brought English Canadians together in a collective national endeavour[4] that ushered in a sustained period of national dominance within the federal system. (The quite different response of French Canadians to the war is discussed in the next chapter.) The war experience and the economic growth it generated, the concentration of political power in Ottawa under the terms of the War Measures Act, and the recognition of Canadian independence that came with the 1926 Balfour Declaration and the 1931 Statute of Westminster all contributed to the growth of both Canadian nationalism and the federal government. During the 1930s, provincial and local governments buckled under the massive economic and social dislocation of the Great Depression. Only the federal government appeared to have the fiscal and administrative

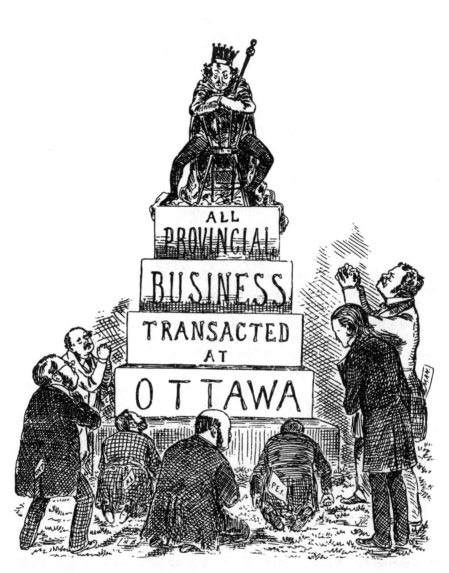

"Centralization"; or "Provincial autonomy abolished." Is this what Sir John is aiming at?

In J.W. Bengough, *A Caricature History of Canadian Politics*, vol. 2 (Toronto: Grip Printing and Publishing, 1886), p. 273.

resources to provide band-aids, though not always solutions, yet Ottawa's response was limited by an ideological disinclination to intervene and by a series of decisions made by the Judicial Committee of the Privy Council, which narrowly defined Parliament's jurisdictional domain. In short, the federal system was not up to the admittedly extraordinary demands of the day. As a consequence, a major overhaul of the federal system was recommended by the Rowell-Sirois Royal Commission on Dominion–Provincial Relations. In its 1940 report the commission called for a restructured federal system in which the federal government would have a greater role in social policy and economic management, and federal–provincial fiscal arrangements would be reformed to provide a more uniform national tax structure and greater federal assistance to the provinces.

Although preoccupation with the Second World War pre-empted any formal governmental response to the Rowell-Sirois recommendations, the war effort itself and the national economic recovery that it engendered moved the federal system along the path outlined by the commission. As a general rule, federal systems tend to centralize during times of military crisis,[5] and Canada was no exception. Provincial government opposition to increased centralization was neutralized when federal politicians campaigned in provincial elections in Ontario and Quebec to defeat governments they depicted as opponents of the nation's war effort. Just as the new federal government had done in 1867, Ottawa attracted "the best and the brightest" to staff the huge bureaucratic machine that regulated, and regulated surprisingly well, virtually every aspect of life during the war years. At the war's end, Garth Stevenson writes,

> the federal government appeared to stand at the height of its power and prestige in relation to the provincial governments. Canada had operated in wartime practically as a unitary state, and the provincial governments had been reduced to insignificance.[6]

During the war years Canadians had come to expect a predominant federal role in social legislation and economic management, a role that the enlarged federal bureaucracy was ready and eager to play in the postwar years. Between 1945 and 1960 the federal government greatly expanded its legislative reach by encroaching on provincial fields of jurisdiction. It did so principally through the spending power, which allowed Ottawa to spend, and thus indirectly to legislate, in provincial fields of jurisdiction. As Donald Smiley explains, "according to the constitutional doctrine that came to prevail, the central government might legally spend revenues as it chose, even on matters within the jurisdiction of the provinces, and could at its discretion fix the circumstances under which a potential recipient ... might receive the federal largesse."[7] Fuelled by tax money from a rapidly growing postwar economy, Ottawa established a series of conditional grant programs in the fields of health care, advanced education, and social welfare.

Conditional grant programs shared a number of characteristics, the most important being that they fell within the jurisdictional domain of the provinces. Program delivery was thus left to the provinces; the federal government's role was largely confined to providing financial support, usually matching provincial expenditures, in return for the imposition of national standards such as universal accessibility. Conditional grant programs and the national standards they embodied enjoyed broad public support in the postwar society. Although the provinces could choose not to participate, as Quebec did in some cases, the political and financial costs of nonparticipation were high. In fact, federal funds were generally welcomed, at least outside Quebec, as the provincial governments faced growing fiscal pressures from postwar electorates demanding enhanced programs in education, health care, and the social services. Caught between rising demand and limited fiscal resources—only Ottawa had the power to raise money "by any Mode or System of Taxation"—the provincial governments had little option but to accept conditional grants from the federal government. However, conditional grant programs were not cost-free. They distorted provincial spending priorities by forcing provincial governments to give highest priority to those programs where matching federal funds were available. Provincial governments raised concerns about the long-term commitment of the federal government to its share of the cost, and about the inflexibility that conditional grant programs imposed on provincial budgets and spending priorities. There was also growing principled resistance, led by Quebec, to federal encroachment onto provincial constitutional turf. Finally, conditional grant programs significantly altered the nature of federal–provincial relations by requiring extensive intergovernmental collaboration and coordination.[8] The name given to this new pattern of intergovernmental relations was "cooperative federalism," a term that often belied the fact that cooperation was largely a one-way street, and that the government paying the piper called the tune.

Ottawa's dominance in the federal system was an established fact to observers at the end of the 1950s. Bora Laskin, who was later to become Chief Justice of the Supreme Court, wrote in 1960 that "never since Confederation have the ideas so cherished by Macdonald for a strong and powerful central government, subordinating the provincial legislatures like so many larger municipal institutions, been so close to realization as they have been in the past ten years."[9] Also writing of the 1950s, J.A. Corry painted a similar scene:

> The most [a province] can hope to hold is its freedom for minor adventure, for embroidering its own particular patterns in harmony with the national design, for playing variant melodies within the general theme ... it is everywhere limited in the distance it can go by having become part of a larger, although not necessarily a better, scheme of things.[10]

And yet, by the early 1960s, the federal government was in retreat across a broad front in the face of resurgent provincial governments; the evolutionary drift toward an Ottawa-centred federal system had been stopped and even reversed. What, then, had changed in order to produce such a dramatic shift in the evolution of federal politics?

Decentralizing Factors

Even during the time of Macdonald's national leadership, the provincial governments had begun to resist what they saw as an excessively centralized federal system. The principal resistance came from the two central Canadian provinces, with Liberal-dominated Ontario being by far the most militant.[11] Although in the early decades after Confederation the provincial governments were unable to muster political and bureaucratic resources comparable to those possessed by Ottawa, their command over such resources would only increase with the passage of time. In this respect they were greatly assisted by a series of judicial interpretations that significantly augmented the powers of the provincial governments and eroded those of the federal government.

Until 1949 the umpire for the Canadian federal system was the Judicial Committee of the Privy Council, a situation that reflected not only Canada's colonial past, but also the fact that the Constitution Act of 1867 was an act of the British rather than of the Canadian Parliament. Thus its adjudication ultimately rested in British rather than Canadian judicial hands. As James Mallory explains, the JCPC

> *originated with the constitutional notion that British subjects in overseas colonies which owed their constitutions to prerogative grants had the right to bring grievances from the local courts to the foot of the throne for satisfaction.*[12]

In the majority of cases in which the JCPC was asked to rule on the federal division of powers, governments themselves were not the protagonists and intergovernmental conflict per se was not the source of the litigation. Most cases were brought forward by private interests trying to stem the growth of government, be it federal or provincial.[13] Canadian governments were nonetheless greatly affected by a series of decisions that over sixty years eroded the constitutional position of the federal government. Without formally altering Sections 91 and 92 of the Constitution Act, the JCPC decisions expanded provincial powers, curtailed those of the federal government, largely transferred residual powers to the provinces (at least in peacetime), reduced the strength of the trade and commerce clause, and cut down federal attempts to regulate natural resource trade with the United States. The "peace, order, and good government" clause was restricted to the enumerated headings of Section 91, to emergency situations, and to matters of national concern or having a "national dimension."[14] During the Great Depression a "judicial massacre" struck down

Prime Minister R.B. Bennett's attempt to impose a Canadian version of President Franklin Roosevelt's "New Deal."[15]

The long-term impact of the JCPC on the evolution of Canadian federalism has been a matter of considerable debate. On the one hand, Donald Smiley describes a consensus among English-speaking scholars that the committee's decisions were "nothing short of calamitous" in their erosion of the federal government's constitutional position.[16] Martha Fletcher concurs, arguing that the JCPC established a legal framework that "operated as a centrifugal force in the federation, dividing jurisdiction and thwarting attempts to centralize control in important areas of economic and social concern."[17] However, Alan Cairns argues persuasively that while the JCPC decisions unquestionably affected the nature of Canadian federalism and did depart from the 1867 formula, they were not out of line with other changes that were also promoting a more decentralized federalism.[18] Social change in the 20th century made the legislative domain of the provinces increasingly important. Whereas in the 1860s many of the matters assigned to the provinces were in reality left to the private sector, by the 1950s they had not only become primary concerns of government, but also involved massive consumption of public funds and programs. Education, hospitals, highways, and social services all fell within the provincial bailiwick, and as a consequence provincial governments grew in both absolute and relative terms as they embraced these new and costly responsibilities. As provincial governments grew, they began to attract a degree of bureaucratic expertise comparable to that traditionally recruited by Ottawa. While this bureaucratic expertise was not to reach full flower in the wealthier provinces until the 1960s and in the poorer provinces until the 1970s, its impact was beginning to be felt by the late 1950s when a reversal in Canada's postwar economic prosperity undercut public support for an expanding federal government. The failure of national policies to provide what were seen as adequate levels of material welfare "projected the provincial administrations into a more active role in economic affairs than they had heretofore assumed,"[19] and it was a role that the provincial governments were unwilling to surrender as the economy roller-coasted its way through the next thirty years. Finally, it should be noted that the federal powers of reservation and disallowance had fallen into disuse. The latter had last been used in 1943, and by the late 1950s both had become constitutional dead letters.

This stew of change in the federal system was brought to a boil by the onset of the Quiet Revolution in Quebec. Before 1960, Quebec had not challenged the fundamental character of the Confederation agreement; Quebec governments had concentrated more on protecting those powers assigned to the provinces and in warding off incursions by the federal government. After 1960, a number of interdependent changes were sought by Quebec, including Ottawa's withdrawal from provincial areas of jurisdiction, the expansion of provincial jurisdiction to provide more autonomous control over cultural and social policy, the conversion of conditional grants to unconditional grants in order to provide greater fiscal autonomy for provincial governments, larger equalization payments, more formalized intergovernmental relations analogous to those between sovereign states, and the right to participate in international relations with respect to matters falling within provincial jurisdiction. At the very least, such changes entailed a fundamental restructuring of the federal system, and to many observers both inside and outside Quebec their realization implied a degree of political autonomy indistinguishable from independence.

Taken alone, the Quebec demands were a major shock to the federal system. The shock then spread as other provincial governments used Quebec as the pointman for their own assault on the federal status quo. In a 1977 speech to the Alberta Progressive Conservative Party, Premier Peter Lougheed drew an explicit parallel between the Alberta and Quebec positions on Confederation:

> *Just as Albertans want more control over their destiny—primarily for economic reasons—Quebecers, I sense, want also more control over their destiny, essentially for cultural and linguistic reasons. Hence, just as Albertans want more government decisions made in Edmonton than in Ottawa, I think Quebecers, for different reasons, but somewhat similar motives, want more government decisions made in Quebec City, and fewer in Ottawa.*[20]

To be sure, no other provincial government went as far as Quebec, or came close to endorsing the extremes of independence or sovereignty-association. There was also considerable variability among the English-Canadian provinces, with Ontario and the Maritime provinces being more supportive of a strong national economic union refereed by a strong federal government than were provincial governments in the West and Newfoundland. Nevertheless, many of Quebec's concerns enjoyed generally enthusiastic governmental support outside Quebec, and across the board provincial governments became more sensitive to jurisdictional issues and more alert to federal encroachments onto their constitutional turf than they had been during the 1950s. In the West, the search for a greater national role for provincial governments was intensified when the elections of 1963, 1965, 1972, 1974, and 1980 produced federal governments with meagre elected representation from the region.

To the extent that there was a broadly shared provincial constitutional strategy, it contained the following elements: (1) the rollback of federal intrusions into provincial fields of jurisdiction, but the retention of the federal funds that had accompanied such intrusions; (2) the erection of more watertight barriers around provincial fields of jurisdiction; (3) the creation of more permeable barriers around federal fields of jurisdiction in order to facilitate greater provincial input into federal policy-making, particularly with respect to economic management; (4) more formalized intergovernmental relations; and (5) expanded provincial jurisdiction in selected fields. Whether the primary emphasis was on greater provincial autonomy or on greater provincial input into national policy, the emerging constitutional strategy necessitated a new style of intergovernmental relations. Thus the quest for reform in the character of intergovernmental relations went hand in hand with the changing dynamics of constitutional politics.

INTERGOVERNMENTAL RELATIONS

For many readers the term "intergovernmental relations" may conjure up images of federal–provincial conflict, for indeed it is difficult to pick up a newspaper or watch the evening news without encountering disputes between Ottawa and the provinces. Federal–provincial conflict is so pervasive it seems to flow into virtually every crack and crevice of the political system. Unfortunately, its very pervasiveness obscures the fact that governments collaborate more than they fight, that a complex web of programs, agreements, committees, and conferences draws the governments together in a common cooperative enterprise. No matter where Canadians might live, many if not most of the government services they receive involve intergovernmental collaboration. Your university or college, for instance, draws financial support from both federal and provincial governments; although Ottawa's support for post-secondary education through transfer payments is less direct and hence less visible than that coming from provincial governments, it is substantial. In addition, numerous federal departments and agencies from National Defence to the Social Sciences and Humanities Research Council are thoroughly entangled in post-secondary education, and even in primary and secondary education.[21]

In large part, the scale of contemporary intergovernmental relations reflects the general growth of government that has occurred since the end of the Second World War. As Chapter 2 describes, the "nightwatchman state," in which government was responsible for little more than the protection of borders and the maintenance of public order, gave way to the welfare state and extensive government intervention in the economy. Governments regulate what we watch and eat, where and what we smoke, when we fish, how we drive, and whom we hire or fire. As Richard Rose points out, the postwar growth of government was not restricted to Canada or to federal systems:

> Government is big in itself, big in its claims upon society's resources and big in its impact upon society. By every conventional measure, government looms large in the life of every Western nation today; governments differ from nation to nation only in their degree of bigness.[22]

In federal states, however, the growth of government takes on added dimensions because growth is seldom even across the various levels of government, and because it has such a marked impact on intergovernmental relations. Governmental growth is accompanied by an increase in intergovernmental contact and interaction, which in turn has resulted in "a large network of cooperative federal–provincial programs, most of which operate unobtrusively and cooperatively and together form a network of government which enables the country to function through the maze of elaborate jurisdictional overlaps that have emerged as government activities have expanded in recent years."[23]

Although cooperation is one product of increased intergovernmental interaction, conflict is another. Almost in a parody of the old western cliché, "this town ain't big enough for both of us," governments within federal states jostle against one another as they grow and necessarily interact. Intergovernmental friction can also stem from a number of other sources. In some fields, such as agriculture, the Constitution assigns concurrent jurisdiction to both orders of government, although in this case federal legislation is given paramountcy should conflict arise. Quite apart from the constitutional provision for concurrent jurisdiction, the two levels of government are both active in a multitude of additional policy domains including such things as environmental protection, public health, aboriginal affairs, transportation, and consumer protection. Thus intergovernmental conflict can arise if the two orders pursue different legislative intentions or regulatory procedures within the same policy domain, or if they compete for the same tax dollar. In policy areas not explicitly addressed in the formal constitutional division of powers, such as regulatory control over cable television, intergovernmental conflict can arise as the federal and provincial governments jockey for constitutional control. As noted above, the federal government may use its spending powers to invade provincial areas of jurisdiction. We also find that the actions of one level of government, even when taken exclusively within its own domain, can have a major impact on programs at the other level. National taxation policies, locational decisions with respect to the siting of federal agencies and military bases, procurement decisions, and regulatory decisions with respect to foreign investment can all have a substantial impact on provincial governments and economies. Conversely, provincial budgets may reinforce or counteract the fiscal policies of the federal government, and thus affect Ottawa's management of the national economy. All of these entanglements necessitate governmental interaction and provide potential ground for intergovernmental conflict.

Environmental protection provides particularly fertile soil for intergovernmental cooperation and conflict. Many environmental concerns, including but by no means limited to water and air pollution, are impervious by their very nature to the federal–provincial division of powers, and indeed to the division of the globe into sovereign nation-states. Problems spill across jurisdictional boundaries in a way that defies unilateral remedies. Yet the fact that effective environmental protection necessitates intergovernmental cooperation does little to ensure that such cooperation will be easy or inevitable. At times conflict may even arise as governments, in the search for votes, try to outdo one another as environmental champions.

Extensive intergovernmental relations are thus characteristic of all modern federal states, but the nature of such relations can vary considerably. In Canada, they have evolved in such a fashion as to take on a higher public profile and a more acrimonious tone than has been the case elsewhere.[24]

The Evolution of Intergovernmental Relations

The only intergovernmental mechanism built into the 1867 Constitution Act was the lieutenant governor, who "was originally envisaged as being a federal officer entrusted with the responsibility of communicating the views of the national government to provincial authorities and, if necessary, making certain that the provincial governments did not step too far off the path deemed correct for them by the national government."[25] It was assumed at the time that the federal and provincial governments would operate within their own constitutional domains and would rarely come into contact. Any federal–provincial interaction that did take place would occur mainly through informal party mechanisms; governmental interaction per se was not institutionally accommodated apart from whatever federal intervention in provincial affairs might occur through the lieutenant governor, and through Ottawa's powers of disallowance and reservation. As a consequence, the very complex intergovernmental infrastructure that we have today, and that has shaped the process and direction of constitutional change over the last two decades, evolved independently of the formal Constitution and did not achieve even parenthetical constitutional recognition until the 1980s. However, its constitutional informality in no way negates its importance. In Canada, as in other federal states, intergovernmental relations are central to the operation of modern government.

The early years following Confederation saw little need for extensive or formalized intergovernmental relations. The governments of the day were largely inactive even within their own legislative domains, and encroachments upon each other's turf were rare. The initial conference of "first ministers"—the Prime Minister of Canada and the provincial premiers—was not held until 1906 when Wilfrid Laurier met with the premiers in Ottawa. Subsequent Dominion–Provincial Conferences, as they were then called, were characterized by a short agenda, poor staff work, and the dominance of the federal government. The major topic of discussion was the perennial bugbear of Canadian federalism, fiscal transfers. The initial Premiers' Conference was held in 1887, followed by meetings in

1902, 1910, 1913, and 1926. The 1887 conference, which was a meeting of predominantly Liberal premiers called to orchestrate a partisan attack on the Conservative government in Ottawa,[26] set the tone for the meetings to follow. Then as now, the premiers dealt less with the coordination of provincial programs and administrative practices than with complaints against the federal government.[27]

The near collapse of provincial governments during the Great Depression increased the tempo of federal–provincial, although not interprovincial, interaction. The first ministers met four times during the 1930s and began to explore the greater institutionalization of federal–provincial relations. Speaking at the 1935 Dominion–Provincial Conference, Prime Minister Mackenzie King stated that "cooperation between the Dominion and the provinces is too vital a matter to be left entirely for intermittent conferences and to correspondence between governments."[28] King's stand was endorsed by the Rowell-Sirois Royal Commission, which recommended that a permanent intergovernmental relations secretariat be established. However, the outbreak of the Second World War pre-empted any such action. The War Measures Act sliced away federal–provincial entanglements, enabling Ottawa to act as if Canada were a unitary rather than a federal state. Moreover, after the initial electoral confrontations between Ottawa and the provincial governments of Quebec and Ontario, the war itself pushed federal–provincial issues from the nation's political agenda and reduced the public's tolerance for intergovernmental conflict.

By 1945 eighteen federal–provincial committees had been established to orchestrate Ottawa's wartime involvement in provincial fields of jurisdiction. This network formed the nucleus of what was to become a huge intergovernmental infrastructure. By the mid-1950s, when cooperative federalism was coming into full flower, more than sixty federal–provincial committees were in place, including a Coordinating Agency on Disease of the Beaver. The most important was the Continuing Committee on Fiscal and Economic Matters, a committee of senior finance officials that Donald Smiley has described as a major breakthrough in the institutionalization of federal–provincial fiscal relations.[29] By 1968 the number of federal–provincial committees, boards, and agencies had risen to 190.[30] In 1972 there were more than 400[31] and by 1975 the total reached almost 800.[32] With the growth in this infrastructure came an increase in the number of federal–provincial conferences, with the first ministers alone meeting approximately twice a year during the 1970s. This was the heyday of what Smiley has termed "executive federalism," a time when intergovernmental affairs overshadowed what seemed to be the more prosaic activities of the federal and provincial governments operating within their own jurisdictional domains. The importance of executive federalism stemmed not only from the frequency with which first ministers, ministers, and senior officials interacted, but also from the fact that such interaction played a critical role in shaping a multitude of government programs and services.

The centrepiece of executive federalism has been the First Ministers' Conference, which brings together the prime minister and the ten premiers.[33] (As we will see, the composition of the FMC has expanded in recent years.) The centrality of the FMC comes from the parliamentary concentration of power in the hands of the political executive and the further concentration of that power in the hands of the respective first ministers. Although the FMC receives passing mention in Sections 37 and 49 of the Constitution Act of 1982, it has no constitutionally derived source of power or authority; it is not a government, but rather a meeting of governments. If consensus reigns, the FMC can be a very powerful policy instrument as the participants can ensure the cooperation of both their cabinet colleagues and legislative assemblies. (The Meech Lake and Charlottetown accords, discussed below, were notable exceptions to this rule.) The first ministers can even shuffle jurisdictional responsibilities without formal constitutional amendment, as long as all participants agree. However, consensus is essential, for there is no decision-making rule apart from unanimous consent. If one of the participants disagrees with the rest, no mechanism exists through which the majority will can be imposed.[34] Decisions are binding only to the extent that participants wish to be bound and only to the extent that they are legislatively enacted. When the first ministers do not agree, as will likely be the case when serious matters are on the agenda, the FMC can become little more than a means of dodging responsibility, of pointing the finger of blame at other governments. It is not government, but political theatre in which first ministers posture for their electorates back home, exchange information, provide impetus for subsequent ministerial negotiations, and at times ratify agreements reached before the meeting began. It is also theatre with a rather large supporting cast; FMCs held over the 1980s averaged more than 200 formal participants over and above the first ministers themselves.

Here it is useful to point out two important features of the FMC. The first is that the participants must play several potentially conflicting roles. The prime minister not only chairs the conference, but is one of the active players, representing his or her government and party. The prime minister is also expected to articulate the national interest, as opposed to the more narrow provincial interests articulated by the premiers, although in another sense the national interest is expected to emerge from the joint deliberations of all eleven first ministers. For their part, the premiers are expected to represent their provinces while at the same time compromising those interests in order to reach an intergovernmental consensus. The second and related feature is that the most productive sessions tend to be those held in private, frequently over dinner and drinks, and away from the television cameras and the glare of publicity. Negotiation and compromise are difficult in a public arena where the forceful defence of one's governmental interests is likely to be of greater electoral value. Over the past few years informality has become almost the norm. Thus the first ministers

TABLE 8.1 *Frequency and Size of First Ministers' Conferences**

Period	# of FMCs	Average # of First Ministers and Advisers
1906–16	1	23
1917–26	1	40
1927–36	6	62**
1937–46	3	165
1947–56	6	103
1957–66	11	136**
1967–76	16	132
1977–87	17	218**

*Data do not include informal meetings, bilateral and regional meetings of first ministers, or meetings of the premiers alone.
**Data unavailable for one or more FMCs; averages based on available data.

Source: Data compiled by Scott McAlpine.

may meet for lunch or for dinner, as they did in Vancouver before Prime Minister Campbell attended her first G7 meeting in Japan. These informal meetings, which are not included in the official tabulation presented in Table 8.1, are more flexible and avoid the increasingly contentious issue of who should attend formal FMCs, and in what capacity. It is now difficult, for example, to exclude aboriginal representatives from formal FMCs, but the invitation list for lunch at the prime minister's residence can be much more restricted.

It should not be surprising that intergovernmental consensus, either between the federal and provincial governments or among the provincial governments themselves, is difficult to achieve. Few of the issues that confront contemporary governments are easily resolved, and the participants at the FMC represent a wide variety of regional, governmental, and partisan interests. Neither should it be surprising that the FMC has come in for a good deal of critical comment. Premier Lévesque and Prime Minister Trudeau, for example, both assailed the 1982 FMC on the economy, Lévesque calling it a "dialogue of the deaf" and Trudeau accusing the premiers of using the conference "to make ten speeches on television blaming the federal government for all the evils of the nation."[35] Garth Stevenson concludes that "despite all the advance preparation, expense and ballyhoo, the record of First Ministers' Conferences in reaching agreements or solving problems is exceedingly poor."[36] The FMC, Stevenson charges, resembles "a meeting of a medieval king with his feudal barons more than it does the government of a modern state."[37]

There is some concern that the symbolic output of the FMC may damage the fabric of federal politics, for more often than not the FMC has been a showcase for conflict and disunity, particularly in the public sessions. Related to this is a fear that the FMC may erode the legitimacy and authority of national parliamentary institutions. This general argument was advanced by Prime Minister Trudeau in a 1981 address:

> *Executive federalism is characterized by the idea that the role of Parliament in governing the country should diminish while premiers should acquire more influence over national public policy. In effect, this theory means that Canada's national government would be a council of first ministers.*[38]

The FMC and executive federalism more generally undercut the importance of cabinet ministers, MPs, and senators as channels of regional representation in the national political system; their role is pre-empted by provincial premiers and governments. Of equal importance, executive federalism undercuts the role of the parliamentary opposition. Opposition parties are not represented around the conference table; if they attend it is as observers only in the public sessions, and any agreements that might result are subjected to the most perfunctory parliamentary scrutiny. Yet, while the perspectives of parliamentary opposition parties may be excluded from the intergovernmental arena, other perspectives are ushered in. As Keith Banting notes:

> *A central role for federal–provincial negotiations diversifies that range of ideologies and interests that are brought to bear on major issues. While regional interests are stoutly defended by provincial champions, partisan and ideological differences also flow into federal–provincial channels.*[39]

FMCs and federal–provincial relations more broadly defined encompass only part of the intergovernmental activity that takes place; they co-exist with and to a degree engender an imposing network of interprovincial relations. Federal–provincial conferences and the interprovincial meetings held in preparation for such conferences provide provincial officials with the opportunity to discuss common interests and to promote interprovincial cooperation, often through the vehicle of federal–provincial programs. Interprovincial conferences quite apart from those linked to federal–provincial conferences are also commonplace. To provide but one example at the ministerial level, the Council of Ministers of Education

Simplifying the World Through the FMC

When countries participate in international affairs, they generally do so as unitary actors, speaking with one voice. Thus we hear that "France protested Y," "the United States backed X," and "Canada argued that Z warranted further study before any action is taken." Yet we know in fact that nation-states are seldom unitary actors, that they encompass a vast array of conflicting views and competing groups. Treating states as unitary actors admittedly simplifies the world, but simplification may also distort our perception of important political realities.

In Canadian politics, some of the same effects may be attributed to the FMC. As governments participate in the quasi-diplomatic environment of the FMC, they take on the attributes of unitary actors. Divisions within a provincial government or governing caucus, divisions that may be readily apparent to provincial residents in other settings, tend to fade as New Brunswick or Manitoba "speaks," "is listened to," or "stalks away from" the FMC. Complex political reality becomes simplified political theatre with a cast of eleven, not thousands.

brings the provincial education ministers together on an annual basis, a pattern followed by most federal and provincial departments. The Premiers' Conference, initiated as an annual affair in 1960 by Quebec's Premier Jean Lesage, brings together the ten premiers and approximately 150 aides, federal observers, spouses, and children for three days of socializing, informal discussions, and rhetorical broadsides at the federal government. The Council of Maritime Premiers brings together the premiers of New Brunswick, Nova Scotia, and Prince Edward Island, the Council of Atlantic Premiers expands to include Newfoundland, and the annual Western Premiers' Conference brings together the four western premiers. There is also, of course, extensive interaction between provincial governments and the local governments falling under their jurisdiction. However, at the present time there is little direct interaction between Ottawa and local governments, a situation unlike that in the United States where the large cities are vigorous congressional lobbyists and where federal programs frequently bypass the state governments to provide federal aid directly to local governments. Although Ottawa established a Ministry of State for Urban Affairs in the early 1970s, the experiment was quickly abandoned.

Table 8.2 provides some indication of the sheer volume of contemporary intergovernmental relations. While the Alberta case may not be typical of all Canadian provinces, the fact that most federal–provincial conferences are multilateral—involving all or most of the provincial

TABLE 8.2 *Intergovernmental Relations: The Case of Alberta*

Since 1974, the Alberta Department of Federal and Intergovernmental Affairs has maintained a detailed record of the province's participation in federal–provincial and interprovincial conferences. While this record may not reflect that of other provincial governments, it does illustrate the scope of intergovernmental relations in the Canadian federal system.

	1980	1981	1982	1983	1984	1985	1986	1987	1988	1989
Frequency of Federal–Provincial Meetings and Conferences										
• Bilateral (Alberta and federal governments only)	12	26	17	27	22	17	23	9	8	16
• Regional (Alberta, one or more of the other western provinces, and the federal government)	9	3	8	2	4	5	3	3	5	2
• Multilateral (all or most of the provinces and the federal government)	41	55	68	55	49	103	112	106	25	35
Total	62	84	93	84	75	125	138	118	38	53
Frequency by Level of Participation										
• First Ministerial	3	2	3	3	2	5	4	9	0	2
• Ministerial	32	47	42	47	54	61	72	64	38	51
• Deputy Ministerial	27	35	48	39	19	59	62	45	*	*
Total	62	84	93	89	75	125	138	118	38	51
Frequency of Interprovincial Meetings and Conferences	58	89	67	47	61	39	32	54	35	45

Note: * = no longer reported.
Source: Annual Reports of the Alberta Department of Federal and Intergovernmental Affairs.

governments—suggests that it is not abnormal. Table 8.2 shows that during the mid-1980s the Alberta government participated in approximately two federal–provincial conferences a week, every week of the year! On top of this, interprovincial conferences and meetings were occurring at an average of once a week. Although the pace of federal–provincial meetings dropped off significantly in the post-Meech period, the table still shows a congested intergovernmental agenda.

The extensive network of intergovernmental relations attests to the fact that most matters of public policy have an intergovernmental dimension. For example, when legislation was first introduced in 1983 to transfer responsibility for national security matters from the RCMP to a new civilian agency, it ran afoul of provincial governments who charged that the proposed legislation would encroach upon the provincial responsibility for the administration of justice. We need only wait for the definitive Canadian spy novel in which lawyers from eleven governments lead the reader in an exciting chase through the Constitution Act in order to determine if the foreign agent is a matter of federal or provincial jurisdiction.

The Institutionalization of Intergovernmental Relations

In a detailed study of the evolution of Canadian intergovernmental relations, Timothy Woolstencroft notes that during the 1950s and early 1960s, when cooperative federalism was in its prime and federal–provincial interaction centred upon shared-cost programs, "a community of interest, cutting across jurisdictional borders, developed among officials which facilitated harmony and cordial relations between the two levels of government."[40] By the late 1960s this community of interest, knit together by federal and provincial program officials who shared similar educational backgrounds, professional norms, and program commitments, came under growing suspicion. Provincial politicians in particular became concerned that bureaucrats were not sufficiently sensitive to jurisdictional issues, and that their commitment to program objectives might lead to the surrender of provincial jurisdiction in exchange for federal funds.[41] Both governments therefore began to create new central agencies through which they could exercise greater political control over the conduct of federal–provincial relations. These central agencies were established to protect their government from jurisdictional intrusions by other governments, and from jurisdictional compromises that might be entertained by program specialists within their own bureaucratic apparatus. They were also a response to the growing scope of intergovernmental relations, to the organizational demands imposed by the constant round of federal–provincial meetings, and to the need for greater expertise in the intergovernmental arena.

The first steps toward institutionalization were taken in Ottawa by the creation of separate federal–provincial divisions within the line departments such as Health and Welfare, Transport, and Agriculture. Here the cornerstone was laid by the 1954 establishment of a federal–provincial relations division in the Department of Finance. In 1968 a special Federal–Provincial Affairs division of the Privy Council Office was established to deal with federal–provincial relations, and by 1975 this had evolved into the Federal–Provincial Relations Office. In 1977 a Federal–Provincial Relations portfolio was established in the federal cabinet, but this was discontinued after the 1980 election; the FPRO then operated under the umbrella of the Prime Minister's Office, and reported to the prime minister through the Secretary to the Cabinet for Federal–Provincial Relations. Following the 1984 election, FPRO was once again granted ministerial representation in the federal cabinet. In 1991 Joe Clark became Minister of Constitutional Affairs, and FPRO fell under his ministerial wing. Then, in June 1993, Kim Campbell folded FPRO into the PCO and assumed direct responsibility for federal–provincial relations. When Jean Chrétien became prime minister, intergovernmental relations regained ministerial representation under Marcel Massé. Mention should also be made of the Intergovernmental Conference Secretariat in Ottawa, staffed by officials seconded from the federal and provincial governments. The secretariat provides liaison for the steady stream of federal–provincial conferences, many of which are held in Ottawa's old Union Station, which has been renovated as the National Conference Centre.

Given that federal–provincial relations touch most program activities of the federal government, the conduct of federal–provincial relations can be centralized to only a limited degree; the line departments handling such matters as agriculture and health care must also maintain a capacity for extensive federal–provincial liaison and policy interaction. At the provincial level, where federal–provincial relations have also been institutionalized, the central control of intergovernmental relations has been more complete. The provincial trend-setter was Quebec, which established a *Ministère des Affaires féderales–provinciales* in 1961. As the Quebec government expanded its international contacts, the mandate of the new ministry was also expanded and its name was changed in 1967 to the *Ministère des Affaires intergouvernementales*. The ministry was divided into two sections covering international and Canadian affairs. In 1984 the two sections were elevated to independent departments, *Affaires internationales* and *Affaires canadiennes*. The latter department maintains offices in Edmonton, Moncton, and Toronto, and contains a special branch to handle liaison with francophone communities outside Quebec. Other provinces soon followed the Quebec example, with the larger provinces going faster and further than the smaller ones. Ontario created a Federal–Provincial and Intergovernmental Affairs Secretariat in 1965. The secretariat was upgraded to a ministry in 1978 and, until 1981, also had responsibility for municipal affairs. In 1971 the Alberta government created the Department of Federal and Intergovernmental Affairs, while in 1973 Newfoundland created an intergovernmental affairs secretariat attached to the premier's office. Saskatchewan created an Office of Intergovernmental Affairs within the Executive Council Office in 1977, and upgraded it to a ministry in 1978. British Columbia created an Office of Intergovernmental Affairs attached to the premier's office in 1976, upgrading it to a full ministry in 1979.

The trend during the late 1970s and 1980s was toward greater institutionalization with independent ministries of intergovernmental relations.[42] However, with the 1992 collapse of the constitutional process, discussed below, and with a growing governmental emphasis on budgetary constraint and smaller cabinets, the more recent trend has been to fold intergovernmental relations back into the premier's office. While distinct bureaucratic organizations often remain, such as Alberta's Department of Federal and Intergovernmental Affairs, in all but the case of Quebec they report through the premier rather than through a separate Minister of Intergovernmental Affairs.

There has been considerable controversy among political scientists as to the impact of institutionalization. Donald Smiley has argued that institutionalization intensifies intergovernmental conflict by shifting federal–provincial relations from line departments to more politicized central agencies where the symbolic, jurisdictional, and electoral stakes are considerably higher. Of particular concern to Smiley was the intergovernmental specialist whose "single-minded devotion to the power of his jurisdiction" makes him or her an agent of jurisdictional aggrandizement rather than a conflict conciliator.[43] However, Timothy Woolstencroft argues that Smiley overstates the impact of and damage from intergovernmental relations specialists. He maintains that their dominance over program officials is far from complete, that when they do influence policy they are not always single-minded province-builders, and that in any event more profound forces than the specialists underlie intergovernmental conflict.[44] Woolstencroft is supported by a study of intergovernmental affairs in Saskatchewan in which Howard Leeson rejects the assertions that "separate departments of intergovernmental affairs result from an expansion of contacts and the consequent need to manage these new relationships."[45] Leeson argues that specific entrepreneurial interests of the provincial state, rather than the simple volume of intergovernmental activity or the abstract need to protect provincial jurisdiction, determine the course of institutionalization. The Saskatchewan study also supports Woolstencroft's assertion that "the impact of intergovernmental specialists in government is not nearly as decisive as other observers have concluded."[46] In any event, the institutionalization of intergovernmental relations has created what Hugh Thorburn describes as "a large and efficient machine" in each province to ward off intrusions from other governments, and "to sustain a status quo situation of watchful defence of individual provincial interests."[47] In this setting, even Woolstencroft describes the intergovernmental relations specialists as "the sentinels of the federal principle."[48]

Factors Affecting Intergovernmental Relations

Intergovernmental relations are often seen by the public to have a very acrimonious tone, and the complaint is often heard that the pervasiveness of "Ottawa-bashing" and "province-baiting" sours public life. However, intergovernmental relations, be they acrimonious or cooperative, should not be seen as an aberration; they are deeply rooted within the institutional fabric of the federal state. One of the most important features of the Canadian political system is the parliamentary concentration of power within cabinets, both in Ottawa and the provinces. As a consequence of the conventions of responsible government, and the party discipline that those conventions foster, cabinets dominate not only the executive arm of government, but also the legislative process. Of equal importance is the federal dispersion of power among the federal or national government, twelve provincial and territorial governments and, in the future, scores of aboriginal governments. The interaction of these two characteristics has produced unique patterns of intergovernmental relations and constitutional politics that set Canadian federal politics apart from the experience of other federal states.

Some of these patterns have already come to light in our previous discussion of intrastate and interstate federalism. An impotent Senate, party cohesion within the House, the secrecy that envelops both cabinet and caucus, and an electoral system that distorts the regional composition of parliamentary parties all impair the representation of territorial interests within the national government. As a consequence, such interests at times may find their primary expression through provincial governments; they are represented *to* rather than within national institutions. Regional conflict and intergovernmental conflict thus blend into and reinforce one another; regional conflict within national institutions becomes supplanted by conflict between powerful governments and their supporting bureaucracies.

In 1972, Richard Simeon introduced the notion of federal–provincial *diplomacy.*[49] The term is an insightful one, acknowledging as it does that federal–provincial relations have taken on many of the trappings of international relations: the importance attached to the symbols of sovereignty; a stress on the formal equality of all actors regardless of the size of the province or the level of government; the conduct of federal–provincial "summit meetings" in an atmosphere laden with pomp and ceremony; the treatment of governments as unitary actors rather than as complex packages of conflicting bureaucratic, partisan, and personal interests; and the use by governments of diplomatic "listening posts" on one another's turf. This diplomatic mode of intergovernmental relations and the broader phenomenon of executive federalism of which it is a part are made possible by the parliamentary concentration of power. Agreements reached by ministers, and particularly first ministers, are usually assured of governmental and legislative support. This means, however, that the participation of the House of Commons and provincial legislatures in federal–provincial relations is reduced to little more than a discussion of actions that have already been taken and the rubber-stamping of deals that have already been made. Given the scope of intergovernmental relations, this can entail a substantial constraint on legislative assemblies.

The limited number of provincial governments also facilitates a diplomatic mode of interaction. With only eleven principal participants at most federal–provincial conferences, albeit principals supported by numerous officials and advisers, everyone gets a chance to be seen and be heard, to know one another, and to garner maximum media coverage from conference events. The norm of formal equality can be maintained, whereas in the United States fifty states and the enormous status gulf between the positions of president and governor preclude anything analogous to the FMC. Incidentally, an implication of the role played by numbers is that the creation of new provinces in the North would seriously disrupt the intergovernmental status quo. Additional northern premiers, some of whom would represent populations equivalent to those found in small southern towns, would erode the diplomatic fiction of provincial equality, reduce the attention paid to any given premier, and as a result, enhance the stature of the prime minister.

There is no question that intergovernmental conflict is at times exploited and exacerbated in election campaigns. Ottawa-bashing is employed by provincial governments who prefer to campaign against the distant federal government rather than against provincial opponents. (Because it is easier to campaign against the federal government when it is of an opposing partisan stripe, provincial governments may offer only lukewarm campaign support for the national wing of their party.) While the opportunities are less frequent, national parties have also featured intergovernmental conflict in their campaigns, with the government party presenting itself as the one party able to stand up against avaricious and fractious provincial governments, and the opposition parties pledging that they will return a spirit of harmony and cooperation to intergovernmental relations. Thus, to a modest degree, intergovernmental conflict can be seen as a campaign artifact. The more important roots, however, draw their nourishment from institutional features of the Canadian federal state.

The style of intergovernmental relations has changed considerably over time as those relations have become more extensive and institutionalized. As mentioned above, intergovernmental relations have permeated virtually every aspect of Canadian public policy. However, it has been within the constitutional arena that intergovernmental relations have received their greatest play and have come under the greatest critical examination.

CONSTITUTIONAL POLITICS

The formal, intergovernmental debate over the amendment of the Constitution began around the time of Canada's centenary, and throughout the late 1960s and 1970s provincial governments moved toward a consensual constitutional vision in which both the formal powers and fiscal resources of provincial governments would be substantially increased. While provinces differed somewhat on their ultimate destination, they were all on the same road toward a more decentralized federal state, and by and large Ottawa's response was one of accommodation. "Opting-out" provisions initiated in 1964 opened the door for provinces to withdraw from joint federal–provincial programs without incurring any financial penalty if analogous provincial programs were established, although it was hoped that only Quebec would walk through. (With respect to the Canada Pension Plan, Quebec exercised its constitutional prerogative under Section 94A of the Constitution Act and did not opt in, establishing instead its own separate but fully compatible Quebec Pension Plan.) Fiscal ground rules were changed as conditional grants gave way to unconditional block grants. Although federal funding of shared-cost programs continued under the terms of the Federal–Provincial Fiscal Arrangements and Established Programs Financing Act of 1977, the level of federal funding was no longer tied to the level of provincial expenditure. In an extended round of constitutional discussions during the 1970s, Ottawa also appeared willing to discuss the devolution of some federal powers to the provinces. Thus despite Pierre Trudeau's image in parts of the country as an unrelenting centralist, his first eleven years in office were marked by an appreciable decentralization of the political system, a trend clearly at odds with that in other Western countries.[50]

This accommodative stance disappeared when the Trudeau Liberals returned to power in 1980 and Ottawa began to reassert the constitutional and fiscal presence of the federal government. Cooperative federalism was devalued and Ottawa became increasingly resistant to provincial encroachments upon its own domain. Federal–provincial conferences, which had provided a highly publicized stage for provincial attacks on the federal government, were de-emphasized as Ottawa tried to recapture the power of unilateral action. Extensive media campaigns were launched to explain what the Government of Canada was doing for, rather than to, Canadians. More subtly, these campaigns were designed to strengthen the bond between individual Canadians and their national government. Ottawa also began to pull back from shared-cost programs, which were consuming a large part of the federal budget and contributing to a growing national debt. The federal government was growing uneasy about a situation in which it was accountable to Parliament for funds spent on such programs even though it had little control over how those funds were spent by the

Regional and Age Variation in Support for Decentralization

There is considerable regional and age variation in the extent to which Canadians would support a more decentralized federal state. In December 1992, Gallup Canada posed the following question to a national sample of 1,021 Canadian respondents:

Some people feel that the provinces should be given more responsibilities in a variety of areas so that programs and services could be tailored to local needs. Others think that the federal government should maintain its current level of power in order to set national standards for programs. Which one of these points of view best reflects your own?

Across the country, 46 percent favoured more provincial control, 33 percent favoured the status quo, 11 percent favoured both, and 10 percent had no opinion. However, support for more provincial control ranged from a low of 36 percent in Ontario to a high of 64 percent in Quebec. In British Columbia 46 percent favoured more provincial control, compared to 42 percent on the prairies and 40 percent in Atlantic Canada.

There was also significant age variation in support for greater decentralization. Among those aged 18 to 29, 53 percent supported more provincial control. This level of support held among respondents aged 30 to 39, of whom 52 percent supported greater provincial control, and then fell to 45 percent for those aged 40 to 49, to 42 percent for those aged 50 to 64, and to only 30 percent for those 65 years of age or older.

Source: *The Gallup Report*, January 11, 1993.

provinces. Of particular importance, however, was the matter of political credit or "visibility." If, for example, Ottawa was to continue to pick up half the cost of advanced education, federal politicians wanted taxpayers to realize that advanced education was not being provided exclusively by the provincial governments. Ottawa did not want to be seen as the government that taxed heavily and did little in return for the average Canadian while provincial governments enjoyed the envious position of supplying popular programs invisibly financed in large part by federal transfer payments. In short, it was "no more Mr. Nice Guy" as a reassertive federal government and unrelentingly assertive provincial governments met in the wake of the 1980 Quebec referendum on sovereignty-association to hammer out a new constitutional framework for the Canadian federal state.

Andy Donato, *The Toronto Sun.*

In a 1982 news conference, Prime Minister Trudeau declared the death of cooperative federalism: "the old type of federalism where we give money to the provinces, where they kick us in the teeth because they didn't get enough ... is finished."

(Cited in Sheilagh M. Dunn, The Year in Review 1982: Intergovernmental Relations in Canada (Kingston: Institute of Intergovernmental Relations, Queen's University, 1982), p. 6.)

The Constitution Act, 1982

The seventeen months following the Quebec referendum witnessed extensive intergovernmental negotiations and public debate. Although the leading actors throughout were the federal and provincial governments, important supporting roles were played by the courts, the Progressive Conservative and New Democratic opposition parties in the House of Commons, the British Parliament, public opinion polls, journalists, academics, innumerable private Canadians participating in countless public debates, and a plethora of organized groups, among which women and native peoples were the most active. Yet despite all the activity, little progress was made until November 1981 when Ottawa and nine of the ten provincial governments—the premier of Quebec, René Lévesque, could not be brought on-side and left the meeting without signing—endorsed a constitutional accord. Five months later, on April 17, 1982, the Constitution Act was proclaimed by Queen Elizabeth II at a ceremony attended by all of the first ministers except Lévesque. After a prolonged, tortuous, and at times bitter process, Canadians had a new Constitution, or what former senator Eugene Forsey has more accurately described as the old Constitution "with knobs on." Let us look first at the knobs.

The Constitution Act of 1982 encompassed a number of important changes. First, the new Constitution included a Canadian amending formula or, more accurately, formulae, built into Part V, Sections 38 through 49, of the Constitution Act. The assent of the British Parliament is no longer needed for constitutional amendment. The basic amendment procedure is defined in Section 38(1):

> An amendment to the Constitution of Canada may be made by proclamation issued by the Governor General under the Great Seal of Canada where so authorized by (a) resolutions of the Senate and House of Commons; and (b) resolutions of the legislative assemblies of at least two-thirds of the provinces that have, in the aggregate, according to the then latest general census, at least fifty per cent of the population of all the provinces.

However, any amendment "that derogates from the legislative powers, the proprietary rights or any other rights or privileges of the legislature or government of a province" requires the consent of each province affected. Any amendment to the amending formula itself, to the office of the Queen, governor general, or lieutenant governor, to the composition of the Supreme Court, to the right of a province to have at least the same number of MPs as it has senators, and to most language guarantees requires the unanimous consent of Parliament and all ten provinces. Finally, the Senate's power in the amendment procedure has been limited to a suspensive veto; under Section 47(1), an amendment can proceed without the need for Senate approval if, after the passage of 180 days from approval by the House of Commons, the House again adopts a resolution in support of the amendment. The 1982 formula made no provision for public participation or consent although, as we shall see, the need for legislative consent opened the door for public involvement.

The most important change introduced by the 1982 act was the constitutionally entrenched Charter of Rights and Freedoms. Prior to 1982, constitutional documents primarily addressed the structure of government institutions and the division of powers among governments. The 1982 act expands the reach of the written Constitution to embrace the relationship between citizens and governments. This is not to suggest that Canadians lacked rights and freedoms in the past, for they did not, nor that such rights and freedoms were devoid of protection in the past, for they were not. However, the Charter enumerates those rights and freedoms, entrenches them within the written Constitution, and transfers the power to determine the practical limits of their application from a political process that is federally divided to a judicial process that is not.[51] The courts can now judge the constitutionality of acts of either Parliament or provincial legislatures on grounds other than the federal division of powers.

Admittedly, there are a number of important formal limits on the extent to which the Charter constrains governments. (There may also be important informal limits if courts and judges prove unwilling to embrace an activist stance toward the Charter and judicial intervention.) Section 1 of the 1982 act states that the Charter "guarantees the rights and freedoms set out in it subject only to such reasonable limits prescribed by law as can be demonstrably justified in a free and democratic society." As discussed in Chapter 3, legislatures can also use the Section 33 "notwithstanding" clause to override some sections of the Charter for a renewable five-year period. The "notwithstanding" clause thus provides a constitutional mechanism of noncompliance with Supreme Court decisions,[52] a mechanism that is available to both orders of government, but that to date has only been employed by the legislative assemblies of Quebec and Saskatchewan. It is one of the most innovative features of the Constitution Act, providing a parliamentary and in some senses a democratic check on judicial activism that departs too radically from the political mainstream; "its existence removes much of the anti-democratic sting from judicial decisions vetoing the acts of the democratically accountable branches of government."[53] For example, if the Supreme Court were to take an overly restrictive or not sufficiently restrictive approach to an issue such as abortion or pornography, legislative assemblies could step in to modify the policy parameters outlined by the court and to "immunize" their legislative response from further court action. The "notwithstanding" clause also reflects the federal character of Canada in that it enables provincial governments to circumvent the universal application of the Charter. In 1988, for example, the Quebec National Assembly was able to use the "notwithstanding" clause to reinstate unilingual sign provisions in the province's language law after those provisions had been struck down by the Supreme Court.

As the ongoing sign debate illustrates, any use of the "notwithstanding" clause is likely to be very contentious. Indeed, the sign debate brought the clause itself under political attack from those who wanted Charter-based rights placed beyond the reach of legislative assemblies. In a speech to the House of Commons on April 6, 1989, Prime Minister Mulroney went so far as to declare that "a constitution that does not protect the inalienable and imprescriptable individual rights of individual

Canadians is not worth the paper it is written on." Mr. Mulroney called on MPs and premiers to amend the Constitution so as to remove the "notwithstanding" clause: "All members ... will want to work together over the next few years as best we can to make sure that the Constitution is improved and that that major flaw [the "notwithstanding" clause] which reduces your individual rights and mine, which holds them hostage, is dealt with collectively by the premiers so that all Canadians have their fundamental rights and know they exist together." This suggestion was not met with any enthusiasm by Quebec Premier Robert Bourassa, who pointed out that Section 38.3 of the amending formula would make it impossible for the "notwithstanding" clause to be removed without Quebec's consent, and that Quebec's consent was not to be expected. Gradually the clause began to drift out of the constitutional debate, and by the time of the 1992 Charlottetown Accord it was no longer an issue.

There is no question that the Charter has had a major impact on Canadian political life, and that its impact is likely to increase in the years ahead. The Supreme Court will ultimately determine what the rights embedded in the Charter mean in practice, and this will to a significant degree politicize the judicial system. The courts now provide an important political resource and arena for groups and individuals who feel their interests have not been adequately taken into account by Parliament and provincial legislatures, or who have lost in the legislative arena. The Charter also weakens the ability of governments to control the political agenda; court action can propel issues back onto the legislative agenda despite the best efforts of governments to keep them off. In the short run, the increased involvement of the courts in the political process may work to the detriment of more conventional political actors and institutions. As Leslie Pal and David Taras point out, Canadians combine an unrealistic view of the courts with a pervasive political cynicism:

> We see judges and courts as above mundane politics. They are lordly, pristine, and they set precedents for our common welfare, unlike the lowly rascals who are elected to political office. This mistake is dangerous because it fails to recognize that when courts get into the rights game, they are no better equipped to decide matters of public policy than are legislatures.[54]

In the longer run, public perceptions of judges and the courts are likely to be corroded as both are drawn further into the political fray. For better or for worse, we can expect a greater "judicialization" of political life,[55] a greater pursuit of political ends through judicial means and within a judicial arena that is national in design and intent.[56] If Charter-related decisions by the courts continue to have a greater impact on provincial legislation than on legislation passed by Parliament,[57] and if the thrust of such decisions is to strike down provincial departures from national norms and standards, then the Charter could also tilt the federal balance by nationalizing Canadian political life. More generally, the Charter will force Canadians to grapple with the complex problems posed by the combination of judicial review and federalism, problems not addressed by the country's founding constitutional document despite a good deal of American precedent.[58]

A more abstract but potentially even greater change may come from the Charter's impact on the political culture, on the norms and values that bond the political community. The Charter focuses our attention on rights shared by all Canadians, and on rights that will receive their definitive form through a national institution, the Supreme Court of Canada. In this sense, the Charter may obscure the nation's federal character and blunt territorial identities by reorienting the political culture to rights shared by all individuals regardless of where they might happen to live. In Pierre Trudeau's words, "the Charter defines the common thread which pulls us together." It can be argued, however, that while a rights-based political culture may blur regional distinctions within Canada, it may also blur the distinction between Canada and the United States. In the words of Pal and Taras, "Canada is moving toward an American-style system in which individual rights are the primal scream of political consciousness."[59] Our political language has become infused with, and perhaps overburdened by, the terminology of rights. Conflicts over matters of public policy are increasingly framed in terms of "rights"; where people used to speak of "interests" or "claims," they now speak in the more absolutist language of rights. Unfortunately, rights provide more barren ground for pragmatic political compromises and trade-offs; they are not easily digested by the political process, and the stakes in relatively routine political decisions are increased as the protagonists are unwilling to accept any decision that might compromise their rights. The Charter provides the foundation for a new rights-based and nationally oriented political culture that does not sit easily with the federally based Constitution formulated in 1867.

In addition to the Charter and the amending formula, four other sections of the 1982 Constitution Act should be mentioned. Section 36 builds in a constitutional commitment to equalization payments, although it is unlikely that this section will have much impact on public policy as the principles that it enshrines are not new to the political community. Section 6 guarantees mobility rights including the right of every citizen to enter, remain in, and leave Canada, and the right of every citizen to take up residence in, and pursue a livelihood in, any province of his or her choice. Section 6(4), however, states that these latter provisions "do not preclude any law, program or activity that has as its object the amelioration in a province of conditions of individuals in that province who are socially or economically disadvantaged if the rate of employment in that province is below the rate of employment in Canada." Thus provincial legislation designed to give employment preference to residents of a particular

Jeffrey Simpson on "The Equality Industry"

The cry for equality, however defined, has been and remains an imperative in Canadian public discourse.

Governments everywhere are pressed daily to render justice to individuals, groups and regions feeling aggrieved. Such cries have been heard often before; nowadays they form the background music for everything that happens in government.

Naturally enough, governments have responded in a variety of ways, including a proliferation of bodies and laws attempting to define equality ... there are now 11 provincial and territorial human rights commissions [plus the Canadian Human Rights Commission], nine provincial ombudsmen, four specialized federal ombudsmen or quasi-ombudsmen, plus a body of statutes governing equal employment. And, of course, there is the Charter of Rights and Freedoms.

We may, therefore, describe these institutions and laws as the bricks and mortar of the equality industry, whose clientele theoretically includes all citizens, though in practice it is made up of minority groups. In the evolution of this industry, persuasion is yielding to regulation and reaction to positive action.

Source: The Globe and Mail, April 7, 1989.

province could be struck down by the courts if passed in Ontario, but not if passed in Newfoundland. Section 92A, which addresses the 1867 division of powers, shores up provincial ownership of and control over nonrenewable natural resources, forestry resources, and electrical energy. Finally, Section 35 defines the aboriginal peoples of Canada to include the Indian, Inuit, and Métis peoples, and states that "the existing aboriginal and treaty rights of the aboriginal peoples of Canada are hereby recognized and affirmed."

In a variety of ways, then, the 1982 Constitution Act undeniably altered Canada's constitutional underpinnings; some of the "knobs" referred to by Senator Forsey are very big knobs indeed. However, the outstanding *federal* characteristic of the act lies in its continuity with the past. There was no formal amendment to the constitutional division of powers, apart from the addition of Section 92A, even though that division was a source of intergovernmental friction throughout most of the 1960s and 1970s. The act did not address institutional constraints on regional representation; although both the amending formula and Section 92A closely matched the stance adopted by the western premiers in the constitutional negotiations, Senate reform and institutional reform more broadly conceived were not addressed. The act did not appeal to popular sovereignty and thereby did not strengthen the identification of individual Canadians with the constitutional apparatus of the federal state. Most importantly, the act did not address, except by its silence, the place of Quebec within the federal state and national political community. Although the federal government had pledged itself to a "renewed federalism" should Quebeckers reject the 1980 referendum on sovereignty-association, the end product of the constitutional negotiations set in motion by that defeat did not alter Quebec's role. Nothing was changed with respect to the jurisdictional authority of the National Assembly or with respect to Quebec's representation in federal institutions. Nor did the act include a preamble within which Quebec's claim to a unique stance within the national community might be acknowledged. For these reasons and more, Donald Smiley denounced the Constitution Act as a betrayal of Quebec:

> The pressure of both government and opposition parties in Quebec provincial politics from 1960 onward has been for an enhanced range of autonomy for the authorities of that province and corresponding restrictions on the power of the federal government over Quebecers. The Constitution Act, 1982 restricts the powers of the Legislature and government of Quebec and was brought into being by a procedure which was opposed by that Legislature and government. Furthermore, the constitutional reform which was effected in the spring of 1982 was an integral part of a general initiative from Ottawa towards a more highly centralized federal system. The pledges of constitutional reform made to the Quebec electorate by the federal Liberal leaders have not been honoured, and it is not too much to say that this electorate has been betrayed.[60]

The proclamation of the 1982 Constitution Act temporarily brought to a close a constitutional process that stretched back to the early 1970s. However, because the act left so many loose ends, because it had not addressed unresolved questions relating to Quebec's status and institutional reform, the pause in constitutional negotiations was bound to be brief. As Alan Cairns observed in 1983:

> In French–English relations, Quebec–Ottawa relations, and federal–provincial relations more generally, there is no resting place, no end to tensions and frustrations. There are no constitutional utopias. We have to be satisfied with the stumbling efforts of imperfect men to keep our problems at bay. From that perspective a restrained half cheer may be suggested as the appropriate response to the new Canadian constitution. It is the only constitution we have.[61]

In the spring of 1987, a very different group of imperfect men met at Meech Lake to address the loose ends of 1982.

The 1987 Meech Lake Accord

In the first few years following the ratification of the 1982 Constitution Act little could be done to overcome Quebec's self-exclusion from the constitutional agreement; movement required, at the very least, a change in players. Then, in early 1984, Pierre Trudeau announced his retirement, and in September 1984, a new Progressive Conservative government led by Brian Mulroney swept to power in Ottawa. In Quebec, René Lévesque also retired, and in the 1985 Quebec provincial election the Parti Québécois government was defeated by the Liberals, led by Robert Bourassa. Thus Canada had a new prime minister determined to solidify his party's still tenuous hold on the Quebec electorate, and Quebec had a new premier determined to prove to nationalist forces in the province that a federalist premier could protect and enhance the political autonomy of Quebec within Canada. Thus the stage was set for another round of constitutional negotiations. The lead was taken by the government of Quebec in 1986 when it announced five conditions that would have to be met if Quebec were to return to the constitutional fold: (1) the constitutional recognition of Quebec as a distinct society; (2) the right to opt out, with full financial compensation, from new federal programs in fields of exclusive provincial jurisdiction; (3) an expanded provincial veto for constitutional amendments; (4) a role in appointments to the Supreme Court of Canada; and (5) the constitutional entrenchment of Quebec's role in immigration, a role that had been expanded over the years through agreements between the Quebec and federal governments. These five conditions were endorsed at the August 1986 Premiers' Conference in Edmonton as the foundation for a resumption in constitutional negotiations. Then, at an informal first ministers' meeting at Meech Lake on April 30, 1987, a tentative constitutional accord was unanimously endorsed by the first ministers. After fine-tuning the following month at a meeting at the Langevin Block in Ottawa, the Meech Lake Accord emerged on the 3rd of June. It was not only endorsed by all eleven first ministers, but received enthusiastic support from opposition leaders in the House.

The accord met Quebec's five conditions, but did so in such a way as to overcome some of the traditional opposition to special constitutional status for Quebec. It expanded Quebec's veto on constitutional change by extending the unanimous consent provisions of the 1982 amending formula to include the powers of the Senate; the method of selecting senators; the number of senators by which a province is entitled to be represented; the principle of proportionate representation of the provinces in the House of Commons; the Supreme Court of Canada; the extension of existing provinces into the territories; and the creation of new provinces. Thus while Quebec's role in the amending formula would be enhanced by the accord, it would be no greater than that of any other province. The accord gave all provinces the right to opt out, with full financial compensation, from new federal programs in areas of exclusive provincial jurisdiction, provided that the opting-out provinces initiated their own programs to meet the national objectives of the federal program. It stated that future appointments to the Supreme Court and to the Senate would be made by the federal government from lists submitted by the provinces, although only in the case of Quebec were three positions on the Supreme Court tied specifically to one province. The accord also gave expanded constitutional recognition to Quebec's role in immigration, recognition that could be extended to other provinces in the future should they request. In these instances, then, Quebec's conditions were universalized to include all ten provinces. Quebec received special, albeit somewhat ambiguous, constitutional status only in the accord's recognition that "Quebec constitutes within Canada a distinct society."

The initial reaction to the accord was generally positive. Although vigorous concerns were expressed by Pierre Trudeau, and although northerners, francophone minorities outside Quebec, Senate reformers, and some women's organizations were uneasy with parts of the accord, it appeared to be a constitutional *fait accompli*. However, the first ministers had allowed three years for the accord's formal ratification by Parliament and the ten provincial legislative assemblies, and this decision allowed opposition to build as the accord was exposed as a target for increasingly critical public inspection. More importantly, the prolonged ratification period meant that some of the first ministers and provincial governments that had initially supported the accord fell by the wayside in the wake of provincial elections. Ratification proceeded quickly in some of the provinces, including Quebec, but at a more leisurely pace in others. As a result, the accord had yet to be ratified in New Brunswick when the incumbent Progressive Conservative government went down to defeat in a provincial election. The incoming Liberal government, led by Frank McKenna, stated that it was opposed to the accord on a variety of grounds, and would not proceed with ratification until public hearings had been held. Whether by design or not, Premier McKenna then became the national spokesperson for those who opposed the accord. The incumbent NDP government in Manitoba also went down to defeat before the accord's ratification. The leader of the new minority Progressive Conservative government, Gary Filmon, initially supported the accord, but the opposition parties were opposed. Then in December 1988, when the Quebec government overrode the Supreme Court's decision on Bill 101, Filmon also came out against the accord. In the spring of 1989, the Progressive Conservative government in Newfoundland, which had secured legislative ratification for the accord, went down to defeat, and the new Liberal premier, Clyde Wells, withdrew that province's support for the accord until changes were made. By so doing, Premier Wells took on the informal national leadership of those opposed to the accord.

By the spring of 1990, when the first ministers met again in Ottawa, public support for the accord had fallen sharply. Ratification was stalled in the Manitoba legislature by aboriginal MLA Elijah Harper, whose opposition to the accord not only crystallized growing aboriginal concern, but also strengthened the resolve of many nonaboriginal Canadians who were uneasy with the bicultural and binational underpinnings of the accord. The five-day meeting in Ottawa failed to provide a way out of the impasse, and on June 23 the constitutional window for ratification closed; the Meech Lake Accord was dead despite its initial endorsement by the eleven first ministers three years earlier.

The primary objective of the accord had been to overcome Quebec's refusal to endorse the 1982 constitutional agreement. As Brian Mulroney said somewhat prematurely when the accord was first signed: "Tonight Canada is whole again, the Canadian family is together again, and the nation is one again." In an editorial calling for ratification of the accord by Manitoba and New Brunswick, *The Globe and Mail* (June 6, 1989) was even more emphatic:

> *Meech Lake is intended almost solely to bring Quebec willingly under the authority of the 1982 Constitution Act. Meech Lake should be immune to criticism for failing to achieve other ends; it was not intended to do so. [emphasis added].*

However, the accord's potential impact was not restricted to Quebec, for it touched upon the power and role of all provincial governments; the nature of federal institutions including the Supreme Court, the Senate, and First Ministers' Conferences; the creation of new provinces; future social programs; and possibly judicial interpretation of the Charter. As Keith Banting notes:

> *The dynamics that would be set in motion by the Accord point to a more regionally diverse pattern of social service initiatives in the future.... Canadians crossing provincial boundaries would notice greater variation in program design than they would otherwise have done.[62]*

The accord was not a narrow document tailored to the specific constitutional interests and aspirations of Quebec; it was a much more sweeping constitutional agreement.

Not surprisingly, supporters and opponents of the accord disagreed on its potential impact on future constitutional change. Supporters argued that although there were other constitutional matters to address, negotiations on such matters could not proceed until the accord had been ratified and Quebec had been brought back to the constitutional table. Opponents argued that once the accord had been ratified, further constitutional change would be very difficult if not impossible to achieve, in part because

Roy Peterson, *Swamped* (Vancouver/Toronto: Douglas and McIntyre, 1987), p. 12.

of the expanded provisions for unanimous consent and in part because Quebec might be indifferent and even hostile to further constitutional change once its own constitutional aspirations had been met.

A good deal of the opposition to the accord was directed to the process that produced it rather than to the contents of the accord per se. Concern was expressed that eleven men, meeting in private, could rewrite the country's basic constitutional parameters. Admittedly, the formal intergovernmental process that produced the initial accord was not significantly different from that that produced the Constitution Act of

1982, and in this latter case there had been little procedural criticism.[63] With the Charter now in place, however, Canadians were more prone to see the Constitution as a contractual agreement between citizens and their governments, and not solely as an agreement among governments. This paradigmatic shift rippled throughout the Meech Lake debate, and found a means of expression because the *ratification procedure* had changed since 1982. The new requirement for legislative ratification over and above endorsation by first ministers opened the door for public hearings and legislative debate. Both were to provide an effective stage for the accord's opponents, who grew in number as the ratification process stretched out over three years.

Here it is interesting to note Alan Cairns's insightful analysis of opposition to the accord. Cairns examined testimony to both the Senate and House committees on the accord, and came to the following conclusion:

> *The bitterness and passion that inform the presentations of the numerous groups objecting to the Accord are not based on a narrow instrumental calculation of its effects on the future flow of material benefits. Their anger is not driven by the fear of tangible gains foregone, but by a more complex battery of emotions. The representatives of women's groups, of aboriginals, of visible minorities, of supporters of multiculturalism, along with northerners and basic defenders of the Charter employ the vocabulary of personal and group identity, of being included or excluded, of being accepted or being treated as an outsider, of being treated with respect as a worthy participant or being cast into the audience as a spectator as one's fate is being decided by others. They employ the language of status—they are insulted, wounded, hurt, offended, bypassed, not invited, ignored, left out, and shunted aside. They evaluate their treatment through the lens of pride, dignity, honour, propriety, legitimacy, and recognition—or their reverse. Their discourse is a minority, outsider discourse. They clearly distrust established governing elites. They are in, but not of the constitution.[64]*

The Meech Lake debate demonstrated the symbolic and emotional salience of constitutional politics. Discussions of constitutional change necessarily embrace the underlying nature of the political community and the direction that community should take in generations to come. They tap deep emotional roots and, in some circumstances, expose deeply ingrained divisions within the political community. Constitution-making is an important form of community expression, and since the arrival of the Charter, Canadians have been less willing to have such expression limited to the first ministers. The extent to which the political culture has been transformed is dramatically illustrated by the round of constitutional politics that followed the death of the Meech Lake Accord.

The Charlottetown Accord and the 1992 Referendum

The constitutional process stalled temporarily after the collapse of the Meech Lake Accord. The first ministers and their constitutional teams had been exhausted by the process and many of the provincial governments had been burned; the defeat of the Liberal government in Ontario on the heels of the Meech debacle was not coincidental. However, there was no avoiding the fact that the country found itself in a serious constitutional crisis. In Quebec, the sense of betrayal instilled in many nationalists by the 1982 Constitution Act was deepened by the collapse of Meech Lake. The government of Quebec was adamant that it would not participate again in a multilateral process, that it would only deal bilaterally with the federal government, and that it would take unilateral action to pursue its own constitutional destiny. Only three months after the death of the accord the Quebec National Assembly established the Commission on the Political and Constitutional Future of Quebec. The committee, chaired by Michel Bélanger and Jean Campeau, was to recommend that a referendum on the best constitutional "offer" from the rest of the country or, lacking such an offer, on sovereignty, be held in Quebec before the end of 1992. Also within Quebec, the Liberal Party released the Allaire Report, which called for exclusive provincial jurisdiction in twenty-two areas and which, to most non-Quebeckers, was indistinguishable from a recommendation for full sovereignty for Quebec. Outside Quebec, the Citizen's Forum on Canada's Future, chaired by Keith Spicer, documented a profound and pervasive public discontent with the political status quo and with the temper of constitutional politics. There was, Spicer noted, "a fury in the land." The Spicer Report presented emphatic demonstration that constitutional unrest was not restricted to Quebec; its more implicit message was that any future constitutional initiative designed to address Quebec's concerns alone was bound to fail.

The constitutional process started again in response to the growing certainty that Quebec would hold a constitutional referendum by the end of 1992 regardless of what happened in the rest of the country. The Quebec deadline in effect set a deadline for the rest of the country; if there was not an offer on the table by the time of the Quebec referendum, then that vote would by default be a vote on sovereignty and the very continuation of Canada. In the rhetoric of the times, "a knife was being held to the throat of English Canada." Ottawa thus began once more to search for a constitutional deal, but this time through a radically different and ultimately far more open process. In the early spring of 1991, Prime Minister Mulroney kicked off the "Canada round" by establishing the Cabinet Committee on Canadian Unity. The CCCU was chaired by the new Minister of Constitutional Affairs, Joe Clark, thereby creating some distance between the committee and the very unpopular prime minister. Its mandate was to come up with a broad set of constitutional proposals by the early fall of

1991, but to do so without engaging in any formal intergovernmental consultation or negotiation, something that was precluded by Quebec's decision not to participate in multilateral forums. The cabinet committee therefore became the sole vehicle through which regional and other perspectives were solicited.

The committee's report, *Shaping Canada's Future Together*, was tabled in the House of Commons on September 24, 1991. It contained twenty-eight recommendations, including the following:

- that Quebec be recognized as a distinct society within Canada, and that the Charter be interpreted in a manner consistent with the preservation and promotion of Quebec as a distinct society;

- that the Constitution be amended to entrench a general justiciable right to aboriginal self-government within the Canadian federation and subject to the Charter of Rights;

- that a "Canada clause" be added to the Constitution that would, among other things, recognize the equality of men and women, the special responsibility borne by Quebec to preserve and promote its distinct society, and a commitment to the free flow of people, goods, services, and capital throughout the Canadian economic union;

- that the Senate be elected, that it provide for "more equitable" provincial and territorial representation than at present, that the Senate's approval be required for most Acts of Parliament, that the Senate not be a confidence chamber, and that Senate seats be reserved for aboriginal Canadians;

- that appointments to the Supreme Court be made by the federal government from lists of nominees submitted by provincial and territorial governments;

- that the Constitution be amended to strengthen the federal government's ability to manage the economic union;

- that the federal government recognize the exclusive jurisdiction of the provinces in the areas of tourism, forestry, mining, recreation, housing, and municipal/urban affairs;

- that labour market training be recognized as an area of exclusive provincial responsibility; and

- that the Constitution be amended to restrict the exercise of the federal spending power in areas of exclusive provincial jurisdiction.

In total, the recommendations reached well beyond the concerns of Quebec and the elements of the Meech Lake Accord to propose a sweeping transformation of the Canadian federal state. Of the major federal institutions, only the House of Commons was left untouched by the package of reforms.

Once *Shaping Canada's Future Together* had been tabled, the constitutional process shifted to a Special Joint Committee of the Senate and House of Commons, which had been put in place in June to receive the constitutional proposals. The committee, chaired eventually by Senator Gérald Beaudoin and MP Dorothy Dobbie, had been designed as the primary vehicle for public input and consultation, and it embarked upon an extensive round of public hearings held across the country. Committee members attended 78 public meetings, heard testimony from over 700 individuals, and received nearly 3,000 written submissions. Yet the committee was generally not well received, and therefore its hearings were supplemented by five major constitutional conferences, initiated and funded by the federal government but privately organized, and held in Halifax, Montreal, Toronto, Calgary, and Vancouver. The conferences each brought together several hundred delegates, largely appointed by governments, but also including constitutional experts, interest group representatives, and a smattering of the general public. The conferences were extensively televised, and their reports fed into the final report of the Beaudoin-Dobbie committee, which was released at the end of February 1992.[65]

The committee's report accepted the broad outlines of the September 1991 proposals and reinforced much of its underlying logic. It asserted that "the recognition of Quebec as a distinct society is in reality the affirmation of a legal, sociological and demographic fact."[66] Thus the distinct society provisions were presented as little more than a codification of the status quo. The report stressed the importance of regional alienation to an unparallelled degree:

> Our hearings have strongly confirmed the need for more effective representation of the outlying regions, and more responsive government. Many Canadians in the West and in the Atlantic provinces have a sense that their needs and concerns routinely lose out in decision-making within the central government. This sense of injustice, in turn, sometimes breeds a generalized suspicion of the centre, and resistance to legitimate demands coming, in particular, from Quebec.[67]

Regional alienation was therefore portrayed as both an intrinsic problem and a strategic problem because it created resistance to Quebec's demands. The solution was to be found in institutional reform:

> We must equip ourselves with the instruments of federalism possessed by virtually every other successful federation: such instruments will allow the people of Canada's regions to have, and to feel that they have, a real voice and influence in the national political life of our country, counter-balancing

in fair and appropriate ways the weight that central Canadians now enjoy through representation by population.[68]

The committee recognized, as the 1991 proposals had done only in part, that "regional representation must be understood as the representation of the people of the provinces and territories, rather than their governments."[69]

The committee did not accept the 1991 recommendations lock, stock, and barrel. The aboriginal right to self-government was strengthened and the application of the Charter to aboriginal self-government weakened, proposed changes to the "notwithstanding" clause were postponed to another round, changes to the Senate were fleshed out in greater detail, and recommendations were made that the House should be able to override a Senate veto, that Quebec be given control over cultural affairs, and that the proposed federal powers to manage the economic union be reduced. In general terms, however, the committee refined and endorsed the September 1991 proposals.

With the release of the committee's report the constitutional process shifted at last to the intergovernmental arena where representatives from the federal government, nine provincial governments, two territorial governments, and four aboriginal associations (the Assembly of First Nations, the Native Council of Canada, the Inuit Tapirisat of Canada, and the Métis National Council) met regularly for close to four months. This round of intergovernmental negotiations was unique in many respects. First, the government of Quebec was not at the table, although it was kept closely informed of any progress being made. Second, the territorial governments were at the table as full participants, and not just as observers as had been the case in the past. Third, aboriginal organizations were also present as full participants in a process that in the past had been restricted to governments.

By July a draft document was ready, and the government of Quebec, despite or perhaps because of serious misgivings about the content of the draft, came back to the table. In August the seventeen negotiating teams met for the last time, and the product was the Charlottetown Accord.[70] As had been the case in 1987, the accord was backed by the federal government and all ten provincial governments. In addition, it was endorsed by the territorial governments and aboriginal organizations that had participated in the negotiations. There was a deal, albeit one that put off a lot of the detailed negotiations until a later time. As Pal and Seidle note:

The original Charlottetown consensus was littered with asterisks indicating the "details" of a given provision would have to be decided in future intergovernmental meetings: most of these were simply rephrased in the legal text as "commitments to convene meetings." ... The potential agenda for future negotiations stretched well beyond view.[71]

The Charlottetown Accord provided a framework for future constitutional negotiations more than it did a new Constitution.

What remained to be decided was how the deal might be ratified. The formal process was clear; the package would have to be ratified through the procedures established by the 1982 amending formula. However, Quebec was committed to a referendum in the fall, both Alberta and British Columbia had passed legislation requiring a provincial referendum on any constitutional amendments before legislative ratification could proceed, and Premier Clyde Wells had said that a Newfoundland referendum was likely. The decision was thus made to hold a national referendum on the package, to roll the provincial referenda into the federal vote, and to avoid a situation where only some Canadians would participate directly in the ratification process. While the vote in Quebec was technically independent of the national vote and was conducted under somewhat different legislative guidelines, it was held on the same day—October 24, 1992— and posed exactly the same question.

The referendum campaign was fought vigorously over September and October. The yes campaign was indirectly spearheaded by the federal and provincial governments, although some of the latter were less than emphatic or enthusiastic in their support. The no campaign brought together a less coherent alliance of opponents, which included the Reform Party, the National Action Committee on the Status of Women, Pierre Trudeau, and a variety of groups whose earlier concerns about the Meech Lake Accord were only reinforced by the latest package. Aboriginal support for the accord was at best mixed and hesitant, even though unprecedented, indeed sweeping, aboriginal gains were woven throughout the Charlottetown Accord. Despite endorsation from all governments, and despite an initially positive public response, the referendum went down to national defeat, and to defeat in Nova Scotia, Quebec, and the four western provinces.[72] The constitutional process stretching back over almost twenty-five years had come to a crashing halt.

Immediately after the referendum Decima Research conducted a survey of 900 voters for *Maclean's* to determine why they had voted as they did.[73] Among respondents outside Quebec, the primary reasons for voting no were that "Quebec got too much" (27 percent), "the agreement is a poor one" (22 percent), "the provinces should not be given more power" (15 percent), and "I am opposed to Brian Mulroney" (8 percent). The primary reasons cited by those respondents who voted yes were "a yes vote will help keep Canada together" (26 percent), "the agreement represents a fair compromise" (22 percent), "it is time to put constitutional matters behind us" (15 percent), "a no vote would be very negative for the country" (13 percent), and "the agreement represents constitutional improvements for Canada overall" (13 percent). Quebec respondents who voted no said that the deal was a poor one (56 percent) and that Quebec failed to get enough concessions from the rest of Canada (44 percent). The most

TABLE 8.3 Results of the 1992 Constitutional Referendum

	Yes	No
Canada	44.6	54.4
Newfoundland	63.2	36.8
Nova Scotia	48.8	51.2
New Brunswick	61.8	38.2
Prince Edward Island	73.9	26.1
Quebec	43.3	56.7
Ontario	50.1	49.9
Manitoba	38.4	61.6
Saskatchewan	44.7	55.3
Alberta	39.8	60.2
British Columbia	31.7	68.3
Northwest Territories	61.3	38.7
Yukon	43.7	56.3

Note: Overall, 1 percent of the ballots were spoiled. The turnout rate was 74.7 percent for Canada as a whole, and ranged from 53.3 percent in Newfoundland to 82.8 percent in Quebec.

popular reason (31 percent) among Quebec voters who supported the accord was that the deal would help keep Canada together. The Decima survey also found that support for the accord was greatest among relatively young respondents, among those with the highest incomes, and among those with the most formal education; university graduates in the sample supported the accord by a margin of 54 percent to 46 percent. There was no significant difference between men and women in their vote on the accord.

The 1992 referendum did not result in a new Constitution, nor is it likely to have brought Canada's prolonged constitutional debate to a close. However, the referendum campaign and the broader constitutional process of which it was a part do suggest a number of conclusions about the future of constitutional politics. First, they demonstrate how difficult it will be in the future to find an agreement. If we look back over the 1982 to 1992 period, we witness a steady expansion in both the scope of the agenda and the number of players. Neither expansion, however, has made the consti-

On October 26, 1992, the people of Canada rejected the government's constitutional package, but their vote cannot be interpreted as a vote for the permanent division of the country. Thus, the Quebec question remains. Even now, fears are growing that a departure of Robert Bourassa from the scene will advance the day when we must all face the constitutional music once again.

When the time comes, Canadians can choose one of two ways to confront the Quebec question: try again to achieve a constitutional compromise inside a pressure cooker and with the ever-present threat of national dissolution in the event of failure; or accept the realities that have emerged from the referendum and from the five futile years of constitutional debate that preceded it and try another way.

The basic reality to emerge from Oct. 26 is that the place of Quebec in Canada cannot ever be constitutionally defined. There are two reasons for this. First, English-speaking Canada has killed special status for Quebec however it might be packaged. This means no "asymmetrical" federalism, no constitutionally defined distinct society, no sovereignty-association. Second, Quebec has killed the notion of Canada as 10 equal provinces, to say nothing of the equality of citizenship in whatever guise these proposals have been raised. This means no Triple-E Senate, no unconditional embrace of the Charter of Rights and Freedoms, and probably no repeal of the notwithstanding clause....

On one level, this is an impasse. No group of politicians who truly represent their constituents will be able to agree on a single set of constitutional principles that a majority of both Quebecers and English-speaking Canadians can support. Despite this impasse, however, neither Quebecers nor English-speaking Canadians want to divide the country. Whether for reasons of emotion, tradition, inertia, fear or raw self-interest, most Canadians, inside and outside Quebec, want Canada to remain one country.

This apparent contradiction cannot be reconciled, but must be accepted as the starting point for an effort to reconfederate Canada. That effort must be political. If it is constitutional, it again will fail....

If a solid majority of both Quebecers and English-speaking Canadians can agree only on the premise that the country must hang together, that is enough common ground for the national parties to be able to broker and balance whatever other aspirations they and other Canadians might have. That, after all, is what they did at Confederation and for most of Canadian history afterward.

So let us all accept that Canadians will never be a single people: not linguistically, not culturally and, therefore, not constitutionally. Let us accept as well that it would be folly to destroy a viable, decent, and well-off country simply because no one group of its citizens or their political leaders will ever be able to agree completely on one set of fundamental constitutional principles.

Source: *The Toronto Star,* February 8, 1993.

tutional process easier to manage, nor a successful outcome more likely. If we look ahead, there is virtually no prospect that the number of players will decrease or that the agenda will be compressed to focus primarily on the concerns of Quebec, as was the case in 1987. Second, and very much related to the first conclusion, the conventions of constitutional amendment have been fundamentally changed even though, in a formal sense, the 1982 amending formulae are still in tact. It will be all but impossible for governments to embark upon significant constitutional change in the future without going to the people in a national referendum. We have, finally and somewhat reluctantly, embraced popular sovereignty with respect to constitutional change.[74] Only extremely courageous (or foolhardy) governments would attempt to elude that embrace in the future.

The third conclusion is that the constitutional process to date has established some firm expectations for the content of any future agreement, although these expectations are not necessarily consistent with one another. Western Canadians are likely to assume that a Triple E Senate and, even more emphatically, the constitutional equality of the provinces have finally been accepted as part and parcel of any deal. For their part, Quebeckers are likely to see the referendum result as a repudiation of the Charlottetown Senate reform package and, even more emphatically, are likely to assume that some form of asymmetrical federalism, incorporating a distinct constitutional status for Quebec, has been accepted as the foundation for constitutional reform. Despite such contradictions, it is likely that any group that gained in the Charlottetown Accord will argue that the accord be seen as the "floor" for any future constitutional negotiations,[75] just as the failed Meech Lake Accord became the foundation upon which the Charlottetown Accord was constructed. This will be particularly true for aboriginal peoples, who gained so much in the process leading up to the 1992 referendum. In essence, the Charlottetown agreement is likely to stand in the minds of intergovernmental negotiators despite its rejection by the Canadian public in the October referendum.

... MY NAME IS BOB, AND I'M AN ASYMMETRICAL FEDERALIST"...

Brian Gable, *The Globe and Mail*; reprinted from Guy Badeaux, ed., *Portfoolio 8* (Toronto: Macmillan, 1992), p. 19.

THE CANADIAN FEDERAL COMMUNITY

In the Confederation agreement a collective decision was reached that Canadians would be served by a federal system, and that the powers of the state would be divided between the federal and provincial governments. The latter in turn have delegated some of their powers to local governments, giving Canadians a three-tiered political system. Over time, this decision has resulted in an extensive network of intergovernmental relations. As governments at all levels expanded in size and extended their regulatory reach further into the economy and society, this network became not only more complex, but also more vital to the provision of government programs and services. To borrow an analogy used by the American political scientist Karl Deutsch, intergovernmental relations can be seen as the nervous system of the modern federal state. Just as the nervous system of an athlete coordinates the various parts of his or her body to produce fluid motion, intergovernmental relations coordinate governments in federal states. And, to extend the analogy further, just as the athlete occasionally stumbles or performs below potential, intergovernmental relations also fail us from time to time.

CANADA

Aislin, *The Gazette* (Montreal)/*The Toronto Star*, reprinted from Guy Badeaux, ed., *Portfoolio 8* (Toronto: Macmillan, 1992), p. 9.

While a great deal of the interaction between governments occurs in a cooperative and productive atmosphere, some intergovernmental friction and conflict is inescapable. Both federal and provincial governments have become large, complex, and ponderous entities, and the task of coordination is inherently difficult. The federal system represents a precarious balance of fiscal resources, jurisdictional responsibilities, and citizen demands. Maintaining this balance in the face of changing economic and social conditions requires no small degree of political skill. Friction is generated by competition among political elites,[76] by conflicting partisan interests, by conflicting bureaucratic ambitions, and by substantive disagreements over the direction of public policy. Such friction is the price we pay for the size and complexity of modern government, and for the adoption of a federal system. While the system can always be fine-tuned and lubricated, intergovernmental friction will never entirely disappear.

Intergovernmental conflict becomes a more serious matter when it serves as an outlet for major societal cleavages, many of which have been present since Confederation. Conflict between Ottawa and the government of Quebec, for example, may go well beyond the intrinsic problems of governmental coordination to a fundamental debate over the place of

Quebec within the Canadian political community. At issue is which government best speaks for Quebec when the two governments pursue quite different political visions. Conflict between Ottawa and the western provinces may go beyond the intergovernmental friction inherent in any modern federal state to regional dissatisfaction with the representational character of national political institutions. Intergovernmental conflict in the energy sector may reflect opposing views on Canada's economic relationship with the United States, and the competing interests of energy-producing and energy-consuming provinces. Intergovernmental conflict over medicare engages basic redistributive principles, as did conflict between Newfoundland and Ottawa over the ownership and control of offshore resources. Not infrequently, then, intergovernmental relations provide the stage upon which we act out the dominant themes in Canadian political life.

It is at this point that intergovernmental conflict becomes more than the inevitable price of federalism. Intergovernmental conflict can seriously disrupt the provision of government services and programs. As Hugh Thorburn observes, "our economy has become balkanized and our politics confrontational, leading us to dissipate our top decision-making resources on struggles of allocation between regions, provinces, industries and so on instead of building a consensus around an agreed-upon program of development."[77] Both Thorburn and Garth Stevenson agree that intergovernmental conflict weakens Canada's international trading position, with Stevenson going on to argue that it distorts the Canadian political agenda: "a lessening of the Canadian obsession with provincial interests and jurisdictional controversies might direct our attention to more significant issues, such as the unequal distribution of wealth, power and opportunity across the population."[78] There is a danger that our political imagination has become too blinkered, too narrowly confined to the intergovernmental arena. By restricting our gaze to visions of which government should do what, we may ignore important ideological questions concerning the role of the state in the Canadian society and economy, the maintenance or dismemberment of the postwar welfare state, and the nature of our relationship with the United States.

Given the general importance of intergovernmental relations and their more specific entanglement with the basic cleavages of Canadian political life, it is not surprising that the call for reform is frequently heard. Suggestions for reform include replacing the Senate with a provincially appointed upper house, redistributing legislative powers so as to provide a more watertight compartmentalization and thereby reduce the need for intergovernmental relations, and creating an elected Senate to strengthen the political authority of the federal government. Richard Simeon, one of Canada's foremost experts on intergovernmental relations, has recommended the establishment of a permanent intergovernmental forum, a Council of Federation that would not have legislative powers and would not serve as a revised Senate, but that would enhance coordination and cooperation among governments. At the same time, however, Simeon argues that

> to rely almost entirely on the intergovernmental mechanism to reconcile centre and periphery, French and English, is to place an intolerable burden on this fragile structure. Thus, while strengthening this mechanism, we must at the same time look elsewhere: and in particular to political parties.[79]

Just as we cannot untangle the "big" issues of Canadian political life from intergovernmental relations, we should not expect an intergovernmental solution to those issues.

SUGGESTED READINGS

1. For an insightful collection of essays on the 1982 Constitution Act, see Keith Banting and Richard Simeon, eds., *And No One Cheered: Federalism, Democracy and the Constitution Act* (Toronto: Methuen, 1983). For a lively account of the process leading up to the Constitution Act, see Robert Sheppard and Michael Valpy, *The National Deal: The Fight for a Canadian Constitution* (Toronto: Fleet Books, 1982).

2. André Bzdera, "Comparative Analysis of Federal High Courts: A Political Theory of Judicial Review," *Canadian Journal of Political Science*, 26:1 (March 1993), pp. 3–29.

3. Alan C. Cairns, "The Governments and Societies of Canadian Federalism," *Canadian Journal of Political Science*, 10 (1977), pp. 695–726.

4. For a comprehensive examination of the Charter of Rights, see Rainer Knopff and F.L. Morton, *Charter Politics* (Toronto: Nelson Canada, 1992).

5. Patrick Monahan, *Politics and the Constitution: Federalism and the Supreme Court of Canada* (Toronto: Carswell/Methuen, 1987).

6. Leslie A. Pal and F. Leslie Seidle, "Constitutional Politics, 1990–92: The Paradox of Participation," in Susan D. Phillips, ed., *How Ottawa Spends: A More Democratic Canada ...?* (Ottawa: Carleton University Press, 1993), pp. 143–202.

7. Roy Romanow, John Whyte, and Howard Leeson, *Canada ... Notwithstanding: The Making of the Constitution, 1976–1982* (Toronto: Methuen, 1984).

8. Peter H. Russell, *Constitutional Odyssey: Can Canadians Be a Sovereign People?* (Toronto: University of Toronto Press, 1992).

9. Donald V. Smiley, *Canada in Question: Federalism in the Eighties*, 3rd ed. (Toronto: McGraw-Hill Ryerson, 1980).

STUDY QUESTIONS

1. Over the course of this term, what federal–provincial conference activity has been reported in the press? What meetings have been held, and who attended—were the participants first ministers, cabinet ministers, or deputy ministers? What coverage were the meetings given in the press, what issues did they deal with, and with what result?

2. This chapter has suggested that the growth of government has been a major factor in the growth of intergovernmental relations, and in the increase in intergovernmental conflict. To what extent do you think this relationship might work in reverse? If the growth of government is brought to a halt or if the size of government is actually decreased, should we expect any corresponding change in intergovernmental relations? What factors might promote or inhibit such change?

3. Make a note of all government programs and services to which you and your family have had access over the past few years. Try to be as inclusive as possible, keeping in mind local services and programs such as medicare and youth allowances. What proportion of these programs and services has been provided by the federal government? By your provincial government? By your local government? What proportion has involved more than one level of government?

4. How does your own province handle federal–provincial relations? Is there a provincial ministry charged with this responsibility, or are they handled through the premier's office? If there is a ministry or department, does your library have its annual report? Can you document the scope of your province's involvement in federal–provincial interaction?

NOTES

1. W.L. Morton, "Confederation, 1870 to 1896," *Journal of Canadian Studies*, 1 (1966), p. 23.

2. For a discussion of Mowat's impact on provincializing the Constitution, see Paul Romney, "The Nature and Scope of Provincial Autonomy: Oliver Mowat, the Quebec Resolutions and the Construction

of the British North America Act," *Canadian Journal of Political Science*, 25:1 (March 1992).

3. Donald V. Smiley, *The Canadian Political Nationality* (Toronto: Methuen, 1967), p. 21.

4. For a discussion of this endeavour and episode in Canadian political life, see John English, *The Decline of Politics: The Conservatives and the Party System, 1901–20* (Toronto: University of Toronto Press, 1977; reprinted 1993).

5. Ivo D. Duchacek, *Comparative Federalism: The Territorial Dimension of Politics* (New York: Holt, Rinehart and Winston, 1970), p. 324.

6. Garth Stevenson, *Unfulfilled Union: Canadian Federalism and National Unity* (Toronto: Macmillan, 1979), p. 138.

7. Smiley, *The Canadian Political Nationality*, p. 41.

8. Donald V. Smiley, *Constitutional Adaptation and Canadian Federalism Since 1945*, Documents of the Royal Commission on Bilingualism and Biculturalism (Ottawa: Information Canada, 1970), p. 28.

9. Bora Laskin, *Canadian Constitutional Law*, 2nd ed. (Toronto: Carswell, 1960), p. 19.

10. J.A. Corry, "Constitutional Trends and Federalism," in J. Peter Meekison, ed., *Canadian Federalism: Myth or Reality* (Toronto: Methuen, 1968), p. 57.

11. Garth Stevenson, "Federalism and the Political Economy of the Canadian State," in Leo Panitch, ed., *The Canadian State: Political Economy and Political Power* (Toronto: University of Toronto Press, 1977), p. 75.

12. J.R. Mallory, *The Structure of Canadian Government*, rev. ed. (Toronto: Gage, 1984), p. 377.

13. Ibid., p. 385.

14. The "national dimension" criterion was established in 1882 by the JCPC ruling in *Russell v. the Queen*. It has since been used to uphold federal legislation relating to aeronautics, broadcasting, the regulation of the National Capital District, and the production of uranium. For a detailed discussion of the judicial interpretation of the "peace, order, and good government" clause, see Donald V. Smiley, *Canada in Question: Federalism in the Eighties*, 3rd ed. (Toronto: McGraw-Hill Ryerson, 1980), pp. 24–25.

15. Frank R. Scott, "Our Changing Constitution," in W.R. Lederman, ed., *The Courts and the Canadian Constitution* (Toronto: McClelland and Stewart, 1967), p. 21.

16. Smiley, *The Canadian Political Nationality*, p. 20.

17. Martha Fletcher, "Judicial Review and the Division of Powers in Canada," in Meekison, *Canadian Federalism*, p. 157.

18. Alan C. Cairns, "The Living Canadian Constitution," in Meekison, *Canadian Federalism*, pp. 86–99.

19. Smiley, *The Canadian Political Nationality*, p. 54.

20. *Calgary Herald*, April 12, 1977, p. 7.

21. For a comprehensive survey, see Ernest D. Hodgson, *Federal Involvement in Public Education* (Toronto: Canadian Education Association, 1988).

22. Richard Rose, *Understanding Big Government: The Programme Approach* (London: Sage, 1981), p. 1.

23. H.G. Thorburn, *Planning and the Economy: Building Federal–Provincial Consensus* (Toronto: James Lorimer, 1984), p. 160.

24. See Roger Gibbins, *Regionalism: Territorial Politics in Canada and the United States* (Toronto: Butterworths, 1982), ch. 4.

25. R.I. Cheffins, *The Constitutional Process in Canada* (Toronto: McGraw-Hill, 1969), p. 140.

26. Stevenson, *Unfulfilled Union*, p. 188.

27. Edwin R. Black, *Divided Loyalties: Canadian Concepts of Federalism* (Montreal: McGill-Queen's University Press, 1975), p. 101.

28. Government of Canada, "Dominion–Provincial Conference 1935," in *Dominion–Provincial Conferences 1927, 1935, 1941* (Ottawa: King's Printer, 1946).

29. Donald V. Smiley, *Canada in Question: Federalism in the Seventies*, 2nd ed. (Toronto: McGraw-Hill Ryerson, 1976), p. 58.

30. Institute of Intergovernmental Relations, *Report: Intergovernmental Relations on Fiscal and Economic Matters* (Ottawa: Queen's Printer, 1969), p. 103.

31. Richard J. Van Loon and Michael S. Whittington, *The Canadian Political System: Environment, Structure, and Process*, 2nd ed. (Toronto: McGraw-Hill Ryerson, 1976), pp. 366–67.

32. V. Seymour Wilson, "Federal–Provincial Relations and the Federal Policy Process," in G. Bruce Doern and Peter Aucoin, eds., *Public Policy in Canada* (Toronto: Macmillan, 1979), p. 198.

33. Prior to 1974, formal meetings between the prime minister and his provincial counterparts were referred to as Dominion–Provincial or Federal–Provincial Conferences.

34. A major but nonetheless isolated exception occurred in the 1981 constitutional negotiations when patriation proceeded without the consent of Quebec. In this case the Supreme Court had ruled that a federal–provincial consensus *but not unanimous consent* was required to amend the Constitution.

35. House of Commons, *Debates*, December 14, 1982, p. 21569.

36. Garth Stevenson, "Federalism and Intergovernmental Relations," in Michael S. Whittington and Glen Williams, eds., *Canadian Politics in the 1980s* (Toronto: Methuen, 1981), p. 288.

37. Ibid., p. 289.

38. Speech at the Liberal Party of Canada fund-raising dinner, Vancouver, November 12, 1981.

39. Keith Banting, "Political Meaning and Social Reform," in K.E. Swinton and C.J. Rogerson, eds., *Competing Constitutional Visions: The Meech Lake Accord* (Toronto: Carswell, 1988), p. 172.

40. Timothy B. Woolstencroft, *Organizing Intergovernmental Relations* (Kingston: Institute of Intergovernmental Relations, Queen's University, 1982), p. 9.

41. Ibid., p. 2.

42. Woolstencroft argues that the degree of institutionalization is related directly to the degree of discontent with the federal status quo. Certainly this relationship appears to be borne out in the cases of Quebec and Alberta; ibid., p. 5.

43. Donald Smiley, "An Outsider's Observations of Federal–Provincial Relations Among Consenting Adults," in Richard Simeon, ed., *Confrontation and Collaboration: Intergovernmental Relations in Canada Today* (Toronto: Institute of Public Administration of Canada, 1979), p. 110.

44. Woolstencroft, *Organizing Intergovernmental Relations*, pp. 79–80.

45. Howard Leeson, "The Intergovernment Affairs Function in Saskatchewan, 1960–1983," *Canadian Public Administration*, 30:3 (Fall 1987), p. 419.

46. Ibid.

47. Thorburn, *Planning and the Economy*, p. 190.

48. Woolstencroft, *Organizing Intergovernmental Relations*, p. 15.

49. Richard Simeon, *Federal–Provincial Diplomacy: The Making of Recent Policy in Canada* (Toronto: University of Toronto Press, 1972).

50. Gibbins, *Regionalism*, pp. 1–3.

51. Peter H. Russell, "The Political Purposes of the Canadian Charter of Rights and Freedoms," *Canadian Bar Review* (1983), pp. 43–46.

52. Rainer Knopff and F.L. Morton, *Nation-Building and the Charter*, Research Report prepared for the Royal Commission on the Economic Union and Development Prospects for Canada, 1984, p. 90.

53. Peter H. Russell, Rainer Knopff, and Ted Morton, *Federalism and the Charter: Leading Constitutional Decisions* (Ottawa: Carleton University Press, 1989), p. 5.

54. Leslie Pal and David Taras, "Better to Tolerate a Practice Than Establish Too Many 'Rights,'" *The Financial Post*, January 12–14, 1989.

55. F.L. Morton, "The Political Impact of the Canadian Charter of Rights and Freedoms," *Canadian Journal of Political Science*, 20:1 (March 1987), pp. 31–56.

56. Knopff and Morton, *Nation-Building and the Charter*, pp. 31–34.

57. F.L. Morton, G. Solomon, I. McNish, and D.W. Poulton, "Judicial Nullification of Statutes Under the Charter of Rights and Freedoms, 1982–1988," Occasional Papers Series 4.3, Research Unit for Socio-Legal Studies, University of Calgary, June 1989.

58. Russell et al., *Federalism and the Charter*, p. 3. As Russell et al. point out, Section 52 of the 1982 Constitution Act establishes an explicit basis for judicial review and veto by declaring that the Constitution is "the supreme law of Canada" and that "any law that is inconsistent with the provisions of the Constitution is, to the extent of the inconsistency, of no force or effect."

59. Pal and Taras, "Better to Tolerate a Practice."

60. Donald V. Smiley, "A Dangerous Deed: The Constitution Act, 1982," in Keith Banting and Richard Simeon, eds., *And No One Cheered: Federalism, Democracy and the Constitution Act*, Toronto: Methuen, 1983), pp. 75–76.

61. Ibid., p. 55.

62. Banting, "Political Meaning and Social Reform," p. 170.

63. For an important exception, see Reginald Whitaker, "Democracy and the Canadian Constitution," in Banting and Simeon, *And No One Cheered*.

64. Alan C. Cairns, "Citizens (Outsiders) and Governments (Insiders) in Constitution-Making: The Case of Meech Lake," *Canadian Public Policy*, 14 Supplement (September 1988), pp. 139–40.

65. Hon. Gérald Beaudoin, Senator, and Dorothy Dobbie, MP, *A Renewed Canada*, Report of the Special Joint Committee of the Senate and House of Commons (Ottawa: February 28, 1992).

66. Ibid., p. 25.

67. Ibid., p. 41.

68. Ibid., p. 17.

69. Ibid., p. 43.

70. *Consensus Report on the Constitution*, Charlottetown, August 28, 1992. The full legal text of the accord was not released until near the end of the referendum campaign.

71. Leslie A. Pal and F. Leslie Seidle, "Constitutional Politics, 1990–92: The Paradox of Participation," in Susan D. Phillips, ed., *How Ottawa Spends: A More Democratic Canada ...?* (Ottawa: Carleton University Press, 1993), p. 161.

72. For detailed assessments of the constitutional referendum, see Casey Vander Ploeg, "The Referendum on the Charlottetown Accord: An Assessment" (Calgary: Canada West Foundation, January 1993) and Shawn Henry, "Public Opinion and the Charlottetown Accord" (Calgary: Canada West Foundation, January 1993).

73. *Maclean's*, November 2, 1992, pp. 16–19.

74. For a full discussion of the evolution of popular sovereignty, see Peter H. Russell, *Constitutional Odyssey: Can Canadians Be a Sovereign People?* (Toronto: University of Toronto Press, 1992).

75. Pal and Seidle, "Constitutional Politics," p. 145.

76. Richard Simeon, "Regionalism and Canadian Political Institutions," in Meekison, *Canadian Federalism*, pp. 301–2.

77. Thorburn, *Planning and the Economy*, p. 242.

78. Stevenson, "Federalism and Intergovernmental Relations," p. 291.

79. Richard Simeon, "Some Suggestions for Improving Inter-governmental Relations," in Paul W. Fox, ed., *Politics: Canada*, 5th ed. (Toronto: McGraw-Hill Ryerson, 1982), p. 102.

THE CANADIAN PARTY SYSTEM

There is no question that political parties play a starring role in democratic politics. Much if not most of what we think of as "politics" entails parties, their leaders, and the competition among both in federal and provincial election campaigns. Elections provide the centrepiece, virtually the defining characteristic of democratic politics, and they are above all else struggles among competing party organizations. Yet, while there is little dispute about the central role of parties in democratic politics, there is much less agreement about the nature of that role. For some, political parties are seen as a means by which the policy preferences of citizens can be conveyed to legislative assemblies. What counts, then, are the policy positions around which parties are organized; election campaigns are seen as a contest among policy options rather than among personalities. Certainly, as this chapter unfolds, we will see examples of issue-based parties and campaigns. At the same time, the democratic ballot in Canada is a very simple, even crude instrument that allows us to do no more than scrawl a single "X" on a piece of paper. As a consequence, elections can unambiguously capture the policy preferences of voters only if the campaign features a single, dominant issue, and only if there are reasonably clear differences among the parties with respect to that issue. Then, and only then, can elections provide a "policy mandate." Parties that differ only as Tweedledum and Tweedledee differ deny citizens the opportunity to direct their governments by providing a mandate for the future.

As we will see in the discussion that follows, successful Canadian party organizations built first and foremost around policy options and political ideals have been relatively rare, as have been elections that have provided a clear policy mandate. It is not surprising, then, that many political scientists discount elections as policy forums and downplay the role of political parties in the articulation of public policy options. Instead, parties are seen primarily as "brokerage" organizations bound together more by the pursuit of power than by any consistent or even distinctive set of ideas, policies, or principles. As Harold Clarke et al. explain:

> *Rather than dividing the electorate among themselves along clear and stable lines of social cleavage, [brokerage parties] constantly compete for the same policy space and the same votes.... They organize around leaders rather than around political principles and ideologies, and expect the leader to work out the multitude of compromises required.*[1]

Within this perspective, elections provide a means by which voters can cast a retrospective judgment on the performance of governments, and through which they can choose representatives but not policies for the future. Campaigns feature the clash of leaders, not ideologies, and are generally fought on the plains of policy consensus rather than from the heights of competing principles. Elections enforce responsible government by allowing voters to throw old rascals out and new rascals in, but they rarely provide an opportunity to choose among policy options. Although Kim Campbell was punished by the voters for being so frank, she may have been right when she said during the 1993 election campaign that elections are not the time for a serious discussion of public policy.

Brokerage parties, and the electoral competition among such parties, can provide important means for bridging cleavages within the political community. As Richard Van Loon and Michael Whittington explain, the brokerage party "must aggregate a wide range of interests into a voting coalition, and in so doing it performs an integrative function for the political

"Of course our party recognizes the fundamental nature of the crisis we find our nation facing.... We have to get elected again."

Len Norris, *27th Annual*; originally published in the *Sun* (Vancouver), March 15, 1978.

system as a whole."[2] This integrative function can be carried out in a number of ways; as David Smith explains:

At different times and under different leaders, national integration has proceeded by various means: the incorporation of people and territory through local patronage supervised personally by leaders like Macdonald and Laurier; the accommodation at the centre of multiple interests and communities by Mackenzie King and St. Laurent; and the nationalization of individual Canadians into a single community (though of two languages and many cultures) through policies enunciated first by John Diefenbaker and late by Pierre Trudeau.[3]

Yet, while Canadian parties have generally tried to build electoral coalitions spanning the linguistic, regional, and class cleavages within the national community, their success has been less than complete. Both the party system and its constituent elements have at times encountered considerable difficulty as vehicles for national political integration. Brokerage aspirations have not ensured brokerage results.

EVOLUTION OF THE CANADIAN PARTY SYSTEM

John Meisel has argued that although party systems are "shaped by a series of specific election outcomes, [they] reflect and respond to a broad spectrum of influences which transcend elections and go to the very roots of society."[4] Those roots, however, are exposed on relatively rare occasions. Only a handful of our thirty-five general elections have had a major impact on the party system, or for that matter on Canadian political life. Only thirteen elections resulted in a change in government,[5] and in some of these cases the change represented little more than a minor ripple in the established political pattern. Between June 1979 and February 1980, for example, the national government changed hands twice, but the nine-month Progressive Conservative government headed by Joe Clark was little more than a temporary deviation from Liberal rule. As Figure 9.1 illustrates, Canada's political history has been marked more by long periods of one-party dominance than it has by the frequent turnover of governments in Ottawa.

National political life was dominated until the 1990s by two parties. The first to emerge was the Conservative Party—it did not become the *Progressive* Conservative Party until 1942—which began to take shape in 1854 as the Liberal–Conservative legislative coalition in the Province of Canada. Led by John A. Macdonald and George-Étienne Cartier, this early legislative coalition brought together the business interests of Montreal and Toronto with the hierarchy of the Catholic Church in Quebec. In the 1867 general election, which was a post-mortem on Confederation fought out

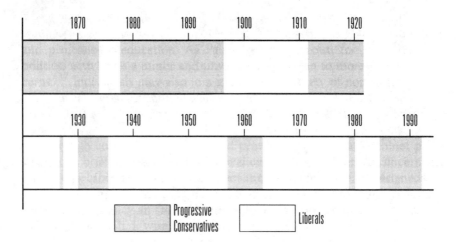

FIGURE 9.1 *Party Forming Federal Government, 1867–1993*

1870	1880	1890	1900	1910	1920

1930	1940	1950	1960	1970	1980	1990

Progressive Conservatives Liberals

among a wide array of candidates in four separate provincial campaigns, the loosely knit Conservatives won 60 percent of the seats and Macdonald became Canada's first prime minister. Although the Conservatives lost the 1874 election, they were returned to power in 1878 and remained in office through the election of 1891, the last fought by Macdonald. Shortly after that election, the party's strength began to unravel with the death of Macdonald, a series of short-lived and generally ineffectual leaders, and the erosion of the party's electoral base in Quebec. The stage was set for the first sustained period of Liberal rule.

The Liberals had first come to power in 1874 under the uncertain leadership of Alexander Mackenzie, when the Pacific Scandal led to the defeat of Macdonald's Conservative government.[6] The Liberal Party provided an umbrella for a variety of groups: the "Clear Grit" agrarian populist reformers from Ontario; anti-clerical francophones from Quebec; anti-confederates from Quebec, New Brunswick, and Nova Scotia; and, more generally, those who supported provincial rights and opposed the centralist and nation-building thrust of the Macdonald Conservatives. It was a "disparate and ineffectual alliance,"[7] easily routed by the Conservatives in 1878. Only after their defeat did the Liberals begin to coalesce as a truly national party, and only under the direction of a new leader, Quebec's Wilfrid Laurier, did they emerge as a serious threat to the dominant Conservatives. Their rise to power came with a reversal of the two parties' fortunes in Quebec. The Liberals, whose association with anti-clerical elements in the province brought on the political wrath of the Catholic Church, won only 16 Quebec seats in the 1884 general election, compared to 49 for the Conservatives. In 1887, following the hanging of Louis Riel and the death of George-Étienne Cartier, Macdonald's powerful Quebec lieutenant, the Liberals captured 32 seats to the Conservatives' 33. In the 1891 election, with Wilfrid Laurier now at the Liberal helm, the Liberals won 37 Quebec seats compared to 28 for the Conservatives, the first in a string of Liberal majorities in Quebec that was not to be broken until 1958. Five years later, in 1896, the Laurier Liberals came to national power, winning 49 of the 65 Quebec seats in the process. The Liberals were to remain in office until 1911, during which time their earlier support for provincial rights gave way to the enthusiastic leadership of nation-building activities in the Canadian West. In 1911 the Liberals went down to defeat after a campaign featuring two issues: a Liberal proposal for greater free trade with the United States (discussed below) and, as war clouds gathered in Europe, Canada's participation in the naval defence of the British Empire. The new Conservative government was led by Robert Laird Borden, who was to steer Canada's passage through the First World War.

The elections of 1917 and 1921 were of critical importance in the evolution of the national party system. The 1917 election, discussed in more detail below, was fought on the single issue of military conscription, which was strongly opposed in Quebec and by the Liberals, but which was generally supported elsewhere in Canada and by the Conservatives. The election had at least three immediate consequences. First, the Liberals were all but purged in Western Canada, winning only 2 of the 56 seats. Second, Quebec was turned into a Conservative wasteland: Conservative candidates won only 3 of Quebec's 65 seats, down from 27 in 1911. (The Liberals, conversely, won 62 of their 82 seats in Quebec.) In combination, the election results in Quebec and the West meant that the two national parties were no longer national in terms of electoral support or representation in the House. Third, the election blurred existing party lines as both the Conservatives and a significant number of pro-conscription Liberals ran under the banner of the Union Government. This in turn set the stage for a new political movement, which held nonpartisanship as one of its leading principles.

The events set in motion by the 1917 election crippled the Conservative and Liberal parties as national organizations and led in 1921 to a fundamental transformation of the national party system. In the 1921 election the incumbent Conservatives, having discarded the wartime umbrella of the Union Government, failed to win a single seat in Quebec or on the prairies. Overall, the Conservatives captured only 50 seats, down from 153 seats for the Union Government in 1917. The Liberals won 116 seats in the 1921 election, including every seat in Quebec. With only 5 seats in the West, the Liberals were able to form only a minority government, Canada's first. The most dramatic outcome came with the emergence of the Progressive Party of Canada, which swept out of the prairies to capture 64

At Last, Women Get the Vote!

Suffragettes in Britain, the United States, and Canada had been campaigning since the late 1800s for the extension of the voting franchise to women. Success, however, was not to come until the First World War.

The war years fundamentally changed the place of women within the Canadian economy and society. The domestic war effort, coupled with the manpower demands of the military, produced a dramatic surge in female participation in the labour force. In turn, this surge brought women's exclusion from the franchise into greater and greater question. The war years were also marked by widespread interest in social reform. Women, through their leadership of reform organizations such as the Women's Christian Temperance Union, were able to place the extension of the franchise near the top of the reform agenda. If the war was being fought to protect democracy, women argued, then surely women were entitled to the vote at home.

The specific impetus for the extension of the franchise came from the Wartime Elections Act. This notorious piece of legislation inflated support for conscription by, among other things, enfranchising the close female relatives of men on active overseas service. The assumption going into the 1917 campaign was that the wives, mothers, sisters, and daughters of servicemen would endorse conscription. The public rationale for extending the vote was that servicemen, who were predominantly English rather than French Canadians, would have trouble finding the time to vote; their female relatives could thus vote in their place. In fact, however, servicemen were given twenty-seven days and every opportunity in which to vote, and few if any were disenfranchised.

In 1921 the federal franchise was extended to all women on the same terms as were applied to men.

seats, including 37 of the 39 prairie seats, 24 seats in Ontario, 3 in British Columbia, and 1 in New Brunswick. Although the Progressives' core support came from agrarian unrest in Western Canada and rural Ontario, the new party was also the vehicle for a more widespread interest in social reform, interest that had been fanned by the war years. The Progressives' nonpartisan approach to politics appealed to those who had supported the wartime Union Government, and support for the Progressives provided a means by which western Canadians could register their growing regional discontent with the partisan and parliamentary organization of political

Nellie McClung was born in Chatsworth, Ontario, in 1873 and moved to Manitoba when she was 7. Trained as a teacher, McClung became a leader in the Women's Suffrage Movement. In 1921 she was elected to the Alberta legislature, becoming the first woman in the British Empire to be elected to a legislative assembly.

Public Archives of Canada/C27674.

life, discontent that transcended agrarian concerns alone. Yet despite these numerous albeit overlapping sources of support, the Progressives faded quickly. In the 1925 general election they won only 24 seats, including 22 from the prairie provinces. In 1926 the Progressives won only 20 seats, including 18 from the prairies, and in 1930 only 12, including 11 from the prairies. In less than a decade the Progressives were driven back to a prairie enclave, and then driven from the political stage.

Figure 9.2 shows that the major parties rebounded quickly after the 1921 debacle. By 1930, when together the Conservatives and Liberals captured 94 percent of the votes cast and 93 percent of the seats, it appeared that the 1921 election had been but a temporary deviation from an enduring pattern of two-party dominance. That pattern, however, was broken conclusively in the 1935 election, fought in the middle of the Great Depression. As voters turned out R.B. Bennett's Conservative government, which had come to power in 1930 just as the Depression was beginning,

Women's political organizations have a long history in Canada. The above photo shows an 1898 meeting of the National Council of Women with the Governor General of Canada, Lord Aberdeen.

Public Archives of Canada/PA28033.

and returned the Liberals to power, they also elected 32 candidates from a variety of third parties, two of which were to leave a permanent mark on the Canadian party system. The Co-operative Commonwealth Federation, a left-of-centre party that brought together the remnants of the Progressive Party, agrarian organizations from Western Canada, elements of the nascent labour movement, and central Canadian left-wing intellectuals grouped under the banner of the League for Social Reconstruction, captured 8.8 percent of the popular vote and 7 seats in the House of Commons. Over the next five federal elections the CCF was to average 11.9 percent of the popular vote and over 19 seats in the House, and in 1944 formed the provincial government in Saskatchewan. The Social Credit Party, also running candidates for the first time in 1935, captured only 4.1 percent of the popular vote, but because its support was more concentrated, won 17 seats, 10 more than the CCF. Across the next five general elections the Social Credit Party averaged 4.2 percent of the popular vote and over 13 seats in the House.[8] The other significant entry in the 1935 election was the Reconstruction Party, a splinter group of Conservative candidates running under the leadership of H.H. Stevens, the Minister of Trade and Commerce in R.B. Bennett's government. Although Reconstruc-

FIGURE 9.2 *Percentage of Seats and Popular Vote Won by the Conservative and Liberal Parties Combined*

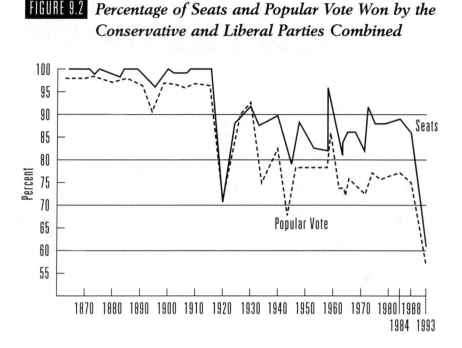

tion candidates captured 8.7 percent of the popular vote, only Stevens was elected and the party vanished without a trace shortly thereafter.

The 1921 and 1935 elections not only marked the end of an uncomplicated two-party system: they also put into place a Liberal dominance of national politics that was to last through to 1984. The Liberals, re-elected in 1935, remained in office until their defeat at the hands of John Diefenbaker in 1957, and then returned to power in 1963. From 1963 to 1984 they dominated the federal scene, apart from the brief Conservative interlude in 1979–80. A quip by Jack Pickersgill, Liberal cabinet minister and party stalwart, took on the appearance of an iron law: "living under a Conservative government is like having a childhood disease—everyone has to experience it once, but never wants to do it again."[9]

The major departure from Liberal dominance came with the "Diefenbaker interlude," which stretched from 1957 to 1963. John Diefenbaker, a prairie populist with a dramatic platform style, transformed the Conservative Party by shifting its centre of gravity westward. The Conservatives had earlier sought western Canadian support in 1942 by enticing John Bracken, the Progressive premier of Manitoba, to lead the national party. Part of that enticement was a change in the party's name to the *Progressive Conservative Party of Canada*. As Table 9.1 shows, however, neither Bracken's leadership nor the change in name greatly improved the party's position in the West. When Bracken was replaced in 1948 by the Conservative

TABLE 9.1 Conservative Support in Western Canada

	% of Popular Vote			Western Canadian Seats	
	All 4 provs.	Prairies only	B.C. only	#	%
1940	21.2%	17.7%	30.5%	7	9.9
1945	23.5	20.7	30.0	10	14.1
1949	20.8	17.6	27.9	7	9.9
1953	16.0	17.0	14.1	9	12.9
1957	30.0	28.6	32.6	21	30.4
1958	53.9	56.2	49.4	65	92.9
1962	38.8	44.9	27.3	48	68.6
1963	38.8	47.0	23.4	45	64.3
1965	36.0	45.3	19.2	45	64.3
1968	33.0	40.8	19.4	25	36.8
1972	42.1	47.5	33.0	42	61.8
1974	47.2	50.6	41.9	49	72.1
1979	49.6	53.0	44.4	57	74.0
1980	46.8	50.6	41.5	49	63.6
1984	51.7	55.3	46.6	58	75.3
1988	40.8	44.5	35.3	48	55.8
1993	13.3	13.2	13.4	0	0.0

premier of Ontario, George Drew, little improvement in the West was to be expected, and none was forthcoming. Diefenbaker was chosen as the new Conservative leader in 1956 after George Drew resigned for reasons of health. In the 1957 campaign, Diefenbaker led his party to a minority government, with strong support in Atlantic Canada (21 seats, up from 5 in 1953) and Ontario (61 seats, up from 33 in 1953), and more modest gains in the West and Quebec. Then, in 1958, the Conservatives rolled up the largest majority ever recorded in a federal election,[10] taking 208 of the 265 seats in the House, including 70 of 75 seats in Western Canada and 50 of the 75 seats in Quebec. The Liberals won only 49 seats overall and were shut out in six provinces; CCF seats were cut from 25 to 8, and no Social Credit candidates were elected.

Although Diefenbaker himself was closely associated with the West, Conservative candidates did well throughout the country, collecting 55 percent of the popular vote in Atlantic Canada, 50 percent in Quebec, 56 percent in Ontario, and 54 percent across the West. It was a truly national victory, foreshadowing Brian Mulroney's victory in 1984, and it marked a new style of accommodative politics. As David Smith notes, Diefenbaker's "one Canada" nationalism was pitched to appeal "to Canadians as Canadians regardless of where they lived or what language they spoke."[11] Yet despite their landslide victory in 1958, the Conservatives retained only a minority government after the 1962 election, and in 1963 they lost power to the Liberals, who formed a minority government under the leadership of Lester Pearson. The 1958 Conservative gains in Quebec had quickly evaporated: 36 of the 50 seats won in 1958 were lost in 1962, with another 6 lost in 1963. Ontario support also faded, with the Conservative seat total falling from 67 in 1958 to 35 in 1962, and only 27 in 1963. What did not evaporate was the Conservative resurgence in Western Canada. As Table 9.1 shows, Diefenbaker not only led the West, and particularly the prairie West, into the Conservative camp; he also kept it there. Although western support for the Conservatives fell in 1968, it quickly rebounded. Thus Diefenbaker's transformation of Western Canada from a Conservative wasteland to the Conservative heartland was a gift to his party that was to last until the 1990s.

The Diefenbaker years touched off a number of other important changes in the party system. The 1958 Conservative rout of the CCF led to that party's collapse and, in 1961, to its reincarnation as the New Democratic Party. The NDP brought together what was left of the CCF's agrarian support in the West with the growing labour movement, led by the Canadian Labour Congress. The new party also reached out more effectively than its predecessor had to white-collar, urban constituencies. Since its first campaign in 1962 the NDP has been a significant player in Canadian national politics even though its support, like CCF support before it, has all but stopped at the Quebec–Ontario border. The 1962 election also marked the rebirth of the Social Credit Party, this time in Quebec under the leadership of Réal Caouette. Although the "Créditistes" were restricted almost exclusively to Quebec, they had a significant impact on the politics of the time, winning 26 federal seats in 1962, 20 in 1963, and 9 in 1965. They continued to survive as a political force in Quebec even during the Liberal hegemony of the Trudeau years, winning 14 seats in 1968, 15 in 1972, 11 in 1974, and 6 in 1979 before being driven from the political stage in 1980.

The national party system was again transformed in 1984 when the Progressive Conservatives, led by Brian Mulroney, captured 211 of the 282 seats in the House of Commons. The Conservative sweep occurred across the country, with Tory candidates taking 25 of the 32 seats in Atlantic Canada, 58 of 75 in Quebec, 67 of 95 in Ontario, 58 of 77 in the West, and all 3 in the North. After more than two decades in which neither the Conservatives nor the Liberals had been able to build a truly *national* electoral coalition, the country once again had a federal government that enjoyed strong support across the land. In Quebec, the magnitude of the electoral change was staggering. The Conservatives, campaigning for the first time with a Quebec leader, increased their share of the popular vote in the province from 12.6 percent in 1980, when only a single Tory candidate was elected, to 50.2 percent in 1984. Conversely, the Liberal share of the Quebec popular vote fell from 68.2 percent in 1980 to only 35.4 percent in 1984. One of the most important constants in Canadian electoral politics—the Liberal fortress of Quebec—had been shattered. The Liberal Party had never done as badly in a federal election as it did in 1984; even in the 1958 Diefenbaker rout, the Liberals retained 49 seats and almost 34 percent of the vote. The party that had come to be known as "the government party" was now out of office, not only in Ottawa, but also across the ten provinces.[12] The NDP withstood the Tory tide more successfully, gaining 8 seats in Ontario to help offset the loss of 9 seats in the West.

Brian Mulroney led his party to an overwhelming victory in 1984 and then, after nine years in office, watched from the sidelines as the Conservatives were decimated in the 1993 election.

The 1988 election largely replicated the 1984 results, albeit with some modifications. The Conservatives remained in office despite the net loss of 42 seats and a drop in the party's share of the popular vote to 43 percent, down from 50 percent in 1984. The Liberals more than doubled their number of seats in the House, while the NDP reached a historic high by winning 43 seats. Quebec support for the Conservatives, which had seemed like an aberration in 1984, actually increased in 1988: the Conservatives won 63 seats compared to 58 in 1984, and received almost 53 percent of the Quebec popular vote, compared to just over 50 percent in 1984. Overall, 32.5 percent of Conservative votes and 37.2 percent of Conservative seats came from Quebec in 1988, up 5 percent and 10 percent respectively.

The 1993 election appears to constitute another watershed in the evolution of the Canadian party system. The Conservatives, led by Prime Minister Kim Campbell, went down to an overwhelming defeat, electing

Although in office for little more than four months, Kim Campbell has left a permanent mark on Canadian political life as the first woman to serve as prime minister.

only two MPs—one each from Quebec and New Brunswick—and capturing only 16 percent of the national popular vote. In Quebec, the Conservatives were swept aside by Lucien Bouchard's Bloc Québécois, which captured 54 seats, 49 percent of the Quebec popular vote, and 13.5 percent of the national popular vote despite running candidates only in Quebec. On its western flank, the Conservatives were swept away by Preston Manning's Reform Party, which captured 18.7 percent of the national popular vote and won 52 seats: 24 in British Columbia, 22 in Alberta, 4 in Saskatchewan, and 1 each in Manitoba and Ontario. The election was also a blow to the New Democrats, whose performance looked good only in contrast to the Conservative debacle. The NDP fell from 43 seats to only 9, and won less than 7 percent of the popular vote. Finally, the 1993 election brought a new Liberal majority government to Ottawa, headed by Jean Chrétien. The Liberals picked up 41.2 percent of the popular vote and 177 of the 295 seats in the House of Commons. Like the Mulroney governments before it, Chrétien's Liberal government enjoys relatively strong representation from across the country; the Liberals have 31 of the 32 seats in Atlantic Canada, 19 of the 75 seats in Quebec, an astounding 98 of 99 in Ontario, and 29 of the 89 seats across Western and northern Canada. Thus the election produced both a broadly representative national government and strong regional opposition from the Bloc in Quebec and the Reform in the West.

PATTERNS IN THE PARTY SYSTEM

At this point it is useful to step back from the historical details of the Canadian party system and look at the general patterns that tie those details together. As we will see, the changes that have occurred have taken place against a backdrop of considerable continuity.

Major Party Dominance

The traditional dominance of the Progressive Conservative and Liberal parties has already been noted in Figure 9.2. Although that dominance was shaken in 1921 and substantially reduced from 1935 onward, the two major parties continued to capture the support of three Canadian voters in four through the 1988 election. Then, in 1993, their combined share of the popular vote fell to 57.2 percent, and their combined share of seats fell to only 60.7 percent. In both instances, however, the decline stemmed almost entirely from the Conservative collapse in the 1993 election.

Figure 9.3 shows that among "third parties" the dominance of the NDP was equally apparent through the 1988 election. With the disappearance of the Créditistes, the NDP's domination of the third-party field was even more complete than the Conservative and Liberal parties' dominance

FIGURE 9.3 *Distribution of the "Third Party" Popular Vote*

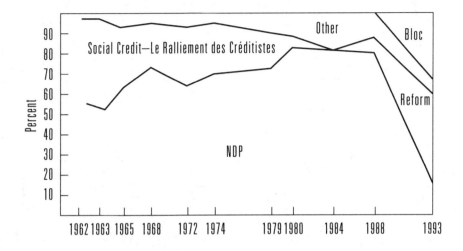

of the national party system. This picture changed dramatically in 1993 when the NDP vote was overshadowed by support for both the Reform Party and the Bloc Québécois. The NDP share of the "third party" vote shrank to only 16.1 percent, whereas the Reform Party and the Bloc captured 43.7 and 31.6 percent respectively. More importantly, and at least for the short term, the 1993 results all but destroy any *contemporary* analytical distinction between "major" and "third" parties. It is true that the Liberals stand well apart from the pack with respect to the size and national character of their electoral support. However, it would appear to make little sense to call the Progressive Conservatives, with only two seats in the House, a major party while at the same time describing the Reform and Bloc as third parties. There is admittedly a lingering utility to this distinction that stems from the historical role that the Conservatives have played in Canadian political life, but it is by no means clear that this role will be enough to resuscitate the Conservatives in the years to come.

The 1993 campaign featured a host of parties that were unquestionably "minor" with respect to the popular vote or seats won. The most prominent of these were the National Party, headed by Mel Hurtig and fielding 171 candidates, and the Natural Law Party, which ran 231 candidates under the banner of transcendental meditation. There were also seven other parties in the campaign: the Abolitionist Party (80 candidates), the Christian Heritage Party (59), the Canada Party (56), the Party for the Commonwealth of Canada (59), the Green Party (79), the Libertarian Party (52), and the Marxist-Leninist Party (51). Another 151 candidates ran as independents. However, as Table 9.2 shows, all of these parties and

TABLE 9.2 *1993 National Election Results*

Party	Number of Candidates	Candidates Elected	Number of Votes	% Total Popular Vote
Liberal	295	177	5,591,031	41.2
Progressive Conservative	295	2	2,175,739	16.0
New Democratic	294	9	933,028	6.9
Reform	207	52	2,535,417	18.7
Bloc Québécois	75	54	1,833,067	13.5
All Other Parties including Independents	989	1	496,226	3.7
Total	2,155	295	13,564,508	100.0

candidates combined left a negligible mark on the political landscape. Only a single independent MP was elected, and he was an incumbent who had lost the Conservative nomination in his riding.

Provincial Variations on the National Theme

One of the most important features of the Canadian party system is that the national cast of party actors is not faithfully replicated across the ten provinces; substantial asymmetry exists with respect to both federal voting behaviour and provincial party systems. As Donald Smiley has discussed at length, this asymmetry is of considerable importance for the political dynamics of the Canadian federal state and the character of executive federalism.[13]

In Atlantic Canada, the Liberal and Conservative parties have dominated both federal and provincial elections to the virtual exclusion of other parties. In the eleven general elections held between 1962 and 1993, Liberal and Conservative candidates captured just under 88 percent of the popular vote across the four Atlantic provinces, compared to 74 percent of the national popular vote. (Even in the 1993 debacle, the Conservatives won 26 percent of the popular vote in Atlantic Canada, which was considerably better than they did elsewhere in the country.) Across those same eleven elections, Liberal and Conservative candidates won 350 of the 355 Atlantic seats (almost 99 percent), losing just 4 seats to the New Democrats and 1 to an independent. The NDP averaged just 11.6 percent of the popular vote in Nova Scotia, 9 percent in Newfoundland, 8.6 percent in New Brunswick, and 5.3 percent in Prince Edward Island. In provincial elections the two major parties have been even more dominant. Thus Atlantic Canada departs significantly from the national pattern with respect to the relative weakness of third-party support across the region.

The national party system is best replicated in Ontario where the Conservatives, Liberals, and New Democrats have all been significant players in federal elections, and where provincial politics have been dominated by the same three parties. Yet, while the party players are the same, their relative strength differs across the federal and provincial arenas. The Conservatives formed the provincial government from 1941 to 1985, but the Liberals have enjoyed the edge federally, winning 541 seats in the eleven elections held between 1962 and 1993 compared to 376 Ontario seats won by the Conservatives. In the 1988 federal election, Conservative candidates won 46 Ontario seats with 38.2 percent of the popular vote, and Liberal candidates won 43 seats with 38.9 percent of the vote. Then, in 1993 the Liberals swept through Ontario, capturing 98 of 99 seats with almost 53 percent of the popular vote. Both the Conservatives and New Democrats were shut out, although the NDP remained in control of the provincial government.

In Quebec, strong provincial parties lacking any federal counterpart have often dominated the provincial stage. The Union Nationale (discussed in Chapter 4), which controlled the provincial government for twenty-four years between 1936 and 1970, did not run federal candidates. The Parti Québécois, in power from 1976 to 1985, did not run federal candidates, although in 1984 it did endorse the Parti Nationaliste and in 1993 endorsed the Bloc. Conversely, the federal Conservative Party has not had a provincial counterpart in Quebec since 1936. Thus federal and provincial campaigns in Quebec are fought along quite different party lines. It should be noted, however, that this has not precluded informal partisan alliances spanning the two levels of the party system. The Union Nationale and the federal Conservative Party had such an alliance in the past, as did the latter and the provincial Liberals in more recent elections. The most dramatic change on the Quebec partisan landscape came in 1993 when 54 of the 75 Quebec seats were taken by the Bloc Québécois, and the Conservatives were reduced to a single seat. The change, moreover, went well beyond the partisan complexion of Quebec; the 1993 election represents the first time that a significant number of MPs—enough to form the Official Opposition in the House of Commons—were elected on the explicit policy platform of dismembering the Canadian state.

The relationship between federal and provincial party systems in Western Canada defies any simple description. The most "deviant" province has been British Columbia where, since 1952, provincial elections have been fought out between the Social Credit Party and the CCF/NDP, with the provincial Liberal and Conservative parties being all but moribund. Only in the most recent election, and with the virtual collapse of Social Credit, was the Liberal Party a significant player. Yet on the federal scene the Liberals and Conservatives, and now Reform, have been both active and successful. Only the New Democrats have been competitive at both levels, while the Social Credit Party has not been active federally since three Socred MPs were elected in 1965.

Alberta provincial politics have been dominated in turn by the Liberals (1905–1921), the United Farmers of Alberta (1921–1935), the Social Credit Party (1935–1971), and from 1971 on, the Progressive Conservatives. Opposition parties of whatever stripe have traditionally been chronically weak, with government control of over 90 percent of the legislative seats being the rule, not the exception. Since Social Credit's defeat in 1971 and its subsequent departure from the provincial stage, Alberta has deviated from the national pattern more in terms of the relative strength of the party players than in the players themselves. It is interesting to note, however, that recent developments appear, at least in part, to be bringing the province more into step with the national party configuration. In the March 1989 provincial election, the Progressive Conservatives retained power, but did so in the face of stiff competition from both the provincial New Democrats and the Liberals. Then in 1993 the New Democrats collapsed and the Conservatives won a relatively close two-party fight with the provincial Liberals. In the 1993 federal election four Liberal MPs were elected in Alberta, the first Liberals to be elected since 1968. At the same time, the election of twenty-two Reform MPs put the province out of step with the national community.

Saskatchewan voters elected North America's first socialist government in 1944 when the CCF broke the Liberals' virtual monopoly in the provincial arena. The CCF remained in office until 1964, when the Liberals were returned to power. The Liberals were then defeated in 1971 by the New Democrats, who were defeated in turn by Grant Devine's Progressive Conservatives in 1982, who were then defeated again in 1991 by the New Democrats. Following Devine's victory in 1982, partisan competition within Saskatchewan, both federal and provincial, was dominated by the Conservatives and New Democrats. In the 1988 federal election, for example, the New Democrats elected 10 MPs, the Conservatives elected 4 MPs, and the Liberals failed to elect any candidates. In 1993, Saskatchewan voters returned the country's most heterogeneous group of MPs, electing 5 Liberals, 5 New Democrats, and 4 Reformers.

Manitoba presents a different picture again. In the midst of the Great Depression the provincial Liberals and Progressives merged to form the nucleus of a nonpartisan and initially all-party administration that was to govern Manitoba until 1958. Over time, however, the government became more Liberal and less nonpartisan as first the CCF members and then a handful of Conservatives left the fold. In the 1958 provincial election the Conservatives came to power and were to remain in power until 1969, when they were defeated by the New Democrats. The Conservatives returned to power in 1977 and then lost again to the New Democrats in 1982. The 1987 election returned the Conservatives to office, but with only a minority government; the official opposition was formed by the provincial Liberals, led by Sharon Carstairs. Unlike the other western provinces, all these major parties remained competitive in the early 1990s.

In summary, the Canadian party system is asymmetrical not only across provinces, but also, in many cases, across the two levels of government within specific provinces.[14] This latter asymmetry is reflected in the growing organizational independence of federal and provincial parties sharing the same party label. Thus Van Loon and Whittington concur with Smiley that "while the Canadian political system can be described as federal, its political parties are at best only confederal."[15]

Party Tenure

The Canadian political system is marked by the longevity of its governments. As Figure 9.1 has shown, it is an unusual federal election in which the government changes hands. This stability is further reflected in Figure 9.4, which plots the proportion of the popular vote received by the Conservative and Liberal parties. What can be seen in this figure is not any regular oscillation in party fortunes, but rather sustained periods of dominance. If anything, Canadian voters have been even *more* steadfast in their support of provincial governments; the tenure of many has been nothing short of remarkable. The Ontario government remained in Conservative hands for forty-two years, from 1943 to 1985. The Social Credit Party was in power from 1935 to 1971 in Alberta, and in British Columbia

FIGURE 9.4 *Percentage of the Popular Vote in General Elections, 1878–1993*

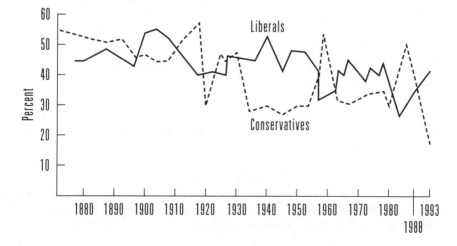

from 1952 to the early 1990s, with the exception of a brief NDP interregnum from 1972 to 1975. Joey Smallwood's Liberal Party controlled the government of Newfoundland from 1949 to 1971.

To illustrate the lengthy tenure of Canadian governments, it is useful to draw upon an American comparison made earlier in Chapter 3. During the time that Pierre Trudeau was prime minister of Canada, Americans experienced five different presidential administrations: those of Lyndon Johnson, Richard Nixon, Gerald Ford, Jimmy Carter, and Ronald Reagan. Each administration, with the possible exception of Ford's, is commonly seen as a unique and distinctive episode in American political life. In Canada, the tempo of change is much slower as voter support for incumbent governments is slow to erode and leaders enjoy lengthy periods in office unknown in the United States, where most political executives, including the president, face constitutional limits on their terms.

Electoral "Distortions"

In the 1993 general election, over thirteen million votes were cast to determine the occupants of 295 seats in the House of Commons. It is the electoral system that translates votes into seats, and thereby determines the partisan composition of the government. That system is based on single-member constituencies, the winner in each constituency being the candidate receiving a plurality of the votes cast within the constituency. Thus to win in what is called a "first-past-the-post" system, one needs only more votes than any other candidate, and not a majority of the votes cast. Given that most ridings are now contested by between five and eight candidates, pluralities well short of majorities are common. The party winner of the election is determined by aggregating the results of the 295 constituency contests; the party with the most seats wins the right to form the next government. While party leaders play a critical role in the national campaign, they do not run as national candidates, but rather seek election as MPs in specific constituencies.

This electoral system is only one of many possible mechanisms that could be used to translate votes into seats. Many countries use systems of proportional representation, designed to ensure that a party's share of seats is roughly proportionate to its share of the popular vote. Such outcomes are not characteristic of the electoral translation that takes place in Canada, for the electoral system tends to overreward the party capturing a plurality of the national vote. In Figure 9.5 we can see that the winning party in national elections consistently receives a much higher percentage of the seats in the House of Commons than its percentage of the popular vote. Indeed, since 1921 the winning party has received a majority of the popular vote on only three occasions. On four occasions—1957, 1962, 1972, and 1979—minority governments were formed by parties receiving less than 40 percent of the popular vote. This tendency of the electoral system

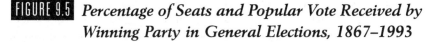

FIGURE 9.5 *Percentage of Seats and Popular Vote Received by Winning Party in General Elections, 1867–1993*

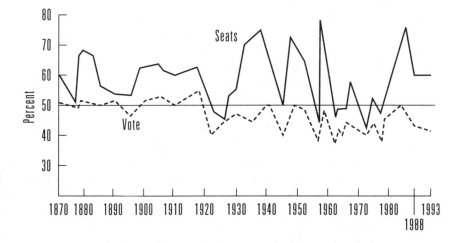

to overreward the leading party, and often to convert a plurality of the popular vote to a majority of the legislative seats, is often seen as a positive distortion, one that increases the probability of a stable majority government despite the lack of a majority preference among Canadian voters.

There is an important caveat to note here. Although it is generally true that the party winning a plurality of the national popular vote also receives a plurality of seats in the House of Commons, this is not always the case. In 1979, for example, the Liberals received 39.8 percent of the popular vote compared to only 35.6 percent for the Conservatives, yet the Conservatives won 136 seats compared to only 114 for the Liberals. Thus it is not the number of votes alone that counts, but also the distribution of those votes.

If winning parties tend to be overcompensated, other parties must be disadvantaged by an electoral system based on simple pluralities, and in fact the second-place finisher receives a smaller proportion of seats than its share of the popular vote. Here again, however, the electoral effects depend upon the distribution of the vote. Parties with a broadly dispersed popular vote tend to fare more poorly than do parties whose vote is regionally concentrated. In the abstract, one can see that a party could win 10 percent or 20 percent of the vote in every constituency across the land without winning a single seat. The NDP, which runs candidates in every federal constituency no matter what the chance of success, received on average 16 percent of the votes cast by Canadians in general elections between 1962 and 1993, but won only 8.8 percent of the seats in the

House of Commons across the board. Conversely, the Social Credit Party received only 4.3 percent of the votes cast in the six general elections held between 1935 and 1957 and yet, because those votes were concentrated in Alberta, managed to capture 5.5 percent of the seats in the House.

The 1993 election produced some major distortions in the translation of votes into seats. If the electoral system had faithfully translated parties' share of the national popular vote into seats in the House of Commons, we would have had a minority Liberal government with 122 Liberals, 55 Reform MPs, 47 Conservatives, 40 Bloc MPs, 20 New Democrats, and 11 MPs elected by a host of smaller parties. Instead, we ended up with a majority Liberal government, and with the electoral collapse of Conservative representation in the House. It is interesting to note, however, that the Liberals and the Bloc fared well with the existing electoral system, and the Reform Party ended up with a share of seats in the House of Commons close to its share of the popular vote. (The most problematic outcome for the Reform Party was in Ontario, where 20 percent of the popular vote netted only a single seat.) The two parties hurt the most by the system, the Conservatives and New Democrats, are also the least well positioned to champion electoral reform.

In most elections, the majority of voters support losing parties and candidates. For example, in the twelve consecutive provincial elections won by the Ontario Conservatives between 1943 and 1981, the party averaged only 43.3 percent of the popular vote. In the eleven federal elections held between 1962 and 1993, 58 percent of Canadians voted for parties that ultimately lost. In the West, the losers averaged 65.1 percent of the electorate compared to 56.3 percent in Ontario, 54.1 percent in Atlantic Canada, and 55 percent in Quebec. The high losing average in the West may not only reflect western alienation, but may also have been a contributing factor to that alienation. It is interesting to speculate in this respect on whether the relative proportion of winners and losers is related to citizen support for political institutions. Might, for example, a system like the one used in American presidential elections, which produces more winners than losers within the electorate, generate higher levels of citizen support and satisfaction? In any event, the fact that more people usually vote against rather than for the winning party should make us wary of election assessments that begin with statements like "*Newfoundlanders* renew the government's mandate." What most people want is not what they get. In 1988 the Progressive Conservatives, who both championed the free trade agreement and won the federal election, received 43 percent of the popular vote; 52 percent of the electorate supported the Liberals and New Democrats in their opposition to the agreement.

As Figure 9.5 shows, minority governments are not uncommon in Canada; five of the last eleven federal governments have been minority governments. They are the consequence, but not the only possible consequence, of a multiparty system. In other countries with multiparty systems, coalition governments are common, governments in which legislators from two or more parties hold cabinet portfolios. In Canada, however, coalition governments have not emerged at the federal level[16] and have been rare in provincial politics.[17] Minority governments behave in essentially the same manner as majority governments, although they may be more cautious and can expect a shorter life. All cabinet ministers come from the party with the plurality of seats.

One of the most frequently raised concerns about the electoral system stems from the fact that the regional composition of parties in the House of Commons often fails to reflect the regional composition of their popular vote. As a consequence, the party system may exacerbate rather than moderate regional cleavages within the electorate, driving the country apart rather than pulling it together. This problem was first addressed in a landmark article by Alan Cairns,[18] and can be illustrated by a brief look at party fortunes during the Trudeau years. This period started well for the Liberal Party in Western Canada. After a severe electoral drought under the leadership of Lester Pearson, the Liberals rebounded in 1968 to win twenty-seven seats and 37 percent of the popular vote across the region. In the ensuing four elections Liberal fortunes waned again as the party's share of the regional popular vote fell to 28 percent in 1972, rose slightly to 30 percent in 1974, and then fell to only 23 percent in 1979 and 1980. The Liberal Party, however, did even worse with respect to seats: 30.7 percent of the regional popular vote across the five Trudeau elections yielded only 14.5 percent of the seats. In the 1980 election, 23 percent of the regional vote produced only two Liberal seats. As a direct consequence, the essential two-way flow of communication between citizens and the government was twice disrupted; there was an insufficient number of Liberal MPs from the West to carry effective regional input into the federal government, and an insufficient number of elected spokespersons for the government to communicate effectively with the West. Western Canadians perceived the national government almost exclusively through the understandably jaundiced viewpoint of opposition MPs. In this respect, then, the electoral system contributed to western alienation.

The Conservatives faced a similar problem in Quebec. Although the Trudeau years were not fruitful ones for the Conservatives in Quebec, the party did average 16.6 percent of the vote across the five elections. Yet this vote yielded only 3.2 percent of the Quebec seats, including just a single seat in 1980. If the Conservatives had won seats in proportion to their share of the popular vote, there is little question that the party would have been more sensitive to the concerns of Quebec, and that the Liberals would not have been able to claim that they alone were the party of national unity. More Conservative seats would probably have produced more Conservative votes, just as a more proportionate share of western seats would have enhanced the Liberals' appeal in the West. Unfortunately, such regional distortions weakened the national parties as vehicles of political integration. In observing the House of Commons in the late 1970s and early 1980s, it was easy to forget that there were Liberal supporters by the hundreds of thousands in the West, just as there were Conservative supporters by the hundreds of thousands in Quebec. In response to this situation, considerable interest in electoral reform developed within the political science community; the challenge was to find an electoral system that would generate parliamentary contingents that more faithfully reflected party shares of the regional popular vote.[19] Given the more national character of the governments elected in 1984, 1988, and 1993, this interest has subsided.

ORGANIZATIONAL CHARACTERISTICS OF CANADIAN POLITICAL PARTIES

Both the Progressive Conservative and Liberal parties find their roots in the organizational imperatives of parliamentary government. The conventions of responsible government require that a group of MPs coalesce under the leadership of a single individual—the prime minister or premier—and that the group assume collective responsibility for the conduct of government. The adversarial format of the House of Commons has the same effect among those left out of the government coalition; power on either side of the House can be wielded more effectively by groups than by individuals. While there is nothing to say that this legislative orchestration of MPs will produce party organizations that are stable over time, this has invariably occurred across Western political systems. In the decades after Confederation, the parliamentary caucuses—the MPs and senators—were the national parties; they chose the party leaders and organized legislative activity in Ottawa. The "extra-parliamentary" parties consisted of little more than a loose assortment of financial backers, fundraisers, backroom advisers, and journalistic supporters unbound by any formal organizational structure. Away from Parliament Hill, the parties were phantom organizations that came briefly to life during election campaigns, and then quickly faded away. Although partisanship was often pervasive and intense in local communities across the country, there was no organizational infrastructure through which the local parts were knit into a coherent national whole.

As time progressed, the extra-parliamentary wings of the two parties came to acquire greater organizational coherence and stability. In 1919, in the case of the Liberals, and 1927 in the case of the Conservatives, the selection of the national party leader passed from the exclusive control of the parliamentary caucus to a national leadership convention in which MPs and senators formed a small, albeit very influential, minority. The national parties began to maintain an organizational presence between election campaigns. In 1932, for example, the National Liberal Federation was formed to provide some organizational coherence independent of the provincial Liberal parties. Constituency organizations became more stable, more formal in their organizational structure, and more extensive in their membership. If we consider today only those individuals who occupy a formal executive position somewhere within the extra-parliamentary organizations of the three major federal parties, be it at the constituency, provincial, or national level, we are looking at close to 10,000 men and women. Thus, while the primary role of extra-parliamentary parties is still to provide campaign support, the extra-parliamentary wings have become significant political players in their own right. This is particularly true for opposition parties.

Most of the third parties that have played on the Canadian political stage have originated outside Parliament or the provincial legislative assemblies. Parties such as the CCF and NDP, the Parti Québécois, the Alberta and British Columbia Social Credit, the Reform Party, and the Créditistes emerged from strains in the broader social fabric and were, at least initially, characterized by relatively strong extra-parliamentary organizations. Even so, there have been no ready Canadian equivalents for some of the mass parties that have existed in Western Europe, parties that have formal memberships running into the millions and that provide a wide array of not only political but also recreational, educational, and social activities for their members. With the exception of small ideological organizations such as the Communist Party in the past, and with the possible exception of the contemporary Reform Party, the Canadian parties are first and foremost electoral organizations. Their memberships swell when election campaigns or leadership conventions are held, and shrink as such activities wind down. Relatively few members are required to keep the national, provincial, and constituency organizations ticking over until their services are called upon again for electoral combat, and thus we find that less than 5 percent of Canadian adults are active party members.[20]

On average, about 75 percent of Canadians vote in federal elections, a turnout that is relatively modest by international standards.[21] Other forms of political participation[22] are engaged in much less frequently. The 1979 Election Study found that with respect to federal politics 43 percent of the respondents said that they often read about politics in the newspapers, 25 percent that they often discussed politics with friends, 8 percent that they often tried to convince friends to vote as they did, 4 percent that they often attended political meetings or rallies, 3 percent that they actively campaigned on behalf of candidates, and 3 percent that they often tried to contact public officials or politicians.[23] (Provincial findings were virtually identical.) In a parallel study of the 1974 campaign, the same authors noted that "the range of participation is wide—from the mere act of voting, which only five percent and ten percent report *never* doing in federal and provincial elections respectively, to working in a campaign, which only seventeen percent report *ever* doing at either level."[24] Overall, high rates of political participation tend to be associated with relatively high levels of income, formal education, and occupational prestige. William Mishler argues that more could be done by the political parties to draw citizens into active participation:

> *Part of the reason that citizens do not participate more extensively in political parties and campaigns may be that many are unaware of the opportunities that exist. Surveys indicate that greater numbers are willing to contribute both time and money, but have never been contacted by parties and candidates and asked to contribute. In Canada, as in the United States, political parties are poorly organized and highly inefficient in recruiting volunteer political activists.[25]*

Mishler nonetheless concludes that "the structure of citizen participation in Canada is surprisingly wide and deep."[26]

Against this participatory backdrop we can sketch in a rough model of Canadian political parties. The apex is formed by the small handful of party members who hold elected *public* office. Such individuals make up a minute percentage of the total party membership, a percentage that is necessarily exaggerated in Figure 9.6. Below them comes a wider but still narrow band of individuals who hold elected *party* office in the national party association, in provincial wings of the national party, or in constitu-

FIGURE 9.6 *The Party Hierarchy*

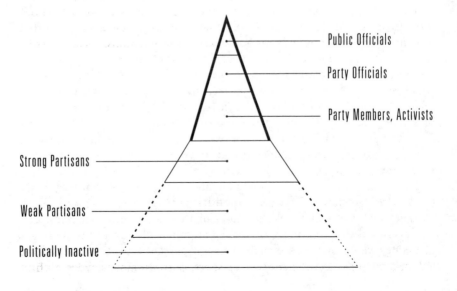

Public Officials

Party Officials

Party Members, Activists

Strong Partisans

Weak Partisans

Politically Inactive

Conflict & Unity

ency associations. Next comes a broader band of party members who do not at the time hold any formal party position but who attend party meetings, rallies, and conventions, and who participate in election campaigns by knocking on doors, giving or raising money, distributing literature, stuffing envelopes, and answering phones. The level of participation within this band, which embraces less than 10 percent of the electorate, can vary from those for whom politics is a major part of their lives to those who are formal but generally inactive party members. Below formal party members are citizens who, while not formal members, nevertheless have a strong partisan identification with one of the parties. These individuals think of themselves as Liberals, New Democrats, Reformers, or Conservatives. They view political life through distinctly partisan spectacles, cheering on "their team" and suffering with it in defeat, and they generally, although not always, vote for their party whenever the opportunity arises.[27]

It is through such partisan attachments that parties reach much further into the electorate than their limited formal memberships would suggest; large numbers of Canadians have a very real emotional stake in the party system even though they may not be card-carrying party members. However, the parties become increasingly wraithlike as we move "down" through the levels of Figure 9.6. As partisanship weakens, so too does the general level of citizen involvement in political life. Thus toward the bottom of Figure 9.6 we find those individuals who not only have a tenuous connection to the party system, but who are also characterized by low levels of political participation and unstable electoral preferences.

The concept of partisanship is an important one in political science; it provides the bridge between formal party organizations, on the one hand, and the electoral behaviour of the majority of citizens, on the other hand, citizens who do not have formal party ties.[28] Partisan identifications are usually acquired early in life, are relatively stable over time, and have a significant impact on a wide range of political perceptions.[29] Partisanship, it should be stressed, is not the same as voting intention or voting behaviour; in any given election many voters will, for a multitude of reasons, abandon "their" party to vote for another party's candidate. Party identification is nonetheless the best predictor of voting behaviour; strong partisans will stick by their party "through hell or high water," believing that nothing could be worse than having the other team win, whereas weaker partisans are more likely to be swayed by the host of short-term factors at work in any election campaign.[30] Partisanship enables us to make sense out of what can be a very complex and confusing political world; it narrows the range of political opinions to which we are exposed, and to which we attribute some credibility. Partisanship simplifies and thereby distorts reality, and yet that very act of simplification is essential for most voters given that the great bulk of their time and energy will be quite properly devoted to nonpolitical activities. In short, partisanship provides a chart and compass with which we can sail our own private ship through the turbulent waters of political life.

Political parties, like most private organizations, have an important social dimension. Although many people join parties in pursuit of policy objectives, many more are drawn in through friends, relations, and business associates, and for a variety of reasons that are more social than political. Brokerage parties, in particular, are held together less by a common set of principles than by the social bonds formed through the intense interpersonal relations characteristic of political activity. In other words, political activity can be socially rewarding in and of itself, and quite apart from its instrumental value. During his 1984 bid for the leadership of the federal Liberal Party, Jean Chrétien was asked why he entered political life. His reply goes to the roots of party politics:

> My dad got me the taste of politics as a game, as a sport. In some ways it was kind of a hobby for him. He had strong convictions but he enjoyed politics as an activity, a social activity.[31]

Political parties differ from other private organizations, however, in that their overriding objective is to capture *public office*. Because they seek to do so through the ballot, which is a public rather than a private instrument, parties come under much closer public scrutiny than do most private organizations. Scrutiny has become particularly intense with respect to the raising and expenditure of party funds.

The financing of political parties in general, and of campaign expenditures in particular, has been a matter of longstanding public concern. The basic fear has been that elections might be "bought" by those with the financial wherewithal to do so, and the electoral process thus distorted to the advantage of monied interests. Public concern has been made more acute by the rising costs of modern election campaigns; extensive reliance on media advertising, prolonged travel by party leaders, and extensive public opinion polls all cost dearly. The major federal legislative response to such concerns came with the 1974 Election Expenses Act, for which legislative counterparts now exist in most provinces.[32] The act and its subsequent amendments regulate the campaign activities of registered political parties and their candidates. (To be registered through the office of the Chief Electoral Officer, parties must present candidates in at least fifty ridings.) The regulations impose campaign spending limits on both national party organizations and local candidates. For the national party organizations these limits amount to approximately 40 cents for each voter in each constituency in which the party is running candidates, or approximately $7 million for parties running full national slates. An individual candidate is allowed to spend up to $1.30 for each of the first 15,000 names on the electoral list in his or her riding, plus $.65 each for the next 10,000 voters and $.33 for each voter thereafter. The average candidate faces an expen-

Brian Gable, *Gable: The Editorial Cartoons of Brian Gable* (Saskatoon, Sask.: Western Producer Prairie Books, 1987), p. 5.

diture ceiling of approximately \$35,000 to \$40,000. The act controls advertising expenditures by prohibiting party advertising during the first twenty-two days of the campaign. It also requires each broadcast outlet to allocate six and a half hours for party advertising during the last four weeks of the campaign. This time is allocated to the parties by the Canadian Radio-television and Telecommunications Commission on the basis of a number of factors including the parties' shares of the popular vote during the last election. Finally, the act requires public disclosure of the total funds raised by the parties and candidates, and the identification of all sources contributing more than \$100. Registered parties must file an annual financial statement and a post-election financial statement with the Chief Electoral Officer. The statements reveal how much money was raised during the year, who it was raised from, and how much was spent.

The Election Expenses Act goes beyond the financial regulation of parties to put in place three forms of public subsidy. First, the federal government now reimburses the parties for one-half of the advertising bill charged by private broadcasters. Second, candidates who receive 15 percent or more of the popular vote are entitled to a federal rebate on campaign expenses, a rebate of more than forty cents per voter in the candidate's constituency. In total, rebates to candidates and parties amount to approximately 50 percent of direct campaign costs. Third, the act

Party Finance

In 1988, the last election year for which figures are available, the national Progressive Conservative Party raised $24.6 million in corporate ($14.4 million) and individual ($10.2 million) donations. Party expenditures during the year totalled $26.6 million, of which $17.8 million went toward the federal campaign.

During the same year the Liberals raised $13.2 million, and spent $6.95 million on the 1988 campaign. Corporate donations to the Liberals outpaced individual donations by a margin of two to one. The NDP, on the other hand, raised only 2.2 percent of its $11.7 million from the corporate sector. The NDP spent $12.1 million on the 1988 campaign.

Of the nine parties submitting returns to the Chief Electoral Officer, the Rhinoceros Party trailed the field with $1,826 from ten individuals.

Source: Chief Electoral Officer, 1988 Annual Report.

encourages financial contributions to the parties by providing tax credits. Seventy-five percent of donations up to $100 can be claimed as a tax credit when the donor computes his or her federal income tax the following year. Donations ranging from $100 to $500 qualify on a sliding scale, with a refund of 55 percent being paid for a donation of $500. (Most provinces now have similar tax provisions.) It should be noted, however, that although the act and similar provincial legislation have opened up party financing to public scrutiny and have broadened the financial base of the parties, they have not reduced the overall cost of elections. Indeed, by making both public and private funds more readily available, they have enabled the parties to spend more rather than less. Spending limits have generally been set well above anticipated expenditures, and thus rarely do the major parties approach their spending limits.

Now that the parties' financial affairs have been brought under public regulation, increased attention is being paid to the gender composition of candidate slates. Although women have been active in party organizations for most of this century, their participation was traditionally channelled through separate women's organizations, parallel to and yet apart from the main party organization. The National Liberal Federation, for example, had three affiliated organizations—the Women's Liberal Federation of Canada (formed in 1928), the Young Liberal Federation, and the Canadian University Liberal Federation—that hived off their constituent groups from the main party.[33] Few women were chosen as candidates, except in ridings where a party was given no chance of winning and thus where male candidates were hard to find, and only a minuscule number were elected either to the House of Commons or to provincial legislatures. In recent years, women have been playing a more active role within the main party organizations. In 1973 the WLFC was disbanded and replaced by the Women's Liberal Commission; the latter was responsible to the women's caucus *within* the national party, and was not an affiliated organization. In 1983 Iona Campagnolo was elected president of the Liberal Party of Canada. At the 1983 Conservative and 1984 Liberal leadership conventions, women delegates were present in great numbers although there were no female candidates. In the 1984 election, women's issues played a major role in the campaigns of all major parties, and more women than ever before ran for election to the House of Commons. Of the 846 candidates from the three major parties, 131 were women, up from 70 in the 1980 campaign. In 1988, 174 women sought office as mainstream party candidates—84 as New Democrats, 53 as Liberals, and 37 as Tories. More women than ever ran in the 1993 campaign, and generally met with

Political Firsts for Women

First MP: Agnes MacPhail, 1921

First senator: Cairine Wilson, 1930

First mayor of a major city: Charlotte Whitton, Ottawa, 1951

First federal cabinet minister: Ellen Fairclough, secretary of state, 1957

First lieutenant governor: Pauline McGibbon, Ontario, 1974

First to run for national leadership: Rosemary Brown, NDP, 1975

First provincial party leader: Alexa McDonough, Nova Scotia NDP, 1980

First on the Supeme Court: Madam Justice Bertha Wilson, 1982

First governor general: Jeanne Sauvé, 1984

First leader of a national party: Audrey McLaughlin, NDP, 1989

First premier: Rita Johnston, British Columbia, 1991

First elected premier: Catherine Callbeck, Prince Edward Island, 1993

First prime minister: Kim Campbell, 1993

Manitoba was the first province (1916) to give women the vote in provincial elections. It was followed by Saskatchewan, Alberta, British Columbia, and Ontario. The last to extend the provincial franchise to women was Quebec, which did so in 1940.

greater success. Of the 64 women candidates who ran in the Liberal Party, 36 were elected; 7 of 20 women in the Reform Party were elected; and 9 of 10 women in the Bloc Québécois were elected. Both the Progressive Conservatives and New Democrats nominated a large number of women candidates, but few were elected: only 1 of 113 for the NDP, and only 1 of 67 for the Conservatives. In total, 54 women were elected in 1993 (18.3 percent of the MPs), compared to 39 (13.2 percent) in 1988 and 28 (10 percent) in 1984. As Table 9.3 shows, the proportion of women MPs in the House of Commons has been less than the similar proportion in provincial legislative assemblies. However, the 1993 election results bring the House more into line with the provincial legislatures.

In summary, political parties are unlike other private organizations in a number of important ways. They extend more broadly and deeply into the society, if not through their formal memberships, then at least through the partisan identifications held by most members of the electorate. Their financial affairs are subjected to extensive public regulation, and their expenditures are heavily subsidized by the public treasury. Their composition, be it in terms of gender, ethnicity, or regional residence, is seen as a legitimate matter of public concern and inquiry. Because they compete through a public ballot for the control of public office, parties are hybrid organizations, both quasi-private and quasi-public.

TABLE 9.3 *Proportion of Women in Canadian Legislative Assemblies, 1992*

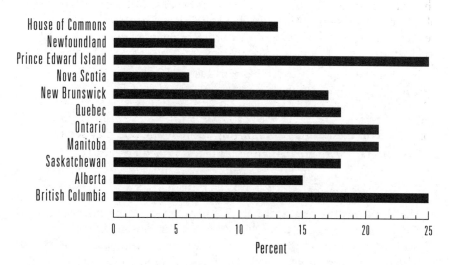

Source: The Globe and Mail, *January 26, 1993, p. A11.*

POLITICAL PARTIES, INTEREST GROUPS, AND PUBLIC OPINION POLLS

In a general election more than thirteen million voters go to the polls, carrying with them multitudinous concerns and interests, policy preferences and principles, inbred prejudices and partisan loyalties. Yet an election makes sense to us only when the thirteen million individual voting decisions are aggregated into a collective decision. In part, this aggregation is achieved through the electoral system, which reduces the individual decisions to 295 constituency decisions, and then from the latter extracts a national government. But because elections are so central to democratic political life, we cannot help but look for some meaning in election outcomes beyond the composition of the next government. We cannot help but look for the *policy mandate* lying behind individual voting decisions.

In the mythology of democratic politics, elections provide an opportunity for citizens not only to choose their government, but also to instruct it. In practice, elections rarely provide citizens with a meaningful vehicle through which to convey policy preferences to those who govern. As noted at the start of this chapter, if elections are to provide a policy mandate there must first be meaningful policy differences among the parties with respect to those issues of concern to voters. However, policy-oriented elections are rare in Canada; the 1988 federal election, with its focus on the proposed free trade agreement, was very much the exception rather than the rule.[34] To the degree that parties do differ, they are likely to do so across an array of issues, thereby raising a second difficulty in determining the policy mandate. I may vote for Party A because I support its policies on abortion even though I do not support its policy on Canadian–American relations. If successful, Party A may, however, interpret its victory as a mandate for its policy on Canadian–American relations, and not abortion.

Consider what may be some of the policy concerns of a typical voter going into the next federal election. She may be particularly concerned about her own employment situation and that of her spouse, along with the employment prospects for her children. Interest rates may well be a concern, with the mortgage coming up for renewal. She may see the election as the opportunity to advance a range of feminist and environmental concerns. She may be concerned that efforts to reduce the national debt may be undermining the continued viability of important social programs. She may have a nagging irritation with policies already in place—bilingualism, the abolition of capital punishment—and a marginal interest in a range of new policy issues—pornography, acid rain, and aboriginal self-government. All of these concerns, however, have to be reduced to a single "X" printed on a ballot, to a choice among parties that may not address her concerns or that may not differ in any meaningful way. Moreover, her policy message must be conveyed through the endorsation of a local candidate whose views on these issues she does not know. In this context, the authors of *The Absent Mandate* conclude that "the persistent failure of major political parties to present voters with distinctive, well-defined policy platforms turns the electoral process into more of a spectator sport for those who enjoy political 'horseraces' than an exercise in informed citizen participation."[35] Yet elections do give the winner the right to articulate a policy mandate, to state what the people meant to say when they elected their government. A new or returning prime minister has the electoral authority to give shape to the election mandate through words and legislation. Admittedly, we have no way of knowing if the mandate that emerges corresponds with what the voters were trying to say, but if the two diverge too markedly the government can be expected to pay the price in the next election.

Fortunately, while parties may be primarily instruments of governance rather than transmission belts for the flow of policy preferences from the electorate to the government, other transmission belts are available. There are, for instance, a number of steps that individuals can take on their own. They can write or phone their provincial member, MP, or the cabinet minister(s) responsible for the policy at issue. They can write letters to the editor and phone in to radio talk shows. They can write to the various departments of the federal and provincial governments that may be involved. However, there are very real limits on the ability of any one individual to move the policy process. What is generally needed is some form of collective action, and it is here that organized interest groups come into play. To illustrate their role, let us look briefly at the interest many people have in protecting whales.

As an individual, I may be very concerned about the fate of the whales, having watched them off the Pacific coast and listened to stereo recordings of their songs. But, again as an individual, there is little direct action that I can take on their behalf. I could refuse to buy products containing whale components, but only if I knew what such products were and only if they were for sale in Canada. I could not set forth from Calgary to try to stop foreign whaling fleets, nor could I expect individual letters sent to the governments of whaling nations to have much effect. In short, as an individual I would be powerless were it not for the existence of organized groups such as Greenpeace. On my behalf, Greenpeace can lobby internationally for the protection of whales, sail small boats in front of the whaling fleets, organize consumer boycotts, and raise concern for whales in newspapers and magazines around the world. Greenpeace becomes my "hired gun" in the fight against the whalers, and yet no more is demanded of me than the thirty seconds it takes to write a small cheque. This very minimal form of individual participation, when aggregated across thousands of individuals, provides the foundation for an effective political organization.

Interest groups, of which Greenpeace is but one example, are private organizations that attempt to influence public officials, and through them, public policy. Unlike political parties, they do not run candidates for public office under their own label. While interest groups may try to influence election outcomes by throwing their weight behind candidates sympathetic to their causes, their primary activity takes place between elections. Their efforts are primarily directed toward cabinet and the government's bureaucratic arm rather than toward the political parties. Given the strictures of party discipline and the cabinet's dominance of the legislative process, interest groups expend relatively little energy lobbying common-garden MPs and provincial legislators. However, with the growing judicialization of politics noted in the last chapter, interest groups are increasingly using the courts to pursue political objectives.

Most interest groups are stable organizations representing longstanding interests within the society. Groups such as the Canadian Medical Association, the Canadian Manufacturers' Association, the Sierra Club, the Canadian Association of University Teachers, the Canadian Broadcasters' Association, the Consumers' Association of Canada, the Canadian Federation of Agriculture, and the Canadian Hospital Association will remain in place no matter who wins a given election. These "institutionalized" groups are concerned about protecting their access to government, and are thus unlikely to become embroiled in election campaigns that might fragment their membership base and disrupt that access.[36] Because they are as interested in the implementation of public policy as they are in its formulation, contacts with the federal and provincial bureaucrats are carefully nurtured. However, there are also "issue-oriented" groups that may pursue a more active electoral role, and that are less concerned with, although not indifferent to, their own organizational survival. At least in theory, their issues are capable of resolution and could potentially be removed from the nation's political agenda. Such issues might include the reinstatement of capital punishment and the legislative prohibition of abortion. While institutionalized groups generally pursue interests that are negotiable—one can have, for example, somewhat more or somewhat less consumer protection or environmental regulation—single-interest groups often pursue non-negotiable interests. Right-to-life groups, for instance, will not settle for fewer abortions. In general, non-negotiable interests are much more difficult for the political system to handle than are issues for which compromises and trade-offs can be struck. Here it should also be noted that we cannot assume that all "interests" within society will find adequate expression through organized groups. Effective organization requires money, leadership skills, and organizational resources, none of which are evenly distributed throughout the population or across the multitude of interests potentially open to political mobilization. Thus interest group politics may extend the political influence of already powerful interests as much as they open up the political arena to a wider array of competing interests.

Although interest groups are important political actors, they are not exclusively or even primarily concerned with political activity. An organization such as the Canadian Medical Association engages in a wide range of nonpolitical activities including medical conferences, research support, group life insurance, travel assistance, legal advice, informational seminars, and professional education. As Paul Pross points out, for many groups political activity "is a minor and unwelcome addition to more general concerns."[37] Individuals may also join groups for a variety of nonpolitical reasons including social functions, access to charter air-fares, and an interest in publications put out by the groups. Yet at some point interest groups will be involved in the political process; they will represent shared group interests through contact with federal and provincial bureaucrats, cabinet presentations, briefs to task forces and royal commissions, letters of concern or support to cabinet ministers, and even media advertisements designed to increase public support for policies in line with the group's interests. Interest groups thus play an essential role in the communication of citizen policy preferences. If I wish to communicate with the government as an academic or as a supporter of whales, the Canadian Association of University Teachers and Greenpeace provide far more effective channels than does the ballot.

Interest groups keep governments informed about the opinion of specific sectors of the electorate, and also provide a vehicle through which governments can get their message out to those sectors. If, however, governments want to know the opinion of the public at large rather than the specific opinions of cattlemen, oilmen, academics, physicians, or manufacturers, they have at their disposal sophisticated public opinion polls. Such polls provide a more precise and less biased reading of the public mood than can be obtained through election results or party organizations. Polling itself can assume many forms. Governments follow the routine polling by commercial firms, much of which we encounter in the daily press. They also commission a great deal of polling research, often "piggy-backing" their questions onto omnibus commercial surveys. Government departments routinely track trends in investor confidence, anticipated consumer spending, and political priorities. In whatever form, polls have become an indispensable tool for keeping governments abreast of the shifting currents of public opinion. They provide a powerful tool that governments can use to dissect the public mood; the ambiguous policy mandate that can be discerned by reading the entrails of election results is supplemented, and to a large degree replaced, by an ongoing diagnosis of the citizen predispositions carried out through public opinion polls. Thus polls provide another, albeit passive, instrument through which citizens can communicate their concerns to governments.

Public opinion polls have been subjected to a great deal of critical commentary. Even if we put aside questions about their accuracy, neutrality, and cost, serious concerns remain. Polls have been accused of having a

Brian Gable, *The Leader Post* (Regina); reprinted in *Calgary Herald*, August 4, 1984.

pernicious impact on campaigning, leading parties and candidates to do little more than echo what the public wants to hear. To argue that polls report but do not shape opinion seems less tenable after the experience of the 1984 election campaign. The 1984 polls, which from early in the campaign indicated a Conservative landslide, arguably had at least three important although not necessarily decisive effects. First, they undercut morale within the Liberal campaign organization, making it difficult to attract financial support and volunteer assistance. Second, they undercut the Liberal campaign strategy in the West; if Western Canada wanted an effective voice in Ottawa, there was little sense in voting for the Liberals given that the Conservatives were expected to win. Third, they assured Quebec voters that a shift to the Conservative Party would not isolate Quebec from the federal government. Perhaps the more general point is that public opinion polls can have a dramatic impact on the strategic calculations of political parties and leaders. Whether they have a similar impact on the more routine determination of public policy is far less certain.

Given the role played by interest groups and opinion polls, it is clear that the parties have been relegated to a secondary role in conveying citizen policy preferences to governments. Nevertheless, parties continue to perform a number of other essential roles. They structure the legislative process, providing reasonably stable governments and a focused legislative opposition. They recruit political leaders. Most importantly, parties enable

POLLBEARERS.

Mayes, *The Edmonton Journal*; reprinted from Guy Badeaux, ed., *Portfoolio 8* (Toronto: Macmillan, 1992), p. 79.

voters to hold governments responsible for their actions. As Richard Van Loon and Michael Whittington point out, "we can vote to 'throw the rascals out' because we can draw a line between 'rascals' and 'non-rascals'; the party labels provide us with this line."[38] Thus, the electoral process enables citizens to cast a retrospective judgment on government performance. The fact that it does not enable citizens to direct or handcuff the course of public policy seems to be of little consequence, given that a profusion of alternative policy instruments exists. If the party system is to be judged, it should be judged on its success or failure in holding the country together, in moderating rather than exacerbating those conflicts that strain the national fabric.

POLITICAL PARTIES AND PATTERNS OF CONFLICT

The preceding chapters have identified some of the major lines of cleavage that run through and across the national political community. Here we turn to a brief discussion of how these cleavages have shaped and have been shaped by party politics.

Linguistic Conflict

In the early decades after Confederation, Macdonald's Conservative Party formed the political bridge between Canada's two linguistic communities. Indeed, the Conservatives' initial dominance of national political life

Ever Wonder Why No One Interviews You?

In a typical Gallup poll, approximately 1,000 respondents are interviewed. Given an adult Canadian population of some seventeen million persons, the odds of any one individual being interviewed are remote. If a Gallup survey were conducted every month and an entirely different set of respondents used each time, any given individual could expect to be interviewed once in every 1,417 *years*!

The odds of being picked as a respondent in any one survey are approximately one in 17,000. The odds of being picked *in your lifetime*, should you live to be 80, are approximately one in twenty-three.

reflected the party's electoral success in both communities, just as the rise to power of the Laurier Liberals reflected the collapse of Macdonald's linguistic coalition. Speaking in 1904, Henri Bourassa described the vision of Canada that underlay the success of both the Macdonald Conservatives and the Laurier Liberals:

> We work for the development of a Canadian patriotism which is in our eyes the best guaranty of the existence of the two races and of the mutual respect they owe each other.... The nation that we wish to see develop is the Canadian nation, composed of French Canadians and English Canadians, that is of two elements separated by language and religion ... but united in a feeling of brotherhood, in a common attachment to a common fatherland.[39]

The mutual respect and brotherhood of which Bourassa spoke were to be severely tested, and found wanting, in the conscription crisis of the First World War, a crisis that led for the first time to the exclusion of one of the linguistic communities from the federal government.

Canada had gone into the First World War with a volunteer army, and prior to 1917, Robert Borden's Conservative government steadfastly maintained that conscription—a military draft—would not be imposed. By 1917, however, the unexpected carnage of trench warfare had created a desperate manpower shortage. Efforts in the first part of that year to recruit additional volunteers were largely futile; in English Canada the manpower pool was all but exhausted, and in Quebec, where the recruiting drive produced only ninety-two volunteers, an earlier enthusiasm for a short European war had evaporated. As Armstrong explains:

> There could not have been any more striking illustration of the indifference and hostility of French Canada to the Dominion's war effort. The

wholehearted enthusiasm of 1914 had turned to bitter mistrust and open opposition by the summer of 1917.[40]

The attempt to recruit French-Canadian volunteers turned into a shambles as anglophone recruiters were sent into Quebec to urge French Canadians to fight, not for Canada, but for England and France. Not surprisingly, their appeal fell on deaf ears. Finally, the government introduced the Military Service Bill on June 11, 1917. The bill's introduction was greeted by massive anti-conscription rallies across Quebec, and its proclamation on August 29 met with violence and riots in Montreal. The bill also touched off a riot by Irish dock workers in Halifax, and was greeted by dismay in the prairie West where farmers were already facing an acute manpower shortage.

French-Canadian opposition to conscription can be traced in part to the isolation of a small linguistic community, cut off from its European roots for 150 years and further isolated on a predominantly anglophone continent. It also reflected French-Canadian anger over the limits placed on Ontario bilingual schools in 1915. Perhaps of greatest importance were the different forms of Canadian nationalism that emerged during the war. While involvement in the British war effort was an expression of Canadian nationalism for most English Canadians,[41] the nationalist horizon of French Canadians stopped at Canadian shores. In the parliamentary debate on the Military Service Bill, "hardly a French Canadian spoke ... who did not insist that his compatriots felt deeply that the only country to which they owed loyalty and service was Canada and that to ask them to rush to the aid of France and England was asking a great deal too much." [42]

Conscription had a profound impact on both the Conservative and Liberal parties. Borden, in an attempt to broaden the political base of support for conscription, formed the Union Government in October 1917. The new cabinet was composed of thirteen Conservative ministers and ten pro-conscription Liberal ministers. The Union Government unquestionably served its intended purpose in English Canada, but it also isolated Quebec. Borden's cabinet included only two weak French-Canadian ministers. In the December 1917 general election, only three Unionist candidates were elected in Quebec. Those Liberals who remained under the leadership of Wilfrid Laurier fought conscription and, in so doing, greatly strengthened what was already a strong electoral position for the Liberal Party in Quebec. Figure 9.7 illustrates the wedge that the 1917 election drove between the two major parties in Quebec. At the same time, Laurier's opposition to conscription caused a deep division within the Liberal Party itself. Many English-Canadian Liberal MPs crossed the floor of the House to support the Union Government, and the party's electoral base in English Canada was severely damaged. Thus the 1917 conscription crisis shattered the party system as a vehicle of political integration across the linguistic divide.

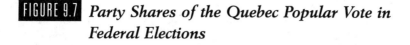

FIGURE 9.7 *Party Shares of the Quebec Popular Vote in Federal Elections*

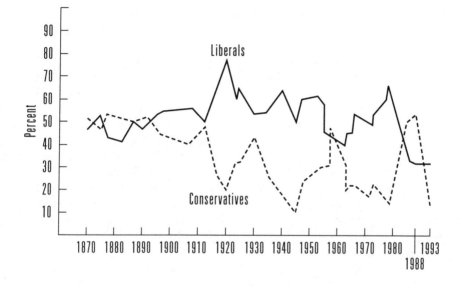

The conscription crisis was played out again in the Second World War. This time Mackenzie King was prime minister. King, who had become leader of the Liberal Party in 1919, was acutely aware how badly both his party and the national fabric had been damaged by the conscription crisis of the First World War. Thus, in a speech to the House of Commons shortly after the Second World War broke out, King promised that Canada's war effort would not entail conscription:

> *I wish to repeat the undertaking I gave in Parliament on behalf of the Government on March 30th last. The present Government believes that conscription of men for overseas service will not be a necessary or effective step. No such measure will be introduced by the present Administration.*[43]

This was the bargain King presented to Quebec in the 1940 general election; Canada would pursue the war at Britain's side, but not at the cost of conscription. In that election, the Liberals captured 61 of Quebec's 65 seats, with 3 seats going to independent Liberals and only 1 to a Conservative candidate.

As the war dragged on, King's promise proved more and more difficult to keep, and the Liberal government began a series of incremental steps toward conscription. In a rare national plebiscite, held in April 1942, King asked voters to release the government from its pledge not to impose conscription. The plebiscite, it should be stressed, was held on the government's pledge and not on conscription per se. The government's policy, King maintained, was "conscription if necessary but not necessarily conscription." The plebiscite quantified the sharp linguistic cleavage that existed on the conscription issue: 72 percent of Quebeckers voted not to release King's government from its pledge, while 80 percent of those outside Quebec, and a national majority overall, voted to do so.[44] Conscription was subsequently introduced, but first only for home defence; conscripted soldiers, or "Zombies" as they came to be called, could not yet be sent overseas. By late 1944, however, the attrition of Canadian forces overseas and the government's inability to raise sufficient replacements through voluntary enlistment forced King to send conscripted men overseas. After five years of war and despite strenuous opposition from Quebec, conscription for overseas service had again been imposed.

This time the impact on the party system was less pronounced. In the 1945 general election, the Liberals lost only eight Quebec seats while the nationalistic and anti-conscriptionist Bloc Populaire elected ten members. As Figure 9.7 shows, the Progressive Conservatives were devastated in Quebec; they elected only one member with a meagre 8.4 percent of the popular vote in their worst showing ever. Although the Liberal government had eventually imposed conscription, King had clearly resisted doing so as long as possible. French Canadians who were nonetheless dissatisfied could hardly throw their support to the Conservatives who had been, after all, much more supportive of conscription than had the Liberals. To vote en masse for the Bloc Populaire was to risk Quebec's isolation from the federal government. Thus the Liberals survived more or less intact in Quebec, while the poor showing by the Conservatives was an extension of, rather than a significant change in, the political status quo. Even though the Liberals lost 48 seats outside Quebec and the Progressive Conservatives gained 26, the Liberals retained both a 7-seat advantage over the Tories outside Quebec and a majority government. The country was not split along linguistic lines as it had been in 1917.

Following the war, the Conservatives found themselves trapped in a vicious circle, or what George Perlin has called the "Tory Syndrome," in Quebec.[45] Because so few Conservatives were elected from Quebec, the party's parliamentary caucus lacked sufficient sensitivity to the province's concerns. Because the party lacked such sensitivity, it tended to come down on the "wrong side" of whatever linguistic conflicts arose, further damaging its electoral prospects in Quebec. Because the party did so poorly in Quebec, it could not compete on equal terms with the Liberals in federal elections; the Liberals were able, with a reasonable degree of veracity, to portray themselves as the only truly *national* party. Successive national defeats led to self-perpetuating internal attacks on the party's leaders, attacks that undermined the party's credibility as an alternative government and thus further weakened its electoral support.

The trend was broken briefly in 1958 when Quebec voters, encouraged by Union Nationale Premier Duplessis, climbed aboard the Diefenbaker bandwagon and elected fifty Progressive Conservative MPs. The Quebec MPs, however, felt ill at ease within the predominantly anglophone Tory caucus. Nor were they a particularly able lot, and the performance of Tory cabinet ministers from Quebec left a great deal to be desired. For his part, Diefenbaker was unable to exploit the Conservative opening in Quebec. As George Grant explains:

> the keystone of a Canadian nation is the French fact.... English-speaking Canadians who desire the survival of their nation have to co-operate with those who seek the continuance of Franco-American civilization. The failure of Diefenbaker to act on this maxim was his most tragic mistake.[46]

In 1962 only fourteen Quebec Tories were re-elected, and in 1963 only eight.

While the Conservatives were mired in Quebec, the Liberals were making the province their own. Mackenzie King retired in 1948 and was replaced by Louis St. Laurent, the Liberals' second French-Canadian leader. St. Laurent was replaced by Lester Pearson in 1957, who was in turn replaced by Pierre Trudeau in 1968. Trudeau was very popular in Quebec, and as discussed in Chapter 4, his leadership came to be identified with the bilingualism policies of the federal government. Although those policies were initiated before Trudeau became prime minister, and were endorsed by the opposition parties, they along with Trudeau formed the basis of a seemingly invincible Liberal fortress in Quebec. (When the Official Languages Act came to a vote, seventeen Conservative MPs, including John Diefenbaker, defied Robert Stanfield and voted against the legislation.) The party's strength in Quebec enabled the Liberals to argue in turn that they alone could form a truly national government spanning the country's two linguistic communities. This was a telling argument at a time when English Canadians were nervous about a growing separatist movement in Quebec.

During Trudeau's leadership, 47 percent of the Liberal seats *came* from Quebec and 84 percent of Quebec's seats *went* to the Liberal Party. The Liberal Party's near monopoly in Quebec gave it a virtual armlock on national power. In the 1972 general election, the Conservatives elected more MPs than the Liberals in eight of the ten provinces, and tied with the Liberals in the ninth. Yet even this was not enough to overcome the Liberal edge in Quebec, where the Liberals won fifty-six seats to only two for the Conservatives. Without a breakthrough in Quebec, the most that the Conservatives could hope for was a minority government, and even that eluded Robert Stanfield by two seats in 1972.

The Conservative resurgence in Quebec began under Joe Clark's leadership. Clark devoted more time and effort to Quebec than any Conservative leader before him, and improved his own grasp of French to the point where he could campaign effectively in the province. Ironically Clark's efforts bore no fruit whatsoever in the short run. In the 1979 general election, the Conservative share of the Quebec popular vote fell from 21.2 percent in 1974 to only 13.5 percent. In the 1980 election it fell again to 12.6 percent, and the Conservatives elected only one Quebec MP.[47] Yet Clark's efforts, in combination with the 1979 minority Conservative government and its 1980 defeat, drove home to Conservatives the necessity of a breakthrough in Quebec. The promise of that breakthrough was the major card played by Brian Mulroney in his successful 1983 bid for the leadership of the Conservative Party.

Mulroney was the first Tory leader to come from Quebec, and the first central Canadian Conservative leader in twenty-seven years. Fluent in both official languages, he proved to be the standard-bearer so badly needed by the Conservative Party in Quebec. In the 1984 campaign Mulroney's personal appeal, along with the retirement of Pierre Trudeau, John Turner's defeat of Jean Chrétien in the Liberal leadership convention, and a weariness in Quebec after a decade of confrontation between nationalists and federalists, produced the long-awaited breakthrough. Tory candidates, often informally backed by the provincial Liberal Party in a manner reminiscent of Duplessis's intervention in 1958, captured 58 Quebec seats, a gain of 57 from 1980. In 1988 Mulroney strengthened the Conservatives' hold in Quebec by taking 63 seats, leaving only 12 seats to Liberal candidates. Back in 1980, only one Tory vote in ten (10.5 percent) had come from Quebec. In the 1984 election, 27.5 percent of the total Conservative vote came from Quebec, a proportion that climbed even further to 32.5 percent in 1988. Then, in 1993, came the collapse: only Jean Charest was elected as a Conservative candidate in Quebec, the party's share of the popular vote in Quebec fell to 13.6 percent, and the proportion of the total Conservative popular vote coming from Quebec fell to 23.2 percent. The Bloc had decisively captured the nationalist support that had found a congenial home in the Conservative Party under Mulroney's leadership.

The national fate of the Conservative and Liberal parties has been largely determined by their success or failure in Quebec. (In the sixteen federal elections since the end of the Second World War, the winning party nationally received a plurality of Quebec seats in twelve of those elections, one less than the number of elections in which the winning party also captured a plurality of Ontario seats.) This has also been the case for the New Democrats, although here the party's Quebec record has been one of unmitigated failure. Since the formation of the NDP in 1962, there has only been a single NDP candidate elected in Quebec. In 1988, the NDP ran a very high profile campaign in the province, in part because public opinion polls taken in 1986 and 1987 had indicated a Quebec surge in

NDP support. However, in the election itself the New Democrats failed again to elect a candidate and finished with only 14 percent of the Quebec popular vote; in 1993, the NDP vote in Quebec fell to 1.5 percent. Without at least an electoral toehold in Quebec, New Democrats will continue to have difficulty convincing Canadians that they have the potential to form a national government. Mr. Mulroney's legacy has been to pass the "Tory Syndrome" to the NDP.

In conclusion, political conflict centred on Quebec and language-related issues has had a profound impact on the party system. Parties that have responded favourably to the concerns of the Quebec electorate have also done well in the pursuit of national power, and parties that have stumbled in Quebec have stumbled nationally. Quite simply, Quebec has been the key to national success. When the Conservatives lost support in Quebec following Macdonald's death, national power shifted to the Liberal Party. The Liberals' domination of national political life over much of the next eighty-five years was strengthened by, first, the party's response to the conscription crisis in the First World War and, second, by the choice of three Quebec leaders (Laurier, St. Laurent, and Trudeau) and by the bilingualism policies associated with Trudeau. The Liberals' hegemony was broken decisively only when the Conservatives selected a Quebec leader, Brian Mulroney, who then went on to strengthen Conservative support in Quebec by initiating a series of constitutional initiatives designed to bring Quebec back into the Canadian constitutional family.

Until recently, then, Quebec has played the determining role in the alternation of power between the Conservative and Liberal parties, and in the lack of national success by the NDP. However, the 1993 election results paint a more confused picture. The Liberals would have won a majority government in the 1993 election without winning any seats in Quebec, although it is also clear that their potential appeal in Quebec was related to the party's national appeal. At the same time, the majority of Quebec seats are now held by neither Liberal nor Conservative MPs. We have in the Reform Party, moreover, a significant national party with little electoral interest or prospects in Quebec, but one that might present that weakness to the rest of the country as a source of strength. Thus while Quebec's role is unlikely to be any less central in elections to come, the province's impact on the national party system has become much harder to predict.

Regional Conflict

Although the emergence of national political parties has been associated with the decline of territorial conflict in many Western countries,[48] this association has been less apparent in Canada. The history of protest parties in Western Canada and the collapse of the Liberal Party in the region between 1968 and 1993 suggest that the party system has been an

Lucien Bouchard's devotion to Quebec nationalism took him from Environment Minister in Brian Mulroney's government to the founding of the Bloc Québécois and, following the Bloc's success in the 1993 election, to being the leader of the Official Opposition.

imperfect vehicle of national political integration. Whether the parties have contributed to regional conflict or have been impaled upon it is more difficult to determine.

Figure 9.8 traces the regional composition of the Liberal and Conservative electoral coalitions from the turn of the century, and that of the NDP from 1962. As discussed above, the contribution of Quebec voters varies considerably across the three parties. While traditionally a core component of the Liberal coalition, they have constituted a more erratic component of the Conservative coalition and a negligible part of the NDP coalition. If we turn to voters from Atlantic Canada, Figure 9.8 shows a modest but generally progressive decline in their contribution to the Conservative and Liberal coalitions. It is not, however, that Atlantic voters are turning away from the two parties; it is simply that Atlantic Canadians constitute a declining proportion of the national electorate and hence a declining proportion of specific party coalitions. There is nothing in Figure

FIGURE 9.8 — Regional Composition of the Party Vote

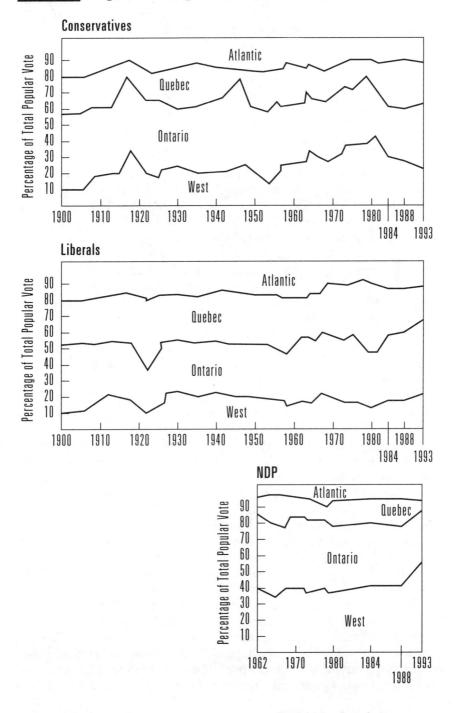

Conservatives

Percentage of Total Popular Vote

Atlantic
Quebec
Ontario
West

1900 1910 1920 1930 1940 1950 1960 1970 1980 1988
                                                    1984 1993

Liberals

Percentage of Total Popular Vote

Atlantic
Quebec
Ontario
West

1900 1910 1920 1930 1940 1950 1960 1970 1980 1988
                                                    1984 1993

NDP

Percentage of Total Popular Vote

Atlantic
Quebec
Ontario
West

1962 1970 1980 1984 1993
                        1988

9.8 to suggest that the regional interests of Atlantic Canadians have found either a clear champion or opponent within the national party system. With the exception of very modest regional support for the NDP, Rawlyk and Brown's discussion of the region in the 1870s applies with equal force to the subsequent century:

> *Throughout the region the disintegration of any political movement which did not correspond to the sole Canadian cleavage of Liberal and Conservative signified the complete political integration of the Maritimes into Canada.... There would be no significant attempts to channel regional protest outside the traditional two-party system.*[49]

Figure 9.8 shows that the Conservatives, Liberals, and New Democrats draw a major portion of their vote from Ontario, as we would expect given that province's share of the national population. It is nonetheless interesting to note that until very recently it was the NDP that drew the largest share of its vote from Ontario. Across the nine elections from 1962 to 1984, 43 percent of the total NDP vote, as opposed to 38.1 percent of the Conservative and 36.9 percent of the Liberal total vote, came from Ontario, a finding that reflects the electoral weakness of the NDP east of the Ontario–Quebec border. In 1988, however, the NDP drew only 35 percent of its total vote from Ontario, compared to 43.3 percent of the Liberal vote and 31.5 percent of the Conservative vote that came from Ontario. In 1993, only 30.9 percent of the total NDP vote came from Ontario. It is also interesting to note that Ontario's contribution to the Conservative vote has declined over time. In the twelve elections held between 1900 and 1945, the Conservatives drew almost 46 percent of their total vote from Ontario. In postwar elections, that proportion fell to just under 40 percent.

The regional composition of the Reform Party vote is relatively easy to dissect. In 1988, its first election, the party only ran candidates in the four western provinces. Then, following a decision in 1990 to expand eastward, the party ran candidates in all provinces but Quebec in the 1993 election. Nonetheless, of the total Reform vote, 57.9 percent came from the four western provinces, and an additional 38.2 percent came from Ontario. The total Reform vote in Atlantic Canada was only half that received by Reform candidates in Calgary alone.

John Diefenbaker's leadership and the elections of 1957 and 1958 initiated a pronounced westward shift in the Conservatives' centre of gravity and an off-setting, although less pronounced, eastward shift for the Liberal Party. The modest 1984 Liberal revival in the West suggested by Figure 9.8 is deceptive; the "revival" is simply an artifact of the Liberal collapse in Quebec. In the 1984 election, Liberal candidates in the West captured only 16.3 percent of the regional popular vote, *down* from 23.4 percent in 1980. In all four western provinces, the Liberal Party finished third. It is

The son of Ernest Manning, former premier of Alberta, Preston Manning led his Reform Party from a shutout in 1988 to 52 seats in the 1993 general election.

thus somewhat ironic that the Liberals emerged from the 1984 election with a party leader, John Turner, representing a Vancouver riding.

Overall, Figure 9.8 suggests a party system that has been reasonably stable in its regional composition. However, there are three important qualifications to any such conclusion. The first is that a more erratic picture would emerge if we looked at the regional distribution of party *seats* rather than *votes*. The difference can be illustrated by a comparison of the regional composition of the Conservative popular vote, shown in Figure 9.8, and the regional composition of Conservative seats in the House of Commons, shown in Figure 9.9. (This latter figure does not, for obvious reasons, include the 1993 results.) The patterns revealed in Figure 9.8 are amplified in Figure 9.9, and the latter figure brings Ontario's pre-Diefenbaker dominance of the party into bold relief. The Conservatives' historical weakness in Quebec is more dramatic, as are the regional shifts that

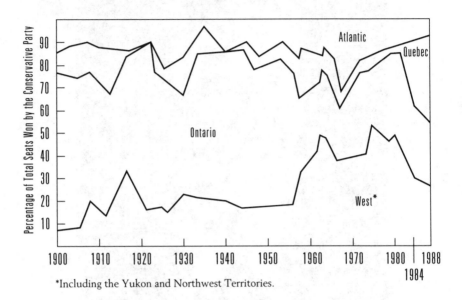

FIGURE 9.9 *Regional Distribution of Conservative Seats in the House of Commons*

*Including the Yukon and Northwest Territories.

occurred in 1984 and following the Diefenbaker sweep in 1958. The second qualification is that Figure 9.8 does not capture the host of protest parties that have arisen in Western Canada since 1921. Certainly it can be argued that parties such as the Progressives, the United Farmers of Alberta, the CCF, Social Credit, and the Reform Party demonstrate the party system's inability to integrate the West into the Canadian political mainstream. As Denis Smith notes, such parties have been sceptical toward the national community since 1921.[50] It can also be argued that the western penchant for third parties does more than reflect western alienation; it may also have contributed to alienation by choking off western input into the only parties forming national governments. If western Canadians have elected MPs to protest rather than to govern, then to a degree they have been architects of their own misfortune. And third, the long-term impact of Reform on the regional composition of the Canadian party system remains to be seen. This impact will depend upon whether the regional, populist, or ideological face of the party comes to the fore.

Class Conflict

The Canadian party system has not been marked by deep or even significant class cleavages among the major parties. There have certainly been parties on the left of the political spectrum, but these have not been "working-class" parties in any conventional sense. The Communist Party and associated factions have been around since the early 1920s, but they have never been nor for that matter have tried to be a significant electoral presence. The Co-operative Commonwealth Federation articulated a forceful social democratic platform that placed it well to the left of the country's ideological centre of gravity, but the CCF's strongest electoral appeal was among the agrarian communities of Western Canada and not among urban, industrial workers. The NDP has enjoyed reasonably significant electoral and financial support from the trade union movement, but its electoral appeal has not been cast along class lines, and it has not succeeded in capturing even a plurality of the trade union vote. Perhaps of greatest importance, there have been virtually no significant or persistent class differences in electoral support for the two historically dominant parties. Whereas the Conservative and Liberal parties have often differed sharply in their regional, religious, and linguistic bases of support, they have not diverged along class lines.

All this is not to say that the party system is without consequence for class or redistributive politics. Indeed, the fact that the parties have not tried to orchestrate class-based electoral support, and that the party system provides no outlet for competing class interests, may have profound consequences for the demobilization of class conflict. The neutrality of the party system may not be neutrality at all, but instead might be seen as a means of reinforcing present inequities in the distribution of income and economic opportunity. However, and for better or for worse, the empirical finding remains that the party system is not organized along class lines. Unfortunately, the explanation for this finding is far from straightforward.

Many suggestions have been advanced as to why class conflict has played such a negligible role in the structural organization of the party system and in the character of electoral competition:

- Class divisions and class consciousness may simply be very weak; voters may not see themselves in class terms, and are therefore unlikely to vote along class lines. This may reflect the complexity of modern social and economic organization, or it may reflect "false consciousness" on the part of many Canadians who "should" but fail to see their situation in class terms.

- Class issues may be salient to many voters, but may be overwhelmed by other issues such as regional and linguistic conflict. Other issues may have forced class conflict down and off the political agenda. Put somewhat differently, people may well have class identities, but these co-exist with other identities based on one's regional residence, language, religion, ethnicity, and gender. When it comes to voting, other identities tend to come to the fore and class identities tend to recede.

- Class cleavages are not reinforced by other lines of political cleavage in the country. Class divisions do not follow regional lines and, since the onset of the Quiet Revolution, have tended not to follow linguistic lines. Other lines of cleavage may cross-cut and suppress those based on social class.

- The lack of a strong, explicit class dimension to American politics may spill over to the way in which Canadians think about politics; we do not see ourselves or act politically in class terms because the American experience to which we are exposed through the mass media does not suggest that these are appropriate ways to think and act.

- Trade unions in Canada have generally followed the American model of "business unionism" in which unions by and large restrict their activities to issues specific to the workplace, and do not engage in the broader political process. Thus unions do not try to mobilize and direct the voting behaviour of their members. While there are exceptions, business unionism has been closer to the general rule than have been highly politicized unions. Only a small proportion of trade union members belong to a local affiliated with the NDP, and even where this connection does exist, more members vote Liberal than vote NDP.[51]

- Class politics may be more pronounced in provincial politics than in federal politics. As Ronald Lambert et al. note, "appeals to regional, ethnic, and other loyalties are more likely to displace social class in federal politics."[52]

- Voters may wish to vote along class lines, but the party system does not provide them with the opportunity to do so. Class conflict is neutralized because the party system, by design or chance, does not provide an outlet. Class differences among competing parties do not exist, or are not seen to exist by voters.[53]

- For whatever reason, Canadians fail to link class issues to those issues that have dominated the campaign agenda. As Jon Pammett notes, "the electorate makes few connections between personal financial circumstances or relations of exploitation in the economic structure and these vast national problems [inflation, unemployment, the deficit]. Without these connections, however, class voting cannot develop."[54]

In short, many Canadian voters may not have politically salient class identities. If they do they may not seek an electoral outlet, and if they do seek an outlet the party system may fail to provide one. The result in any event is a party system that is not organized along class lines and that does not orchestrate class interests. If the party system has an impact on class conflict, it is to depoliticize that conflict.

Canadian–American Relations

Issues surrounding Canada's relationship with the United States have not been a constant feature of federal election campaigns, but from time to time they have played a central and even dramatic campaign role. Certainly the economic relationship between Canada and the United States played such a role in the 1891 and 1911 general elections, and the military relationship between the two countries played a significant if less central role in the 1963 election. Throughout the 1970s and early 1980s issues relating to economic and cultural nationalism, and to the tone of the relationship, played an ongoing if less than decisive role in federal election campaigns. Then, in 1988, Canada's economic relationship with the United States was the central and virtually only issue in a federal election fought on the proposed free trade agreement. This dispute was to ripple through to the 1993 election when the expanded North American Free Trade Agreement was an element, but not a very significant element, in a more complex campaign.

In 1891, Sir John A. Macdonald's Conservative government appeared to be on the brink of collapse. Macdonald himself was ailing, the country had been unable to shake a prolonged economic depression, and the government was plagued by scandal and the acrimonious Manitoba schools dispute. The Liberal opposition moved to the attack with a proposal for the reciprocal removal of trade barriers between Canada and the United States, a policy that would be called free trade in contemporary usage and that at the time was termed *unrestricted reciprocity*. By so doing, the Liberals handed Macdonald the issue that was to save his Conservative government. Reciprocity, Macdonald argued, would reduce the national government's revenues and necessitate an annual per capita tax of $15 to make up for the loss. More importantly, Macdonald portrayed reciprocity as a threat to Canada's British ties and to the very survival of Canada. He accused the Liberals of "veiled treason which attempts by sordid means and mercenary proffers to lure our people from their allegiance."[55] There was, he concluded, "a deliberate conspiracy by force, by fraud or by both to force Canada into the American union."[56] This was strong language indeed, and was reinforced by Macdonald's ringing statement that "a British subject I was born, and a British subject I shall die."

The campaign engaged the country's major economic interests; the farming community endorsed reciprocity, but the major transportation, financial, and manufacturing interests opposed it, and carried more weight in the campaign. Of greatest importance, however, were the emotional loyalties brought into play. In Quebec, the Conservative Party argued that reciprocity would launch French Canadians down the slippery slope to absorption into American secular materialism. In the Maritimes, the threat to the British connection was emphasized. The *Halifax Morning Herald*, planting the Red Ensign on its masthead for the duration of the campaign, proclaimed that the Canadian people were being brought to a parting of the ways: Would they choose to be bound in vassalage to their foreign foes—the Americans—or to continue to prosper as part of the greatest empire the world had ever seen?[57] Under the emotional barrage of Macdonald's campaign, the Liberals and the reciprocity proposal went down to defeat.

In 1911 the Liberals, now in power, once again ventured into the reciprocity thicket. In January 1911, a reciprocity agreement had been reached between Canada and the United States, and had been approved by the American Congress. Prime Minister Wilfrid Laurier, however, decided to go to the Canadian people in a general election before introducing the reciprocity legislation in Parliament. Again, the farming community supported reciprocity, and again reciprocity was opposed by the major transportation, financial, and manufacturing interests. As in 1891, the purely economic debate was soon obscured by an emotional debate over the future of Canada. The Conservatives' campaign slogan was "No Truck Nor Trade with the Yankees," a slogan coined in the advertising department of a wholly American-owned subsidiary.[58] Premier McBride of British Columbia summed up the emotional stakes with a simple placard that superimposed "Which?" over pictures of the Union Jack, on the one side, and the Stars and Stripes on the other. As in 1911, the Liberals had the wrong emotional end of the issue and went down to defeat. Taken together, the 1891 and 1911 campaigns demonstrated that the Canadian–American relationship could engage deeply felt emotions and national insecurities. Twice burned, the Liberals were never again to campaign for free trade, although significant support for the notion persisted in the party until at least the mid-1980s.

When the issue of Canadian–American relations entered the 1963 campaign, the focus was upon Canada's military relationship with the United States. During John Diefenbaker's term of office, the Conservative government had purchased a considerable stock of military hardware that, to be effective, required tactical nuclear warheads. By early 1963, however, the warheads had yet to be acquired and the cabinet, badly split on the issue, vacillated on whether to proceed with their acquisition. The government's indecision was openly criticized by the American government and was made a central issue by the Liberal opposition in the 1963 general election campaign. The Liberal leader, Lester Pearson, argued that Canada must acquire nuclear weapons to fulfil its alliance commitments to the United States and NATO. The Conservatives remained badly divided on the issue, and it is likely that the party's internal disarray hurt it as much at the polls as did Diefenbaker's opposition to nuclear weapons. George Grant argues that Diefenbaker faced the "full power of the Canadian ruling class, the American government and the military," and that in the unequal contest Canadian nationalism was dealt a lethal blow.[59] In any event, the minority Conservative government went down to defeat, to be replaced by a minority Liberal government.

Over the next twenty-five years, the substance of Canadian–American relations intruded less vigorously into federal election campaigns. In an extensive analysis of issue-voting in Canadian elections, the authors of *Absent Mandate* concluded that debate over important Canadian–American issues in the 1970s "occurred outside the electoral arena, as did any conflict resolution."[60] To the extent that Canadian–American relations played a significant role, the focus was on the tone rather than the substance of the relationship. Thus, for example, in the 1984 campaign the Conservatives called for an improved and friendlier relationship without specifying what an altered relationship might entail. Admittedly, the federal parties differed among themselves with respect to the Canadian–American relationship. The NDP staked out a clear position on the nationalist end of the continuum, the Liberal Party was the architect of the nationalist policies embedded in the Foreign Investment Review Agency and the National Energy Program, and the Conservatives favoured a more hospitable environment for American investment. However, neither the Liberals nor the Conservatives sought to move Canadian-American relations to the top of the electoral agenda.

This situation changed dramatically when the Mulroney government announced its intention to negotiate a free trade agreement with the United States. When the legislation to implement the FTA was blocked in the Senate, the Conservatives had no choice but to go to the people in a general election. The historical irony of the 1988 campaign was that the Conservatives, who had traditionally opposed closer integration with the United States, championed the FTA while the Liberals, who had traditionally been the party of free trade, opposed the agreement. The FTA dominated the campaign, and as had happened in the past, emotional arguments played a central role. When it became difficult to sort through the largely hypothetical economic arguments, the impassioned political debate turned to the potential impact of the FTA on national unity, on Canadian culture, on social programs such as medicare, and indeed on the very survival of Canada. When the election came, the Conservatives carried the day; although more Canadians appeared to oppose than support the FTA, the opposition vote was divided between the Liberals and New Democrats. The FTA legislation was reintroduced into Parliament immediately after the election, was passed this time by both the House and Senate, and came into effect on January 1, 1989.

Intergovernmental Relations and Constitutional Politics

In the complex world of federal–provincial relations, conflict among governments has often been overlaid with partisan conflict. The first meeting of provincial premiers, held in 1887, was called by the predominantly Liberal premiers to orchestrate a partisan attack on the then-Conservative federal government. As the Great Depression descended in 1930, Prime Minister

King declared in the House of Commons that his government would not give a nickel in federal relief to provincial governments controlled by Conservative administrations. During the latter part of the Trudeau era, when the Liberals controlled the federal government but all ten provincial governments were in non-Liberal hands, intergovernmental conflicts frequently took on a partisan air. Certainly the energy conflicts between the Government of Canada, on one side, and the governments of Alberta and Newfoundland, on the other, appeared to be sharpened by the partisan conflict between the federal Liberals and the provincial Conservatives.

Despite such examples, however, there is a general consensus within the political science literature that partisanship plays a modest role in the bargaining positions and outcomes of federal–provincial negotiations,[61] and that it affects the tone more than the substance of intergovernmental relations. This consensus has been pulled together by Donald Smiley, who notes that political parties "appear to be of diminishing importance in the aggregation and articulation of citizen interests and the conversion of these into public policy."[62] While this diminished importance is a general phenomenon, it has been particularly evident in federal–provincial relations. In First Ministers' Conferences, Smiley argues, cleavages "are on axes other than partisan ones: between 'have' and 'have-not' provinces; between governments which put an urgent priority on bilingual and bicultural matters and those which do not; between Quebec and other jurisdictions; between the heartland of Ontario and Quebec and the peripheral provinces."[63] The provinces have enduring characteristics including their size, wealth, resource base, and regional location that persist no matter which party forms the provincial government, and that will tend to be of primary importance in shaping intergovernmental relations. Partisanship may shape the tone of and strategy employed in such relations, but provincial interests and concerns are relatively immutable.

In federal states, political parties have a potentially important role to play in the operation of the federal system. Highly centralized party systems, in which the national parties dominate those in the states or provinces, may centralize the federal system far beyond what we might expect from the constitutional framework by acting as a solvent on the constitutional division of powers.[64] In the Canadian case, however, the party system has, if anything, reinforced the division of powers. In part, this reinforcement stems from an asymmetrical party system, with quite different parties being dominant at the federal and provincial levels. This very asymmetry precludes political parties serving as effective bridges across the constitutional division of powers and among the governmental actors in executive federalism. The situation that arose after the 1984 election, in which a single party was in power both nationally and in seven of the ten provinces, has not been typical of the Canadian experience.

The impression should not be left that intergovernmental relations are completely divorced from party politics. The atmosphere within which intergovernmental relations are conducted can be affected by the partisan mix of governments and first ministers. "Ottawa-bashing" can often play an important role in provincial election campaigns as government parties wage electoral combat with the federal government rather than with provincial opponents. Federal–provincial relations can enter federal campaigns, as they did in the 1979 and 1980 campaigns when Trudeau offered his leadership as the country's best defence against voracious provincial premiers, and in 1984 when both Brian Mulroney and John Turner pledged that their administrations would bring renewed harmony to federal–provincial relations. Nonetheless, party influences operate primarily at the margins of intergovernmental relations, acting more as either a lubricant or grit within intergovernmental machinery that is driven by an array of forces largely removed from the partisan arena.

The political parties for the most part have not been active players in the country's prolonged constitutional debate. The Conservative, Liberal, and New Democratic parties all supported the 1987 Meech Lake Accord, and little attempt was made during the 1988 federal election campaign to mobilize growing opposition to the accord. The party strategies corresponded closely to the consociational model discussed in Chapter 4; the parties acted so as to neutralize constitutional unrest as an election issue. The three major parties also locked arms in support of the 1992 Charlottetown Accord, albeit with less enthusiasm this time around, and pooled resources for the yes side in the national referendum campaign. In this case, however, the Reform Party broke ranks and played a central role in the no campaign. It should also be noted that the constitutional visions of party leaders have certainly played an important role in recent constitutional politics even if the party organizations per se were not involved in the debate. There is no question that Joe Clark, Brian Mulroney, and Pierre Trudeau, and to a lesser extent Preston Manning, have been key players, and that their constitutional visions have been thoroughly entangled in their parties' electoral strategies.

PARTIES, LEADERSHIP, AND NATIONAL INTEGRATION

John Meisel, writing in 1975, argued that "in the absence of national and nationalizing nonpolitical institutions ... parties and the party system have become important factors in nation building and in the evolution and preservation of national unity."[65] Although the parties have not had an unblemished record as vehicles of national integration, there is little doubt that they have generally pursued brokerage strategies designed to knit together the often disparate elements of the Canadian political community. In such strategies, the party leaders have played a pivotal role. Smith suggests that leaders from the time of John Diefenbaker and Lester Pearson have adopted a pan-Canadian leadership style that cuts across regional and linguistic cleavages. In so doing, they have helped build a national consciousness and community.

Leaders at both the provincial and federal level have left an indelible mark on the political life of their country. It is difficult to imagine, for example, Newfoundland politics without Joey Smallwood; Nova Scotia politics without Richard Hatfield; New Brunswick politics without Louis Robichaud; Quebec politics without Maurice Duplessis, René Lévesque, and Robert Bourassa; Saskatchewan politics without Tommy Douglas; Alberta politics without Ernest Manning and Peter Lougheed; or British Columbia politics without W.A.C. Bennett and William Bennett, his son. At the national level, leaders such as Macdonald, Laurier, Diefenbaker, Trudeau, and Mulroney did more than ride the political currents of their times; they shaped their political environment as much as they took shape from it.

In contemporary electoral politics, the party leader is so central to the campaign, so much the focus of media coverage and campaign advertising, that the party and leader have almost fused into a single entity.[66] The importance of the leader, however, extends well beyond the electoral process. As the late Walter Young noted, the contemporary importance of leadership is a response to the growth of government:

> *Instead of the vast and faceless bureaucracy, there is a prime minister who speaks for and to the nation. At a time when the engine of the state at both the federal and provincial levels is large and complicated, the existence of a single individual as the functioning head of the apparatus provides credibility and a much needed focus. The need for such a figure increases with the growth of the machine, and the power of such a figure increases accordingly.[67]*

Leaders help personify the political system, and thus provide us with handles on a reality that might otherwise be overwhelming in its complexity.

Phrases such as "the Macdonald era," "the Trudeau years," and the "Mulroney Conservatives" capture the central role that leaders have played in the life of both their party and nation. Given this importance, the constitutional framework of the Canadian state is somewhat at odds with political reality. Although voters across the country in the 1993 Conservative campaign were urged to "vote for Kim Campbell," only the voters in Vancouver-Centre in fact had the opportunity to do so, just as only the voters in St-Maurice had the opportunity to vote directly for or against Jean Chrétien. Although party leaders dominate both federal and provincial campaigns, the format of the ballot restricts voters to a choice among local candidates. Nor is the public at large involved in the selection of party leaders in the first place. While the national conventions that selected Jean Chrétien in 1990 and Kim Campbell in 1993 were each attended by three to four thousand party members, those in attendance

Jean Chrétien arrived in Ottawa as a freshman MP in 1963, served as a cabinet minister under Pierre Trudeau, was elected to lead the Liberal Party in 1990, and went on to win a majority government in the 1993 election.

constituted a minuscule proportion of the national electorate. In a somewhat contradictory fashion, the constitutional framework fails to recognize the central role of party leaders while at the same time the parliamentary concentration of power in the hands of the political executive contributes much to the power leaders wield, and to their ability to shape the political landscape.

Consensus as to the importance of leaders should not imply any consensus on what distinguishes good leadership from bad. Indeed, Canadians may hold quite contradictory leadership expectations, as Ron Graham illustrates in his 1983 comparison of the public's reaction to Joe Clark and Pierre Trudeau:

For seven years Clark had suffered in comparison with Pierre Trudeau, although most agreed that Clark was a better human being, more sympathetic, more dedicated, more open-minded, perhaps more complex and courageous. But Trudeau was what Canadians really wanted to be—intellectual, suave, worldly, independent, and unpredictable—while Clark was what they feared they were—earnest, nice, competent, unimaginative, honest and rather dull.... Joe Clark wasn't good enough. They wanted to be something greater.[68]

In democratic countries, there is a special tension to leadership expectations. A leader is expected to lead and yet to follow the people, to rise above the narrow views of the electorate while remaining its servant.

Canada has certainly experienced leaders who have been charismatic in character, who have risen above the confines of party politics to capture, if only momentarily, a national vision that touched not only the minds but also the hearts of the electorate. There is little question, for example, that René Lévesque accomplished this in Quebec, just as John Diefenbaker and Pierre Trudeau were able to do in the 1958 and 1968 campaigns. Yet it should also be noted that some of Canada's most successful leaders have been marked by very different political styles. Although few political commentators described Bill Davis, Ontario's premier from 1971 to 1985, as a charismatic leader, his low-keyed search for the middle ground was coupled with daunting electoral success. Robert Bourassa's long-running success in Quebec has been attributed by very few to his charismatic character.

Canada's most famous example of successful noncharismatic leadership is provided by William Lyon Mackenzie King. Although often defeated himself at the polls—as a consequence representing ridings in Ontario, Saskatchewan, and Atlantic Canada—King led his party to victory in 1921, narrowly lost to the Conservatives yet clung to power in 1925, won in 1926, lost in 1930, and then piled up impressive wins for the federal Liberals in 1935, 1940, and 1945. King was cautious in the extreme, arguing that "in the course of human history far more has been accomplished for the welfare and progress of mankind in preventing bad actions than in doing good ones."[69] As Joseph Wearing notes, King was not devoid of principles, but he "was not one to let his ideals lead him into precipitate action."[70] A poor speaker with a cool and aloof public presence, King has been widely and harshly criticized. F.R. Scott, who was closely associated with the CCF during King's leadership of the Liberal Party, summed up King's style in a poem, "W.L.M.K.," written shortly after King's death:

He blunted us.
We had no shape
Because he never took sides,
And no sides
Because he never allowed them to take shape.
He skilfully avoided what was wrong
Without saying what was right,
And never let his on the one hand

Know what his on the other hand was doing....
He seemed to be in the centre
Because we had no centre,
No vision
To pierce the smokescreen of his politics.
Truly he will be remembered
Whenever men honour ingenuity,
Ambiguity, inactivity, and political longevity.[71]

Whitaker describes King's government as "the defender of the people against the big interests and the defender of the big interests against the people."[72]

Nonetheless, King has a legitimate claim to being Canada's most successful prime minister. His party enjoyed significant electoral support across the country; in the seven national campaigns in which King was leader, the Liberals won 913 seats compared to only 541 for their Conservative opponents. He reinforced the Liberal base in Quebec, even though he himself was unilingual, while maintaining a substantial electoral base in Western Canada. He steered Canada through the Second World War, during which the country's impressive military contribution abroad was combined with economic growth and, more so than during the First World War, political tranquillity at home. His career stands as a monument to political craftsmanship. He may not have lifted the hearts and souls of Canadians, but the party he led commanded their electoral support.

Whether the party system in the years to come will meet the challenges posed by a fractious political community remains to be seen. We have now had three consecutive federal elections in which the winning party secured a broad national mandate with sizable representation from all regions of the country. Yet, in the 1993 election, we also witnessed the virtual collapse of two long-established national parties, and the emergence of two powerful parties with regional bases of support. In the face of competition from the Bloc in Quebec and the Reform in the West, and to a significant degree Ontario, will the Liberals be able to knit together the political community? Will the Reform Party expand beyond its regional heartland to replace the Conservatives, or will the latter arise Phoenix-like from the ashes of the 1993 campaign? Will the NDP survive, and will the Bloc succeed in advancing a nationalist agenda for Quebec? The answers to these questions are closely linked not only to the future direction of Canada, but to our survival as a national community.

SUGGESTED READINGS

1. Ivan Avakumovic, *The Communist Party in Canada: A History* (Toronto: McClelland and Stewart, 1975); and *Socialism in Canada:*

A Study of the CCF-NDP in Federal and Provincial Politics (Toronto: McClelland and Stewart, 1978).

2. Sylvia B. Bashevkin, Toeing the Lines: Women and Party Politics in English Canada, 2nd ed. (Toronto: Oxford University Press, 1993).

3. Janine Brodie and Jane Jenson, "The Party System," in Michael S. Whittington and Glen Williams, eds., Canadian Politics in the 1990s, 3rd ed. (Scarborough: Nelson, 1989), pp. 249–67.

4. William Christian and Colin Campbell, Political Parties and Ideologies in Canada, 2nd ed. (Toronto: McGraw-Hill Ryerson, 1983).

5. Harold D. Clarke, Jane Jenson, Lawrence LeDuc, and Jon H. Pammett, Political Choice in Canada (Toronto: McGraw-Hill Ryerson, 1979); and Absent Mandate: The Politics of Discontent in Canada (Toronto: Gage, 1984).

6. John English, The Decline of Politics: The Conservatives and the Party System, 1901–20 (Toronto: University of Toronto Press, reprinted 1993).

7. Alain-G. Gagnon and A. Brian Tanguay, eds., Canadian Parties in Transition (Scarborough: Nelson, 1989).

8. Richard Johnston, André Blais, Henry E. Brady, and Jean Crête, Letting the People Decide: Dynamics of a Canadian Election (Montreal and Kingston: McGill-Queen's University Press, 1992).

9. John Laschinger and Geoffrey Stevens, Leaders and Lesser Mortals: Backroom Politics in Canada (Toronto: Key Porter Books, 1992).

10. Patrick Martin, Allan Gregg, and George Perlin, Contenders: The Tory Quest for Power (Scarborough: Prentice-Hall, 1983).

11. Sydney Sharpe and Don Braid, Storming Babylon: Preston Manning and the Rise of the Reform Party (Toronto: Key Porter Books, 1992).

12. Jeffrey Simpson, Discipline of Power: The Conservative Interlude and the Liberal Restoration (Toronto: Personal Library Publishers, 1980).

13. Hugh G. Thorburn, ed., Party Politics in Canada, 6th ed. (Scarborough: Prentice-Hall, 1991).

14. Joseph Wearing, ed., The Ballot and Its Message: Voting in Canada (Toronto: Copp Clark Pitman, 1991).

15. Walter D. Young, The Anatomy of a Party: The National CCF, 1932–1961 (Toronto: University of Toronto Press), 1969.

STUDY QUESTIONS

1. In order to explore the concepts of partisanship and party identification, ask yourself the following questions. Do you find that you have an emotional loyalty for one party rather than another, that you tend to identify with one particular partisan camp? If so, has your identification always been with one party, or has it changed over time? If it has changed, how would you account for the change? Do you identify with the same or different parties in federal and provincial politics? Which level of government commands the strongest partisan loyalties in your case? Can you identify the partisanship of your parents? How evident were partisan affiliations in your environment when you were growing up? Is your own partisanship in line with, or at odds with, that of your parents?

2. Divide a piece of paper into three columns, labelling the first Reform–Liberal, the second Liberal–NDP, and the third Reform–NDP. Now jot down, in the appropriate column, those aspects of public policy for which you feel significant party differences exist. How many differences can you identify? Which two parties are the most clearly distinquishable from each other, and which two are the least so?

3. If the federal government were to change hands over night, what difference would you expect for people like yourself? Jot down any significant differences on a piece of paper. Now pose the same question for your provincial government; what changes would you expect if the government were to change hands? In examining your answers, determine your perceptions of party differences, and the policy significance of election outcomes for people such as yourself.

NOTES

1. Harold D. Clarke, Jane Jenson, Lawrence LeDuc, and Jon H. Pammett, *Absent Mandate: The Politics of Discontent in Canada* (Toronto: Gage, 1984), p. 10.

2. Richard J. Van Loon and Michael S. Whittington, *The Canadian Political System: Environment, Structure and Process*, 3rd ed. (Toronto: McGraw-Hill Ryerson, 1981), p. 307.

3. David E. Smith, "Party Government, Representation and National Integration in Canada," in Peter Aucoin, Research Coordinator, *Party Government and Regional Representation in Canada* (Toronto: University of Toronto Press, 1985), p. 52.

4. John Meisel, "The Party System and the 1974 Election," in Howard R. Penniman, ed., *Canada at the Polls: The General Election of 1974* (Washington, D.C.: American Enterprise Institute for Public Policy Research, 1975), p. 1.

5. The 1925 and 1926 elections are not included in this total. On October 29, 1925, the incumbent Liberals elected only 99 MPs compared to 116 for the Conservatives. Yet, because neither party could form a majority government, the Liberal prime minister, William Lyon Mackenzie King, decided to stay in power until late June 1926, when King sought a dissolution of the House. The governor general, Lord Byng, refused and instead asked the leader of the Conservative Party, Arthur Meighen, to form a government. The Meighen government lasted only three days before it was defeated in the House. Meighen was then granted a dissolution, a general election was called for September 14, 1926, and the Liberals won a majority government with 128 seats, compared to 91 for the Conservatives.

6. The Pacific Scandal exposed financial entanglements among Macdonald, the Conservative Party, and the builders of the new Canadian Pacific Railway.

7. Meisel, "The Party System," p. 14.

8. Seventy-six of all eighty-four seats won by Social Credit candidates came from Alberta, where the party overwhelmingly dominated provincial politics from 1935 to 1971.

9. Cited in Joseph Wearing, *The L-Shaped Party: The Liberal Party of Canada, 1958–1980* (Toronto: McGraw-Hill Ryerson, 1981), p. 1.

10. The Conservatives captured 78.5 percent of the House seats, whereas the 211 Conservative seats in 1984 constituted 74.8 percent of the seats in a slightly larger House of Commons.

11. Smith, "Party Government," p. 27.

12. The term "government party" comes from Reginald Whitaker's *The Government Party: Organizing and Financing the Liberal Party of Canada, 1930–58* (Toronto: University of Toronto Press, 1977).

13. Donald J. Smiley, *Canada in Question: Federalism in the Eighties*, 3rd ed. (Toronto: McGraw-Hill Ryerson, 1980), ch. 5.

14. For a detailed analysis of the relationship between federal and provincial party support, see Wearing, *The L-Shaped Party*, pp. 81–86.

15. Van Loon and Whittington, *The Canadian Political System*, p. 319.

16. The Union Government is a unique case in that the Conservative Party had a clear parliamentary majority before embarking upon the Union coalition with pro-conscription Liberals.

17. Brian H. Coulter, *Coalition Governments in Canada: A Comparative Analysis of Four Case Studies* (University of Calgary: Unpublished M.A. Thesis, 1982).

18. Alan C. Cairns, "The Electoral System and the Party System in Canada, 1921–1965," *Canadian Journal of Political Science*, 1 (1968), pp. 55–80.

19. For example, see William P. Irvine, *Does Canada Need a New Electoral System?* (Kingston: Institute of Intergovernmental Relations, Queen's University, 1979).

20. William Mishler, "Political Participation and Democracy," in Michael S. Whittington and Glen Williams, eds., *Canadian Politics in the 1980s*, 2nd ed. (Toronto: Methuen, 1984), p. 178.

21. Clarke et al., *Absent Mandate*, p. 35.

22. Mishler defines political participation as "voluntary activities by citizens which are intended to influence the selection of government leaders or the decisions they make." "Political Participation," p. 175.

23. Clarke et al., *Absent Mandate*, p. 37.

24. Harold D. Clarke, Lawrence LeDuc, Jane Jenson, and Jon H. Pammett, *Political Choice in Canada* (Toronto: McGraw-Hill Ryerson, 1979), p. 87.

25. Mishler, "Political Participation," pp. 179–80.

26. Ibid., p. 190.

27. It is among individuals with strong party identifications but without formal party memberships that we find the greatest overlap between federal and provincial parties sharing the same label.

28. For a useful discussion of partisanship, see Clarke et al., *Political Choice*, ch. 5.

29. Ibid., p. 136.

30. Considerable debate exists as to the general strength and stability of partisan identifications in Canada. In summarizing this debate, Jon Pammett concludes that the majority predisposition is toward *flexible partisanship*, that about 60 percent of voters "develop party loyalties that are either weak, changeable over time or different at the two levels of the federal system." See "Elections" in Whittington and Williams, *Canadian Politics*, p. 276.

31. *The Globe and Mail*, National Edition, June 2, 1984, p. 1.

32. For an overview of both federal and provincial legislation, see Khayyam Z. Paltiel, "Canadian Election Expense Legislation: Recent Developments," in Hugh G. Thorburn, ed., *Party Politics in Canada*, 4th ed. (Scarborough: Prentice-Hall, 1979), pp. 100–110.

33. Wearing, *The L-Shaped Party*, p. 216.

34. For a general and informative discussion of the policy mandates of Canadian elections, see Clarke et al., *Absent Mandate*.

35. Ibid., p. 34.

36. For a discussion of the distinction between institutionalized and issue-oriented interest groups, see Paul Pross, "Pressure Groups: Adaptive Instruments of Political Communication," in Pross, ed., *Pressure Group Behaviour in Canadian Politics* (Toronto: McGraw-Hill Ryerson, 1975), pp. 8–18.

37. Pross, *Pressure Group Behaviour*, p. 3.

38. Van Loon and Whittington, *The Canadian Political System*, p. 313.

39. Cited in Mason Wade, *The French Canadians, 1860–1967*, vol. II (Toronto: Macmillan, 1968), pp. 524–25.

40. Elizabeth Armstrong, *The Crisis of Quebec, 1914–1918* (Toronto: McClelland and Stewart, 1937; reprinted 1974), p. 166.

41. For a discussion, see John English, *The Decline of Politics: The Conservatives and the Party System, 1901–20* (Toronto: University of Toronto Press, 1977).

42. Ibid., p. 187.

43. House of Commons, *Debates*, September 8, 1939, p. 36.

44. Although the voting returns did not distinguish between the two linguistic communities in Quebec, it is clear that the no vote among francophones alone was even higher.

45. George C. Perlin, *The Tory Syndrome: Leadership Politics in the Progressive Conservative Party* (Montreal: McGill-Queen's University Press, 1980).

46. George Grant, *Lament for a Nation: The Defeat of Canadian Nationalism* (Toronto: McClelland and Stewart, 1965), p. 20.

47. In the 1980 election, 102 ridings contained a francophone population of 10 percent or more. Of these, the Liberals won 100 and the Conservatives won 2. As Mulroney argued in his 1983 leadership bid, "give the Liberals a 100 seat lead and they'll beat you ten times out

of ten." Patrick Martin, Allan Gregg, and George Perlin, *Contenders: The Tory Quest for Power* (Scarborough: Prentice-Hall, 1983), p. 84.

48. Stein Rokkan, "Electoral Mobilization, Party Competition, and National Integration," in Joseph LaPalombara and Myron Weiner, eds., *Political Parties and Political Development* (Princeton: Princeton University Press, 1966), pp. 241–66; and Seymour Martin Lipset and Stein Rokkan, "Cleavage Structures, Party Systems, and Voter Alignments: An Introduction," in Lipset and Rokkan, eds., *Party Systems and Voter Alignments: Cross-National Perspectives* (New York: The Free Press, 1967), pp. 1–64.

49. G.A. Rawlyk and Doug Brown, "The Historical Framework of the Maritimes and Confederation," in G.A. Rawlyk, ed., *The Atlantic Provinces and the Problems of Confederation* (Breakwater Press: 1979), p. 16.

50. Denis Smith, "Political Parties and the Survival of Canada," in R. Kenneth Carty and W. Peter Ward, eds., *Entering the Eighties: Canada in Crisis* (Toronto: Oxford University Press, 1980), p. 140.

51. For a fuller discussion, see Keith Archer, "The Failure of the New Democratic Party: Union, Unionists, and Politics in Canada," *Canadian Journal of Political Science*, 17:2 (June 1985), pp. 353–66.

52. Ronald D. Lambert, James E. Curtis, Steven D. Brown, and Barry J. Kay, "Social Class, Left/Right Political Orientations, and Subjective Class Voting in Provincial and Federal Elections," *Canadian Review of Sociology and Anthropology*, 24:2 (1987), pp. 526–49.

53. Richard Nadeau and André Blais found that Canadian voters were able to detect significant and reasonably stable differences among the three major parties with respect to international relations and national unity, but not with respect to class issues. See "Do Canadians Distinguish Between Parties? Perceptions of Party Competence," *Canadian Journal of Political Science*, 23:2 (June 1990), pp. 317–33.

54. Jon H. Pammett, "Class Voting and Class Consciousness in Canada," *Canadian Review of Sociology and Anthropology*, 24:2 (1987), p. 287.

55. For a discussion of the 1891 and 1911 campaigns, see J.M. Beck, *Pendulum of Power* (Scarborough: Prentice-Hall, 1968), pp. 57–68 and 120–33.

56. Ibid., p. 64.

57. Ibid., p. 68.

58. Ramsay Cook, *The Maple Leaf Forever* (Toronto: Macmillan, 1971), p. 212.

59. Grant, *Lament for a Nation*, p. 12 and ch. 3.

60. Clarke et al., *Absent Mandate*, pp. 20–21.

61. Ibid., p. 12.

62. Smiley, *Canada in Question*, p. 146.

63. Ibid., p. 148.

64. This point is developed in a comparative context by Ivo D. Duch-
acek, *Comparative Federalism: The Territorial Dimension of Politics*
(New York: Holt, Rinehart and Winston, 1970), p. 329 and William
H. Riker, *Federalism: Origin, Operation, Significance* (Boston: Little,
Brown, 1964), p. 129.

65. Meisel, "The Party System," p. 2.

66. In the 1980 post-election study, the following rather difficult question was posed to respondents: "Take a moment to think over all the
reasons why you decided to vote the way you did, and just briefly tell
me the things that were most important to you." More respondents—
30 percent—named a party leader or leadership than identified any
other single factor. Twenty-three percent named a party, while only 9
percent cited local candidates. Clarke et al., *Political Choice*, p. 273.

67. Walter D. Young, "Leadership and Canadian Politics," in John
Redekop, ed., *Approaches to Canadian Politics*, 2nd ed. (Scarborough: Prentice-Hall, 1983), pp. 269–70.

68. Ron Graham, "The Legacy of Joe Clark," *Saturday Night*, September
1983, p. 30.

69. Cited in Peter C. Newman, *The Distemper of Our Times* (Toronto:
McClelland and Stewart, 1968), p. 57.

70. Wearing, *The L-Shaped Party*, p. 4.

71. F.R. Scott, "W.L.M.K.," from *Selected Poems of F.R. Scott* (Oxford
University Press, 1966), pp. 60–61.

72. Whitaker, *The Government Party*, p. 141.

LOOKING AHEAD

One of the underlying themes of this text has been the stress on patterns of continuity in Canadian politics. The argument has been made that since Confederation, national politics have been repeatedly energized by a recurrent set of issues and concerns: by linguistic tensions, by regional conflict, by debate over the appropriate relationship with the United States, by a highly conditioned and somewhat subdued debate on redistributive politics, and of somewhat more recent vintage, by the quest for constitutional reform. It is this very continuity that makes an understanding of the past so important; not only is the political present anchored in the past, but our future options are also constrained by decisions already taken and roads already travelled. Thus we must come to grips with patterns of continuity if we are to comprehend the present and look ahead with some measure of confidence in our ability to understand the future unfolding of Canadian political life.

In large part, the continuity in Canadian politics is reflected by a widespread concern with boundary maintenance, with the protection of borders both around and within the national political community. This is certainly the case, for example, in the ongoing debate over Canada's relationship with the United States, a debate in which the physical, economic, and cultural aspects of boundary maintenance have been of great importance. In the case of Quebec, the protection of the francophone community has often entailed the defence of the province's jurisdictional and constitutional borders from intrusions, both real and perceived, from the broader Canadian community. The protection of jurisdictional boundaries relating to the ownership and control of natural resources has been of perennial concern in Western Canada. Boundary maintenance has also been a more general intergovernmental concern for federal and provincial governments in their running and frequently abrasive battle over the jurisdictional boundaries between the two orders of government, and over federal incursions across those boundaries. In short, boundary maintenance has been a pervasive structural theme in Canadian political life.

However, it is important to stress that the political environment is far from static, that while there have been recurrent themes and impressive patterns of continuity, there are at the same time significant changes that are beginning to transform the political landscape. These changes are of interest in their own right. For example, the dynamics of environmentalism and feminism, to name but two, have a compelling attraction that reaches well beyond the domain of Canadian politics. Yet they are also of more immediate interest to the present discussion in that they threaten to erode the very boundaries that have been so important in the past, the jurisdictional "lines on maps" that have preoccupied generations of Canadian political leaders. Environmentalists and feminists, by arguing for national programs, national standards, and the universal application of human rights and environmental principles, threaten to erode the importance and public policy significance of the national boundary between Canada and the United States, and of jurisdictional boundaries within the country. In so doing, they challenge the constitutional and institutional underpinnings of the Canadian federal state.

What, then, are these changes that are beginning to transform the political landscape? The first is the freer international flow of trade and financial resources associated with global economic change. It is widely assumed that global economic change is eroding the importance of those political boundaries that, in the past, channelled the flow of trade and investment. To the extent that the world economy is in fact being globalized, nations are losing their capacity to direct domestic and foreign investment, to determine where corporations might locate, and with whom they might trade. Clearly the FTA and NAFTA are part of this pattern of globalization, albeit on a continental scale. Their anticipated impact is equally clear; they are designed to minimize the importance of national boundaries within the continental economy. They will also, as a consequence, make it increasingly difficult to maintain economic boundaries between units within the federal states of North America. In the Canadian case, interprovincial barriers to trade and, as discussed in Chapter 6, regional economic development incentives will be very difficult to sustain within the context of continental free trade and a globalized economy. Thus the general impact of globalization, and the specific impact of the FTA and NAFTA, will be to make political boundaries within Canada and the political boundary between Canada and the United States less important. Given the emphasis we have traditionally placed on boundary maintenance, this is a transformation that is close to revolutionary in its potential impact.

The second change is related less to the flow of capital and investment than it is to the flow of human resources, and more specifically to changing patterns of immigration. Immigration, of course, has always been of critical importance to Canada. Apart from the aboriginal peoples, we are in a very fundamental sense an immigrant society. It is clear, moreover, that immigration will continue to be of critical importance as the demographic profile of the population changes, as the society ages, and as the domestic birthrate continues to be below that needed to maintain the current level of population. However, in recent years, and not coincidentally as more and more immigrants have come from Asia and the Third World, immigration policy has become increasingly contentious. The points of contention range from which level of government should handle the reception and integration of immigrants—an issue of considerable importance in both the Meech Lake and Charlottetown accords—to the status of political refugees and the level, and ethnic composition, of immigrant flows. Opinion polls have shown relatively high levels of public concern about current levels of immigration. For example, in a Gallup national survey of 1,032 respondents conducted in May 1992, 46 percent of respondents felt that Canada should accept fewer immigrants at this time, 37 percent supported existing levels of immigration, and only 13 percent would favour increasing the level of immigration.[1] Support for reducing the level of immigration ranged from a low of 35 percent in Quebec to 46 percent on the prairies, 47 percent in British Columbia, 50 percent in Ontario, and 58 percent in Atlantic Canada.[2]

Immigration may also begin to pose a significant challenge to the federal sinews of the Canadian state. The dramatic changes over the past two decades in the national origin of immigrants have led to growing and politically engaged ethnic communities within which territorial affiliations

The Limits of Tolerance

Changing patterns of immigration have brought the level of tolerance in the Canadian society into question. There is some evidence to suggest that the growing proportion of immigrants from non-white and non-European countries has been associated with growing racial intolerance within the country. For example, a February 1993 Angus Reid/Southam News telephone poll of 1,501 randomly selected respondents from across the country found the following:

- 57 percent said that "minority groups should try to be more like other Canadians rather than maintain their native language and culture";

- 47 percent of the respondents felt that Canada was taking in too many immigrants;

- 26 percent believed that non-whites could "damage the fabric of Canadian society";

- 24 percent said that more white and fewer non-white immigrants should be taken in by Canada; and

- 13 percent believed that "Canada would be better off if all recent immigrants went back to their home countries."

There is no evidence that racial intolerance and opposition to immigration are characteristic of the majority of Canadians. At the same time, both sentiments show surprising and disturbing strength within the electorate.

with provincial communities are relatively weak. Powerful new ethnic communities are emerging that do not have a territorial base, and that are unlikely to foster strong political identifications with provincial governments and communities. Such communities are more likely to challenge the constitutional division of powers by asserting the primacy of Charter guarantees and by promoting national values and programs. These new Canadians may be less federal in their political values and orientations than are Canadians who are more deeply entrenched in the traditional political culture.

The third change is feminism, which seeks to transform the social, economic, and political underpinnings of Canadian society. The point to stress in this particular instance is that feminism rests uneasily with the federal principles that, to the present time, have guided the evolution of the Canadian political system. (Feminism also rests uneasily with other traditional aspects of the political culture, but this is another story.) Feminists tend to support national social programs and standards, to argue that the principles of gender equality should be applied in the same manner regardless of provincial residence. Federalism, however, implies that public policies and programs should be tailored to fit regional differences in priority and taste, that their application in Saskatchewan might not be the same as their application in Quebec or Nova Scotia. This is a difficult point to sell to those who argue that gender equality, and human rights more broadly defined, should be universal in their application and impact. In this narrow sense, then, feminists challenge the federal underpinnings of the Canadian state.

The fourth change is environmentalism, which also poses a significant transformative challenge to the institutional status quo. Environmentalists are not opposed to federalism in principle, and indeed many environmental theorists favour a highly decentralized political system that would maximize local control. However, environmentalists also tend to support national environmental programs, and tend to be relatively intolerant of provincial differences in environmental standards. As environmentalists confront problems that spill across provincial and national borders, they also express some frustration with jurisdictional boundaries, with the political lines-on-maps that often have little correspondence to natural divisions in the ecosystem. Thus, if environmentalism continues to transform our political agenda, it is likely as a consequence to have a significant impact on the evolving nature of Canadian federalism.

The above-noted changes are similar in that they all challenge the importance of jurisdictional boundaries and they all promote, albeit to varying degrees, citizen identities that are at the same time more national—less constrained by provincial boundaries—and more international—less constrained by national boundaries. However, these are by no means the only forces of social and political change at work on the contemporary political landscape. Others also have the potential to radically transform that landscape, although their impact on federalism per se is more difficult to predict.

The growing institutionalization of aboriginal self-government will require a fundamental change in the political relationship between aboriginal peoples and the existing national, provincial, and local governments. The introduction of self-government will have its most immediate and direct impact on reserve-based communities, and will pose a major challenge to the representation of those communities within the larger institutions and intergovernmental frameworks of the federal state. Over the longer term, the quest for self-government will extend to aboriginal communities without sharp territorial definition, including the large aboriginal populations within urban centres. This will challenge our political imaginations as we try to come up with new forms of governance and representation that are not based on territorially defined communities.

A somewhat related change is taking place with the rapid evolution of territorial government in the Canadian North.[3] To this point, the North has had a limited impact on national politics. While it has certainly infused our imaginations, and while images drawn from the North have played an important role in the definition of our national identity, the region itself has had too small a population base to leave a significant mark on national political life. However, this situation is unlikely to continue as the northern territories move toward provincial status, and as those territories become more fully integrated into the institutional matrix of the Canadian federal state. Thus we already find, for example, that the territories have all but full representation within the forums of executive federalism. In the years to come they may well transform those forums by expanding the number of players, something that aboriginal representatives have also done, and thereby undermining some of the norms of participant equality that undergird executive federalism. For instance, the equality of provinces will become an increasingly difficult diplomatic fiction to maintain with northern premiers representing populations as small as 20,000 people, or roughly 1/500 of Ontario's population. It will also be interesting to see how the amending formula might be changed to incorporate evolutionary developments in the North.

The last decade has witnessed a growing public interest in direct democracy, in moving the levers of political power closer to the electorate. This interest was particularly evident during the 1992 constitutional referendum, and has been addressed not only by parties that explicitly challenge the institutional status quo, such as the Reform Party, but also by parties that embody the status quo, such as the Progressive Conservatives when led by Kim Campbell. A common theme in this reform agenda is discontent with parliamentary institutions and with the broader conventions of representative democracy. There is growing emphasis on giving individual legislators more freedom of action with respect to party discipline, and on giving voters more power through the more frequent use of

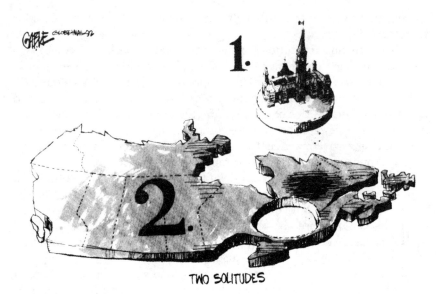

TWO SOLITUDES

Brian Gable, *The Globe and Mail*, October 29, 1992.

referenda and a variety of other consultative mechanisms. Now it may be that Canadians have sufficiently vented their frustration with parliamentary institutions and representative democracy, and that with the defeat of the constitutional referendum we will return to a general acceptance of existing institutional conventions. However, and with the success of the Reform Party in the 1993 election, it is more likely that the populist impulse for institutional reform will continue to ripple through the political system for some time to come. It is unlikely, for example, that the conventions of executive federalism that guided intergovernmental relations for most of the past three decades will remain in tact in the face of the populist challenge.

And finally, of course, there are concerns with the deficit and debt. While it is not clear that these concerns will transform the constitutional or institutional underpinnings of the Canadian federal state, they have already transformed the terms of political debate across the country. Challenges ranging from aboriginal self-government to environmentalism and pay equity will be seen through the prisms of debt and deficit, and our capacity to respond, and indeed our political imaginations, will be increasingly constrained as a consequence. The debate over deficits and debt is also tied to a more longstanding ideological debate over the size and scope of government. This latter debate brings into play the programs of the welfare state and the redistributive policies pursued, or not pursued, by Canadian governments.

All of this suggests that the Canadian political landscape is far from static, and that the patterns of continuity outlined in this text will face significant challenges in the years ahead. This is not to predict, of course, that any particular challenge will be successful. Existing institutional arrangements have proven to be resilient in the face of challenge in the past, and it is by no means clear that the issues that have dominated the political agenda to this point—linguistic conflict, regional conflict, and Canada's relationship with the United States—will be easily deposed. However, the contemporary challenges are so strong, and come from so many directions, that it is unlikely that the political landscape at the turn of the century will be the same as it was in the early 1990s. As the 1993 election results have demonstrated, we face exciting times as we move toward the 21st century.

NOTES

1. *The Gallup Report*, June 9, 1992.

2. Ibid. A parallel study by Gallup's American affiliate found that 69 percent of Americans believed that too many immigrants were entering the United States from Latin America, 58 percent believed that too many were entering from Asia, 47 percent that too many were entering from Africa, and 36 percent that too many were entering from Europe.

3. For a summary of this evolution, see Mark O. Dickerson, *Whose North? Political Change, Political Development, and Self-Government in the Northwest Territories* (Vancouver: University of British Columbia Press, 1993).

APPENDIX A

Constitution Act, 1982

Part I
Canadian Charter of Rights and Freedoms

Whereas Canada is founded upon principles that recognize the supremacy of God and the rule of law:

GUARANTEE OF RIGHTS AND FREEDOMS

Rights and Freedoms in Canada

1. The *Canadian Charter of Rights and Freedoms* guarantees the rights and freedoms set out in it subject only to such reasonable limits prescribed by law as can be demonstrably justified in a free and democratic society.

FUNDAMENTAL FREEDOMS

Fundamental freedoms

2. Everyone has the following fundamental freedoms:
   (a) freedom of conscience and religion;
   (b) freedom of thought, belief, opinion and expression, including freedom of the press and other media of communication;
   (c) freedom of peaceful assembly; and
   (d) freedom of association.

Democratic rights of citizens

3. Every citizen of Canada has the right to vote in an election of members of the House of Commons or of a legislative assembly and to be qualified for membership therein.

Maximum duration of legislative bodies

4. (1) No House of Commons and no legislative assembly shall continue for longer than five years from the date fixed for the return of the writs at a general election of its members.

Continuation in special circumstances

(2) In time of real or apprehended war, invasion or insurrection, a House of Commons may be continued by Parliament and a legislative assembly may be continued by the legislature beyond five years if such continuation is not opposed by the votes of more than

one-third of the members of the House of Commons or the legislative assembly, as the case may be.

Annual sitting of legislative bodies

5. There shall be a sitting of Parliament and of each legislature at least once every twelve months.

MOBILITY RIGHTS

Mobility of citizens

6. (1) Every citizen of Canada has the right to enter, remain in and leave Canada.

Rights to move and gain livelihood

(2) Every citizen of Canada and every person who has the status of a permanent resident of Canada has the right

(a) to move to and take up residence in any province; and

(b) to pursue the gaining of a livelihood in any province.

Limitation

(3) The rights specified in subsection (2) are subject to

(a) any laws or practices of general application in force in a province other than those that discriminate among persons primarily on the basis of province of present or previous residence; and

(b) any laws providing for reasonable residency requirements as a qualification for the receipt of publicly provided social services.

Affirmative action programs

(4) Subsections (2) and (3) do not preclude any law, program or activity that has as its object the amelioration in a province of conditions of individuals in that province who are socially or economically disadvantaged if the rate of employment in that province is below the rate of employment in Canada.

LEGAL RIGHTS

Life, liberty and security of person

7. Everyone has the right to life, liberty and security of the person and the right not to be deprived thereof except in accordance with the principles of fundamental justice.

Search or seizure

8. Everyone has the right to be secure against unreasonable search or seizure.

Detention or imprisonment

9. Everyone has the right not to be arbitrarily detained or imprisoned.

Arrest or detention	10. Everyone has the right on arrest or detention *(a)* to be informed promptly of the reasons therefor; *(b)* to retain and instruct counsel without delay and to be informed of that right; and *(c)* to have the validity of the detention determined by way of *habeas corpus* and to be released if the detention is not lawful.
Proceedings in criminal and penal matters	11. Any person charged with an offence has the right *(a)* to be informed without unreasonable delay of the specific offence; *(b)* to be tried within a reasonable time; *(c)* not to be compelled to be a witness in proceedings against that person in respect of the offence; *(d)* to be presumed innocent until proven guilty according to law in a fair and public hearing by an independent and impartial tribunal; *(e)* not to be denied reasonable bail without just cause; *(f)* except in the case of an offence under military law tried before a military tribunal, to the benefit of trial by jury where the maximum punishment for the offence is imprisonment for five years or a more severe punishment; *(g)* not to be found guilty on account of any act or omission unless, at the time of the act or omission, it constituted an offence under Canadian or international law or was criminal according to the general principles of law recognized by the community of nations; *(h)* if finally acquitted of the offence, not to be tried for it again and, if finally found guilty and punished for the offence, not to be tried or punished for it again; and *(i)* if found guilty of the offence and if the punishment for the offence has been varied between the time of commission and the time of sentencing, to the benefit of the lesser punishment.
Treatment or punishment	12. Everyone has the right not to be subjected to any cruel and unusual treatment or punishment.

Self-incrimination	13. A witness who testifies in any proceedings has the right not to have any incriminating evidence so given used to incriminate that witness in any other proceedings, except in a prosecution for perjury or for the giving of contradictory evidence.
Interpreter	14. A party or witness in any proceedings who does not understand or speak the language in which the proceedings are conducted or who is deaf has the right to the assistance of an interpreter.

EQUALITY RIGHTS

Equality before and under law and equal protection and benefit of law	15. (1) Every individual is equal before and under the law and has the right to the equal protection and equal benefit of the law without discrimination and, in particular, without discrimination based on race, national or ethnic origin, colour, religion, sex, age or mental or physical disability.
Affirmative action programs	(2) Subsection (1) does not preclude any law, program or activity that has as its object the amelioration of conditions of disadvantaged individuals or groups including those that are disadvantaged because of race, national or ethnic origin, colour, religion, sex, age or mental or physical disability.

OFFICIAL LANGUAGES OF CANADA

Official languages of Canada	16. (1) English and French are the official languages of Canada and have equality of status and equal rights and privileges as to their use in all instructions of the Parliament and government of Canada.
Official languages of New Brunswick	(2) English and French are the official languages of New Brunswick and have equality of status and equal rights and privileges as to their use in all institutions of the legislature and government of New Brunswick.
Advancement of status and use	(3) Nothing in this Charter limits the authority of Parliament or a legislature to advance the equality of status or use of English and French.
Proceedings of Parliament	17. (1) Everyone has the right to use English or French in any debates and other proceedings of Parliament.

Proceedings of New Brunswick legislature

(2) Everyone has the right to use English or French in any debates and other proceedings of the legislature of New Brunswick.

Parliamentary status and records

18. (1) The statutes, records and journals of Parliament shall be printed and published in English and French and both language versions are equally authoritative.

New Brunswick statutes and records

(2) The statutes, records and journals of the legislature of New Brunswick shall be printed and published in English and French and both language versions are equally authoritative.

Proceedings in courts established by Parliament

19. (1) Either English or French may be used by any person in, or in any pleading in or process issuing from, any court established by Parliament.

(2) Either English or French may be used by any person in, or in any pleading in or process issuing from, any court of New Brunswick.

Communications by public with federal institutions

20. (1) Any member of the public in Canada has the right to communicate with, and to receive available services from, any head or central office of an institution of the Parliament or government of Canada in English or French, and has the same right with respect to any other office of any such institution where

(a) there is a significant demand for communications with and services from that office in such language; or

(b) due to the nature of the office, it is reasonable that communications with and services from that office be available in both English and French.

Communications by public with New Brunswick institutions.

(2) Any member of the republic in New Brunswick has the right to communicate with, and to receive available services from, any office of an institution of the legislature or government of New Brunswick in English or French.

Continuation of existing constitutional provisions

21. Nothing in sections 16 to 20 abrogates or derogates from any right, privilege or obligation with respect to the English and French languages, or either of them, that exists or is continued by virtue of any other provision of the Constitution of Canada.

Rights and
privileges
preserved

22. Nothing in sections 16 to 20 abrogates or derogates from any legal or customary right or privilege acquired or enjoyed either before or after the coming into force of this Charter with respect to any language that is not English or French.

Language of
instruction

23. (1) Citizens of Canada
  (a) whose first language learned and still understood is that of the English or French linguistic minority population of the province in which they reside, or
  (b) who have received their primary school instruction in Canada in English or French and reside in a province where the language in which they received that instruction is the language of the English or French linguistic minority population of the province,

have the right to have their children receive primary and secondary school instruction in that language in that province.

Continuity of
language
instruction

(2) Citizens of Canada of whom any child has received or is receiving primary or secondary school instruction in English or French in Canada, have the right to have all their children receive primary and secondary school instruction in the same language.

Application
where numbers
warrant

(3) The right of citizens of Canada under subsections (1) and (2) to have their children receive primary and secondary school instruction in the language of the English or French linguistic minority population of a province
  (a) applies wherever in the province the number of children of citizens who have such a right is sufficient to warrant the provision to them out of public funds of minority language instruction; and
  (b) includes, where the number of those children so warrants, the right to have them receive that instruction in minority language educational facilities provided out of public funds.

Enforcement of guaranteed rights and freedoms

24. (1) Anyone whose rights or freedoms, as guaranteed by this Charter, have been infringed or denied may apply to a court of competent jurisdiction to obtain such remedy as the court considers appropriate and just in the circumstances.

Exclusion of evidence bringing administration of justice into disrepute

(2) Where, in proceedings under subsection (1), a court concludes that evidence was obtained in a manner that infringed or denied any rights or freedoms guaranteed by this Charter, the evidence shall be excluded if it is established that, having regard to all the circumstances, the admission of it in the proceedings would bring the administration of justice into disrepute.

GENERAL

Aboriginal rights and freedoms not affected by Charter

25. The guarantee in this Charter of certain rights and freedoms shall not be construed so as to abrogate or derogate from any aboriginal treaty or other rights or freedoms that pertain to the aboriginal peoples of Canada including

(a) any rights or freedoms that have been recognized by the Royal Proclamation of October 7, 1763; and

(b) any rights or freedoms that may be acquired by the aboriginal peoples of Canada by way of land claims settlement.

Other rights and freedoms not affected by Charter

26. The guarantee in this Charter of certain rights and freedoms shall not be construed as denying the existence of any other rights or freedoms that exist in Canada.

Multicultural heritage

27. This Charter shall be interpreted in a manner consistent with the preservation and enhancement of the multicultural heritage of Canadians.

Rights guaranteed equally to both sexes

28. Notwithstanding anything in this Charter, the rights and freedoms referred to in it are guaranteed equally to male and female persons.

Rights respecting certain schools

29. Nothing in this Charter abrogates or derogates from any rights or privileges guaranteed by or under the Constitution of Canada in respect of denomination, separate or dissentient schools.

Application to territories and territorial authorities	30. A reference in this Charter to a province or to the legislative assembly or legislature of a province shall be deemed to include a reference to the Yukon Territory and the Northwest Territories, or to the appropriate legislative authority thereof, as the case may be.
Legislative powers not extended	31. Nothing in this Charter extends the legislative powers of any body or authority.

APPLICATION OF CHARTER

Application of Charter	32. (1) This Charter applies (a) to the Parliament and government of Canada in respect of all matters within the authority of Parliament including all matters relating to the Yukon Territory and Northwest Territories; and (b) to the legislature and government of each province in respect of all matters within the authority of the legislature of each province.
Exception	(2) Nothwithstanding subsection (1), section 15 shall not have effect until three years after this section comes into force.
Exception where express declaration	33. (1) Parliament or the legislature of a province may expressly declare in an Act of Parliament or of the legislature, as the case may be, that the Act or a provision thereof shall operate notwithstanding a provision included in section 2 or sections 7 to 15 of this Charter.
Operation of exception	(2) An Act or a provision of an Act in respect of which a declaration made under this section is in effect shall have such operation as it would have but for the provision of this Charter referred to in the declaration.
Five year limitation	(3) A declaration made under subsection (1) shall cease to have effect five years after it comes into force or on such earlier date as may be specified in the declaration.
Re-enactment	(4) Parliament or the legislature of a province may re-enact a declaration made under subsection (1).
Five year limitation	(5) Subsection (3) applies in respect of a re-enactment made under subsection (4).

Citation

34. This Part may be cited as the *Canadian Charter of Rights and Freedoms.*

Part II
Rights of the Aboriginal Peoples of Canada

Recognition of existing aboriginal and treaty rights

35. (1) The existing aboriginal and treaty rights of the aboriginal peoples of Canada are hereby recognized and affirmed.

Definition of "aboriginal peoples of Canada"

(2) In this Act, "aboriginal peoples of Canada" includes the Indian, Inuit and Métis peoples of Canada.

Part III
Equalization and Regional Disparities

Commitment to promote equal opportunities

36. (1) Without altering the legislative authority of Parliament or of the provincial legislatures, or the rights of any of them with respect to the exercise of their legislative authority, Parliament and the legislatures, together with the government of Canada and the provincial governments, are committed to
(a) promoting equal opportunities for the well-being of Canadians;
(b) furthering economic development to reduce disparity in opportunities; and
(c) providing essential public services of reasonable quality to all Canadians.

Commitment respecting public services

(2) Parliament and the government of Canada are committed to the principle of making equalization payments to ensure that provincial governments have sufficient revenues to provide reasonably comparable levels of public services at reasonably comparable levels of taxation.

Part IV
Constitutional Conference

Constitutional conference

37. (1) A constitutional conference composed of the Prime Minister of Canada and the first ministers of the provinces shall be convened by the Prime Minister of Canada within one year after this part comes into force.

Participation of aboriginal peoples	(2) The conference convened under subsection (1) shall have included in its agenda an item respecting constitutional matters that directly affect the aboriginal peoples of Canada, including the identification and definition of the rights of those peoples to be included in the Constitution of Canada, and the Prime Minister of Canada shall invite representatives of those peoples to participate in the discussions on that item.
Participation of territories	(3) The Prime Minister of Canada shall invite elected representatives of the governments of the Yukon Territory and the Northwest Territories to participate in the discussion on any item on the agenda of the conference convened under subsection (1) that, in the opinion of the Prime Minister, directly affects the Yukon Territory and the Northwest Territories.

Part V
Procedure for Amending Constitution of Canada

General procedure for amending Constitution of Canada	38. (1) An amendment to the Constitution of Canada may be made by proclamation issued by the Governor General under the Great Seal of Canada where so authorized by *(a)* resolutions of the Senate and House of Commons; and *(b)* resolutions of the legislative assemblies of at least two-thirds of the provinces that have, in the aggregate, according to the then latest general census, at least fifty per cent of the population of all the provinces.
Majority of members	(2) An amendment made under subsection (1) that derogates from the legislative powers, the proprietary rights or any other rights or privileges of the legislature or government of a province shall require a resolution supported by a majority of the members of each of the Senate, the House of Commons and the legislative assemblies required under subsection (1).
Expression of dissent	(3) An amendment referred to in subsection (2) shall not have effect in a province the legislative assembly of which has expressed its dissent thereto by resolution supported by a majority of its members

prior to the issue of the proclamation to which the amendment relates unless that legislative assembly, subsequently, by resolution supported by a majority of its members, revokes its dissent and authorizes the amendment.

Revocation of dissent

(4) A resolution of dissent made for the purposes of subsection (3) may be revoked at any time before or after the issue of the proclamation to which it relates.

Restriction on proclamation

39. (1) A proclamation shall not be issued under subsection 38(1) before the expiration of one year from the adoption of the resolution initiating the amendment procedure thereunder, unless the legislative assembly of each province has previously adopted a resolution of assent or dissent.

Idem

(2) A proclamation shall not be issued under subsection 38(1) after the expiration of three years from the adoption of the resolution initiating the amendment procedure thereunder.

Compensation

40. Where an amendment is made under subsection 38(1) that transfers provincial legislative powers relating to education or other cultural matters from provincial legislatures to Parliament, Canada shall provide reasonable compensation to any province to which the amendment does not apply.

Amendment by unanimous consent

41. An amendment to the Constitution of Canada in relation to the following matters may be made by proclamation issued by the Governor General under the Great Seal of Canada only where authorized by resolutions of the Senate and House of Commons and of the legislative assembly of each province:

(a) the office of the Queen, the Governor General and the Lieutenant Governor of a province;

(b) the right of a province to a number of members in the House of Commons not less than the number of Senators by which the province is entitled to be represented at the time this Part comes into force;

(c) subject to section 43, the use of the English or the French language;

(d) the composition of the Supreme Court of Canada; and

(e) an amendment to this Part.

Amendment by general procedure

42. (1) An amendment to the Constitution of Canada in relation to the following matters may be made only in accordance with subsection 38(1):

(a) the principle of proportionate representation of the provinces in the House of Commons prescribed by the Constitution of Canada;

(b) the powers of the Senate and the method of selecting Senators;

(c) the number of members by which a province is entitled to be represented in the Senate and the residence qualifications of Senators;

(d) subject to paragraph 41(*d*), the Supreme Court of Canada;

(e) the extension of existing provinces into the territories; and

(f) notwithstanding any other law or practice, the establishment of new provinces.

Exception

(2) Subsections 38(2) to (4) do not apply in respect of amendments in relation to matters referred to in subsection (1).

Amendment of provisions relating to some but not all provinces

43. An amendment to the Constitution of Canada in relation to any provision that applies to one or more, but not all, provinces, including

(a) any alteration to boundaries between provinces, and

(b) any amendment to any provision that relates to the use of the English or the French language within a province, may be made by proclamation issued by the Governor General under the Great Seal of Canada only where so authorized by resolutions of the Senate and House of Commons and of the legislative assembly of each province to which the amendment applies.

Amendments by Parliament

44. Subject to sections 41 and 42, Parliament may exclusively make laws amending the Constitution of Canada in relation to the executive government of Canada or the Senate and House of Commons.

Amendments by provincial legislatures

45. Subject to section 41, the legislature of each province may exclusively make laws amending the constitution of the province.

Initiation of amendment procedures

46. (1) The procedures for amendment under sections 38, 41, 42 and 43 may be initiated either by the Senate or the House of Commons or by the legislative assembly of a province.

Revocation of authorization

(2) A resolution of assent made for the purposes of this Part may be revoked at any time before the issue of a proclamation authorized by it.

Amendments without Senate resolution

47. (1) An amendment to the Constitution of Canada made by proclamation under section 38, 41, 42 or 43 may be made without a resolution of the Senate authorizing the issue of the proclamation if, within one hundred and eighty days after the adoption by the House of Commons of a resolution authorizing its issue, the Senate has not adopted such a resolution and if, at any time after the expiration of that period, the House of Commons again adopts the resolution.

Computation of period

(2) Any period when Parliament is prorogued or dissolved shall not be counted in computing the one hundred and eighty day period referred to in subsection (1).

Advice to issue proclamation

48. The Queen's Privy Council for Canada shall advise the Governor General to issue a proclamation under this Part forthwith on the adoption of the resolutions required for an amendment made by proclamation under this Part.

Constitutional conference

49. A constitutional conference composed of the Prime Minister of Canada and the first ministers of the provinces shall be convened by the Prime Minister of Canada within fifteen years after this Part comes into force to review the provisions of this Part.

Part VI
Amendment to the Constitution Act, 1867

Amendment to Constitution Act, 1867

50. *The Constitution Act, 1867* (formerly named the *British North America Act, 1867*) is amended by adding thereto, immediately after section 92 thereof, the following heading and section:

Laws respecting non-renewable natural resources, forestry resources and electrical energy

92A. (1) In each province, the legislature may exclusively make laws in relation to

(a) exploration for non-renewable natural resources in the province;

(b) development, conservation and management of non-renewable natural resources and forestry resources in the province, including laws in relation to the rate of primary production therefrom; and

(c) development, conservation and management of sites and facilities in the province for the generation and production of electrical energy.

Export from provinces of resources

(2) In each province, the legislature may make laws in relation to the export from the province to another part of Canada of the primary production from non-renewable natural resources and forestry resources in the province and the production from facilities in the province for the generation of electrical energy, but such laws may not authorize or provide for discrimination in prices or in supplies exported to another part of Canada.

Authority of Parliament

(3) Nothing in subsection (2) derogates from the authority of Parliament to enact laws in relation to the matters referred to in that subsection and, where such a law of Parliament and a law of a province conflict, the law of Parliament prevails to the extent of the conflict.

Taxation of resources

(4) In each province, the legislature may make laws in relation to the raising of money by any mode or system of taxation in respect of

(a) non-renewable natural resources and forestry resources in the province and the primary production therefrom, and

(b) sites and facilities in the province for the generation of electrical energy and the production therefrom,

whether or not production is exported in whole or in part from the province, but such laws may not authorize or provide for taxation that differentiates between production exported to another part of Canada and production not exported from the province.

"Primary production"

(5) The expression "primary production" has the meaning assigned by the Sixth Schedule.

Existing powers or rights

(6) Nothing in subsection (1) to (5) derogates from any powers or rights that a legislature or government of a province had immediately before the coming into force of this section."

Idem

51. The said Act is further amended by adding thereto the following Schedule:

"The Sixth Schedule
PRIMARY PRODUCTION FROM NON-RENEWABLE NATURAL RESOURCES AND FORESTRY RESOURCES

1. For the purposes of section 92A of this Act,
   (a) production from a non-renewable natural resource is primary production therefrom if
      (i) it is in the form in which it exists upon its recovery or severance from its natural state, or
      (ii) it is a product resulting from processing or refining the resource, and is not a manufactured product or a product resulting from refining crude oil, refining upgraded heavy crude oil, refining gases or liquids derived from coal or refining a synthetic equivalent of crude oil; and
   (b) production from a forestry resource is primary production therefrom if it consists of sawlogs, poles, lumber, wood chips, sawdust or any other primary wood product, or wood pulp, and is not a product manufactured from wood."

Part VII
General

Primacy of Constitution of Canada

52. (1) The Constitution of Canada is the supreme law of Canada, and any law that is inconsistent with the provisions of the Constitution is, to the extent of the inconsistency, of no force or effect.

Constitution of Canada	(2) The Constitution of Canada includes *(a)* the *Canada Act 1982*, including this Act; *(b)* the Acts and orders referred to in the schedule; and *(c)* any amendment to any Act or order referred to in paragraph (*a*) or (*b*)
Amendments to Constitution of Canada	(3) Amendments to the Constitution of Canada shall be made only in accordance with the authority contained in the Constitution of Canada.
Repeals and new names	53. (1) The enactments referred to in Column I of the schedule are hereby repealed or amended to the extent indicated in Column II thereof and, unless repealed, shall continue as law in Canada under the names set out in Column III thereof.
Consequential amendments	(2) Every enactment, except the *Canada Act, 1982*, that refers to an enactment referred to in the schedule by the name in Column I thereof is hereby amended by substituting for that name the corresponding name in Column III thereof, and any British North America Act not referred to in the schedule may be cited as the *Constitution Act* followed by the year and number, if any, of its enactment.
Repeal and consequential amendments	54. Part IV is repealed on the day that is one year after this Part comes into force and this section may be repealed and this Act renumbered, consequentially upon the repeal of Part IV and this section, by proclamation issued by the Governor General under the Great Seal of Canada.
French version of Constitution of Canada	55. A French version of the portions of the Constitution of Canada referred to in the schedule shall be prepared by the Minister of Justice of Canada as expeditiously as possible and, when any portion thereof sufficient to warrant action being taken has been so prepared, it shall be put forward for enactment by proclamation issued by the Governor General under the Great Seal of Canada pursuant to the procedure then applicable to an amendment of the same provisions of the Constitution of Canada.
English and French versions of certain constitutional texts	56. Where any portion of the Constitution of Canada has been or is enacted in English and French or where a French version of any portion of the Constitution is enacted pursuant to section 55, the English

and French versions of that portion of the Constitution are equally authoritative.

English and French versions of this Act

57. The English and French versions of this Act are equally authoritative.

58. Subject to section 59, this Act shall come into force on a day to be fixed by proclamation issued by the Queen or the Governor General under the Great Seal of Canada.

Commencement of paragraph 23(1)(a)

59. (1) Paragraph 23(1)(a) shall come into force in respect of Quebec on a day to be fixed by proclamation issued by the Queen or the Governor General under the Great Seal of Canada.

Authorization of Quebec

(2) A proclamation under subsection (1) shall be issued only where authorized by the legislative assembly or government of Quebec.

Repeal of this section

(3) This section may be repealed on the day paragraph 23(1)(a) comes into force in respect of Quebec and this Act amended and renumbered, consequential upon the repeal of this section, by proclamation issued by the Queen or the Governor General under the Great Seal of Canada.

Short title and citations

60. This Act may be cited as the *Constitution Act, 1982*, and the *Constitution Acts 1867 to 1975* (No. 2) and this Act may be cited together as the *Constitution Acts, 1867 to 1982*.

APPENDIX B

Excerpts from the Constitution Act, 1867

The federal division of powers is set forth in a number of sections of the Constitution Act, 1867. The most general treatment is contained in Sections 91 and 92, while subsequent sections deal in more detail with particular powers.

VI. Distribution of Legislative Powers

POWERS OF PARLIAMENT

91. It shall be lawful for the Queen, by and with the advice and consent of the Senate and House of Commons, to make laws for the peace, order, and good government of Canada, in relation to all matters not coming within the classes of subjects by this Act assigned exclusively to the Legislatures of the Provinces; and for greater certainty, but not so as to restrict the generality of the foregoing terms of this section, it is hereby declared that (notwithstanding anything in this Act) the exclusive Legislative Authority of the Parliament of Canada extends to all matter coming within the classes of subjects next hereinafter enumerated, that is to say:—

1. The amendment from time to time of the Constitution of Canada, except as regards matters coming within the classes of subjects by this Act assigned exclusively to the Legislatures of the Provinces, or as regards rights or privileges by this or any other Constitutional Act granted or secured to the Legislature or the Government of a Province, or to any class of persons with respect to schools or as regards the use of the English or the French language or as regards the requirements that there shall be a session of the Parliament of Canada at least once each year, and that no House of Commons shall continue for more than five years from the day of the return of the Writs for choosing the House: provided, however, that a House of Commons may in time of real or apprehended war, invasion or insurrection be continued by the Parliament of Canada if such continuation is not opposed by the votes of more than one-third of the members of such House.

1A. The Public Debt and Property.

2. The regulation of Trade and Commerce.

2A. Unemployment insurance.

3. The raising of money by any mode or system of Taxation.

4. The borrowing of money on the public credit.

5. Postal service.
6. The Census and Statistics.
7. Militia, Military and Naval Service, and Defence.
8. The fixing of and providing for the salaries and allowances of civil and other officers of the Government of Canada.
9. Beacons, Buoys, Lighthouses, and Sable Island.
10. Navigation and Shipping.
11. Quarantine and the establishment and maintenance of Marine Hospitals.
12. Sea Coast and Inland Fisheries.
13. Ferries between a Province and any British or Foreign country or between two Provinces.
14. Currency and Coinage.
15. Banking, incorporation of banks, and the issue of paper money.
16. Savings Banks.
17. Weights and Measures.
18. Bills of Exchange and Promissory Notes.
19. Interest.
20. Legal tender.
21. Bankruptcy and Insolvency.
22. Patents of Invention and Discovery.
23. Copyrights.
24. Indians and lands reserved for the Indians.
25. Naturalization and Aliens.
26. Marriage and Divorce.
27. The Criminal Law, except the Constitution of Courts of Criminal Jurisdiction, but including the Procedure in Criminal Matters.
28. The establishment, maintenance, and management of Penitentiaries.
29. Such classes of subjects as are expressly excepted in the enumeration of the classes of subjects by this Act assigned exclusively to the Legislatures of the Provinces.

And any matter coming within any of the classes of subjects enumerated in this section shall not be deemed to come within the class of matters of a local or private nature comprised in the enumeration of the classes of subjects by this Act assigned exclusively to the Legislatures of the Provinces.

EXCLUSIVE POWERS OF PROVINCIAL LEGISLATURES

92. In each Province the Legislature may exclusively make laws in relation to matters coming within the classes of subjects next hereinafter enumerated, that is to say,
1. The amendment from time to time, notwithstanding anything in this Act, of the Constitution of the Province, except as regards the Office of Lieutenant-Governor.

2. Direct Taxation within the Province in order to the raising of a Revenue for Provincial purposes.

3. The borrowing of money on the sole credit of the Province.

4. The establishment and tenure of Provincial offices and the appointment and payment of Provincial officers.

5. The management and sales of the Public Lands belonging to the Province, and of the timber and wood thereon.

6. The establishment, maintenance, and management of public and reformatory prisons in and for the Province.

7. The establishment, maintenance, and management of hospitals, asylums, charities, and eleemosynary institutions in and for the Province, other than marine hospitals.

8. Municipal institutions in the Province.

9. Shop, saloon, tavern, auctioneer, and other licenses, in order to the raising of a revenue for Provincial, local, or municipal purposes.

10. Local works and undertakings other than such as are of the following classes,—

    a. Lines of steam or other ships, railways, canals, telegraphs, and other works and undertakings connecting the Province with any other or others of the Provinces, or extending beyond the limits of the Province;

    b. Lines of steam ships between the Province and any British or Foreign country;

    c. Such works as, although wholly situate within the Province, are before or after their execution declared by the Parliament of Canada to be for the general advantage of Canada or for the advantage of two or more of the Provinces.

11. The incorporation of companies with Provincial objects.

12. The solemnization of marriage in the Province.

13. Property and civil rights in the Province.

14. The administration of justice in the Province, including the constitution, maintenance, and organization of Provincial Courts, both of civil and of criminal jurisdiction, and including procedure in civil matters in those Courts.

15. The imposition of punishment by fine, penalty, or imprisonment for enforcing any law of the Province made in relation to any matter coming within any of the classes of subjects enumerated in this section.

16. Generally all matters of a merely local or private nature in the Province.

EDUCATION

93. In and for each Province the Legislature may exclusively make laws in relation to education, subject and according to the following provisions:—

1. Nothing in any such law shall prejudicially affect any right or privilege with respect to denominational schools which any class or persons have by law in the Province at the Union.

2. All the powers, privileges, and duties at the Union by law conferred and imposed in Upper Canada on the separate schools and school trustees of the Queen's Roman Catholic subjects shall be and the same are hereby extended to the dissentient schools of the Queen's Protestant and Roman Catholic subjects in Quebec.

3. Where in any Province a system of separate or dissentient schools exists by law at the Union or is thereafter established by the Legislature of the Province, an appeal shall lie to the Governor-General in Council from any Act or Decision of any Provincial authority affecting any right or privilege of the Protestant or Roman Catholic minority of the Queen's subjects in relation to education.

4. In case any such Provincial law as from time to time seems to the Governor-General in Council requisite for the due execution of the provisions of this section is not made, or in case any decision of the Governor-General in Council on any appeal under this section is not duly executed by the proper Provincial authority in that behalf, then and in every such case, and as far only as the circumstances of each case require, the Parliament of Canada may make remedial laws for the due execution of the provisions of this section and of any decision of the Governor-General in Council under this section.

...

OLD AGE PENSIONS

94A. The Parliament of Canada may make laws in relation to old age pensions and supplementary benefits, including survivors' and disability benefits irrespective of age, but no such law shall affect the operation of any law present or future of a provincial legislature in relation to any such matter.

AGRICULTURE AND IMMIGRATION

95. In each Province the Legislature may make laws in relation to Agriculture in the Province, and to Immigration into the Province; and it is hereby declared that the Parliament of Canada may from time to time make laws in relation to Agriculture in all or any of the Provinces, and to Immigration into all or any of the Provinces; and any law of the Legislature of a Province relative to Agriculture or to Immigration shall have effect in and for the Province as long and as far only as it is not repugnant to any Act of the Parliament of Canada.

...

VIII. Revenues; Debts; Assets; Taxation

...

109. All lands, mines, minerals, and royalties belonging to the several provinces of Canada, Nova Scotia and New Brunswick at the Union, and all sums then due or payable for such lands, mines, minerals, or royalties, shall belong to the several Provinces of Ontario, Quebec, Nova Scotia, and New Brunswick in which the same are situate or arise, subject to any trusts existing in respect thereof, and to any interest other than of the Province in the same.

...

APPENDIX C
Writing a Term Paper

Instructors vary considerably in what they expect from student term papers. The following notes are therefore intended to provide guidelines which can be adapted to fit the requirements of your course and instructor.

1. PAY ATTENTION TO THE SPECIFIC ASSIGNMENT

All term paper assignments are *not* the same. The nature of the assignment will differ across departments within your university, and across courses and instructors within departments. Therefore it is essential to pay close attention to the *specific* assignment. Do not assume that a paper format that has worked well for you in the past will necessarily work this time around.

2. GET AN EARLY START

The sooner you start on the paper assignment, the more likely you are to find research material. Library resources will invariably be strained toward the end of the term. If you give yourself enough lead time, useful material is likely to emerge from newspaper and magazine articles, from other sources, from conversations with friends, and from random thoughts and observations that you might have.

3. SOURCES

There are a number of leads that can be pursued in trying to locate research material for your paper. Use the suggested readings in this and other recent texts, and work backward from the footnotes. Use the card catalogue in your library. Use the *Canadian Periodicals Index*, and go through the recent and as yet unindexed issues of journals such as the *Canadian Journal of Political Science*, *Canadian Public Policy*, and the *Journal of Canadian Studies*. Keep a close eye on the newspapers, and on magazines such as *Maclean's*, *Saturday Night*, and *Canadian Forum*. When you find one useful source, plunder its footnotes and bibliography for other leads.

4. DO NOT REINVENT THE WHEEL

Your paper should draw upon the existing social science literature, as a term paper in an introductory course can carry only a limited amount of original research. What counts is your ability to apply existing knowledge and theories to the particular subject under examination in your paper.

5. CREATE A MEMORY BANK

Set up a file folder or large envelope for each assignment you face during the term. Then, whenever you have a thought or insight into the assignment, whenever you encounter a possible source of research material, jot it down on a piece of paper and file it away in the folder or envelope. Whenever you encounter something that might be useful, be it in a text, journal article or newspaper, take notes (including the source of the information) and file them away. All the relevant material for each assignment will then be gathered together in one place, ready to be dumped out on your desk when the writing begins. Less material will be lost from a paper memory than from a mental one.

6. RESPECT DEADLINES AND PAGE LIMITS

Take deadlines seriously, and frame your assignment within the page limits set by your instructor. After all, in the "real world" projects have to be done on time and within specified limits. If you are asked for a fifteen-page synopsis by Friday, your employer will not expect a thirty-page synopsis by the following Thursday.

7. WRITE AT LEAST TWO DRAFTS

Do not expect to product a good paper on the first draft. Allow enough time that you can write a rough draft and let it sit for a few days. Then go through the draft as dispassionately as possible, pretending, if you like, that someone else wrote it. Rewrite the sections that are rough, add in new material, and correct problems of style, substance, and interpretation. Remember that rewriting in the early stages often entails substantial reorganization of the material, not merely correcting spelling and grammatical errors. Writing is a cognitive process, a way of thinking about your material and discovering what you want to say. Thus do not be surprised if your paper changes considerably from one draft to the next.

8. A RESEARCH PAPER IS NOT AN ESSAY

A research paper must do more than present your own viewpoint. It should explore a particular theme or question through a marshalling of the available evidence. While it is acceptable to be argumentative, you should stray beyond the bounds of the existing evidence. The argument should be derived from the evidence, or at least supported by it, rather than an expression of one's own beliefs.

9. THE THEMATIC STRUCTURE

A good paper pursues an explicit theme or thesis. This should be laid out as early as possible, perhaps in the introductory paragraph. The main body of the paper should then develop this thesis or theme, and the concluding paragraph should link back to the introductory paragraph. There is, then, a circular structure to the paper: you state what it is you intend to do, you got out and do it, and then you conclude by summarizing what you did, answering the questions posed in your introductory paragraph.

10. PAY ATTENTION TO STYLE AND ORGANIZATION

In the famous words of Marshall McLuhan, "the medium is the message." How you communicate your ideas will have a critical impact on their reception. Do not expect your instructor to sift through awkward sentences, indifferent organization, and a sloppy style searching for intellectual gold. Good ideas poorly presented are indistinguishable from poor ideas poorly presented.

11. DO NOT RUSH TO THE ATTACK

It is relatively easy and at times satisfying to attack, to condemn and deplore. However, while a moralistic stance *may* enrich a paper, your primary task is to *understand* the phenomenon, event, or personality under investigation. Why did something happen? What were the alternatives? Why were some options pursued and others avoided? Once you understand the complexities of the issue, then and only then are you in a position to render some judgment.

12. AVOID LOADED WORDS

Be careful in your use of words like genocide, lie, murder, deceive, catastrophic, and disaster. Strong words in a research paper are analogous to swear words in more common discourse; if overused, they lose their impact. If you call something a disaster, be sure that you really mean a *disaster* and not merely an unfortunate or unpleasant event. Readers are more impressed by firm but *reasonable* statements supported by evidence than by fervently held beliefs expressed in highly charged language.

13. DO NOT PLAGIARIZE

To plagiarize means to pass off the words *or ideas* of others as your own. In many schools, plagiarism can lead to automatic failure and even expulsion. If you use the words of other writers, enclose them within quotation marks and provide their source in a footnote. If you paraphrase other writers, you must still indicate the source of the material. There is no problem in using the work of other people, and indeed this is what much of the research enterprise is all about—building upon an existing body of knowledge and insights. However, where the work of others is used, *it must be acknowledged.*

14. PARAGRAPHING

A good paragraph has its own internal structure and coherency. It explores a single theme or issue, and the break between paragraphs is used to signify a shift in analysis or emphasis. (A good check on the coherence of a paragraph is to read the first and last sentences; they should make sense together and should contain the essence of the paragraph.) Be wary of very long paragraphs—I once received a paper with a paragraph that stretched over five and a half pages! Paragraphs of over a page in length suggest an indifference on the part of the writer to organization.

15. SUBHEADINGS

Subheadings can be used to impose an organizational structure upon your paper. They break up the paper into more easily digested chunks, and convey the impression that you have paid attention to the structural form and coherency of your argument. It is essential, however, to provide some transition between the sections of your paper. Subheadings emphasize points of transition; they do not provide a substitute for transitions in the body of your text.

16. DO NOT ASSUME SHARED KNOWLEDGE

Students are often unsure whether to include information that they feel will be "obvious" to the marker. Often when I have criticized students for failing to include certain information they have replied "I just assumed you knew that." The problem is that it is difficult for a marker to assume that the writer indeed knows information that is not contained in the paper. You may well assume that I know that John A. Macdonald was the leader of the Conservative party, but I have less grounds for assuming that you know. Therefore it pays to err on the side of including what you may assume to be shared or common knowledge. Write less for your instructor than for some other, impartial audience that is not privy to what has gone on in your course.

17. AVOID LONG QUOTES

Excessively long quotes suggest an overreliance on the work of others, and a reluctance on the writer's part to come to grips with the ideas behind the quote. Your job, after all, goes well beyond *presenting* the works of others. When quotes of more than one sentence in length are used, they should be set off from the main body of the paragraph and they should be introduced. Phrases like "As Smith has observed…" and "Jones elaborates upon this point at some length" can be useful in introducing long quotes.

18. AVOID TERMINOLOGICAL CONFUSION

A good argument can be obscured by terminological confusion. Be careful, for example, not to confuse Parliament with the Government of Canada, or French Canadians with the Québécois, or Nova Scotia with the Government of Nova Scotia. Be sure to define the key terms and concepts in your paper. In doing so, do not rely on an English language dictionary. A dictionary of political science or an encyclopedia of social sciences provides a much better source.

19. FOOTNOTES

Footnotes provide the linkage between your text and the research material that you have employed. Whatever footnote style you adopt—and some institutions specify a particular format—apply it consistently. Footnotes are not peripheral to a good research paper; they are an intrinsic part of it and should not be passed over lightly. It should be possible for a reader to reconstruct the paper from the footnotes, and thus to verify your findings.

20. BIBLIOGRAPHY

A bibliography should be included to acknowledge the sources that you consulted, and in particular those sources that have been of general use but to which specific reference has not been made either in the text or in the footnotes. Do not pad your bibliography by throwing in material that you have *not* looked at.

21. END WITH AN EMPHATIC CONCLUSION

Avoid a paper that fizzles out at the end, that creates the impression that you ran out of things to say and just stopped. The conclusion should not simply review the main points in the paper. It should tie the paper together, looping back to the introduction in order to demonstrate that you have done what you set out to do. Admittedly, a conclusion is often not easy to write, but it is the conclusion that pulls the research enterprise together and answer the question, "so what?"

22. HAND-WRITTEN PAPERS

Most universities and colleges have regulations which state that students are not penalized for hand-written papers. The fact remains, however, that poor handwriting will lessen the impact of your paper. If the reader has to struggle through, word by word and sentence by sentence, there is a good chance that at the end of the paper he or she will have little appreciation of the paper's broader theme and argument. Poor handwritting *will* hurt you, no matter how hard the marker tries to keep to the spirit of institutional regulations.

23. PROOFREAD

Always proofread your paper and, better still, have a friend do it also. Pay particular attention to grammar and spelling, and to the agreement between subjects and verbs. A paper that has not been proofread suggests sloppiness and indifference on the part of the author. A careful proofreading ensures that your paper is as good as it can be, that the marker will not be distracted from your argument and ideas by a progression of typos, spelling mistakes, and grammatical errors.

24. GOOD LUCK!

INDEX

Abolitionist Party, 377
Aboriginal peoples, 218, 242
Aboriginal rights, 75, 348
Aboriginal self-government, 346,
  435, 436
Acid Rain Treaty, 282, 284
Act of Union (1840), 12, 13, 14,
  22
Agricultural and Rural Develop-
  ment Act (1965), 246
Agricultural Rehabilitation and
  Development Act (1961), 246
Alberta Heritage Savings and Trust
  Fund, 243
Allaire Report, 345
Amending formula. *See* Constitu-
  tional Act (1982)
Amending procedure, 59
American Revolution, 23, 261,
  262
American War of Independence,
  261
Annexation manifesto, 17, 295
Anti-Americanism, 296, 298
Asbestos strike (1949), 127
Atlantic Accord, 165
Atlantic Canada, 157–168
  and Confederation, 157
  historical perspective,
    157–165
  interregional conflict with
    West, 159–161
  opposition to Confederation,
    17–18, 20
  regional political culture,
    165–168
Atlantic Canada Opportunities
  Agency (ACOA), 248
Autopact (1965), 266–267
Baie Comeau policy, 277
Balfour Declaration (1926), 22,
  310

Beaudoin, Gérald, 347
Beaudoin-Dobbie Special Joint
  Committee, 11, 347
Belanger, Michel, 345
Bennett, R.B., 315, 369, 370
Bennett, W.A.C., 420
Bennett, William, 420
Bilingualism, 13, 107–108, 110,
  122–124, 130, 136, 139, 142,
  143, 170, 175–176, 405, 407
  provincial response to,
    120–124
  regional variation in support
    of, 118
Bill 22 (Quebec's Official Lan-
  guage Act), 136, 139
Bill C-72, 111, 119
Bill 86, 142
Bill 101 (*Charte de la langue
  française*), 139–143, 341
Bill 178, 141, 143
Bloc Populaire, 404
Bloc Québécois, 376, 377, 379
Borden, Robert Laird, 367, 401,
  402
Border disputes, 280–283
Bouchard, Lucien, 376, 408
Bourassa, Henri, 117, 401
Bourassa, Robert, 135, 336, 340,
  420, 422
Bracken, John, 371
British North America Act (BNA
  Act). *See* Constitution Act,
  1867
Brokerage parties, 363–365
Brown, George, 14, 22
Brown, Rosemary, 393
Bush, George, 282
Cabinet, 62–71
  collective responsibility of, 45
  committees, 69–70
  provincial cabinets, 65
  provincial experience of
    ministers, 67–68
  representation, 65, 196, 197

To the owner of this book

We hope that you have enjoyed *Conflict & Unity: An Introduction to Canadian Political Life,* and we would like to know as much about your experiences with it as you would care to offer. Only through your comments and those of others can we learn how to make this a better text for future readers.

School _____ Your instructor's name _____

Course _____ Was the text required? _____ Recommended? _____

1. What did you like the most about *Conflict & Unity?*

_____

_____

_____

2. How useful was this text for your course?

_____

_____

_____

3. Do you have any recommendations for ways to improve the next edition of this text?

_____

_____

_____

4. In the space below or in a separate letter, please write any other comments you have about the book. (For example, please feel free to comment on reading level, writing style, terminology, design features, and learning aids.)

_____

_____

_____

Optional

Your
name _____ Date _____

May Nelson Canada quote you, either in promotion for *Conflict & Unity* or in future publishing ventures?

Yes _____ No _____

Thanks!

- FOLD HERE -

MAIL ⮞ POSTE

Canada Post Corporation / Société canadienne des postes

Postage paid
if mailed in Canada

Port payé
si posté au Canada

Business Reply

Réponse d'affaires

0107077099   01

TAPE SHUT

TAPE SHUT

0107077099-M1K5G4-BR01

Nelson

Nelson Canada
College Editorial Department
1120 Birchmount Rd.
Scarborough, ON M1K 9Z9

PLEASE TAPE SHUT. DO NOT STAPLE.